the complete Beatles chronicle

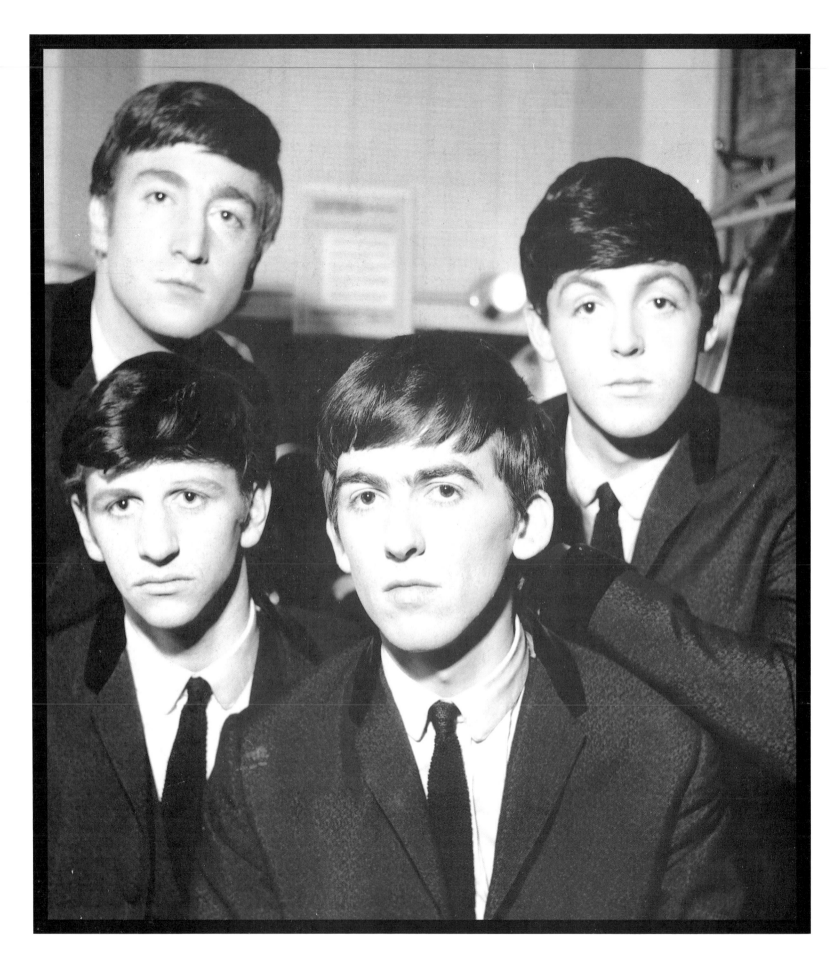

the
complete
Beatles
chronicle

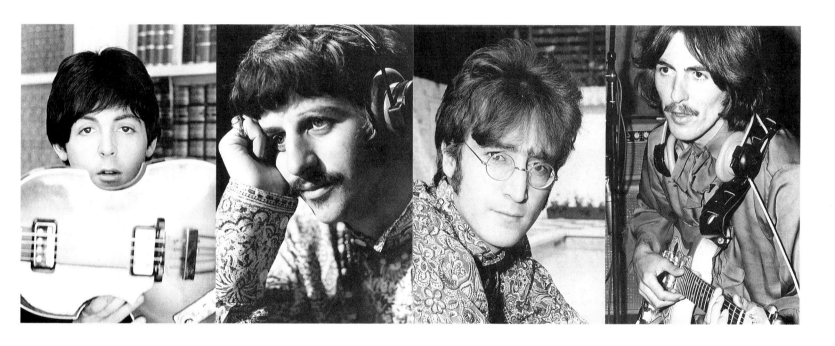

Mark Lewisohn

Harmony Books / New York

AUTHOR'S ACKNOWLEDGEMENTS

This book being the result of, in effect, 12 years' research,
there are a huge amount of people to thank for information,
assistance and the like. So without any more ado . . .

Published by Harmony Books,
a division of Crown Publishers Inc.,
201 East 50th Street, New York, New York 10022.
Member of the Crown Publishing Group.

Originally published in 1992 in Great Britain
by Pyramid Books, an imprint of
Reed Consumer Books Limited
Michelin House, 81 Fulham Road, London SW3 6RB
and Auckland, Melbourne, Singapore and Toronto

Reprinted 1992

HARMONY and colophon are trademarks of
Crown Publishers Inc.,

Printed in the United States of America

Library of Congress Cataloging-in-Publication Data
is available upon request.

ISBN 0-517-58100-0
10 9 8 7 6 5 4 3 2

For copyright reasons this edition may not be sold
outside the United States of America

For assistance in the research and reporting of the Beatles' live appearances, thanks to John Askew (Johnny Gentle), Neil Aspinall, Tony Barrow, Art Barry, the late Mona Best, Rod Bleackley, Albert Bonici, Brian Bowman, Johnny "Guitar" Byrne, Roy Carr, John Cochrane, Ray Coleman, Joe Collins, Mark Cousins, Pat Daniels, Hunter Davies, Rod Davis, Harry Dickinson, Peter Doggett, Tony Elwood, Walter Eymond, Jack Fallon, Stan Fishman, Dave Forshaw, Neil Foster, Bill Fraser Reid, Danny Friedman, Bob Gannon, Debbie Geoghegan, Nigel Greenberg, Jim Gretty, Johnny Gustafson, Arno Guzek, Maurice Haigh, Colin Hanton, Roger Howell, Liz and Jim Hughes, Douglas Jenkins, Hilary Kay, Leslie Kearney, Fred Keight, Brian Kelly, Spencer Leigh, Monty Lister, Charlie McBain Jr, Mike McCartney, Eric MacKenzie, Tony Meehan, David Moores, Chas Newby, Jos Nicholl, Jimmy Nicol, Jos Remmerswaal, Geoff Rhind, Mike and Elizabeth Robbins, Charles Roberts, Brian Roylance, Eileen Ruane, Sir Jimmy Savile OBE, the late Roger Scott, Helen Simpson, Keith Sluchansky and Eddie Suarez, David J Smith, the late John Smith, Peter and Coral Stringfellow, Pauline Sutcliffe, Derek Taylor, Chas Tranter, René van Haarlem, John Walker, Ron Watson CBE, Bob Woodward, Graham Wootton, and all those who wrote offering nuggets of new information after publication of *The Beatles Live!* in May 1986.

For assistance in the research and reporting of the Beatles' recording sessions, thanks to Malcolm Addey, Terri Anderson, Kenny Baker, the late John Barrett, Norman Bates, Martin Benge, Pete Best, Anil Bhagwat, Leo Birnbaum, Chris Blair, Peter Blake, John Blocher, Bob Boast, Peter Bown, Jerry Boys, Tony Bramwell, Alan Brown, Jack Brymer, John Burden, Barrie Cameron, Jenny Caswell, Clem Cattini, George Chkiantz, the late Alan Civil, Tony Clark, Frank Clarke, Peter Coe, Ray Coleman, Terry Condon, Hunter Davies, Malcolm Davies, Bryan Dunn, Ruth Edge, Stuart Eltham, Geoff and Nicole Emerick, Kenneth Essex, Jack Fallon, Eric Ford, Jim Foy, Francisco Gabarro, Brian Gibson, Tony Gilbert, Laurie Gold, Keith Grant, Richard Hale, Dave Harries, Derek Healey, Mike Heatley, Sarah Hobbs, Alan Holmes, David Hughes, Ted Huntley, Bill Jackman, Jeff Jarratt, Philip Jones OBE (the musician), Jenny Keen, Harry Klein, Bobby Kok, John Kurlander, Richard Langham, Richard Lush, Paul McCartney MBE, Phil McDonald, Linda Mallarkey, George Martin CBE, David Mason, Peter Mew, Mo Miller, Barry Morgan, Rex Morris, Harry Moss, Sarah Murgatroyd, Mitch Murray, Piers Murray Hill, Cris Neal, Alan Parsons, Ron Pender, Bill Povey, Ron Richards, Christine Russell, Mike Sammes, Sidney Sax, John Scott, Ken Scott, Mike Sheady, Stephen Shingles, Kenneth Sillito, John Skinner, Keith Slaughter, Norman Smith, Tracie Smith, Brian Southall, Bob Street, Derek Taylor, Chris Thomas, Eddie Thornton, John Timperley, Ken Townsend, Kathy Varley, Peter Vince, Tony Wadsworth, Nick Webb, Andy White, and all those who wrote offering information after publication of *The Complete Beatles Recording Sessions* in September 1988.

For assistance from 1988 to 1991 regarding research into the Beatles' radio, television, film and video work, thanks to John Bauldie, David Bellan, Roy Benson, Tony Bilbow, Billy Blaney, Tony Bramwell, Jack Breckon, Richard Buskin, Ed Butcher, Adrian Cairns, Richard Carraro, Ray Coleman, Roy Corlett, Ivor Cutler, Peter Doggett, Jo Durden-Smith, Frank Elliott, Naomi Fairbairn, Michael Fentiman, Nicholas Ferguson, Denise Fraser, Rune Hallberg, Tommy Hanley, Andy Hitchcock, Kevin Howlett, Philip Jones OBE (the TV executive), Shelagh Jones, Julia Kent, Dave Lee, Richard Lester, Michael Lindsay-Hogg, Mike Lowson, Jennie McClean-Cooke, Joe McGrath, Barrie MacDonald, George and Judy Martin, Stephen Maycock, Andrew Milton, Desmond Morris, Denis O' Dell, Staffan Olander, Stuart Payton, Wally Podrazik, Clive Reed, Mark Rigby, Tim Ritchie, Susan Rolling, Norman Rossington, Brian Roylance, Neil Shand, John Sheppard, Roger Simons, Adam Smith, Jim Smith, David Stark, Harry Storey, Caroline Tipple, JacquesVolcouve, Jeff Walden, Carey Wallace, Scott Wheeler, Mary Wilcock, Muriel Young.

Without wishing to appear to undervalue those who kindly rendered special assistance with the *Live!* and *Sessions* aspects of the overall work – but who've already had merit mentions in those previous publications – here is the "special thanks to" bit for the radio, television, film and video element of this book, and for other noteworthy help in recent years: to George Martin for his lovely foreword; to Jon Keeble at ITC Library Sales for finding and enabling me to view rare film; to Bill Parker at Thames Television, preserver of the ABC/Thames written archive and optimist that it goes to a safe home come January 1993; to Sylvia Cowling, film and tape librarian at Granada Television and the remarkably patient Denise Carlin in Granada's written archive; to Ruth Edge, Jenny Keen and Sarah Hobbs at EMI for always friendly help, tea, and uncovering a bulging boxfile of hitherto unseen recording sessions documents; to Jamie Leasing for sleuthing the addresses of so many long gone US concert venues; to Piet Schreuders for inspiration, information and much, much else; to Allan Kozinn for always being at the end of a fax line at 3.00 am New York time, audio/video tapes, advice and, with lovely wife Johanna, fine hospitality; to Fred Vincent for untold help and answering hundreds of questions before I even needed to ask; and to Nell Burley at Apple Corps for being a friendly and helpful aide, and for sharing the fruits of her marvellous research, soon to be seen on a video machine near you. Grateful thanks go to my agent, Bill Hamilton of A M Heath & Company, and to Piers Murray Hill, David Heslam, Mike Evans, Anna Smith, Bryan Dunn and Ashley Western (a real Fixer Upper) at Reed Consumer Books.

♥ Most of all, infinite love and thanks to Tarja, Oliver and Thomas, who have so patiently put up with a stressed, tired, preoccupied and all too rarely present husband/father.

This book is dedicated, with love, to my late mother, who instilled in me a keen appreciation of talent and all the other fine things in life – especially the Beatles.

PICTURE CREDITS

The Abergavenny Chronicle: 113 bottom
Apple/Hulton-Deutsch Collection: 193 left, 199 right, 200 bottom, 204 right, 206 right, 207, 210, 211 top, 221, 222, 223, 225 bottom, 226, 239 bottom, 243, 262 bottom, 264 left, 264 bottom right, 265 top right, 267 top, 267 bottom, 271
Apple/Walter Shenson Films: 138, 149, 150 top left, 185 right, 186, 192
Aquarius Picture Library: 9 bottom right, 11 bottom and bottom centre
Art Barry: 50 right
Laurie Asprey: 336
BBC Photo Library: 107, 119, 120, 133, 134, 177
Beatle City: (letter) 13 top
Ken Beaton/John Askew collection: 19 bottom
Bedford Record: 86
Albert Bonici: 95
Bootle Times: 26
Tony Bramwell: 284
Johnny Byrne: 58 bottom right
Camera Press: 7 top right, 106, 211 centre, 227 bottom, 236, 246 bottom, 312, 346
Camera Press/Apple: 331
Cheniston Roland/Mark Lewisohn collection: 19 top
Christie's: 9 bottom left, 32 top, 35 top left, 45 bottom, 62 top, 63 left, 90 top, 97, 151, 155 left, 201 centre, 213 right, 245, 265 left, 291 left, 319 bottom
The Cincinnati Enquirer: 140 top, right of centre
The Cleveland Press: 140 top, left of centre
Colorific!: 194
Commonwealth United Films: 314 bottom, 319 right
Coventry Evening Telegraph: 82
The Daily Cinema: 165 top, 198
Daily Herald: 92 bottom, 94 top
Daily Mail: 241 right
Darwen Advertiser: 98 top
Hunter Davies: 70 top
Robert Ellis: 308 right
EMI: 7 top left, bottom left and right, 54, 55 (all except centre picture), 61 bottom left, 70 bottom, 77 left, 79, 80 left, 90 bottom, 91, 92 top, 94 bottom, 99 bottom, 102, 103, 104 bottom, 115 (all pictures), 117, 129, 146, 147, 148 top, 148 centre, 168 left, 168 right, 170, 172, 174, 175 right, 180, 183 bottom, 184, 195 left, 204 left, 209, 216 bottom, 217, 218, 219, 224, 233, 234, 235, 238 top, 242 bottom, 244, 246 top, 248, 249, 250, 251, 252 top, 253 left, 256, 257, 259, 260, 262 top, 288, 289, 191 right, 292, 293, 294 right, 299, 300, 303, 308 left, 313, 315 left, 319 left, 321, 322, 325, 327, 330 top, 330 right, 332 bottom, 334, 339 bottom, 342, 343, 344, 345, 349 left
Paul Fender: 36
Dave Forshaw: 67 right
Granada Television: 59, 130
Nigel Greenberg: 76 right
Maurice Haigh: 96
Richard Hale: 294 left, 295
Heswall and Neston News and Advertiser: 19 right, 27 top right
Hong Kong Tiger Standard: 162
Home Counties Newspapers: 140 bottom
David Hughes/Mark Lewisohn collection: 13 bottom
Hulton-Deutsch Collection: 9 top right, 22 right, 22 left, 89 bottom, 100, 131 left, 132 top left, 135 right, 136 right, 137 top, 142 bottom, 143, 159, 161 left, 167 left, 169, 188, 232, 237 bottom, 252 bottom, 261, 263, 266 bottom, 277 top, 279, 298, 305 bottom, 317, 318
Inverness Courier: 27
The Japan Times: 211 right
Peter Kaye: 62 bottom
Leslie Kearney/Mark Lewisohn collection: 15 left, 58 top right

Jon Keeble: 131 right
Allan Kozinn: 145 top right, 216 top left
Richard Langham: 123
Richard Lester: 137 bottom, 190 top
Liverpool Echo: 15 right, 16 top, 41, 42, 43, 49, 63 right, 64 right, 75 bottom, 81 right, 163 bottom right, 197, 213 left, 230 left
Liverpool Weekly News: 52 right, 58 left
London Features International: 9 top left, centre and centre right, 11 top, 110 bottom, 145 top, 145 bottom right, 156 bottom, 178, 179 top right, 183 top
Linda McCartney: 314 top, 324, 329 bottom, 330 bottom,
The Maidenhead Advertiser: 193 right
Manchester Evening News: 17 top
The Manila Chronicle: 212
Albert Marrion/Mark Lewisohn collection: 37 bottom, 52 left
Dick Matthews: 34, 44, 45 top, 50 top, 50 bottom left
The Melbourne Age: 163 left
Mersey Beat: 55 centre
Graham Moyle: 163 top right
New Musical Express: 225 top, 238 bottom, 275 right
Staffan Olander: 126 top
Peterborough Standard: 85
Phillips: 39, 51, 80 right, 88
Radio Times: 239 top, 268 top
Record Retailer/Spotlight Publications: 60, 61 bottom right
Relay Photos: 264 right, 276 right, 339 top
The *Reporter* Group (South Lancashire Newspapers): 101
Rex Features: 2, 3 all pictures, 11 top centre, 124 bottom, 181, 214 right
Geoff Rhind: 14 right
Rhyl Journal and Advertiser: 73
Richmond, Twickenham and Barnes Herald: 189
Charles Roberts: 14 right
The San Francisco Chronicle: 201 right
The San Francisco Examiner: 140 top left
Scope Features: 114 top, 165 bottom, 166, 187,
Keith Sluchansky at Revolver: 48 left, 145 centre left, 167 right, 182 left, 182 centre, 201 top left, 227 top, 229
David J Smith: 24 left, 32 bottom
Somerset County Gazette: 265 bottom right
Sotheby's: 18, 23, 24 right, 25, 28 bottom, 29, 31 top, 31 bottom right, 35 bottom right, 37 top, 48 right, 56, 57, 65, 69 left, 69 right, 71 right, 88, 89 top, 116, 132 top right, 136 left, 154 right, 220, 237 right, 286 left, 332 top
Southport Visiter: 64 left
Stroud News and Journal: 68
Times Newspapers: 122, 127 bottom
TV Times: 127 top
Don Valentine: 82
Victoria and Albert Theatre Museum: 108 bottom
Wallasey News: 20, 27 bottom right, 28 top
West Derby Reporter: 16 top
The West London Observer: 155 right
Yorkshire Evening Post: 114 bottom

Other illustrations courtesy Mark Lewisohn, with grateful thanks to Apple Corps Ltd for their assistance in providing a number of the pictures used in this book.

Every effort has been made to acknowledge correctly and contact the source and/or copyright holder of each illustration, and Pyramid apologises for any unintentional errors or omissions, which will be corrected in future editions of this book.

CONTENTS

FOREWORD

Normally I do not wallow in nostalgia; life is too short to keep looking back. But a recent reappraisal of old Beatles masters at Abbey Road has enabled me to delve into the past without too much of a guilt complex. I have listened again to the original tapes that we made all those years ago. Can it really be 30 years since I introduced the Fab Four to the strange and wonderful world of recording at EMI Studios in London? Even in 1962 they were experienced performers, although their genius for creating brilliant music and songs had yet to emerge. Certainly they were no strangers to hard work, and the years that followed saw them plunge into a whirlwind of concerts, broadcasts, feature-films, TV appearances, press conferences and photo calls that would have broken lesser men. Make no mistake about their lives then; there was little glamour in their goldfish bowl, and far too many demands were made on them.

As one of those behind the scenes urging them on, I had to stake my claim on their time for recording, which they fortunately enjoyed. In the studio their inventiveness and quest for new sounds is well known. They were quick learners, and in no time the master found himself becoming the student. Once the studio became their priority – from 1966 on – their horizons were limitless. Always curious, they insisted on finding new sounds and newer ways of achieving them.

Of course, there were moments when I could cheerfully have strangled one or other of them, and no doubt the feeling sometimes was reciprocated, but my enduring memory of those times is the enormous fun it all was. We really did not think about material success and the fortunes that they were earning. Our only consideration was to achieve the very best that we could, and we were completely united in that aim. If I inwardly believed we were developing an art form that would last for decades I kept it to myself. The value of what we were doing was never discussed. But we all knew that something really worthwhile was emerging.

Of all the chroniclers who have studied the lives of John, Paul, George and Ringo, Mark Lewisohn stands supreme. His dedication in getting all the true facts and cataloguing them, coupled with a style of writing that is most readable, leaves him with no rival. Time and again he has proven that he knows far more about what we did and when we did it than any of us. His book on the Beatles' recording sessions is an authoritative journal that I find invaluable. So many other books have been written about the lives of the Beatles that are less than truthful and a great deal of misinformed rubbish has been avidly devoured. We are fortunate to have Mark's scholarship. We need have no fears about his latest work, *The Complete Beatles Chronicle*; it will be as accurate as it is detailed.

GEORGE MARTIN

INTRODUCTION

During a recent visit to the United States I was struck by just how much the Beatles have become a part of everyday popular culture. Barely a few hours went by without their name coming up in the news, in a film or television script, in advertisements, in conversation or, more obliquely, via some quote or headline (so and so "has got his ticket to ride"; will this or that country "give peace a chance"?). Although perhaps less so, the same can also be said for Britain, my home country. As a group they split up more than 20 years ago but interest in the Beatles remains remarkably high and their image and music continue to illustrate not only the 1960s but the latter half of the 20th century.

Of course, no one could possibly have predicted this – least of all the Beatles themselves who, as this book shows, began humbly and never aspired to be the world leaders and mighty voice they became. Their talent and personalities took them right to the top, though, and now their place in history is not only assured but already a fact: pick up any modern encyclopedia or reference book and you'll find a potted history of the Beatles.

Strangely for such a recent event, however, the story of the Beatles' career is frequently mis-reported, with errors of all kinds creeping in and distorting the truth. In 1979, with a vague plan of sifting fact from fiction, I set about establishing a complete list of the group's live appearances, from the Quarry Men skiffle era of the late 1950s through to 1966, when the Beatles stopped giving concerts. To my surprise there was no existing catalogue and no short cut: the research took seven long years and the result was published in 1986 as the book *The Beatles Live!*

Soon afterwards I received the invitation of a lifetime from EMI Records: to be the only person outside of the Beatles, George Martin and a handful of studio staff to go into Abbey Road and listen to the company's entire collection of Beatles recording session tapes, then to interview virtually everyone involved in their making and write a book about it all, published in 1988 as *The Complete Beatles Recording Sessions*. No one was more astonished than me to see it enter the best-seller lists and shift something over 150,000 copies. I should have remembered the power of the Beatles.

Shortly before publication of *Recording Sessions* the *Live!* book went out-of-print and no copies were around to meet renewed demand. While I was considering a reprint edition it was suggested that I combine the live performance material with a condensed version of *Recording Sessions* and all-new research and text covering the Beatles' work in radio, television, film and video.

This is that book. It's called *The Complete Beatles Chronicle* because that's what it is: a complete, chronological summary of the group's entire *oeuvre* – their live performances from 1957, their sessions and other recording studio activities, their appearances on the small and large screen and on radio. I'm happy to report that the *Live!* and *Recording Sessions* aspects of the story incorporate all of the relevant new information that came to light following those previous publications, helping to make the account as accurate as possible.

So watch those videos, play those discs, read the book and savour the experience, once again, of a 20th century phenomenon that we now know will run and run and run.

Mark Lewisohn
Hertfordshire,
England,
December 1991

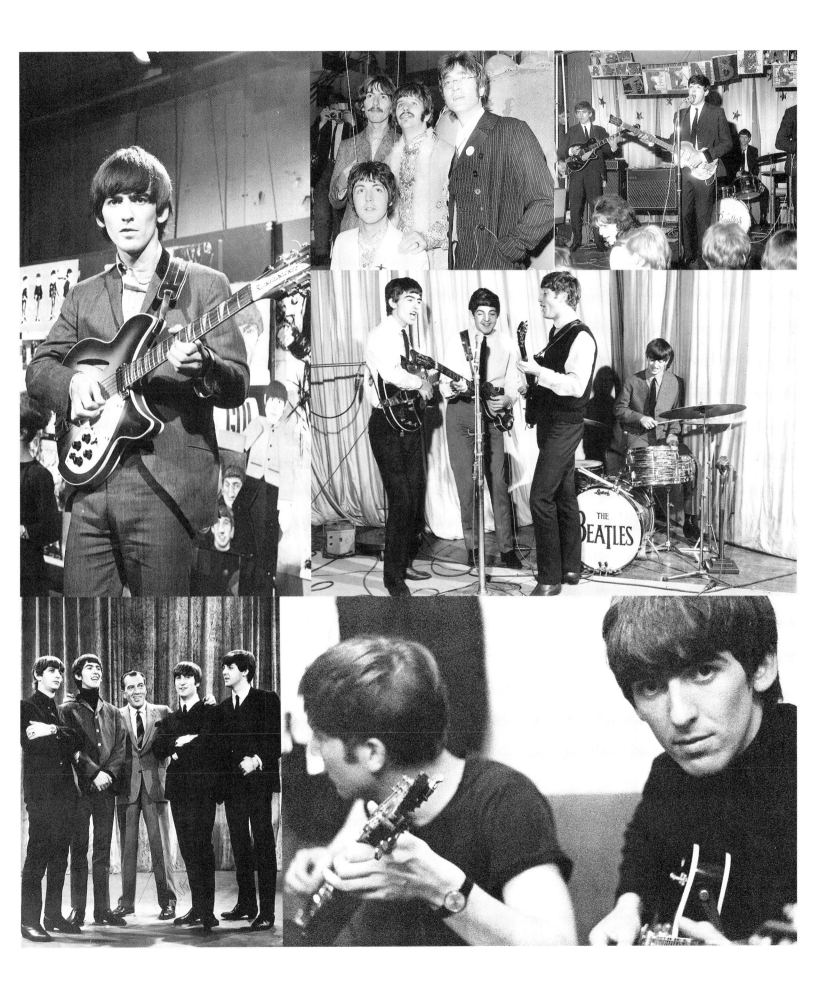

G U I D A N C E   N O T E S

A live performance before a paying audience. It is important to recognise that few such performances until 1963, and not even all of them in that year, could be classified as concerts. In those pre-discotheque days the Beatles were mostly booked to provide music for dancing, and to entertain, in ballrooms or other venues without seating.

A Beatles recording session, or recording audition, or an occasion when an overdub was taped onto one of their recordings, although perhaps without their personal involvement.

A mix session, in which a Beatles recording was mixed down from a multi-track tape to a two-track, quarter-inch tape whether for reference purposes or the cutting of acetate discs or mastering. (See also adjacent note.)

An engagement for the purposes of a radio broadcast, either live or recorded for subsequent transmission.

An engagement for the purposes of a television broadcast, either live or filmed/taped for subsequent transmission.

A formal rehearsal with a TV crew which takes place on a day different from the actual filming/taping/live transmission. Rehearsals taking place immediately before filming/taping/live transmission are *not* subjected to a separate symbol.

An activity expressly connected with filming or video-taping – either the actual shooting or post-production work – that leads to a short or feature-film, promotional video/film clip, or an independently made film/video for subsequent television broadcast, but *not*, however, filming expressly for or by a TV company. (Example: filming of *The Beatles At Shea Stadium* and *Magical Mystery Tour* is shown with the clapperboard symbol; filming by the BBC for its documentary *The Mersey Sound* is denoted by a TV symbol.)

AN IMPORTANT NOTE
ABOUT MIXING

Despite the thoroughness with which staff noted the details of the Beatles' work at EMI Studios, there is no possible means of proving the participation, or lack of it, of the group in their mixing sessions. Generally, it is true that the Beatles attended few mix sessions during their early years at EMI, from 1962 through to and including, say, mid-1965. Indeed, engagements elsewhere often prevented their direct involvement even if they desired it. George Martin and his balance engineer, or just the latter, would be left alone to oversee this important element in the recording process.

From mid-1965, and especially from 1966, however, through to 1970, the Beatles took a much greater personal interest in mix sessions. Even still, one cannot say for certain which ones they attended (or which of the group was present) and which sessions they were content to leave solely in the hands of the EMI balance engineers and George Martin. During the production of *Sgt Pepper's Lonely Hearts Club Band*, for example, the Beatles are said to have taken a hands-on approach with the mono mixing yet left the task of stereo mixing almost entirely to others.

Because of the importance of this ill-defined area this book will detail most mixing sessions with the appropriate symbol and address, *assuming* the presence of one or more of the group.

Only where their non-involvement is beyond doubt – if they were known to be elsewhere at the time, for example – will the symbol and address not show at the head of a diary entry.

In October 1962, when the Beatles first appeared on television, 15 programme companies comprised Britain's Independent Television (ITV) network, the commercial rival to the BBC. These companies had then, and have still, a three-fold purpose: to provide programming for the region in which they are based; to also make programmes suitable for broadcast in other regions; and, similarly, to broadcast the best non-local programmes made by other companies.

So, some Beatles' appearances on ITV were broadcast only by the local company concerned; some were broadcast by that company and also, perhaps, by a few surrounding companies; others were "networked" – that is, fed to all (or virtually all) of the 14 other ITV companies for nationwide transmission. Even with this latter situation, however, the different companies may have broadcast a particular programme at different times, perhaps even on a different day from each other. For all of the Beatles' ITV appearances, this book gives a specific transmission date and start/finish time – it should be recognised by the reader that these could vary from region to region. Usually, the timings local to the relevant ITV production company are shown; for networked programmes the book gives London-area timings.

OTHER POINTS

Many of the Beatles' live appearances, principally those from 1964, were illegally recorded by spectators on basic (amateur) portable equipment, leading to a proliferation of illegal "bootleg" records in the 1970s and beyond. To a much lesser degree a few were filmed in this manner, too. This book details only *legal* activities.

In the realm of radio and television, this book includes everything the Beatles did except for a) news broadcasts, b) press conferences, and c) material for origination outside of Britain except in special circumstances. For example, the Beatles' principal activities in the USA are always noted, in full. The book does not, however, because no book possibly could, track down and report full recording/transmission details for the hundreds of other, minor interviews they gave to local stations across that or any other continent.

The full postal address of every live appearance venue, radio, TV or film studio, and any other relevant location, is shown on the first occasion it arises in the book, written as it was written at the time. Subsequently, abbreviations are used. To avoid unnecessary and unsightly repetition in the early stages of the book, the county in which Liverpool was geographically located in those years, Lancashire, is not listed where it should be shown.

In the realm of recording activities, this book details everything done by any of the Beatles up to April 1970 except for involvement as a guest musician/producer/adviser on other artist's material. It should also be recognised that the group members often taped song material away from the recording studio – at home, in hotel rooms, etc – and that as no details, specifically dates, are available for this type of private material, they do not show in the book.

Country · Western · Rock 'n' Roll · Skiffle

The Quarry Men

LEOSDENE.
VALE ROAD, WOOLTON,   OPEN FOR ENGAGEMENTS
LIVERPOOL.

ROCK 'N' ROLL   SKIFFLE

The Quarry Men

OPEN FOR ENGAGEMENTS   MANAGER
                           GATEACRE 1715

Two different examples of the Quarry Men's visiting card, as distributed among club proprietors in the hope of a booking. The address/phone number belonged to occasional bass player and "manager" Nigel Whalley.

WHEN 24-year-old Lonnie Donegan burst into the limelight in January 1956 he could scarcely have imagined the dramatic and spiralling effect he would have on British youth and culture. After all, his version of the old Huddie (Leadbelly) Ledbetter song 'Rock Island Line' was not that different from the original, aeons-old black blues version. And besides, even his recording was already 18-months-old.

And yet this very record, credited to the Lonnie Donegan Skiffle Group, started a craze among teenagers, predominantly male, that swept through Britain in 1956 and 1957. Skiffle wasn't really new at all, since its roots were embedded in the negro jazz and folk music of the 1920s American Depression. Even in Britain, Ken Colyer had incorporated a special skiffle section within his jazz band as early as 1949.

But what made skiffle so attractive to British teenagers was not its history but its very structure – it was basic and easy to play. Anyone, without even much imagination, talent or money, could form a group. All one needed was a cheap (often Spanish) acoustic guitar, a household washboard and, an inspirational invention, the tea-chest bass. This was a crude copy of a stand-up bass, made by poking a broom-handle through a hole in an upturned tea-chest and tensing a piece of cord to form a sounding string. More instruments could be added if one was particularly flush with money – a banjo, or a set of drums, perhaps – but these were superfluous to the core of the group.

It would not be an exaggeration to say that in the wake of Donegan's success – and, though to a lesser degree, the knock-on success of others like Tommy Steele, the Vipers, Chas McDevitt and Nancy Whiskey, and Johnny Duncan – there were upwards of 5000 skiffle combos in existence around Britain during 1956 and 1957. In Liverpool alone there were, quite literally, several hundred.

John Winston Lennon, a bright but unruly 16-year-old living in Woolton, a comfortable village bordering Liverpool city centre, had been particularly smitten with "teenagers' music" since May 1956, when he had been overawed by the power and grace of Elvis Presley's 'Heartbreak Hotel'. In March 1957, having finally persuaded his guardian, Aunt Mimi, to buy him a £17 guitar, he decided to form a skiffle group. Fun and laughter were their chief aims, with the prospect of subsequent money and fame, although not entirely unconsidered, by no means the overriding concern.

For their first week, Lennon named the group – comprising at this point just himself and his crony Pete Shotton – the Black Jacks, but since they both attended the Quarry Bank High School for Boys, and its school song contained the line "Quarry Men, strong before our birth", it was decided that they should re-name themselves the Quarry Men instead.

Band members quickly joined and just as quickly departed; to compile a full personnel list would be impossible since some lasted for just one rehearsal or performance, and the line-up was in a continual state of flux. Certainly John and Pete's Quarry Bank classmate Bill Smith was the first new member, playing tea-chest bass. Other early personnel included Rod Davis (banjo), Eric Griffiths (guitar), Len Garry, Ivan Vaughan and Nigel Whalley (more bassists) and Colin Hanton (drums). John Lennon was guitarist and, since it was his group, the vocalist, while Pete Shotton briefly played the washboard. Undocumented early engagements consisted mainly of friends' parties and the ten-a-penny skiffle contests which sprang up at almost every dance hall or ballroom during the boom months. They even entered a talent contest run by "Mr Star-Maker" Carroll Levis, at Liverpool Empire Theatre, but failed miserably, not even passing the initial audition.

On Saturday 6 July 1957, while they were playing at the summer fête of St Peter's Parish Church in Woolton – a booking secured by Pete Shotton's mother – the Quarry Men were watched by a chubby 15-year-old lad from nearby Allerton, James Paul McCartney. On that day the seed of a partnership that would rock the entertainment world was sown: John Lennon and Paul McCartney.

Having been brought up in a musical family – his father Jim had led a local combo, Jim Mac's Jazz Band, in the early 1920s – Paul initially learnt the trumpet and piano, but then he saw Lonnie Donegan perform in concert at the Liverpool Empire on 11 November 1956 and became besotted with the guitar. He was evidently a quick learner for – after the Quarry Men had come off the outdoor stage that day at the fête and were setting up for the post-fête evening dance in the church hall – Paul grabbed a guitar and displayed to them his versions of Eddie Cochran's recently released 'Twenty Flight Rock' and Gene Vincent's 'Be-Bop-A-Lula'. Both were great favourites of John's but he was unable to remember the lyrics and would often resort to making up his own. Recalling lyrics was one of Paul's strong points and he obligingly jotted them down and handed them to the young Lennon. As if this wasn't impressive enough, Paul then showed John and Eric Griffiths his most recent accomplishment, the art of tuning a guitar. Unable to do this, the two guitarists had been taking their instruments to a man in Kings Drive, Woolton, who did it for them for a small fee.

After Paul had cycled home John was left to make a tough decision. Should he strengthen and improve the group, his group, by inviting this comparatively talented new boy to join up – thus challenging his own undoubted superiority – or should he let the group plough on into probable oblivion without him, but with his own supremacy intact? After careful consideration he chose the first option.

Two weeks later, Pete Shotton chanced upon Paul McCartney while cycling in Woolton, and on behalf of John and the group invited him to join up. Paul thought for a while and agreed that, yes, he would. But although he rehearsed with them regularly thereafter he didn't make his public début with the Quarry Men until Friday 18 October 1957 at the New Clubmoor Hall (Conservative Club). He missed the group's first-ever engagement at the Cavern Club on 7 August because he was away at scout camp in the Peak District village of Hathersage with his brother Michael.

Paul's arrival in the Quarry Men coincided not only with the death throes of skiffle, which departed almost as suddenly as it had (seemingly) arrived, but also with the career embarkation of several Quarry Men. While John had left Quarry Bank school for Liverpool College of Art, and so was free to continue much as before, other group members began to drift into full-time employment. By early 1958 the group was down to a hard core of just five – John, Paul, Len Garry, Eric Griffiths and Colin Hanton – although they were occasionally supplemented by others, like pianist John Lowe, nicknamed "Duff".

In March 1958 Paul wrote a letter to a family contact, Mike Robbins, employed at a Butlin's holiday camp, asking for work for the group during the school summer holiday. It was signed on behalf of himself, John and Len Garry – Hanton and Griffiths clearly having no intention of giving up jobs for such an engagement. Although the request wasn't successful, the letter also mentioned a young guitarist they had recently met. His name was George Harrison.

George was even younger than his school buddy Paul McCartney, having just turned 15. So despite his keen ability as a guitarist – formed after hours of finger-tearing graft – John, in particular, felt that George was little more than a child, their two-and-a-half-year age gap being a veritable chasm in one's early teens. But George was persistent, following the group around a couple of party engagements and eventually ingratiating himself sufficiently to become a fully-fledged member of the Quarry Men.

Despite their newly strengthened line-up, bookings became sparse throughout the remainder of 1958 and all of 1959, and their only engagements were at private parties. It was around this time that John and Paul began to write songs together, filling a school exercise book with uncomplicated tunes like 'I Lost My Little Girl', 'That's My Woman', 'Thinking Of Linking' , 'Years Roll Along', 'Keep Looking That Way', 'Just Fun' and 'Too Bad About Sorrows', as well as instrumentals like 'Looking Glass' and 'Winston's Walk'. Several songs from this early period were later to emerge: 'Love Me Do', 'The One After 909', 'Hello Little Girl', 'When I'm Sixty-Four', 'Hot As Sun', 'Catswalk' and others.

The Quarry Men even made a demonstration record in mid-1958, recorded in the back room of a house at 53 Kensington, Liverpool, owned by an old gentleman named Percy Phillips. The lads – John, Paul, George and John Lowe; Colin Hanton did not participate – cobbled together 17s 6d (87½p) and made a two-sided shellac disc. John sang lead on both recordings: on the top side they taped Buddy Holly's 'That'll Be The Day' and on the other performed a Harrison-McCartney composition, 'In Spite Of All The Danger', sung

in late-1950s "doo-wop" style. On another occasion, the Quarry Men tried to court fame via the world of the small screen, auditioning for ABC Television at their studios in Didsbury, Manchester, but failing.

By early 1959 the group was drifting, aimlessly. Drummer Colin Hanton had a furious row with the other three after an engagement in Prescot – the night had turned into drunken chaos when there was a slim chance that a good performance might impress the manager of a local cinema and provide them interval bookings. On the way home, still in an alcoholic haze, Hanton – inexplicably, though somehow symbolically – hauled himself and his drums off the bus before his usual stop. He neither saw nor heard from the Quarry Men again. Even George Harrison began to play with other groups, particularly with the Les Stewart Quartet, and for several months in 1959 the Quarry Men seem to have ceased existence altogether. But on 29 August fate intervened.

The Les Stewart Quartet had been promised an engagement at the opening night of a new youth venue, the Casbah Coffee Club, located in the cellar of a large Victorian house in the West Derby district of Liverpool. On the day of the opening, Stewart and Ken Brown, the Quartet's bass player, had a fierce argument which ended with Stewart walking out, vowing never to return. In desperation, Brown asked George if he knew of any mates who could help out. George rounded up Paul and John, and the Quarry Men played at the Casbah that night and every Saturday night thereafter.

They had been rescued from the brink of oblivion, and Brown was invited to become a part of the revitalised Quarry Men. He was to last no more than six weeks, however, quitting when a row developed after a Casbah appearance, probably on 10 October 1959, when he was suffering from a heavy cold and couldn't perform. At the end of the evening, when club owner Mona Best gave Brown his 15 shilling (75p) share of the group's customary £3 fee, Paul could see no earthly reason why Brown should receive the dividend if he hadn't played. After a brief discussion, John, Paul and George closed ranks and walked out on him and the club.

Although the Casbah engagements had dried up, the trio felt sufficiently buoyed to have another crack at Carroll Levis's talent contest, temporarily ditching the Quarry Men moniker in favour of Johnny and the Moondogs. They successfully came through two Liverpool auditions and were invited to contest a further heat in Manchester – success there would guarantee them a two-minute spot on Levis's ATV show *Discoveries*. But although George was in proper employment (as an electrician), John and Paul were still at school and had no money. So having got to Manchester and performed on stage, when the evening ran over time they simply couldn't afford to stay in town for the night. Before the audience came to vote for the winning act (measured by the volume of their applause), Johnny and the Moondogs were halfway back to Liverpool aboard the last train.

Their one chance of success dashed, the future of the group looked particularly bleak at the end of 1959. But though they certainly couldn't have known it, the embryo Beatles had reached the end of the first phase of their long and arduous apprenticeship. The tough times were by no means over but from 1960 they were never to look back.

The Quarry Men at the Casbah Coffee Club in September 1959: George, Paul, Ken Brown, John. "The rhythm's in the guitars," they would respond when asked why they had no drummer.

Sunday 9 June

Empire Theatre, Lime St, Liverpool

This local qualifying audition for "Mr Star-Maker", Carroll Levis, marked the first official engagement of the Quarry Men. Levis ran these "TV Star Search" shows all over Britain, providing not only low-budget theatre entertainment (grateful for the opportunity, artists did not generally receive a fee) but also a steady source of acts for his season of television shows on ATV: ventriloquists, budgerigars, jugglers, musical-saw players and, especially in 1957, skiffle hopefuls.

The Quarry Men did not even qualify from this 3.00 pm preliminary audition, won by the Sunnyside Skiffle Group, a Speke combo which featured a 19-year-old 4ft 6in Nicky Cuff on vocals and tea-chest bass. Literally, because Cuff stood on the tea-chest while playing it.

The twice-nightly finals were held at the Empire, without the Quarry Men, between 17 and 23 June.

Right: this is how Paul McCartney first saw John Lennon: the Quarry Men performing at Woolton Parish Church Fête, 6 July 1957, a photo taken by Quarry Bank schoolboy Geoff Rhind and reproduced here from the original negative. L to R: Eric Griffiths, Colin Hanton, Rod Davis, John, Pete Shotton, Len Garry.

Saturday 22 June

Rosebery St, Liverpool

An unusual engagement, even by Quarry Men standards, playing from the back of a stationary coal lorry in the afternoon and evening during street celebrations for the 750th anniversary of King John issuing a Royal Charter "inviting settlers to take up burgages or building plots in Liverpool, and promising them all the privileges enjoyed by free boroughs on the sea".

The party was a typical community effort. Mrs Marjorie Roberts, at number 84, was principal organiser, and her son Charles, who was a friend of Colin Hanton (it was Roberts who designed the group's logo on Hanton's bass drum), invited the Quarry Men along to play, although they did not live locally. The lorry from which they played was supplied by the man at number 76, who also ran the microphone lead through his front-room window.

The only blemish on the occasion was when a group of louts from neighbouring Hatherley Street threatened to beat up the group, and in particular "that Lennon", so as soon as their spot finished the musicians wasted little time in diving for the sanctuary of Mrs Roberts' house, where she served them tea until the danger had passed.

The *Liverpool Post and Echo* newspaper group awarded Rosebery Street the prize for the best-decorated street outside of the city centre, so the residents celebrated with a second party, at which the more prestigious Merseysippi Jazz Band performed. The Quarry Men were not invited back.

Saturday 6 July

Garden Fête, St Peter's Church, Church Rd, Woolton, Liverpool

A truly historic date.

The Quarry Men played during the afternoon on a makeshift stage in the field behind the church, and also – with the exception of Colin Hanton – at the evening dance in the church hall over the road (commencing at 8.00 pm, admission two shillings [10p]), alternating with the more traditional George Edwards Band. It was while the Quarry Men were setting up their instruments in the hall during the early evening that occasional tea-chest bass Quarry Man Ivan Vaughan introduced to John and the others his classmate from Liverpool Institute, 15-year-old Paul McCartney.

PROGRAMME

STALLS — SIDESHOWS — ICE CREAM — LEMONADE

Teas and Refreshments in large Marquee situated behind the hut.

2-00 p.m. PROCESSION leaves Church Road, via Allerton Road, Kings Drive, Hunt's Cross Avenue; returning to the Church Field. Led by the Band of the Cheshire Yeomanry. Street Collection by the Youth Club during the procession.

3-00 p.m. CROWNING OF THE ROSE QUEEN (Miss Sally Wright) by Mrs. THELWALL JONES.

3-10 p.m. FANCY DRESS PARADE.
Class 1. Under 7 years.
Class 2. 7 to 12 years.
Class 3. Over 12 years.
Entrants to report to Miss P. Fuller at the Church Hall before the procession.

3-30 p.m. MUSICAL SELECTIONS by the Band of the
to Cheshire (Earl of Chester) Yeomanry. Band-
5-00 p.m. master: H. Abraham.
(By permission of Lt.-Col. G. C. V. Churton, M.C., M.B.E.).

4-15 p.m. THE QUARRY MEN SKIFFLE GROUP

5-15 p.m. DISPLAY by the City of Liverpool Police Dogs. By kind permission of the Chief Constable and Watch Committee.

5-45 p.m. THE QUARRY MEN SKIFFLE GROUP

8-0 p.m. *GRAND DANCE in the CHURCH HALL*
GEORGE EDWARDS BAND also *The Quarry Men Skiffle Group*
TICKETS 2/-
REFRESHMENTS AT MODERATE PRICES.

Wednesday 7 August

Cavern Club, Mathew St, Liverpool

The Cavern Club, named after Le Caveau Français Jazz Club in Paris, had been officially opened by the Earl of Wharncliffe on Wednesday 16 January 1957. The owner,

Alan Sytner, was the son of a doctor who played at the same golf club, Lee Park, as Nigel Whalley, who was now an apprentice golf professional. Via this labyrinthine route, the Quarry Men booking was made. Despite being a jazz venue, skiffle, with its jazz origins, was just about acceptable in the Cavern Club, although rarely as anything more than an interval attraction. But having performed the most acceptable 'Come Go With Me', John Lennon's brash attempt to follow with Elvis Presley's 'Hound Dog' and 'Blue Suede Shoes' was met with much disdain by the Quarry Men's folk purist Rod Davis, and also by Alan Sytner who promptly dispatched a terse note to the stage, "Cut out the bloody rock!" Paul McCartney did not play with the Quarry Men on this occasion because he was away at scout camp.

Friday 18 October

New Clubmoor Hall (Conservative Club)

(Back) Broadway, Norris Green, Liverpool

In addition to his "strict tempo" evenings, south Liverpool dance promoter Charlie McBain – known as Charlie Mac – ran regular rock and skiffle nights at his venues, including Wilson Hall, Garston; the Garston Swimming Baths (known locally as the Blood Baths because of the fierce gang fights which took place there); Holyoake Hall, Wavertree; and Wavertree Town Hall. This one, at the Conservative Club's New Clubmoor Hall in Norris Green, marked the début of Paul McCartney with John Lennon and the Quarry Men.

Playing lead guitar on this one occasion, Paul's first-night nerves proved insurmountable and he made an unqualified

abortion of his solo during a version of Arthur Smith's 1946 hit 'Guitar Boogie'.

McBain's only recorded comment on the Quarry Men this evening was an ambiguous "Good & Bad", scribbled in pencil on their visiting card.

Thursday 7 November

Wilson Hall, Speke Rd, Garston, Liverpool

The first of four known Quarry Men performances at this rough, tough venue, built by Francis Wilson opposite the Garston bus depot. Charlie Mac ran "Rhythm Nights" here every Thursday.

Saturday 16 November

Stanley Abattoir Social Club, East Prescot Rd,

Old Swan, Liverpool

Undoubtedly the most peculiar Quarry Men engagement of all: a dance for the social club members of the massive Stanley Abattoir. Various slaughter-house personnel, meat porters and their wives, saw two – allegedly cacophonous – sets by the combo either side of an interval. They were not re-booked.

Saturday 23 November

New Clubmoor Hall, Norris Green, Liverpool

A return visit to the Conservative Club.

The Quarry Men skiffling at New Clubmoor Hall, 23 November 1957. L to R: Colin Hanton, Paul McCartney, Len Garry, John Lennon, Eric Griffiths, all resplendent in bootlace ties.

DECEMBER

Saturday 7 December

Wilson Hall, Garston, Liverpool

A slightly more prestigious Saturday-night booking.

WILSON HALL (Opposite Garston Bus Depot).
To-night Rockers, Quarrymen Before 8. 2/6
Saturday. Always Gay. 4/- before 8.20 3/-
CARNIVAL NEXT WEEK CARNIVAL

Friday 10 January 1958

New Clubmoor Hall, Norris Green, Liverpool

The Quarry Men were originally booked for a dance the previous night at Wilson Hall, Garston, but promoter Charlie McBain switched the engagement.

Friday 24 January

Cavern Club, Liverpool

Thursday 6 February

Wilson Hall, Garston, Liverpool

This date almost certainly marked the first meeting of 14-year-old George Harrison with the Quarry Men. George

KASBAH HAS A NEW MEANING FOR LOCAL TEENAGERS

"Come with me to the Kasbah," is a sentence familiar to Charles Boyer fans, but for teenagers in West Derby it has taken on a new meaning.

The Kasbah is a club which was opened recently by an enterprising mother, Mrs. Mona Best, Haymans Green, West Derby, in the cellars of her home.

"The house was like a railway station," Mrs. Best told the Reporter, "then my sons had the idea of turning the cellars into a 'den' for their friends. They began by papering the walls, but of course with it being a cellar it wouldn't stay up, so they became downhearted."

Mrs. Best decided that the job should be done properly so, after a conference with 18-years-old Peter. Rory (aged 15) and some of their friends, they decided to form a club. For two months Mrs Best helped the boys to paint the walls and stain the boards that now give the club its Eastern atmosphere. Their pride and joy is a large dragon which is painted along the length of one wall.

GUITAR GROUP

Three of the boys, Kenneth Brown, 149, Storrington Avenue, Norris Green, David Hughes, 119, Blackmoor Drive, West Derby, and Douglas Jenkins, 28, Cottesbrook Road, Norris Green, went to the cellars from their jobs each evening and helped with the conversion at weekends.

Kenneth Brown is also a member of a guitar group which entertains the club members on Saturday nights. The other members of the group, who call themselves "The Quarrymen," travel from the south end of the city to play. They are: John Lennon, Menlove Avenue, Woolton, Paul McCartney, Forthlin Road, Allerton, and George Harrison, Upton Green, Speke. During the week members take their own records or play those provided by Mrs Best. There is even room for the energetic who wish to dance.

The club has only been open a few weeks but already membership has exceeded 280. "I enjoy having them here," said Mrs. Best And although her husband was sceptic about the idea at first he now admits that it is a great success.

MISSIONARY WORK

The speaker at last week's meeting of the Church of the Good Shepherd Mothers Union. West Derby, was Miss J. Troughton, who took as her subject "Missionary work."

Two of the teenagers chat with Rory Best. (B1563/1)

Three "cool cats" listen to "The Quarrymen." (B1565)

himself remembers seeing them for the first time at this venue although drummer Colin Hanton recalls that George was introduced to them one night at the Morgue Skiffle Cellar (see 13 March), and George's mother remembered that they met in a local chip shop. Pete Shotton (who had long since left the Quarry Men) reckons that the lads, led by George's school friend Paul McCartney, made their way over to the Harrisons' council house at 25 Upton Green, Speke, and met him there.

Thursday 13 March

The Morgue Skiffle Cellar, 'Balgownie', Oakhill Park, Broadgreen, Liverpool

The opening night of a club run by 18-year-old Alan Caldwell who had his own group, Al Caldwell's Texans (with, from 25 March 1959, Ringo Starr on drums). Caldwell later took the stage name Rory Storm, and his Texans became the Hurricanes.

Several local groups, including the Texans and the Quarry Men, played from 7.30 on the opening night of this aptly named club, situated in the cellar of an enormous Victorian house at 25 Oakhill Park, latterly a home for retired nurses. It held 100 people and had no facilities. A single bare, blue bulb and one white fluorescent strip light provided the only source of illumination, and one electric fan supplied the only "fresh" air.

Not surprisingly, because of the illegality and danger in holding meetings in such an apparently decrepit environment, its existence was short-lived. On 1 April police halted the proceedings and on 22 April the venue closed for ever. Club nights at the Morgue cellar took place on Tuesdays and Thursdays, though no records exist to indicate which groups played when. One can safely assume, though, that the Quarry Men attended on at least a handful of occasions.

Saturday 20 December

Upton Green, Speke, Liverpool

If regular, paid, bookings had dried up, the Quarry Men could always be called upon to provide free and willing entertainment at family functions. Between 1957 and 1959 they played at several such affairs, although only one date – this, at the wedding reception of George Harrison's brother Harry, and his bride Irene McCann, at the Harrison household, can be positively researched.

Thursday 1 January 1959

Wilson Hall, Garston, Liverpool

Not a Charlie McBain promotion but the rather belated Christmas 1958 party of the Speke Bus Depot Social Club. Harry Harrison, George's father, was chairman of the club, hence the booking of the Quarry Men for this afternoon affair. Fortunately, the lads were all on school holidays so there was no need for truancy.

Saturday 24 January

Woolton Village Club, Allerton Rd, Woolton, Liverpool

Yet another, even later, Christmas party. Chosen because of their local availability, the Quarry Men played a ten-minute selection of skiffle numbers.

Saturday 29 August

**Casbah Coffee Club, Hayman's Green,
West Derby, Liverpool**

The opening night of a new teenagers' social club in the extensive cellars of a large Victorian house at 8 Hayman's Green, owned by Mrs Mona Best. The Quarry Men played at the Casbah Coffee Club every Saturday night from 29 August until, probably, 10 October, when they had the disagreement with Ken Brown (see Introduction) – a total of seven engagements in all. They were not to play the club again until – as the Beatles – they returned from Hamburg on 17 December 1960.

Saturday 5 September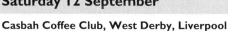

Casbah Coffee Club, West Derby, Liverpool

Saturday 12 September

Casbah Coffee Club, West Derby, Liverpool

Saturday 19 September

Casbah Coffee Club, West Derby, Liverpool

Saturday 26 September

Casbah Coffee Club, West Derby, Liverpool

Saturday 3 October

Casbah Coffee Club, West Derby, Liverpool

Saturday 10 October

Casbah Coffee Club, West Derby, Liverpool

Sundays 11, 18 or 25 October

Empire Theatre, Liverpool

More than two years after the Quarry Men's dismal 1957 failure, the group – John, Paul and George but not Ken Brown, who had left after the disagreement at the Casbah Coffee Club – again performed an audition for "Mr Star-Maker", Carroll Levis, re-christening themselves Johnny and the Moondogs especially for the event.

Preliminary qualification rounds took place on these three consecutive Sundays, although the Moondogs would have appeared only once, probably on 18 October. One qualifier from the 11 October audition was Jett (later Rory) Storm and the Hurricanes with Ringo Starr on drums.

This time John Lennon and his friends were more successful, and they qualified for the finals.

Monday 26 – Saturday 31 October

Empire Theatre, Liverpool

The local finals of the Carroll Levis "TV Star Search" were held throughout the week at the Empire, and Johnny and the Moondogs appeared on at least two occasions (precise dates not known). They did not win the contest (that prize went to a group called the Connaughts, ironically the same combo, albeit with a new name, as the 1957 winners, the Sunnyside Skiffle Group, with Nicky Cuff) but were placed sufficiently high to qualify for the final hurdle of auditions, to be held at the Hippodrome Theatre in Manchester. Qualification from that would guarantee the trio a brief spot on Levis's ATV show, with resultant "fame" surely just around the corner.

Sunday 15 November

**Hippodrome Theatre, Hyde Rd, Ardwick Green,
Ardwick, Manchester, Lancashire**

The final round of Levis's north-west "TV Star Search" for 1959, marking the first non-Merseyside appearance of the group later to become the Beatles.

Although they put in a reasonable performance, the actual judging of the contest was based mostly on the strength of audience applause after a brief on-stage reappearance by each act in the finale. Unfortunately, this took place very late in the evening and the three Liverpool lads, with drastically insufficient funds to stay in town overnight, were long gone – along with their chance of fame – back to Merseyside by the time the MC came to announce their turn.

IF, **FOR** the three members of the Quarry Men, 1960 started with the same mood of despondency evident at the end of 1959, it certainly ended with their career at its highest point so far. The 12 months of 1960 saw many major career developments: the invention and employment of the names the Beatals, Silver Beats, Silver Beetles, Silver Beatles, and eventually – by the middle of August – Beatles; it saw the group's first tour, their first fully-professional engagements, their first and probably most beneficial trip to Hamburg, the realisation that they might be able to eke a living from rock music, and the first, embryonic, Beatlemania, three years before Britain and the rest of the world caught on.

The man responsible for many of these occurrences was 29-year-old Allan Williams, a stockily-built opportunist who, from May 1960 until April 1961, became the group's occasional booking agent and quasi-manager. Williams ran the Jacaranda, a small coffee bar typical of the era, at 23 Slater Street in the centre of Liverpool. The Quarry Men could often be found there, idling away their lunch hours and evenings and, in true coffee-bar style, making a single sixpenny espresso last at least two hours.

In January 1960 the Quarry Men's ranks had been swollen to four by yet another guitarist, John's close friend from art college, Stuart Fergusson Victor Sutcliffe. A brilliant and original artist, the 19-year-old Scottish-born Sutcliffe held no musical ambition or talent but saw the life of a musician as a vital counterpoint to his brooding artistic persona. Between 17 November 1959 and 17 January 1960 the second biennial John Moores Exhibition had taken place at the illustrious Walker Art Gallery in Liverpool, and one of Sutcliffe's canvases had been selected to hang. Indeed, Moores himself was so impressed with the work that at the end of the two-month exhibition he bought the painting for £65, a huge sum of money – then as now – to an art student struggling along on a meagre grant. But instead of ploughing the money back into his artistic career, as his parents wished, Sutcliffe – with a great deal of enthusiastic encouragement from John Lennon – bought himself a Hofner President bass guitar and joined the Quarry Men. He was never to learn beyond the basic, rudimentary skills, however, so would often stand with his back to the audience, hiding his inadequacy.

INTRODUCTION

1960

AND DIARY

During the week of 14–20 March 1960, Eddie Cochran and Gene Vincent spearheaded a pop package show at the Liverpool Empire, promoted by the top pop impresario in Britain, Larry Parnes. It was a huge success and Allan Williams, to use his own words, "could smell money... lots of it". After the shows Williams wrote and then telephoned Parnes and arranged for the two headlining stars and some of the support artists to return to Liverpool on 3 May for a joint Parnes-Williams one-night promotion at Liverpool Stadium, a boxing and wrestling venue in Bixteth Street, behind the city's Exchange Station. On the extensive bill were Cochran, Vincent, Davy Jones (not the Monkee-to-be but a black American rock and roll singer), the Viscounts, Colin Green and the Beat Boys (including Georgie Fame), Peter Wynne, Lance Fortune and Nero and his Gladiators, plus Liverpool groups Cass and the Cassanovas (Cassanovas deliberately mis-spelt after the name of the group's leader, Brian Cassar) and Rory Storm and the Hurricanes.

Tickets began to sell and all was running smoothly when tragedy struck. On Sunday 17 April, bound for London Airport from a concert in Bristol, Cochran was killed in a road crash just outside of Chippenham, Wiltshire. Already deformed from a motor-cycle accident in his youth, Vincent suffered additional injury, including a broken collar-bone. The Liverpool concert was just 16 days away but Parnes wouldn't speak of cancellation. Instead, upon receiving word from Parnes that Vincent would still be able to fulfil the engagement, Williams set about padding the already crowded bill even further with two other Parnes artists – Julian 'X' and Dean Webb – and more local acts: Gerry and the Pacemakers, Wallasey group Bob Evans and his Five Shillings, Mal Perry, and the Connaughts.

The Quarry Men, now re-named Beatals by Stuart Sutcliffe in honour of Buddy Holly's Crickets, were drummerless as usual so were not invited to play, although they did attend the show, sitting in the audience amid scenes of mayhem which were a foretaste of the years to come. At this time the only occasion Williams had engaged the group was to decorate the ladies' lavatory at the Jacaranda Coffee Bar.

Parnes was impressed by the prowess of the Merseyside rock and rollers and realised that he had stumbled upon a large array of untapped talent. Back at the Jacaranda after the show he explained to Williams that he needed groups to back his "stable" of solo singers on tour, all of whom he had re-christened with tempestuous stage names: Billy Fury, Duffy Power, Tommy Steele, Dickie Pride, Georgie Fame, Johnny Gentle, Nelson Keene, Lance Fortune, Marty Wilde and Vince Eager. Fury, in particular, was on the eve of a nationwide tour and was in desperate need of a backing group, so it was arranged that exactly one week later Parnes would return to Liverpool with Fury and audition a few hopefuls.

The vital changeover from Quarry Men to Beatals is captured in this richly worded early-1960 letter drafted, as "manager", by Stuart Sutcliffe.

Allan Williams

Dear Sir, As it is your policy to present entertainment to the habitués of your establishment, I would like to draw your attention to a band the Star "Beatals". This is a promising group of young musicians who play all music for all tastes, preferably rock and roll. They have won many competitions, including Carroll Levis' and auditions for A.T.V. Unfortunately pedagogical activities have hindered them from devoting full themselves full time to the world of entertainment.

I hope you find time if necessary the group will give you an groups prepared for an audition, I hope you will be able to engage them.

Yours sincerely
Stu Sutcliffe (Manager).

Sometime during that week, around Thursday 5 May, acting on advice from Brian Cassar, Williams secured the Beatals a drummer, Tommy Moore. He was considerably older than the others, but a drummer was a drummer, they reasoned, so he was welcomed into the group. Cassar also declared, in rather earthy terms, that the name Beatals was "ridiculous". He suggested they call themselves Long John and the Silver Beetles, and although John Lennon refused to be called Long John, for want of anything better they stuck with the name the Silver Beetles.

The audition before Parnes and Fury was held between 10.30 am and 4.30 pm on Tuesday 10 May at the Wyvern Social Club, 108 Seel Street, in premises newly acquired by Allan Williams for a night club he was to call the Blue Angel. Several of Liverpool's top beat groups turned out to perform before the star and The Big Man From London, among them Cass and the Cassanovas, Derry and the Seniors, Gerry and the Pacemakers, and Cliff Roberts and the Rockers. The Silver Beetles were there too, more or less making up the numbers, or so it was thought. But when their turn came to play they were missing Tommy Moore, who was somewhere across town collecting his drum equipment from a club, so Johnny Hutchinson, the burly drummer from the Cassanovas, sat in with them until Moore appeared halfway through their ten-minute, four-song audition.

Precisely what happened next is in doubt. According to Williams, Parnes and Fury both loved the Silver Beetles but were put off by Stuart Sutcliffe's awkward back-turned fumblings on bass; he says that Parnes' attempt to prise Stuart out of the group by dangling the offer of the tour before the four remaining members was met by a flat and loyal refusal. Parnes himself remembered nothing of the sort, only that he was slightly discouraged by the sight of Tommy Moore, who arrived late and flustered.

A backing group for Billy Fury was not found that day, but Parnes did offer to use two of Williams' groups to support other, less important, artists on ballroom tours of north-east England and Scotland. The Silver Beetles were the first in line and on Wednesday 18 May they gratefully accepted a nine-day seven-engagement Scottish tour backing 20-year-old Liverpudlian and one-time apprentice carpenter Johnny Gentle, at £18 per man per week, part-expenses paid. They had just two days to prepare and certainly didn't bother to inform promoter Brian Kelly of their unavailability for a Saturday-night booking he'd generously given them, at Lathom Hall in Seaforth. Hurriedly, George and Tommy Moore arranged time off work, Paul persuaded his father that the rest away from home would make it easier to revise for his forthcoming A-level exams, and John and Stuart cut college.

Before setting out for this first-ever tour, three of the Silver Beetles decided to adopt stage names. Paul became Paul Ramon, George became Carl Harrison (after American rockabilly musician Carl Perkins) and Stuart became Stuart de Stael (after the Russian artist Nicholas de Stael). So, with visions of their name in lights, money, fame, and girls chasing them, the group set out from Liverpool Lime Street station for Alloa.

In reality, the tour was not only dismally disappointing but it was poorly planned. After Alloa, the other six dates were scheduled along the north-east coast, from Inverness to Peterhead, a distance of 112 miles. But Parnes and his Scottish intermediary, an elderly chicken farmer from Dumfries named Duncan McKinnon, arranged the dates without much care for geography and the group spent the week unnecessarily ferrying back and forth along the

The Silver Beetles auditioning for Larry Parnes and Billy Fury, 10 May 1960. Note Stuart Sutcliffe's side-on stance and the apparent boredom of guest drummer Johnny Hutchinson, filling in for the yet-to-arrive Tommy Moore.

Johnny Gentle on stage in Alloa, backed by the Silver Beetles. He had evidently bought or borrowed a pair of their matching shoes.

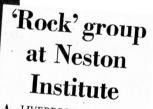

'Rock' group at Neston Institute

A LIVERPOOL rhythm group "The Beatles," made their debut at Neston Institute on Thursday night when north-west promoter, Mr. Les Dodd, presented three and a half hours of rock 'n' roll.

The five strong group, which has been pulling in capacity houses on Merseyside, comprises three guitars, bass and drums.

John Lennon, the leader, plays one of the three rhythm guitars, the other guitarists being Paul Ramon and Carl Harrison. Stuart Da Stael plays the bass, and the drummer is Thomas Moore. They all sing, either together, or as soloists.

Recently they returned from a Scottish tour, starring Johnny Gentle, and are looking forward to a return visit in a months time.

Among the theatres they have played at are the Hippodrome, Manchester; the Empire, Liverpool and the Pavilion, Aintree.

Highland roads, clocking up 300 miles. On 23 May Johnny Gentle himself was driving the van from Inverness across to Fraserburgh, relieving the regular driver, Gerry Scott, who wanted a rest. Tired, and perhaps a little the worse for alcohol, Gentle drove straight into the rear of a stationary Ford Popular at a crossroads outside of Banff. Although two old women who were sitting in the car were badly shaken, and Gentle later received an endorsement on his licence, the worst casualty was Tommy Moore, who felt the full impact of a flying guitar in his face. That evening, as he lay sedated in hospital, concussed and without several front teeth, the manager of the Dalrymple Hall in Fraserburgh, led by John Lennon, arrived at Moore's side, hauled him out of bed and insisted that he take his place on stage behind the drum kit.

As the week dragged on so the tour disintegrated. In the claustrophobic van, tempers easily frayed, especially those of Tommy and Stuart who were both on the receiving end of John's unceasingly acerbic and often downright nasty wit. To make matters worse, funds were running out fast. Meals became infrequent, and cadged from anyone foolish enough to admit to having money. Larry Parnes recalled receiving a frantic reverse-charges telephone call from John – "Where's the bloody money?" – on 23 May, just three days after they'd been paid. On one occasion, the group slipped out of an hotel, the Royal Station in Forres, without settling their bill.

The Silver Beetles arrived back in Liverpool on 29 May, bedraggled, poor, hungry and desperately disappointed, though certainly a little wiser about the "glamorous" rock and roll business. For a while there remained a notion that they would return to Scotland in mid-July to back Dickie Pride around the same north-east ballroom circuit, but this failed to materialise. Happily, while they were away, Williams had secured them their first fully professional local engagements at £10 a time (£2 each) with Les Dodd, a Wallasey promoter. Dodd ran dances at the Grosvenor Ballroom in Liscard, Wallasey and at the Institute Hall in Neston, venues renowned more for violence than for entertainment. On one evening in Neston a boy was almost kicked to death while the Beatles were playing on stage.

In return for a Coca-Cola and beans on toast – but no money – Williams also allowed the group to play on Monday nights in the tiny downstairs area at the Jacaranda Coffee Bar, when his resident four-man Royal Caribbean Steel Band had their night off. The cellar had no microphone stands so girlfriends had to sit at the feet of the group holding upside-down broomsticks and mops with microphones crudely tied to the tops. It was on one of these occasions, probably 13 June, that Tommy Moore played his last date with the group. Under constant but undoubtedly valid criticism from his girlfriend for wasting his time with the group when he could be out earning proper money, he had also endured far more of John Lennon than he could stand.

Moore intended to leave the Silver Beetles in the lurch after their 9 June date at Neston Institute, and so failed to turn up at the Jacaranda Coffee Bar on 11 June, as arranged, before setting out for a date at the Grosvenor Ballroom in Wallasey. The group piled into Williams' car and screeched their way around to Moore's house in Fern Grove, Toxteth, only to find his girlfriend leaning out of an upstairs window shouting, "You can go and piss off! He's not playing with you any more; he's got a job at Garston bottle works on the night shift!" Off they sped to the Window Lane works, to find a sullen Moore in white overalls, perched high aboard a forklift truck.

Despite the group's pleas, Moore wouldn't climb down so the group had to go on at the Grosvenor with a drum kit but no drummer. To assuage the ballroom's tough patrons, known to launch into unbridled attack for lesser cause than a group without a drummer, John stepped up to the microphone, smilingly explained the situation and rhetorically enquired if someone in the audience could help out. The joke misfired disastrously when a huge hulking Teddy boy called Ronnie, who led the local gang but had patently never been within a hundred yards of a drum kit in his life, clambered up on to the stage and sat, beaming at his new-found mates, from behind Moore's precious hire-purchase kit. A frantic though surreptitious interval phone call from John brought Williams back across to the Grosvenor and somehow he managed to extricate the group and their equipment from the alarming predicament before ruthless Ronnie "volunteered" to join up on a permanent basis – or else.

With Moore's brief membership over, the group were back in their familiar drummerless state. For a short while they continued without one, although they were ever careful not to lumber themselves with another Ronnie episode. But apart from a season of Saturday-night dates at the Grosvenor Ballroom, no one else would book them.

Around this time, probably in early July, Williams provided the now re-named Silver Beatles with their oddest engagement. Along with a West Indian gentleman known as Lord Woodbine, so nicknamed because of the cigarette always dangling from his lower lip, Williams opened up an illegal strip club, the New Cabaret Artistes, in the dingy cellar of a terraced Victorian house at 174a Upper Parliament Street, Liverpool 8, the so-called "vice" area of the city, where brothels and shebeens operated under cover of darkness.

One particular week, Williams was sent "Janice", who was quite spectacularly endowed in the bust department. Janice promised to bring in good business but, she insisted to Williams, would strip only if backed by a live band. Records, she made sadly clear, were inappropriate.

Since Janice was certain to send Williams' profits booming he reluctantly agreed, and – because they were the only group without daytime jobs – approached the Silver Beatles. At first they flatly refused, but the eventual promise of ten shillings (50p) per man per night proved irresistible and they accepted. So for one week, four Silver Beatles – all with guitars and amplifiers – and Janice, crowded onto a stage just seven-feet square and performed their act before assorted groaning men in grimy raincoats. The stripper carefully gave her backing group printed sheet music of Beethoven and Khachaturian but that was futile because they couldn't read notation. So instead they played old standards like 'Harry Lime (*Third Man* Theme)', 'Summertime', 'Moonglow And The Theme From *Picnic*', 'September Song', 'It's A Long Way To Tipperary' and 'Begin The Beguine'. It was, quite simply, the nadir of their career.

Shortly after the strip club débâcle, the group acquired another drummer, Norman Chapman. A picture-framer and renovator by trade, Chapman's interest in drums was purely a hobby, and he used to practise on a hire-purchase kit kept in an office in Slater Street, virtually opposite the Jacaranda. One summer evening, as dusk was slowly falling, Williams and the Silver Beatles heard the sound of Chapman's drumming drifting through the streets and were so impressed that they set about trying to trace its source. It took some time but eventually they found Chapman and offered him the vacant drummer's position in the group. He accepted, but fulfilled no more than three Saturday engagements with them at the Grosvenor Ballroom before he was conscripted for two years' national service in Kenya and Kuwait – his career with the Silver Beatles at an end.

In late June, unbeknown to Allan Williams, his resident Royal Caribbean Steel Band were lured away, kettle drums and all, to a dockside club in Hamburg by a visiting West German businessman. Feeling no remorse over their moonlight flit, one or two members of the band guilelessly wrote back to Williams exclaiming about the high life, the fast money and the even faster women to be found in Hamburg, particularly on the notorious and wickedly naughty Reeperbahn, the city's red-light area. "Why don't you come over," they wrote, "have a look, and maybe bring some groups to play?" So Williams, ever on the look-out for an enterprising scheme, made the journey across together with the ennobled Lord Woodbine and a party of local businessmen out for a dirty weekend, flying to Amsterdam on a rickety Dakota plane chartered by Williams. Rather characteristically, the duo then donned top hats as they wended their tired and emotional way by rail on to Hamburg.

Before they had left Liverpool, Williams had invited the Silver Beatles, Gerry and the Pacemakers, Cass and the Cassanovas, the Spinners folk group, and Noel Walker's Stompers (a local trad jazz outfit) to record some songs onto a tape which he would use to try to sell their music. But when he produced the 7½ ips, two-track reel midway through his hard-sell act before Bruno Koschmider, the owner of a Grosse Freiheit night club called the Kaiserkeller, the only sound to emanate from it was unintelligible gibberish. Somehow, somewhere along Allan Williams' eventful plane and train journey across Europe, the tape had become demagnetised.

Williams returned to Liverpool downhearted, his plan of exporting rock groups to Hamburg in tatters. But fate intervened, in the shape of Larry Parnes. The London impresario had promised Williams that he could provide a group or two with work, backing his singers during summer seasons at Blackpool and Great Yarmouth. With this offer in mind, the members of Derry and the Seniors had quit their jobs. Then,

out of the blue, Parnes wrote cancelling the engagement. The group were livid, and their saxophonist, a large youth named Howie Casey, was threatening extensive bodily damage to lots of people, most especially to Parnes. Out of sheer desperation, Williams put the group in his van and took them down to the Two I's Coffee Bar in London, the Soho venue where Tommy Steele and others had been discovered. The Two I's was managed by Tommy Littlewood, an acquaintance of Williams's, so upon their arrival at the club he was happy to allow the Liverpool group onto his famous stage to run through a set. By sheer, remarkable coincidence, sitting in the club at that precise moment, quietly sipping coffee, was Bruno Koschmider, owner of the Kaiserkeller in far-off Hamburg.

Koschmider had been impressed by Williams' visit to him a few weeks earlier, boasting that his groups were the best in the world and playing garbled tapes. So when he didn't hear from him again he decided to take a trip to England to see these wonder groups for himself, heading, not unnaturally, for London, the pop music capital, instead of Liverpool. As Koschmider was unable to speak English, one Herr Steiner – an Austrian – was fetched from the next door coffee bar, the Heaven and Hell, to act as translator. Through the mouthpiece, a booking for the evidently impressive Derry and the Seniors was drawn up there and then, with Koschmider offering 30DM (Deutsche Marks) each man per day. This was 24 July. By 31 July the boys were on stage at the Kaiserkeller.

Like the Royal Caribbean Steel Band before them, Derry and the Seniors wrote back exuberant and enthusiastic letters to Williams. After just two days Koschmider wrote too. Business at the Kaiserkeller was booming and he intended to open a second music venue nearby, the Indra, presently a strip club. Could Williams send across a second group? Williams could, but wasn't sure whom. Mindful of the Silver Beatles' drummerless state he thought first of Rory Storm and the Hurricanes, but they were midway through a summer season at Butlin's in Pwllheli, north Wales. And Cass and the Cassanovas were still up in Scotland backing Duffy Power. Williams then offered the opportunity to Gerry and the Pacemakers but they weren't keen on the idea, although they were to go a few months later. Reluctantly, Williams concluded that the Silver Beatles would have to go, but only – he insisted – if they first found themselves a drummer. Williams wrote Derry and the Seniors a courtesy letter informing them of the Silver Beatles' impending arrival, and Howie Casey – with signatures from all the Seniors except Derry Wilkie – wasted little time in returning a none-too-subtle howl of protest, adding that it would spoil the scene for everyone if he sent over such a bum group.

It just so happened that on 6 August 1960 the Silver Beatles' regular Saturday-night engagement at the Grosvenor Ballroom in Liscard was cancelled by the Wallasey Corporation, finally bowing to protests from local residents about the deplorable noise and hooliganism from the more vociferous members of the ballroom's teenage clientele. At a loss for somewhere to play, the four guitar players trooped over to the West Derby area of the city and presented themselves at the Casbah Coffee Club, a place

1960

they hadn't visited for some months. They found the venue thriving and a quartet called the Blackjacks in residence. Guitarist in the group was none other than Ken Brown who, less than a year previously, had been dumped from the Quarry Men over the £3 booking-fee squabble. And on drums, sitting proudly behind his gleaming new kit, was 18-year-old Randolph Peter Best, known to all as Pete, the son of club owner Mona Best. The other members of the Blackjacks were Chas Newby and Bill Barlow. A shy boy, Pete had just left the Collegiate grammar school and was planning a full-time, professional career as a drummer, although with whom he wasn't too sure since the Blackjacks were on the verge of breaking up, its members having reached that age where careers beckon greater than playing "silly music". Brown, for example, moved down to London that summer and was never heard from again. Newby, after taking a job in Harlow, Essex, returned north to pursue a course of further education at a college in St Helens.

Shrewdly eyeing the imminently unemployed drummer and, moreover, his beautiful new kit, and mindful of the Hamburg opportunity, the Silver Beatles swiftly offered Pete the chance to join their group. On Friday 12 August, after a simple and almost superfluous audition at the Wyvern Social Club which he could hardly have failed to pass (the group, after all, did not want him to fail), Pete was in and Hamburg was beckoning.

Four days later, on 16 August, after hastily arranging passports and visas, though conveniently forgetting to apply for time-consuming work permits (this was left to Koschmider, who also "forgot"), the five Silver Beatles, now re-named simply the Beatles, along with their equipment, Allan Williams and his wife Beryl, her brother Barry Chang, and Lord Woodbine, set out in Williams' green Austin van for Hamburg. After stopping briefly in London to pick up yet another passenger, the interpreting Herr Steiner from the Heaven and Hell, they sauntered onward to Harwich and caught the ferry over to the Hook of Holland. From there the

overcrowded van slowly but surely made its way across country and over the border into West Germany.

They pulled into Hamburg at dusk on 17 August, the time when the red-light area comes to life. On both sides of the Grosse Freiheit, even over their heads, flashing neon lights screamed out the various entertainments on offer, while scantily clad women sat unabashed in shop windows waiting for business opportunities to arise. At the Kaiserkeller, Derry and the Seniors were about to go on stage for the night and gave the Beatles a decidedly cool reception, scarcely masking their disapproval.

But whereas the Kaiserkeller, at 36 Grosse Freiheit, was a fairly plush night spot, with an unusual nautical theme and good lighting, the Indra – along the strasse at 58 – where the Beatles were to play, was quite the opposite. Koschmider had clearly spent little or no money adapting the tatty strip club into a bar for music and dancing. The place was small, poky and threadbare, and it still boasted typical strip club décor, with its tiny stage, heavy drapes, carpeted floors and small tables with little red lampshades. The Beatles' living quarters were to prove even gloomier: on their second day in Hamburg – they spent the first night in Bruno Koschmider's flat – he took them to a grubby little cinema he also owned, the Bambi-Filmkunsttheater at 33 Paul-Roosen Strasse. Unaware of quite why they were being led around a deserted cinema which showed old American westerns, the Beatles blithely followed Koschmider to a small, filthy room behind the yellowing screen. "This," he explained through the interpreter amid the noise of gun-totin' heroes and wagon trails, "is where you will sleep. And there," he said, pointing back behind him to the cinema toilet, "is where you may wash." It was of only little consolation to the Beatles to discover later that, despite the Kaiserkeller's comparative luxury as a club, even Derry and the Seniors were having to endure similarly awful living conditions.

Before the Beatles went on stage at the Indra one trifling business matter had to be concluded – a contract. It was drawn up to run for two months, from 17 August to 16 October, at 30DM (£2.50) per musician per day, payable every Thursday. In addition to this, Koschmider was to deposit a weekly German equivalent of £10 agents' commission in Williams' newly-opened account with the Commerzbank in St Pauli, Hamburg. In return, the Beatles would play for four-and-a-half hours every weekday night

(8.00–9.30, 10.00–11.00, 11.30–12.30, 1.00–2.00) and for six hours a night on Saturdays (7.00–8.30, 9.00–10.00, 10.30–11.30, 12.00–1.00, 1.30–3.00) and Sundays (5.00–6.00, 6.30–7.30, 8.00–9.00, 9.30–10.30, 11.00–12.00, 12.30–1.30). An additional clause, part of "the small print", forbade the group from playing at any other place of entertainment within a radius of 25 miles (40 kilometres) unless they had the written consent of Bruno Koschmider's *Betriebe* (agency).

When the five Beatles eventually took to the stage in Hamburg on 17 August, without much food or sleep since leaving Liverpool the previous day, they were so exhausted that they could barely move. Just a handful of customers turned up. And it wasn't too long before trouble reared its head in the shape of an old woman who lived in a flat above the club. She was prepared to put up with striptease beneath her but not noisy rock and roll music. She complained to Koschmider and she complained to the police. Their solution, to decrease the volume of the Beatles' already feeble and battered amplifiers, was a disaster: 'Long Tall Sally' wasn't written to be whispered. On 4 October, just 48 nights after Koschmider had opened the Indra to beat music, he closed it down and moved the Beatles on to the bustling Kaiserkeller.

The only problem the Beatles faced at the Kaiserkeller was caused by the huge, though rotting, stage. Aside from John, Paul and George's four five-minute Carroll Levis auditions in Liverpool and Manchester a year previously, the group had never played on such a large podium. It made the Indra's platform look like a matchbox by comparison. The Beatles' stage movements froze until, on 10 October, Allan Williams – who was making a return visit to Hamburg – could stand it no longer. "Make a show boys!" he exhorted. Koschmider and the Kaiserkeller club regulars soon took up the chant in their best pidgin-English. "Mach schau" they would shout whenever the group looked like flagging during the long nights.

The Beatles' reply to this encouragement was incredible, the four guitarists – though particularly John – launching into exaggerated contortions and writhings, strongly resembling Gene Vincent's genuinely crippled movements at Liverpool Stadium. Virtually overnight the Beatles began to go down very big with the rumbustious Hamburg club audiences. Very often a crate or two of beer, bought by customers, would be sent onto the stage for the group to drink while playing. Realising the criminal nature of many of the club regulars, the Beatles understood it was wise to oblige. One typical cry from a man in the audience might be "Two crates if you sing 'Hound Dog'!" The effect of the alcohol was devastating, especially when combined with the variety of multi-coloured pills the group – except Pete Best who never participated – were liberally swallowing to keep themselves awake and maintain energy during the long nights on stage. If the customers wanted the Beatles to "mach schau" there seemed no limit to which they wouldn't go to please. John was soon calling the audience "fucking nazis", wearing swastikas and performing Sieg Heils and goose-steps on stage – all illegal in Germany just 15 years after the war had ended.

On 2 October, Derry and the Seniors' contract with

The Beatles "mach schau" during an early appearance at the Top Ten Club.

Koschmider expired, and after hanging around town for a while they returned to England. In their place, on 1 October, came Rory Storm and the Hurricanes, fresh from their summer season at Butlin's. From 4 October the Beatles and Rory's group played welcome split shifts at the Kaiserkeller, and for a while the two groups enjoyed a fierce contest to see which of them would be the first to demolish the club's rotten and increasingly precarious stage. Eventually Rory managed it, executing an athletic leap and one final, deliberately heavy-footed landing during a performance of 'Blue Suede Shoes' . He was severely chastised by Koschmider and had 65DM docked from his wages to pay for the damage.

The Beatles made another amateur record in 1960. On Saturday 15 October, while Allan Williams was in Hamburg, they got together with two members of Rory Storm's Hurricanes, drummer Ringo Starr and singer/bass player Walter Eymond (stage name Lou Walters, nickname Wally), in a small studio, the Akustik, situated at 57 Kirchenallee, behind Hamburg's central railway station. Pete Best was not present so, excluding Eymond, for one brief moment John, Paul, George and Ringo were together for the first time. They recorded one song, a version of George Gershwin's 'Summertime', and it was cut onto a 78-rpm disc, the other side of which comprised a salesman's message about leather handbags and shoes. In all, nine discs were cut, only one of which is known to have survived the years.

On 16 October the Beatles' contract with Koschmider was extended until 31 December and there was even talk of the group moving on to West Berlin on 7 January 1961 for a month's work there. Then, at the end of October, a new club – the Top Ten – opened at 136 Reeperbahn, situated in the Hippodrome, a former sex-circus. The new owner, Peter Eckhorn, clearly intended to hit the Kaiserkeller and immediately wooed away Bruno Koschmider's chief bouncer – an absolute necessity in Hamburg's tough clubland – former boxing champion Horst Fascher, and contracted performer Tony Sheridan (born Anthony Esmond Sheridan McGinnity), an accomplished English singer/guitarist who had several British record releases and TV appearances to his credit. The Beatles held Sheridan in very high esteem and would often leave the Kaiserkeller during their half-hour breaks to nip across to the Top Ten. Naturally, it was only a matter of time before they were up on stage jamming with Sheridan and his London group, the Jets.

News of their defection soon reached Koschmider who, already livid with the Beatles and Rory Storm over the broken-stage incident, decided that enough was enough. Citing the clause in their agreement which stipulated that they could not play elsewhere within a radius of 25 miles without his permission, he handed the Beatles a month's termination of contract notice. Somehow, word also found its way to the police authorities that George Harrison was under 18 and, therefore, under West German law, was not allowed to stay, let alone work, in a night club after midnight.

The Beatles played out their notice period under a pall of gloom, while – on Monday 21 November – George was deported by the authorities for deliberately flouting the law. He returned home alone, a perilous 24-hour journey, spending all of his savings on train fares, porters' tips, and taxis. The remaining Beatles struggled on without him, spending only the barest minimum of time in the Kaiserkeller, preferring instead – whenever possible – to socialise and play their music at the Top Ten. Peter Eckhorn offered them bunk-bed accommodation in the attic above his club, not exactly luxurious accommodation but a five-star hotel compared to their atrocious quarters behind the screen at the Bambi-Filmkunsttheater.

One day at the end of November, probably around the 29th, Paul McCartney and Pete Best were back at the Bambi surreptitiously packing their belongings. The cinema was closed and in darkness and as there were no torches or candles the two Beatles fiendishly decided to set light to the rotting, peeling tapestry hanging from the wall, in order to see their way around. A dull glow soon appeared and Paul and Pete packed their clothes and left, deliberately ignoring, in their contempt for Koschmider, their makeshift lighting arrangement. The glowing cord was eventually extinguished by the dampness in the wall.

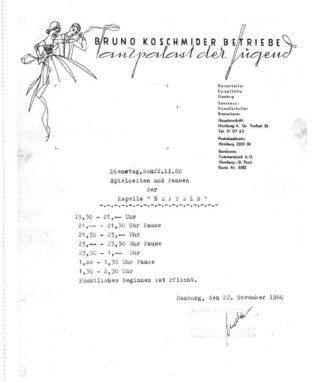

Within the hour, Koschmider received word that the two Beatles "had attempted to set fire to the Bambi" and he decided that it was a matter for the police. Paul was arrested and thrown into the jail at St Pauli police station on a charge of suspected arson, and very soon Pete Best was with him in the cell too. Both were held overnight and released the following morning. Feeling tired after their detention they went to their new lodgings above the Top Ten to sleep, but a few hours later, early in the afternoon, were awoken by a heavy banging on the door. When Pete Best sleepily slid back the bolt and opened the door he was greeted by two plain-clothes policemen. The two Beatles were ordered to dress without delay and were then bundled into a car and sped to the Hamburg *Kriminal* police headquarters where the officer in charge, Herr Gerkins, announced that they were being deported on a midnight airplane back to London. The police escorted Best and McCartney back to the Top Ten and gave them five minutes to re-pack their belongings. Pete had to leave his drums behind, Paul carried his guitar over his shoulder. Then it was back to the jail until nightfall and an escort to the airport. Bemused by the language difficulties, and therefore not entirely comprehending the situation, the two Beatles asked for permission to telephone the British Consul. This was refused, and a few hours later they were touching down at London Airport. They had just enough money for an early-morning bus to Euston Station and the train home to Liverpool. It was Thursday 1 December.

One other thing happened on 30 November before Best and McCartney were deported. The Beatles provisionally negotiated with Peter Eckhorn a one-month booking at the Top Ten Club for the following April, subject to the lifting of their various deportation bans. Allan Williams was unaware of these dealings, which would sever his link with the group.

Three of the five Beatles were now back in Britain, deported, and the West German police were soon after John Lennon and Stuart Sutcliffe too. On the morning of 10 December John voluntarily set out on the long train journey back to England, his precious amplifier strapped to his back in case someone tried to steal it. Stuart, meanwhile, had gone into temporary hiding, aided by a Hamburg girl named Astrid Kirchherr with whom he had fallen in love and become engaged. (An imaginative photographer, Astrid took some stunning shots of the Beatles during this visit and became a good friend to them all.) Stuart eventually flew home to Liverpool in late-February 1961.

For a short while George, Pete and Paul were unaware that John had also made it home. Indeed they didn't see or hear from him until 15 December. But once reunited, the group decided to try to find some local bookings, although their first priority, in Sutcliffe's absence, was to find a new bass player. Pete Best thought of the Blackjacks' bassist Ken Brown, but he was now living in London, and besides, the Beatles didn't want him back in the group after his short spell in the Quarry Men had ended in disharmony. Best then remembered Chas Newby, rhythm guitarist with the Blackjacks, and phoned him at his home in Everton. As it was mid-December Newby was on Christmas holiday from his college course and agreed to help out. Chas Newby shared two things in common with Paul McCartney: both were born on 18 June (Newby in 1941, McCartney in 1942) and both were left-handed. What Newby didn't have was a bass guitar and a leather jacket to match the Beatles' Hamburg uniform, but he borrowed both and joined up. However, he was to play only four dates with the group before returning to his college course early in January, and henceforth into obscurity.

On 17 December the five-man Beatles gave their first post-Hamburg performance, at the Casbah Coffee Club, and they played a return booking there on New Year's Eve. Meanwhile, on 19 December, Allan Williams booked the group into a Christmas Eve dance at their old stamping ground, the Grosvenor Ballroom in Wallasey. But it was on

27 December, at the Town Hall ballroom in Litherland, when it all came together, when the Beatles truly became rock and roll kingpins of Merseyside in one fell swoop.

The man responsible for getting them this date was Bob Wooler, a 28-year-old erudite figure who, until recently, had been a railway office clerk. He had resigned from his steady job to become disc-jockey and compere at a new, unlicensed cabaret-type venue opened by Allan Williams on Thursday 1 December: the Top Ten Club, situated at 100 Soho Street near the centre of Liverpool. Williams had evidently returned from Hamburg with grandiose ideas. Pop luminaries Terry Dene and Garry Mills were there for the opening week, supported by prominent local groups, and bookings for the following four weeks included Davy Jones, Danny Rivers, Michael Cox and Don Fox. But at 11.30 pm on Tuesday 6 December, just after the last customer had left, the club mysteriously burnt down, almost certainly – although nothing was proven – the result of arson.

Now out of work, Wooler was idling away time in the Jacaranda when he got talking to the Beatles. Could he find them any engagements they wondered? Wooler said yes, he would try to find them a date with promoter Brian Kelly, for whom he was an occasional compere. He telephoned Kelly then and there from the Jacaranda. Kelly was loath to book the Beatles again, remembering the occasion just seven months previously when they had let him down by dashing off to Scotland, unannounced, after he had given them a booking. Kelly was even more disgruntled when, through Wooler, the Beatles asked for an £8 fee. Kelly offered £4 and, after protracted haggling, they settled on £6. More than anything else, the booking was a special favour to Wooler since Kelly already had three groups engaged for the evening – the Del Renas, the Searchers, and the Deltones.

As the Beatles' addition to the night's fare was too late for Kelly to include their name in his standard advertisement in the *Bootle Times*, promotion of their appearance was restricted to routine stage announcements at Kelly's three other dances over the Christmas period – at Lathom Hall, Seaforth and at Alexandra Hall, Crosby – and on the hastily re-designed amateur posters which were now emblazoned with an extra legend, stuck on with flour and water: "Direct From Hamburg, The Beatles!" So few people in north Liverpool had heard of the group, bearing in mind that they had performed only once in the area up to that time (an unadvertised audition at Lathom Hall on 14 May), that most of the Litherland Town Hall clientele, upon looking at the poster, concluded that the Beatles were a German group.

As the curtains shuffled open and Paul launched himself into Little Richard's 'Long Tall Sally', everyone suddenly and spontaneously crushed forward to the front of the stage, swept away by the group's sheer magnetism. Five hundred hours on stage in Hamburg had forged the style that would conquer the world. The five-man Beatles – John, Paul, George, Chas Newby and Pete – were an absolute powerhouse, creating an inexplicable and unprecedented frenzy among the spellbound teenagers. As the Beatles blasted out their Hamburg night-club repertoire they too were bewildered by the incredible scene they were invoking. Beatlemania was enjoying its birth pangs.

The Beatles

SOLE DIRECTION:
A. WILLIAMS
TEL. ROYAL 7943

BOOKINGS:
TEL. STANLEY 1556

Saturday 23 April

The Fox and Hounds, Gosbrook Rd, Caversham, Berkshire

During the college/school Easter holidays, John and Paul took off for a short break in the south of England, staying for a few days with Paul's cousin Bett (Elizabeth) Robbins and her husband Mike, who had recently left their employment as Butlin's Redcoats and were the new tenants of the Fox and Hounds public house in Caversham.

In return for working behind the bar during the week, Mike Robbins gave John and Paul the opportunity to perform live on the Saturday night, calling them the Nerk Twins and drawing-up hand-made posters which he pinned to the saloon bar door.

The Nerk Twins played in the newly decorated taproom, perched high on two bar stools, acoustic guitars in hand, without microphones. Stuck for an opening song, Robbins suggested 'The World Is Waiting For The Sunrise', an old variety number, and Butlin's favourite, which John and Paul knew from the 1953 Les Paul and Mary Ford recording. Amid much laughter the Nerk Twins managed to struggle through and complete the song, before continuing with numbers in their more familiar C&W/rock vein.

Sunday 24 April

The Fox and Hounds, Caversham

Before setting off on the long trek north to Liverpool, the Nerk Twins made their second and last appearance during the Sunday lunchtime pub session, 12.00 noon to 2.00 pm.

Saturday 14 May

Lathom Hall, Lathom Ave, Seaforth, Liverpool

The Silver Beetles' (or Silver Beats as they were called on this one occasion) first proper engagement was for Crosby-based promoter Brian Kelly, who ran dances at forbidding-looking halls and institutes in north Liverpool. Kelly was one of the first to spot the surging beat boom on Merseyside, promoting his first live dance/jive session at the Savoy Hall in Bath Street, Waterloo on 11 May 1959, and quickly adding to his roster such illustrious venues as Lathom Hall, Seaforth; Town Hall, Litherland; the Institute, Aintree; and Alexandra Hall, Crosby.

The Silver Beats were not advertised for this date, which featured Cliff Roberts and the Rockers, the Deltones and King Size Taylor and the Dominoes, but played a few songs in the interval by way of an audition for Kelly. Two reports on how they fared differ enormously. One suggests that they were so bad that Kelly ordered them off stage after their second song. But the local *Bootle Times* newspaper reported that they were "sensational". The truth probably lies somewhere in between, although the group must have shown sufficient promise for Kelly to re-book them for the following Saturday's dance, 21 May, actually headlining over King Size Taylor.

For reasons that became apparent halfway through this week, however, the Silver Beats/Beetles were unable to fulfil the engagement. Rather typically, they omitted to inform Kelly of this, who had to face patrons without his advertised attraction.

Friday 20 May

Town Hall, Marshill, Alloa, Clackmannanshire

The first night of the Silver Beetles' tour backing Johnny Gentle. It was the only date fixed for the south of Scotland, the remaining six all taking place along the north-east coast, well into the Highlands. The Silver Beetles and Gentle had their first and only rehearsal – lasting just 30 minutes – before they took to the stage at the Town Hall this Friday evening.

Saturday 21 May

Northern Meeting Ballroom, Church St, Inverness, Inverness-shire

The Johnny Gentle troupe moved on 152 miles north to Inverness, "capital of the Highlands". As the travelling musicians were quickly discovering, the tour was by no means all they had envisaged. Indeed, on this occasion they had the ignominious task of playing in an upstairs hall while downstairs the more traditional Lindsay Ross Band kept the older townsfolk happy with old-tyme dancing.

And for this, the Silver Beetles had skipped their first-ever official, advertised engagement, back at Lathom Hall in Seaforth, Liverpool.

Monday 23 May

Dalrymple Hall, Seaforth St, Fraserburgh, Aberdeenshire

The first advertisement for a Beatles performance, billed here as the Silver Beats, 21 May 1960. But they were in Scotland and missed the show.

BEEKAY presents

JIVE AT LATHOM HALL

Every SATURDAY

THIS WEEK — SILVER BEATS, DOMINOES, DELTONES.
7-30 — 11-30.   Admission 4/-.   Members 3/6

FRIDAY TO-NIGHT — Transferred to ALEXANDRA HALL (L1, L3, L30 to door). 7-30—11 p.m. Admission 3/-

EVERY MONDAY 7-30 — 11 p.m.   Admission 2/6
THIS MONDAY — CLUBMEN

NORTHERN BORDER DANCES PROUDLY PRESENT

To-morrow (Saturday), 21st MAY, 7.30 to 11.30 p.m.

UPSTAIRS — Modern Dancing to **THE BEAT BALLAD SHOW** introducing another TV and Decca Recording Star, JOHNNY GENTLE and his Group, and RONNIE WATT and the CHEKKERS Rock Dance Band.

DOWNSTAIRS — Old tyme Dancing to **LINDSAY ROSS** and his Famous Broadcasting Band

ADMISSION - Before 8 p.m. 3/- After 8 p.m. 5/-
(Limited Numbers — Right of Admission Reserved)

Wednesday 25 May

St Thomas' Hall, Chapel St, Keith, Banffshire

Thursday 26 May

Town Hall, High St, Forres, Morayshire

Despite the fact that the Silver Beetles played here, the town may well be happier with its mention in Shakespeare's *Macbeth*.

Friday 27 May

Regal Ballroom, Leopold St, Nairn, Nairnshire

Saturday 28 May

Rescue Hall, Prince St, Peterhead, Aberdeenshire

The seventh and final date of the Johnny Gentle tour.

Monday 30 May

Jacaranda Coffee Bar, Slater St, Liverpool

The first of several Silver Beetles engagements at this city-centre venue owned by Allan Williams. When they weren't otherwise engaged the group played here on Mondays, when the club's resident Royal Caribbean Steel Band had their night off.

Note: a full listing of the Beatles' performances at this venue cannot be compiled since they were neither noted down nor advertised at the time. They probably numbered around 12.

Thursday 2 June

The Institute, Hinderton Rd, Neston, Wirral, Cheshire

The first of six consecutive Thursday-night engagements at this venue, situated on the west side of the Wirral, close to north Wales. Paramount Enterprises, alias promoter Les Dodd, had been running "strict tempo" evenings at this venue – and also at the Grosvenor Ballroom in Liscard, Wallasey – since 1936, but had, rather grudgingly, come to the conclusion that rock and roll/jive sessions were more lucrative. On this evening Dodd paid the Silver Beetles £10, out of which they gave £1 commission to Allan Williams.

Saturday 4 June

Grosvenor Ballroom, Grosvenor St, Liscard, Wallasey, Cheshire

Saturday night became "big beat" night at Les Dodd's other venue, the Grosvenor Ballroom. But while Dodd advertised for people to "see this new all-star outfit in a swing session", many local youths preferred to use the ballroom as a place to swing their fists. Bloody dance-floor skirmishes would be watched with horror by the Beatles, valiantly playing on despite the mêlée beneath them.

Monday 6 June

Grosvenor Ballroom, Liscard, Wallasey

To celebrate the Whitsun "bank holiday", Les Dodd presented a special Monday jive and rock session, booking the two groups who would eventually become Liverpool's most successful, the Silver Beetles and Gerry and the Pacemakers. This was the first of many occasions that they appeared together on a bill.

'ROCK' NIGHT IS THURSDAY

Cass and his Cassanovas, a rhythm group making a name for themselves in Neston, will be missing from the Thursday "rock" nights in the Institute for the next few weeks. They are going on tour with Billy Fury, one of the top teenage idols of the day.

In their place the teenagers—and older—of Neston and district will be able to dance to the music of the Silver Beetles. This new five-piece group has made a terrific impact on Merseyside, pulling in capacity houses wherever they appear.

North western promoter Mr. Les Dodd, of Paramount Enterprises, has satisfied a long felt need of the district by providing an evening of "rock and jazz" for the teenagers' enjoyment.

★

Big 'beat' night

Paramount Enterprises, in complete contrast to their Tuesday "Plus 21" Night, are presenting two of the star 'Rock' groups in the North West, at the Grosvenor Ballroom on Whit Monday.

Pride of place goes to the Silver Beetles, who are returning to Merseyside after a successful tour with Johnny Gentle. Supporting them on the same programme will be another new group to Wallasey —Gerry and the Pace-Makers. Both these groups are jive and rock specialists.

★

GROSVENOR BALLROOM

The Grosvenor Ballroom to-night introduces a new series of summer Saturday evening dances for youthful patrons, when the all-star outfit The Silver Beetles will be playing.

★

the unannounced arrival at the Grosvenor of Johnny Gentle, making the most of a rare weekend without engagements to return to his home in Litherland, north Liverpool. Keen to look up his recent backing group, Gentle and his father arrived at Allan Williams' Jacaranda Coffee Bar, was informed of the Silver Beetles' date in Liscard, and went across to surprise them. The reunion was a good one, with Gentle leaping up on stage to sing a few numbers.

Thursday 9 June

The Institute, Neston, Wirral

Saturday 11 June

Grosvenor Ballroom, Liscard, Wallasey

Almost certainly the night of the "Ronnie" episode (see Introduction).

Monday 13 June

Jacaranda Coffee Bar, Liverpool

After letting down the Silver Beetles on 11 June, Tommy Moore made one last appearance with the group on this occasion.

Thursday 16 June

The Institute, Neston, Wirral

Saturday 18 June

Grosvenor Ballroom, Liscard, Wallasey

The night of Paul's 18th birthday.

Thursday 23 June

The Institute, Neston, Wirral

Saturday 25 June

Grosvenor Ballroom, Liscard, Wallasey

Thursday 30 June

The Institute, Neston, Wirral

Saturday 2 July

Grosvenor Ballroom, Liscard, Wallasey

What looked like being just another run-of-the-mill Saturday-night performance was considerably brightened by

Thursday 7 July

The Institute, Neston, Wirral

Saturday 9 July

Grosvenor Ballroom, Liscard, Wallasey

Saturday 16 July

Grosvenor Ballroom, Liscard, Wallasey

Saturday 23 July

Grosvenor Ballroom, Liscard, Wallasey

Saturday 30 July

Grosvenor Ballroom, Liscard, Wallasey

The Silver Beatles' run of Saturday-night performances at the Grosvenor came to a grinding halt after this, the ninth occasion. By the end of July the violence and rowdiness before, during and after each dance had grown so bad that the local residents lodged a complaint with Grosvenor's lessors, the Wallasey Corporation, giving them little alternative but to cancel the season forthwith and resume "strict tempo" dances. (The Grosvenor did re-open for rock sessions later in the year but the Corporation itself assumed control of the proceedings, relieving, albeit temporarily, Les Dodd's Paramount Enterprises of the dubious – though certainly remunerative – pleasure.)

Wed 17 August – Mon 3 October

Indra Club, Grosse Freiheit, Hamburg,
West Germany

Forty-eight nights. The first 200-plus hours that the Beatles played in Hamburg, ending after a constant stream of noise complaints.

Tues 4 October – Wed 30 November

The Kaiserkeller, Grosse Freiheit, Hamburg,
West Germany

Fifty-eight nights. Unable to put them on at the Indra, Bruno Koschmider moved the Beatles into his other club, the Kaiserkeller. Here they shared the bill with fellow

Liverpudlians Rory Storm and the Hurricanes and for the next eight weeks, until the end of November, played alternate shifts through the long, long nights.

Saturday 17 December

Casbah Coffee Club, West Derby, Liverpool

The Beatles' first engagement following their return from Hamburg. It also marked the first of four consecutive appearances with the group by temporary bassist Chas Newby. Pete Best's mother Mona, who ran the Casbah, and Neil Aspinall, Pete's trainee-accountant friend, covered the club with hand-drawn "Return of the Fabulous Beatles!" posters and virtually a full-house saw the performance.

Saturday 24 December

Grosvenor Ballroom, Liscard, Wallasey

With either the threat of violence slightly decreased, or memories dimmed, rock dances returned to the Grosvenor with the Wallasey Corporation in charge. Playing their first true public performance after Hamburg (the Casbah being a strictly members-only club), the Beatles shared the bill with Derry and the Seniors, the two groups each receiving ten guineas (£10.50).

Tuesday 27 December

**Town Hall Ballroom, Hatton Hill Rd,
Litherland, Liverpool**

If any one live performance in the Beatles' career could be described as *the* turning point it would be this, their penultimate engagement in 1960. Their career was not without hiccups in the future, but, really, the group never looked back after this night.

Saturday 31 December

Casbah Coffee Club, West Derby, Liverpool

The last occasion that Chas Newby played guitar with the Beatles.

THE SIGHT of Beatles-inspired hysteria among his customers at the Town Hall ballroom in Litherland on 27 December 1960 sent promoter Brian Kelly scurrying for his engagements diary before anyone else could beat him to the group. He booked them for 36 dances, for around £6 to £8 each, between January and March 1961, and it was these bookings, above all others, which established the Beatles as the premier rock combo and number one attraction on Merseyside.

With Chas Newby back at college, the bass position within the group fell vacant once again. This time, though, a permanent move was made and after George refused an invitation from John to take up the instrument, Paul did so, switching from his position on rhythm guitar and/or piano. Initially he played a cheaply-constructed Solid 7 model, strung with three strings surreptitiously snipped from a convenient piano, but when the Beatles next returned to Hamburg he saved enough money to purchase an unusual Hofner model, shaped like a violin.

The hectic life for the Beatles in the 12 months of 1961 was in dramatic contrast to the uncertainties and tribulations of the previous year, a fact proven by the course of their live bookings. On their return from Hamburg in December 1960, aside from the last handful of dates procured for the group by Allan Williams, responsibility for finding and negotiating bookings fell to Pete Best and his mother Mona. (Both were adept at the task because Pete's father, Johnny Best, was a locally famous boxing promoter, with a regular column on the sport in the *Liverpool Echo*.) On a great many occasions, the Bests had no alternative but to double- or even triple-book the Beatles in a single day, such was the demand. And these weren't just 20-minute sessions. The group might play two three-hour shows in one evening just hours after a long lunchtime session.

Of course, none of the groups in those heady days had very much equipment to handle. In early 1961 the Beatles had just three guitars, three amplifiers (sometimes) and one drum kit. More often than not, they would use microphones supplied by a promoter which he, in turn, would hire if he couldn't afford to own them himself. None of the apparently sophisticated equipment of the present day had been invented back then; in Liverpool in 1961 you just turned the volume knob on the (often home-made) amplifier to maximum.

Nonetheless, the frequency of the bookings, the distance between the halls, and the late finishing times, made the need for a van and, if possible, a regular driver, nothing short of essential if the group was to progress. It was here that Neil Aspinall, friend of Pete Best, first proved invaluable to the Beatles. Rapidly tiring of his correspondence course in accountancy, Aspinall found the life, comparative excitement and cash-in-hand existence of "road managing" more attractive than preparing a trial balance. For £80 he bought

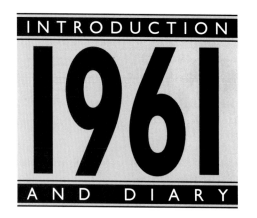

INTRODUCTION 1961 AND DIARY

an old Commer van and became the group's permanent assistant.

One thing that hadn't changed since 1960 or, for that matter, in decades, was the rumbustious and (sometimes literally) razor-sharp atmosphere at some Merseyside dance halls. Although the Teddy boy era was on the wane, the violent thuggery at these gatherings was still little short of terrifying, and most of the venues the Beatles played in 1961 were no place for the meek or faint-hearted. Neil Aspinall and Paul McCartney both remember, with some trepidation, those days of old, particularly at one beat venue, the Hambleton Hall in Huyton, where Paul and George were beaten-up one night. Aspinall had the odious duty of loading and unloading the Beatles' van there, under the watchful eyes and heavy breath of the local toughs, who would have been only too pleased to wade into action at the drop of a wrong word. Every time Aspinall humped gear into the hall he had to lock the van carefully, in case he returned to find the remaining equipment, indeed even the van, gone. Paul McCartney has since recalled that whenever they played 'Hully Gully' there it would end in fighting. One night rival gangs even turned fire extinguishers upon each other, in addition to their usual array of coshes, knives, chains and knuckle-dusters.

One place remarkably free of such violence was the dingy cellar underneath number 10 Mathew Street, Liverpool city centre, known as the Cavern Club, a venue played by the Quarry Men in 1957 and 1958. Since that time it had changed hands, and was now owned by Ray McFall, formerly the accountant to Alan Sytner, the club's previous owner. McFall had taken over the reins on 3 October 1959, at the birth of the massive trad jazz boom in Britain, so he was happy to maintain Sytner's pro-jazz, anti-beat policy for the club. But by mid-1960 McFall began to look further afield for his entertainment – even to rock and roll. For a short while a few top Liverpool beat groups played the club as interval attractions – though not always to the liking of the jazz audience – until eventually, on Wednesday 25 May 1960, while the Silver Beetles were up in Scotland backing Johnny Gentle, the Cavern Club held its first all-beat night, headlined by Cass and the Cassanovas and Rory Storm and the Hurricanes.

It took some nine months for the Beatles to gain playing access to the Cavern, but they did so through the efforts of Mona Best and Bob Wooler, the local dance compere now resident at the club, who championed the Beatles' cause in the ear of McFall. Mrs Best was also very persistent, and had first telephoned McFall about "her son's group" on 4 December 1960, just three days after Pete had returned home, deported, from Hamburg.

The Beatles made their début at the Cavern Club at the lunchtime session on Tuesday 9 February 1961, three-and-a-half years after John Lennon and his Quarry Men cronies had skiffled their way through an August 1957 evening there, and six weeks prior to the Beatles' first night-time appearance at the venue, as guests of that curious jazz/rock hybrid, the Swinging Bluegenes. Until August 1963, the Cavern was like the Beatles' second home and, in Liverpool at least, the two names were synonymous.

There can be no denying the role of the Cavern Club in the history of the Beatles. It was here, in a former fruit and vegetable warehouse 18 stone steps below street level, that they honed their precocious talent. And it was here that they formed an incredible rapport with their audience. For an initial fee of £15 a night, or £5 a lunchtime session, the Beatles rocked the city from their grimy underground lair, and went from nobodies to the biggest entertainment phenomenon Britain has produced.

The Cavern Club was a health inspector's nightmare, though. It had no ventilation, no dramatic lighting other than a set of 60-watt white bulbs starkly pointing down at the stage, woefully inadequate toilet arrangements, no tables, no curtains, no carpets, no booze, no fights – and most certainly no room. For Beatles performances hundreds would squeeze into the claustrophobic, subterranean hothouse, where the sweat would stream down the bare-brick walls and arches, and where the stench and steam would hang in the air, endangering the lives of the electric guitar heroes perched on the creaky wooden stage. This, in itself, was just two feet off the ground, and the same distance from the outstretched arms of the kneeling, clamorous girls who made up the front row.

The Cavern Club girls idolised and romanticised about the Beatles. At each and every performance they would desperately strive to attract the attention of one or other of the group in the hope of an acknowledgement or perhaps even a date. Two minutes before the Beatles took to the stage there would be a mass, final preening session among the girls. The dust of compact powder would clog the air, hair curlers and rollers would be removed and frantic back-combing take place. Many of these fans even formed themselves into little groups or cliques, like the Cement Mixers, the Bulldog Gang or the Woodentops, and it was not unusual for a nominated leader to telephone either Paul on GAR 6922, George on GAR 4596, John on GAT 1696 or Pete on STA 1556 to

request a certain song for a certain show. Far from being annoyed, the Beatles encouraged this kind of rapport and yearned for such intimate contact in later years when they were playing venues so vast and cold that they were 200 yards or more away from the nearest fan.

Another important effect of the Cavern Club on the Beatles in 1961 was the way it helped to shape and define the differing personalities within the group. It was here that John's sharp, cutting edge, his imperious personality, his defiant stage stance – legs astride, head back, guitar thrust high on chest – all took shape. While girls were never quite sure how to handle John, his apparent arrogance was much modelled by the Cavern Club's male clientele. Paul, meanwhile, attracted the girls' eyes with his good looks, charming stage patter and earnest politeness. George remained mostly in the background but his youthful features, lop-sided smile and droll humour did not go without their female admirers. Mostly though, the girls went for Pete Best, the self-effacing, almost painfully reticent drummer who would quietly, and without expression, provide the Beatles' solid beat. His natural air of detachment and monotone voice would send the hearts of the female Cavernites a-fluttering.

Shortly after their Cavern Club début, the Beatles were off for their second trip to Hamburg. Coming just three months after George, Paul and Pete's enforced departure from the country, it was no easy matter to arrange, and a great many promises of good behaviour were made in a series of letters from Pete and Mona Best to the West German authorities. Fortunately the Beatles now had allies in Hamburg working on their behalf. Bass player Stuart Sutcliffe, who had returned to Liverpool long after the others, in late February 1961, had gone back again on 15 March to pursue his blossoming romance with Astrid Kirchherr and an artistic career at the city's fine State College of Art. Another ally was Peter Eckhorn, owner of the Top Ten Club, who had made the hurried agreement with the Beatles on 30 November 1960 for a month's engagement in April.

With this collective help, the breakthrough finally came in a letter to Pete Best from the West German Immigration Office which gave him and Paul a one-year lifting of the deportation ban by "special concession of the Foreign Department". As an advance against their forthcoming weekly wages, Eckhorn paid 158DM to the authorities on

Call your favourite Beatle with a request: extracts from the 1961 Liverpool telephone directory. Pete Best was listed under J (after his father, Johnny); Paul McCartney under J (after his father, James); and John Lennon under G T Smith (after his late Uncle George, husband of Aunt Mimi). George Harrison's family was ex-directory but keen fans traded the GARston 4596 number.

Klaus Voormann, Astrid Kirchherr and Stuart Sutcliffe at the Top Ten Club, 1961.

behalf of Pete and Paul – the cost of sending them home the previous winter – and with George now turned 18-years-old the way was finally clear for the group to return.

A few days before leaving Liverpool they got together at the Best household and telephoned Eckhorn to negotiate the final contract. It was a standard gruelling Hamburg engagement – they were required on stage from 7.00 pm until 2.00 am Mondays to Fridays, and from 7.00 pm until 3.00 am weekends, always with a 15-minute break in every hour. The salary was a modest 35DM (£3) per man per day. Eckhorn's all-in accommodation, though dingy – old army bunk-beds in the attic four flights above the club – was certainly superior to the behind-the-cinema-screen lodgings proffered the previous year by Bruno Koschmider, however. At the end of March, the Beatles set off from Lime Street station on the long train and boat journey to Hamburg. They took to the stage on 1 April and happily began the 13-week haul through a twice-extended contract until 1 July.

Now domiciled permanently in Hamburg, Stuart's playing days with the Beatles were all but over, although he did perform the occasional evening with them for old times' sake and also played on one or two occasions with other visiting Merseyside groups. Perhaps it was because of his ex-Beatle status that Stuart was assigned on the group's behalf the unpleasant task of writing back to Allan Williams in Liverpool, announcing that as they themselves had negotiated the booking with Eckhorn, they were refusing to pay Williams a commission. Williams was livid, claiming that he had first taken the Beatles to Hamburg, that he had arranged the Eckhorn contract, and had helped quash Paul and Pete's deportation ban. On 20 April he wrote a tersely-worded letter to the group threatening to exact damaging retribution if they went ahead and reneged on their, regrettably verbal, agreement. This he could probably have done should he have felt so disposed but, as time passed, the situation cooled.

Hamburg was Hamburg, the same as before. Uproarious, immoral, clamorous, a veritable hotbed of vices *verboten* and yet, somehow, charming too. The Beatles were glad to be back, and this time they even had a small but élite following, mostly friends of Astrid Kirchherr. Although Stuart had effectively left the Beatles, he and Astrid attended the Top Ten Club on most evenings and Astrid continued to photograph them whenever she could. It was during this Hamburg visit that she cut Stuart's hair into the style which would eventually become known as the Beatle-cut – long, clean, brushed forward, and with a fringe. At first, the mere sight of Stuart was enough to send the four Beatles into paroxysms of laughter, but after a while they grew to like it and, within a few months – with the exception of Pete Best – they re-styled their rock and roll quiffs in the same way.

Without a doubt, the highlight of this second Hamburg jaunt was the Beatles' first professional recording session, which led to the release of their début disc. At the Top Ten

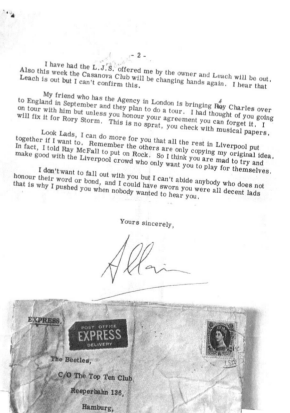

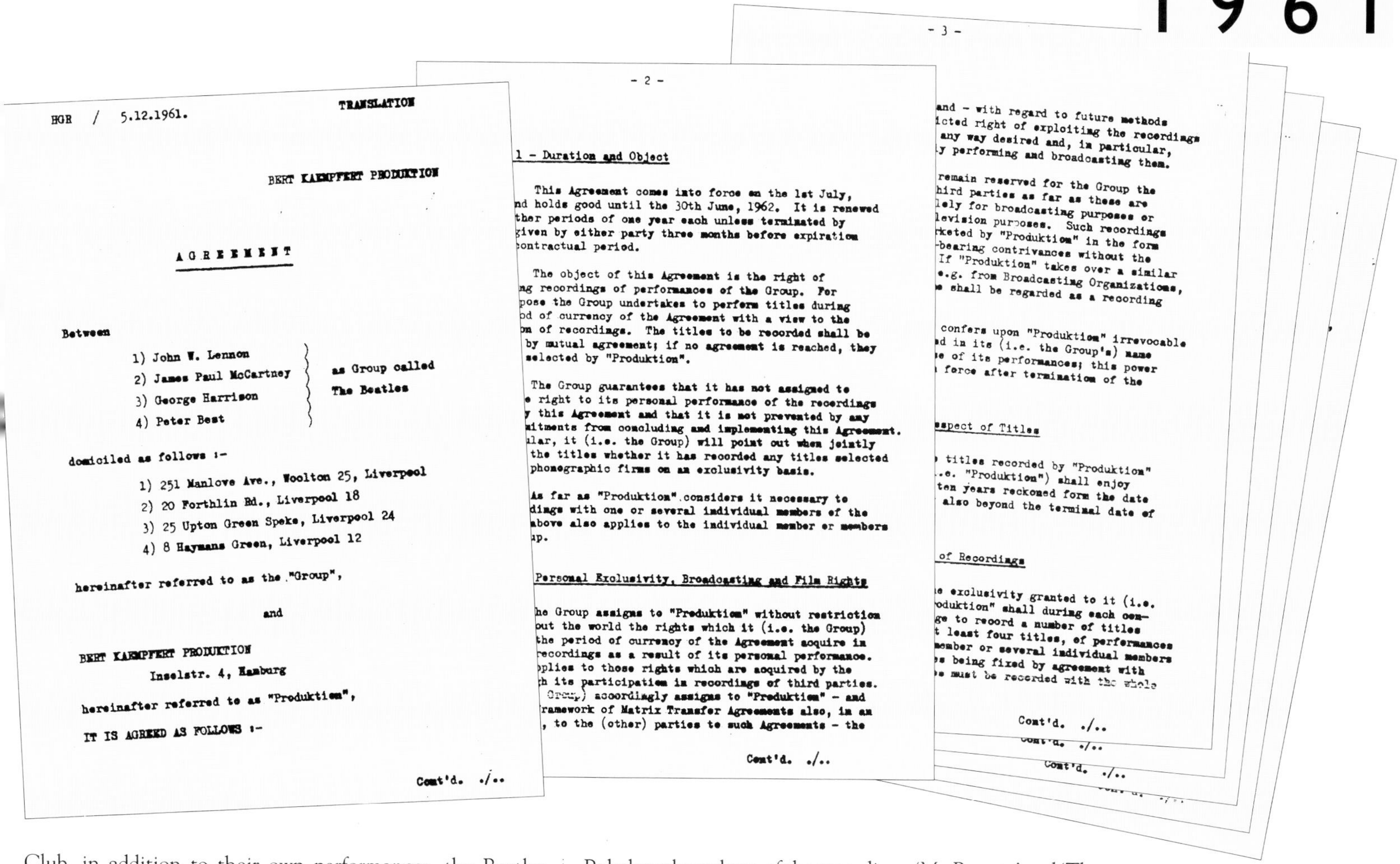

HGR / 5.12.1961.

TRANSLATION

BERT KAEMPFERT PRODUKTION

AGREEMENT

Between

1) John W. Lennon
2) James Paul McCartney
3) George Harrison
4) Peter Best

as Group called The Beatles

domiciled as follows :-

1) 251 Manlove Ave., Woolton 25, Liverpool
2) 20 Forthlin Rd., Liverpool 18
3) 25 Upton Green Speke, Liverpool 24
4) 8 Haymans Green, Liverpool 12

hereinafter referred to as the "Group",

and

BERT KAEMPFERT PRODUKTION
Inselstr. 4, Hamburg

hereinafter referred to as "Produktion",

IT IS AGREED AS FOLLOWS :-

Cont'd. ./..

- 2 -

1 - Duration and Object

This Agreement comes into force on the 1st July, nd holds good until the 30th June, 1962. It is renewed ther periods of one year each unless terminated by given by either party three months before expiration contractual period.

The object of this Agreement is the right of ng recordings of performances of the Group. For pose the Group undertakes to perform titles during od of currency of the Agreement with a view to the on of recordings. The titles to be recorded shall be by mutual agreement; if no agreement is reached, they selected by "Produktion".

The Group guarantees that it has not assigned to e right to its personal performance of the recordings y this Agreement and that it is not prevented by any mitments from concluding and implementing this Agreement. ular, it (i.e. the Group) will point out when jointly the titles whether it has recorded any titles selected phonographic firms on an exclusivity basis.

As far as "Produktion" considers it necessary to dings with one or several individual members of the above also applies to the individual member or members up.

Personal Exclusivity, Broadcasting and Film Rights

he Group assigns to "Produktion" without restriction out the world the rights which it (i.e. the Group) the period of currency of the Agreement acquire in recordings as a result of its personal performance. pplies to those rights which are acquired by the h its participation in recordings of third parties. Group) accordingly assigns to "Produktion" – and ramework of Matrix Transfer Agreements also, in an , to the (other) parties to such Agreements – the

Cont'd. ./..

- 3 -

and – with regard to future methods icted right of exploiting the recordings any way desired and, in particular, y performing and broadcasting them.

remain reserved for the Group the hird parties as far as these are lely for broadcasting purposes or levision purposes. Such recordings rketed by "Produktion" in the form -bearing contrivances without the If "Produktion" takes over a similar e.g. from Broadcasting Organizations, shall be regarded as a recording

confers upon "Produktion" irrevocable d in its (i.e. the Group's) name e of its performances; this power force after termination of the

espect of Titles

titles recorded by "Produktion" .e. "Produktion") shall enjoy ten years reckoned form the date also beyond the terminal date of

of Recordings

e exclusivity granted to it (i.e. oduktion" shall during each con- ge to record a number of titles t least four titles, of performances member or several individual members s being fixed by agreement with e must be recorded with the whole

Cont'd. ./..

Cont'd. ./..

Cont'd. ./..

An English translation (made in December 1961 for Brian Epstein by an EMI employee) of the Beatles' German recording contract with Bert Kaempfert.

Club, in addition to their own performances, the Beatles regularly backed Tony Sheridan, the young veteran of British TV pop shows whose presence in Hamburg the previous November had tempted the starry-eyed Beatles to break their contract with Bruno Koschmider by playing at a rival venue. In Germany, Sheridan was contracted to make records with Deutsche Grammophon, under the auspices of its popular music label Polydor, and one night in April 1961 Alfred Schacht, the European director of co-ordination for the Aberbach music publishing organisation, walked into the Top Ten to speak with Sheridan, and saw the Beatles. Schacht was impressed by the Sheridan/Beatles union and later discussed with his friend Berthold (Bert) Kaempfert – the 37-year-old German orchestra leader/composer who had recently scored an American number one hit with 'Wonderland By Night' – the possibility of recording them together for Polydor. The Beatles were invited to Kaempfert's office to discuss a recording and publishing contract and willingly agreed to sign up.

One morning, probably on 22 June, not long after the group had wearily climbed the four flights of stairs from the Top Ten Club to their beds in the attic, two taxis arrived to take them and their equipment to the recording studio. Despite Kaempfert's prestige, this was no more than an infant's school, and the recording took place on the main hall stage, with the curtain closed. They backed Sheridan on five numbers and then had two to themselves: 'Ain't She Sweet' and 'Cry For A Shadow', the latter a guitar instrumental composed by the unique team of Lennon-Harrison.

In August, after the Beatles had returned to Liverpool, Polydor released two of the recordings, 'My Bonnie' and 'The Saints' (as they titled them) on a single, credited to Tony Sheridan and the Beat Brothers, and it eventually reached number five on the local hit parade, selling a reputed 100,000 copies in the process. The label had been afraid to use the word Beatles in case it was confused with the similar-sounding "peedles", north German slang for penis.

Their second Hamburg stint completed, the Beatles rejoined the fast and furious merry-go-round of Merseyside engagements on 13 July. There was no doubt now that they were something really quite special, yet nothing seemed to be happening for them. Liverpool might just as well have been the North Pole as far as London pop impresarios were concerned, and the Beatles felt there was a real danger that fame and fortune might elude them. The group were uncrowned kings of Merseyside, in great demand at all the dance halls and they had made a record. Yet they were also quickly growing tired and restless with the monotony of appearance after appearance at the Cavern, much as they all loved the venue. It was a dead end, Liverpool was a dead end, and they had no idea how to escape.

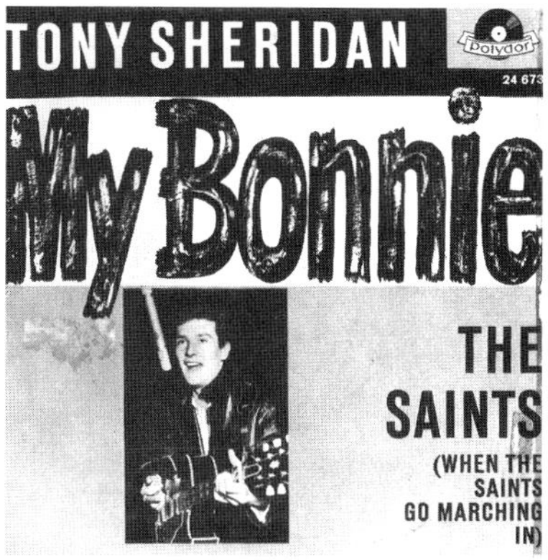

As far as they were concerned, the only real excitement to hit the local rock and roll scene at this time was the launching of *Mersey Beat*, its own bi-weekly newspaper, by Bill Harry, John and Stuart's former art college friend. For several months Bill Harry and his fiancée Virginia Sowry had been visiting local jive halls, talking to groups and making notes about the burgeoning beat scene. They had

quickly realised how parochial it was: groups in one area of town had little or no knowledge of groups or opportunities in other areas. With this in mind they hit upon the idea of a special newspaper. Harry was quick to promote his friends and page two of the first issue, 6–20 July 1961, carried a witty article by John Lennon, written before the Beatles had gone to Hamburg in March, entitled 'Being A Short Diversion On The Dubious Origins Of Beatles'. It was his first printed prose, and the same style was to be fêted three years later when In His Own Write, his book of similarly inspired lunacy, topped the best-sellers.

Two weeks before John's 21st birthday on 9 October he received a very generous coming-of-age gift of £100 from his Aunt Elizabeth in Sutherland, Scotland. To the annoyance of George and Pete, he and Paul immediately decided to take off for Paris for a fortnight's break. In a letter from Hamburg, Stuart had mentioned to John that Jurgen Vollmer would be in Paris. Jurgen was a friend of Astrid and one of the small band of Beatles followers in Hamburg, who had also photographed them on numerous occasions at the Top Ten Club. John and Paul were keen to meet him again and wasted little time in getting there. Although they spent most of the trip lounging around left-bank cafés until their money ran out (forcing them to abandon a planned foray into Spain), John and Paul also observed the typically French music scene, attending a Johnny Hallyday concert at the Olympia Theatre in Paris, and a rock music club in Montmartre. One other retrospectively-important event happened during this trip – Jurgen finally persuaded John and Paul to re-style their hair permanently like his own, and Stuart Sutcliffe's, indeed, like most French teenagers'. The "Beatle haircut" was here to stay.

On Thursday 9 November 1961 the Beatles' lunchtime session at the Cavern Club had a rather curious visitor, the well-spoken and dapper 27-year-old manager of NEMS (an acronym for North End Music Stores), a prosperous record store situated in nearby Whitechapel, one of the main thoroughfares in Liverpool city centre. His name was Brian

Samuel Epstein, and quite what he was doing there even he was really at a loss to explain. Nor, for that matter, has it ever become crystal clear how he came to discover the place, or seek out the Beatles.

One school of thought – supported by Epstein's own autobiography – follows this theory: Stuart Sutcliffe sent a few copies of 'My Bonnie' across from Hamburg to Liverpool, and George had given a copy to Bob Wooler one Saturday night in August, on a bus en route for the Aintree Institute. Bob plugged the disc relentlessly at his almost-nightly circuit of disc-jockey/compere engagements on Merseyside, constantly urging people to demand the disc at record shops in the hope of persuading a company to import officially a few copies from West Germany. One youth who heard Wooler's promotion of the disc, at Hambleton Hall, was 18-year-old Raymond Jones from Huyton, and – so the account continues – at 3.00 in the afternoon of Saturday 28 October, sporting a leather jacket and jeans, Jones walked into NEMS in Whitechapel and asked manager Brian Epstein for the disc. Epstein was nonplussed, having – so he said – heard of neither the record nor the group. But he promised to do some research and, if possible, order Jones a copy. On the following Monday morning two girls made a similar enquiry, and Epstein determined to find out why a disc should be in demand when he knew nothing about it and when it hadn't been listed in the industry publication Record Retailer.

He placed telephone calls to specialist record importers but no one seemed to have heard of the disc. On the verge of giving up, Epstein met Bill Harry and casually mentioned his problem. The editor of Mersey Beat surprised Epstein by revealing that the Beatles were a Liverpudlian group and not, as Epstein had quite reasonably assumed, German. He further pointed out that they were regularly to be found less than two hundred yards away from NEMS, in a place called the Cavern Club.

Harry himself remembers the situation differently. He says that Epstein had been one of the chief vendors of Mersey Beat since its inception four months previously and, furthermore, had taken great interest in its content. He says that Epstein sold 12-dozen copies of the paper's second issue, in which the bold headline "Beatles Sign Recording Contract!" followed by an article (about the Polydor deal) and a photograph of the group dominated the front page. Harry also points out that Epstein wrote a regular record review column in the paper, commencing with issue three. Although he may well have been uninterested in rock and roll, it is, nonetheless, hard to believe that he would have failed to read, or even casually glance through, the rest of each issue.

But one thing is for certain. On 9 November, wearing a neatly pressed pin-striped suit, and tie, with his attaché case tucked under his arm, and flanked by his similarly-attired assistant Alistair Taylor, Brian Epstein descended the 18 stone steps into the Cavern Club and another world opened up for him. In a 1964 BBC radio interview he recalled the events of that day:

"It was pretty much of an eye-opener, to go down into this darkened, dank, smoky cellar in the middle of the day, and to see crowds and crowds of kids watching these four young men on stage. They were rather scruffily dressed – in the

Throughout the remainder of November Brian found himself returning to the Cavern Club whenever the Beatles were on, always managing to grab a few hurried words with them. No immediate friendship seems to have been struck but the Beatles were slightly flattered by his attentions. As the days passed though, and Epstein discovered more and more about them, a vague idea of somehow "fathering" the group germinated. It was of course preposterous – as everyone to whom he mentioned it hastened to inform him. Nevertheless, he began to quiz record company sales reps and London record store managers about the intricacies of pop music management, and he even went to the Blue Angel night club and sought out Allan Williams to ask his advice. "What should I do?" enquired Epstein, to which Williams – still bitter over the recent Hamburg episode – memorably replied, "Brian, don't touch 'em with a fucking bargepole."

nicest possible way or, I should say, in the most attractive way: black leather jackets and jeans, long hair of course. And they had a rather untidy stage presentation, not terribly aware, and not caring very much, what they looked like. I think they cared more even then for what they sounded like. I immediately liked what I heard. They were fresh and they were honest, and they had what I thought was a sort of presence and, this is a terribly vague term, star quality. Whatever that is, they had it, or I sensed that they had it."

In short, then, Epstein had witnessed a typical 1961 Beatles' Cavern Club performance – in which the group might smoke, eat, swear, tell private jokes and laugh among themselves, turn their backs on the audience or suddenly stop a song midway through – and he was transfixed. It has

Although still uncertain about precisely what he was going to propose to the Beatles, Brian Epstein invited them to a meeting in his shop on Sunday 3 December at 4.30 pm. Paul was very late but when, eventually, he did arrive, the party retired to a local milk bar to discuss matters to their mutual advantage. The Beatles' reaction was not unfavourable, and another meeting was set for the following Wednesday afternoon,

since been revealed that Brian Epstein was homosexual but whether this can explain his fascination with the Beatles will always be conjecture and is, for the purposes of this book, entirely irrelevant. The fact remains that after the lunchtime session was over Epstein struggled through the sweaty teenage hordes to the Cavern Club's minuscule bandroom to meet the Beatles. He had, after all, theoretically gone there on business – to find out more about their record backing Tony Sheridan, so that he could import 200 copies. He first encountered George, and a slightly sarcastic jibe: "What brings Mr Epstein here?" Brian explained about the enquiries for their record, found the answers he required, heard the disc (courtesy of Cavern Club DJ Bob Wooler) and left.

6 December. In those intervening three days Epstein sought advice from his family's solicitor, E Rex Makin. It was all negative – Makin, who had known Brian all his life, was sceptical about what he saw as another scheme in which the young Epstein would surely lose interest before too long.

But Epstein was not to be deterred, and when Wednesday afternoon arrived he put his proposals and terms to the Beatles. He would require 25 per cent of their gross fees on a weekly basis. In return, he would assume responsibility for arranging their bookings which, he stressed, would be better organised, more prestigious and in uncharted areas further afield than Liverpool. He further vowed that the group would never again play a date for less than £15 – a bold and rather rash promise to make in 1961 – except for Cavern Club lunchtime sessions, where he would ensure their £5 fee was doubled to £10. But more than all of this he dangled before the Beatles the biggest carrot of all – he would extricate them from their recording contract with Bert Kaempfert and would then use his influence as one of the north-west's biggest record retailers to gain the Beatles a decent deal with a major British recording company.

Coming from a man who had no previous pop management experience, going to a provincial group which up until then had taken their musical career comparatively lightly, this was pretty strong talk. There was an awkward silence while the four Beatles pondered the proposals. Then John, on behalf of the group, blurted, "Right then, Brian. Manage us. Now where's the contract, I'll sign it." But there was no contract – yet. The one Brian had been given by a friend in

the business – a typical management/artist document of the time – had so disgusted him with its meanness and exploitation, and enslavement of the artist, that he steadfastly refused to utilise it. Instead, using it as a guide, he modified and adapted the terms to draw up a much fairer agreement.

Another meeting was held four days later, on Sunday 10 December, this time at the Casbah Coffee Club, where the Beatles usually congregated before going out for their night's work. John, Paul, George and Pete all agreed in principle to the contract and vowed that, subject to Brian attempting to carry through his promises, they would eventually sign. This duly happened in the NEMS office after the Beatles' Cavern Club lunchtime session on 24 January 1962. Interestingly though, while Alistair Taylor lawfully witnessed the contract by countersigning it in five places, only four other signatures graced the document; Brian Epstein did not add his own. Perhaps, in his own mind at least, ever the gentleman, Brian still wanted to prove himself to the group before he was seen to be "capturing" them. In fact, he wasn't to sign for a further nine months, until October 1962. The group, though, were oblivious to this triviality – nor would it have mattered to either party or affected their relationship. To all intents and purposes, from that moment, on the afternoon of Wednesday 24 January 1962, Brian Epstein was the Beatles' first, and only, real manager.

An example of the Gargantuan task that Epstein was voluntarily taking on can be seen from the reaction – or lack of it – to "Operation Big Beat", promoter Sam Leach's mighty dance presentation at the New Brighton Tower Ballroom on 10 November 1961. Over 3000 paying customers turned up to see the top beat groups on Merseyside in a marathon five-and-a-half-hour session. And yet not only was the event predictably ignored by all of the blinkered London-based musical papers, but the two daily Liverpool newspapers, the *Post* and *Echo*, and even the two local weekly papers, the *Wallasey News* and *Birkenhead News*, ignored it too. Not one single mention anywhere, neither before the night nor after. But Epstein did it: he transformed this pulsating but insular scene into the biggest popular music boom Britain has ever seen. Within just two short years, all five of the groups participating in "Operation Big Beat" would have major recording contracts with London companies.

The one concession the *Liverpool Echo* did make to popular music at this time was a disc review column entitled "Off The Record" which ran every Saturday, written, mysteriously, under the pen name Disker. Early in December 1961, Epstein wrote to Disker in the hope of soliciting a favourable mention for the Beatles in the column. But when the reply arrived it came not from the *Echo* but from London and, strangely, from someone at Decca Records. Disker, it transpired, was the *nom de plume* of Tony Barrow, a London-based Liverpudlian who, in addition to being a freelance journalist, was a full-time sleevenote writer for Decca. Barrow's reply was not discouraging and Epstein travelled to London to meet him. But when they met, and Epstein played Barrow a crudely-recorded, scratchy acetate of the Beatles playing in the Cavern Club, Barrow was visibly unimpressed, and he further disappointed Epstein by emphasising that "Off The Record" was precisely that – a column in which new records were reviewed. He could not deviate from this and mention a group which didn't have a release.

But there was something about Epstein and his group that nagged away at Barrow, so after Epstein had left his office he made a couple of internal telephone calls around Decca. One of these was to the sales division which, as Barrow expected, in turn contacted the A&R (artists and repertoire) department and explained that an important company client was touting a group. It would be tactful, they suggested, if Decca gave them a try-out.

The head of Decca A&R was Dick Rowe, and he had been in the game long enough to know that it would be bad for company business if he refused. So it was that on Wednesday 13 December 1961 Rowe's young assistant, Mike Smith, was dispatched to Liverpool to witness a full Beatles performance in the group's best possible surroundings, the Cavern Club. There was great excitement in the Cavern that night – for the first time ever, an A&R man would be in attendance. It was a major coup for Brian Epstein. Smith liked what he saw – not enough to warrant an immediate contract, admittedly, but sufficiently to arrange a second audition quickly, this time to take place in a real recording studio, Decca's own, in north London.

The date was set for 1 January 1962.

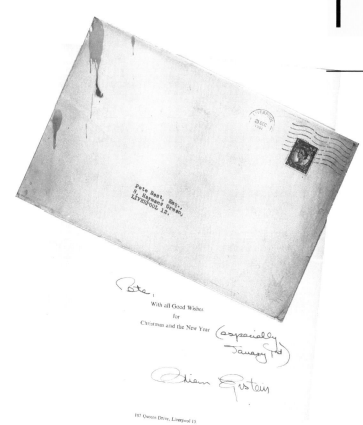

Thursday 5 January

Town Hall, Litherland, Liverpool

The first of 36 Beatles engagements between this date and 11 March for promoter Brian Kelly, who ran "Beekay" dances at various halls in north Liverpool. Many were booked immediately after their sensational appearance for Kelly at this hall on 27 December 1960. On this occasion, the group's fee was £7 10s (£7.50).

In the audience this evening were Johnny Guitar and Ringo Starr from Rory Storm and the Hurricanes. They had returned from Hamburg on 4 January.

Friday 6 January

St John's Hall, Oriel Rd, Bootle, Lancashire

The organiser of this dance, 17-year-old Dave Forshaw, was the only promoter other than Brian Kelly to enter the Beatles' dressing-room after the Litherland show on 27 December. He swiftly booked them for three monthly dates, on this first occasion paying them £6 10s (£6.50), a fee easily recouped since the hall was filled almost to capacity. Clearly, word of the Beatles' prowess was spreading fast.

Saturday 7 January

Aintree Institute, Longmoor Lane, Aintree, Liverpool
and Lathom Hall, Seaforth, Liverpool

The first of 31 Beatles appearances at the Aintree Institute, situated – as promoter Brian Kelly almost always pointed out in his advertisements – behind the Black Bull pub, not far from the famous Aintree racecourse (the home of the annual Grand National steeplechase). The favourite pastime among one faction at the Institute was to lob chairs at all and sundry, even at the group on stage.

The second part of this evening's double-header for "Beekay" meant a return to the location of the Silver Beats' (Silver Beetles) first booking, on 14 May 1960.

Friday 13 January

Aintree Institute, Aintree, Liverpool

Saturday 14 January

Aintree Institute, Aintree, Liverpool

Sunday 15 January

Casbah Coffee Club, West Derby, Liverpool

Wednesday 18 January

Aintree Institute, Aintree, Liverpool

The Beatles were paid £8 10s (£8.50) for this appearance.

Thursday 19 January

Alexandra Hall, College Rd, Crosby, Liverpool

Another "Beekay" promotion.

Friday 20 January

Lathom Hall, Seaforth, Liverpool

Saturday 21 January

Lathom Hall, Seaforth, Liverpool
and Aintree Institute, Aintree, Liverpool

The Aintree appearance was unadvertised.

Wednesday 25 January

Hambleton Hall, St David's Rd, Page Moss, Huyton, Liverpool

The first of 16 engagements for promoters Wally Hill and Vic Anton at this desperate-looking municipal building on the eastern edge of Liverpool.

LOOK!
THREE TOP GROUPS AGAIN
NEXT WEDNESDAY NIGHT
AT HAMBLETON HALL
Page Moss, Huyton

— What a terrific line up for —
WEDNESDAY, 25th JANUARY 1961

● The Sensational Beatles ●
● Derry & The Seniors ●
● Faron & The Tempest Tornadoes ●

YES! You must come along early
and bring your friends!

PAY AT THE DOOR 2/6 before 8 p.m. 3/- afterwards
NOTE! No admission after 9-30 p.m.

Thursday 26 January

Town Hall, Litherland, Liverpool

Friday 27 January

Aintree Institute, Aintree, Liverpool

Saturday 28 January

Lathom Hall, Seaforth, Liverpool
and **Aintree Institute, Aintree, Liverpool**

Sunday 29 January

Casbah Coffee Club, West Derby, Liverpool

Monday 30 January

Lathom Hall, Seaforth, Liverpool

The Beatles were again paid £8 10s (£8.50) for their night's work.

Wednesday 1 February

Hambleton Hall, Huyton, Liverpool

Thursday 2 February

Town Hall, Litherland, Liverpool

Friday 3 February

St John's Hall, Bootle

The second of Dave Forshaw's bookings, for which the Beatles were paid an increased fee of £7 10s (£7.50).

Saturday 4 February

Lathom Hall, Seaforth, Liverpool

Sunday 5 February

Blair Hall, Walton Rd, Walton, Liverpool

The Beatles' first engagement with Peak Promotions, a company which ran jive dances at four venues: Holyoake Hall in Wavertree, the David Lewis Club in Great George Place, the Columba Hall in Widnes, and this one. The Beatles played all but Columba Hall.

Monday 6 February

Lathom Hall, Seaforth, Liverpool

The Beatles' third appearance here in a week.

Tuesday 7 February

Merseyside Civil Service Club,
Lower Castle St, Liverpool

The first of five Beatles engagements at this venue – the others took place in November 1961. Their fee on this occasion was £5.

Wednesday 8 February

Aintree Institute, Aintree, Liverpool
and **Hambleton Hall, Huyton, Liverpool**

Dances for two different promotions in one evening. The venues are several miles apart so newly-acquired road manager Neil Aspinall had his work cut out.

Thursday 9 February

Lunchtime **Cavern Club, Liverpool**

Although the Quarry Men had skiffled here more than three years previously, this was the Beatles' début – albeit an unadvertised one – at the club they would swiftly come to dominate. Their fee was £5.

Friday 10 February

Aintree Institute, Aintree, Liver ool
and **Lathom Hall, Seaforth, Liverpool**

Saturday 11 February

Lathom Hall, Seaforth, Liverpool
and **The Cassanova Club, Sampson and Barlow's
New Ballroom, London Rd, Liverpool**

The second of these two evening bookings was the first of a great many they were to undertake for local promoter Sam R Leach. The Cassanova Club had moved to these premises from its previous location in Temple Street on 9 February.

Sunday 12 February

Casbah Coffee Club, West Derby, Liverpool

John in action at the Casbah, 1961.

Tuesday 14 February

Cassanova Club, Liverpool
and **Town Hall, Litherland, Liverpool**

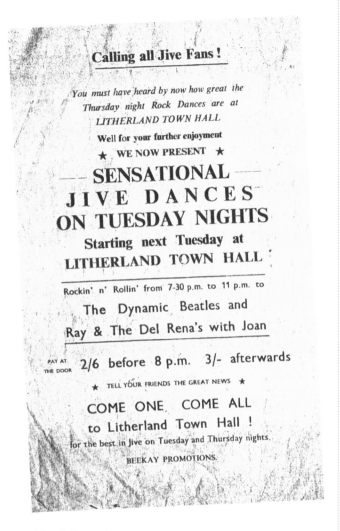

Handbills and posters for the Cassanova Club booking credited the Beatles as originators of "The Atom Beat", a dance involving much foot stomping.

The Litherland engagement was a special event, to mark St Valentine's Day. When Paul sang the Elvis Presley *GI Blues* film song (and imminent British hit single) 'Wooden Heart', he wore just such a large item on his coat, covered in satin and embroidered with the four names "John", "Paul", "George", "Pete". The heart was then raffled, with the lucky winner also promised a kiss from Paul. But when the victorious girl went on stage to collect her prize, dozens of others did so too, squealing. In the mêlée, John was knocked to the floor and the others were generally mobbed, until bouncers rescued them, the curtain was closed and the showstopped until calm had been restored.

Wednesday 15 February

Aintree Institute, Aintree, Liverpool
and **Hambleton Hall, Huyton, Liverpool**

Thursday 16 February

Cassanova Club, Liverpool
and **Town Hall, Litherland, Liverpool**

Friday 17 February

St John's Hall, Snaefell Ave, Tuebrook, Liverpool

Mona Best, mother of Pete and owner of the Casbah Coffee Club, also ran some dances at this venue, not far from her home in West Derby. Receiving preferential treatment, the Beatles were paid the handsome sum of £20.

Saturday 18 February

Aintree Institute, Aintree, Liverpool

What would have been a two-dance evening was reduced to one when the Beatles were withdrawn from an engagement at the Cassanova Club, re-scheduled for the 28th.

Sunday 19 February

Casbah Coffee Club, West Derby, Liverpool

Tuesday 21 February

Lunchtime **Cavern Club, Liverpool**
Night **Cassanova Club, Liverpool**
and **Town Hall, Litherland, Liverpool**

The first of many occasions when the Beatles performed three engagements in a day.

Wednesday 22 February

Aintree Institute, Aintree, Liverpool
and **Hambleton Hall, Huyton, Liverpool**

For the Aintree appearance the Beatles received £7 2s (£7.10).

Friday 24 February

Grosvenor Ballroom, Liscard, Wallasey

The Beatles' first engagement across the Mersey in 1961.

Saturday 25 February

Aintree Institute, Aintree, Liverpool
and **Lathom Hall, Seaforth, Liverpool**

A far from easeful way for George to spend his 18th birthday.

Sunday 26 February

Casbah Coffee Club, West Derby, Liverpool

Tuesday 28 February

Lunchtime **Cavern Club, Liverpool**
Night **Cassanova Club, Liverpool**
and **Town Hall, Litherland, Liverpool**

Three engagements, each for a different promoter: Ray McFall at the Cavern, Sam Leach at the Cassanova Club and Brian Kelly in Litherland.

Wednesday 1 March

Aintree Institute, Aintree, Liverpool

Thursday 2 March

Town Hall, Litherland, Liverpool

Friday 3 March

St John's Hall, Bootle

Saturday 4 March

Aintree Institute, Aintree, Liverpool

Sunday 5 March

Casbah Coffee Club, West Derby, Liverpool

Monday 6 March

Lunchtime **Cavern Club, Liverpool**
Night **Liverpool Jazz Society, Temple St, Liverpool**

The LJS date marked the Beatles' first appearance at what had previously been and would eventually re-emerge as the famous Iron Door Club.

Tuesday 7 March

Cassanova Club, Liverpool

Wednesday 8 March

Lunchtime **Cavern Club, Liverpool**
Night **Aintree Institute, Aintree, Liverpool**
and **Hambleton Hall, Huyton, Liverpool**

Friday 10 March

Lunchtime **Cavern Club, Liverpool**
Night **Grosvenor Ballroom, Liscard, Wallasey**
and **St John's Hall, Tuebrook, Liverpool**

The Wallasey dance was the last date arranged for the Beatles by Allan Williams. (He hadn't booked them anywhere other than at this hall since their return from Hamburg three months previously.)

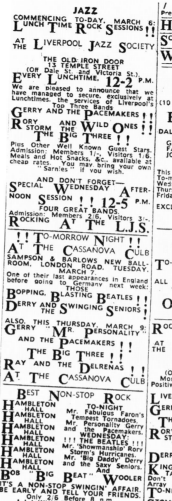

Saturday 11 March

Aintree Institute, Aintree, Liverpool
and **Liverpool Jazz Society, Liverpool**

The LJS engagement was a true innovation on the part of Sam Leach, certainly the most adventurous and ambitious rock dance promoter in the Merseyside area: a 12-group, 12-hour, all-night session, commencing at 8.00 Saturday night and finishing at 8.00 Sunday morning. The admission price was just 6s 6d (32½p) for Liverpool Jazz Society members and 7s 6d (37½p) for non-members. Although the attendance capacity of the Temple Street cellar was 1000, approximately 2000 people saw at least some part of the show.

Leach was to hold many similar marathon "Big Beat Sessions" over the next two years at several different venues, most (although not all) of which featured the Beatles as the main attraction.

Sunday 12 March

Casbah Coffee Club, West Derby, Liverpool
and **Cassanova Club, Liverpool**

1 9 6 1

M A R C H

A typical 1961 extract from the Liverpool Echo classifieds, the Beatles being advertised for appearances at Hambleton Hall and at the Cavern (including, here, their night-time début at the club, 21 March, as guests of the Swinging Bluegenes).

Monday 13 March

Lunchtime **Cavern Club, Liverpool**
Night **Liverpool Jazz Society, Liverpool**

Tuesday 14 March

Lunchtime **Cavern Club, Liverpool**

Wednesday 15 March

Lunchtime **Cavern Club, Liverpool**
Afternoon **Liverpool Jazz Society, Liverpool**

After the Beatles' lunchtime spot at the Cavern Club (12.00 noon–1.00 pm on this occasion), they shifted their equipment over Victoria Street and into the Liverpool Jazz Society for a five-hour afternoon session alternating with Rory Storm and the Wild Ones (Rory plus assorted guest musicians) and Gerry and the Pacemakers. The Beatles' first appearance was at 2.00 pm.

Thursday 16 March

Cavern Club, Liverpool

Friday 17 March

Mossway Hall, Moss Way, Croxteth, Liverpool
and **Liverpool Jazz Society, Liverpool**

The Mossway Hall booking was the Beatles' one and only engagement for Messrs McIver and Martin who, under the name of Ivamar, promoted at three venues in north Liverpool at this time: St Luke's Hall in Crosby (aka The Jive Hive), the Ivamar Club (Masonic Hall) in Skelmersdale, and this one.

Sunday 19 March

Casbah Coffee Club, West Derby, Liverpool

The usual Sunday engagement for Mrs Best and the youthful patrons of her basement coffee club.

Monday 20 March

Lunchtime **Cavern Club, Liverpool**
Night **Hambleton Hall, Huyton, Liverpool**

Tuesday 21 March

Night **Cavern Club, Liverpool**

The night-time début of the Beatles in Mathew Street.

Wednesday 22 March

Lunchtime **Cavern Club, Liverpool**

Friday 24 March

Lunchtime **Cavern Club, Liverpool**

Sunday 26 March

Casbah Coffee Club, West Derby, Liverpool

The Beatles' last engagement before journeying to Hamburg for their second visit.

Saturday 1 April - Saturday 1 July

Top Ten Club, Reeperbahn, Hamburg, West Germany

A twice-extended contract led to the Beatles staying 13 weeks at the Top Ten Club, playing a staggering total of 503 hours on stage over 92 nights.

It was little wonder then that, just as the Beatles found with their first German trip, their stamina and musical versatility improved dramatically as the visit wore on. When they returned to Liverpool in July they were simply untouchable.

Thursday 22 - Friday 23 June

Friedrich Ebert Halle, Hamburg, West Germany

The *probable* dates of the Beatles' recordings with producer Bert Kaempfert. Little can be stated for certain about this entire episode because what scant information exists is contradictory.

These dates, and the recording venue, were supplied with a December 1984 compact disc reissue of the Tony Sheridan/Beatles material, however some of the other data given on the same sheet is clearly wrong, so this may be incorrect too – especially considering that the Beatles' contract with Bert Kaempfert (they signed with him as an independent producer, he in turn assigned the recordings to the Polydor label) came into effect on 1 July 1961. It seems odd that he contracted them *after* rather than before this session. (The contract was drawn up to run for one year, until 30 June 1962, renewable on application.)

Four Beatles played on the sessions: Stuart Sutcliffe did not participate although he attended as an observer and saw the Beatles back Sheridan on five numbers. The first, popular in the Top Ten Club as a request often submitted by visiting seamen, was a rock version of 'My Bonnie Lies Over The Ocean'. George played the opening lead guitar sequence but Sheridan played the middle-eight solo section. Paul is clearly evident, shouting in the background.

The second recording was of another old standard, 'When The Saints Go Marching In', the third was Sheridan's own ballad composition 'Why (Can't You Love Me Again)', the fourth was Hank Snow's country number 'Nobody's Child' and the fifth was Jimmy Reed's 'Take Out Some Insurance On Me, Baby' (aka 'If You Love Me Baby'). The CD information states that this latter song, alone among the material, was recorded the following day, 24 June, at Studio Rahlstedt in Hamburg. Since it's hard enough to believe that this was even a two-day session, this seems particularly unlikely.

The Beatles made two recordings without Sheridan. The first was 'Ain't She Sweet', with John singing lead vocal. The other was a Lennon-Harrison guitar instrumental – this didn't have a title to begin with and 'Beatle Bop' was among the names considered until they finally plumped for 'Cry For A Shadow', a play on the Shadows, Cliff Richard's instrumental backing group.

Information about "takes", mixes and the sessions' start/finish times has not come to light. And details are even murkier for an occasion when the Beatles again recorded with Sheridan and Kaempfert, in spring 1962 (see 23-27 April 1962).

Thursday 13 July

St John's Hall, Tuebrook, Liverpool

The Beatles travelled home to Liverpool during Sunday 2 and Monday 3 July and had given themselves a holiday from the 4th to the 12th. This first return date was for Mrs Best at St John's Hall.

Friday 14 July

Lunchtime **Cavern Club**, Liverpool
Night **Cavern Club**, Liverpool

Saturday 15 July

Holyoake Hall, Smithdown Rd,
Wavertree, Liverpool

Aside from the Quarry Men engagements here and at St Barnabas Church Hall in 1957, this was, geographically, the closest the Beatles came to playing in Penny Lane, the road made world famous in their 1967 recording.

Sunday 16 July

Blair Hall, Walton, Liverpool

The first of three consecutive Sunday-night dates at this venue for Peak Promotions.

Monday 17 July

Lunchtime **Cavern Club**, Liverpool
Night **Town Hall**, Litherland, Liverpool

Wednesday 19 July

Lunchtime **Cavern Club**, Liverpool
Night **Cavern Club**, Liverpool

Thursday 20 July

St John's Hall, Tuebrook, Liverpool

Friday 21 July

Lunchtime **Cavern Club**, Liverpool
Night **Aintree Institute**, Aintree, Liverpool

Saturday 22 July

Holyoake Hall, Wavertree, Liverpool

Sunday 23 July

Blair Hall, Walton, Liverpool

Monday 24 July

Town Hall, Litherland, Liverpool

Tuesday 25 July

Lunchtime **Cavern Club**, Liverpool
Night **Cavern Club**, Liverpool

Wednesday 26 July

Night **Cavern Club**, Liverpool

Thursday 27 July

Lunchtime **Cavern Club**, Liverpool
Night **St John's Hall**, Tuebrook, Liverpool

Also on the bill with the Beatles at St John's Hall were the Big Three – the remains of Cass and the Cassanovas after Brian Cassar had left the group and gone to London. On this night they also backed a young girl who occasionally sang with them, Cilla White – later to become world famous as Cilla Black.

Friday 28 July

Aintree Institute, Aintree, Liverpool

Saturday 29 July

Blair Hall, Walton, Liverpool

Sunday 30 July

Blair Hall, Walton, Liverpool

Monday 31 July

Lunchtime **Cavern Club**, Liverpool
Night **Town Hall**, Litherland, Liverpool

Wednesday 2 August

Lunchtime **Cavern Club**, Liverpool
Night **Cavern Club**, Liverpool

1961

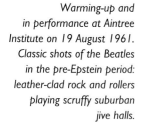

Jive Fans This Is It!

MEET THE BEATLES
every Saturday at
AINTREE INSTITUTE
BUSES 70, 71, 72, 58, 92, 95, 19, 11 & 100 TO BLACK BULL, NEXT DOOR
YES! PAUL, JOHN, GEORGE AND PETE
will be playing for you exclusively at Aintree Institute,
every Saturday, starting 12th August 1961.
You must be there, too!
Come early and bring your friends!
Jiving from 7-30 to 11 p.m.   Admission 4/-
Aintree Institute Your Saturday Dance Date

*Warming-up and
in performance at Aintree
Institute on 19 August 1961.
Classic shots of the Beatles
in the pre-Epstein period:
leather-clad rock and rollers
playing scruffy suburban
jive halls.*

Thursday 3 August

St John's Hall, Tuebrook, Liverpool

Friday 4 August

Lunchtime **Cavern Club, Liverpool**
Night **Aintree Institute, Aintree, Liverpool**

Saturday 5 August

Night **Cavern Club, Liverpool**

An all-night session in which the Beatles shared the bill with noted jazz trumpeter Kenny Ball.

Sunday 6 August

Casbah Coffee Club, West Derby, Liverpool

Monday 7 August

Town Hall, Litherland, Liverpool

Tuesday 8 August

Lunchtime **Cavern Club, Liverpool**

Wednesday 9 August

Night **Cavern Club, Liverpool**

Thursday 10 August

Lunchtime **Cavern Club, Liverpool**
Night **St John's Hall, Tuebrook, Liverpool**

Friday 11 August

Night **Cavern Club, Liverpool**

Saturday 12 August

Aintree Institute, Aintree, Liverpool

The first of seven consecutive Saturday-night engagements for the Beatles at Aintree Institute, promoted by Brian Kelly.

Sunday 13 August

Casbah Coffee Club, West Derby, Liverpool

Monday 14 August

Lunchtime **Cavern Club, Liverpool**

Wednesday 16 August

Night **Cavern Club, Liverpool**

Thursday 17 August

St John's Hall, Tuebrook, Liverpool

During this evening the Beatles played as a five-man outfit, augmented by Johnny Gustafson, good-looking bassist with the Big Three, who were also on the night's bill. In frivolous mood, Paul moved around the stage and among the audience singing into a microphone *sans* guitar, in the style of the solo singers of the day.

Friday 18 August

Lunchtime **Cavern Club, Liverpool**
Night **Aintree Institute, Aintree, Liverpool**

Saturday 19 August

Aintree Institute, Aintree, Liverpool

Sunday 20 August

Hambleton Hall, Huyton, Liverpool

Monday 21 August

Lunchtime **Cavern Club, Liverpool**

Wednesday 23 August

Lunchtime **Cavern Club, Liverpool**
Night **Cavern Club, Liverpool**

Thursday 24 August

St John's Hall, Tuebrook, Liverpool

Friday 25 August

Lunchtime **Cavern Club, Liverpool**

Night **MV** *Royal Iris*, **River Mersey**

The first of four floating Beatles performances, aboard the infamous Mersey vessel the *Royal Iris* colloquially known as "The Fish And Chip Boat".

During the summer months Ray McFall, owner of the Cavern Club, occasionally booked the ferry for "Riverboat Shuffles", always providing a cross-section of entertainment in order to attract as many customers as possible. Heading the bill on this occasion, and drawing in a large following, was Acker Bilk, clarinetist and spearhead of the trad jazz boom. Providing the beat music, and attracting a more youthful audience, were the Beatles. The three-and-a-quarter-hour jaunt began and ended at the Pier Head.

Saturday 26 August

Aintree Institute, Aintree, Liverpool

Sunday 27 August

Casbah Coffee Club, West Derby, Liverpool

Monday 28 August

Lunchtime **Cavern Club, Liverpool**

Tuesday 29 August

Lunchtime **Cavern Club, Liverpool**

Wednesday 30 August

Night **Cavern Club, Liverpool**

Thursday 31 August

St John's Hall, Tuebrook, Liverpool

Friday 1 September

Lunchtime **Cavern Club, Liverpool**

Night **Cavern Club, Liverpool**

Saturday 2 September

Aintree Institute, Aintree, Liverpool

Sunday 3 September

Hambleton Hall, Huyton, Liverpool

Tuesday 5 September

Lunchtime **Cavern Club, Liverpool**

Early Cavern Club newspaper advertisements listed the Beatles to perform during this evening's session too, but they were withdrawn before the event and played instead the following evening.

Wednesday 6 September

Night **Cavern Club, Liverpool**

THE CAVERN PRESENTS
A RIVERBOAT SHUFFLE
FRIDAY, 25TH AUG. 1961
ABOARD THE
"M.V. ROYAL IRIS"
WITH
MR. **ACKER BILK'S**
PARAMOUNT JAZZ BAND
and **THE BEATLES**
BOAT SAILS AT 7.45 P.M.
FROM LIVERPOOL LANDING STAGE
RETURNING AT 11.0 P.M.
Tickets **8'6**

Thursday 7 September

Lunchtime **Cavern Club, Liverpool**
Night **Town Hall, Litherland, Liverpool**

Friday 8 September

St John's Hall, Tuebrook, Liverpool

Saturday 9 September

Aintree Institute, Aintree, Liverpool

Sunday 10 September

Casbah Coffee Club, West Derby, Liverpool

Monday 11 September

Lunchtime **Cavern Club, Liverpool**

Wednesday 13 September

Lunchtime **Cavern Club, Liverpool**
Night **Cavern Club, Liverpool**

Thursday 14 September

Town Hall, Litherland, Liverpool

Friday 15 September

Lunchtime **Cavern Club, Liverpool**
Night **Grosvenor Ballroom, Liscard, Wallasey**
and **Village Hall, East Prescot Rd, Knotty Ash, Liverpool**

Two evening engagements for the Beatles on different sides of the Mersey, following a lunchtime session at the Cavern Club. The Wallasey date was the Beatles' first appearance "across the water" in six months, while the Knotty Ash dance, promoted by Mona Best, marked their début at this fine, mock-Tudor village hall in the area made famous as the home of comedian Ken Dodd, and his "jam butty mines".

Saturday 16 September

Aintree Institute, Aintree, Liverpool

Sunday 17 September

Hambleton Hall, Huyton, Liverpool

Tuesday 19 September

Lunchtime **Cavern Club, Liverpool**

Wednesday 20 September

Night **Cavern Club, Liverpool**

Thursday 21 September

Lunchtime **Cavern Club, Liverpool**
Night **Town Hall, Litherland, Liverpool**

A memorable evening before a capacity crowd in Litherland, promoter Brian Kelly booking Liverpool's top three outfits for one dance: the Beatles, Gerry and the Pacemakers and Rory Storm and the Hurricanes. Three-and-a-half "rocking hours" for just three shillings (15p).

Friday 22 September

Village Hall, Knotty Ash, Liverpool

Saturday 23 September

Aintree Institute, Aintree, Liverpool

Sunday 24 September

Casbah Coffee Club, West Derby, Liverpool

Monday 25 September

Lunchtime **CaverncClub, Liverpool**

Wednesday 27 September

Lunchtime **Cavern Club, Liverpool**
Night **Cavern Club, Liverpool**

Thursday 28 September

Town Hall, Litherland, Liverpool

Friday 29 September

Lunchtime **Cavern Club, Liverpool**
Night **Village Hall, Knotty Ash, Liverpool**

The Beatles' last performance before John and Paul took off for their two-week trip to Paris.

Sunday 15 October

Afternoon **Albany Cinema, Northway, Maghull, Liverpool**
Night **Hambleton Hall, Huyton, Liverpool**

The Maghull booking was the Beatles' first engagement (and a most unusual one at that) following John and Paul's return from Paris.

Jim Gretty – a C&W guitarist since the 1930s, a variety agent specialising in charity work and also a part-time guitar salesman at Hessy's music store in Liverpool (it was Gretty who sold John Lennon his first guitar in 1957) – put on this Sunday afternoon charity concert in Maghull, a sleepy village north of Aintree. All proceeds went to the local

JIM GRETTY

presents

STAR MATINEE

with your compere ARTHUR SCOTT introducing . . .

1. The Dusty Road Ramblers	10. The Beatles
2. Les Arnold	11. Dennis Horton and Gladys
3. Joe Cordova	Ambrose
4. Dunn and Markey	12. Jackie Owen and the Joe Royal
5. Bob McGrady	Trio
6. Lennie Rens	13. Edna Bell
7. Shirley Gordon	14. Jim Gretty
8. Bert King	15. Denis Smerdon
9. The Eltones	16. KEN DODD
Interval	

At the Lowry Organ—BERT SMITH

At the piano Maurice Ley and Joe Royal

Production and Stage Management - George Martin and Jim Gretty

THE BEATLES.

We are fortunate in having secured the services of The Beatles as they have only just arrived back from Germany. They are in England for only a short time before embarking upon another European tour. All four are Liverpool born, and great favourites with the teenagers all of whom are of one voice in describing them as "FABULOUS." What more can we say ?

branch of the St John Ambulance Brigade. Topping the 16-act three-hour bill was comedian Ken Dodd, supported by tenors, an organist, trad jazz and C&W outfits and a singer of operatic arias.

Hopelessly out of place on such a bill – and performing before an audience that included the local mayor, councillors and civic dignitaries – the Beatles closed the show with a ten-minute thrash.

Monday 16 October

Lunchtime **Cavern Club, Liverpool**

Tuesday 17 October

David Lewis Club, Great George Place (Nile St entrance), Liverpool

The Beatles' only appearance at this city-centre venue was also the first commercial venture by their one-month-old fan club.

Wednesday 18 October

Lunchtime **Cavern Club, Liverpool**

Night **Cavern Club, Liverpool**

Thursday 19 October

Town Hall, Litherland, Liverpool

Booked as well as the Beatles on this typical Thursday-night "Beekay" bill were Gerry and the Pacemakers. Midway through the evening someone suggested that, as a break from routine, the two groups should join forces for one night to become, as it were, the Beatmakers. This they then did – George on lead guitar, Paul on rhythm, Pete Best sharing his drum kit with Freddy Marsden, Les Maguire on saxophone, Les Chadwick on bass, John Lennon at the piano and Gerry Marsden on lead guitar and vocals. Karl Terry, leader of the group Karl Terry and the Cruisers, also on the bill, joined in the singing.

The union was not intended to be permanent, indeed it was never attempted again, despite frequent opportunities for the two groups to do so.

Friday 20 October

Lunchtime **Cavern Club, Liverpool**

Night **Village Hall, Knotty Ash, Liverpool**

Saturday 21 October

Night **Cavern Club, Liverpool**

This booking could really be counted as two engagements, with the Beatles playing both before and after midnight during this Cavern Club all-night session.

Sunday 22 October

Casbah Coffee Club, West Derby, Liverpool

Tuesday 24 October

Lunchtime **Cavern Club, Liverpool**

Wednesday 25 October

Night **Cavern Club, Liverpool**

Thursday 26 October

Lunchtime **Cavern Club, Liverpool**

Friday 27 October

Village Hall, Knotty Ash, Liverpool

Saturday 28 October

Aintree Institute, Aintree, Liverpool

Sunday 29 October

Hambleton Hall, Huyton, Liverpool

Monday 30 October

Lunchtime **Cavern Club, Liverpool**

Tuesday 31 October

Town Hall, Litherland, Liverpool

Wednesday 1 November

Lunchtime **Cavern Club, Liverpool**
Night **Cavern Club, Liverpool**

Friday 3 November

Lunchtime **Cavern Club, Liverpool**

Saturday 4 November

Night **Cavern Club, Liverpool**

Tuesday 7 November

Lunchtime **Cavern Club, Liverpool**
Night **Merseyside Civil Service Club, Liverpool**
and **Cavern Club, Liverpool**

The first of four consecutive Tuesday appearances at the Merseyside Civil Service Club.

MERSEYSIDE CIVIL SERVICE CLUB

THE FABULOUS BEATLES

On Tuesday, 7th November, 1961

Guest's Ticket 3/-

The member whose name appears on the reverse of this ticket must accompany the bearer and sign the Visitor's Book at the time of admission

Wednesday 8 November

Night **Cavern Club, Liverpool**

Thursday 9 November

Lunchtime **Cavern Club, Liver ool**
Night **Town Hall, Litherland, Liverpool**

Perhaps the most important date in the Beatles' early years, for in attendance amid the predominantly young and female lunchtime Cavern Club throng, conspicuous in his pin-striped suit, was local record store owner, 27-year-old Brian Epstein.

By a complete coincidence, though certainly symbolic of Epstein's later influence over them, this date also marked the last appearance by the Beatles at the shabby ballroom of Litherland Town Hall.

Friday 10 November

Tower Ballroom, Promenade, New Brighton, Wallasey, Cheshire
and **Village Hall, Knotty Ash, Liverpool**

A spectacularly busy evening for the Beatles. Main attraction was undoubtedly the Tower Ballroom engagement, the first of many occasions they played at this huge hall, capable of holding a 5000 audience.

Over 3000 were packed in to witness this, the first "Operation Big Beat" in Liverpool, run on a grand American-style scale by ambitious promoter Sam Leach. (Leach had previously tested the water with a run of July 1961 "Big Beat Sessions" at the Civic Hall in Ellesmere Port, Cheshire, in which the Beatles had not participated.)

Between 7.30 pm and 1.00 am five top groups played alternate shifts on stage. The Beatles' first spot was at 8.00 pm, after which they dashed back, via the Mersey tunnel, to appear at Knotty Ash Village Hall. The evening was rounded off in fine style back at the Tower with a second spot at 11.30 pm, and a frantic car race with Rory Storm and the Hurricanes back under the River Mersey to Liverpool city centre, which very nearly resulted in a bloody and premature end to the lives of the latter group's members.

Note: the first advertisement for the Tower Ballroom show in the *Liverpool Echo*, carried in the 27 October edition, included NEMS among the various ticket outlets. This predates by 24 hours Brian Epstein's first knowledge of the group's name as he described their discovery.

Saturday 11 November

Aintree Institute, Aintree, Liverpool

After the performance, the Beatles headed for the Liverpool Jazz Society to attend a party thrown by Sam Leach to celebrate the success of the previous evening at the Tower Ballroom.

Sunday 12 November

Hambleton Hall, Huyton, Liverpool

Monday 13 November

Lunchtime **Cavern Club, Liverpool**

Tuesday 14 November

Night **Merseyside Civil Service Club, Liverpool**
and **Cavern Club, Liverpool**

Wednesday 15 November

Lunchtime **Cavern Club, Liverpool**
Night **Cavern Club, Liverpool**

Friday 17 November

Lunchtime **Cavern Club, Liverpool**
Night **Village Hall, Knotty Ash, Liverpool**

Saturday 18 November

Night **Cavern Club, Liverpool**

Sunday 19 November

Casbah Coffee Club, West Derby, Liverpool

Tuesday 21 November

Lunchtime **Cavern Club, Liverpool**
Night **Merseyside Civil Service Club, Liverpool**

Wednesday 22 November

Night **Cavern Club, Liverpool**

Thursday 23 November

Lunchtime **Cavern Club, Liverpool**

Friday 24 November

Casbah Coffee Club, West Derby, Liverpool
and **Tower Ballroom, New Brighton, Wallasey**

After fulfilling their Casbah engagement, the Beatles moved on to New Brighton for another Sam Leach presentation, "Operation Big Beat II".

The Beatles' 11.00 pm spot was considerably enlivened by the surprise appearance in the ballroom of two top black singers of the day, Britain's Emile Ford and America's UK-domiciled Davy Jones. Jones joined the Beatles on stage for two numbers while Ford performed with Rory Storm and the Hurricanes.

Sunday 26 November

Hambleton Hall, Huyton, Liverpool

Monday 27 November

Lunchtime **Cavern Club, Liverpool**

Tuesday 28 November

Merseyside Civil Service Club, Liverpool

Wednesday 29 November

Lunchtime **Cavern Club, Liverpool**
Night **Cavern Club, Liverpool**

Friday 1 December

Lunchtime **Cavern Club, Liverpool**
Night **Tower Ballroom, New Brighton, Wallasey**

The Beatles headed this five-and-a-half-hour, six-group "Big Beat Session" at the Tower, attended by 2000 people.

Saturday 2 December

Night **Cavern Club, Liverpool**

Sunday 3 December

Casbah Coffee Club, West Derby, Liverpool

Tuesday 5 December

Lunchtime **Cavern Club, Liverpool**

Wednesday 6 December

Night **Cavern Club, Liverpool**

*Cavern Club, 8 December 1961:
all eyes on Davy Jones.*

Friday 8 December

Lunchtime **Cavern Club, Liverpool**
Night **Tower Ballroom, New Brighton, Wallasey**

A big day for the Beatles, with Sam Leach booking Davy Jones to headline his seven-act bill at the Tower, and Ray McFall booking him for a lunchtime Cavern Club session. The Beatles backed Jones at both venues as well as performing their own sets.

South African-born singing star Danny Williams, at number four on the hit parade with 'Moon River' (and destined for the top position three weeks later), was in Liverpool for a week's engagement at the Cabaret Club so he too was added to the New Brighton bill just days before the event.

Saturday 9 December

Palais Ballroom, Queens Rd, Aldershot, Hampshire
and **The Blue Gardenia Club, St Anne's Court,**
off Dean St/Wardour St, London

The Beatles' first live performance in the south of England, followed by their first in London. Not that southerners knew much about it: the Aldershot date, owing to a major blunder, was unadvertised and attracted a mere 18 customers, while the London performance was a spur-of-the-moment whim to jump on stage in a semi-illicit Soho club/café run by an old friend.

If the minute attendance at the Aldershot engagement suggests an air of impetuous planning then certainly the idea was a good one. Liverpool promoter Sam Leach had shrewdly come to realise that as no London agents or record company executives would ever come to Liverpool, he would, instead, take the Liverpool groups to see them. Fine, in principle; in reality, Leach's geographical familiarity with the south of England was somewhat wayward, and instead of choosing a venue in Greater London he ended up booking five consecutive Saturday nights at the Palais Ballroom in Aldershot, a military outpost 37 miles south-west of the capital. Not surprisingly, his optimistic invitations to London's top pop impresarios went unheeded.

This, the first of the bookings, was billed on posters and handbills as a "Battle Of The Bands" between the Beatles and the totally unknown London combo Ivor Jay and the Jaywalkers (unrelated to the hit group Peter Jay and the Jaywalkers). Leach claims that he also placed a substantial advertisement in the local newspaper, the *Aldershot News*, proudly announcing the event. But unfortunately, Leach says, the paper refused to accept his cheque since he was not a regular advertiser, and nor could they contact him because he hadn't thought to give them his home address. The advert did not appear.

*An all-out effort for the
Aldershot 18 – Paul entertains
the few, 9 December 1961.*

Come the day of the dance, tired and aching from the nine-hour van journey down from Liverpool, the group discovered – much to their horror – that they faced the prospect of playing to an empty hall. Their only solution was to rush around the town's two coffee bars, and pubs, shouting, "Hey! There's a dance on at the Palais tonight" and offer free admission. Eighteen people turned up. To their credit, the Beatles valiantly played on, while Sam Leach went out among the dancers imploring them to spread out so as to look more numerous. The event was captured for posterity by Leach's photographer friend Richard Matthews.

At the end of the evening the Liverpudlian entourage drowned their sorrows in southern Watney's brown ale, played a soccer match with bingo balls on the dance floor and generally made a nuisance of themselves. The police ordered them out of town.

In their youthful exuberance, at 1.00 am and with nowhere to stay overnight, they headed for the bright lights of London, and a club run by their old friend Brian Cassar, former leader of Cass and the Cassanovas. The Soho club was small and very obscure, and the few late-night drinkers scarcely raised a collective eyebrow when the Beatles (minus George, who did not participate) jumped on stage to perform an impromptu set.

The following Saturday, 16 December, Leach escorted south Rory Storm and the Hurricanes for a "Battle Of The Bands II" with Ivor Jay. This time the advertisement did appear in the *Aldershot News* and 210 paying customers turned up. But despite the encouraging attendance Leach, by this time, was disgruntled and dissatisfied with the Aldershot experience and cancelled his booking for the three remaining dances.

Sunday 10 December

Hambleton Hall, Huyton, Liverpool

The Beatles' return north, in those pre-motorway days, was long and arduous, and they arrived very late for their appearance in Huyton. So late, in fact, that they had time to play only a 15-minute set. For the promoters, still expected to meet the £15 fee, this was deplorable behaviour. For Brian Epstein, waiting at Hambleton Hall to watch them perform, it highlighted how hard he would have to work to stamp out the group's carefree attitude over bookings.

Monday 11 December

Lunchtime **Cavern Club, Liverpool**

Wednesday 13 December

Lunchtime **Cavern Club, Liverpool**
Night **Cavern Club, Liverpool**

Mike Smith, A&R assistant at Decca Records, came up from London and attended this night-time Cavern Club session with a view to signing the Beatles to their prized British recording contract.

Friday 15 December

Lunchtime **Cavern Club, Liverpool**
Night **Tower Ballroom, New Brighton, Wallasey**

Another typical Sam Leach presentation – five groups providing five-and-a half hours' entertainment for the Tower Ballroom customers. Added to the bill at the last moment were Cass and the Cassanovas, a one-night reunion of Brian Cassar and the Big Three.

Saturday 16 December

Night **Cavern Club, Liverpool**

Sunday 17 December

Casbah Coffee Club, West Derby, Liverpool

Monday 18 December

Lunchtime **Cavern Club, Liverpool**

Tuesday 19 December

Lunchtime **Cavern Club, Liverpool**

Wednesday 20 December

Night **Cavern Club, Liverpool**

Thursday 21 December

Lunchtime **Cavern Club, Liverpool**

Saturday 23 December

Night **Cavern Club, Liverpool**

Another all-night session.

Tuesday 26 December

Tower Ballroom, New Brighton, Wallasey

Wednesday 27 December

Night **Cavern Club, Liverpool**

This engagement was advertised as "The Beatles' Xmas Party".

Friday 29 December

Night **Cavern Club, Liverpool**

Saturday 30 December

Night **Cavern Club, Liverpool**

A T 11.00 am on Monday 1 January 1962 – a cold and icy New Year's Day – John Lennon, Paul McCartney, George Harrison and Pete Best sat in the reception area at Decca Studios in West Hampstead, north London, and waited for the summons that would take them into the big time. While Brian Epstein had travelled down by train and stayed overnight with an aunt, for the four Beatles it had been an uncomfortable ten-hour journey, hunched in a van already crowded with their equipment and battling against heavy New Year's Eve snowstorms which caused road manager Neil Aspinall to lose his way near Wolverhampton.

Mike Smith, the A&R man who had seen the Beatles at the Cavern Club on 13 December 1961, and who would be supervising the audition, was late, following an all-night New Year's party. The Beatles were fidgety and Brian Epstein angry, sensing that Smith's delay was a slight on their importance. But eventually Smith did arrive and shepherded the motley Liverpudlians into the studio. There was an immediate problem: Smith was aghast at the state of the Beatles' amplifiers, battered and ragged veterans of more than 300 tough Merseyside dance dates and long Hamburg nights, and insisted the group use unfamiliar studio equipment instead.

Eventually, everyone readied themselves, the red light went on and the session began. With so much at stake, the Beatles were ill at ease and restrained, but they soldiered on, recording 15 songs chosen with care by Brian Epstein to highlight their versatility. At the end of the session, Smith hurried them out of the studio because he was running late for a second audition he was to supervise, with Brian Poole and the Tremeloes, a group from Barking, Essex. But Smith seemed pleased with the Beatles, and the chance of them landing a prized recording contract looked favourable. They returned to Liverpool to await the good news.

In that first week of the year, the Beatles' horizon looked decidedly bright. On 4 January, three days after the Decca audition, *Mersey Beat* published the result of its first group popularity poll. The Beatles were clear winners over their nearest rivals Gerry and the Pacemakers, the Remo Four, Rory Storm and the Hurricanes, and Johnny Sandon and the Searchers. The following day, Friday 5 January, saw the official British release by Polydor of Tony Sheridan and the (now correctly named) Beatles' single 'My Bonnie', a move prompted by Brian Epstein. The likelihood of it being a chart hit was remote, as Epstein realised, but the prestige to be gained from having a British record release was quite considerable: the Beatles added it to their stage repertoire, John singing lead vocal, while Epstein added such phrases as "Polydor Recording Artistes!" or "Hear The Beatles Play Their New Record" to dance advertisements, posters and handbills.

By the end of January – after, unofficially, just one month and, officially, just one week, under Brian Epstein's direction – the Beatles had a decent and fair management contract, a record in the shops, a possible contract with the mighty Decca organisation in the offing, an audition with BBC radio lined up for 12 February, a much superior Hamburg engagement to fulfil in the spring, money in their pockets, and a rota of new and vastly-improved venues to play. Out went the great majority of the Beatles' 1961 live venues, deemed unsuitable by Epstein for his group, out went the Beatles' uncaring attitude, their childish stage antics and reputation for poor punctuality. And out, too, went the group's hit-and-miss music presentation, to be replaced by one or two precise, pre-arranged sets of never more than 60 minutes.

But perhaps the most significant transformation of all was contained in the brown paper bags carried by each of the Beatles into the Playhouse Theatre in Manchester on Wednesday 7 March, about to rehearse and then record their début radio appearance for the BBC. For inside each bag was a brand-new £40 grey, brushed-tweed lounge suit, with pencil-thin lapels and matching tie, all bought from bespoke tailor Beno Dorn in Grange Road West, Birkenhead, for which they had been measured and paid a £3 deposit on 29 January. From that very moment, out forever went the Beatles' dishevelled stage appearance: the black leather outfits or jeans and the plimsolls. If the group really wanted to make it to the top, Epstein continually reminded them, they had to have a professional attitude and a presentable appearance. The Beatles threw up only temporary resistance before bowing to the logic of Epstein's argument. They had enjoyed their own, unique way for two years yet remained unknown outside of Liverpool and Hamburg. If wearing suits would enable them to have a stab at national success, so be it.

But even the suits came too late to prevent the unexpected; the rejection of the Beatles by Decca, news of which

INTRODUCTION 1962 AND DIARY

They're hoping for a hit record

Three local guitarists, who are members of Merseyside's most popular beat group, are to have their first record released tomorrow (Friday).

The guitarists, all members of "The Beatles" group together with 20-years-old drummer Pete Best, 8 Haymans Green, West Derby, are John Lennon, 251 Menlove Avenue, Woolton, George Harrison, 25 Upton Green, Speke, and Paul McCartney, who lives at 20 Forthlin Road, Allerton.

The record which the group have made was recorded in Germany while they were appearing at a Hamburg club, and their manager, Mr. Brian Epstein,

believes that it made a showing in the German popularity charts.

Now the record, backing singer Tony Sheridan, is to be released in England, and it is their hope that their own records will make the British charts later next year.

Twenty - one - years - old John Lennon plays the guitar and sings, and writes articles in "beat" language, while 19-years-old Paul plays the guitar, sings and writes songs in conjunction with John.

The boys have always been full-time musicians, ever since they left school, and are making quite a name for themselves locally. Who knows it might not be long before they achieve nation-wide acclaim.

came through at the beginning of February. If the Beatles were disillusioned at their failure, Brian Epstein was positively smarting. The capture of a recording contract was the essential ingredient in his master plan to establish the Beatles, and it had seemed such a formality. Mike Smith had seen the group on two occasions and been enthusiastic both times. The reasons now put forward: that they sounded too much like the Shadows and that "guitar groups are on the way out" were folly.

Epstein vowed to pursue the matter and travelled to London to meet Dick Rowe (head of singles A&R) and Sidney Arthur Beecher-Stevens (sales manager) at Decca's HQ on the Thames embankment. But the executives would not be budged – kindly, but somewhat high-handedly, they sniffed, "The Beatles won't go, Mr Epstein. We know these things. You have a good record business in Liverpool, why not stick to that?" The red-faced Epstein quickly lost his remaining cool. "You must be out of your minds," he ranted, "these boys are going to explode. I am completely confident that one day they will be bigger than Elvis Presley!" The important Decca men afforded themselves a wry smile; they heard that one every day from every manager of every struggling pop band in the land.

Still, Epstein had a foot in Decca's door and was reluctant to withdraw it and allow that door to close. He toyed with the idea of offering to buy 3000 copies of any Beatles single released by the company, then decided against it. He also, the next day, had a meeting with Tony Meehan, the former Shadows drummer turned independent producer, with a view to buying studio time at a cost of £100 and having Meehan produce a single. But, wrote Epstein later, Meehan kept him waiting and when the meeting started was disparaging towards the Beatles, viewing them as another no-hope group taking up his valuable time. Indignant, Epstein dropped the matter, severing the Beatles' last link with Decca in a letter dated 10 February.

While in London on this same failed mission Brian Epstein wasted no opportunity to ply his group around other major record companies. Armed with the only fruitful outcome of the Decca audition – two reel-to-reel tapes containing 15 songs – he went first to Pye and then to Oriole and at both places the reply was the same: a polite, or impolite, but emphatic "No". So, around Thursday 8 February, desperate in a straw-clutching way, Epstein walked into the prestigious EMI-owned HMV record shop in Oxford Street. One year before, as manager of NEMS, Epstein had been to Hamburg (ironically) on a record retail management course run by Deutsche Grammophon, and there had befriended Bob Boast, HMV's genial manager. Now, in the nicest sense, he was going to exploit that friendship for all he could. After a little chatting, he played Boast extracts from the Decca tapes. Boast listened but explained, as Epstein must have known, that he was in no position to help – other than to suggest that it might be better if Epstein hawked around discs rather than cumbersome tapes. Epstein agreed and so Boast led him to a small studio on the first floor of the store, where customers could make 78rpm demonstration records.

While the engineer, Jim Foy, was cutting discs from Epstein's tapes, he remarked that the group sounded inter-esting. Epstein added, proudly, that three of the songs had actually been written by members of the group, uncommon in those days. Foy asked if they had been published and Epstein replied that they hadn't. Foy then informed Epstein that the office of Ardmore & Beechwood, a music publishing subsidiary of EMI, was located on the top floor of the shop. A flicker of hope must have raced across Epstein's mind as Foy fetched down to the small studio Ardmore & Beechwood's general manager, Sid Colman. He, too, liked the sound and wanted to discuss acquiring the group's music publishing rights. When Foy finished the disc cutting Epstein and Colman retired to Colman's office.

Sid Colman's expression of interest was undoubtedly pleasing but Epstein made his real quest clear: the Beatles first and foremost needed a recording contract, not a music publishing deal. Colman understood and made a call to George Martin, the head of A&R at Parlophone, an EMI record label. Parlophone was EMI's joker in the pack, and not just because it released many comedy records. In terms of budget, hits and prestige it was the poor relation of the company's powerful labels, Columbia and HMV.

When the telephone rang in George Martin's office on the fourth floor of EMI's nearby Manchester Square headquarters, Judy Lockhart-Smith, his secretary, answered it. Martin wasn't there but Epstein arranged a meeting with him for Tuesday 13 February. Beforehand, at 10.30 am on 9 February, Colman and Martin met up to discuss – probably among other things – Epstein's quest.

The following Tuesday Brian Epstein went to Manchester Square and met George Martin for the first time. He was unlike any A&R man Epstein had come across before. Although well-spoken and educated he was witty, intelligent and approachable. Epstein began his sales pitch, saying how huge the Beatles were on Merseyside, and then expressing great – and by now well-practised – mock-surprise when Martin said that he hadn't heard of them. Then Epstein played Martin the newly-cut discs and held his breath.

There was something in the music, a certain indefinable quality, which appealed to George Martin as to no other A&R man before him. He wasn't over-impressed, admittedly, but was curious, seeming to enjoy 'Hello Little Girl' and 'Till There Was You', commenting favourably upon George's guitar playing and identifying Paul as a possible group leader. Martin concluded that it might be worth his while seeing the Beatles; heartened by this news, although not yet with an actual meeting date written into his diary,

Die Not hat ein **Ende!**
Die Zeit der Dorfmusik ist vorbei!
Am Freitag, dem 13. April
eröffnet
★ **Star-Club**
die Rock n' Twist-Parade 1962
mit The Beatles   Tex Roberg   Roy Young   The Graduates   The Bachelors
zusätzlich ab Mai: Tony Sheridan-Quartett und Gerry and the Pacemakers
Eine Ballung der Spitzenklasse Europas
Hmb.-St.Pauli, Gr. Freiheit 39

C/2/SFA   7th December, 1961.

Mr. B. Epstein,
Nems Limited,
12-14 Whitechapel,
LIVERPOOL, 1,
Lancs.

Dear Mr. Epstein,

    I return herewith the original of the contract you gave to me in confidence a few days ago and thought you might like to have a translation to save you the bother of having it done.

    Now that I see that their contract expires quite soon with Kaempfert I will certainly ask our Artistes Managers if they are interested in the Group. I think you should note that it is necessary to give three months notice of termination before the 30th June 1962 if you are to obtain their services.

    Please feel assured that I will have the material assessed very carefully and will write to you again as soon as possible.

    Yours very truly,

    R.N. WHITE
    General Marketing Manager.

NEMS LTD.

TELEVISION · RECORDS · DOMESTIC APPLIANCES

12-14 WHITECHAPEL	70-72 WALTON ROAD	HEAD OFFICE
LIVERPOOL 1	LIVERPOOL 4	50 GT. CHARLOTTE STREET
Tel. ROYal 7895	Tel. NORth 3221	LIVERPOOL 1
		Tel. ROYal 7895

Our Ref: BE/BA: Your Ref: Replies to Whitechapel

8th December 1961

Dear Mr. White,

As I'm somewhat disappointed at not having heard from you with regard to the matter we discussed last week, I thought I'd write and attempt to impress you once again with my enthusiasm for, and belief in, the potential success of 'The Beatles'.

If I didn't mention that they were so much better in reality than on the disc it was because I may have assumed that "you'd heard it before". This point has been confirmed during the last few days by various persons that I'd persuaded to come from London to see them. Earlier this week the group were seen by representatives of Deutsche Grammophon (in connection with the record they are issuing in January) who were very impressed, and now feel that the release will be worth summoning all the efforts and promotional activities that D.G. can muster in this country.

Next week the Group will be seen by A. & R. men from Decca. I mention this because, (as you may appreciate), if we could choose it would certainly be E.M.I. These four boys who are superb instrumentalists, also produce some exciting and pulsating vocals. They play mostly their own compositions and one of the boys has written a song which I really believe to be the hottest material since 'Living Doll'. This is a Group of exceptional talents and appealing personalities.

Cont..../

SERVICE ENQUIRIES Telephone ANField 2616

NEMS LTD.

TELEVISION · RECORDS · DOMESTIC APPLIANCES

12-14 WHITECHAPEL	70-72 WALTON ROAD	HEAD OFFICE
LIVERPOOL 1	LIVERPOOL 4	50 GT. CHARLOTTE STREET
Tel. ROYal 7895	Tel. NORth 3221	LIVERPOOL 1
		Tel. ROYal 7895

Our Ref: BE/BA: Your Ref: Replies to Whitechapel

-2-

8th December 1961

I look forward to hearing from you.

Yours sincerely,
Brian Epstein.

P.S. With regard to the German contract they had signed (a copy of which I left with you) I understand that if pressed Deutsche Grammophon in Germany would probably be willing to negotiate the possibility of their breaking same at an earlier date than stated.

R.N. White, Esq.,
Messrs. E.M.I. Records Ltd.,
20, Manchester Square,
LONDON W.1

SERVICE ENQUIRIES Telephone ANField 2616

12-14, Whitechapel, Liverpool 1

BE/BA:

27th March 1962

Dear Mr. Kaempfert,

Thank you very much for your letter dated March 3rd concerning The Beatles Agreement with yourself.

As it happens the particular recording Company with whom we have negotiated are unable to record the group until they return from Germany and in any event prefer to wait until their existing contract with yourself has expired.

In the circumstances therefore I would like to give you formal notice of our wish to terminate the contract at the end of this contractual period (30th June 1962).

With regard to their recording when in Germany I would myself be very pleased to discuss this with you as I shall be arriving in Hamburg on April 9th - a few days in advance of the group. I will, therefore contact you then and possibly we can settle details of their actual recording sessions.

Yours sincerely,
Brian Epstein. Manager
for and on behalf of The Beatles.

Bert Kaempfert, Esq.,
Bert Kaempfert Produktion,
Inselstr 4,
Hamburg,
GERMANY

                        7th July, 1958.

George Martin, Esq.,
Parlophone Artiste's Manager,
E.M.I. Records Limited,
8-11, Great Castle Street,
LONDON, W.1.

Dear Mr. Martin,

    You are cordially invited to cocktails in the Oak Room, Trocadero Restaurant, Shaftesbury Avenue, W.1., on Wednesday, July 9th, at 6.30pm - 7.30pm, for the purpose of meeting Mr. Sid Colman, the new General Manager for Ardmore and Beechwood, Ltd., and associates.

    Yours sincerely,

    JOSEPH E. ZERGA

                3429

APPLICATION FOR ARTISTES' CONTRACT

To: Miss E. F. Harwood,
Administration,
E.M.I. Records Limited, Hayes.

Will you please have a contract prepared between:-

THE PARLOPHONE   Company Limited
and
Name of Artiste .... THE BEATLES .... Group of Instrumentalists
Professional name (if any) ....
Address .... c/o N.E.M.S. LTD.
      12-14 Whitechapel, Liverpool 1.
If a Minor -
  Name of Parent ....
      OR
  Name of Guardian ....
Address of Parent or Guardian ....
Nationality of Artist
(British or not British) .... British
Period of Contract .... 1 year
Commencing date of Contract .... 6th June, 1962.
Number of Titles Per Annum .... 6 titles
Flat Fee .... None
Rate of Royalty .... 1d per d/s
Advance Royalty .... None
Royalty to be paid to
(one name only) .... Brian Epstein (on behalf of The Beatles)
Option .... 1st year royalty increasing 1d.
Special Clauses .... 2nd year royalty increasing 1d.
Date .... 18th May, 1962.   Signed ... For George H. Martin.

Ref. 4450   C.F.

Inter-departmental MEMORANDUM   Date May 25th. 1962.

To Miss E. Harwood.   C/S9/JLS
  Administration.
  Hayes.

Re: THE BEATLES/PARLOPHONE.

Thank you for your memo' of May 24th. enclosing the Contract for the Beatles.

In point of fact, I will pay the musicians the ordinary M.U. fee but I did not think that it was necessary to include this in the Contract.

G.H. Martin.
E.M.I. Records Ltd.

Ref. 4450   H.P.W.

Inter-departmental MEMORANDUM   Date June 5th. 1962.

To Miss Harwood.   C/S9/JLS.
  Administration.
  Hayes.

Re: THE BEATLES.

I am returning herewith Contract for the above artist duly signed.

G.H. Martin.
E.M.I. Records Ltd.

Encl.

                    18th June 1962

MR.G.H.MARTIN

BRIAN EPSTEIN / THE BEATLES

Herewith agreement between the above parties. This has been signed by the Secretary and witnessed, and is for the artists retention.

Evelyn F. Harwood,
Administration

C/H/EFH/F

Document 1 (top left):

C/2/AJS

18th December, 1961

Brian Epstein, Esq.,
NEMS Limited,
12-14 Whitechapel,
LIVERPOOL, 1.

Dear Mr. Epstein,

Thank you for your letter of the 8th December in connection with "The Beatles".

I am sorry that I have been so long in giving you a decision but I have now had an opportunity of playing the record to each of our Artistes Managers.

Whilst we appreciate the talents of this group, we feel that we have sufficient groups of this type at the present time under contract and that it would not be advisable for us to sign any further contract of this nature at present.

Please accept my sincere apologies and also thanks for letting us have the opportunity of first refusal.

I return the original of the German contract herewith.

With best wishes for Christmas and the New Year.

Yours sincerely,

R.N. WHITE.
General Marketing Manager.

Document 2 (top middle):

NEMS LTD.

TELEVISION RECORDS RADIO DOMESTIC APPLIANCES

12-14 WHITECHAPEL, LIVERPOOL 1   Telephone ROYAL 7895 (5 lines)

RS/Ed.

10th February 1962

Dear Mr. Rowe,

I am writing to thank you for your kind offer of co-operation in assisting me to put the Beatles on records. I am most grateful for your own and that of your colleagues consideration of this Group and whilst I appreciate the offer of Mr. Meehan's services I have now decided not to accept.

The principal reason for this change of mind is that since I saw you last the Group have received an offer of a recording contract from another Company.

Kindest regards,

Yours sincerely,
Brian Epstein.

Dick Rowe, Esq.,
Messrs. Decca Record Co.Ltd.,
Decca House,
9, Albert Embankment,
LONDON S.W.1

Copies to :- S.A. Beecher Stevens Esq., A.J. Kelland, Esq.,

Document 3 (top right):

BERT KAEMPFERT PRODUCTION   Hamburg 20, den 21. März 196

Klaus Reimann

Mr.
Brian Epstein

12-14 Whitechapel

Liverpool 1 / England

Dear Mr. Epstein,

with reference to your letter dated February 20, 1962 I should like to inform you that it was agreed upon with "THE BEATLES" that they would return to Germany around February 1962 and that recording should be made with them at that time. My understanding is that "THE BEATLES" are to come to Hamburg again in April of this year. I am in principle willing to release this group from their agreement before the official expiration of their contract. However, I would appreciate if a way could be found that they are still recording for the Polydor label during their stay in Hamburg in April or May. I do not want to spoil the chance of the group to get recording contracts elsewhere, but I do think that we should have the chance to make recordings with the group for the Polydor label whilst they are in Hamburg.

Very truly yours,

Bert Kaempfert

Bert Kämpfert

Document 4 (middle left):

24th May, 1962.

MR. G. MARTIN

THE BEATLES/PARLOPHONE (Manager Mr. Brian Epstein)

Enclosed please find copy of this contract for despatch to Mr. Epstein so that he can sign and return it to us.

Brian Epstein is getting a royalty and I asked specially whether any provision was to be made for payment of M.U. rates to musicians at the recording sessions, but I was told no, they would not get any such payment. I hope this is correct !

Evelyn F. Harwood
Administration
EMI Records Ltd.

C/E/EFH/JMH

Document 5 (center telegram):

POST OFFICE TELEGRAM

Charges to pay ____ s. ____ d.   RECEIVED

Prefix. Time handed in. Office of Origin and Service Instructions.

195   ROY 0033

At ____ m.   From ____   By ____

+G166 12.40 PRIMROSE TS 26

MERSEY BEAT ROYAL 0003 LIVERPOOL=
HAVE SECURED CONTRACT FOR BEATLES TO RECORDED
FOR EMI ON PARLAPHONE LABEL 1ST RECORDING
DATE SET FOR JUNE 6TH= BRIAN EPSTEIN +

0003 6TH + 1ST + 1   TS 0

For free repetition of doubtful words telephone "TELEGRAMS ENQ' at office of delivery. Other enquiries should be accompanied by this form.

Document 6 (bottom left):

C/2/SPA   26th June, 1962.

Brian Epstein, Esq.,
NEMS Limited,
12-14 Whitechapel,
LIVERPOOL, 1.

Dear Mr. Epstein,

I was nonplussed and somewhat embarrassed to see details of a contract going through for "The Beatles" especially in view of my letter to you of the 18th December, 1961 when I told you that our Artiste Managers did not feel we could use them.

I hasten to say that I am very pleased that a contract is now being negotiated as I felt that they were very good but our Artiste Managers who heard the record felt at that time that they had the greatest difficulty in judging their quality from the record.

George Martin tells me that he has been suitably impressed with them and has made certain suggestions to you which in his view may improve them still further and it is for this reason that he has offered a contract.

My only reason for writing is to endeavour to explain what must appear to you to be an anomaly in our Organisation. I can assure you that the Artistes Managers did hear the record but I know you will appreciate that even Artistes Managers are human and can change their minds !

With best wishes,

Yours sincerely,

R.N. WHITE.
General Marketing Manager.

Document 7 (bottom middle):

NEMS ENTERPRISES LTD

DIRECTORS: B. AND C. J. EPSTEIN

12-14 WHITECHAPEL, LIVERPOOL, 1   TELEPHONE ROYal 7895

RS/BA:

29th June 1962

Dear Mr. White,

Thank you very much for your letter of the 26th instant regarding The Beatles. In the circumstances your attitude and remarks are greatly appreciated. As you will probably realise it is a great pleasure for me to be associated with all this manner. I am very much looking forward to the issue of the groups' first disc which I expect should be towards the end of August - although I have not heard from George Martin recently.

Thank you again, kindest regards.

Yours sincerely,
Brian Epstein.

R.N. White, Esq.,
Messrs. E.M.I. Records Ltd.,
E.M.I. House,
20, Manchester Square,
LONDON W.1

Document 8 (bottom right):

17th December, 1963.
C/I/SB

MR. R. DAWES

THE BEATLES

I hear so many different stories about how the Beatles came to E.M.I. that I thought I ought to set down on paper the true facts.

a) A Beatles Polydor recording was submitted by Brian Epstein to Mr. R.N. White.

b) Mr. R.N. White submitted this disc to Mr. Ridley and to Mr. Newell. Both turned it down on the basis that it sounded like a bad recording of The Shadows - and apparently it did!

c) Epstein then took the Polydor disc to Decca. Their "pop" A. & R. Manager, Dick Rowe, was in America, so his deputy decided to give the Beatles a test, and in fact did so.

d) Dick Rowe returned from America and the test recording was played to him. His reaction was that electric guitars were now 'old hat' and he was not interested in the Beatles.

e) A depressed Brian Epstein then sent to our private recording department in the Oxford Street Store a tape of some of the Beatles own compositions which he wanted transferred to disc.

f) The engineer at Oxford Street was quite impressed with some of the compositions and referred them to Syd Colman.

g) Colman then phoned George Martin, said he ought to hear the tape, and Martin agreed.

h) Brian Epstein then took the tape to George who agreed to give the Beatles a recording test - Martin took the test himself - was impressed with what he heard, signed them to a contract and the rest is public knowledge.

L.G. WOOD
E.M.I. RECORDS LTD.

The Beatles

Business & Personal Manager:
BRIAN EPSTEIN
12-14 WHITECHAPEL
LIVERPOOL 1
ROYal 7895

Epstein returned to Liverpool. There the Parlophone situation rested for almost three months, however: the ever-busy Martin did not hurry in re-establishing contact.

While the Beatles, John in particular, were convinced that Epstein had lost them their chance of a Decca contract by selecting their audition material and so interfering in what they knew best, the music, their next trip to Hamburg came along. The seeds of the visit, their third, had been sown in late-December 1961 when Peter Eckhorn, accompanied by Tony Sheridan, journeyed to Liverpool to sign up some groups for the Top Ten Club. Epstein asked for 500DM (£44.50) per man per week but Eckhorn offered only 450DM (£40) and so left Liverpool on 30 December without the Beatles' contract. Three weeks later, accompanied by musician Roy Young, Horst Fascher – former bouncer at both Bruno Koschmider's Kaiserkeller and Eckhorn's Top Ten clubs – arrived in Liverpool. He was now working for Manfred Weissleder, a prominent Hamburg club owner planning to open the Star-Club at 39 Grosse Freiheit. He offered 500DM per man (along with an additional one-off "under the table" 1000DM) and a contract was drawn up engaging the Beatles from 13 April until 31 May 1962.

The Beatles' train-travelling days were over, with Epstein extravagantly arranging for the group to fly to Hamburg. On 11 April, John, Paul and Pete flew out of Manchester destined for Germany. George, who was unwell, flew out the following day with Brian Epstein. But when the first entourage arrived in Hamburg they were met at the airport by a distraught Astrid Kirchherr. Her fiancé Stuart Sutcliffe, the truly gifted artist, former Beatles bass player and John's closest friend, was dead, aged 21. He had died of a brain haemorrhage the previous day. John, Paul, George and Pete were devastated by the loss of their friend. On Friday 13 April, the same day that they opened at the Star-Club, Stuart's grieving mother arrived in Hamburg to undergo the dreadful task of formally identifying her dead son, and to take home his body for burial in Liverpool.

Having overseen the Beatles' safe arrival in Hamburg, met Manfred Weissleder and observed the opening nights of the Beatles' seven-week stint at the Star-Club, Brian Epstein flew back to England and prepared himself for one last onslaught on the London record companies.

One door that hadn't yet been slammed in his face was at Parlophone, where, back on 13 February, George Martin had made encouraging noises about seeing the Beatles in person, even though, subsequently, he had done nothing about it. Pushed into doing so, however, by Sid Colman at Ardmore & Beechwood (he intended directing Epstein to EMI rival Philips if the Parlophone opportunity fizzled out), George met Brian a second time, at 11.30 am on Wednesday 9 May, on this occasion at EMI Studios in Abbey Road, St John's Wood.

Although contradictory to all other published accounts of the story, what happened next – the facts supported by unassailable EMI paperwork – was that George Martin promptly offered Brian Epstein's group a recording contract without first seeing them in person. He wasn't *guaranteeing* the Beatles a contract, just offering them their best chance yet. But he agreed to process the relevant paperwork within EMI so that, should he consider the group worthy of a deal after actually seeing them – the date of 6 June was promptly set for the Beatles' first trip to Abbey Road – EMI would have only to add its signature to an otherwise completed contract to consummate the deal.

Thus on 18 May Martin sent an "Application For Artiste' [*sic*] Contract" form to EMI's administration department, stating the details and terms upon which the department was to draw up the contract. On 24 May the typed contract – post-dated 4 June – was returned to George Martin for his dispatch to Brian Epstein. (Martin acknowledged receipt of this on 25 May.) Then on 5 June – the day before he first met the Beatles – Martin received back the contract from Epstein, signed and witnessed, and returned it to administration ready for the all-important, legally binding EMI signature if he decided that he liked them.

From an historian's perspective, the 18 May contract request finally explains why the Beatles thought that the 6 June session was arranged so that they could record their début single, not merely audition for the company. (In fact the session fulfilled both purposes: they auditioned a good many songs which were not recorded, and then performed four which were.) It explains why they expected this début record to be issued in July. It explains why the documentation for the 6 June session is readable in such a way that the Beatles were already under contract. And it explains why, around 12.30 pm on Wednesday 9 May 1962, Epstein left EMI Studios and went direct to the Post Office on nearby Wellington Road to telephone his parents and then send two telegrams. The first, to the Beatles in Hamburg, read, "Congratulations boys. EMI request recording session. Please rehearse new material." The second, to Bill Harry at *Mersey Beat*, read "Have secured contract for Beatles to recorded [*sic*] for EMI on Parlaphone [*sic*] label. 1st recording date set for June 6th."

That the Beatles should have ended up with EMI was, anyway, highly ironic. In December 1961, before any other company had turned down the group, before even the Decca audition, they had been rejected by post by the A&R managers at EMI labels Columbia and HMV. This was after Brian Epstein had sent a copy of the 'My Bonnie' single to the company's general marketing manager, Ron White. White had played it to both A&R men but they felt, understandably, that there was little to impress them in the backing behind Tony Sheridan's vocal (which they were requested to ignore).

The Beatles' seven-week engagement at the Star-Club came to an end on 31 May and they flew home to England on 2 June. Four days later, on Wednesday 6 June, they arrived at EMI Studios in Abbey Road for the first time. All but the ever-reticent drummer Pete Best got on famously with George Martin. He himself impressed the Beatles by revealing that he had produced the solo comedy records by Goons members Peter Sellers and Spike Milligan. John and George, particularly, counted these among their personal favourites. The Beatles, meanwhile, impressed Martin with their irreverent humour and apparent ease in what were usually nerve-racking conditions. "I've got nothing to lose," he concluded, and duly sanctioned the addition of a binding EMI signature to the Beatles' recording contract.

The Beatles rejoined the Merseyside nightly engagements scene on 9 June, their popularity undimmed despite a two-month absence. At a "Welcome Home" night at the Cavern, the club's record attendance figure was shattered. Long queues, stretching the length of Mathew Street, would now form hours before Beatles appearances there, even for lunchtime sessions. On 11 June a coach-load of fan club members, with the Beatles on board, travelled to the Playhouse Theatre in Manchester for the group's second BBC radio recording session. Afterwards, Beatles hysteria spread to the nearby Manchester streets and, in the mêlée, the coach returned to Liverpool without Pete Best, left stranded and alone. It was to prove a symbolic moment for the Beatles' drummer.

That summer of 1962 Brian Epstein was booking the Beatles into ever-improving local venues and slowly but surely – though sometimes with a dash of naivety – securing them invaluable out-of-town dates too, in such places as Stroud, Northwich, Rhyl, Doncaster, Swindon, Morecambe and Lydney. On 7 June Brian and his brother Clive put down a share capital of £100 on NEMS Enterprises, a new venture designed to channel Brian's show-business aspirations. Then on 28 June the Beatles made their début at the Majestic Ballroom in Birkenhead, not in itself a particularly auspicious event but, put into its proper perspective, a landmark, and one which illustrates perfectly the way in which Brian Epstein was handling the Beatles in the crucial middle months of 1962.

The Majestic was a Top Rank venue, one of 28 ballrooms dotted around Britain that belonged to the company. From Bill Marsden, manager at Birkenhead, Epstein ascertained the name of the company's theatre division manager, L B (Len) Fancourt, and wrote to him praising the Beatles and announcing their availability to Top Rank. Fancourt filed this with the dozens of similar letters received every week from hopeful pop-group managers. He sent Epstein the standard reply – the names and addresses of every ballroom operated by Top Rank, accompanied by a short note to the effect of "try them yourself". Epstein did just that – from Aberdeen to Plymouth and Crewe to Kilburn, each and every ballroom manager received an immaculately-typed letter, on newly-designed NEMS Enterprises notepaper, beginning with the opening gambit, "L B Fancourt has personally suggested I write to you concerning the possible engagement of my group, the Beatles..." These letters invariably included a line like "I must tell you that the group is very heavily booked as far ahead as October (or whatever month was three months after the post date) but I might just be able to squeeze you in..." Amazingly, it worked, and the Beatles were to play 12 of the 28 Top Rank ballrooms within a year of the Birkenhead début.

During the Beatles' first eight weeks back in England after Hamburg, from 6 June to 31 July, they fulfilled a staggering total of 62 live engagements, plus two recording sessions –

one for EMI and the other for the BBC. Every week Brian would give each Beatle and Neil Aspinall neatly-prepared "accounts statements" showing precise details of the past seven days' bookings with fees, expenses and commission all calculated to the last penny, and also giving details and relevant instructions for the coming week's engagements. Here Brian would stress the need for punctuality and smart appearance and underline – often literally – why each and every performance was of particular importance to the group. The week's bookings would invariably include a Wednesday-night session and a quota of two or three lunchtime shows at the Cavern Club (usually in the form of Monday, Wednesday, Friday one week, Tuesday and Thursday the next), plus at least one "major" appearance, either in Southport, on the Wirral or out of town. At these engagements Epstein would break the Beatles' one-hour stage spot into two separate half-hour sets, to tantalise the audience and also prepare the group for the big time. This, after all, was how the *stars* appeared live.

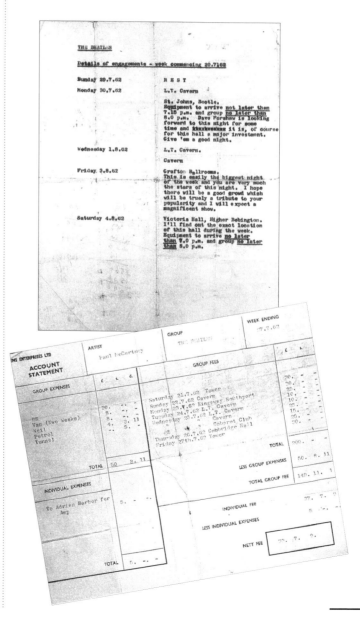

1962

In Skegness, Lincolnshire, 161 miles from Liverpool across the breadth of Britain, one of the most incredible strokes of good fortune in show-business history was about to touch a small-built, sad-eyed, 22-year-old Liverpudlian earning a meagre summer wage playing drums with a group called Rory Storm and the Hurricanes at the resort's Butlin's holiday camp. His name was Richard Starkey, known as Ritchie to his friends and Ringo Starr on stage, and on 14 August 1962 he was plucked from almost certain obscurity to the bosom of the Beatles and lifelong fame in one fell swoop.

The Beatles had been contemplating the dismissal of Pete Best for some considerable time and, in their own deliberate way, were gradually divorcing him from their activities. For example, Best did not learn of the group's failure at the Decca audition for some time after the others because they "forgot" to tell him. A plan was hatching in the minds of John, Paul and George to oust him – it was based largely on jealousy of his good looks and the way that he attracted the most girls, but it also went deeper than this. His drumming ability, though adequate, was quite limited and was almost certainly unsuitable for recording purposes, a point which George Martin made quite clear to Brian Epstein on 6 June. Best's personality was also markedly different to the others' – they were witty, brash and exuberant, he was painfully shy and reserved. He had also refused to re-style his hair into the fringe-style the Beatles would make famous and, as a consequence, looked out of place, too. George in particular was keen to see Best out and Ringo Starr in, and had visited Ringo's house to ask his parents if the Beatles could approach him about joining up. Then John and Paul made a secret trip to Skegness to discuss it with Ringo, but when Rory and the other Hurricanes asked Ringo why they'd come he refused to comment.

Despite his alleged shortcomings, it was still shabby treatment for Pete, who had served the group unstintingly from their hapless, drummerless Silver Beatles days through three lengthy Hamburg seasons and over 200 Cavern Club performances. He had shared in the heartaches and the headaches, had controlled the Beatles' bookings before Epstein took over, and had made his home – the Casbah – their home. The Beatles had had two years in which to dismiss him but hadn't done so, and now – as they were beginning to reap the rewards for their long, hard slog, with money rolling in and an EMI recording contract secured – he was out. It was the most underhand, unfortunate and unforgivable chapter in the Beatles' rise to monumental power.

Being their manager, John, Paul and George gave Brian Epstein the odious task of breaking the news to Pete Best, and he summoned him to a meeting in his office at NEMS' Whitechapel shop at 11.00 am on Thursday 16 August. Half an hour later a dumbstruck Best, along with his buddy Neil Aspinall, was drowning his anger in Liverpool ale. Within hours the news leaked out and there was a minor uproar among Beatles fans, among many of whom Pete Best was the favourite. Epstein needed protection to walk down Mathew Street for a few days, and his new Ford Zephyr was scratched.

Another time there were scuffles outside the Cavern Club and George received a shining black left eye.

As it transpired, Ringo had been unsettled with Rory Storm and the Hurricanes for some time. After graduating through the Eddie Clayton Skiffle Group in 1957 and 1958, he first drummed with the Raving Texans (the embryo Hurricanes) on Wednesday 25 March 1959 at the Mardi Gras club in Mount Pleasant, Liverpool, although he didn't join the group on a permanent basis until that November, by which time, via two other name changes, they had become Rory Storm and the Hurricanes. (The others were Al Storm and the Hurricanes and Jett Storm and the Hurricanes.)

In May 1960 the band secured a valuable summer season engagement at Butlin's in Pwllheli, north Wales, to commence 4 June, but Ringo announced that he wasn't going; he was getting married that same month. But the wedding was cancelled and Ringo went to Butlin's instead and then, in October, on to Hamburg with the group to play at the Kaiserkeller. It was here that Ringo first came into regular contact with the Beatles and the two parties took an almost immediate liking to one another – it was Starr, not Pete Best, who accompanied Walter Eymond and the Beatles to the tiny Akustik studio to record 'Summertime' that 15 October.

A year later, in October 1961, after a second summer engagement at Butlin's in Pwllheli, Ringo became restless again. He had long been enamoured with American Wild West movies so he wrote to the Houston Chamber of Commerce, in Texas, expressing interest in emigration. But

Mementos from Ringo Starr's pre-Beatles career: performing stand-up drumming with the Eddie Clayton Skiffle Group at Wilson Hall, Garston, 23 May 1957; far-left in the nattily dressed Rory Storm and the Hurricanes, about to set the Butlin's ballroom buzzing, Pwllheli, summer 1960; and a rare South Liverpool Weekly News item, 25 August 1960.

RICHARD REALISES A BOYHOOD AMBITION

RICHARD STARKEY always wanted to be a drummer. From when he was a small boy he was always tapping his fingers.

He has been in hospital twice, and has had 12 operations, several of them major ones.

When he came out last time after two years spent mostly in bed, he looked around for something to do—and started his fingers tapping again.

So he saved up and spent £10 on a second-hand drum kit and set about teaching himself to play.

After two months' hard practice he joined a group. And now, with a new drum kit costing £125, he is entertaining hundreds of teenagers at a Pwllheli (North Wales) holiday camp as a member of Rory Storm's Hurricanes.

All five of them Liverpool lads, are packing the camp's rock and calypso ballroom each evening for three-hour jive sessions.

Working a 16-hour week they spend their spare time joining in all the fun of the camp, swimming, sport and sunbathing.

"It's as good as a holiday—and we get paid for it," said 20-years-old Richard — he lives in Admiral Grove, Dingle—during a break in the rock session. His suntanned face broke into

a smile as he added: "It's fabulous."

PROFESSIONAL CAREER

Richard—he plays under the name of Ringo Starr—is the second ex-pupil of St. Silas C. of E. School, Dingle, to make a professional career in rock and roll.

The first—Ronnie Wycherley now carving a niche for himself as Billy Fury.

It is the group's biggest contract so far; before they filled dates at Liverpool jazz clubs and had a spot in a rock show at Liverpool Stadium in May, which starred Gene Vincent and was to have featured Eddie Cochran.

Led by ex-cotton sampleman Rory Storm (his real name is Alan Caldwell) whose home is at 54 Broadgreen Road, Stoneycroft, the group has been playing together for just 10 months.

The other members — Lou Walters, 22 (bass guitar and vocal), Ty Brian, 19 (lead guitarist), Johnny Guitar, 20 (rhythm guitar and vocal) and Richard, all belonged to other groups before that.

When they finish their 13-week engagement at Pwllheli in a few days, the lads plan a holiday in London.

And later they hope to go on the Continent to seek dates there.

Said Richard: "There is too much competition here. Rock and roll is beginning to wane."

He added: "But I like the life. I certainly don't want to give it up."

while the reply was not unfavourable, Ringo became disheartened by the sight of so many application forms and abandoned the idea. Nevertheless, three months later, he did quit the Hurricanes to work overseas, though not in Houston but in Hamburg. On 30 December 1961 he left Lime Street station with Peter Eckhorn and Tony Sheridan to be the drummer behind Sheridan in the house-band at the Top Ten Club. But by February 1962 Ringo had grown tired of the argumentative Sheridan, quit Hamburg and rejoined Rory Storm in time for a working holiday in France and a third summer season at Butlin's, this time at Skegness.

When John telephoned there on Tuesday 14 August and confirmed Ringo's invitation to join the Beatles, Rory Storm and his group were just 15 days away from completing their three-month stint at the holiday camp. But the Beatles' need was urgent and, as Ringo had been keen to join them for some time – he had even sat in with them for two engagements on 5 February, when Pete Best was ill – he gave Rory three days' notice and on Saturday 18 August 1962 took his place behind the drum kit at the Hulme Hall in Port Sunlight, near Birkenhead. On that night the Fab Four was born.

The Best-Starr controversy had one further complication – Neil Aspinall. Neil was a friend of the Best family and lived with them at 8 Hayman's Green. But he was also the Beatles' loyal and hard-working road manager, and a good one at that. When Pete Best was sacked from the group Aspinall was left to decide where his loyalty lay. To Brian Epstein's

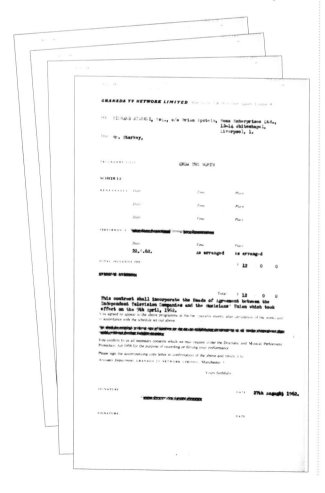

and the remaining Beatles' everlasting relief, he opted to stay with them.

On 22 August, four days after Ringo joined, a camera crew from Granada Television came to Liverpool and captured not just the only film of the Beatles playing in the Cavern but also the first of hundreds of TV appearances the group would make. And still this hectic August week was not over, for on Thursday 23 August John Lennon married Cynthia Powell at the Mount Pleasant Register Office in Liverpool. He spent that evening with the Beatles, however, playing at the Riverpark Ballroom in Chester.

Although the Beatles' had recorded four songs at EMI on 6 June none was considered worthy of release for their first single, so on 4 September John, Paul, George and Ringo flew down to London to take part in a second session. Two numbers were taped this day, 'Love Me Do', and 'How Do You Do It', the latter composed by Mitch Murray. The Beatles thoroughly resented having to perform a song that they didn't like and hadn't chosen themselves, although this was established procedure in the 1950s and 1960s, and they made little attempt to disguise their unhappiness.

Still George Martin remained dissatisfied, and he summoned the Beatles for a third session one week later, on 11 September. Rarely had so much time and money been invested in a début single. This time Martin booked in a session drummer, Andy White, to take the place of a dismayed Ringo Starr, left to shake a tambourine and a maraca. Three more numbers were recorded, all Lennon-McCartney compositions: an early version of 'Please Please Me', 'Love Me Do' and 'PS I Love You'. At last George Martin was happy, and for the Beatles' first single he chose the 4 September version of 'Love Me Do' as the A-side (later re-pressings substituted the second version of the song, with Ringo just on tambourine), and the 11 September recording of 'PS I Love You' as the flip-side.

On Friday 5 October 1962 the great event happened – the Beatles' début single was released and one week later it crept into the *Record Retailer* chart at 49. There was a strong suspicion in Liverpool and in the record industry as a whole, hotly denied by Brian Epstein, that he hyped the disc by buying up 10,000 copies between October and December 1962. Certainly the single led an unusually erratic, up and down chart career. (Before it peaked at 17 on 27 December it showed at 49, 46, 41, 32, 37, 29, 23, 21, 26, 19 and 22.) Nonetheless, it was a most encouraging début, and three days prior to its release, on 2 October, Brian Epstein and the Beatles signed a five-year management contract – this time Epstein even added his own signature.

As 'Love Me Do' slowly climbed the charts so the Beatles began to fulfil bookings further afield. At noon on Sunday 28 October, just hours before they made their début at the prestigious Liverpool Empire theatre, Brian Epstein made a trunk telephone call down to Peterborough in Northamptonshire. Quite by chance, he had discovered the home telephone number of Arthur Howes, Britain's leading concert promoter who ran "package shows" at virtually every major variety theatre (or cinema with a stage) in Britain. When Howes answered the phone Brian launched into his usual sales pitch, now backed with the added weight of a chart record,

BRITAIN'S TOP 50

record retailer and music industry news

December 27, 1962

#	Title	Artist	Label
1	RETURN TO SENDER	(1) Elvis Presley	R.C.A. RCA 1320
2	NEXT TIME	(2) Cliff Richard	Columbia DB 4950
3	DANCE ON!	(11) The Shadows	Columbia DB 4948
4	DANCE WITH THE GUITAR MAN	(6) Duane Eddy	R.C.A. RCA 1316
5	LOVESICK BLUES	(3) Frank Ifield	Columbia DB 4913
6	ROCKIN' AROUND THE CHRISTMAS TREE	(7) Brenda Lee	Brunswick 05880
7	SUN ARISE	(4) Rolf Harris	Columbia DB 4888
8	TELSTAR	(9) The Tornados	Decca F 11494
9	BOBBY'S GIRL	(5) Susan Maughan	Philips 326544 BF
10	LET'S DANCE	(12) Chris Montez	London HLU 9596
11	DESAFINADO	(18) Stan Getz & Charlie Byrd	H.M.V. POP 1061
12	SWISS MAID	(8) Del Shannon	London HLX 9609
13	YOUR CHEATING HEART	(25) Ray Charles	H.M.V. POP 1099
14	DEVIL WOMAN	(10) Marty Robbins	C.B.S. AAG 114
15	IT ONLY TOOK A MINUTE	(13) Joe Brown	Piccadilly 7N 35082
16	THE MAIN ATTRACTION	(14) Pat Boone	London HLD 9620
17	LOVE ME DO	(22) The Beatles	Parlophone R 4949
18	WE'RE GONNA GO FISHIN'	(27) Hank Locklin	R.C.A. RCA 1305
19	A FOREVER KIND OF LOVE	(19) Bobby Vee	Liberty LIB 10046
20	ME AND MY SHADOW	(32) Frank Sinatra and Sammy Davis Jnr.	Reprise-R 20128
21	MUST BE MADISON	(24) Joe Loss and His Orch.,	H.M.V. POP 1075
22	UP ON THE ROOF	(26) Kenny Lynch	H.M.V. POP 1090
23	BABY TAKE A BOW	(30) Adam Faith	Parlophone R 4964
24	ISLAND OF DREAMS	(34) The Springfields	Philips 326557 BF
25	SHERRY	(17) The Four Seasons	Stateside SS 122
26	HE'S A REBEL	(40) The Crystals	London HLU 9611
27	LOVE ME TENDER	(15) Richard Chamberlain	M-G-M MGM 1173
28	GO AWAY LITTLE GIRL	(39) Mark Wynter	Pye 7N 15492
29	LIKE I DO	(20) Maureen Evans	Oriole CB 1760
30	I REMEMBER YOU	(36) Frank Ifield	Columbia DB 4856
31	JAMES BOND THEME	(16) John Barry and His Orch.,	Columbia DB 4898
32	VENUS IN BLUE JEANS	(23) Mark Wynter	Pye 7N 15466
33	LIMBO ROCK	(37) Chubby Checker	Cameo-Parkway P 849
34	HEARTACHES	(35) Patsy Cline	Brunswick 05878
35	GOSSIP CALYPSO	(38) Bernard Cribbins	Parlophone R 4961
36	THE MADISON	(43) Ray Ellington	Ember S 102
37	SUSIE DARLIN'	(41) Tommy Roe	H.M.V. POP 1092
38	ONWARD CHRISTIAN SOLDIERS	(44) Harry Simeone Chorale	Ember S 144
39	DEAR LONELY HEARTS	(49) Nat 'King' Cole	Capitol CL 15280
40	JINGLE BELL ROCK	(46) Chubby Checker & Bobby Rydell	Cameo-Parkway C 205
41	DESAFINADO	(—) Ella Fitzgerald	Verve VS 502
42	I CAN'T HELP IT	(—) Johnny Tillotson	London HLA 9642
43	NO ONE CAN MAKE MY SUNSHINE SMILE	(21) Everly Brothers	Warner Bros. WB79
44	LOCO-MOTION	(28) Little Eva	London HL 9581
45	BECAUSE OF LOVE	(29) Billy Fury	Decca F 11508
46	CAN CAN '62	(31) Peter Jay and the Jay Walkers	Decca F 11531
47	RAMBLIN' ROSE	(33) Nat 'King' Cole	Capitol CL 15270
48	OH LONESOME ME	(45) Craig Douglas	Decca F 11523
49	LET'S GO	(—) The Routers	Warner Bros. WB 77
50	DON'T HANG UP	(—) The Orlons	Cameo-Parkway C 231

Title		Title	
Baby Take A Bow	23	Heartaches	34
Because Of Love	45	He's A Rebel	26
Bobby's Girl	9	I Can't Help It	42
Can Can '62	46	I Remember You	30
Dance On	3	Island Of Dreams	24
Dance With The Guitar Man	4	It Only Took A Minute	15
Dear Lonely Hearts	39	James Bond Theme	31
Desafinado	11, 41	Jingle Bell Rock	40
Devil Woman	14	Let's Dance	10
Don't Hang Up	50	Let's Go	49
Forever Kind Of Love	19	Like I Do	29
Go Away Little Girl	28	Limbo Rock	33
Gossip Calypso	35	Loco-motion	44

Title		Title	
Love Me Do	17	Rockin' Around The Christmas Tree	6
Love Me Tender	27	Return To Sender	1
Lovesick Blues	5	Sherry	25
Madison, The	36	Sun Arise	7
Main Attraction, The	16	Susie Darlin'	37
Me And My Shadow	20	Swiss Maid	12
Must Be Madison	21	Telstar	8
Next Time	2	Up On The Roof	22
No One Can Make My Sunshine Smile	43	Venus In Blue Jeans	32
Oh, Lonesome Me	48	We're Gonna Go Fishin'	18
Onward Christian Soldiers	38	Your Cheating Heart	13
Ramblin' Rose	47		

R.R. & M.N. 27/12/62

'Love Me Do' is issued and, in December, peaks at 17 on the Record Retailer chart. The release was heralded by the Beatles signing a new, revised management contract with Brian Epstein, and by the issue of an independent press release written for NEMS by Tony Barrow – "a hard fact driven into every sentence".

MAY WE INTRODUCE ...

The Beatles play original rock'n'roll

THINGS really happened for The Beatles on December 27, 1960, at a suburban town hall in Liverpool. It was their first important public appearance since their formation in mid-1958 and followed local club and ballroom dates as semi-pros.

As Liverpool critic Bob Wooler wrote shortly after: "Here again, in The Beatles, was the stuff that screams are made of . . . rugged yet romantic, appealing to both sexes, with calculated naivete and an ingenious throwaway approach to their music, effecting indifference to audience response and yet always saying 'thank-you'".

The Beatles, who have achieved their success as singers *and* instrumentalists, were further described by Mr. Wooler as "musically authoritative and physically magnetic". And, after explaining how they had exploded on a jaded scene, he went on to attribute their success to—the 'resurrection' of original-style rock 'n' roll music.

GOT TOGETHER

It was at the Liverpool Institute that John Lennon (rhythm guitar), Paul McCartney (bass guitar) and George Harrison (lead guitar) got together to form The Beatles. They were joined later by drummer Pete Best who left the group in the summer of 1962 and was replaced by Ringo Starr.

Before the town hall engagement The Beatles scored a spectacular success—in Germany. They left their native Liverpool not long after their formation to appear at the 'Top Ten' Club in Hamburg. In the spring of 1961 they returned there to Germany a short time in May and June, 1962, for a six-week stint at the Star Club in Hamburg.

While there in Germany they were asked to accompany British singer Tony Sheridan on a record of "My Bonnie", made by a German company. Personal manager Brian Epstein takes up the story:

FIRST RECORD

"They made this record and then the German company asked them to record as solo artistes. But I decided to turn down the offer because I wanted them to record for a British company". This they did in September, 1962, when they recorded their own compositions, "Love me do" and "P.S. I love you" for

E.M.I's Parlophone label (45-R4949).

"*The first time I submitted demo discs of The Beatles I was told there was already too much of that type of material", says Brian Epstein. "Then I went into the H.M.V Record Shop in Oxford Street to get some tapes transferred to disc. As soon as the people there heard the tapes they advised me to get in touch with George Martin, Parlophone's A & R manager"*

THE FOUR

JOHN LENNON, born October 9, 1940, in Liverpool, is 5 ft. 11 ins. tall, has brown eyes and brown hair, attended Quarry Bank High School in Liverpool, and Liverpool College of Art.

PAUL McCARTNEY, born in Liverpool on June 18, 1942, is 5 ft. 11 ins. tall, has brown eyes, dark brown hair, and attended the Liverpool Institute. He likes the colour black, steak and chips, the work of Ray Charles, Peggy Lee, Dinah Washington, Chuck Berry, Little Richard, Carl Perkins and Fats Waller.

GEORGE HARRISON, born February 25, 1943, in Liverpool, is 5 ft. 11 ins. tall, has hazel eyes and dark brown hair, and attended the Liverpool Institute. He likes the colours blue/black, enjoys egg and chips, Carl Perkins and Eartha Kitt, and wants nothing more than to retire with lots of money.

RINGO STARR, born July 7, 1940, in Liverpool, is 5 ft. 8 ins. tall, has blue eyes and brown hair. He went to St. Silas and Dingle Vale Secondary Modern School, likes the colour black, steak and chips, Ray Charles and Dinah Washington, Paul Newman and Brigitte Bardot, and sleek suits and ties.

MEET THE BEATLES

JOHN LENNON (harmonica, rhythm guitar, vocal) Born Liverpool, 9 October 1940
PAUL McCARTNEY (bass guitar, vocal) Born Liverpool, 18 June 1942
GEORGE HARRISON (lead guitar) Born Liverpool, 25 February 1943
RINGO STARR (drums) Born Liverpool, 7 July 1940

BEATLES DRIVE
the quickie story-finding game with a hard fact driven into every sentence.

THE BEATLES...

...were voted the North West's Top Group by readers of the Liverpool publication "Mersey Beat".

...have written over 100 original songs, many of which they use in their 60 minute stage presentation. Recently they added LOVE ME DO and P.S. I LOVE YOU to their act so that a ready-made Merseyside advance order of some thousands awaits the Parlophone release of these titles on Friday 5 October.

...took on a new drumming man - RINGO STARR - earlier this year. Ringo was in the same class as Billy Fury at Dingle Vale Secondary Modern School.

...have played on package bills alongside such top-liners as Bruce Channel, Joe Brown (who thought they were fab), Mike Berry, Gene Vincent, Mr. Acker Bilk, and Kenny Ball on their extensive tours (Aldershot to Fleetwood, Manchester to Birmingham).

...drew a record-splintering crowd of over 900 at Liverpool's famous Cavern basement on 9 June 1962. The occasion was a Welcome Home show put on to celebrate the group's return from their third fantastically successful season in Hamburg and it broke Cavern attendance records set up by The Shadows and The Temperance Seven.

...have made two broadcasts on the BBC Light Programme (Teenagers Turn) with a third lined up for Friday 26 October.

...were filmed at the Cavern Granada Television; a screening date is to be fixed within the next few weeks.

...explain their group name via this unqualified statement from JOHN LENNON "It came to us in a vision. A man descended unto us astride a flaming pie and spake these words unto us saying 'From this day on you are The Beatles with an A'. Thus it did come to pass thus".

...FAN CLUB, organised after an immensely successful "The Beatles for their Fans" presentation last April, has a paid-up membership of well over 1000 with fresh applications flooding in from all parts of the country.

...will appear with Little Richard at the Tower Ballroom, New Brighton on Friday 12 October and at the mammoth Liverpool Empire later in the month with Little Richard, Craig Douglas, Jet Harris and Kenny Lynch.

...brought forth this praise from Liverpool compere/deejay BOB WOOLER: "The biggest thing to hit the Liverpool scene in years...the hottest property any promoter could hope to encounter. Musically authoritative and physically magnetic, THE BEATLES are rhythmic revolutionaries with an act which is a succession of climaxes.

and opportunistically asked for some dates. There and then, amazingly, Howes provisionally booked the Beatles onto a Helen Shapiro package set for February 1963 and, to see what they were like, onto a one-night bill at the Embassy Cinema in Howes' home town of Peterborough headed by the yodelling Australian Frank Ifield. Although he offered the group only £30 a night for the Shapiro tour, and wouldn't pay them at all for the Ifield date beyond travelling expenses, Brian showed his gratitude by giving Howes first option on all future Beatles tours. Though the Peterborough date was

something of a disaster for the group, Howes then booked them into a second package tour, with American stars Tommy Roe and Chris Montez, set for March 1963.

Before all that could happen, two separate fortnight engagements at the Star-Club, Hamburg, arranged many months previously, still had to be fulfilled. And in between the two, on 26 November, the Beatles made their fourth visit to EMI Studios, recording their second single (A-side 'Please Please Me') which was scheduled for release early in January. After the long wait, suddenly it was all happening for the Beatles. In addition to their ever-increasing schedule of non-Liverpool dates, there was a sudden rush of radio and television appearances to promote 'Love Me Do'. They topped the second *Mersey Beat* popularity poll with consummate ease and were even voted fifth in an end-of-year national *New Musical Express* poll for the Best British Vocal Group, and seventh in the Best British Small Group category, a remarkable achievement on the strength of one single by an "unknown" northern combo.

It was with the greatest reluctance, then, that the Beatles returned to Hamburg for the fifth and final time on 17 December. From the moment they arrived they could think of little else but getting back home and working hard to consolidate their small foothold on the ladder to fame.

A serious, private, mid-afternoon rehearsal at the Cavern Club, crafting the sound that would rock 1963.

Monday 1 January

Decca Studios, Broadhurst Gardens, London

Then a "bank holiday" only in Scotland, the Beatles undertook their most important assignment to date this fresh New Year's Day morning: their first formal audition for a British record company, Decca.

Recording at the company's London studio – situated less than two miles from rival EMI's in Abbey Road – the Beatles nervously taped 15 songs, chosen by Brian Epstein to show off every facet of their talent. The likely order of performance was: 'Like Dreamers Do', 'Money (That's What I Want)', 'Till There Was You', 'The Sheik Of Araby', 'To Know Her Is To Love Her', 'Take Good Care Of My Baby', 'Memphis, Tennessee', 'Sure To Fall (In Love With You)', 'Hello Little Girl', 'Three Cool Cats', 'Crying, Waiting, Hoping', 'Love Of The Loved', 'September In The Rain', 'Besame Mucho' and 'Searchin''. In other words, three Lennon-McCartney compositions ('Like Dreamers Do', 'Hello Little Girl' and 'Love Of The Loved'), two eccentric arrangements of old standards, seven cover versions of 1950s material – encompassing rock and roll, R&B and C&W – two soft ballads and a contemporary chart hit.

It's unlikely that the Beatles were given any opportunity to perform more than one take of any song, and each was recorded strictly live onto two-track mono tape, no overdubbing permitted. Decca's A&R assistant Mike Smith was in the control room – it was he who had seen the Beatles at the Cavern Club 19 days earlier – and the audition began around 11.00 am, ending approximately an hour later.

Had they done enough to pass? Smith promised to let Epstein know.

> available everywhere within the next few days.
> ● Latest episode in the success story of Liverpool's instrumental group The Beatles: Commenting upon the outfit's recent recording test, Decca disc producer Mike Smith tells me that he thinks The Beatles are great. He has a continuous tape of their audition performances which runs for over 30 minutes and he is convinced that his label will be able to put The Beatles to good use. I'll be keeping you posted . . .
> ● The first three singles to appear in this country on the American Liberty label

Wednesday 3 January

Lunchtime **Cavern Club, Liverpool**
Night **Cavern Club, Liverpool**

Friday 5 January

Lunchtime **Cavern Club, Liverpool**

Saturday 6 January

Night **Cavern Club, Liverpool**

Sunday 7 January

Casbah Coffee Club, West Derby, Liverpool

Tuesday 9 January

Lunchtime **Cavern Club, Liverpool**

Wednesday 10 January

Night **Cavern Club, Liverpool**

Thursday 11 January

Lunchtime **Cavern Club, Liverpool**

Friday 12 January

Night **Cavern Club, Liverpool**
and **Tower Ballroom, New Brighton, Wallasey**

Another two-performance night for the Beatles. Their spot at the Tower Ballroom took place at 11.30 pm, as makeshift headliners of the show, Screaming Lord Sutch – billed as the top act of the night – having failed to arrive.

Saturday 13 January

Hambleton Hall, Huyton, Liverpool

The Beatles' last appearance here – much, one would imagine, to their relief. This certainly was not the type of venue Brian Epstein wanted his group to be seen in.

Sunday 14 January

Casbah Coffee Club, West Derby, Liverpool

Monday 15 January

Lunchtime **Cavern Club, Liverpool**

Wednesday 17 January

Lunchtime **Cavern Club, Liverpool**
Night **Cavern Club, Liverpool**

The only published account of the Beatles' audition at Decca appeared in the Liverpool Echo *on 27 January, written, before they were rejected, by Tony Barrow (as Disker). Decca pressed up a handful of acetate discs from the audition recordings prior to saying no.*

1962

Friday 19 January

Lunchtime **Cavern Club, Liverpool**

Night **Tower Ballroom, New Brighton, Wallasey**

Saturday 20 January

Night **Cavern Club, Liverpool**

Sunday 21 January

Casbah Coffee Club, West Derby, Liverpool

Monday 22 January

Lunchtime **Cavern Club, Liverpool**

Night **Kingsway Club, Promenade, Southport, Lancs**

The lunchtime spot at the Cavern Club was the first of five experimental one-hour sessions, half the usual duration. The admission price was one shilling (5p).

The Southport venue was a good illustration of Brian Epstein's first influence over the Beatles' direction. No longer would they be seen in the scruffy and violent suburban jive halls of 1961 but in respectable, civilised clubs, places with a real stage, curtains, dressing-rooms and even carpets, befitting their elevated status. There was also considerable emphasis on promotion, with cleverly structured advertisements exaggerating the Beatles' achievements, and a news release/article and photograph of the group sent to the local newspaper in advance of the engagement.

THE
BEATLES
Come and meet
" PETE, PAUL, JOHN and GEORGE "
The Group Everyone has been asking for — Now they're here, at the
KINGSWAY
NEXT MONDAY — ONLY 2/6
Come and hear them play their latest record, It's Sensational

Wednesday 24 January

Lunchtime **Cavern Club, Liverpool**

Night **Cavern Club, Liverpool**

Friday 26 January

Lunchtime **Cavern Club, Liverpool**

Night **Cavern Club, Liverpool**

and **Tower Ballroom, New Brighton, Wallasey**

Saturday 27 January

Aintree Institute, Aintree, Liverpool

The Beatles' last engagement at this venue, and for promoter Brian "Beekay" Kelly. For Brian Epstein, who ferried the group to and from the dance in his car, the evening ended in red-faced fury when Kelly paid the Beatles' £15 fee in handfuls of loose change. Epstein was angered at what he saw as a slight on the group's importance and ensured that they never played for Kelly again, and he remained sufficiently piqued to mention the incident in his autobiography two years later.

Sunday 28 January

Casbah Coffee Club, West Derby, Liverpool

Monday 29 January

Kingsway Club, Southport

The second of three consecutive, block-booked appearances at this venue. As the club was licensed to sell alcohol, beat groups had to play in an upstairs ballroom, without a bar, so that under-18s could be admitted.

Tuesday 30 January

Lunchtime **Cavern Club, Liverpool**

Wednesday 31 January

Night **Cavern Club, Liverpool**

Thursday 1 February

Lunchtime **Cavern Club, Liverpool**

Night **Thistle Café, Banks Rd, West Kirby, Wirral, Cheshire**

The West Kirby date was the first booking against which Brian Epstein took a commission, and the engagement perfectly encapsulates the manner of his managerial handling at this time.

The venue was a dance instruction hall behind and above a café in a sleepy dormitory village on the River Dee, ten miles from Liverpool. It was not a regular haunt for beat groups so Epstein was able to persuade the lessor of the hall, somewhat magnanimously, into calling it "The Beatle

GRAND OPENING OF
THE BEATLE CLUB
THISTLE CAFE, Banks Road, West Kirby
To-morrow, Thursday Feb. 1. 7.30-11.30.
Starring Merseyside's Premier Beat Group
THE BEATLES
and STEVE DAY & THE DRIFTERS.
Tickets 4/6, Strothers.   Membership
forms available.

Club", a true misnomer since, after this engagement, the group never returned there! This, anyway, was billed as the "Grand Opening Night" and the Beatles' fee was quite substantial for the time – £18. Epstein's commission, to cover petrol, oil and other miscellaneous expenses, was just 10% – especially reduced for this celebratory occasion.

Friday 2 February

Oasis Club, Lloyd St, Manchester, Lancashire

The Beatles' first professionally organised out-of-town date – Epstein's influence was clearly beginning to show. Tony Stuart, manager of the Oasis on behalf of the owners, Kennedy Street Enterprises, booked the Beatles into the club on three further occasions over the next year.

1. The Hippy Hippy Shake
2. Sweet Little Sixteen
3. The Sheik of Araby
4. September In the Rain
5. Dizzy Miss Lizzie
6. Take Good Care of My Baby
7. 'Til There Was You
8. Memphis Tenessee
9. What A Crazy World We Live In
10. Like Dreamers Do
11. Money
12. Young Blood
13. Honeymoon Song
14. Hullo Little Girl
15. So How Come (Everly's)
16. Oo My Soul
17. To Know Her is to Love Her or Bully Gully
18. Roll Over Beethoven
19. The Love of the Loved
20. Dance/Twist In the Streets
21. Dream
22. Searchin.

Saturday 3 February

Night **Cavern Club, Liverpool**

Sunday 4 February

Casbah Coffee Club, West Derby, Liverpool

Monday 5 February

Lunchtime **Cavern Club, Liverpool**

Night **Kingsway Club, Southport**

When Ringo Starr joined the Beatles on 18 August 1962 he had already known the group for two years, since Rory Storm and the Hurricanes shared with them the long nights of autumn 1960 at the Kaiserkeller in Hamburg. But he had also drummed with them, too – on this day. Pete Best was unwell and unable to take his place in the Beatles for these two engagements, and John, Paul and George's first choice as temporary replacement was Ringo, the Hurricanes enjoying a rare day-off.

Wednesday 7 February

Lunchtime **Cavern Club, Liverpool**

Night **Cavern Club, Liverpool**

Friday 9 February

Lunchtime **Cavern Club, Liverpool**

Night **Cavern Club, Liverpool**

and **Technical College Hall, Borough Rd, Birkenhead, Cheshire**

The first of three consecutive Friday-night engagements for the Technical College.

Saturday 10 February

Youth Club, St Paul's Presbyterian Church Hall, North Rd, Tranmere, Birkenhead, Cheshire

Another unusual Beatles venue booked by Brian Epstein, not half-a-mile from the technical college where they had played the previous evening.

Sunday 11 February

Casbah Coffee Club, West Derby, Liverpool

Monday 12 February

Broadcasting House, Piccadilly, Manchester, Lancashire

Brian Epstein was quick to explore all means of furthering the Beatles' career. The first and most important method was to obtain for them a recording contract. Meanwhile, as these pages show, he also booked the group into better live venues, smartened their appearance and promoted press attention.

Another route to fame was via broadcasting, and on 10 January 1962 Epstein returned to the BBC's Manchester HQ an assiduously completed three-page "Application For An Audition By Variety Department", hopeful of securing the group an opportunity of testing before radio producers.

The application was approved and on this day, 12 February, the Beatles travelled to Broadcasting House in Manchester to audition before Peter Pilbeam, producer of "teen" radio programmes made in the north-west, although broadcast all over the nation.

The Beatles performed four songs at the audition: Paul singing his own composition 'Like Dreamers Do' and also Peggy Lee's 'Till There Was You', and John singing Chuck Berry's 'Memphis, Tennessee' and his own composition 'Hello Little Girl'. Pilbeam's opinions, written on the back-page of the audition application, were a "No" for Paul and a "Yes" for John. He then gave his overall view of the Beatles: "An unusual group, not as 'Rocky' as most, more C&W with a tendency to play music".

Pilbeam's concluding statement was the vital one, however: "Yes. Booked for TT's 7 March 1962" – the Beatles had passed their audition and had been booked for their first radio appearance, on *Teenager's Turn*, to be recorded on Wednesday 7 March. A contract for this was issued by the BBC on Tuesday 20 February.

Tuesday 13 February

Lunchtime **Cavern Club, Liverpool**

Wednesday 14 February

Night **Cavern Club, Liverpool**

Thursday 15 February

Lunchtime **Cavern Club, Liverpool**
Night **Tower Ballroom, New Brighton, Wallasey**

With a "Panto Ball" set for the following evening, this Tower Ballroom booking was a "Pre-Panto Ball". Terry Lightfoot and his New Orleans Jazz Band shared the bill with the Beatles, watched by 3500 customers.

Friday 16 February

Technical College Hall, Birkenhead
and **Tower Ballroom, New Brighton, Wallasey**

A double booking across the River Mersey.

Saturday 17 February

Night **Cavern Club, Liverpool**

Sunday 18 February

Casbah Coffee Club, West Derby

Monday 19 February

Lunchtime **Cavern Club, Liverpool**

Tuesday 20 February

Floral Hall, Promenade, Southport, Lancashire

Probably the Beatles' biggest engagement under Epstein to date: the Floral Hall was actually a theatre, with gold lamé curtains and tiered seats.

To attract the largest possible audience, the evening was billed as a "Rock 'n' Trad Spectacular". In addition to the Beatles, four other rock groups were on the bill, including Gerry and the Pacemakers and Rory Storm and the Hurricanes, while the trad element was supplied by the Chris Hamilton Jazzmen.

Wednesday 21 February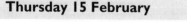

Lunchtime **Cavern Club, Liverpool**
Night **Cavern Club, Liverpool**

Friday 23 February

Lunchtime **Cavern Club, Liverpool**
Night **Tower Ballroom, New Brighton, Wallasey**
and **Technical College Hall, Birkenhead**

Two separate Beatles appearances at the Tower, at 9.00 and 10.45 pm. In between, the group had time to slip away for a half-hour set at the college.

Saturday 24 February

Night **YMCA, Birkenhead Rd, Hoylake, Wirral, Cheshire**
and **Cavern Club, Liverpool**

The YMCA engagement was not, surprisingly, an Epstein booking, but the result of much perseverance by club organiser Charles Tranter, who, eager to book the Beatles – he had first asked them to fulfil a date on 8 September 1961 but they were already booked elsewhere – arrived at Mona Best's house and offered a generous £30 fee for this one date. Unfortunately, the YMCA audience did not share his enthusiasm for the Beatles, grew dissatisfied with their over-long introductions between songs, and booed them off stage.

The Cavern appearance took place after midnight, during another of the club's all-night sesssions.

Sunday 25 February

Casbah Coffee Club, West Derby, Liverpool

Monday 26 February

Kingsway Club, Southport

Tuesday 27 February

Lunchtime **Cavern Club, Liverpool**

Wednesday 28 February

Night **Cavern Club, Liverpool**

Thursday 1 March

Lunchtime **Cavern Club, Liverpool**
Night **Storyville Jazz Club, Temple St, Liverpool**

The Beatles had already played the Storyville premises when the venue was known as the Liverpool Jazz Society. In September 1962 it would become the Iron Door Club.

Friday 2 March

St John's Hall, Bootle
and **Tower Ballroom, New Brighton, Wallasey**

The Bootle date was a slight reversion to habitats of old: inglorious jive halls. But it was played because young promoter Dave Forshaw always saved and worked hard so that occasionally he could present a top-line act for his clientele.

Later in the evening the Beatles went across the Mersey for another Tower booking, billed on this occasion as a "Mad March Rock Ball".

Saturday 3 March

Night **Cavern Club, Liverpool**

Sunday 4 March

Casbah Coffee Club, West Derby, Liverpool

Monday 5 March

Lunchtime **Cavern Club, Liverpool**
Night **Kingsway Club, Southport**

Tuesday 6 March

Night **Cavern Club, Liverpool**

Wednesday 7 March

Playhouse Theatre, St John's Rd, Hulme, Manchester, Lancashire

No concert this day for the Beatles; instead – having passed their 12 February audition – they went to the Playhouse Theatre in Manchester to record their radio début, for the BBC Light Programme show *Teenager's Turn – Here We Go*. It was broadcast the following afternoon, Thursday 8 March, between 5.00 and 5.29 pm.

The Beatles rehearsed for the programme from 3.45 pm and then, dressed for the first time ever in suits, took their place among the other artists – Brad Newman, the Trad Lads, and the Northern Dance Orchestra directed by Bernard Herrmann – for the recording which ran from 8.00 to 8.45 in front of a teenage audience. Interspersed by the other acts, the Beatles performed three songs on the show, all cover versions: 'Dream Baby (How Long Must I Dream?)', 'Memphis, Tennessee' and 'Please Mister Postman'.

Thursday 8 March

Storyville Jazz Club, Liverpool

Friday 9 March

Lunchtime **Cavern Club, Liverpool**
Night **Cavern Club, Liverpool**

Saturday 10 March

Youth Club, St Paul's Presbyterian Church Hall, Tranmere, Birkenhead

A return date, one month after the first appearance.

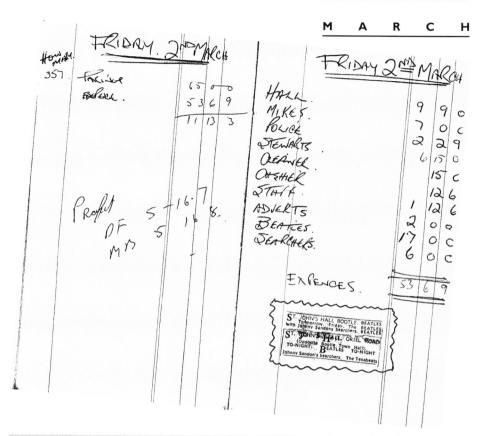

Sunday 11 March

Casbah Coffee Club, West Derby, Liverpool

Monday 12 March

Kingsway Club, Southport

The first of two consecutive but unadvertised Monday-night Kingsway dates.

Promoter Dave Forshaw's personal diary for 2 March 1962, documenting the Beatles' £17 fee, £6 paid to support act the Searchers, an attendance of 357 and profit of over £11.

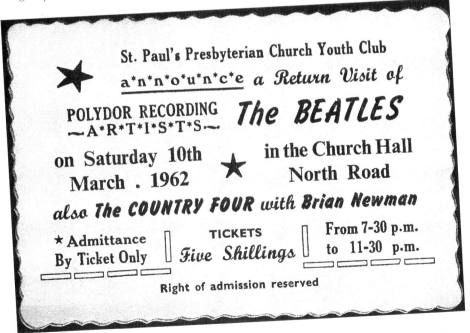

St. Paul's Presbyterian Church Youth Club a*n*n*o*u*n*c*e a *Return Visit* of POLYDOR RECORDING ~A*R*T*I*S*T*S~ **The BEATLES** on Saturday 10th March . 1962 in the Church Hall North Road *also* **The COUNTRY FOUR** with *Brian Newman* ★ Admittance By Ticket Only TICKETS *Five Shillings* From 7-30 p.m. to 11-30 p.m. **Right of admission reserved**

Tuesday 13 March

Lunchtime **Cavern Club, Liverpool**

Wednesday 14 March

Night **Cavern Club, Liverpool**

Thursday 15 March

Lunchtime **Cavern Club, Liverpool**

Night **Storyville Jazz Club, Liverpool**

The Storyville date was titled "The Beatles' Farewell Party".

Friday 16 March

Night **Cavern Club, Liverpool**

Saturday 17 March

Village Hall, Knotty Ash, Liverpool

A special event for promoter Sam Leach: his engagement night. He had taken over the responsibility of promoting beat nights at this venue after Mona Best declined her option.

Billing the evening as a "St Patrick's Night Rock Gala", Leach booked the Beatles and Rory Storm and the Hurricanes in order to attract a bumper crowd and pay for his engagement party in Huyton, which began after the evening's rock and roll proceedings had ended. Both groups attended the party which, in true Liverpool style, did not end until the following afternoon.

Sunday 18 March

Casbah Coffee Club, West Derby, Liverpool

Monday 19 March

Kingsway Club, Southport

Tuesday 20 March

Night **Cavern Club, Liverpool**

Wednesday 21 March

Lunchtime **Cavern Club, Liverpool**

Thursday 22 March

Night **Cavern Club, Liverpool**

Friday 23 March

Lunchtime **Cavern Club, Liverpool**

Night **Cavern Club, Liverpool**

Saturday 24 March

Heswall Jazz Club, Barnston Women's Institute, Barnston Rd, Heswall, Wirral, Cheshire

The first of three Beatles' bookings at this unusual venue.

Sunday 25 March

Casbah Coffee Club, West Derby, Liverpool

Monday 26 March

Lunchtime **Cavern Club, Liverpool**

Wednesday 28 March

Lunchtime **Cavern Club, Liverpool**

Night **Cavern Club, Liverpool**

Thursday 29 March

Odd Spot Club, Bold St, Liverpool

The Beatles' first appearance at this city-centre night club which had opened on 9 December 1961.

Friday 30 March

Lunchtime **Cavern Club, Liverpool**

Night **Cavern Club, Liverpool**

Saturday 31 March

Subscription Rooms, George St, Stroud, Glos

Preceded only by Sam Leach's Aldershot débâcle in December 1961, this was the Beatles' second southern engagement, their first under Brian Epstein.

Actually, Epstein's choice of southern venue was equally as wayward as Leach's, although at least this date was booked through a reputable London company, the Cana Variety Agency. In company with Bill Fraser Reid, John (Jack) Fallon, who runs Cana, also promoted dances – predominantly in the western counties – under another company, Jaybee Clubs, hence the booking. The Beatles were to play four different "Jaybee" venues in all. (See also 12 July 1968.)

SUBSCRIPTION ROOMS ———— STROUD
SATURDAY, MARCH 31   8.30 - 11.45
JAYBEE CLUBS present Liverpool's top vocal and instrumental
group—stars of Polydor records — the
SENSATIONAL
B E A T L E S
Plus the REBEL ROUSERS
At the request of the Council—No Teddy Boys and Ladies please
do not wear stiletto heels.
NEXT WEEK — LEE ATKINS

Sunday 1 April

Casbah Coffee Club, West Derby, Liverpool

Monday 2 April

Lunchtime **Cavern Club**, Liverpool

Night **Pavilion Theatre**, Lodge Lane, Liverpool

The Pavilion date was an unusual booking, the Beatles sharing the bill with the Royal Waterford Showband, especially flown in from Ireland for the occasion. The evening was promoted by local variety agent Jim Gretty and it marked the Beatles' only appearance at the "Pivvy", long established as Liverpool's foremost striptease theatre, although the Quarry Men did play here in late-1950s skiffle contests.

Wednesday 4 April

Lunchtime **Cavern Club**, Liverpool

Night **Cavern Club**, Liverpool

Thursday 5 April

Night **Cavern Club**, Liverpool

A special appearance, presented by the Beatles' fan club. For old time's sake, the group played first in their black leather outfits and then changed into their new Beno Dorn suits and ties for the second-half.

Friday 6 April

Lunchtime **Cavern Club**, Liverpool

Night **Tower Ballroom**, New Brighton, Wallasey

The Tower date was a two-and-a-half-hour "Beatles Farewell Ball", prior to their imminent Hamburg trip. They shared the bill with Emile Ford and the Checkmates.

Saturday 7 April

Night **Casbah Coffee Club**, West Derby, Liverpool
and **Cavern Club**, Liverpool

The Beatles' last three Liverpool performances until June – these two and the Casbah booking the next day – took place without George, who was unwell. Mindful of the impending Hamburg engagement, Brian Epstein would not allow him to perform.

Sunday 8 April

Casbah Coffee Club, West Derby, Liverpool

Friday 13 April – Thursday 31 May

Star-Club, Grosse Freiheit, Hamburg, West Germany

Seven weeks at the Star-Club, Hamburg's newest rock venue. The Beatles were required to play four hours one

A snapshot from the fan club night at the Cavern Club on 5 April 1962: Paul takes to the drums while Pete Best moves centre-stage for a performance of Lennon-McCartney's unreleased 'Pinwheel Twist'.

night, and three the next, with a one-hour-on, one-hour-off rota. For two of the seven weeks they shared the bill with Gene Vincent. The only day off was 20 April, Good Friday.

By 31 May, at the end of their third lengthy Hamburg stint within two years, another 172 hours' stage time had been toiled, over 48 nights. The Beatles left Hamburg mid-afternoon on Saturday 2 June, flying Lufthansa to London Airport. They then caught a connecting flight to Manchester, arriving at Ringway at 7.25 pm, and were driven home to Liverpool. On the 3rd and 4th they rehearsed in private at the Cavern Club (approximately 3.00–6.30 pm the first day, beginning at 7.00 pm the second), and on Tuesday 5 June they drove south, to London.

Monday 23 – Friday 27 April

Hamburg (venue not known)

Before producer Bert Kaempfert was prepared to allow the Beatles an early escape from his exclusive recording agreement with them, set to expire on 30 June, he informed Brian Epstein that he wished to make two further recordings with the group.

Although it certainly took place between 23 and 27 April, the exact date, and venue, of this one 1962 session – in which, as in the previous year, they backed Tony Sheridan – has proven impossible to research, and was certainly not detailed along with the (possibly inaccurate) 1961 information supplied with a 1984 CD reissue of the Sheridan/Beatles recordings. (See 22-23 June 1961.) Indeed, the date it does give for one of the songs known for certain to have been recorded in spring 1962, 'Sweet Georgia Brown', is 21 December 1961 and the Beatles were not in Hamburg then.

The second song recorded in this new session was either 'Swanee River' (as reported in *Mersey Beat* in May 1962) or 'Skinny Minny' (as reported by Pete Best in his biography *Beatle!*), neither of which is included on the supposedly complete 1984 CD. The backing on 'Skinny Minny' does not sound like the Beatles' at all; the backing on 'Swanee River' does – except, that is, for a saxophone break which may well have been overdubbed later, perhaps at the same time that Sheridan re-recorded his lead vocal for 'Sweet Georgia Brown', in early 1964.

Precisely what the Beatles recorded with Sheridan, and when and where, may never be clearly determined.

Wednesday 6 June

Studio Two, EMI Studios, Abbey Rd, London

Another historic date: the Beatles' first visit to EMI Studios, situated at 3 Abbey Road in the quiet St John's Wood suburb of London, although less than three miles north of the bustling central area. It was also Pete Best's only EMI session – by the time they next returned here, on 4 September, Ringo Starr had been installed as the Beatles' drummer.

From EMI paperwork uncovered in 1991 it is clear that this session – now known to have been held in studio two from 7.00 until 10.00 pm – was not only an audition but also

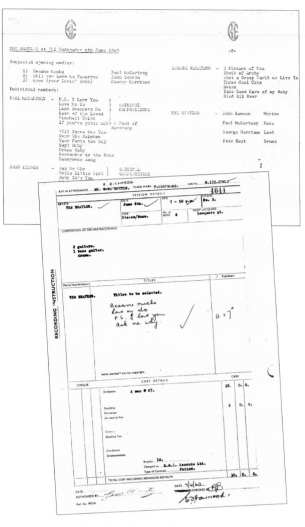

a proper recording date, the Beatles' first under their 4 June contract with the company. So after performing a large selection of material, and gaining the metaphorical thumbs-up, four actual recordings were made, of 'Besame Mucho' and three Lennon–McCartney numbers 'Love Me Do', 'PS I Love You' and 'Ask Me Why'. (They were taped in this order, although more precise information, such as "take" details, no longer exists.) None was commercially issued, however, although the studio paperwork confirms that sample lacquer discs were cut.

The session began under the charge of Ron Richards, George Martin's assistant. Martin only became involved when the interest of balance engineer Norman Smith was aroused by 'Love Me Do'; he prompted tape op Chris Neal to fetch Martin who then stayed for the rest of the evening – and, indeed, for the remainder of the Beatles' career.

Meanwhile, the group returned to Liverpool on 7 June and waited for word of their progress as recording artists.

Saturday 9 June

Night **Cavern Club, Liverpool**

This "Beatles Welcome Home Show" appearance smashed the Cavern's attendance record, 900 vociferous youngsters cramming themselves into the underground sweatbox to see the group.

For the next 12 days the Cavern Club had the Beatles under exclusive contract.

Monday 11 June

Playhouse Theatre, Manchester

The Beatles' second radio recording and another trip to the Playhouse Theatre in Manchester for *Teenager's Turn – Here We Go*. They had a rehearsal at 4.00 pm and then took part in the recording between 8.45 and 9.30 pm, singing 'Ask Me Why' – the first broadcast of a Lennon-McCartney composition – 'Besame Mucho' and 'A Picture Of You', before a studio audience.

The programme was broadcast on Friday 15 June, between 5.00 and 5.29 pm on the BBC Light Programme.

THE BEATLES FAN CLUB

90 Buchanan Road,
Wallasey.

Dear Fans,

As you probably know The Beatles will be returning sometime this coming weekend and their first re-appearance in this country will take place at the Cavern Club on Saturday June 9th. We hope that as many of you as possible will be able to attend this special 'Welcome Home' performance. We are enclosing a list of their engagements which follow this appearance and also leaflets giving details of the Bruce Channel and the Joe Brown shows. (Incidentally Joe Brown also appears at the Cambridge Hall Southport with the boys on July 26th.) We hope particularly that these shows will be a tremendous success and that the boys will receive a great reception. As they look like being very exciting events we recommend that you buy your tickets early!

We are running two coach trips in connection with special appearances that The Beatles are making, and would like any of you who are interested to either send a postal order accompanied by a stamped addressed envelope to the above address or you may purchase your tickets from the book counter at Nems Limited, Whitechapel, Liverpool, 1.

Coach Trip No. 1. to the BBC Recording Studios in Manchester on Whit Monday 11th June 1962. The coach will leave from Nems Whitechapel at 6.0.p.m. and will return at approximately 10.30. p.m.
Tickets will cost 10/6d. (inclusive.)

Coach Trip No. 2. to the Plaza Ballroom St. Helens on Monday June 25th. The coach will depart from Nems Whitechapel at 7.15.p.m. returning at approximately 11.15.p.m.
Tickets will cost 5/3d (inclusive of admittance to Ballroom)

Looking forward to seeing you.

Yours sincerely,
Miss. R. Brown,
Secretary.

Tuesday 12 June

Lunchtime **Cavern Club, Liverpool**

Night **Cavern Club, Liverpool**

The first of three two-in-a-day Cavern bookings this week.

Wednesday 13 June

Lunchtime **Cavern Club, Liverpool**

Night **Cavern Club, Liverpool**

Friday 15 June

Lunchtime **Cavern Club, Liverpool**

Night **Cavern Club, Liverpool**

Saturday 16 June

Night **Cavern Club, Liverpool**

Tuesday 19 June

Lunchtime **Cavern Club, Liverpool**

Night **Cavern Club, Liverpool**

Wednesday 20 June

Lunchtime **Cavern Club, Liverpool**

Night **Cavern Club, Liverpool**

Thursday 21 June

Tower Ballroom, New Brighton, Wallasey

Although it wasn't advertised as such, this was the first of many occasions in the second half of 1962 that Brian Epstein booked a top-line act to appear on Merseyside, in order that the Beatles could be seen to support them on the bill, or maybe even upstage them. On this occasion it was Bruce Channel who headlined, just five weeks after scoring a Top Ten hit with 'Hey! Baby'.

An early Beatles Fan Club letter from its first secretary, Roberta (Bobbie) Brown. Clearly, Brian Epstein had already realised the advantages of close fan co-operation.

The evening was of further, unexpected benefit. Channel's harmonica player, Delbert McClinton, so inspired John Lennon that his influence would be clearly heard on much of the Beatles' recorded output through to 1964.

Friday 22 June

Lunchtime **Cavern Club, Liverpool**

Night **Cavern Club, Liverpool**

Saturday 23 June

(Victory) Memorial Hall, Chester Way, Northwich, Cheshire

The first of six Beatles appearances at this up-market venue in Northwich, a famous Cheshire salt-mining town 25 miles south-east of Liverpool. The promoter, Lewis Buckley, ran beat music dances all over Britain, so an impressive performance was important.

Sunday 24 June

Casbah Coffee Club, West Derby, Liverpool

The Beatles' final appearance at the Casbah – which, approaching three years' activity – closed down at the end of June after a death in the Best family.

Monday 25 June

Lunchtime **Cavern Club, Liverpool**

Night **Plaza Ballroom, Duke St, St Helens, Lancashire**

The St Helens date was the Beatles' first booking with Whetstone Entertainments, a company which ran two other ballrooms in the Merseyside area, the Orrell Park in Liverpool and the Riverpark in Chester.

Before the engagement, for which they were paid £25, Brian Epstein wrote a note to the Beatles stating that Whetstone "control 16 venues in the Northwest" but this was a careful fabrication to chivvy his group. He well knew that 13 of the 16 were devoted exclusively to bingo.

Wednesday 27 June

Lunchtime **Cavern Club, Liverpool**

Night **Cavern Club, Liverpool**

Thursday 28 June

Majestic Ballroom, Conway St, Birkenhead, Cheshire

Not just the first of 17 Beatles appearances at this venue but also, more importantly, their first booking with Top Rank, Britain's premier entertainment organisation of the era, owning theatres, cinemas, ballrooms and bingo clubs. Twenty-eight Top Rank ballrooms – mostly named Majestic

– featured live beat music and the Beatles played 12 of them in the ensuing year.

Friday 29 June

Lunchtime **Cavern Club, Liverpool**

Night **Tower Ballroom, New Brighton, Wallasey**

Following his two successful ventures the previous winter, and an unnumbered occasion on 9 March without the Beatles, Sam Leach presented "Operation Big Beat III" at the Tower this evening. Ten local groups, headed by the Beatles, performed in a "cavalcade of rock 'n' twist" during the five-and-a-half-hour show.

Saturday 30 June

Heswall Jazz Club, Barnston Women's Institute, Heswall, Wirral

HESWALL J·A·Z·Z CLUB

★ AN ALL STAR SHOW

Merseyside's Joy

The Fabulous ●

BEATLES

PARLOPHONE RECORDING ARTISTES

★ PLUS **THE BIG THREE** One of L'Pool's TOP 5 GROUPS

PLUS Current TOP 20 Records

BARNSTON WOMEN'S INSTITUTE

BARNSTON ROAD ● NEAR HESWALL

SATURDAY JUNE 30

7/6 By Ticket Only

DOORS OPEN 7-30   No admission after 9-45 p.m.

The Gazette Press, 266/268, Borough Road, Birkenhead. COPYRIGHT. Genuine Letterpress re-print by F. W. Cooper from original type and equipment used by him in 1962.

Sunday 1 July

Night **Cavern Club, Liverpool**

Also appearing on the Cavern Club bill this evening was Gene Vincent, with whom the Beatles had met and become friendly during their spring visit to Hamburg.

Monday 2 July

Plaza Ballroom, St Helens

The second of the Beatles' four consecutive Monday-night bookings at this venue.

Tuesday 3 July

Lunchtime **Cavern Club, Liverpool**

Wednesday 4 July

Night **Cavern Club, Liverpool**

Thursday 5 July

Majestic Ballroom, Birkenhead

Friday 6 July

MV *Royal Iris*, River Mersey

Another "Riverboat Shuffle" aboard the "The Fish And Chip Boat", presented by the Cavern Club. Once again the Beatles shared the bill with Acker Bilk, whose single 'Stranger On The Shore' (an especially apt title to perform on this occasion) was still in the Top Ten more than six months after release.

Whether he handed them out to all of his support acts or just to the Beatles is not known, but Bilk presented John, Paul, George and Pete with a black bowler-hat each during the evening, this being an essential ingredient in his own stage apparel.

Saturday 7 July

Hulme Hall, Bolton Rd, Port Sunlight,
Birkenhead, Cheshire

The first of four Beatles appearances at this venue, situated in the unusual village of Port Sunlight, created by Viscount Leverhulme in 1888 for the employees of his soap business, now the thriving multinational Unilever. The official attendance capacity of Hulme Hall was 450 but, unofficially, 500 paying customers would be squeezed in on Beatles nights. This engagement was a dance for the local golf club.

Sunday 8 July

Night **Cavern Club, Liverpool**

Monday 9 July

Plaza Ballroom, St Helens

Tuesday 10 July

Lunchtime **Cavern Club, Liverpool**

Wednesday 11 July

Night **Cavern Club, Liverpool**

Thursday 12 July

Lunchtime **Cavern Club, Liverpool**
Night **Majestic Ballroom, Birkenhead**

Friday 13 July

Tower Ballroom, New Brighton, Wallasey

Saturday 14 July

Regent Dansette, High St, Rhyl, Flintshire

The Beatles' first performance in Wales. It took place in a ballroom which – like so many snooker and billiards clubs of the day – was situated above a branch of Burton's tailoring empire.

Sunday 15 July

Night **Cavern Club, Liverpool**

Monday 16 July

Lunchtime **Cavern Club, Liverpool**
Night **Plaza Ballroom, St Helens**

Tuesday 17 July

McIlroy's Ballroom, Havelock Square,
Swindon, Wiltshire

The Beatles' third southern date and their second for Jaybee Clubs, in which they performed two separate 60-minute sets.

Wednesday 18 July

Lunchtime **Cavern Club, Liverpool**
Night **Cavern Club, Liverpool**

Thursday 19 July

Majestic Ballroom, Birkenhead

The Beatles' Thursday-night season at this venue, booked to run over three weeks, from 28 June to 12 July, was extended for one more week owing to popular demand.

Friday 20 July

Lunchtime **Cavern Club, Liverpool**
Night **Bell Hall, Orford Lane, Warrington, Lancashire**

The evening date was the Beatles' one and only appearance in Warrington, a town 18 miles west of Liverpool.

Saturday 21 July

Tower Ballroom, New Brighton, Wallasey

Sunday 22 July

Night **Cavern Club, Liverpool**

Monday 23 July

Kingsway Club, Southport

Tuesday 24 July

Lunchtime **Cavern Club, Liverpool**

Wednesday 25 July

Lunchtime **Cavern Club, Liverpool**
Night **Cavern Club, Liverpool**
and **Cabaret Club, Duke St, Liverpool**

The Cabaret Club booking was a curious one – an apparent (and ill-judged) attempt by Brian Epstein to break the Beatles into the cabaret circuit. Although the group received a £15 fee, this unadvertised performance was akin to an audition – which they failed miserably. The co-manager of the club at the time, Bob Woodward, remembers the audience response as nil, and the Beatles playing so loud that they set the windows rattling. He didn't engage them again.

Thursday 26 July

Cambridge Hall, Lord St, Southport, Lancashire

The first of two consecutive evenings, promoted by Brian Epstein's NEMS Enterprises, showcasing Joe Brown and his Bruvvers, and the Beatles. At the time, Brown stood at number three in the charts with 'A Picture Of You', one of Epstein's favourite pop records and also a new feature of the Beatles' own stage act, sung by George.

Friday 27 July

Tower Ballroom, New Brighton, Wallasey

Saturday 28 July

Night **Cavern Club, Liverpool**
and **Majestic Ballroom, Birkenhead**

Monday 30 July

Lunchtime **Cavern Club, Liverpool**
Night **St John's Hall, Bootle**

Another return to the 1961 stamping ground in Bootle, rewarding the efforts of promoter Dave Forshaw who always saved hard to afford the Beatles whenever possible. By this time, he'd given the St John's Hall its own name for rock nights, the Blue Penguin Club.

Wednesday 1 August

Lunchtime **Cavern Club, Liverpool**
Night **Cavern Club, Liverpool**

Friday 3 August

Grafton Rooms, West Derby Rd, Liverpool

The first rock show at this pre-war *palais de danse*, promoted by local man Albert Kinder. The Beatles headed the bill above Gerry and the Pacemakers and the Big Three. The Quarry Men performed here in late-1950s skiffle contests.

Saturday 4 August

Victoria Hall, Village Rd, Higher Bebington, Wirral, Cheshire

Another unusual venue. So few groups had played here that, initially, not even Brian Epstein knew how to find the hall.

Sunday 5 August

Night **Cavern Club, Liverpool**

Tuesday 7 August

Lunchtime **Cavern Club, Liverpool**
Night **Cavern Club, Liverpool**

Wednesday 8 August

Co-op Ballroom, St Sepulchre Gate, Doncaster, Yorks

The Beatles were excused their regular Cavern Club Wednesday-night appearance (this time they would have shared the bill with Shane Fenton – later Alvin Stardust – and the Fentones) so that they could fulfil a booking in Doncaster, 86 miles away across the Pennines.

Thursday 9 August

Lunchtime **Cavern Club, Liverpool**

Friday 10 August

MV *Royal Iris*, River Mersey

A little more than a month after floating down river with Acker Bilk, the Cavern Club presented the Beatles with Johnny Kidd and the Pirates, two years after their chart number one 'Shakin' All Over'. Also participating in this "Riverboat Shuffle" were the Dakotas, the instrumental group from Manchester later teamed up with Billy J Kramer by Brian Epstein.

Saturday 11 August

Odd Spot Club, Liverpool

Sunday 12 August

Night **Cavern Club, Liverpool**

Monday 13 August

Lunchtime **Cavern Club, Liverpool**
Night **Majestic Ballroom, High St, Crewe, Cheshire**

The Crewe date was the first of two consecutive Monday Beatles appearances at this Top Rank venue, which billed its beat nights as "The Biggest Rock Since Blackpool Rock"!

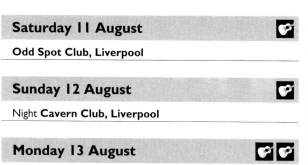

Wednesday 15 August

Lunchtime **Cavern Club, Liverpool**
Night **Cavern Club, Liverpool**

The night-time Cavern date was Pete Best's final appearance with the Beatles, two years and three days after he had joined them.

Thursday 16 August

**Riverpark Ballroom, Union St/Love St,
Chester, Cheshire**

What should have been one of the Beatles' more successful evenings, with the first of four (unconsecutive) Thursday-night bookings in this splendid Cheshire town, was marred by the non-appearance of Pete Best, dismissed from the group by Brian Epstein a few hours beforehand. At the time, Best had said that he would fulfil the Chester engagement but, hardly surprisingly, he later decided against it. Johnny Hutchinson of the Big Three was drafted in as replacement.

Friday 17 August

Majestic Ballroom, Birkenhead
and **Tower Ballroom, New Brighton, Wallasey**

Once again Johnny Hutchinson stood in for Pete Best, playing at both engagements. Oddly, the Big Three also had a booking on this date, at Orrell Park Ballroom, so *they* had to find a replacement.

Saturday 18 August

Hulme Hall, Port Sunlight, Birkenhead

The first engagement of the new-look Beatles: John, Paul, George and Ringo. The four had a two-hour rehearsal before taking to the Hulme Hall stage shortly after 10.00 pm, the closing attraction in the local Horticultural Society's 17th annual dance.

Sunday 19 August

Night **Cavern Club, Liverpool**

Monday 20 August

Majestic Ballroom, Crewe

Wednesday 22 August

Lunchtime **Cavern Club, Liverpool**
Night **Cavern Club, Liverpool**

The lunchtime session was a momentous occasion – the first time that television cameras were focused upon the Beatles.

As a direct result of Beatles fans' letters, producers from the Manchester-based Granada Television had watched the group in action at Cambridge Hall in Southport on 26 July and again in the Cavern Club on 1 August. Impressed by what they had seen, a crew was dispatched this lunchtime to film them in live performance for a programme entitled *Know The North*. They sang two songs, 'Some Other Guy' and 'Kansas City'/'Hey-Hey-Hey-Hey!'. Coming less than a week after the controversial dismissal of Pete Best, the Granada microphone also caught one male fan's shout at the end of 'Some Other Guy', "We Want Pete!".

But the murky Cavern Club conditions were scarcely conducive to good filming, and the end result was largely unsatisfactory; the footage was shelved, deemed unfit for use, and was only exhumed for broadcast much later on, when the Beatles were famous. The first transmission of 'Some Other Guy' (only) was on Wednesday 6 November 1963, on Granada's evening magazine programme *Scene At 6.30*, (6.30–7.00 pm) and it has been widely shown ever since.

Although just this 'Some Other Guy' performance and other assorted off-cuts have survived the passing years, this Granada film nonetheless remains the only existing footage of the Beatles before they achieved national fame, and of them playing in the Cavern Club.

Note: acetate discs of 'Some Other Guy', as recorded by Granada's film unit, were later circulated in Liverpool, pressed locally at the instigation of Brian Epstein and distributed from his NEMS store. Proving that the Beatles had performed the song more than once for the cameras, the acetates feature a version slightly different from that which accompanies the footage.

Thursday 23 August

Riverpark Ballroom, Chester

This was how John Lennon spent his wedding night: playing with the Beatles in Chester.

Friday 24 August

Lunchtime **Cavern Club, Liverpool**
Night **Majestic Ballroom, Birkenhead**

Saturday 25 August

Marine Hall Ballroom, Esplanade, Fleetwood, Lancs

The Beatles' only appearance in this northern coastal town famous for its fishing industry.

Sunday 26 August

Night **Cavern Club, Liverpool**

Also appearing this night was Mike Berry, the solo singer who had enjoyed a Top 30 hit in October 1961 with 'Tribute To Buddy Holly'.

Tuesday 28 August

Night **Cavern Club, Liverpool**

An irregular Tuesday-night Cavern Club date for the Beatles, switched in mid-August in order that they could fulfil a booking in Morecambe on the 29th.

Wednesday 29 August

Floral Hall Ballroom, Promenade, Morecambe, Lancs

The first of two performances given by the Beatles at this north-west seaside resort.

Thursday 30 August

Lunchtime **Cavern Club, Liverpool**
Night **Riverpark Ballroom, Chester**

Friday 31 August

Town Hall, Town Hall Chambers, Church Rd,
Lydney, Gloucestershire

The first of a Friday/Saturday double-engagement with Jaybee Clubs.

Saturday 1 September

Subscription Rooms, Stroud

A return to the venue played on 31 March.

Sunday 2 September

Night **Cavern Club, Liverpool**

Monday 3 September

Lunchtime **Cavern Club, Liverpool**
Night **Queen's Hall, Victoria Rd, Widnes, Lancashire**

The first of three consecutive Monday-night NEMS presentations in Widnes, the industrial town on the Mersey 12 miles south of Liverpool. The Beatles, naturally, headlined each one and, although the support groups varied from week to week, Rory Storm and the Hurricanes – home from their latest Butlin's stint on 1 September – appeared on the first two occasions, initially bearing malice over the hijacking of their drummer, Ringo Starr, although this soon passed.

The first shots of the Beatles at Abbey Road: rehearsing in studio three on 4 September 1962. Photographer Dezo Hoffmann was requested to snap George Harrison from the right-side only because he sported a blackened left eye after a Cavern Club kerfuffle.

Tuesday 4 September

Studios Three/Two, EMI Studios, London

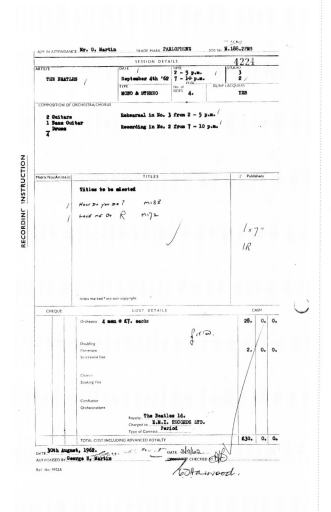

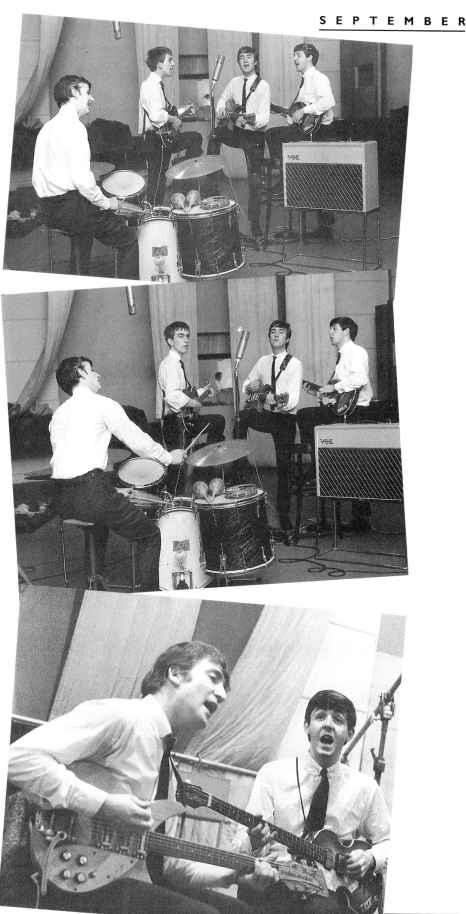

Ninety days after their 6 June session, the Beatles returned to EMI for another attempt at recording their début single. They flew down from Liverpool airport in the morning, checked into a small Chelsea hotel and arrived at Abbey Road shortly after lunch.

Between 2.00 and 5.00 pm Ron Richards put the Beatles through a vigorous rehearsal in studio three, running through six songs, from which two were selected for recording in the evening session, booked for 7.00–10.00 yet running overtime to 11.15. One of these was already selected – 'How Do You Do It', composed by Mitch Murray (real name Lionel Michael Stitcher) – which, in the apparent absence of any stronger original material, George Martin was insisting would be the group's first single. 'Love Me Do' and 'Please Please Me' were among the five other numbers rehearsed during the afternoon.

Interesting information has recently come to light about the Beatles' recording of 'How Do You Do It'. Most surprising is the discovery that they considerably re-arranged Mitch

Murray's composition. George Martin had mailed the group an acetate-disc of the original demo and they must have spent some time adapting it to suit their particular style. (Taped and cut at Regent Sound Studios in Denmark Street, central London, in summer 1962, the demo was sung by another aspiring songwriter Barry Mason, backed by the then unknown London group the Dave Clark Five. It was intended to interest Adam Faith and, as a consequence, was performed in a light, skipalong style.) Later, when the Beatles' recording was passed over and the song was given instead to Gerry and the Pacemakers, it was their re-arrangement which Gerry copied, not Murray's original.

Mitch Murray's diary for 1962 shows that on Wednesday 5 September, the day after this session, he was informed by Ron Richards that his song had "Come off best last night". Two days later, the diary shows, Murray heard the recording for the first time. But on the 12th he was informed that they had taped another song ('PS I Love You') and that 'How Do You Do It' would not be released by the Beatles.

There can be no doubt that this decision pleased the Beatles immensely. Apart from the fact that the song was far too "white" for their liking, being devoid of any resemblance to R&B, there was nothing especially wrong with 'How Do You Do It' – indeed, it would rise to number one in the charts for Gerry and the Pacemakers – but John and Paul were anxious that the group release their own compositions as singles. (This wish was realised throughout their career, for although some Beatles albums included "cover versions", A- and B-sides of singles were always occupied by Lennon-McCartney or Harrison compositions.) So while the group on this occasion were prepared to tape 'How Do You Do It', they did so grudgingly and with little ambition. George Martin got the message and, showing great foresight in the midst of what he considered to be their present mediocrity, was prepared to give Lennon-McCartney songs a chance. Dick James thought the Beatles' version worse than the demo.

George took the Beatles to dinner between 5.00 and 7.00 pm, returning for the evening recording session which saw them tape an unknown number of takes of 'How Do You Do It' and in excess of 15 of 'Love Me Do'. Paul was nervous at having to sing one of the lines that he'd never had to sing in rehearsal or on stage, and Ringo employed a curious drumming technique, attempting to play several percussion instruments simultaneously even if it meant hitting the hi-hat with a maraca instead of a drum stick.

Studio documentation shows that 'How Do You Do It' and 'Love Me Do' were mixed by George Martin and balance engineer Norman Smith before the evening was out, and that acetates of the two titles were cut for Martin and Brian Epstein to listen to the next morning.

Wednesday 5 September

Night **Cavern Club, Liverpool**

Anticipating an uncertain return time following the London recording session, this day's lunchtime engagement at the Cavern Club was switched in advance to Thursday. By the evening, however, they were back in Liverpool.

Thursday 6 September

Lunchtime **Cavern Club, Liverpool**
Night **Rialto Ballroom, Upper Parliament St/ Stanhope St, Toxteth, Liverpool**

The Rialto date was a Sam Leach promotion, although it was at a Top Rank ballroom. It was also the Beatles' début at the venue, although the Quarry Men performed here once or twice in late-1950s skiffle contests.

Friday 7 September

Newton Dancing School, Village Hall, Thingwall Rd, Irby, Heswall, Wirral, Cheshire

Another inauspicious Beatles booking.

Saturday 8 September

YMCA, Whetstone Lane, Birkenhead, Cheshire and **Majestic Ballroom, Birkenhead**

Sunday 9 September

Night **Cavern Club, Liverpool**

Also on the bill was Clinton Ford, the British singer with two Top 30 singles to his credit. His appearance was re-arranged from the previous Sunday.

Monday 10 September

Lunchtime **Cavern Club, Liverpool**
Night **Queen's Hall, Widnes**

Tuesday 11 September

Studio Two, EMI Studios, London

A swiftly-scheduled return to Abbey Road for yet a third attempt to record the first single. This time, George Martin was taking no chances: in place of the studio-inexperienced Ringo Starr he engaged seasoned session drummer Andy White to provide the percussion, leaving a dejected Ringo to shake maracas on 'PS I Love You' – at this point prime candidate for the A-side – and tambourine on 'Love Me Do'.

Recently uncovered EMI documents give the actual time of this studio two session as 5.00 to 6.45 pm, although it had been booked for 4.45–6.30. Ron Richards took charge, George Martin only arriving midway through. Ten takes of this first re-make of 'PS I Love You' were taped, and 18 of this second re-make of 'Love Me Do'. Additionally, still with Andy White on drums, an attempt was made at recording 'Please Please Me' (an unspecified number of takes). After the session, George Martin told the Beatles that the song would work better if they increased the tempo and worked out some tight harmonies.

'Love Me Do' and 'PS I Love You' were mixed into mono

immediately after the recordings were completed and EMI proceeded to manufacture the two tracks, in that order, as the A- and B-sides of the Beatles' début single. It was issued on Friday 5 October. (Curiously, initial pressings featured the 4 September recording of 'Love Me Do', with Ringo on drums [so the 11 September re-make could not have been regarded as a significant improvement after all], although later pressings and releases – the version on the LP *Please Please Me*, for example – had the Andy White recording.)

Wednesday 12 September

Night **Cavern Club, Liverpool**

As well as performing their customary set, the Beatles also backed a 16-year-old singer, Simone Jackson. On the bill, too, were Manchester group Freddie and the Dreamers.

Thursday 13 September

Lunchtime **Cavern Club, Liverpool**
Night **Riverpark Ballroom, Chester**

The Beatles' fourth and final Thursday-night appearance at this venue.

Friday 14 September

Tower Ballroom, New Brighton, Wallasey

Sam Leach's "Operation Big Beat V". Six groups, the Beatles heading the bill, played a five-and-a-half-hour session. ("Operation Big Beat IV" had taken place on 3 August, while the Beatles were playing at the Grafton.)

Saturday 15 September

(Victory) Memorial Hall, Northwich

Sunday 16 September

Night **Cavern Club, Liverpool**

Monday 17 September

Lunchtime **Cavern Club, Liverpool**
Night **Queen's Hall, Widnes**

The last of the three Monday night NEMS Enterprises bookings in Widnes.

Wednesday 19 September

Night **Cavern Club, Liverpool**

Thursday 20 September

Lunchtime **Cavern Club, Liverpool**

Friday 21 September

Tower Ballroom, New Brighton, Wallasey

A special five-group evening to celebrate Rory Storm's birthday.

Saturday 22 September

Majestic Ballroom, Birkenhead

Sunday 23 September

Night **Cavern Club, Liverpool**

Tuesday 25 September

Heswall Jazz Club, Barnston Women's Institute, Heswall, Wirral

A midweek engagement at the WI.

Wednesday 26 September

Lunchtime **Cavern Club, Liverpool**
Night **Cavern Club, Liverpool**

Friday 28 September

Lunchtime **Cavern Club, Liverpool**

Night **MV *Royal Iris*, River Mersey**

The Beatles' third and last "Riverboat Shuffle" of the summer season, headlining with Lee Castle and the Barons.

Saturday 29 September

Oasis Club, Manchester

A return visit to the scene of the Beatles' first major engagement under Brian Epstein.

Sunday 30 September

Night **Cavern Club, Liverpool**

Tuesday 2 October

Lunchtime **Cavern Club, Liverpool**

Wednesday 3 October

Night **Cavern Club, Liverpool**

Thursday 4 October

Lunchtime **Cavern Club, Liverpool**

Saturday 6 October

Hulme Hall, Port Sunlight, Birkenhead

Prior to this third engagement in Port Sunlight, a dance promoted by the local Horticultural Society, the Beatles put in a personal appearance at Dawson's Music Shop in Widnes, signing copies of 'Love Me Do', released the previous day.

Sunday 7 October

Night **Cavern Club, Liverpool**

Monday 8 October

EMI House, Manchester Square, London

The Beatles' lunchtime booking in the Cavern Club this day was cancelled because they were headed for London, for their début appearance on Radio Luxembourg.

In the early 1960s, airtime on the influential Luxembourg station, which had a medium- and short-wave service beamed directly at Britain and aimed at the British audience, could be bought by UK record companies for exclusive promotion of their artists and discs. Among other shows, EMI had *The Friday Spectacular*, for which this début appearance by the Beatles was recorded, taped on a Monday evening in front of an audience of more than 100 sitting or dancing youngsters gathered inside a small ground-floor studio inside EMI's central London headquarters. Despite the presence of the artists, however, only records were played on the show, so that radio listeners would hear the actual disc release, augmented – for good effect – by natural applause. The artists would also be interviewed.

In this particular programme, broadcast on Friday 12 October, 10.00–11.00 pm (British time), listeners (many of whom, according to the Luxembourg legend, would have been under their bed-covers) heard 'Love Me Do' and 'PS I Love You' as well as the interview.

The Beatles did not have any engagements on John's birthday, 9 October. Instead, they stayed over in London, visiting freelance music journalists and the weekly pop papers to promote 'Love Me Do'.

Wednesday 10 October

Lunchtime **Cavern Club, Liverpool**

Night **Cavern Club, Liverpool**

Thursday 11 October

Rialto Ballroom, Liverpool

Billed as a "Rock 'n' Twist Carnival", this evening was organised by Liverpool University.

Friday 12 October

Lunchtime **Cavern Club, Liverpool**

Night **Tower Ballroom, New Brighton, Wallasey**

The Tower Ballroom date was Brian Epstein's most ambitious promotional venture yet: a five-and-a-half-hour, 12-act presentation spearheaded by the great American rocker Little Richard. The evening was an enormous success, and

Epstein re-booked Richard to top the bill at another NEMS presentation scheduled for the Empire Theatre, Liverpool, on 28 October.

For the Beatles, the experience of playing second on a 12-act bill to Little Richard was enormous. Enormous is also the word to describe their embarrassment when they bumped into Pete Best backstage at the Tower Ballroom. He was there in his new role as drummer with Lee Curtis and the All-Stars.

Saturday 13 October

Night **Cavern Club, Liverpool**

Monday 15 October

Majestic Ballroom, Birkenhead

Tuesday 16 October

La Scala Ballroom, High St, Runcorn, Cheshire

The first of two Beatles appearances in Runcorn, the industrial town situated on the River Mersey, 14 miles south of Liverpool.

Wednesday 17 October

Lunchtime **Cavern Club, Liverpool**
Evening **Studio Four, Granada TV Centre, Quay St, Manchester, Lancashire**
Night **Cavern Club, Liverpool**

In between this day's two Cavern Club engagements the Beatles made their television début, appearing live on Granada's local magazine programme *People And Places*, broadcast only in the north and north-west of England, 6.35–7.00 pm.

They rehearsed before the cameras between 3.00 and 4.00 and then again from 4.15 to 6.00, and sang two songs in this important first transmission, 'Some Other Guy' and 'Love Me Do'.

Friday 19 October

Lunchtime **Cavern Club, Liverpool**

Saturday 20 October

Majestic Ballroom, Witham, Hull, Yorkshire

Another Top Rank venue, and at 128 miles from Liverpool the furthest one from home that the Beatles had played to date. They returned here four months later - see 13 February 1963.

Sunday 21 October

Night **Cavern Club, Liverpool**

Monday 22 October

Queen's Hall, Widnes

Another NEMS showcase for the Beatles. Also on the bill were Lee Curtis and the All-Stars, entailing another encounter with Pete Best.

Thursday 25 October

Playhouse Theatre, Manchester

The Beatles' third recording for the BBC radio Light Programme show *Here We Go* (the prefix title *Teenager's Turn* had been dropped by this time). It meant another trip to Manchester, where the group rehearsed from 4.00 pm and recorded between 8.00 and 8.45, before a studio audience.

The programme was broadcast on Friday 26 October, from 5.00 to 5.29 pm, featuring three numbers by the Beatles, 'Love Me Do', 'A Taste Of Honey' and 'PS I Love You', not split up as before but performed in one mid-programme block. A fourth recording, of Tommy Roe's song 'Sheila', was edited out of the broadcast tape to keep the show within its 29-minute transmission slot.

Friday 26 October

Lunchtime **Cavern Club, Liverpool**
Night **Public Hall, Lune St, Preston, Lancashire**

The Beatles' début in this major Lancashire town 30 miles north-west of Liverpool.

Public Hall, Preston — Friday, 26th October
The Preston Grasshoppers Rugby F.C. present the
1962 Rock & Beat Spectacular
featuring the Top H.M.V. Recording Star
MIKE (Tribute to Buddy Holly) BERRY
The First Visit to Preston of That Sensational Group **THE OUTLAWS**
The First Visit to Preston of Merseyside's Fabulous Combination **THE BEATLES**
The North's Top Big Band
The Syd Munson Orchestra
Licensed Bar — Running Buffet — Late Transport
Non-Stop Dancing 8-0 p.m. to 2 a.m. — TICKET 6/-

Saturday 27 October

Hulme Hall, Port Sunlight, Birkenhead

The Beatles' fourth and final appearance at this venue, topping the bill in a dance promoted by the local Recreations Association.

At 8.45 pm, prior to going on stage, they recorded a radio interview for the patients of local hospitals Cleaver and Clatterbridge, quizzed by Monty Lister and two teenage

EXIT

friends, Malcolm Threadgill and Peter Smethurst. The item was broadcast on the closed-circuit radio station within the hospitals, the first occasion being the next day on Lister's regular show *Sunday Spin*.

The Beatles taped another hospital radio interview on 29 November 1963 (see entry) and may well have done others.

Sunday 28 October

Empire Theatre, Liverpool

A most important engagement for the Beatles, for not only were they part of an eight-act, big-name, non-Mersey groups bill, but this was also their first appearance (barring the Quarry Men's auditions) at the top theatre in Liverpool, the Empire, and their first "pop package show", with two separate "houses", at 5.40 and 8.00 pm.

Heading the NEMS presentation bill, once again, was Little Richard, while the other acts included Craig Douglas (whom the Beatles actually backed, in addition to perform-

ing their own set), Jet Harris (the ex-Shadows bass player), Kenny Lynch and Sounds Incorporated. Epstein had hoped to book Sam Cooke too, but he was unavailable.

To their dedicated Liverpool fans, the Beatles had really hit the big time.

Monday 29 October

Studio Four, Granada TV Centre, Manchester

The Beatles' second appearance on the Granada Television magazine programme *People And Places* was taped this day and transmitted from 6.30 to 7.00 pm on Friday 2 November, by which time they were in Hamburg.

The group rehearsed and recorded from 11.00 am to 1.00 pm, singing 'Love Me Do' and 'A Taste Of Honey'. In a most unusual stage-setting, while George played acoustic guitar, Paul the bass and Ringo the drums, all standing, John sat – without an instrument – astride the set, singing 'Love Me Do' as would a solo singer fronting a support group. For

'A Taste Of Honey' he donned an acoustic guitar and rejoined the front line, although for this number the four removed their suit jackets to perform in waistcoats.

The next morning, 30 October, they flew to Hamburg.

Thurs 1 – Wed 14 November

Star-Club, Hamburg, West Germany

A brief, 14-night return to the Star-Club, the first time the Beatles had officially played in the same Hamburg venue on successive trips. Their fee was an increased 600DM (£53.50) per man per week and they were happy, once again, to share billing with Little Richard, as they had twice done in Liverpool in the previous three weeks.

Add another 49 stage hours to the Hamburg experience.

Friday 16 November

EMI House, London

The Beatles' second appearance on Radio Luxembourg, recorded this evening at EMI in front of an audience and transmitted on that company's show *The Friday Spectacular* on 23 November, 10.00–11.00 pm. Once again, they were on-hand for an interview, around which was played both sides of their début disc, 'Love Me Do' and 'PS I Love You'.

Saturday 17 November

Matrix Hall, Fletchamstead Highway, Coventry, Warwickshire

This Coventry booking was the Beatles' first performance in the Midlands region. Though incorrectly recalling the venue (he remembered it as De Montfort Hall in Leicester, a place

they were shortly to play), Paul referred to this date in a candid 1969 conversation with John (seen in the film *Let It Be*) describing it as "the worst first-night ever" after a return from Hamburg.

Sunday 18 November

Night Cavern Club, Liverpool

Another highly successful "Welcome Home" night.

Monday 19 November

Lunchtime Cavern Club, Liverpool
Night Smethwick Baths Ballroom, Thimblemill Rd, Bearwood, Smethwick, Staffordshire
and Adelphi Ballroom, New St, West Bromwich, Staffordshire

This return visit to the Midlands, for an evening double-header, necessitated an 85-mile afternoon dash down from Liverpool. (Smethwick Baths was also known locally as Thimblemill Baths.)

Tuesday 20 November

Floral Hall, Southport

Another two "house" theatre appearance.

Wednesday 21 November

Lunchtime Cavern Club, Liverpool
Night Cavern Club, Liverpool

The lunchtime session, originally slated for the Remo Four, was played by the Beatles in a hurried swap for their lunch booking on the 23rd, which they had to miss owing to a London appointment.

Thursday 22 November

Majestic Ballroom, Birkenhead

Friday 23 November

Lunchtime St James's Church Hall, Gloucester Terrace, London
Night Tower Ballroom, New Brighton, Wallasey

The lunchtime slot at the Cavern Club this day was played by the Remo Four because the Beatles were in London for an audition with BBC Television, arranged so that their TV potential could be assessed.

Surprisingly, the audition came about not through the endeavours of Brian Epstein but through two persuasive letters sent to the Corporation by one of the Beatles' fans, David John Smith of Preston, who wrote asking for the group to be featured on BBC programmes. Assuming that Smith managed the group, the BBC wrote back to him offering them an audition in London on 6 November. Smith passed on the letter to NEMS Enterprises, from where Clive Epstein (brother Brian was with the Beatles in Hamburg) re-arranged this 23 November date.

The ten-minute audition took place at 12.20 pm in a central London church hall. Four days later, Brian Epstein received a non-committal "don't call us, we'll call you" letter from Mr Ronnie Lane, Light Entertainment Auditioner. It would only be when the Beatles had enjoyed a number one record that they would make their BBC TV début. (See 13 April 1963.)

After the audition, the Beatles sped back to Merseyside for an unusual engagement at the Tower Ballroom, the 12th annual "Lancashire And Cheshire Arts Ball". Sharing the bill with the Beatles were Billy Kramer and the Coasters (prior to Epstein's signing Kramer to a management contract, adding the spurious middle initial J and severing the Coasters link in favour of Manchester group the Dakotas) the Llew Hird Jazz Band and the Clan McCleod Pipe Band.

Saturday 24 November

Royal Lido Ballroom, Central Beach,
Prestatyn, Flintshire

Only the Beatles' second engagement in Wales, following the début in nearby Rhyl four months earlier.

Sunday 25 November

Night Cavern Club, Liverpool

Monday 26 November

Studio Two, EMI Studios, London

With the modest success of 'Love Me Do', the Beatles were invited to return to EMI to record a second single. 'Please Please Me', first aired in the studio on 11 September, was completed during this session, booked for 7.00–10.00 pm but which finished 15 minutes ahead of time, at 9.45. The group arrived at Abbey Road at 6.00 pm and had a short rehearsal prior to the session proper.

Including overdubs of John's distinctive harmonica wailing, 'Please Please Me' was recorded in 18 takes and was chosen as the A-side. Then, after a short break, six takes of a re-make of 'Ask Me Why' were taped (the first version having been recorded on 6 June), and the best was selected for the B-side. The Beatles also played to George Martin a third Lennon-McCartney number, 'Tip Of My Tongue', but George was unhappy with the arrangement and said that it would have to be held over for another time. In fact, the Beatles never revived it, and it wasn't until July 1963 that it was recorded – by another Epstein artist, Tommy Quickly.

Tuesday 27 November

BBC Paris Studio, Regent Street, London

The Beatles' first BBC radio session in London. It took place at the Corporation's confusingly-named Paris Studio – situated not in France but just south of Piccadilly Circus in the heart of the West End.

The recording was for the Light Programme show *The Talent Spot*, broadcast on Tuesday 4 December between 5.00 and 5.29 pm. Rehearsals ran from 4.00 pm and recording before a live studio audience from 7.00 to 8.00. Among the other acts appearing on this programme – "who make our guests for today and the stars of tomorrow," as programme host Gary Marshal announced at the start of the show – was Elkie Brooks, who also went on to achieve fame, albeit several years hence.

The Beatles performed three songs on this programme, 'Love Me Do', 'PS I Love You' and 'Twist And Shout'.

Wednesday 28 November

Night Cavern Club, Liverpool
and 527 Club, Lewis's, Ranelagh Street, Liverpool

Two engagements in one night, the second of which was a "Young Idea Dance" for the staff of Lewis's, the premier department store in Liverpool, held on the top floor of the shop.

Thursday 29 November

Majestic Ballroom, Birkenhead

Friday 30 November

Lunchtime Cavern Club, Liverpool
Night Town Hall, Market St, Earlestown,
Newton-le-Willows, Lancashire

The Earlestown engagement, billed as "The Big Beat Show No 2", was presented by T&T Vicars Sports and Social Club (Football Section).

Mono mixes of 'Please Please Me' and 'Ask Me Why' for the Beatles' second single were produced this day at Abbey Road by George Martin (session time unknown). The Beatles themselves weren't present; apart from a few isolated incidences, they only began to attend – and participate in – mix sessions much later, around 1965/66. The new single was issued by EMI on Friday 11 January 1963.

Saturday 1 December

(Victory) Memorial Hall, Northwich
and Tower Ballroom, New Brighton, Wallasey

The Beatles were added to the New Brighton bill a day before the show in order to boost flagging ticket sales. It meant a hurried journey up from Northwich and a very late-night spot on stage.

Sunday 2 December

Embassy Cinema, Broadway, Peterborough, Northants

This fine piece of Epstein opportunism backfired disastrously when the Beatles bombed on this Frank Ifield package bill, and in both the "houses" too. The experience may have been good, but damage to the group's collective ego was extensive. About the only positive aspect of these Peterborough concerts was the Beatles' dressing-room discovery of theatrical make-up, showed to them by genial guitar-player Ted Taylor, leader of the much admired Ted Taylor Four. (The Beatles went on to teach the art of stage make-up to Mick Jagger who used it more liberally than ever before and whose own influence in this area has been widespread. Ted has a lot to answer for.)

Ray McFall at the Cavern Club graciously waived his contracted Beatles engagement for this night.

I'll remember Frank Ifield

— says Lyndon Whittaker

IT IS EASY TO SEE why Frank Ifield has been so popular in this country. No pseudo American accent; no sulky Presley look. Frank Ifield is himself and he flashed many a happy smile as he breezed through a confident performance at the Embassy on Sunday.

As expected his well-known hit songs "I remember you," "Lovesick blues" and "She taught me how to yodel" were sung in addition to "Lonesome Me" and "Lucky devil".

Ifield came well up to expectations, but the supporting artists failed to please. Just a year ago, Billy Fury, Eden Kane, Karl Denver, The Allisons and Chas. McDevitt all appeared on the same show. Since then there has been a gradual decline in the standard of supporting artists.

"The exciting Beatles" rock group quite frankly failed to excite me. The drummer apparently thought that his job was to lead, not to provide rhythm. He made far too much noise and in their final number "Twist and Shout" it sounded as though everyone was trying to make more noise than the others. In a more mellow mood, their "A taste of honey" was much better and "Love me do" was tolerable.

Young vocalist Susan Cope seemed more confident than when she last appeared at the Embassy on the Bobby Vee Show, and she introduced a little piano playing into her act this time. However she still looked immature. With a few more years experience Miss Cope could develop into a top-line entertainer.

The Tommy Wallis and Beryl xylophone team tried to show versatility. Mr. Wallis's solo "Bumble boogie", a hotted-up version of the classic "Flight of the bumble bee", was very good. His xylophone playing pleased.

He then demonstrated his 'versatility' by blasting on the drums and blowing on the saxophone. He should stick to the xylophone!

Beryl, who assisted Tommy in xylophone duets and played the mouth organ a little, was really little more than an ornament, and I fail to see the necessity for her to appear half naked.

Bad timing

The Lana Sisters, clad in pink, added a welcome feminine flavour. "Much better than those Beatles" I heard one gentleman remark.

The Ted Taylor Four were an ordinary run-of-the-mill backing group — nothing special about them at all.

Joe Black was not a very inspiring compère — nor was he very original. But his job was made difficult by some bad timing. On a couple of occasions the stage had not been set behind the curtains by the time Mr. Black had finished and he was left stranded, fighting to fill in time.

Once he announced the next act, and a voice back-stage bawled: "Not yet". Joe passed the time by telling an incomplete joke. On another occasion he just pranced around the stage for a couple of minutes until the curtains were ready to be raised.

Something else which has not been seen at previous Embassy shows was a constant moving and billowing of the curtain in between acts.

Looking back I can say that the show was not as good as we have become accustomed to, and Frank ("I remember you") Ifield is the only one I shall remember.

Monday 3 December

TWW Television Centre, Bath Rd, Bristol, Somerset

Another ITV appearance, produced by TWW (Television Wales and the West) and seen only in that and other nearby regions.

The programme was a weekly pop music show with the very 1960s (and aptly Welsh sounding) title *Discs A Gogo*, supposedly set – using the original meaning of the word – in "the gayest coffee bar in town". The Beatles appeared on it just this once, miming to 'Love Me Do' from TWW Television Centre in this live 7.00–7.30 pm broadcast.

The Monday 26 July 1965 edition of this series screened the promotional film for 'Help!' (see 22 April 1965).

Tuesday 4 December

Studio Four, Wembley Studios, Wembley Park Drive, Wembley, Middlesex

The Beatles made their London-area television début with this spot on the children's programme *Tuesday Rendezvous*, transmitted by the capital's weekday ITV station, Associated-Rediffusion.

It was a live appearance, broadcast from the company's Wembley Studios, just along the road from the Empire Pool arena where the Beatles would perform in concert on four occasions, 1963–66. The programme went out from 5.00 to 5.55 pm, the Beatles miming to all of 'Love Me Do' and 45 seconds of 'PS I Love You'. They also took part in rehearsals, 1.30–5.00 pm.

Among the other acts appearing in this edition of the weekly series – co-hosted, as was Radio Luxembourg's *The Friday Spectacular*, by the lovely Muriel Young – were guitar virtuoso Bert Weedon, folk singer Wally Whyton (formerly a member of the Vipers Skiffle Group, produced by George Martin) and glove puppets Fred Barker and Ollie Beak.

Wednesday 5 December

Lunchtime **Cavern Club, Liverpool**
Night **Cavern Club, Liverpool**

Thursday 6 December

Club Django, Queen's Hotel, Promenade, Southport, Lancashire

As the name implies, Club Django was a jazz venue, but its management was too aware of the Beatles' escalating prominence to pass up an opportunity of booking the group.

Friday 7 December

Lunchtime **Cavern Club, Liverpool**
Night **Tower Ballroom, New Brighton, Wallasey**

The Beatles headed a seven-group line-up at the Tower.

Saturday 8 December

Oasis Club, Manchester

Sunday 9 December

Night **Cavern Club, Liverpool**

George Martin and his assistant Judy Lockhart-Smith attended this performance, a year less four days after Decca's Mike Smith had done the same.

Monday 10 December

Lunchtime **Cavern Club, Liverpool**

Tuesday 11 December

La Scala Ballroom, Runcorn

The Beatles' second Runcorn date, although – unlike the first – this was a NEMS presentation.

Wednesday 12 December

Lunchtime **Cavern Club, Liverpool**
Night **Cavern Club, Liverpool**

Thursday 13 December

Corn Exchange, St Paul's Sq, Bedford, Bedfordshire

Another southern engagement, arranged following the withdrawal of Joe Brown, originally advertised to appear.

Love me do, Parlophone Recording

THE BEATLES

Also

ROBIN HALL

and

JIMMIE MACGREGOR

with

SUPPORTING GROUP

CORN EXCHANGE, BEDFORD

December 13, 8 to 11.30 p.m.

Owing to non-appearance of Joe Brown

Admission 3/-

Friday 14 December

Music Hall, The Square, Shrewsbury, Shropshire

A major booking with promoter Lewis Buckley. Most top acts of the day played here.

Saturday 15 December

Majestic Ballroom, Birkenhead

Two entirely separate engagements in one night. During the evening the Beatles performed a standard Majestic booking. Then, at midnight, the first-ever *Mersey Beat* poll awards show (for 1962) began. As winners of the poll – and for the second year in succession, too – the Beatles closed the show at 4.00 am and were also presented with a handsome plaque.

The poll runners-up, on stage immediately prior to the Beatles, were Lee Curtis and the All-Stars, so there was another encounter with Pete Best.

Sunday 16 December

Night **Cavern Club, Liverpool**

Monday 17 December

Studio Four, Granada TV Centre, Manchester

The Beatles' third appearance on the Granada Television programme *People And Places*, transmitted live this time between 6.35 and 7.00 pm.

They performed two numbers, 'Love Me Do' and 'Twist And Shout', as rehearsed from 3.00 to 4.00 pm and again from 4.15 to 6.00.

Tuesday 18 – Monday 31 December

Star-Club, Hamburg, West Germany

The Beatles grudgingly left England and their chart record, radio, TV and increasingly prestigious live bookings, for an undesirable fifth and final club trip to Hamburg, playing for 13 nights. Despite the increased fee of 750DM (£67) per man per week, all the four Beatles could think about was getting back home to capitalise on their success.

Their only night off was on Christmas Day, 25 December, and their final performances, on New Year's Eve, were taped on amateur equipment and released for the first time in 1977 against the Beatles' own wishes. Though extremely low-fidelity, they are fascinating recordings, and have been reissued extensively.

The Beatles' final 42 hours on the Star-Club stage brought the group's gruelling Hamburg experience to a total of approximately 800 hours. Quite how valuable the work tied up in this remarkable statistic was to prove was, at this point, beyond comprehension. The Beatles had served their apprenticeship, and served it the hard way. They were now ready to take on whatever the world could throw at them.

LEFT
JOHN LENNON

RIGHT
PAUL McCARTNEY

BOTTOM LEFT
GEORGE HARRISON

BOTTOM RIGHT
RINGO STARR

1962 the BEATLES

YEAR OF ACHIEVEMENT

★ WON "MERSEY BEAT" POPULARITY POLL (2nd YEAR)

★ VOTED FIFTH IN NEW MUSICAL EXPRESS POLL FOR BEST BRITISH VOCAL GROUP

★ E.M.I. RECORDING CONTRACT

★ FOUR B.B.C. BROADCASTS

★ FOUR T.V. APPEARANCES

★ TWO LUXEMBOURG BROADCASTS

★ TWO HAMBURG ENAGEMENTS

★ ENTERED THE TOP FIFTY WITHIN TWO DAYS OF "LOVE ME DO" RELEASE

★ HIT NO 21 IN THE CHARTS WITH "LOVE ME DO" THEIR FIRST DISC

★ APPEARED WITH LITTLE RICHARD, FRANK IFIELD, JOE BROWN, JET HARRIS, GENE VINCENT, JOHNNY AND THE HURRICANES, CRAIG DOUGLAS and many others.

★ APPEARED AT LIVERPOOL (EMPIRE), BIRMINGAM, MANCHESTER, HULL, DONCASTER, CREWE, STROUD, COVENTRY, SHREWSBURY, BEDFORD, PETERBOROUGH, PRESTON, BLACKPOOL, etc., etc.

AND IN 1963

★ **'Please, Please Me'**
Released by Parlophone
JANUARY 11th

★ Appearances in 'Thank Your Lucky Stars,' 'Saturday Club,' and B.B.C. T.V. (January).

★ **Scottish Tour**
(JANUARY)

★ **Helen Shapiro Tour**
(FEBRUARY)

★ **'Love Me Do'**
RELEASE AMERICA, CANADA AND GERMANY

TOMMY ROE/CHRIS MONTEZ TOUR (MARCH)

AND WHO KNOWS !

Sole Direction:
Brian Epstein,
Nems Enterprises Ltd.,
12/14 Whitechapel,
Liverpool, 1
ROYal 7895

Recording Manager:
George Martin,
EMI Records Limited,
20, Manchester Square,
London W.1

Press Representative:
Tony Calder Enterprises
15, Poland Street,
London W. 1

Road Manager:
Neil Aspinall

Fan Club Secretary:
Miss R. Brown
90, Buchanan Road,
Wallasey, Cheshire

THE YEAR that it all went berserk, 1963, started in a fairly quiet fashion, with the Beatles on a five-date tour of Scotland during the worst British winter weather in decades. But a few days later, on Friday 11 January, the group's second single, 'Please Please Me', was released and on 17 January it followed 'Love Me Do' into the charts.

Whereas their first single had led an erratic up and down run on the "hit parade", 'Please Please Me' ran the more traditional course: a key television appearance (the Beatles' début on the networked *Thank Your Lucky Stars*) and favourable press reviews leading to precious radio airplay and healthy sales, importantly this time not just in Liverpool but

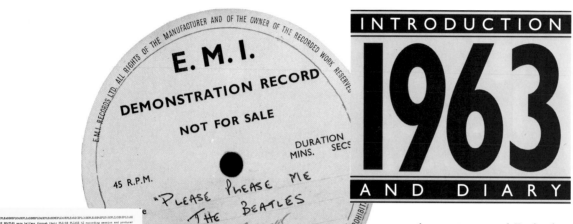

everywhere. Indeed, many of the Beatles' most dedicated home-town fans, naturally possessive of the group after two years' exclusive ownership, realised that buying the disc might well take the Beatles out of their grasp and into wider circulation.

And this is exactly what happened. As 'Please Please Me' took a firm grip on the charts so too the Beatles' circle of engagements grew ever larger and their Liverpool appearances ever fewer. They gave six performances at the Cavern Club in January, only three in February and none at all in March. And the many demands on their time soon necessitated residence in London.

But the Beatles had worked hard for this situation, driven relentlessly with style by Brian Epstein. In the 12 months of 1963 the group slogged their way through the most uncompromising schedule of concert tours, one-night ballroom appearances, EMI recording sessions, BBC radio sessions, television appearances, photographic sessions and press interviews. They dodged no one and no assignment. Everyone could have access to the group, no reasonable demand was refused. Never before, it seems, had any pop group exerted themselves quite so much.

After a rapid climb, 'Please Please Me' hit the prized and once so unattainable number one spot on the *New Musical Express* chart in the week ending 22 February, initially sharing the position with Frank Ifield's 'The Wayward Wind' but then, a week later, occupying the summit alone. The Beatles and Brian Epstein, their friends, families, associates and

employees were absolutely ecstatic. The group were about to start on the second phase of their comparatively low-key package tour with Helen Shapiro when word of the number-one placing came through in a telegram from the *NME*. In the Cavern Club on 19 February, just as the Beatles were due on stage, compere Bob Wooler announced the news. It was met with silence by the faithful – their fears had been realised. But throughout the rest of Britain, in the audiences on the Shapiro tour, the Beatles became the main attraction.

Rapturous receptions greeted the group on the tour that immediately followed, this one starring two American singers, Tommy Roe and Chris Montez. Neither was particularly big in Britain, having scored just a couple of chart hits, but they were *American*, and no British act had yet superseded an American act. The Beatles did, and they were both pleased and embarrassed by it at the same time, having – by audience demand – to assume top-billing.

The tour with Roe and Montez concluded at the end of March but there was no respite in the Beatles' barrage of Britain. Throughout April, as the deeply-packed snow finally began to thaw, the group covered England north, south, east and west on a nightly rota of ballroom appearances. Their third single, 'From Me To You', was released on the 11th so there were a few radio and TV appearances to be slotted in too, promoting themselves and the disc.

It is clear from the local newspaper coverage that Beatles-inspired hysteria had definitely begun by the late spring, some six months before it was brought to national attention by Fleet Street newspapers. Why the mayhem started, and why it was necessary to those causing it, will forever remain a mystery, defying social psychologists and historians then as now. Certainly the Beatles were not the first to be subjected to such vocal adulation. Frank Sinatra, in his prime, had sent the bobby-soxers swooning and screaming. Johnny Ray too, in the mid-1950s. And in the yet-young rock and roll era Elvis Presley in the USA and Cliff Richard in Britain had already inspired similar scenes without ever knowing how or why. Ability was not the only answer, witness the meteoric

Another Tony Barrow press release, this time for 'Please Please Me', clearly reflecting the Beatles' growing stature. A number of publications ran the mini-stories virtually verbatim.

The four English pretenders flanking American tourists Chris Montez (left) and Tommy Roe (right).

subsequent rise of so many lesser talented acts. The Beatles were as baffled by it as anyone else, and – initially at least – more than a little flattered. But this was to turn to resentment before very long as they became stifled by the very madness of it all.

When 'From Me To You' entered the *New Musical Express* chart at number six, set for a lengthy spell at the top within a further week, it was clear to all that here really was something bright, fresh and new on the British music scene. Ironically the Beatles had for some time been attempting to gauge what the next pop music fad might be. Might it be Latin-beat, calypso-rock, a resurgence of twist music? What they hadn't considered, of course, was that they themselves created the next and most resounding boom of all.

The Beatles' breakthrough had some quite remarkable side-effects. Unfashionable Liverpool suddenly became *El Dorado*. Scores of agents, managers, tour promoters and record company executives rushed up to Merseyside waving pens and pointing to dotted lines, and it wasn't long before

Liverpool had broken the long-established London stranglehold and taken over the charts, with Gerry and the Pacemakers, Billy J Kramer, Cilla Black, the Searchers, the Fourmost, the Swinging Blue Jeans (re-named from the Swinging Bluegenes) and the Merseybeats all following in the wake of the Beatles. To say that they all owed their success to the Beatles would not be wrong, for without Brian Epstein and the Beatles opening the metaphorical floodgates it is highly unlikely that any of them would have even been allowed a stab at national success.

Few of them lasted the distance anyway, and those that did were largely (though not all) the ones managed by Brian Epstein. For after the Beatles had established a foothold with 'Love Me Do', Epstein had begun to expand his NEMS Enterprises roster to encompass the Big Three, Gerry and the Pacemakers, Billy J Kramer with the Dakotas, the Fourmost, Cilla Black and Tommy Quickly. Not all were successes but those that were, often fuelled by exclusive Lennon-McCartney tunes, swamped the British charts in 1963. In the 52 charts published during the year by *Record Retailer* three of these acts between them scored a total of 45 weeks in the top ten. Combined with the Beatles' own tally of 40 weeks, Brian Epstein's groups accounted for 85 top ten placings that year. In December 1961 he had been a record-store owner, by December 1963 he had orchestrated the biggest-ever revolution in the British record and music industry.

A second side-effect of the Beatles' staggering success was the way that it dramatically and so speedily altered the grass-roots level of British music. From as early as March/April 1963, throughout the length and breadth of Britain, the concept of beat/rock and roll music radically altered. Huge numbers of new clubs and venues opened to cater for this sudden upsurge in interest – almost every town of medium-to-large population had one – and to fill these clubs were formed thousands of leaderless groups composing their own material, many later to swamp the once all-American British charts, indeed even the all-American American charts.

Pop music had always been treated with disdain and condescension by the British press but, now, suddenly, newspapers became interested, from about May 1963 on a localised scale and then, when the message had percolated through, on a national basis.

By the early summer of 1963 the Beatles were astride all the echelons of a suddenly burgeoning pop business. After a stream of appearances on various radio shows, the BBC offered them their own 15-week series, *Pop Go The Beatles*. The four weekly music papers – *Melody Maker*, *New Musical Express*, *New Record Mirror* and *Disc* – gave the Beatles' activities blanket coverage while the numerous weekly teenage girls' magazines, from *Boyfriend* to *Valentine*, were running regular features, colour pin-up posters and "interviews" with the Beatles. A publisher named Sean O'Mahony had already launched *Beat Monthly* with great success, a magazine predominantly featuring the Beatles and other Liverpool acts, and his preparations for the group's own glossy magazine, *The Beatles Monthly Book*, were almost complete, with the initial issue going to press in early July.

Television too, particularly the commercial network, had felt the changing mood quite early. ABC screened an all-

On stage at the Majestic Ballroom, Birkenhead.

Liverpool edition of *Lucky Stars (Summer Spin)* (the summer version of *Thank Your Lucky Stars*), headed by the Beatles, on 29 June. And on the charts the Beatles reigned supreme. Their début LP *Please Please Me*, a refreshing change from the below-par albums usually released by artists after a hit single, cracked the top of the *Record Retailer* chart on 11 May and remained immovable for 30 straight weeks… until it was dislodged by the Beatles' own follow-up.

From 18 May to 9 June the Beatles toured Britain again – their third nationwide package in as many months. The tour had been conceived in March as a vehicle for American guitarist Duane Eddy, but problems beset his visit and Ben E King and the Four Seasons were lined up to replace him. When they too fell through it was announced that the great Roy Orbison would be the tour's top attraction. But he wasn't – the Beatles, who admired and were influenced by Orbison in their formative years, completely dominated the tour and relegated the American to second fiddle.

Suddenly, Brian Epstein was besieged with offers for the Beatles. A garden fête appearance here, a merchandising endorsement there. And as for live bookings, there wasn't a promoter in the land who didn't want to engage them for a show. What a difference a year can make! As in all such cases

Facing page, top left: about to begin their third package tour of the year, and it's only May: the Beatles in their dressing-room at Slough with Gerry and the Pacemakers and the tour's supposed headliner Roy Orbison.

Other photographs: unused EMI publicity shots of the Beatles horsing on the Abbey Road steps on 5 March 1963, the day they recorded third single 'From Me To You'.

Inter-departmental MEMORANDUM

Ref. 4410   H.P.W. 55042

Date May 28th. 1963.

C/E9/JLS.

To   Mr. L.G. Wood.

Copy to: Miss Harwood.

Re: THE BEATLES.

Last week I saw the Manager of the Beatles and told him the glad news that on signing the option we intended to double the royalty of the Beatles raising it to 2d. for coming year.

He was delighted with this and it has made the Beatles very happy people. This is particularly timely as their third record has just topped the half million mark. Unfortunately he cannot grant us the options that we require as he does not have them under contract himself for this period.

I did not pursue the matter any further as I felt it would take the gilt off the gingerbread. I am sure that this move is a wise one.

G.H. Martin.
E.M.I. Records Ltd.

of sudden fame, it actually took quite some time for Epstein and the Beatles to reap financial gain from the situation. In June and July they were still fulfilling dates contracted back in the spring at fees ridiculously small compared with what they could now command. In similar circumstances, it was not uncommon for whingeing managers to claim that their artist had suddenly been taken ill and could not fulfil certain bookings. Brian Epstein would have none of this and, although he did attempt to buy the Beatles out of a booking on one or two occasions – especially if he considered the venue was unable to guarantee their safety – he never reneged on a signed contract. Almost every agent or promoter consulted during the researching of this book spoke, without any prompting, of his scrupulously fair business dealings.

In July the Beatles began a lengthy series of summer bookings in seaside resorts, including weekly "residencies" in Margate, Weston-super-Mare, the Channel Islands, Llandudno, Bournemouth and Southport, as well as one-nighters in four other towns. In between these dates were packed other club and ballroom appearances, BBC radio sessions and more recordings at EMI. On 1 July the Beatles taped their fourth single, the epochal 'She Loves You', while throughout the rest of the month they somehow found time to squeeze in most of the recording sessions for their second LP, to be titled *With The Beatles*. EMI chose to delay its release until sales of *Please Please Me* began to subside.

On 3 August the Beatles gave their final performance at the Cavern Club and an historic era was brought to an end. The Cavern could no longer contain their fast-growing legions of fans, nor for that matter could Liverpool contain the Beatles. In the remaining three years that the group gave concerts they performed in Liverpool on just four occasions.

By now, the clamorous scenes before, during and after every single Beatles engagement had become little short of maniacal, and dangerous for all concerned – fans and Beatles alike. The worst part was the continual problem of how the group could be smuggled into a venue, then later effect an escape from stage-door to van, shielded as best he could by the none-too-large frame of road manager Neil Aspinall, and thence get from the car park out onto the open road. Two important decisions were made: Neil Aspinall, and the Beatles, would have a second assistant: Mal Evans, a former bouncer at the Cavern Club and latterly a Post Office engineer. The likeable "Big Mal" became an essential part of the Beatles' working lives from 11 August when he met them on their return from a five-night stint in the Channel Islands.

The second decision had the typical Epstein touch. The Beatles, he vowed, would accept only theatre bookings, there would be no more clubs, no more ballrooms. While undoubtedly a matter of prestige, the decision was forced upon Epstein by the frenetic scenes at the Beatles' summer shows, and the horrifying thought that one of "the boys" might be physically hurt if they continued to play such venues.

As far as the national press was concerned, Beatlemania (in itself a Fleet Street term coined at this time) first occurred on Sunday 13 October when the group appeared on the ATV programme *Val Parnell's Sunday Night At The London Palladium*, a long-running British variety show broadcast live each week from the famous theatre in central London. The next day's newspapers happily reported the riotous scenes that had greeted the Beatles' arrival in a chauffeured Austin Princess (an Epstein-orchestrated touch of which beat van-travelling any day). Good heavens above, the teenagers even screamed *inside* the hallowed theatre.

Then, only two days later, came the news that, back in late-August, the group had accepted an invitation from impresario Bernard Delfont to appear before the Queen Mother and Princess Margaret at the annual Royal Command Performance. (What the public never discovered was that, every year after 1963, the Beatles were invited back and always said no.)

After more engagements, all feverishly covered by the press, and a recording session at EMI in which they taped the two sides of their next single ('I Want To Hold Your Hand' and 'This Boy'), the Beatles took off to Sweden for their first foreign tour. This was no less gruelling than a typical British itinerary, with nine concert performances and radio and TV dates crammed inside a week. Sweden too, judging by press and public reaction, succumbed to the Beatles as Britain had done, Beatlemania engulfing even the non-English-speaking among the country's teenagers. At a Stockholm show George was all but dragged from the stage by adoring fans.

Ironically, the Swedish tour is best remembered today for the Beatles' homecoming, when they flew into London Airport on 31 October from Arlanda, Stockholm. Despite a heavy rainstorm, several hundred screaming fans, many sporting the now famous "Beatle haircut" – fashioned,

Siege of the Beatles

WHAT A SUNDAY NIGHT AT THE PALLADIUM!

HERALD REPORTER

NEARLY 2,000 teenage girls, screaming "We Want The Beatles," battled through a panting police cordon outside the London Palladium last night.

The battle reached its climax minutes after the curtain came down at the close of I T V's Sunday Night at the Palladium.

SMUGGLED

Since mid-morning, Liverpool's Beatles group — John Lennon, Paul McCartney, George Harrison and Ringo Starr — had been prisoners in the Palladium while the teenagers surged outside.

Extra police stood at the gangways while more sealed off the stage door.

But when the Beatles, with their bobbed haircuts, finished their 12-minute act, the trouble really started.

Screaming girls launched themselves against the police —sending helmets flying and constables reeling.

Police vans sealed off the front of the theatre so that the Beatles could be smuggled out.

seemingly, so long before by Astrid Kirchherr in Hamburg – thronged the rooftop gardens of the Queen's Building and created a din so piercing that it drowned the noise of the jet engines. Representatives from all of the national newspapers and the BBC were out in force too, with 50 photographers and as many journalists jostling around the four surprised Beatles as they descended the steps of the plane and witnessed the first of a hundred so-called "airport receptions".

The celebrated Royal Command Performance took place on Monday 4 November at the Prince of Wales Theatre in London. There were the by-now-expected scenes of Beatlemania outside the theatre: hordes of screaming teenagers being held valiantly in check by rows of arm-linked strong British bobbies. For once, the arrival of the Royals was overshadowed, and by four young men from Liverpool who played rock and roll music – had the country gone mad? Inside the theatre the Beatles wooed and won over their bejewelled audience as quickly and effectively as they once, long ago, had captured a Cavern Club assembly. Performing on the same bill as Pinky and Perky may not have been the Beatles' idea of fame – nor, for that matter, was playing for socialites and débutantes – but their natural talent and impudent wit carried them through. Before launching into 'Twist And Shout' – hardly, one would think, a suitable choice of song for so austere an occasion, or so sedentary an audience – John stepped up to the microphone. "For our last number I'd like to ask your help," he said. "Would the people in the cheaper seats clap your hands? And the rest of you, if you'll just rattle your jewellery."

Sitting proudly in his tuxedo amid the royal gathering, Brian Epstein was overcome with relief that John hadn't said what, backstage, he was threatening to say. "I'll just tell 'em to rattle their fuckin' jewellery," was the genesis of the famous ad-lib.

Real, unstoppable, all-conquering Beatlemania followed. All 100,000 tickets for "The Beatles' Christmas Show", an enterprising Epstein-conceived seasonal extravaganza encompassing music and comedy, sold out within 25 days of going on sale. And all over Britain teenagers in their thousands queued overnight in wintry conditions, causing scenes of mayhem reported daily on front pages, just to get tickets for the Beatles' autumn tour when box-offices opened. This one had been announced back in June, and it was the group's fourth package tour around Britain in ten months, visiting 34 towns, two "houses" per night.

The Beatles' second album, *With The Beatles*, largely recorded back in the relative calm of July, was released on Friday 22 November to record advance orders of 270,000. One week later sales topped the half-million mark, a then astonishing achievement. On 13 August the Beatles' EP release *Twist And Shout* became the first of its kind to sell 250,000 copies and qualify for a silver disc. Then 'She Loves You', more than a million copies sold and number one since August, was finally displaced in the first week of December by the Beatles' fifth single, 'I Want To Hold Your Hand'. Record-splintering British advance orders of one million copies did not, as was feared in the Beatles' camp, temper the disc's eventual sales, and it stayed put at number one for six weeks, right through the Christmas period. On 5 November,

just one day after its release was announced, and 24 days before it was issued, EMI had received orders for 500,000 copies.

In the newspapers boys were being sent home from school all over the country for sporting "Beatle haircuts", a Beatle ballet was being planned, a trendy vicar and numerous politicians were using the Beatles' name to garner personal publicity, and questions were being raised in Parliament about the cost of the police protection afforded the group in London – protection, it was screamingly obvious, that was nothing short of essential if the limbs of John, Paul, George and Ringo were to remain intact.

For the Beatles themselves it was already getting beyond a joke. Having to wear elaborate disguises to walk in public; being victims of an attempted joke kidnap; their families and homes in a permanent state of siege; having guitars and clothes stolen from dressing-rooms; and Brian Epstein having to appeal to fans not to hurl missiles onto the stage – mostly jelly-babies, or whole packets of jelly-babies, because George had once jokingly remarked that they were his favourite brand of confection. Being smuggled into and out of each town on the autumn tour was more akin to an army exercise than a rock group on the road. And once inside a theatre they could do nothing but remain cooped up in dingy dressing-rooms, prisoners of their own fame.

On stage it was no better – performing 20-25 minute sets before audiences so uncontrollable that the screaming not only ruled out the chance of any musical sound being heard in the audience but prevented the Beatles themselves, in those days of primitive amplification equipment, from hearing their own voices, harmonies or instrumentation. After six years of musical progression on stage, the Beatles now became more stilted with every concert they played.

The tumultuous year of 1963 ended with the name of the Beatles, as one newspaper reported in a special Beatles edition, "engraved upon the heart of the nation". They completely dominated the newspapers, magazines, radio and television. The charts were positively swamped with Beatles records, not only by them but about them. *Record Retailer* announced that the British had paid £6,250,000 for Beatles records during the year.

Satisfied that the group were now established, never again would Brian Epstein put them through such a punishing year. At least, not domestically. The horizons were broadening: at the end of July the Beatles had been booked into the Olympia Theatre in Paris for a three-week run in January 1964. On the evening of 29 October, while the Beatles were in Sweden, Brian Epstein and film company United Artists concluded an agreement for their first feature-film, shooting to commence in March 1964. And in mid-December Epstein signed an agreement for the Beatles to tour Australia and New Zealand the following June.

1963

Beatles deny break-up story

Rumours that the Beatles are splitting up were denied last night by George Harrison, one of the group. He said: "We know that on our own we would be useless."

On Tuesday 5 November, the day after the Beatles' appearance in the Royal Command Performance, Epstein took Billy J Kramer to the USA for a promotional visit. While there, Epstein met Ed Sullivan, host of America's top-rated, networked TV variety programme *The Ed Sullivan Show*. Sullivan happened to have witnessed Beatlemania first-hand when he was delayed at London Airport only a few days earlier, on 31 October, because of the Beatles' return from Sweden, and he thought it would be amusing for his country to see this latest, crazy British fad. But he and his producer Bob Precht were flabbergasted when Epstein insisted that his group, unknown in the USA, receive promi-

nent billing on the show, and they only conceded when they learned that, in order to achieve this accolade, Epstein was willing to trade a hefty cut in their appearance money.

So it was that on the evening of 11 November 1963, in Sullivan's New York home/office suite at the Delmonico Hotel, the impresarios reached agreement. For what, in US terms, was a trifling $10,000, the Beatles would make three appearances on *The Ed Sullivan Show*, two of them live – on 9 and 16 February 1964, the first from New York, the second from Miami, worth $3500 each – and one taped for transmission on the 23rd, worth $3000. (A top act would usually earn $7500 from *one* performance on *The Ed Sullivan Show* at this time.) Sullivan would also pay the Beatles' round-trip air fares and their hotel bills in New York and Miami. It was probably the best investment that either man ever made.

While in New York Epstein also met with Brown Meggs, the director of eastern operations at Capitol Records, EMI's North American subsidiary, and was delighted to learn that, upon releasing the single 'I Want To Hold Your Hand' on 13 January 1964, Capitol was at last planning to push the Beatles in the USA. On four previous occasions – 'Love Me Do', 'Please Please Me', 'From Me To You' and 'She Loves You' – this major US label had declined its option to release the group's singles, which had instead been issued there – with very little success – by small independent companies.

Because of substantial consumer demands following early radio airplay, however, Capitol decided to bring forward the release by 17 days, to 26 December …

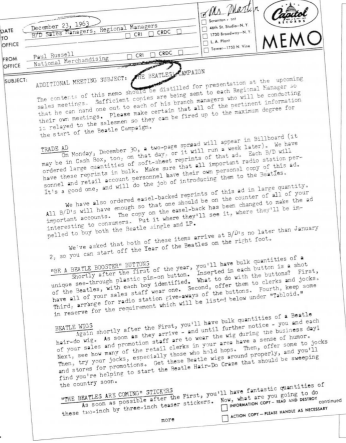

Wednesday 2 January

Longmore Hall, Church Rd, Keith, Banffshire (cancelled)

This opening night of a five-date booking in Scotland and the Beatles' first proper tour – also a return visit to the town played as support to Johnny Gentle on 25 May 1960 – was cancelled owing to the terrible weather conditions which had the whole of Scotland in an icy grip. Snowdrifts made virtually all of the Highlands roads impassable, and the Beatles hadn't a chance of getting through to Keith in time to fulfil the engagement.

The tour had got away to a bad start even before this set-back. Thanks to the inclement weather, the Beatles' flight from London to Edinburgh during the morning of 2 January (the group had flown to London from Hamburg on 1 January and spent the night there) was switched at the last moment to land at Aberdeen – too late to notify Neil Aspinall who turned up to meet them at Edinburgh with the van.

Safe in the knowledge that they had nothing to do until the evening of the 3rd, John then flew home to Liverpool for a few hours, returning to Scotland early in the morning.

Thursday 3 January

Two Red Shoes Ballroom, South College St, Elgin, Morayshire

At last the tour got under way. This ballroom was slightly L-shaped, which meant that some of the dancers were unable to see the Beatles on the stage.

Friday 4 January

Town Hall, High St, Dingwall, Ross and Cromarty

Saturday 5 January

Museum Hall, Henderson St, Bridge of Allan, Stirlingshire

Sunday 6 January

Beach Ballroom, Sea Beach, Aberdeen, Aberdeenshire

The last night of the five-date Scottish tour.

Tuesday 8 January

Scottish Television, Theatre Royal, Hope Street, Glasgow, Lanarkshire

The Beatles remained north of the border after the Aberdeen date and travelled down to the Scottish Television studios in Glasgow for an appearance on the children's magazine programme *Roundup*, presented by Paul Young and Morag Hood and broadcast (locally only) live from 5.00 to 5.55 pm. The Beatles' contribution was to mime to their forthcoming single, 'Please Please Me'.

Thursday 10 January

Grafton Rooms, Liverpool

The Beatles' first home-town engagement in nearly a month, heading a five-act bill. The evening was a resounding success, with a record-breaking attendance crowding into the large Grafton Rooms. One enterprising local stole 100 tickets a few days beforehand only to find that they were numbered and declared invalid.

Friday 11 January

Lunchtime **Cavern Club, Liverpool**
Night **Plaza Ballroom, Halesowen Rd, Old Hill, nr Dudley, Staffordshire**
and **Ritz Ballroom, York Rd, King's Heath, Birmingham, Warwickshire** (postponed)

Although the Beatles successfully made the hazardous afternoon journey south from Liverpool to Old Hill, blizzards ensured that they were unable to drive the 11 miles from there to King's Heath to fulfil the second part of a double booking in the Midlands. It was the coldest night in the area for seven years. The King's Heath date was re-arranged for 15 February.

Saturday 12 January

Invicta Ballroom, High St, Chatham, Kent

The Beatles' southernmost engagement to date.

Sunday 13 January

**Alpha Television Studios, Aston Rd North,
Aston, Birmingham, Warwickshire**

Secured for them by music publisher Dick James – a coup which, in turn, secured him immense fortune because it won his company the group's song copyrights from 'Please Please Me' onwards – this was far and away the Beatles' most important television appearance to date, a taping for the very popular and – most importantly of all – almost fully networked *Thank Your Lucky Stars*. Most of Britain's teenage population saw this weekly pop programme, in which top acts of the day mimed to their latest record releases. For most viewers, it was their first sight of the Beatles.

Thank Your Lucky Stars was made by ABC Television, the ITV franchise supplying weekend programming for the Midlands and the north (and some for networking), and this day's taping took place at Alpha Television Studios in Birmingham, jointly owned by ABC and ATV (which broadcast in the Midlands on weekdays and in London at weekends).

Bottom of a seven-act bill, the Beatles performed one song, 'Please Please Me', closing the first half of the programme, prior to the commercial break, during the 5.50–6.30 pm broadcast on Saturday 19 January.

Monday 14 January

**Civic Hall, Whitby Rd, Ellesmere Port,
Wirral, Cheshire**

The Beatles' only engagement in Ellesmere Port, the industrial town 19 miles south of Liverpool. A capacity crowd of 700 packed the Civic Hall for this Wolverham Welfare Association Dance.

Wednesday 16 January

Studio Four, Granada TV Centre, Manchester
and **Playhouse Theatre, Manchester**

A double Manchester media booking for the Beatles, appearing live on the Granada Television show *People And Places* and then recording a BBC radio appearance for *Here We Go*. Their afternoon/evening schedule went like this:

3.00–4.00   Rehearsal in studio four at Granada TV Centre.

4.30–5.30   Rehearsal at the Playhouse Theatre for the BBC.

6.35–7.00   Back to Granada for live transmission of *People And Places*, miming to 'Ask Me Why' and 'Please Please Me'.

8.45–9.30   Recording of *Here We Go* at the Playhouse, for broadcast on the BBC Light Programme, 5.00–5.29 pm, on Friday 25 January. The Beatles sang four numbers: 'Chains', 'Please Please Me', 'Three Cool Cats' and 'Ask Me Why', but 'Three Cool Cats' was omitted from the edited transmission tape.

Thursday 17 January

Lunchtime **Cavern Club, Liverpool**
Night **Majestic Ballroom, Birkenhead**

Every ticket for the Majestic dance was sold in advance, much to the disappointment of an extra 500 fans outside the venue.

Friday 18 January

Floral Hall Ballroom, Morecambe

Saturday 19 January

**Town Hall Ballroom, Pauls Moss, Dodington,
Whitchurch, Shropshire**

The Beatles and fans at the Floral Hall Ballroom, Morecambe, 18 January 1963.

Sunday 20 January

Night **Cavern Club, Liverpool**

Monday 21 January

EMI House, London

The Beatles' third appearance on EMI's *The Friday Spectacular*, broadcast by Radio Luxembourg on 25 January, 10.00–11.00 pm, chatting to series hosts Shaw Taylor (later responsible for the crime-solving TV programme *Police Five*) and Muriel Young, and witnessing the broadcast of 'Please Please Me' and 'Ask Me Why'. The show was recorded, as usual, before an audience of 100 teenagers inside EMI House in central London.

Tony Barrow referred to this particular appearance in his sleevenote for the Beatles' soon-to-be-recorded début album *Please Please Me*.

Tuesday 22 January

BBC Paris Studio, London
and **Playhouse Theatre, Northumberland Ave, London**
and **BBC Paris Studio, London**

A remarkably busy day for the Beatles, in which they appeared live on one BBC radio programme and recorded sessions for two others.

First stop was a return to the Paris Studio in Regent Street where, to accompany the broadcast of new single 'Please Please Me', the Beatles chatted on the live lunchtime show *Pop Inn*, broadcast on the Light Programme between 1.00 and 1.45 pm. (The disc-playing/artist-interview structure was similar to EMI's *The Friday Spectacular* on Radio Luxembourg.) Among the other guests were Joan Regan, Jon Pertwee (the future Dr Who) and Shane Fenton (the future Alvin Stardust).

Second stop was the Playhouse Theatre, situated near Charing Cross. Here the Beatles rehearsed from 2.30 pm and recorded from 4.00 to 5.00 for their first appearance on the top pop radio programme of the era *Saturday Club*, as influential on radio as *Thank Your Lucky Stars* was on TV, and both were presented by the same man, Brian Matthew.

The Beatles recorded five songs in the *Saturday Club* session, 'Some Other Guy', 'Love Me Do', 'Please Please Me', 'Keep Your Hands Off My Baby' and 'Beautiful Dreamer'. The programme was broadcast on 26 January, between 10.00 am and 12.00 noon, the second half-hour (actually 10.31–10.59) of the two-hour show being simultaneously transmitted on short-wave frequencies by the BBC's General Overseas Service (now World Service) to Australasia, Africa, the Far East, the Middle East, south-east Asia and the Mediterranean area. Of the five Beatles songs in this particular programme, 'Some Other Guy' and 'Love Me Do' occurred in the GOS section. (During British Summer Time it was the fourth half-hour of *Saturday Club*, 11.31–11.59 am, which was aired by the GOS. BST in 1963 was 21 April to 6 October, in 1964 it was 22 March to 25 October.)

The third and final session took place back at the Paris Studio where, before an audience, the Beatles recorded another contribution to the Light Programme show *The Talent Spot*, for broadcast between 5.00 and 5.29 pm on Tuesday 29 January, an appearance arranged for them by music publisher Dick James. Rehearsing from 5.30 and recording between 7.00 and 8.00 pm, they sang 'Please Please Me', 'Ask Me Why' and 'Some Other Guy'. Among the other guests on the show was young guitarist Rog Whittaker, destined to make a name for himself as Roger Whittaker.

Wednesday 23 January

Night **Cavern Club, Liverpool**

The Beatles began their drive north to Liverpool during Wednesday morning and arrived just in time for the night-time Cavern Club engagement after an appalling journey by road. Their van's windscreen had shattered and, in bitterly cold conditions, deputy (and later permanent) assistant road manager Mal Evans – Neil Aspinall had remained in Liverpool, being unwell – had no choice but to drive on without a screen while the Beatles conserved any remaining vestiges of warmth by laying on top of one another in the back.

Thursday 24 January

Assembly Hall, High St, Mold, Flintshire

Before setting off to north Wales for this engagement the Beatles made a personal appearance at NEMS' central Liverpool record store, 12-14 Whitechapel, signing copies of their 'Please Please Me' single and giving a brief acoustic performance from the foot of the staircase leading from the ground floor (popular records) to the first floor (classical records, television, radio and recording equipment).

Friday 25 January

Co-operative Hall, Market St, Darwen, Lancashire

A dance promoted by the local Baptist church youth club.

BAPTIST YOUTH CLUB

INVITE YOU TO

The Greatest Teenage Dance !

FEATURING —

THE BEATLES

SUPPORTED BY — THE ELECTONES   THE MIKE TAYLOR COMBO

THE MUSTANGS with RICKY DAY

IN THE CO-OPERATIVE HALL,

FRIDAY NEXT, JANUARY 25th

NON-STOP DANCING 7-30 to 11-30 p.m.

TICKETS 6/-   Right of Admission Reserved   BUFFET

ADMISSION BY TICKET ONLY!

WARNING — Tickets for the above Dance have been Sold faster than expected
A few Only are available from :- NIGHTINGALES RECORD SHOP ; CO-OP TRAVEL
AGENCY ; WALSH'S CYCLE SHOP, Bridge-street ; NELSON'S GROCER SHOP,
458, Blackburn-road   BUY YOURS NOW

Saturday 26 January

**El Rio Club, El Rio Dance Hall, Queen Victoria St,
Macclesfield, Cheshire**
and **King's Hall, Glebe St, Stoke-on-Trent, Staffordshire**

Twenty-one miles separated this double booking. At the El Rio dance, first arranged for 19 January but subsequently moved to this date, the Beatles were supported by local combo Wayne Fontana and the Jets, Fontana later finding fame with the Mindbenders.

Backstage at Stoke, John and Paul began writing 'Misery', a song they intended donating to Helen Shapiro, whom the Beatles would meet a week later. On stage, they performed a song this night for the first and only time, a cover of 'Walk Right In', just breaking in Britain as a hit for the US act the Rooftop Singers, and already a number one in their homeland.

Sunday 27 January

Three Coins Club, Fountain St, Manchester, Lancashire

A return visit to the club part-owned by radio disc-jockey Jimmy Savile (first played by the Beatles soon after it opened in late-1961 – see Other Engagements Played appendix).

Monday 28 January

**Majestic Ballroom, Westgate Rd,
Newcastle-upon-Tyne, Northumberland**

Wednesday 30 January

Lunchtime **Cavern Club, Liverpool**

Thursday 31 January

Lunchtime **Cavern Club, Liverpool**
Night **Majestic Ballroom, Birkenhead**

Such was the ticket demand for the Majestic date that the Beatles gave two entirely separate "houses", at 8.00 and 11.00 pm. Though standard practice in theatres/cinemas, this was an unheard-of arrangement for a ballroom.

Friday 1 February

Assembly Rooms, Corporation St, Tamworth, Staffs
and **Maney Hall (St Peter's Church Hall), Maney Hill Rd,
Maney, Sutton Coldfield, Warwickshire**

Another double engagement in the Midlands, the venues this time eight miles apart.

Saturday 2 February

Gaumont Cinema, New Victoria St, Bradford, Yorks

The opening night of the Beatles' first nationwide tour, bottom of a six-act bill headed by 16-year-old Londoner Helen Shapiro, voted Best British Female Singer in 1961 and 1962.

The Beatles' repertoire on this first night was 'Chains', 'Keep Your Hands Off My Baby', 'A Taste Of Honey' and 'Please Please Me'. Two others, 'Love Me Do' and 'Beautiful Dreamer', were used during the remaining dates as prepared alternatives. After this date, the tour resumed on 5 February.

Sunday 3 February

Night **Cavern Club, Liverpool**

The Beatles headed an eight-hour eight band "Rhythm And Blues Marathon".

Monday 4 February

Lunchtime **Cavern Club, Liverpool**

The Beatles' last lunchtime session at the Cavern.

Tuesday 5 February

Gaumont Cinema, Hallgate, Doncaster, Yorkshire

Resumption of the Shapiro package tour.

Wednesday 6 February

**Granada Cinema, St Peters Street,
Bedford, Bedfordshire**

Thursday 7 February

Regal Cinema, Kirkgate, Wakefield, Yorkshire

Friday 8 February

ABC Cinema, Warwick Rd, Carlisle, Cumberland

Probably the highlight of an otherwise uneventful tour happened after these two "houses", when the Beatles, Helen Shapiro and Kenny Lynch were ejected from a Carlisle Golf Club dance at the Crown and Mitre Hotel in the town centre. Offence was taken after the Beatles had been admitted to the ballroom wearing leather jackets.

Saturday 9 February

Empire Theatre, High St, Sunderland, Durham

For the Beatles, these Sunderland shows marked the last night of the Shapiro tour's first leg, to be resumed on 23 February. They did not participate in two 10 February "houses" at the Embassy Cinema in Peterborough (where their place on the bill was temporarily filled by Peter Jay and the Jaywalkers) because they had to be in London first thing in the morning of 11 February, fresh and ready for a recording session…

Monday 11 February

Studio Two, EMI Studios, London

It was not *so* unusual in 1963 for pop groups to record an entire album in one day – quality and care were forsaken but budgets were adhered to. What *was* unusual was the Beatles' ability to turn out a brilliant début album under these circumstances. *Please Please Me*, the 14-track LP for which all ten new recordings were made this day, remains a first-class collection of great performances. There can scarcely have been 585 more productive minutes in the history of recorded music.

Remarkably, only two sessions – 10.00 am–1.00 pm and 2.30–5.30 pm – were originally booked; in reality, this second session ended at 6.00 and a third, 7.30–10.45, was added. The Beatles weren't even fully fit, John suffering from a bad cold which affected his singing voice. Tea, milk, cigarettes and "Soothing and Comforting" Zubes lozenges saw them through the long day.

A basic run-down of the day looks like this: between 10.00 am and 1.00 pm they recorded ten takes of 'There's A Place' and nine of a song at this point titled 'Seventeen' (later changed to 'I Saw Her Standing There').

From 2.30 to 6.00 pm: seven takes of 'A Taste Of Honey', eight of 'Do You Want To Know A Secret', three more of 'There's A Place', three more of 'I Saw Her Standing There' and 11 of 'Misery'.

From 7.30 to 10.45 pm: 13 takes of 'Hold Me Tight' (this song would remain unreleased until a re-make recorded on 12 September 1963 was included on the group's second album *With The Beatles*), three takes of 'Anna (Go To Him)', one of 'Boys', four of 'Chains', three of 'Baby It's You' and, finally, the closing number to end all closing numbers, two takes of 'Twist And Shout' (the first of which was chosen for the album).

An article in the 22 February edition of *New Musical Express*, and also a little later in *Pop Weekly* (probably the work of the same author), suggested that the Beatles also recorded a version of 'Keep Your Hands Off My Baby' at this session. But the complete set of the day's recording sheets do not mention this title, nor does it appear in the tape library log.

Please Please Me was released in Britain on Friday 22 March 1963, where it was the best-selling LP for 30 straight weeks – until it was dislodged by *With The Beatles*.

Tuesday 12 February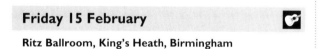

Azena Ballroom, White Lane, Gleadless, Sheffield, Yorkshire
and **Astoria Ballroom, King St, Oldham, Lancashire**

Wednesday 13 February

Majestic Ballroom, Hull

Thursday 14 February

Locarno Ballroom, West Derby Rd, Liverpool

A special dance to mark St Valentine's Day. It was the Beatles' first appearance at this prominent Liverpool ballroom, although the Quarry Men did perform here once or twice in late-1950s skiffle contests.

Friday 15 February

Ritz Ballroom, King's Heath, Birmingham

The re-arranged engagement, postponed from 11 January. The situation was ideal for the Ritz promoters who presented a group now featuring in the top three of the singles chart at the same cost as when they were a comparatively unknown act.

Saturday 16 February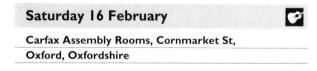

Carfax Assembly Rooms, Cornmarket St, Oxford, Oxfordshire

A one-nighter at this city-centre venue and the Beatles' first booking with John Smith, one of the top London promoters.

Sunday 17 February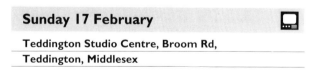

Teddington Studio Centre, Broom Rd, Teddington, Middlesex

The Beatles' second appearance on ABC Television's *Thank Your Lucky Stars*, the most influential TV pop programme in Britain before *Top Of The Pops*, taped this time at the company's Teddington Studio Centre south-west of London. They were called for rehearsal at 11.00 am and recorded the programme later in the afternoon, miming to one song, 'Please Please Me'. It was transmitted across most of the UK on Saturday 23 February, between 5.50 and 6.30 pm. They had now ascended to third placing on the seven-act bill, the

star of this particular edition being fellow Liverpudlian Billy Fury, for whom the amateur Silver Beetles had auditioned on 10 May 1960.

A brief extract from this performance was repeated in the Saturday 2 March edition of *ABC At Large* (see that date).

Monday 18 February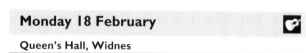

Queen's Hall, Widnes

Another NEMS Enterprises' showcase, with two separate "houses". Both were sell-outs.

Tuesday 19 February

Night **Cavern Club, Liverpool**

The Beatles' first Cavern Club performance in more than a fortnight. The queue for admission formed *two days* beforehand. Also on the bill were Lee Curtis and the All-Stars. This was the last time that any of the Beatles set eyes on Pete Best in person.

Wednesday 20 February

Playhouse Theatre, London
and **Swimming Baths, St James Street, Doncaster, Yorkshire**

The Beatles were not present at Abbey Road for a 10.30 am–1.00 pm overdub session in studio one, which saw George Martin add piano to 'Misery' and celeste and piano to 'Baby It's You'. (The latter piano piece was never used.)

Instead, after concluding their Tuesday-night engagement in Liverpool they drove down to London through the night in order to appear on the live lunchtime radio show

Parade Of The Pops, broadcast by the BBC Light Programme direct from the Playhouse Theatre between 12.31 and 1.30 pm. (They also took part in a prior rehearsal, at 11.15 am.) The group performed two songs, 'Love Me Do' and 'Please Please Me'.

After the show, while probably pondering whether a total airtime of 4 mins 10 secs on the BBC had been worth the effort, the Beatles quickly returned 160 miles north to fulfil their evening date in Doncaster.

Thursday 21 February

Majestic Ballroom, Birkenhead

Once again there were two separate "houses", the Beatles appearing at 7.30 and 11.30 pm.

Friday 22 February

Oasis Club, Manchester

Saturday 23 February

Granada Cinema, West Gate, Mansfield, Notts

So began part two of the Helen Shapiro package tour. Before going on stage for the first of the two "houses" the Beatles crowded into Helen's dressing-room and watched their latest appearance on *Thank Your Lucky Stars*, taped the previous Sunday. Being the headliner, Shapiro had the only TV set among the artists.

Sunday 24 February

Coventry Theatre, Hales St, Coventry, Warwickshire

After this date there was a one-day break from the tour, which resumed on the 26th.

Monday 25 February

Casino Ballroom, Lord St, Leigh, Lancashire

In the Beatles' absence once again, George Martin and his team produced the mono and stereo masters of the *Please Please Me* album, mixing and banding the 14 tracks in 10.00 am–1.00 pm and 2.30–5.45 pm sessions in studio one at EMI.

The group, meanwhile, were in a van on their way to Leigh for a NEMS Enterprises dance booking.

Tuesday 26 February

Gaumont Cinema, Corporation St, Taunton, Somerset

Back to the package tour. In the unceasingly terrible winter weather, Helen Shapiro was struck down with a cold and was forced to miss this date. Danny Williams assumed top-of-the-bill status and Billie Davis, currently charting with 'Tell Him', was drafted in to pad out the line-up.

Wednesday 27 February

Rialto Theatre, Fishergate, York, Yorkshire

Once again Helen Shapiro had to bow out of the proceedings owing to illness.

Thursday 28 February

Granada Cinema, Castle Gates, Shrewsbury, Shropshire

While travelling this day between York and Shrewsbury, on the coach containing the entire Shapiro entourage, John and Paul wrote the Beatles' next single, 'From Me To You'.

With this date Helen Shapiro resumed her role as headliner, and Billie Davis left the tour.

Friday I March

Odeon Cinema, Lord St, Southport, Lancashire

Saturday 2 March

City Hall, Barker's Pool, Sheffield, Yorkshire
and **Studio Two, Didsbury Studio Centre, Parrs Wood Road, Manchester, Lancashire**

After finishing the second Shapiro "house" at Sheffield, the Beatles drove 38 miles to Manchester, to appear live on the ABC TV news-magazine programme *ABC At Large*, broadcast in the Midlands and north regions only from the company's Didsbury Studio Centre between 11.00 and 11.50 pm.

Together with Brian Epstein, they participated in a lengthy interview with David Hamilton (later a top radio DJ), answering questions about their sudden fame and pondering why they had succeeded where hundreds of other groups – from Liverpool and elsewhere – had not done so.

Backstage at the Casino Ballroom, Leigh, 25 February 1963.

1 9 6 3

With George Martin in the EMI canteen and in the studio, 5 March 1963. Many of their recording sessions, especially the early ones, began with the Beatles demonstrating their material to George while he sat on a high stool.

The feature also included interviews with pop fans and an appearance by Gerry Marsden of Gerry and the Pacemakers.

The Beatles did not perform music on this programme, although a brief clip of a mimed 'Please Please Me' from their most recent appearance on ABC's *Thank Your Lucky Stars* (taped 17 February, transmitted 23 February) was shown again.

Sunday 3 March

Gaumont Cinema, Piccadilly, Hanley, Staffordshire

The final night of the Helen Shapiro package tour. By this time the Beatles had been elevated on the bill from playing the ignominious first spot to the final act in the first-half.

Monday 4 March

Plaza Ballroom, St Helens

The Beatles' first £100 booking.

Tuesday 5 March

Studio Two, EMI Studios, London

Five days after writing it on the Helen Shapiro coach, the Beatles recorded 'From Me To You' this day at EMI. It began the session as the B-side of their third single; during the session, however, it was promoted to premier status over the previously preferred 'Thank You Girl', also taped this day (under the working title 'Thank You Little Girl') which became the new B-side. The Beatles worked in studio two between 2.30 and 9.00 pm – although the session had been booked for 2.30–5.30 and 7.00–10.00 – recording 13 takes of

'From Me To You' and the same number of 'Thank You Girl'. The single was issued by EMI on Thursday 11 April.

With some studio time remaining, the Beatles were keen to record two more Lennon-McCartney titles, 'The One After 909' and 'What Goes On' – although, in the end, it was possible only to tape the former. Five takes were recorded but the result was deemed unsatisfactory and this version remains unissued. The Beatles returned to the song during the *Get Back* sessions (see 28–30 January 1969) hence its inclusion on the album *Let It Be*, and they returned to 'What Goes On' for *Rubber Soul* (see 4 November 1965).

Wednesday 6 March

Playhouse Theatre, Manchester

A return trip to the Playhouse in Manchester for the Beatles' fifth and final appearance on the BBC Light Programme radio show *Here We Go*, produced by Peter Pilbeam, the man who had auditioned and broadcast the group before they had an EMI recording contract.

The Beatles inside and outside EMI's central London HQ on 5 March 1963. Music publisher Dick James (in glasses) joined George Martin and Brian Epstein (not shown) for the photo session.

After a 4.00 pm rehearsal, the group took part in the recording from 8.00 to 8.45, performing 'I Saw Her Standing There', 'Misery', 'Do You Want To Know A Secret' and 'Please Please Me', although 'I Saw Her Standing There' was edited out of the broadcast tape, transmitted from 5.00 to 5.29 pm on Tuesday 12 March.

Thursday 7 March

Elizabethan Ballroom, Co-operative House,
Parliament St, Nottingham, Nottinghamshire

An inspirational idea on the part of Brian Epstein: a one-night stand featuring his fast-growing stable of artists, all beginning to enjoy great success. The Beatles, Gerry and the Pacemakers, the Big Three, and Billy J Kramer with the Dakotas all appeared, as did the Cavern Club compere Bob Wooler. On this occasion the entire entourage travelled down from Liverpool on two coaches run by NEMS Enterprises, joined by 80 fans who paid an all-in fare of 25 shillings (£1.25).

This was the first of six such engagements over the following three months, concluding on 16 June. It became known as the "Mersey Beat Showcase" tour.

Friday 8 March

The Royal Hall, Ripon Rd, Harrogate, Yorkshire

Saturday 9 March

Granada Cinema, Barking Rd, East Ham, London

A mere five days after concluding the Helen Shapiro tour – five days in which they had fulfilled three live engagements, a recording session for EMI and a radio session for the BBC – the Beatles set off gallivanting around a still-snowbound Britain on a second theatre package tour. Top billing this time was shared by two American individuals, Tommy Roe and Chris Montez, although both were very quickly superseded – on the first "house" of the first night, in fact – by the increasingly all-conquering Beatles.

Their repertoire on this tour was 'Love Me Do', 'Misery', 'A Taste Of Honey', 'Do You Want To Know A Secret', 'Please Please Me' and 'I Saw Her Standing There'.

Sunday 10 March

Hippodrome Theatre, Hurst St, Birmingham, Warks

After this date, the tour resumed on the 12th.

Monday 11 March

EMI House, London

The Beatles spent the evening of the one-day Monday respite from the tour inside the small ground-floor studio within EMI House, making their fourth and last appearance on the company's *The Friday Spectacular*, broadcast on Radio Luxembourg on 15 March, 10.00–11.00 pm. Once again, they chatted about themselves and their work, around which 'Please Please Me' and 'Ask Me Why' were transmitted.

Tuesday 12 March

Granada Cinema, Bedford

Back to the Roe/Montez tour. This was a three-man Beatles performance because a heavy cold kept John in bed. The songs, particularly 'Please Please Me', were re-arranged so that George and Paul could take over his vocal lines.

Wednesday 13 March

Studio Two, EMI Studios, London
and **Rialto Theatre, York**

The Beatles travelled from Bedford to York for this evening's two Roe/Montez "houses" via EMI Studios in London, where

they participated in a 10.00 am–1.00 pm harmonica over-dubbing session for 'Thank You Girl', recording takes 14–28. When complete, the song was edited and then mixed into mono and stereo. It was just as well that no vocals were required, for John was still voiceless and didn't play at York.

Thursday 14 March

Gaumont Cinema, Snow Hill, Wolverhampton, Staffs

Editing, mono mixing and stereo mixing of 'From Me To You' by George Martin and team took place this day at EMI Studios, 10.00 am–1.00 pm. The Beatles were absent, still travelling south from York to Wolverhampton for another night's work without John Lennon.

Friday 15 March

Colston Hall, Colston St, Bristol

John returned to the Beatles' line-up for these two "houses".

Saturday 16 March

Studio 3A, Broadcasting House, Portland Pl, London
and City Hall, Sheffield

Owing to their Radio Luxembourg commitment, and John's cold, the Beatles had been forced to cancel an 11 March session for this day's BBC Light Programme radio show *Saturday Club* (recording had been arranged for the Playhouse Theatre in London between 5.30 and 6.30 pm).

Instead, they made their contribution live from Broadcasting House, the central London HQ of domestic BBC radio. The group arrived by taxi in time for a 9.00 am rehearsal and then performed six songs live, interspersed throughout the 10.00 am to 12.00 noon broadcast: 'I Saw Her Standing There' and 'Misery', 'Too Much Monkey Business', 'I'm Talking About You', 'Please Please Me', and 'The Hippy Hippy Shake'. Only 'Too Much Monkey Business' was included in the 10.31–10.59 am section broadcast simultaneously by the General Overseas Service.

After the programme was over, the Beatles sped 158 miles north in order to be at the City Hall in Sheffield in time for the first Roe/Montez tour "house" at 6.10 pm.

Sunday 17 March

Embassy Cinema, Peterborough

Monday 18 March

Regal Cinema, St Aldate Street,
Gloucester, Gloucestershire

Tuesday 19 March

Regal Cinema, St Andrews Street,
Cambridge, Cambridgeshire

Wednesday 20 March

ABC Cinema, South St, Romford, Essex

Thursday 21 March

Studio One, BBC Piccadilly Studios,
Piccadilly, London
and ABC Cinema, London Rd, West Croydon, Surrey

Between 1.00 and 2.00 pm, following a 10.00 am rehearsal, the Beatles recorded a BBC radio session for *On The Scene*, broadcast in the Light Programme from 5.00 to 5.29 pm on Thursday 28 March. They performed three songs: 'Misery', 'Do You Want To Know A Secret' and 'Please Please Me', working for the first time at Piccadilly Studios, at 201 Piccadilly in central London.

After the session, the group drove south, to Croydon, to continue the Roe/Montez tour.

Friday 22 March

Gaumont Cinema, Doncaster

Saturday 23 March

City Hall, Northumberland Rd,
Newcastle-upon-Tyne, Northumberland

Sunday 24 March

Empire Theatre, Liverpool

A celebrated return to the Beatles' home-town, their first Liverpool performance in more than a month.

The Beatles spent the tour's one-day break on the 25th at a number of local locations with photographer Dezo Hoffmann, with both stills and 8mm mute colour home-movie footage resulting. They later repeated the exercise in Weston-super-Mare – see 22-27 July 1963.

Tuesday 26 March

Granada Cinema, Mansfield

Wednesday 27 March

ABC Cinema, Abingdon Square,
Northampton, Northamptonshire

Thursday 28 March

ABC Cinema, London Inn Square,
Exeter, Devonshire

Friday 29 March

Odeon Cinema, Loampit Vale,
Lewisham, London

Saturday 30 March

Guildhall, The Square, Portsmouth, Hampshire

Sunday 31 March

De Montfort Hall, Granville Rd,
Leicester, Leicestershire

The final night of the tour with Tommy Roe and Chris Montez.

Monday 1 April

Studio One, BBC Piccadilly Studios, London

On this day the Beatles recorded contributions to two programmes in the weekly BBC Light Programme radio series *Side By Side*, hosted by staff announcer John Dunn, later a top presenter. Inclusive of rehearsal time, the sessions took place from 2.30 to 5.30 and 6.30 to 10.30 pm.

Side By Side featured two groups each week, one being the resident Karl Denver Trio. Together, they and their guest act would open the show singing 'Side By Side' (written by Harry Woods, first recorded in 1927 by the Paul Whiteman Orchestra); thereafter, the two groups would alternate until the end of the show half-an-hour later.

The afternoon recording was transmitted between 5.00 and 5.29 pm on Monday 22 April, the Beatles contributing 'I Saw Her Standing There', 'Do You Want To Know A Secret', 'Baby It's You', 'Please Please Me', 'From Me To You' and 'Misery', as well as the 'Side By Side' duet with Denver's trio.

The evening recording was transmitted between 5.00 and 5.29 pm on Monday 13 May, the Beatles contributing 'From Me To You', 'Long Tall Sally', 'A Taste Of Honey', 'Chains', 'Thank You Girl' and 'Boys', together with a repeat of the 'Side By Side' duet with Denver.

Wednesday 3 April

Playhouse Theatre, London

The Beatles' first recording for the BBC Light Programme radio show *Easy Beat*, hosted by the ubiquitous Brian Matthew and taped weekly in front of an enthusiastic teenage audience at the Playhouse.

The Beatles rehearsed from 5.30 pm and took part in the continuous recording from 8.30 to 9.45; the programme was then transmitted between 10.31 and 11.30 am on Sunday 7 April. Their contribution was three songs: 'Please Please Me', 'Misery' and 'From Me To You'.

As well as performing music, two of the Beatles – John and Paul – took part in the programme's record-review panel spot "Going Up?" (along with Laura Lee and Clare O'Rourke), giving their opinions of new singles by Bert Weedon, Cleo Laine, the Vernons Girls, and Tommy Roe. For undertaking this work, each panel member received one guinea (£1 1s, now £1.05) in cash before leaving the studio.

Thursday 4 April

BBC Paris Studio, London
and Roxburgh Hall, Stowe School, Stowe, Bucks

Having taped sessions for two programmes in the Light Programme radio series *Side By Side* only the previous Monday, the Beatles returned to the BBC this day, 11.00 am-2.00 pm, to record a third. (An option for a fourth appearance in the series, to have been taped between 2.00 and 6.00 pm this day, was not taken up, however.)

The Beatles and the Karl Denver Trio did not bother to re-record their duet of 'Side By Side', the BBC using the 1 April tape for this transmission, which took place between 5.00 and 5.29 pm on Monday 24 June. (It was unusual for the Corporation to keep recordings so long before broadcast, and this was certainly the longest any Beatles tape remained "in the can".) Listeners to the show heard the group perform 'Too Much Monkey Business', 'Love Me Do', 'Boys', 'I'll Be On My Way' and 'From Me To You'.

'I'll Be On My Way' is of particular interest for it was the Beatles' only studio-environment recording and known public performance of a Lennon-McCartney song given exclusively to Billy J Kramer with the Dakotas for record release: they taped their version at EMI Studios on 14 March and released the track on 26 April as the B-side of 'Do You

Rocking the Roxburgh Hall underneath the hallowed Latin: the Beatles perform for the self-restrained boys at Stowe School, 4 April 1963.

Want To Know A Secret', another – though not so exclusive – Lennon-McCartney original.

The late-afternoon live engagement at Stowe, the boys' public school, was probably the Beatles' most unusual concert appearance of all, and was booked as a direct result of one Liverpudlian boy's interest in his home-town group.

Friday 5 April

Swimming Baths, High Rd Leyton, Leyton, London

Earlier in the evening, prior to the date at Leyton Baths, the Beatles gave a private live performance for record company executives at EMI House in central London, during a presentation ceremony to celebrate the award of their first silver disc, for the single 'Please Please Me'.

Saturday 6 April

**Pavilion Gardens Ballroom, St John's Rd,
Buxton, Derbyshire**

Sunday 7 April

**Savoy Ballroom, South Parade, Southsea,
Portsmouth, Hampshire**

Tuesday 9 April

**BBC Paris Studio, London,
and Studio Four, Wembley Studios, Wembley
and Ballroom, Gaumont State Cinema,
Kilburn High Rd, Kilburn, London**

Another busy day: a live radio interview at lunchtime, a live (but mimed) television appearance at tea-time, live in concert at night.

The BBC's Pop Inn *crowd, 9 April 1963. The 1960s rock revolution brought a swift end to variety-led pop radio line-ups like this: the Beatles with Paul and Paula, British music-hall star Arthur Askey, Shani Wallis, Winifred Atwell and DJs David Jacobs and Keith Fordyce.*

The radio appearance occurred on the BBC Light Programme lunchtime chat show *Pop Inn*, the Beatles going along to the Paris Studio for a 12.30 pm rehearsal and live broadcast between 1.00 and 1.45. The interview was accompanied by the playing of their imminent new single 'From Me To You'. Among the other guests on the show were disc-jockey David Jacobs, veteran comedian Arthur Askey, and popular pianist Winifred Atwell.

The television appearance, also live, was a return booking on the Associated-Rediffusion children's magazine programme *Tuesday Rendezvous*, broadcast in London and some other ITV stations between 5.00 and 5.55 pm. (The Beatles also attended the rehearsal, from 2.00 to 5.00 pm.) They mimed to 'From Me To You', played in its entirety, and to 50-seconds of 'Please Please Me', played over the closing titles. Among the other guests on the show were ever-present puppets Ollie Beak and Fred Barker, naturalist Grahame Dangerfield and cookery couple Fanny and Johnnie Cradock.

The Gaumont State cinema in Kilburn, scene of the evening engagement, is only a short distance from Wembley, and closer still to EMI Studios in Abbey Road.

Wednesday 10 April

Majestic Ballroom, Birkenhead

The Beatles' last appearance at this venue.

Thursday 11 April

Co-operative Hall, Long St, Middleton, Lancashire

Friday 12 April

Night **Cavern Club, Liverpool**

A special Good Friday return to the Cavern Club, spearheading another eight-hour "Rhythm And Blues Marathon".

Saturday 13 April

**Studio E, Lime Grove Studios, Lime Grove,
Shepherd's Bush, London**

After 11 appearances on British independent television, this – at last – was the Beatles' début on the national BBC network, a video recording for *The 625 Show*, transmitted from 6.25 to 6.50 pm on Tuesday 16 April and billed as featuring "up and coming young talent".

The recording took place at the Corporation's Lime Grove Studios in west London, a 10.30 to 11.30 am band call, 11.30 am to 1.00 pm and 2.15 to 3.45 camera rehearsal and 4.30 to 6.00 final rehearsal preceding the 7.30 to 8.15 pm taping. (There's nothing like being prepared.)

The Beatles performed three songs on the programme, 'From Me To You', 'Thank You Girl' and 'Please Please Me'. The latter song closed the show and so the Beatles were enjoined by the entire cast: compere/singer Jimmy Young, singers/guitarists Rolf and Tino, singer Bobbi Carrol, singer/guitarist Hank Locklin, guitarist Wout Steenhuis, a four-piece orchestra led by Micky Greeve, pianist Johnny Pearson and musical conductor Edwin Braben.

This taping of *The 625 Show* precluded the Beatles from making an advertised personal appearance – though they weren't scheduled to perform – at a football club dance held this night at the Civic Hall in Uppermill, near Oldham, Lancashire. Instead, the Beatles stayed local to London, going to a party thrown at his North Harrow home by the Shadows' guitarist Bruce Welch. Here they met Cliff Richard for the first time.

Sunday 14 April

Teddington Studio Centre, Teddington

Taping of the Beatles' third appearance on the ABC Television programme *Thank Your Lucky Stars*, broadcast across most of the ITV network on Saturday 20 April, 5.50–6.30 pm.

In this edition the group were called for an 11.00 am rehearsal and took part in the continuous taping during the afternoon, miming to one song, 'From Me To You'. The Beatles were third on the bill, other guests including the not yet successful Dave Clark Five, the Vernons Girls, Bert Weedon and, topping the line-up, visiting American Del Shannon, with whom the Beatles would work again the next Thursday.

After the *TYLS* taping the Beatles drove to the nearby town of Richmond-upon-Thames to see, for the first time, another up-and-coming new group, the Rolling Stones, in live action at the Crawdaddy Club in the town's Station Hotel pub.

Monday 15 April

Riverside Dancing Club, Bridge Hotel, Teme St, Tenbury Wells, Worcestershire

Tuesday 16 April

Studio Four, Granada TV Centre, Manchester

The Beatles' first appearance on Granada Television in three months was this live (mimed) performance of 'From Me To You' on *Scene At 6.30*, a new half-hour news-magazine programme for the north of England, succeeding from *People And Places*. Following 3.00–4.00 and 4.15–6.00 pm rehearsals, it was broadcast between 6.30 and 7.00 pm, clashing with the Beatles' taped BBC TV appearance on *The 625 Show* which went out from 6.25 to 6.50 (see Saturday 13 April).

Wednesday 17 April

Majestic Ballroom, Mill St, Luton, Bedfordshire

Thursday 18 April

Royal Albert Hall, Kensington Gore, London

During the first half of 1963 the BBC presented, and broadcast live, three concerts direct from this famous venue, each performed in front of an audience. The Beatles appeared on only this occasion, in a show titled *Swinging Sound '63*, alongside a host of other artists, including Del Shannon, the Springfields, Lance Percival, Rolf Harris, the Vernons Girls, Kenny Lynch, Shane Fenton and the Fentones, and George Melly.

The concert was a fairly complicated affair, taking place in two distinct halves, 8.00 to 8.50 and 9.10 to 10.15 pm, with an interval in between. Only the second half was broadcast; the first was not even recorded – so, in essence, this could be classified as a Beatles concert appearance and the second half a live radio appearance. Further, the BBC's General Overseas Service beamed a simultaneous broadcast across much of the globe between 9.15 and 10.00 pm, which meant that overseas listeners missed out on the Beatles by seconds, since they did not play in the second-half until 10.02 pm.

This was the Beatles' first appearance at the Royal Albert Hall – a venue they would remember in their 1967 song 'A Day In The Life' – and they spent virtually the entire day there, mostly in dressing-room 5A. They were called at 10.15 am for a 10.45 to 11.30 rehearsal, and again at 12.45 pm for a 1.00 to 1.30 rehearsal of the concert's finale.

Fellow Liverpudlian, jazz singer and arts critic George Melly introduced the Beatles on stage during both halves of the concert. In the first, at around 8.40 pm, they played two songs, 'Please Please Me' and 'Misery', with only the briefest of pauses in between.

In the second-half, broadcast live, the group sang 'Twist And Shout' and 'From Me To You', again segued. They had

18 April: rocking the Albert Hall...

planned on opening with 'Thank You Girl', duly rehearsed earlier, but switched it to the more upbeat 'Twist And Shout' at the last moment, unbeknown to the BBC producers Terry Henebery and Ron Belchier. In the grand finale, all the acts on the bill, including the Beatles, crowded onto the stage for an instrumental blast of 'Mack The Knife', which they played for over three minutes, until the Light Programme broadcast was faded down at 10.15. (Written in 1928 by Kurt Weill for *The Three Penny Opera*, 'Mack The Knife' has since been recorded by hundreds of artists.)

After the broadcast Paul first met his fiancée-to-be, aspiring young actress and "teen" TV personality Jane Asher, who – earlier in the evening – had posed, screaming for the Beatles, for a photographer from *Radio Times*, the BBC's weekly listings journal.

Friday 19 April

King's Hall, Stoke-on-Trent

The second "Mersey Beat Showcase" date (see 7 March 1963).

Saturday 20 April

Ballroom, Mersey View Pleasure Grounds, Overton Hills, Frodsham, Cheshire

The Beatles' only appearance at this north-west venue although other top Liverpool groups had played here regularly since 1961.

...and, 21 April, rolling the Empire Pool.

Sunday 21 April

Empire Pool, Empire Way, Wembley, Middlesex and Pigalle Club, Piccadilly, London

The afternoon performance at Wembley marked the Beatles' biggest concert date yet, both in stature and size of venue, a reported 10,000 pop fans crowding into the arena to see a 14-act bill, headed by Cliff Richard and the Shadows, in the *New Musical Express* 1962–63 Annual Poll-Winners' All-Star Concert. Although the Beatles hadn't actually won any of the readers' polls, which had been conducted before the end of 1962, the *NME* slotted them in as the show's penultimate act by virtue of their two recent number one singles. They performed four songs, 'Please Please Me', 'From Me To You', 'Twist And Shout' and 'Long Tall Sally'.

The evening booking at the Pigalle Club was an odd one, and the Beatles' only appearance at this fashionable central London restaurant/night club later to become the "in"

with the compliments of

THE NEW **MUSICAL EXPRESS**

23 DENMARK STREET, LONDON, W.C.2

Telephone : COVent Garden 2266 (5 lines)

meeting place for the Mod movement. On this evening almost the entire audience was Jewish, the only advertisement for the engagement having appeared in the weekly newspaper *Jewish Chronicle*.

Tuesday 23 April
Floral Hall, Southport

Wednesday 24 April
Majestic Ballroom, Seven Sisters Rd,
Finsbury Park, London

Another of NEMS' "Mersey Beat Showcase" presentations. This Top Rank ballroom was situated close by the Finsbury Park Astoria cinema where the Beatles would play on many future occasions. Two thousand people attended this evening.

Thursday 25 April
Ballroom, Fairfield Hall, Park Lane, Croydon, Surrey

This "Mersey Beat Showcase" date was arranged by promoter John Smith back in January, before the Beatles had a hit with 'Please Please Me' and before Gerry and the Pacemakers, Billy J Kramer and the Big Three had emerged out of Liverpool. Concerned that he might not fill the ballroom for one "house", let alone two, Smith engaged star singer/actor John Leyton to top the bill.

Three months later, however, on the day of the shows, Leyton fell ill and was unable to fulfil the booking. But when Smith posted notices to this effect outside the ballroom's main entrance there was great cheering. No one had come to see him.

Friday 26 April
Music Hall, Shrewsbury

The first of two consecutive bookings for promoter Lewis Buckley.

Saturday 27 April
(Victory) Memorial Hall, Northwich

The day after this performance, on 28 April, Paul, George and Ringo took off for a 12-day holiday in Santa Cruz, Tenerife. John and Brian Epstein flew to Spain.

Saturday 11 May
Imperial Ballroom, Carr Road, Nelson, Lancashire

Mayhem hit this northern industrial town in a big way as 2000 frantic teenagers crammed into the enormous Imperial Ballroom to see the Beatles.

Sunday 12 May
Alpha Television Studios, Aston, Birmingham

A return visit to Aston for the Beatles' first bill-topping appearance on the ABC Television show *Thank Your Lucky Stars*, taped this afternoon for transmission six days later, Saturday 18 May, between 5.55 and 6.35 pm.

For the first time, the Beatles mimed to more than one song in a *TYLS* broadcast: 'From Me To You' and also LP track 'I Saw Her Standing There'.

Tuesday 14 May
Rink Ballroom, Park Lane, Sunderland, Durham

Wednesday 15 May
Royalty Theatre, City Road, Chester, Cheshire

The Beatles' repertoire on this night comprised 'Some Other Guy', 'Thank You Girl', 'Do You Want To Know A Secret', 'Please Please Me', 'You Really Got A Hold on Me', 'I Saw Her Standing There' and 'From Me To You'.

Thursday 16 May
Television Theatre, Shepherd's Bush Green, London

The Beatles' second appearance on national BBC TV was in the children's series *Pops And Lenny*, broadcast live, in front of an enthusiastic audience, from the Television Theatre in west London. The title said it all: the show mixed pop music with glove-puppet fun in the shape of Lenny the Lion ("Oh don't embawass me"), as manipulated by cohort Terry Hall.

The Beatles arrived at Television Theatre in time for a 1.30 pm rehearsal and performed two songs in the 5.00–5.30 broadcast, 'From Me To You' and a shortened (1 min 5 secs) version of 'Please Please Me'. They also joined resident musicians the Bert Hayes Octet and the other members of the cast – Terry Hall, the Raindrops, Patsy Ann Noble, and, of course, Lenny the Lion – for the finale, a one-minute version of 'After You've Gone', the Creamer/Layton standard written in 1929 and since performed by scores of artists.

Friday 17 May
Grosvenor Rooms, Prince Of Wales Rd,
Norwich, Norfolk

A £250 booking, arranged in mid-April through London promoter Barry Clayman.

Saturday 18 May
Adelphi Cinema, Bath Rd, Slough, Buckinghamshire

The opening night of the Beatles' third nationwide package tour in as many months. Although Roy Orbison, whom the

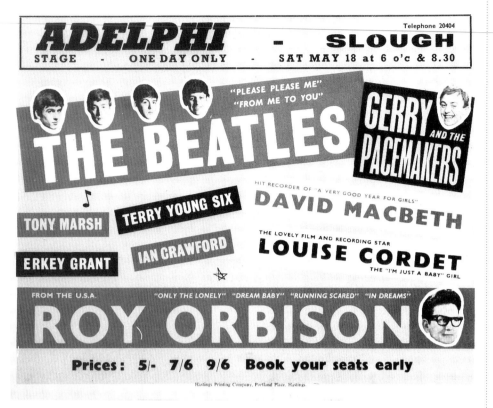

ADELPHI - SLOUGH
Telephone 20404
STAGE - ONE DAY ONLY - SAT MAY 18 at 6 o'c & 8.30

"PLEASE PLEASE ME"
"FROM ME TO YOU"

THE BEATLES

GERRY AND THE PACEMAKERS

HIT RECORDER OF "A VERY GOOD YEAR FOR GIRLS"
DAVID MACBETH

TONY MARSH   TERRY YOUNG SIX

THE LOVELY FILM AND RECORDING STAR
LOUISE CORDET
THE "I'M JUST A BABY" GIRL

ERKEY GRANT   IAN CRAWFORD

FROM THE U.S.A.   "ONLY THE LONELY" "DREAM BABY" "RUNNING SCARED" "IN DREAMS"
ROY ORBISON

Prices: 5/- 7/6 9/6 Book your seats early

Hastings Printing Company, Portland Place, Hastings.

Ringo reading a listener's request at the Saturday Club microphone with the Beatles' old mate Brian Matthew.

Beatles much admired, initially began as bill-topper, the Beatles very quickly – by audience demand – assumed this position.

Their repertoire on this tour comprised 'Some Other Guy', 'Do You Want To Know A Secret', 'Love Me Do', 'From Me To You', 'Please Please Me', 'I Saw Her Standing There' and 'Twist And Shout'.

Sunday 19 May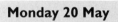

Gaumont Cinema, Hanley

Monday 20 May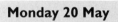

Gaumont Cinema, Commercial Rd,
Southampton, Hampshire

After this date the Orbison tour took a one-day break, resuming on the 22nd.

Tuesday 21 May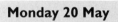

Playhouse Theatre, London

Two separate sessions for BBC radio – hardly, then, a rest day from the rigours of nationwide touring.

The first session was for *Saturday Club*, a special occasion in that it was the Beatles' first top-of-the-bill appearance on this prestigious programme. It began with a rehearsal from 2.30, the actual recording taking place between 5.30 and 6.30 pm. The tape was then inserted into the next edition of

the series, broadcast on the Light Programme between 10.00 am and 12.00 noon on 25 May.

In addition to some witty conversation with host Brian Matthew, the Beatles performed six songs: 'I Saw Her Standing There', 'Do You Want To Know A Secret', 'Boys', 'Long Tall Sally', 'From Me To You' and 'Money (That's What I Want)'. The last three numbers fell within the last half-hour of the programme, simultaneously broadcast by the BBC's General Overseas Service.

After a 45-minute break for dinner, the Beatles returned to the Playhouse to rehearse (from 7.15) and record (10.00 to 11.15 pm) a new show for the Light Programme, *Steppin' Out*, broadcast on "bank holiday" Whit Monday, 3 June, between 10.31 and 11.30 am. Before playing their first couple of numbers, host of the show, Diz Disley, introduced the Beatles – "We have here four young fellas who, since they emerged from the trackless interior of Merseyside a mere matter of months ago, have been laying 'em in the aisles all over the Isles – from Land's End to John O' Groats – so mind your backs, wacks, for it's the earth-shaking sounds of *the Beatles!*" Unfortunate *double-entendre* aside, this was typical "hip" radio speak for pop radio and TV programmes of the day.

Before a very enthusiastic audience, the Beatles performed six songs: 'Please Please Me', 'I Saw Her Standing There', 'Roll Over Beethoven', 'Twist And Shout', 'Thank You Girl' and 'From Me To You'. 'Twist And Shout' was edited out of the broadcast tape, however.

Wednesday 22 May

Gaumont Cinema, St Helen's Street,
Ipswich, Suffolk

The resumption of the Orbison package tour.

Thursday 23 May

Odeon Cinema, Angel Row, Nottingham, Notts

Friday 24 May

Studio Two, Aeolian Hall, New Bond St, London
and **Granada Cinema, Hoe St, Walthamstow, London**

Proof positive of the Beatles' meteoric rise to fame, the visit to the BBC's Aeolian Hall premises in central London saw them record the first programme in their very own radio series, *Pop Go The Beatles*. For a group which, only a year previously, had still to record for EMI, and had only enjoyed two number one records, it was a remarkable coup – and also a brave move for the Corporation.

The series was born out of a suggestion made by Vernon Lawrence, a young studio manager within radio Light Entertainment, who tabled his idea in a 30 April memo to Donald MacLean, his assistant head of department. MacLean approved and initiated the series, commending Lawrence for his judgement. (Lawrence was clearly cut out for higher things, being a senior executive at Yorkshire

Television in 1991.) Within four weeks a series title had been decided, recording and broadcast dates booked, and a £100 per programme budget allocated to producer Terry Henebery (who, truth be told, was a jazz fanatic and didn't care too highly for pop).

Initially, four programmes were commissioned, with an option for a further 11 if these proved successful. The format was typical of the times: as resident stars, the Beatles would have a guest act each week, chosen by the BBC and taped – except on this opening occasion – in a separate session. There would also be a resident compere: radio actor and occasional disc-jockey Lee Peters held this post for the first four programmes – in keen Reverend Spooner fashion the Beatles called him "Pee Litres" when away from the microphone – and he would joust with the Beatles, giving them ample opportunity to crack jokes, be mildly naughty and generally send things up while answering his questions and reading listeners' song requests. The show was transmitted every Tuesday on the Light Programme from 5.00 to 5.29 pm, a proven slot for pop.

The programme also had a theme tune, a rocked-up variation of the nursery rhyme 'Pop Goes The Weasel', especially re-arranged by one Mr Patrick. The Beatles recorded it at this initial session – though, reputedly, they had some trouble doing so and were aided in the task by the first programme's guest group the Lorne Gibson Trio. Each show in the series opened and closed with this 24 May recording, usually around 20-seconds' worth at the start and of variable length at the end, faded to suit broadcast needs and sometimes running to more than a minute.

The Beatles and the Lorne Gibson Trio recorded this programme together, 2.00–6.00 pm inclusive of rehearsal time, and the end result, broadcast on Tuesday 4 June, had the Beatles performing 'From Me To You', 'Everybody's Trying To Be My Baby', 'Do You Want To Know A Secret', 'You Really Got A Hold On Me', 'Misery' and 'The Hippy Hippy Shake'.

The BBC's Audience Research Department published a report on this first programme which estimated that 5.3 per cent of the British population tuned in, something like 2.8 million people, a typical figure for this time of the day; reactions varied from the ecstatic "really with it" to the unimpressed "they make an obnoxious noise", giving an overall, surprisingly below-average Appreciation Index of 52 (out of a maximum 100).

In the evening, after all the BBC excitement, the Beatles continued the Roy Orbison package tour with two "houses" at the Walthamstow Granada in north London.

Saturday 25 May

City Hall, Sheffield

Sunday 26 May

Empire Theatre, Liverpool

The Beatles' first home-town appearance in more than six weeks. They were fast outgrowing the city.

Monday 27 May

Capitol Cinema, Dock St, Cardiff, Glamorganshire

Tuesday 28 May

Gaumont Cinema, Foregate St, Worcester, Worcs

Wednesday 29 May

Rialto Theatre, York

Thursday 30 May

Odeon Cinema, Oxford St, Manchester, Lancashire

This concert was reviewed in the *Daily Express* by its northern show-business correspondent, Derek Taylor, who subsequently became Brian Epstein's personal assistant and then the Beatles' and Apple Records' press officer.

Friday 31 May

Odeon Cinema, High St, Southend-on-Sea, Essex

Saturday 1 June

BBC Paris Studio, London
and **Granada Cinema, Mitcham Rd, Tooting, London**

Another hectic day for the Beatles: eight hours inside a BBC radio studio followed by two separate "houses" at the Tooting Granada with the Roy Orbison package tour.

The BBC session was for both the second and third editions in their own series *Pop Go The Beatles*. Curiously, programme three was taped first, between 9.30 am and 1.30 pm; number two was then recorded between 1.30 and 5.30. (A rehearsal element was included in these timings.) The Beatles' guests in programme three were Carter-Lewis and the Southerners, and in programme two the Countrymen.

Before the series began, the Beatles let it be known that they would use the privileged BBC airtime to broadcast songs that had formed the backbone of their pre-fame live repertoire. An article in the *New Musical Express* of 24 May 1963 stated, "The Beatles will sing five or six numbers in each presentation [programme]. R&B material will be strongly featured." It was an interesting decision, for although they did play a few Lennon-McCartney numbers, they certainly could have featured them much more. Instead, the Beatles opted for versatility, letting the British public hear the songs they could no longer perform in live concerts now restricted to 20–25 minutes and hit material.

It was because of this decision that people have been able to hear – and preserve – studio environment, often live in-one-take recordings of rare Beatles performances, a huge cache of remarkable material.

In programme three, broadcast in the Light Programme between 5.00 and 5.29 pm on Tuesday 18 June, the group sang 'A Shot Of Rhythm And Blues', 'Memphis, Tennessee',

'A Taste of Honey', 'Sure To Fall (In Love With You)', 'Money (That's What I Want)' and 'From Me To You'.

In programme two, transmitted in the Light Programme between 5.00 and 5.29 pm on Tuesday 11 June, the Beatles performed 'Too Much Monkey Business', 'I Got To Find My Baby', 'Youngblood', 'Baby It's You', 'Till There Was You' and 'Love Me Do'.

Sunday 2 June

Hippodrome Theatre, Middle St, Brighton, Sussex

Monday 3 June

Granada Cinema, Powis St, Woolwich, London

Tuesday 4 June

Town Hall, Congreve St, Birmingham, Warwickshire

Wednesday 5 June

Odeon Cinema, The Headrow, Leeds, Yorkshire

Friday 7 June

Odeon Cinema, Renfield St, Glasgow, Lanarkshire

The first of five concert visits by the Beatles to Glasgow, a city they always enjoyed playing because of its remarkably enthusiastic audiences.

Saturday 8 June

City Hall, Newcastle-upon-Tyne

Sunday 9 June

King George's Hall, Northgate, Blackburn, Lancashire

The last date in the Roy Orbison package tour begun in Slough on 18 May.

Monday 10 June

Pavilion, North Parade, Bridge Rd, Bath, Somerset

Wednesday 12 June

Grafton Rooms, Liverpool

A special concert, arranged back in February, in aid of the children's charity NSPCC. The Beatles gave their services free. Jeffrey Archer, later a major Conservative politician and author, helped organise the event.

Thursday 13 June

Palace Theatre Club, Turncroft Lane, Offerton, Stockport, Cheshire
and Southern Sporting Club, The Corona, Birch St, Hyde Rd, Manchester, Lancashire

A most unusual double booking – two northern variety/cabaret night-clubs, ten miles apart.

Friday 14 June

Tower Ballroom, New Brighton, Wallasey

A sensational final return to an old stamping ground – always one of the Beatles' favourite venues – to play another in the "Mersey Beat Showcase" series presented by NEMS Enterprises.

Saturday 15 June

City Hall, Fisherton St, Salisbury, Wiltshire

A surprise date with Jaybee Clubs, the promotion which had booked the Beatles into the historically important 31 March 1962 Stroud engagement. This show was arranged in April 1963 for the huge fee of £300 but, as the date approached, Brian Epstein began to have serious misgivings about the Beatles' safety in such a venue. He offered Jaybee £200 to cancel the booking but was turned down. Over 1500 people crowded into the City Hall.

Sunday 16 June

Odeon Cinema, South St, Romford, Essex

The final date in the "Mersey Beat Showcase" series, promoted this time by John Smith. Five more dates in the series, planned for 17-20 and 23 June, were scrapped by Brian Epstein.

This was a truly remarkable booking for, in what may be the only time in popular music history, the show's three main acts – the Beatles, Billy J Kramer with the Dakotas, and Gerry and the Pacemakers – occupied numbers one, two and three in that week's British singles charts.

Monday 17 June

Studio Five, Maida Vale Studios, Delaware Rd, London

The fourth and, for now, final recording in the BBC Light Programme radio series *Pop Go The Beatles*. It was taped at the BBC's Maida Vale studios, not far from EMI's studio in Abbey Road. The Beatles rehearsed and recorded their contribution between 10.30 am and 1.00 pm, after which they took lunch in the BBC staff restaurant and then went out into Delaware Road with photographer Dezo Hoffmann

(who had been with them all morning, taking session and restaurant pictures) to give the birthday bumps to Paul McCartney, 21-years-old the next day.

For this programme the Beatles recorded 'I Saw Her Standing There', 'Anna (Go To Him)', 'Boys', 'Chains', 'PS I Love You' and 'Twist And Shout'. It was broadcast on Tuesday 25 June between 5.00 and 5.29 pm, the guest group in this edition being the Bachelors.

Wednesday 19 June

Playhouse Theatre, London

Life was certainly hectic for the Beatles at this time. After their 17 June BBC session in London the group drove to Liverpool in time for Paul's 21st birthday party the evening of the 18th, held in a marquee in the back-garden of an aunt's house in Huyton. A few hours later they were heading south again, to be back in London in time for their second appearance on the BBC Light Programme radio show *Easy Beat*, taped in front of a screaming audience at the Playhouse Theatre between 8.45 and 9.45 pm.

The recording, broadcast on Sunday 23 June between 10.31 and 11.30 am, featured the Beatles performing 'Some Other Guy', 'A Taste Of Honey', 'Thank You Girl' and 'From Me To You'.

Friday 21 June

Odeon Cinema, Epsom Rd, Guildford, Surrey

Saturday 22 June

Television Theatre, London
and Ballroom, Town Hall, Cross St, Abergavenny, Monmouthshire

While George, Paul and Ringo travelled to Wales in the van with road manager Neil Aspinall, John stayed on in London to tape an appearance on the BBC Television show *Juke Box Jury*, an extraordinarily popular programme at this time, in which new singles came up for "Hit" or "Miss" judgement, signified, respectively, by either the pinging of a bell or the sounding of a klaxon.

This particular edition was transmitted the following Saturday, 29 June, from 6.35 to 7.00 pm, hosted, as ever, by genial DJ David Jacobs. The four-person "jury" was usually chosen to represent different walks of show business so along with John Lennon on this occasion there was TV personality Catherine (Katie) Boyle, actor Bruce Prochnik and actress Caroline Maudling.

Typically, John's appearance caused something of a stir, in that he openly stated negative views of every single one of the discs up for review, whereas panel members customarily couched any such comments in quasi-positive, non-offensive terms. The records reviewed in this edition were 'Southend' by Cleo Laine, 'So Much In Love' by the Tymes; 'Devil In Disguise' by Elvis Presley (John said of his former idol that he now sounded like Bing Crosby), 'The Click Song' by Miriam Makeba, 'On Top Of Spaghetti' by Tom Glaser, 'Flamenco' by Russ Conway, 'First Quarrel' by Paul and Paula and 'Don't Ever Let Me Down' by Julie Grant. Thanks to John's influence, the panel voted every one of them a "Miss" except for the Presley single. (Three other songs were taped but omitted from the broadcast, 'Lies' by Johnny Sandon and the Remo Four, 'Too Late To Worry' by Richard Anthony, and 'Just One Look' by Doris Troy. Sandon and the Remo Four were Liverpool contemporaries of the Beatles, and Doris Troy would one day be signed to their Apple record label.)

The *Juke Box Jury* session kept John in London until well into the evening: there was a camera rehearsal from 7.45 to 8.00, a sound and vision test between 8.00 and 8.30 and the recording itself ran from 8.30 to 9.15. Immediately after this John was driven to Battersea Heliport from where he flew to Wales in a helicopter especially chartered by Brian Epstein at a cost of £100. He touched down at the Penypound football ground in Abergavenny at 9.50 pm, just in time for the £250 engagement.

Sunday 23 June

Alpha Television Studios, Aston, Birmingham

In February 1964, the sensational success of the Beatles would open the floodgates of the North American record market, allowing scores of other British groups an opportunity to move in and enjoy major hits.

In the summer of 1963, the sensational success of the Beatles opened the floodgates within the British record market for groups from Liverpool. They were dominating the UK

A Pop Go The Beatles recording session at the BBC's Maida Vale Studios, 17 June 1963. Presenter Lee Peters ("Pee Litres") is on the left, jazz-loving producer Terry Henebery stands mid-group, Brian Epstein and (sitting) Jane Asher silently spectate.

GUITAR PLAYER WILL ARRIVE BY HELICOPTER

Will land on local football ground

ONE MEMBER OF THE BEATLES, THE POPULAR MUSICAL GROUP WHO ARE APPEARING AT THE TOWN HALL DANCE TOMORROW NIGHT, WILL ARRIVE IN ABERGAVENNY BY HELICOPTER ONLY AN HOUR OR SO BEFORE THE PERFORMANCE STARTS.

Jonn Lennon, the group's composer and guitarist, will travel from the B.B.C. television studios in London, and make his landing at the Thursdays' football field in Penypound.

Dance organiser Mr. Eddie Tattersall told the Abergavenny Chronicle last night : " I had a letter from the group's agent asking me if i could put them on at the Town Hall as late as possible.

" The reason is that John Lennon is to sit on the panel of the television programme, Juke Box Jury, tomorrow night, and arrangements will be made to fly him to Abergavenny immediately afterwards."

When the helicopter touches down at Penypound, a car will be waiting nearby to rush the "pop" star to the Town Hall, where The Beatles are due on stage at about 10.30 p.m.

MAYOR'S WELCOME

This Saturday's performance of Juke Box Jury will be tele-recorded, and will not be seen by viewers until the following Saturday, June 29.

On the same day. The Beatles will be seen on the I.T.V. programme, " Thank Your Lucky Stars," and on the Sunday after the Town Hall show they will be heard on " Easy Beat," the popular radio disc show.

When the members of the group arrive at the Town Hall they will be met by the mayor and mayoress, Councillor and Mrs. J. F. Thurston, who will give them a civic welcome.

Afterwards, the group will sign hundreds of autographs — at three-pence each — proceeds of which will be donated to the local committee of the Freedom from Hunger Campaign.

Mr. Tattersall has already received many autograph books from enthusiasts who want to make sure of collecting the signatures of their favourite pop stars.

All tickets for the dance, described by Mr. Tattersall as one of the town's greatest-ever attractions, were sold a week ago. A capacity audience of about 600 is expected.

Court. Magistrates at Abergavenny Court on Wednesday were the chairman (Mr. A. E. Howells), Mrs. G. Shackleton, Dr. W. D. C. Thomas, and Mr. A. C. Higgs (chairman, Abergavenny R.D.C.).

After a 2.30 pm rehearsal, the Beatles taped this session between 5.30 and 6.30 at the Playhouse Theatre in London, performing 'I Got To Find My Baby', 'Memphis, Tennessee', 'Money (That's What I Want)', 'Till There Was You', 'From Me To You' and 'Roll Over Beethoven'. The last two songs were included in the final 29 minutes of the programme, broadcast simultaneously by the BBC's General Overseas Service.

Tuesday 25 June

Astoria Ballroom, Wilson St, Middlesbrough, Yorks

Wednesday 26 June

Majestic Ballroom, Newcastle-upon-Tyne

The Beatles' last performance in a Top Rank ballroom, although they were to continue utilising the company's extensive cinema and theatre network.

After the show, in their Newcastle hotel room, John and Paul wrote the A-side of the Beatles' next single, 'She Loves You'.

Friday 28 June

Queen's Hall, Sovereign St, Leeds, Yorkshire

Three thousand, two hundred people crammed into the vast Queen's Hall to see the Beatles share the bill with Acker Bilk and his Paramount Jazz Band.

Sunday 30 June

ABC Cinema, Regent Rd, Gt Yarmouth, Norfolk

The first date in a ten-week run of engagements at seaside resorts. On this night the Beatles' repertoire comprised 'Some Other Guy', 'Thank You Girl', 'Do You Want To Know A Secret', 'Misery', 'A Taste Of Honey', 'I Saw Her Standing There', 'Love Me Do', 'From Me To You', 'Baby It's You', 'Please Please Me' and 'Twist And Shout'. The compere was Ted Rogers.

Monday 1 July

Studio Two, EMI Studios, London

Composed in Newcastle-upon-Tyne the previous Wednesday, 'She Loves You' – which was to become the Beatles' first million-selling single, yielding the "yeah yeah yeah" catchphrase so loved by the media – was recorded during a 345-minute session this day at EMI, as was its B-side, 'I'll Get You' (known at this point by its working title 'Get You In The End').

The session was arranged for 2.30–5.30 pm, instead it ran from 5.00–10.45; however, existing EMI paperwork does not document the number of "takes" it took for the two songs to be recorded.

Girl bites steward at Leeds dance

charts at this time: Gerry and the Pacemakers, Billy J Kramer with the Dakotas, the Fourmost, the Searchers and others, with people like Cilla Black waiting in the wings. To celebrate the "Mersey Beat" boom, an entire edition of ABC Television's *Lucky Stars (Summer Spin)* – the summer title of *Thank Your Lucky Stars* – was given over to Liverpool acts. Hosted not by Brian Matthew but by Pete Murray, it was taped during this afternoon and transmitted on Saturday 29 June between 6.05 and 6.45 pm on most of the ITV network. More than six million people tuned in, although Beatles fans had a dilemma in that the last ten minutes overlapped with John's appearance on the BBC's *Juke Box Jury*.

The Beatles, naturally, topped the bill, and therefore closed the show, miming to 'From Me To You' and 'I Saw Her Standing There'.

Monday 24 June

Playhouse Theatre, London

Another recording for *Saturday Club*, broadcast in the BBC radio Light Programme between 10.00 am and 12.00 noon on Saturday 29 June.

'She Loves You' was issued by EMI on Friday 23 August; British sales passed the half-million mark on 3 September and the million milestone on 27 November. The single also achieved the very rare feat of enjoying two separate spells at number one, originally occupying the summit for four weeks, spending a further seven in the top three and then returning to the top for two more.

Tuesday 2 July

Studio Five, Maida Vale Studios, London

The four-week trial of *Pop Go The Beatles* had been a success, and the BBC booked another run, a further 11 programmes, making 15 in total. These additional shows ran after only a two-week absence and featured a new host, Rodney Burke, replacing Lee Peters. The Beatles' disregard for names continued: whereas, off-air, they had called Lee Peters "Pee Litres", on-air, at the start of this programme, when the host said "My name's Rodney Burke" John piped up "That's your fault!" (And actually it was, for Burke was Rodney's personally selected professional surname.)

The Beatles taped their contribution to the fifth edition on this day, to be broadcast in the Light Programme on Tuesday 16 July, between 5.00 and 5.29 pm. Rehearsal and recording took place at Maida Vale Studios between 6.30 and 9.30 pm. From the standpoint of musical versatility, no other Beatles session for BBC radio could match this: they began with a cover of Elvis Presley's 'That's All Right (Mama)' and followed with their own 'There's A Place', Chuck Berry's 'Carol', Arthur Alexander's 'Soldier Of Love (Lay Down Your Arms)', Carl Perkins' 'Lend Me Your Comb' and the Jodimars' 'Clarabella'. Yet more songs were recorded but not broadcast: the Coasters' 'Three Cool Cats', Chuck Berry's 'Sweet Little Sixteen' and their own 'Ask Me Why'.

The Beatles' guest act in this edition was Duffy Power with the Graham Bond Quartet.

Wednesday 3 July

Playhouse Theatre, Manchester

This BBC radio session, for the Light Programme's *The Beat Show*, was recorded at the Playhouse Theatre in Manchester, scene of the Beatles' first sessions for *Here We Go* in 1962. In fact, *The Beat Show* featured much the same content as *Here We Go*: the BBC Northern Dance Orchestra directed by Bernard Herrmann, and the Trad Lads. Only the presenter and producer were different, the host being Gay Byrne, also the affable link-man on the Granada TV programme *Scene At 6.30* on which the Beatles had featured.

After a 4.00 pm rehearsal, the programme was recorded live, in front of an audience, between 8.00 and 9.00, the Beatles performing 'From Me To You', 'A Taste Of Honey' and 'Twist And Shout'. It was broadcast the next lunchtime, 1.00–1.30 pm on Thursday 4 July.

Perhaps fearing over-exposure for the Beatles, and certainly now in a position to pick and choose their appearances with ever-greater care, Brian Epstein cancelled several BBC radio contracts at this time. This spot on *The Beat Show* only came about after he had turned down 17 June, 18 June and 3 July recordings for *Here We Go*; three more *Side By Side* sessions were cancelled too, to have taken place on 2 July, 10 July and 23 August.

Thursday 4 July

Studio Two, EMI Studios, London

Mono mixing by George Martin of 'She Loves You' and 'I'll Get You', 10.00 am–1.00 pm. The Beatles were *probably* absent, although they were certainly in London in the evening, popping along to the Scene Club in Soho for a second view of the Rolling Stones in live performance. They were accompanied this time by Peter Asher, brother of Jane and, later, half of the successful duo Peter and Gordon.

Photos from 1 July 1963, inside and outside EMI Studios. Their July session dates having been publicised in advance by the weekly pop papers, police twice had to be summoned to Abbey Road when the Beatles came to record, so many were the fans outside. One girl managed to penetrate studio two before the 'She Loves You' session, almost reaching John (seen here chatting to balance engineer Norman Smith).

Friday 5 July

Plaza Ballroom, Old Hill

The Beatles' second appearance at this venue, and a long-arranged date which Brian Epstein would have preferred to cancel but would not renege upon.

Also on the bill was local combo Denny and the Diplomats, led by Denny Laine, future member of the Moody Blues and, eventually, Paul's post-Beatles group, Wings.

Saturday 6 July

(Victory) Memorial Hall, Northwich

Prior to this performance, all four Beatles attended – and brought chaos to – the annual Northwich Carnival at Verdin Park, Northwich. Paul even crowned the new carnival queen. All good PR.

Sunday 7 July

ABC Theatre, Church St, Blackpool, Lancashire

Compere for this and the following four Beatles engagements at this venue over the next two months was *Carry On* film actor Jack Douglas.

Monday 8 – Saturday 13 July

Winter Gardens, Fort Crescent, Margate, Kent

Wednesday 10 July

Studio Two, Aeolian Hall, London

Six consecutive nights in Margate, two "houses" each, for which the Beatles' repertoire comprised 'Roll Over Beethoven', 'Thank You Girl', 'Chains', 'Please Please Me', 'A Taste Of Honey', 'I Saw Her Standing There', 'Baby It's You', 'From Me To You' and 'Twist And Shout'.

With the commitment of their BBC Light Programme radio series *Pop Go The Beatles*, the group were obliged to return to London early in the morning of Wednesday 10 July to record two shows, for transmission on Tuesdays 23 and 30 July respectively, both from 5.00 to 5.29 pm. Programme six was rehearsed and recorded from 10.30 am to 1.30 pm, programme seven from 1.30 to 3.30 pm. After that, the group made a mad dash back to Margate, in order to appear in the first "house" of the evening at the Winter Gardens.

In programme six the Beatles performed 'Sweet Little Sixteen', 'A Taste Of Honey', 'Nothin' Shakin' (But The Leaves On The Trees)', 'Love Me Do', 'Lonesome Tears In My Eyes' and 'So How Come (No One Loves Me)'.

In the seventh show they played 'Memphis, Tennessee', 'Do You Want To Know A Secret', 'Till There Was You', 'Matchbox', 'Please Mister Postman' and 'The Hippy Hippy Shake'.

The Beatles' guests in these two programmes were Carter-Lewis and the Southerners and the Searchers respectively.

Sunday 14 July

ABC Theatre, Blackpool

Tuesday 16 July

BBC Paris Studio, London

A testament to their stamina – and that of the BBC's studio staff: the Beatles taped three editions of their Light Programme radio series *Pop Go The Beatles* in this one day.

Working at the Paris Studio they rehearsed and recorded show eight between 3.00 and 5.30 pm, nine between 6.00 and 8.30 and ten between 8.45 and 10.30; transmissions were on 6, 13 and 20 August, each between 5.00 and 5.29 pm. (Guest groups in the three shows were, respectively, the Swinging Blue Jeans, the Hollies, and Russ Sainty and the Nu-Notes.)

The severity of this schedule was actually down to the Beatles themselves: they failed to meet the appointed time of 10.30 am for the first recording (which would have been at the Playhouse Theatre in London) and then opted to make three shows this day rather than leave the recording of programme ten until the 17th, for when it had been scheduled at the Playhouse between 10.00 am and 1.00 pm.

In programme eight they performed 'I'm Gonna Sit Right Down And Cry (Over You)', 'Crying, Waiting, Hoping', 'Kansas City'/'Hey-Hey-Hey-Hey!', 'To Know Her Is To Love Her', 'The Honeymoon Song' and 'Twist And Shout'.

In the ninth show they featured 'Long Tall Sally', 'Please

Please Me', 'She Loves You', 'You Really Got A Hold On Me', 'I'll Get You' and 'I Got A Woman'.

In programme ten the Beatles played 'She Loves You' (although the broadcast actually repeated the version from the ninth show), 'Words Of Love', 'Glad All Over', 'I Just Don't Understand', '(There's A) Devil In Her Heart' and 'Slow Down'.

Justifiably, the Beatles' 11 February 1963 recording session at EMI has gone down in popular music history, the group taping all ten new tracks for their début album in one day. But on this day, 16 July, in less time, the group actually taped 18 new tracks, with only one repetition, and considerable on-mike conversation, too. A remarkable feat.

Wednesday 17 July

Playhouse Theatre, London

Yet another BBC radio recording, this time for the Sunday morning pop show *Easy Beat*, transmitted in the Light Programme on 21 July between 10.31 and 11.30 am.

The programme was taped between 8.45 and 9.45 pm before its usual teenage audience. The Beatles performed four songs, 'I Saw Her Standing There', 'A Shot Of Rhythm And Blues', 'There's A Place' and 'Twist And Shout'.

Thursday 18 July

Studio Two, EMI Studios, London

Originally booked for 6.00 to 10.00 pm, the Beatles recorded in EMI studio two from 7.00 to 10.45, beginning sessions for their second album with the taping of four songs, all cover versions – 'You Really Got A Hold On Me' (11 takes), 'Money (That's What I Want)' (seven), '(There's A) Devil In Her Heart' (six) and 'Till There Was You' (three).

Such sessions for this second album – as yet untitled – revealed the maturity which the Beatles had already gained inside the recording studio, the cover of Smokey Robinson and the Miracles' 'You Really Got A Hold On Me' being a superb reading of another artist's work.

Friday 19 and Saturday 20 July

Ritz Ballroom, Promenade, Rhyl, Flintshire

Two sold-out nights by the Beatles in north Wales, a year after their inglorious Rhyl/Wales début in the ballroom above Burton's tailor shop. The group returned to Liverpool immediately after the second of the Saturday "houses".

Sunday 21 July

Queen's Theatre, Bank Hey St, Blackpool, Lancashire

Monday 22 – Saturday 27 July

Odeon Cinema, The Centre,
Weston-super-Mare, Somerset

Visiting from London, Dezo Hoffmann spent one of these six days with the Beatles, taking photographs and colour (mute) 8mm home-movies of the group at their hotel and on location on the beach at nearby Brean Down, where they dressed in Victorian bathing-costumes and also went go-karting.

Sunday 28 July

ABC Cinema, Great Yarmouth

Tuesday 30 July

Studio Two, EMI Studios, London
and Playhouse Theatre, London
and Studio Two, EMI Studios, London

The Beatles spent the morning and evening at EMI recording more material for their second LP, either side of an afternoon's work at the BBC.

The morning session began at 10.00 and saw the group first tape a cover of the Marvelettes' 'Please Mister Postman', completed in nine takes, and then tackle the first Lennon-McCartney song for the LP, the superb 'It Won't Be Long'. Ten takes were recorded but it remained unfinished when the session halted at 1.30 pm, half an hour later than scheduled.

The Beatles taped two BBC radio recordings during the afternoon, the first an interview for the "Pop Chat" section of the show *Non Stop Pop*, broadcast in the Light Programme from 5.00 to 5.29 pm on Friday 30 August; the second was a session for *Saturday Club*, broadcast, again in the Light Programme, from 10.00 am to 12.00 noon on Saturday 24 August.

The short interview for *Non Stop Pop* was conducted by bandleader Phil Tate and was recorded just after 2.30 pm, when the Beatles arrived at the Playhouse Theatre to rehearse and record the *Saturday Club* session.

The *Saturday Club* recording took place immediately afterwards (much earlier than the contracted time of 5.30–6.30), the Beatles taping six numbers, 'Long Tall Sally', 'She Loves You', 'Glad All Over', 'Twist And Shout', 'You Really Got A Hold On Me' and 'I'll Get You'. The last three of these fell within the final 29 minutes of the domestic broadcast, simultaneously aired by the BBC's General Overseas Service.

Resuming at EMI on time at 5.00 pm, George Martin overdubbed a piano track onto the previously taped 'Money (That's What I Want)', they taped a five-take remake of 'Till There Was You' and an eight-take recording of Chuck Berry's rock classic 'Roll Over Beethoven'. They then resumed work on 'It Won't Be Long', moving it on to take 23, and, finally, recorded Paul's 'All My Loving', certainly his best and most complex piece of songwriting yet – this was completed in 13 takes. The session ended at 11.00 pm, an hour later than scheduled.

Wednesday 31 July

Imperial Ballroom, Nelson

Another riotous appearance in Nelson.

Thursday 1 August

Playhouse Theatre, Manchester

Two more sessions for *Pop Go The Beatles* – editions 11 and 12 – broadcast in the BBC radio Light Programme on Tuesdays 27 August and 3 September between 5.00 and 5.29 pm. (The Beatles' guests were Cyril Davies' Rhythm & Blues All-Stars featuring Long John Baldry, and Brian Poole and the Tremeloes.)

The recordings were made at the Playhouse Theatre in Manchester (without an audience, like all the shows in the series). They arrived at 12.00 noon for a rehearsal and then taped programme 11 between 1.30 and 4.00 and programme 12 from 4.00 to 6.00 pm.

In the eleventh the Beatles performed 'Ooh! My Soul', 'Don't Ever Change', 'Twist And Shout', 'She Loves You', 'Anna (Go To Him)' and 'A Shot Of Rhythm And Blues'.

For programme 12 the group taped 'Lucille', 'From Me To You', 'I'll Get You', 'Money (That's What I Want)', 'Baby It's You', 'There's A Place', 'Honey Don't' (John singing lead vocal) and 'Roll Over Beethoven'. 'Lucille' and 'Baby It's You' were omitted from the broadcast, however.

Friday 2 August

Grafton Rooms, Liverpool

The Beatles returned to Merseyside after a seven-week absence to play for the last time at the Grafton.

Saturday 3 August

Night Cavern Club, Liverpool

After close-on 300 Beatles appearances at the Cavern Club, spanning two-and-a-half years, this was the last. The venue had played perhaps *the* vital role in preparing them for The Big Time and now that time had come. Bob Wooler, the Cavern Club compere, remembers Brian Epstein promising that one day the Beatles would be back, but it was not to be.

Tickets for the performance went on sale on 21 July at 1.30 pm and by 2.00 pm were sold-out. The Beatles' fee was £300 – they had first played at the Cavern for £5.

Sunday 4 August

Queen's Theatre, Blackpool

There were so many fans outside the Queen's, blocking all entrances front and back, that the Beatles had to go through a builder's yard, up across some scaffolding and across to the roof of the theatre, from which they were lowered into the wings through a trap in the roof.

Monday 5 August

Urmston Show, Abbotsfield Park, Chassen Road, Urmston, Lancashire

An interesting engagement: the Beatles headed a four-act bill playing inside a huge marquee at this annual south Manchester "bank holiday" event, compered by David Hamilton.

Tuesday 6 and Wednesday 7 August

Springfield Ballroom, Janvrin Rd, St Saviour, Jersey, Channel Islands

The first two of four nights in Jersey, promoted by John Smith. The Beatles' five nights in the Channel Islands earned them £1000.

Thursday 8 August

Auditorium, Candie Gardens, Candie Rd, St Peter Port, Guernsey, Channel Islands

The Beatles made the 30-mile journey across from Jersey to Guernsey in a 12-seater plane while their equipment was transported by ferry.

Friday 9 and Saturday 10 August

Springfield Ballroom, St Saviour, Jersey

Back to Jersey for the last two nights of the Tuesday to Saturday Channel Islands engagement.

Sunday 11 August

ABC Theatre, Blackpool

Monday 12 – Saturday 17 August

Odeon Cinema, Gloddaeth Ave, Llandudno, Caernarvonshire

Wednesday 14 August

Studio Four, Granada TV Centre, Manchester

Six nights in concert on the north Wales coast, two "houses" each. After the second show on Tuesday the Beatles returned to Liverpool and the next morning drove across to the Granada TV Centre in Manchester, where – dressed not in suits but, unusually, in black polo-neck sweaters and jeans – they taped two separate song performances for broadcast in Granada's north-area news-magazine programme *Scene At 6.30*. The first, 'Twist And Shout', was transmitted this day (6.30–7.00pm). The second, 'She Loves You', was retained for broadcast on Monday 19 August (same times).

Following the taping, the Beatles nipped back to Wales for the first Llandudno "house" of the evening.

Sunday 18 August

Alpha Television Studios, Aston, Birmingham
and **Princess Theatre, Torbay Rd, Torquay, Devonshire**

The Beatles drove south from Llandudno to Torquay, where they played two shows this evening, by way of the Alpha Television Studios in Aston, Birmingham. Here, late in the morning, they rehearsed and then taped an appearance on ABC Television's *Lucky Stars (Summer Spin)*, hosted by Pete Murray and transmitted across most of Britain on Saturday 24 August, 6.05–6.45 pm. They mimed to both sides of their forthcoming single, 'She Loves You' and 'I'll Get You'.

Monday 19 – Saturday 24 August

Gaumont Cinema, Westover Rd, Bournemouth, Hants

Wednesday 21 August

Studio Three, EMI Studios, London

Thursday 22 August

Southern Independent Television Centre, Northam, Southampton, Hampshire

Six nights in Bournemouth, two shows each. It was during this week, at their hotel in town, the Palace Court, that photographer Robert Freeman took the "half-shadow" cover photo for their next album, *With The Beatles*.

On the Wednesday, editing and mono mixing for the new LP took place back at EMI Studios, of songs '(There's A) Devil In Her Heart', 'Money (That's What I Want)', 'You Really Got A Hold On Me', 'Please Mister Postman', 'Till There Was You', 'Roll Over Beethoven', 'All My Loving' and 'It Won't Be Long'. The work was carried out from 10.00 am to 1.00 pm and 2.00–5.30 pm; although it is not possible to be certain, the Beatles may have been present during the first session and part of the second, but they would have left by mid-afternoon to be back in Bournemouth by the evening.

At around lunchtime on the Thursday, the Beatles (again with Freeman) drove across to the Southampton studios of Southern Television, where – miming to 'She Loves You' – they taped an appearance on Southern's local news-magazine programme *Day By Day*, broadcast that same evening between 5.55 and 6.40 pm.

Sunday 25 August

ABC Theatre, Blackpool

Monday 26 – Saturday 31 August

Odeon Cinema, Southport

Tuesday 27 – Friday 30 August

Location filming in Southport, Manchester and Liverpool

A six-night residency – two "houses" per night – in Southport, just up the coast from Liverpool. The Beatles' repertoire comprised 'Roll Over Beethoven', 'Thank You Girl', 'Chains', 'A Taste Of Honey', 'She Loves You', 'Baby It's You', 'From Me To You', 'Boys', 'I Saw Her Standing There' and 'Twist And Shout'.

From Tuesday through to Friday, the Beatles filmed a number of contributions to a 30-minute sociological documentary being made by Manchester-based BBC TV producer Don Haworth, aiming to capture the essence and atmosphere of the "Mersey Beat" boom. After initial talks with Brian Epstein, Haworth had met the Beatles on 21 July and discussed the production, promising them the opportunity, which they certainly desired, of being able to discuss themselves more seriously than in the somewhat flip fashion typical of the usual pop TV programmes. After a meeting with Epstein on 6 August, Haworth duly captured the Beatles' contract, which also precluded them from appearing

in *Beat City*, an equally thorough, though perhaps not as serious, rival documentary on the subject being made at the same time by ITV company Associated-Rediffusion.

The Beatles' first filming took place from 9.30 am on **Tuesday 27 August**. Requiring live action footage of the group, yet aware of the enormous difficulties filming amid the bedlam of an actual live Beatles concert, Don Haworth booked time at the Little ·Theatre in Hoghton Street, Southport, where the group played on stage without an audience. The film was then intercut with hysterical audience footage shot the previous night at the Beatles' Odeon show. This morning the Beatles performed 'Twist And Shout' and 'She Loves You', dressed in typical-of-the-day grey collarless suits. Then, in black collarless suits and with a curtain behind them (to lend the appearance of a separate shoot), they played 'Love Me Do', although the EMI disc recording was later dubbed onto the film, replacing the live music performance.

On **Wednesday 28 August**, again from 9.30 am, the Beatles were filmed in a dressing-room at the BBC's Dickenson Road premises in Manchester, frankly discussing their past and their aims and hopes for the future, considering that the present boom probably couldn't last much longer. They were also filmed applying theatrical make-up, as if they were about to go on stage for the previous day's "concert" shoot, and intently walking around backstage with their guitars, as if they were about to make a BBC television appearance.

On **Thursday 29 August**, the Beatles were filmed walking on the top deck of a ferry boat travelling between Liverpool Pier Head and Wallasey, signing autographs and looking over the bow. They then shot footage at Speke Airport, south Liverpool, where they acted out an airport arrival, descending the steps of an airplane.

On **Friday 30 August**, shooting took place outside Ringo's house, 10 Admiral Grove, Liverpool 8. Ringo was filmed coming out through the front door, battling his way through a horde of kids (most of whom looked around seven-years-old, and seemed to have been put there by the TV crew) and getting into George's open-top sports car, which then sped away with kids hanging onto the back. (Paul and John were at this shoot too, but did not participate in the sequence used.) Ringo then shot a solo scene, in which – to realise his oft-stated long-term aspiration to become a ladies'

hairdresser – he was filmed walking along a line of women sitting under hairdryers in the salon situated within Horne Bros clothing store in Lord Street, Liverpool city centre.

During production, the documentary went under the working title *The Beatles* but this was altered before transmission to *The Mersey Sound*, a more accurate reflection of its content, which also featured footage of and interviews with many other groups and participants in the local beat scene. The first broadcast of Don Haworth's film was on Wednesday 9 October 1963, between 10.10 and 10.40 pm, although it was screened only in London and the north on this occasion. A national transmission then took place on Wednesday 13 November, between 7.10 and 7.40 pm. Executives of the commercial station ATV were upset at the scheduling of the 9 October broadcast, being only four days before the Beatles would star in that company's live variety show *Val Parnell's Sunday Night At The London Palladium*, and they made their anger clear to Brian Epstein.

The Mersey Sound was well received as a sharply-observed documentary by critics and public alike, and at least two requests for copy prints were received, and complied with, one being presented to the Lord Mayor of Liverpool for preservation in the city archive, the other going to what has since become known as the National Film Archive, in London. Extracts have also been fed into numerous subsequent programmes and documentaries around the world. And sound-only excerpts from the Beatles' speech element were also broadcast on radio – in the Home Service programme *Pick Of The Week* on Friday 11 October 1963 (1.10–2.00 pm, repeated Saturday 12 October 3.10–4.00 pm) and in *The Week In The North* broadcast in the North of England Home Service on 12 October (9.30–9.50 am).

One further extract transmission from *The Mersey Sound* was made in January 1964 – a very important one, for it served as the Beatles' television début in the USA, outside of news coverage (see 16 November 1963). The BBC's New York Office sold a clip of 'She Loves You' to NBC for use in *The Jack Paar Show*. Brian Epstein was furious about this, claiming (though he knew it not to be so) that it would jeopardise his exclusive Beatles contract with Paar's CBS-TV rival Ed Sullivan. A considerable flurry of national and international letters, telexes and telephone calls followed in the wake of Epstein's wrath, the BBC trying to rescind its sale of the clip. But Paar resisted any such move and broadcast it regardless in his show on Friday 3 January (10.00–11.00 pm, EST). Characteristically, a piqued Epstein threatened – but failed to carry through – a vow to prevent any future BBC TV appearances by the Beatles, which would have harmed him and the group as much as the Corporation, and he certainly accepted the £225 fee that came with the sale.

Ironically, though, Paar's transmission of the clip did the Beatles good service in the United States, boosting interest considerably – and this despite Paar's sarcastic comment after the film, "It's nice to know that England has finally risen to our cultural level …," and *New York Times* television writer Jack Gould concluding the next morning "It would not seem quite so likely that the accompanying fever known as Beatlemania will also be successfully exported. On this side of the Atlantic it is dated stuff."

Sunday 1 September

Studio One, Didsbury Studio Centre, Manchester

A Sunday TV taping for ABC Television, but not this time for *Thank Your Lucky Stars* – this appearance was on the variety show *Big Night Out*, hosted by Mike and Bernie Winters. (It was the first of four Beatles TV engagements with the comedian brothers – see also 23 February and 19 July 1964, and 1 August 1965.) Fellow guests in this edition included Billy Dainty, Patsy Ann Noble and Lionel Blair.

Following daytime rehearsals, the show was taped during the evening on the main stage at ABC's Manchester studio, before an audience of 600, the Beatles miming to three songs – 'From Me To You', 'She Loves You' and 'Twist And Shout'. It was transmitted across most of the ITV network, 7.40–8.30 pm, on Saturday 7 September.

Note: the Beatles had originally been requested to tape their *Big Night Out* début on Sunday 18 August, for Saturday 24 August transmission, but their diary could not accommodate this.

Tuesday 3 September

Studio Two, Aeolian Hall, London

Recordings for the final three editions of the 15-part BBC Light Programme radio series *Pop Go The Beatles*, taped in one long session. The first of the three was produced, as usual, by Terry Henebery, but the final two were handled by Ian Grant.

Including rehearsal time, programme 13 was recorded between 2.00 and 4.30 pm, the Beatles performing 'Too Much Monkey Business', 'Till There Was You', 'Love Me Do', 'She Loves You', 'I'll Get You' and 'The Hippy Hippy Shake'. During later editing, 'A Taste Of Honey' (taped while making programme 14) was additionally inserted after 'I'll Get You', making a total of seven Beatles performances in this show rather than the usual six. It was broadcast between 5.00 and 5.29 pm on Tuesday 10 September, with separately taped guest act Johnny Kidd and the Pirates.

After a half-hour break, the fourteenth edition was recorded between 5.00 and 7.30 pm, the Beatles performing 'Chains', 'You Really Got A Hold On Me', 'Misery', 'A Taste Of Honey' (transferred to the previous programme), 'Lucille', 'From Me To You' and 'Boys'. This show was broadcast between 5.00 and 5.29 pm on Tuesday 17 September, with guests the Marauders.

After another 30-minute breather the Beatles launched into the third part of the session, for programme 15. Songs recorded were 'She Loves You', 'Ask Me Why', '(There's A) Devil In Her Heart', 'I Saw Her Standing There', 'Sure To Fall (In Love With You)' and 'Twist And Shout'. This final programme in the series was broadcast between 5.00 and 5.29 pm on Tuesday 24 September, with guests Tony Rivers and the Castaways, the nucleus of what would later become the Beatles' Apple Publishing group Grapefruit, who contributed such old country numbers as John Loudermilk's 'Abilene', a contemporary US hit for George Hamilton IV.

Wednesday 4 September

Gaumont Cinema, Worcester

The first of a four-night run promoted by John Smith. Brian Epstein granted him this mini-tour because of the earlier cancellation of several "Mersey Beat Showcase" dates. The Beatles' fee was £250 per night.

Thursday 5 September

Gaumont Cinema, Taunton

Friday 6 September

Odeon Cinema, Dunstable Rd, Luton, Bedfordshire

Saturday 7 September

Playhouse Theatre, London
and Fairfield Hall, Croydon

Before travelling to Croydon for their evening's work, the Beatles stopped off at the Playhouse Theatre in London to record a BBC radio session for *Saturday Club* – a special edition, its fifth birthday show, 262 shows after the first broadcast on 4 October 1958, to be transmitted in the Light Programme on 5 October between 10.00 am and 12.00 noon. Quite apart from the world audience during the programme's last 29 minutes, recent editions in the series had achieved a British audience of around nine million, a remarkably high figure.

Including rehearsal time, this session took place from 1.00 to 4.00 pm, the Beatles performing 'I Saw Her Standing There', 'Memphis, Tennessee', 'Happy Birthday Saturday Club', 'I'll Get You', 'She Loves You' and 'Lucille'. 'Happy Birthday Saturday Club' was the group's short though appropriate ode to the anniversary, the composer details being officially noted on the programme report as "Trad arr Lennon". The last three of the six songs were included in the simultaneous broadcast by the BBC's General Overseas Service, 11.31–11.59 am.

After the *Saturday Club* recording, Paul gave a short solo interview to BBC radio producer Rosemary Hart for a programme in her Home Service series *A World Of Sound*. It was broadcast on Thursday 21 November, 4.30–5.00 pm, in an edition sub-titled 'Liverpool: A Swinging City'.

Sunday 8 September

ABC Theatre, Blackpool

Wednesday 11 September

Studio Two, EMI Studios, London

Back to EMI for more work on the second album, to be released as *With The Beatles*. From 2.30–6.00 pm the group recorded three new Lennon-McCartney numbers: one take

Superb studio studies of the Beatles at work, Abbey Road, 11 September 1963.

of 'I Wanna Be Your Man', Ringo's vocal vehicle on the album (the previous day, John and Paul had also given it to the Rolling Stones; they taped their version on 7 October, released it on 1 November and it was their first Top 20 hit within a month), two takes of 'Little Child' and 15 takes of 'All I've Got To Do'.

In the evening session, 7.00–10.15 pm, nine takes were recorded of another Lennon-McCartney song, 'Not A Second Time', and the first seven of 'Don't Bother Me', George Harrison's début as a composer.

Thursday 12 September

Studio Two, EMI Studios, London

It wasn't only in Britain that the Beatles were enjoying tremendous record sales. On 5 July Brian Epstein verbally agreed to the group undertaking a June 1964 concert tour of Australia, and on 2 December the contract was formally signed. Now though, to satisfy demands from Australian radio, the group recorded four messages for broadcast there, three addressed directly to Bob Rogers (a DJ at the Sydney station 2SM) and one "open-message", to be used by any station. These semi-scripted, semi-spontaneous lines consisted of typically witty Beatles chatter and were the first of a number of speech items the group taped at EMI over the years.

The recordings were made between 2.30 and 6.30 pm along with ten takes of a re-make of 'Hold Me Tight', first attempted for *Please Please Me* on 11 February but completed more successfully this time around.

Between 7.00 and 11.30 pm, which meant running 90 minutes over the booked time of 10.00, the Beatles set about another re-make, of George's 'Don't Bother Me', with ten takes needed to complete the recording, and then resumed work on two songs begun the previous day, taping 16 more takes of 'Little Child' and six more of 'I Wanna Be Your Man'.

Friday 13 September

Public Hall, Preston

After this show, Paul drove 25 miles to the Imperial Ballroom in Nelson, arriving just after midnight, to appear on a panel judging the "Imperial Miss 1963" contest, part of the annual "Young Ones' Ball", sponsored by the local newspaper the *Nelson Leader*.

Saturday 14 September

(Victory) Memorial Hall, Northwich

Sunday 15 September

Royal Albert Hall, London

The Beatles headed this afternoon show, the annual "Great Pop Prom" promoted by *Valentine*, *Marilyn* and *Roxy* magazines in aid of the Printers' Pension Corporation. Eleven other acts appeared, including the Rolling Stones. DJ Alan Freeman was the compere.

On 16 September the Beatles took off for holidays. John and his wife Cynthia travelled to Paris, where they were joined by Brian Epstein; George, with his brother Peter, visited his sister Louise in the USA, who had emigrated to Benton, Illinois in 1954; Paul and Ringo went to Greece.

Monday 30 September

The Beatles were still away on holidays when a 10.00 am–1.15 pm editing, overdubbing and mixing session took place this day in studio two at Abbey Road. 'Little Child' and 'Hold Me Tight' were edited, George Martin recorded additional keyboard passages for 'Money (That's What I Want)' and 'I Wanna Be Your Man', and then 'All I've Got To Do', 'Don't Bother Me', 'Little Child', 'Hold Me Tight' and 'Not A Second Time' were mixed into mono.

Thursday 3 October

Studio Three, EMI Studios, London
and **NEMS Enterprises, Monmouth Street, London**

All of the Beatles but George arrived back in England on Wednesday 2 October. He returned this day although after this 10.00 am–1.00 pm session at EMI which saw Ringo overdub a new vocal onto 'I Wanna Be Your Man' and John and Paul do likewise for 'Little Child'.

During the mid-afternoon, with George, the Beatles made the first of three appearances on the ahead-of-its-time BBC radio programme *The Public Ear*, a spoken-word magazine for which the Beatles' contributions were always of the interview variety. It was a series to which the group keenly listened when on tour.

This interview – taped by the programme's features assistant Michael Colley at NEMS' 13 Monmouth Street office – went into the edition transmitted in the Light Programme from 3.00 to 4.00 pm on Sunday 3 November, as part of a fascinating, almost-12 minute feature devoted to them and the "Mersey Beat" boom. Interviews with Bill Harry, Pete Best, Millie Sutcliffe (mother of the late Stuart), "beat poet" Royston Ellis (whom the Beatles had backed at the Jacaranda Coffee Bar in Liverpool one night in May 1960) and members of the public were also featured. The item was narrated by broadcaster Tony Hall, a much respected figure in the British record industry and personal friend and central London neighbour of the Beatles.

Note: *The Public Ear* was considered such an interesting programme that some editions were re-broadcast in revised form on the Home Service as *In The Public Ear*. The Beatles' interview elements from Colley's feature were included in such a programme on 14 January 1964, 9.00–9.30 pm. (See also 18 March 1964.)

Ringo left the NEMS office immediately the interview was over and drove to Southend to see a package show concert at the Odeon Cinema featuring the Everly Brothers, Bo Diddley and the Rolling Stones.

Friday 4 October

Studio Nine, Television House, Kingsway, London

The Beatles' début on the television show most synonymous in Britain with the so-called "Swinging Sixties", and equally synonymous – in London, at least – with Friday evenings ('The Weekend Starts Here!') – *Ready, Steady, Go!*

This edition of *RSG!*, like most until 26 March 1965, was broadcast live (although the performers always mimed) from studio nine at the Television House headquarters of London's weekday ITV franchise Associated-Rediffusion, situated by the Aldwych. The series had begun on 2 August although, for the first few months, it was not fully networked around Britain.

Following an afternoon camera rehearsal, the Beatles performed three songs, 'Twist And Shout', 'I'll Get You' (proof of the miming was especially evident here, since neither John nor anyone else was playing the clearly-audible harmonica) and 'She Loves You'.

Teenagers danced around the Beatles' small podium while they performed. They were also interviewed by show host Keith Fordyce and by singer Dusty Springfield, a decidedly cheeky affair with, at one point, John asking Dusty to reveal her scabs. The programme was transmitted from 6.15–7.00 pm.

The 8 November edition of *Ready, Steady, Go!* (also 6.15–7.00 pm) carried a repeat of this 'She Loves You' performance while a special edition on 31 December (subtitled 'The New Year Starts Here!'), 11.15 pm–12.15 am, repeated this entire three-song set.

Saturday 5 October

Concert Hall, Argyle St, Glasgow, Lanarkshire

The first of a three-night mini-tour of Scotland, promoted by Albert Bonici under his exclusive north-of-the-border agreement with Brian Epstein.

Sunday 6 October

Carlton Theatre, Arcade Halls, Sinclairtown,
Kirkcaldy, Fifeshire

A concert presented by the management of Kirkcaldy's Raith Ballroom, unable to use their own premises because of Brian Epstein's new ruling that, where possible, the Beatles would perform only in proper theatres. Fifteen hundred people attended each of the two "houses".

EMI Studios' second engineer/tape op Richard Langham with the now almost completely fab Four, during a session for With The Beatles.

Monday 7 October

Caird Hall, City Square, Dundee, Angus

Wednesday 9 October

BBC Paris Studio, London

This BBC radio session was not for a pop programme but for *The Ken Dodd Show*, a 30-minute collection of comedy sketches and sound effects starring Liverpudlian comedian Ken Dodd – on whose charity bill at the Albany Cinema in Maghull the scarcely known Beatles had inappropriately belted out rock and roll numbers only two years previously.

The Beatles did not participate in any of Dodd's comedy sketches: their sole contribution was to perform the show's one musical interlude, 'She Loves You'. It was taped in the middle of the programme, before a studio audience at the Paris, between 10.00 and 11.00 pm. (The Beatles had also participated in the rehearsal, from 6.30 pm.)

The show was broadcast in the Light Programme on Sunday 3 November between 2.30 and 3.00 pm (any listener staying tuned to this waveband would have heard the Beatles in the following programme too, *The Public Ear* – see 3 October) and was repeated on Wednesday 6 November (8.00–8.30 pm) and again on Saturday 1 February 1964 (1.10–1.40 pm).

Friday 11 October

Ballroom, Trentham Gardens, Stone Rd, Trentham, Staffordshire

Sunday 13 October

London Palladium, Argyll St, London

The Beatles' first booking with one of the leading ITV companies, Associated TeleVision, headed by Lew Grade, for so long a powerful figure in British show business. And what a début – on the top-rated entertainment programme of them all, *Val Parnell's Sunday Night At The London Palladium*, fully networked live from the prestigious theatre in the heart of London and seen by 15 million viewers at peak-time, 8.25 to 9.25 pm. An appearance on SNALP – especially as bill-toppers, as were the Beatles this night – was a major event and, for so many artists, the pinnacle of a career, even if, today, one almost wonders what the fuss was about.

All the same, it was certainly a remarkable appearance. The London Palladium, so-called "home of the stars", had never before witnessed the screaming fans who made themselves very audible not only inside but outside the theatre too, blocking Argyll Street and delighting photographers with ready-made front-page picture-stories for the next morning. The word Beatlemania was coined by Fleet Street writers to describe the scenes, and it remains in use today, and probably will for ever more.

The youth element in the theatre was teased right from the start when, against tradition, the Beatles, though top-of-the-bill, appeared at the beginning of the show – albeit only for a few seconds. Compere Bruce Forsyth then announced, "If you want to see them again they'll be back in 42 minutes..."

When they came back, to close the hour-long show, Forsyth rose above the screams to count down "5-4-3-2-1" before the Beatles struck up 'From Me To You'. Thereafter they went into their by now well-oiled stage routine (even still, they had had a private rehearsal the previous evening). Paul tried to introduce the next number ('I'll Get You'), John sent him up. Then John, Paul and George all spoke the next announcement together, stopping together and re-starting together, until George carried it off alone, introducing 'She Loves You'. Then Paul tried to announce the closing number, John shouted at the screamers to "Shut up!", the adults among the audience applauded, Paul asked people to clap their hands and stamp their feet, John went into his spastic imitations, and the group finally launched into 'Twist And Shout'.

The show ended, as ever, with the bill-toppers joining the other acts (Brook Benton, Des O'Connor, host Bruce Forsyth) on the revolving stage, waving at the audience and cameras while the resident Jack Parnell Orchestra played the theme tune 'Startime'.

The Beatles were clearly becoming a phenomenon – this TV appearance was actually covered by the late-evening ITN news, which had cameras in the group's Palladium dressing-room.

Tuesday 15 October

Floral Hall, Southport

Wednesday 16 October

Playhouse Theatre, London

The Beatles' fourth and last session for the Sunday morning BBC radio Light Programme pop show *Easy Beat*. Owing to the incredible demands on their time, and fearing for their safety, Brian Epstein told the BBC that he would no longer permit the group to appear in audience radio shows – just as he had decided that, for British concerts, they would play only theatres or venues with fixed seating, no more ballrooms. An instant casualty of this decision was a fifth booking for *Easy Beat*, which would have taken place on Wednesday 4 December for transmission on the 8th. (Epstein had recently cancelled a BBC television booking too, for the programme *Kindly Leave The Stage*, to have been taped on Sunday 15 September and transmitted on the 22nd.)

This show was recorded at the Playhouse Theatre from 9.00 to 10.00 pm, with a prior rehearsal from 4.00 pm. The Beatles performed 'I Saw Her Standing There', 'Love Me Do', 'Please Please Me', 'From Me To You' and 'She Loves You', the last four songs being the group's singles to date, in the correct order. It was broadcast on Sunday 20 October, 10.31–11.30 am.

While at the Playhouse, the Beatles were also interviewed by reporter Peter Woods about the announcement, made the previous day, that they had been invited to perform in the Royal Variety Show on 4 November. The interview, in which the group cleverly parried Woods' clearly condescending tones, was broadcast on the Light Programme's main evening news bulletin (7.00–7.31 pm) *Radio Newsreel*.

Thursday 17 October

Studio Two, EMI Studios, London

Two sessions, 2.30–5.30 and 7.00–10.00 pm, saw the Beatles cater for three different projects: they attempted to improve a recording for the new album, they taped the A- and B-sides of their fifth single, and also recorded some wacky horseplay for 'The Beatles' Christmas Record', to be distributed free-of-charge exclusively to members of their Official Fan Club on 9 December. This was the first of seven such discs they would make.

These sessions also marked the dawn of a new era for the Beatles at EMI: four-track recording, ushering in entirely new recording processes and allowing the group to use the facility more experimentally. No longer would they need to record all instruments live in the studio – although, on occasions, they did continue to do just this.

The two sides of the next single, 'I Want To Hold Your Hand' and the exquisite three-part harmony song 'This Boy', both of them progressive Lennon-McCartney numbers, were the first to benefit from four-track and each was perfected in 17 takes. Later, though, despite the better facilities, they gave up trying to perfect 'You Really Got A Hold On Me' after attempting one final take, its 12th.

The new single was issued in Britain on Friday 29

November, crashing into the chart while 'She Loves You' was enjoying its second spell at the top. Within a week it had replaced its predecessor, and the Beatles were holding numbers one and two, in addition to numbers one and two in the LP chart. 'I Want To Hold Your Hand' was also critically important in another direction: it broke the group into the US market, paving the way for a 1964 that would eclipse even 1963 in terms of record sales and all-encompassing Beatlemania.

Friday 18 October

Studio Four, Granada TV Centre, Manchester

Another appearance on *Scene At 6.30*, taped during the early afternoon at Granada Television and transmitted in this evening's programme, 6.30–7.00 pm. The Beatles mimed to 'She Loves You'.

Saturday 19 October

Pavilion Gardens Ballroom, Buxton

Sunday 20 October

Alpha Television Studios, Aston, Birmingham

Another bill-topping appearance on ABC Television's *Thank Your Lucky Stars*, taped during the afternoon and transmitted 5.50–6.35 pm on Saturday 26 October.

In this edition they mimed to an unprecedented three numbers, one more than usual, two more than most other acts – 'All My Loving', 'Money (That's What I Want)' and 'She Loves You'. The first two formed an exclusive glimpse of *With The Beatles*, not issued until 22 November. *TYLS* producer Philip Jones had acquired advanced acetate pressings of some of the album tracks and persuaded Brian Epstein to allow him first opportunity to plug them.

Monday 21 October

Studio One, EMI Studios, London

Mono mixing and editing of 'This Boy' and mono and stereo mixing of 'I Want To Hold Your Hand', effected by George Martin from 10.00 am to 1.00 pm. The Beatles may well have attended.

Wednesday 23 October

Studio Two, EMI Studios, London

The Beatles' final input to their second album, recording the 16th take of 'I Wanna Be Your Man' and then watching as George Martin and Norman Smith mixed this, 'Little Child' and 'Hold Me Tight' into mono, all done between 10.00 am and 1.00 pm.

After lunch, the group flew to Sweden for their first foreign tour.

TELSTAR PRESENTERAR:

THE
BEATLES

EUROPAS POPULÄRASTE POP BAND
-:-:-:-:-:-:-:-:-:-:-:-:-:-:-:-

JERRY WILLIAMS
THE VIOLENTS
TRIO ME' BUMBA
THE TELSTARS
MONA SKARSTRÖM
JACK DAILEY m. fl.
Konferencier: CARL EIVAR

I AFTON
29 OKT. — ESKILSTUNA
SPORTHALLEN — Kl. 19.00

FÖRKÖP: EK-Centralen. Kassan i Sporthallen öppnas föreställningsdagen kl. 12.

Thursday 24 October

Karlaplansstudion, Karlaplan, Stockholm, Sweden

The Beatles' first duty in Sweden was to record a radio appearance at the Karlaplansstudion, situated in the centre of Stockholm. The title of the programme was *The Beatles pupgrupp från Liverpool på besök i Stockholm* – which, translated, means "The Beatles pop group from Liverpool visiting Stockholm", a neatly descriptive title.

Clearly exuberated at playing before the Swedish audience, perhaps pleased at having to work harder to win them over (the British teenage public having long lapsed into adoration), the Beatles put in a terrific performance, playing live an exciting set of seven songs, 'I Saw Her Standing There', 'From Me To You', 'Money (That's What I Want)', 'Roll Over Beethoven', 'You Really Got A Hold On Me', 'She Loves You' and 'Twist And Shout'. Between 'Money' and 'Roll Over Beethoven' the Beatles took a break while local group Hasse Rosen and the Norsmen played three numbers.

Produced by Klas Burling, who had called Brian Epstein and booked the Beatles by phone for this appearance, the session was recorded from 5.00 pm (without prior rehearsal) and broadcast on channel one of Sveriges Radio (Swedish National Radio) on Monday 11 November, 10.05–10.30 pm.

Friday 25 October

Nya Aulan, Sundsta Läroverk, Sundstavägen, Karlstad, Sweden

Not seven months after their concert at Stowe, it was very much "back to school" for the Beatles as they kicked-off their £140-a-night Swedish concert tour in the unlikely setting of the new hall of a secondary school in the tiny town of Karlstad.

The Beatles' repertoire for the two "houses" here, at 7.00 and 9.00 pm, and for the remainder of the short tour, comprised 'Long Tall Sally', 'Please Please Me', 'I Saw Her Standing There', 'From Me To You', 'A Taste Of Honey', 'Chains', 'Boys', 'She Loves You' and 'Twist And Shout'.

Despite a wildly enthusiastic reception from screaming Swedish Beatlemaniacs, one man not so impressed was "Johnny", the pop reviewer from local Karlstad newspaper *Nya Wermlands Tidning*. He thought the Beatles terrible, their music corny and their playing out of rhythm, adding that the group should have been grateful the fans' screams helped drown out their awful performance, and then he concluded by stating that the Beatles were of no musical importance whatsoever and that their local support group, the Phantoms, decidedly outshone them.

Saturday 26 October

Kungliga Tennishallen, Lidingövägen, Stockholm, Sweden

Two shows, at 5.00 and 8.00 pm, in which – theoretically at least, because the audience clearly demanded otherwise – the Beatles were second on the bill to Joey Dee and the Starliters.

Sunday 27 October

Cirkus, Lorensbergsparken, Göteborg, Sweden

The Beatles gave *three* shows, at 3.00, 5.00 and 8.00 pm, here in the city known to the English as Gothenburg.

Monday 28 October

Boråshallen, Bockasjögatan, Borås, Sweden

One performance, at 7.30 pm, preceded by a half-hour spot during the mid-afternoon signing records at the Waidele record shop in Borås.

Tuesday 29 October

Sporthallen, Hamngatan, Eskilstuna, Sweden

A few hours before the Beatles concluded their concert tour of Sweden with one final performance, George Martin – back at EMI Abbey Road – was overseeing the entire set of stereo mixes, edits and banding for their second album, all done in a single three-hour session, 10.00 am–1.00 pm. The tracks were worked on in the order that George had devised for the finished disc: 'It Won't Be Long', 'All I've Got To Do', 'All My Loving', 'Don't Bother Me', 'Little Child', 'Till There Was You', 'Please Mister Postman', 'Roll Over Beethoven', 'Hold Me Tight', 'You Really Got A Hold On Me', 'I Wanna Be Your Man', '(There's A) Devil In Her Heart', 'Not A Second Time' and 'Money (That's What I Want)'. Only this 14th and final track would require more, later attention.

Wednesday 30 October

Narren-teatern, Gröna Lund, Stockholm, Sweden

Abbey Road activity this day saw the production of another stereo mix for 'Money (That's What I Want)', overseen by George Martin in a 2.30–5.30 pm session. To avoid any further generational loss caused by more tape-to-tape copying, two separate two-track mono mixes were used for the stereo album, one for each channel.

This was the final item of preparation for *With The Beatles* and the album was issued on Friday 22 November 1963, precisely eight months after *Please Please Me*, to astonishing British advance orders of 300,000. Domestic sales swiftly passed the half-million mark and in 1965 topped one million. The album even earned a brief placing in the singles chart, which – since LP sales were, theoretically, so comparatively few in number in the early 1960s – was calculated at that time on sales of any record, irrespective of diameter.

Meanwhile, in Sweden, the evening before flying home to England and their first "airport reception", the Beatles returned to Stockholm to tape an appearance on the

Sveriges Television pop show *Drop In*, broadcast from 7.00 to 7.30 pm on Sunday 3 November.

The recording was made before a live audience at Narrenteatern, a small theatre within the Stockholm amusement park Gröna Lund, and it began at 7.00 pm, following afternoon rehearsals. Although intending to perform only two songs, 'She Loves You' and 'Twist And Shout', presenter Klas Burling persuaded the Beatles to extend their repertoire to four, these two in the same order plus 'I Saw Her Standing There' and 'Long Tall Sally'. Very clearly enjoying themselves, although they'd not eaten all day, the Beatles also enthusiastically joined in with handclapping during the programme's closing theme tune, named, appropriately enough, 'Drop In'.

On 31 October the group took the morning flight back to London Airport.

Friday I November

Odeon Cinema, Winchcombe St, Cheltenham, Gloucestershire

The opening night of "The Beatles' Autumn Tour", their fourth trek around Britain inside nine months, earning them £300 a night. Identical for every performance, the Beatles' repertoire for this one comprised 'I Saw Her Standing

1. THE RHYTHM & BLUES QUARTET
2. Frank Berry introduces THE VERNONS GIRLS
3. FRANK BERRY
4. THE BROOK BROTHERS
5. FRANK BERRY
6. PETER JAY & THE JAYWALKERS
   interval
7. THE RHYTHM & BLUES QUARTET
8. THE KESTRELS
9. FRANK BERRY
10. **THE BEATLES**

There', 'From Me To You', 'All My Loving', 'You Really Got A Hold On Me', 'Roll Over Beethoven', 'Boys', 'Till There Was You', 'She Loves You', 'Money (That's What I Want)' and 'Twist And Shout'.

But the screaming was so loud that no one – not even the Beatles – could hear more than a few notes of it.

Saturday 2 November

City Hall, Sheffield

Sunday 3 November

Odeon Cinema, Leeds

A few minutes of one of the Beatles' two "houses" this evening was recorded for use in a court case involving the Performing Right Society. The tape no longer exists.

After this night the tour resumed on the 5th.

Monday 4 November

Prince Of Wales Theatre, Coventry St, London

The Beatles' famous Royal Command Performance, in the presence of the Queen Mother and Princess Margaret, with Lord Snowdon. Though appearing seventh on a 19-act bill, they were undoubtedly the night's main attraction.

As they had done on *Val Parnell's Sunday Night At The London Palladium* on 13 October, the group put all of their tried-and-trusted stage tricks into the performance: they began playing the opening number, 'From Me To You', before the curtain parted, then John and Paul simultaneously moved their microphone stands closer to the audience at its end; they bowed at the close of the second song, 'She Loves You'; Paul – clearly nervous – cracked a joke about Sophie Tucker being their "favourite American group" before third song 'Till There Was You'; before the fourth and last number, John and Paul returned their mike stands to their original positions, and then John waited for the applause to die away before uttering his notorious jewellery-rattling witticism as an introduction to 'Twist And Shout'; finally, Ringo came down from his drum podium to join John, Paul and George, the curtain closed behind them,

they bowed to the audience, then to the royal box, and then – to show youthful exuberance – sprinted off the stage.

Historically, televising of the Royal Command Performance has alternated between the BBC and ITV; this year it fell to the latter. Pictures were networked across Britain by ATV the following Sunday, 10 November, 7.28–10.30 pm, with the Beatles' entire four-song performance included. However, when the BBC radio Light Programme transmitted highlights from the show (also on 10 November, 7.35–8.30 pm), it omitted 'She Loves You'.

Tuesday 5 November

Adelphi Cinema, Slough

In the late-morning the Beatles had an engagement with a TV crew from Associated-Rediffusion, which had decided to dedicate half of the next edition of its 30-minute current affairs series *This Week* to the subject of the Beatles and Beatlemania.

The group consented to an interview, filmed in the back of a hire car driving around London. Owing to the cramped conditions it wasn't possible for all four Beatles to be in camera at the same time, so George and Ringo were filmed together, then John and Paul.

Exactly nine minutes of interview footage, cut from the 10 mins 40 secs that was shot, made it into the finished programme and this was supplemented by more than 20 Beatles photo stills and also by a studio conversation about (though not with) the group, inserted live into the Thursday 7 November transmission, 9.10–9.40 pm.

In the evening the Beatles resumed their nationwide package tour with two "houses" at Slough. ("Oh, that's near us," the Queen Mother had remarked to the group when, during their presentation to Her Majesty after the Royal Command Performance the previous evening, she had asked them where they'd next be playing. Slough is only two miles from Windsor.)

Wednesday 6 November

ABC Cinema, Northampton

Thursday 7 November

Dublin Airport, Dublin, Eire
and Adelphi Cinema, Middle Abbey St, Dublin, Eire

The Beatles' only appearance in Ireland. On their arrival at Dublin Airport they were interviewed by reporter Frank Hall for the RTE (Radio Telefis Eireann) news-magazine television programme *In Town*, transmitted this same evening, 7.55–8.00 pm.

The Beatles' first feature-film *A Hard Day's Night* – though it was five months away from gaining that title – first took shape on this day, when screenwriter Alun Owen, appointed by the film's producer Walter Shenson at the group's suggestion, began a three-day observation of the Beatles and their increasingly chaotic lifestyle. He flew into Dublin with the group from London Airport and stayed with them up to and including their engagement at East Ham on the 9th.

Friday 8 November

Studio 8, Broadcasting House, Ormeau Ave, Belfast
and Ritz Cinema, Fisherwick Place, Belfast

En route from Dublin to Belfast, near to the Irish border, the Beatles stopped at a pre-arranged spot to be interviewed for Ulster Television (the ITV franchise for Northern Ireland) by reporter Jimmy Robinson. The item was included in this evening's edition of *Ulster News*, 6.25–6.35 pm.

Then, on their 2.00 pm arrival in Belfast, the Beatles went to the BBC's local television studios, at Broadcasting House, where they taped an interview with Sally Ogle for the Corporation's rival to *Ulster News*, the magazine programme *Six Ten*, broadcast, hardly surprisingly, at 6.10, until 6.31. The interview was taped at 3.00 pm. The Beatles had been also contracted to sing (mime) one song, but this they did not do.

Saturday 9 November

Granada Cinema, East Ham, London

Backstage before the show, with news hot from EMI, George Martin announced to the Beatles that their forthcoming single 'I Want To Hold Your Hand' looked likely to sell one million copies in advance of release. Later on, still before the release date, sales did actually top the million mark – the first time this feat had been achieved in Britain.

Sunday 10 November

Hippodrome Theatre, Birmingham

Tuesday 12 November

Guildhall, Portsmouth (postponed)

Hampshire's teenage population went into veritable mourning when a gastric flu virus hit Paul McCartney and caused postponement of the Beatles' Portsmouth shows this evening. They were soon re-scheduled for Tuesday 3 December, however.

Not postponed but cancelled (that is, never re-arranged) was a mimed musical appearance on the Southern Television magazine programme *Day By Day*, scheduled to have been taped during the early afternoon at the company's Southampton studios and transmitted this evening, 6.05–6.45 pm. Instead, in the Guildhall dressing-room, they gave a short interview to reporter Jeremy James which was broadcast in the same programme.

The Beatles also appeared on this evening's local BBC TV magazine programme *South Today*, 6.10–6.30, in an interview with reporter John Johnston taped earlier at their Southsea hotel, the Royal Beach.

Wednesday 13 November

Westward Television Studios, Derry's Cross, Plymouth, Devonshire
and **ABC Cinema, George St, Plymouth, Devonshire**

Being that they were in Plymouth, the Beatles consented to an approach from Westward Television (which then held the ITV franchise for programming south-west England) to give a brief interview to presenter Stuart Hutchison for the local teenage programme *Move Over, Dad* (billed as "A gay new show with the accent on the beat of the young"). It was included in the next edition of the series, Saturday 16 November (5.15–5.45 pm).

But such was the chaos outside the ABC Cinema, where the group were ensconced in their dressing-room, that they had to be smuggled out of a side-door and into a side-door of the adjacent Athenaeum Theatre. Westward occasionally used the theatre as an annexe studio, and direct access could be gained to the company's main studio block, in Derry's Cross, via a connecting tunnel. The Beatles followed this route in order to appear on *Move Over, Dad*, and then repeated the exercise in the other direction, back to the ABC for the night's two "houses".

Thursday 14 November

ABC Cinema, Exeter

Friday 15 November

Colston Hall, Bristol

Saturday 16 November

Winter Gardens Theatre, Exeter Rd, Bournemouth, Hampshire

News of Beatlemania was beginning to spread abroad. Three different camera teams from the major North American television networks – NBC, ABC and CBS – filmed parts of this Beatles performance and the audience hysterics. Reports went into US television news programmes on 18, 19 and 21 November, and 7 December.

In the CBS item, reporter Alexander Kendrick was particularly condescending. Talking of the group's fans he declared, "Some of the girls can write" and spoke of the Beatles' "dish-mop hairstyles". The Beatles were seen entering the Winter Gardens Theatre and playing 'She Loves You' on stage (the disc version was overdubbed for TV); John and Paul also gave a short interview with another reporter, Josh Darsa. In punning, lofty fashion, Kendrick then concluded, "They symbolise the 20th century non-hero, as they make non-music, wear non-haircuts and give none-mersey".

Sunday 17 November

Coventry Theatre, Coventry

Tuesday 19 November

Gaumont Cinema, Wolverhampton

Monday 18 November had not been a day of rest for the Beatles as it had for the other acts on their package tour. Instead, they attended a ceremony at EMI House in London where they received a clutch of presentation discs: silver LPs for *Please Please Me* and *With The Beatles* – the latter in advance of release – from EMI Ltd chairman Sir Joseph Lockwood; a miniature silver EP each for *Twist And Shout* from George Martin; and a silver EP and single for *Twist And Shout* and 'She Loves You' respectively from Gerald Marks, editor of weekly pop paper *Disc*. They also stayed for a cocktail party and then a formal lunch in the boardroom, with company executives and privileged guests.

Wednesday 20 November

ABC Cinema, Stockport Rd, Ardwick Green, Ardwick, Manchester, Lancashire

Trading their exclusive permission for a share of the proceeds, the Beatles permitted Pathé News to film two songs from their first "house" this evening, 'She Loves You' and 'Twist And Shout'. (A disc recording of 'From Me To You' played under other footage.)

Together with backstage sequences, scenes of the hysterical audience and typically pun-filled commentary, this combined to make an eight-minute "Techniscope" colour newsreel *The Beatles Come To Town*, distributed around selected British cinemas for a week from 22 December. (Two years on, Pathé incorporated the footage into a 70-minute feature-film titled *Pop Gear*, released to British cinemas on 18 April 1965. Memorably, the US title of this release was *Go Go Mania*.)

Granada TV also had a crew shooting backstage at the ABC Ardwick, covering much the same sequences as Pathé and also conducting an exclusive interview in which the Beatles talked of their first US visit set for the following February. These items were first transmitted in the Monday 6 January 1964 edition of *Scene At 6.30* (6.30–7.00 pm).

The Beatles and Brian Epstein join George Martin and EMI Records executives (including managing director Len Wood, behind Ringo, and group chairman Sir Joseph Lockwood, centre) for lunch in the Manchester Square boardroom, 18 November 1963.

And BBC radio was also backstage at the Ardwick: a two-minute interview with the Beatles by Michael Barton was broadcast this evening, 20 November, in the North Home Service programme *Voice Of The North*, 6.10–6.30 pm. Additionally, Barton taped a brief interview with George alone for *Wacker, Mach Schau*, a programme about the relationship between the Liverpool and Hamburg rock scenes, broadcast on the North Home Service on 27 November, 8.00–8.30 pm.

Thursday 21 November

ABC Cinema, Carlisle

Friday 22 November

Globe Cinema, High St, Stockton-on-Tees, Durham

Saturday 23 November

City Hall, Newcastle-upon-Tyne

Sunday 24 November

ABC Cinema, Ferensway, Hull, Yorkshire

Monday 25 November

Studio Four, Granada TV Centre, Manchester

Re-arranged from an original booking for 27 November, the Beatles spent the afternoon at Granada Television taping a music sequence and interview for use part on 27 November on the 11.45–12.00 pm local programme *Late Scene Extra* (a production from the *Scene At 6.30* team)

and part on Friday 20 December in *Scene At 6.30* itself, 6.30–7.00 pm.

They taped two music sequences, miming to 'I Want To Hold Your Hand' and its B-side 'This Boy', performing on an unusual set comprising enlarged fictitious *Daily Echo* newspaper headlines. ('I Want To Hold Your Hand' was broadcast on the 27th, 'This Boy' was held back to 20 December.)

For the interview (shot on the same set), done with programme host Gay Byrne, the Beatles were joined by comedian Ken Dodd. Dodd turned the proceedings into an ad-libbers delight. At one point, when he suggested inviting ideas for an earthy name, so that he might form a rock group, George quipped "sod". It wasn't edited from the 27 November broadcast, nor indeed from a repeat of the whole Beatles appearance, 'This Boy' included, in the Boxing Day (Thursday 26 December) edition of *Scene At 6.30*, again 6.30–7.00 pm.

Tuesday 26 November

Regal Cinema, Cambridge

Before their two "houses" this evening, the Beatles appeared live on the local BBC TV news-magazine programme *East At Six Ten*, broadcast – oddly – from 6.38 to 7.01 pm, being interviewed in their Regal dressing-room by reporter Jean Goodman.

Wednesday 27 November

Rialto Theatre, York

Thursday 28 November

ABC Cinema, Saltergate, Lincoln, Lincolnshire

Friday 29 November

ABC Cinema, Market St, Huddersfield, Yorkshire

Between "houses" at the ABC, the Beatles were visited in their dressing-room by a representative from the Huddersfield Tape Recording Society, there to obtain an interview with each of the group, and have them read record requests, for *Music Box*, a monthly programme the Society produced for closed-circuit broadcast within several local hospitals in the area. The representative, meek and humble, was Gorden Kaye, 20 years later to achieve great popularity in Britain as René, the star of sitcom *'Allo 'Allo!*

Saturday 30 November

Empire Theatre, Sunderland

Sunday 1 December

De Montfort Hall, Leicester

After this date the tour resumed on the 3rd.

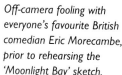

TR/6010   5

Morecambe and Wise have The Beatles as their guest stars in this edition of their series, and the fabulously popular group not only hold the screen with their own numbers but join in with the two comedians to add to the laughter. In turn, Morecambe and Wise try to join up with The Beatles. At any rate, they can do the "Yeah, yeah, yeah" bit!

Regular viewers of the "Morecambe and Wise Show" will be well aware that the two comics have a strong addiction to birds. They are usually of the shapely human variety. But this time, the bird they introduce is of ornithological interest - to wit (if Eric Morecambe can be believed), a South American purple oggled warbler. He claims that the "POW" gets lonely without him, sulks, loses its feathers and regards Eric as his mother. It's therefore essential that he should be in the programme, and Eric has some remarkable information to impart to Ernie Wise about the habits of his pet.

Those who have listened to two people simultaneously trying to explain what a film is all about will understand how Sid Green and Dick Hills feel when Morecambe and Wise try to do just this.

And for good measure in this programme, Eric and Ernie are found in a kitchen, assuming the disguise of two famous food connoisseurs who are about to demonstrate how to make an omelette flambeau.

Monday 2 December

Studio C, Elstree Studio Centre, Eldon Ave, Borehamwood, Hertfordshire
and **Ballroom, Grosvenor House Hotel, Park Lane, London**

The Beatles spent the period from mid-morning to late-afternoon at Associated TeleVision's Elstree Studio Centre (not to be confused with the nearby Elstree Film Studio, where feature-films were made), the object – very successfully achieved – being to rehearse and shoot an appearance on *The Morecambe And Wise Show*, hosted by the much-loved British comedy double-act Eric Morecambe and Ernie Wise. It was networked by ATV on Saturday 18 April 1964 (8.25–9.00 pm) and repeated on Saturday 24 July 1965 (as *The Best Of Morecambe And Wise*, 9.20–10.00 pm).

Performing live before a minimal studio audience, the Beatles initially sang two numbers, 'This Boy' and 'All My Loving', and then returned after more Eric and Ernie comedy sketches to sing a third, 'I Want To Hold Your Hand'.

After this last song, John, Paul and George put down their instruments and stepped forward to where Morecambe and Wise had walked on. (Ringo stayed at the back, on his drum podium.) What followed next was fine comedy, Morecambe calling the three Beatles "the Kaye Sisters" (a British female trio of the late 1950s), shouting up to Ringo, "Heeellllo Bungo!", and then engaging in witty and apparently ad-lib (though scripted) repartee, including an especially funny moment with John Lennon. Wise and the three Beatles next suggested they join forces for a number. While they kitted themselves out with boaters and striped jackets and launched into 44 seconds of 'Moonlight Bay' (written in 1912 by Madden/Wenrich and popularised by Doris Day in the 1951 film *On Moonlight Bay*), Morecambe rushed on in Beatles wig and collarless jacket, screaming "Yeah yeah yeah" and, unforgettably, "I Like It!" (Gerry and the Pacemakers' hit). This item closed the show, the end credits appearing over vision of Ringo finally stepping down from his kit. Though the Beatles appeared on television with a number of comedians, the end result was never better than this.

The night's Grosvenor House concert appearance was a most unusual live booking, and not a part of the current package tour – a cabaret floor-show (in aid of a spastics charity) before an evening-dressed audience at the prestigious London hotel. The Beatles were not altogether happy about it and were never again booked for this type of engagement.

In cabaret at the Grosvenor House, 2 December; Paul's handwritten set list includes the between-songs jokes which were a familiar part of the Beatles' repertoire at this time.

Tuesday 3 December

Guildhall, Portsmouth

The concert re-arranged from Tuesday 12 November. From 4 to 6 December the Beatles enjoyed a clear break.

Saturday 7 December

Empire Theatre, Liverpool
and **Odeon Cinema, London Rd, Liverpool**

The Beatles' first home-town concerts in four months were part of an exceedingly hectic day. The afternoon was a special affair, a concert at the Empire Theatre before 2500 members of the group's Northern Area Fan Club, though the rest of Britain had a chance to view the action when BBC

No misses here. With programme host David Jacobs before the taping of Juke Box Jury.

Television, in an unprecedented move, screened 30-minutes of the show later the same evening in a special peak-time programme entitled *It's The Beatles!*

Earlier the same afternoon at the Empire, utilising the same fan club audience, the BBC also taped a special edition of its weekly *Juke Box Jury*, with the panel comprising all four Beatles. This too was transmitted that same day – not for nothing were sceptics moaning that the BBC really stood for Beatles Broadcasting Corporation.

Juke Box Jury came first, being taped from 2.30 to 3.15 pm for broadcast between 6.05 and 6.35 in the evening – when it was viewed by 23 million Britons. Chaired as usual by David Jacobs, 13 new singles were reviewed in this particular edition – 'I Could Write A Book' by the Chants, 'Kiss Me Quick' by Elvis Presley, 'The Hippy Hippy Shake' by the Swinging Blue Jeans, 'Did You Have A Happy Birthday' by Paul Anka, 'The Nitty Gritty' by Shirley Ellis, 'I Can't Stop Talking About You' by Steve & Eydie, 'Do You Really Love Me Too' by Billy Fury, 'There! I've Said It Again' by Bobby Vinton, 'Love Hit Me' by the Orchids, 'I Think Of You' by the Merseybeats, 'Broken Home' by Shirley Jackson, 'Where Have You Been All My Life' by Gene Vincent and 'Long Time Ago' by the Bachelors. The last three were omitted from the broadcast, however, in order that it did not over-run. The Beatles voted all to be hits except for Paul Anka, Shirley Ellis, Bobby Vinton and the Orchids.

The concert, taped for *It's The Beatles*, took place between 3.45 and 4.30 pm, the group singing a shortened 'From Me To You' then full versions of 'I Saw Her Standing There', 'All My Loving', 'Roll Over Beethoven', 'Boys', 'Till There Was You', 'She Loves You', 'This Boy', 'I Want To Hold Your Hand', 'Money (That's What I Want)', 'Twist And Shout' and a reprise of 'From Me To You'. It was broadcast from 8.10 to 8.40 pm.

Unfortunately for the BBC, vast technical difficulties created by the dearth of rehearsal time (a mere 15 minutes for *Juke Box Jury* only 20 for *It's The Beatles*) and, worse still, the incessant ear-perforating screams from the audience, drowning out the director's instructions to his cameramen and sound recordists, all but ruined both programmes. There was considerable consternation about this within the higher echelons of the Corporation, executives feeling that the coup it had achieved in presenting the Beatles so exclusively to the nation had somewhat rebounded against them in that the technical shortcomings were obvious and embarrassing.

And still the Beatles had one more duty for the BBC: they recorded a two-minute interview for broadcast on radio on Christmas Day in the Light Programme show *Top Pops Of 1963*, a 90-minute special (6.00–7.30 pm) in which disc-jockey Alan Freeman played the year's number one chart singles, interspersed with interviews with some of the artists.

After their activities at the Empire the Beatles dashed the 50 yards down a specially closed and police-reinforced Pudsey Street to the Odeon Cinema where they gave two more performances as part of the continuing package tour (this date was added to the tour itinerary after the initial press announcement).

Sunday 8 December

Odeon Cinema, Lewisham, London

Monday 9 December

Odeon Cinema, Southend-on-Sea

Once again, a TV news crew, this time from the BBC, interviewed the Beatles in their dressing-room. It was becoming a regular occurrence.

Tuesday 10 December

Gaumont Cinema, Doncaster

In their dressing-room at the Gaumont, sometimes straining to make themselves heard above the din of shouting and singing fans outside, the Beatles gave an entertaining inter-

view to a British-domiciled Australian broadcaster, Dibbs Mather, for overseas distribution by the BBC's Transcription Service (and not for domestic broadcast). Extracts from the interview – which also featured John reading 'Neville Club', a piece of poetry to be published three months later in his first book *In His Own Write* – were included in the 61st edition of *Dateline London* and also in the 453rd edition of *Calling Australia*, sent to any radio station in that country which paid the BBC's nominal subscription.

Wednesday 11 December

Futurist Theatre, Foreshore Rd, South Bay, Scarborough, Yorkshire

Thursday 12 December

Odeon Cinema, Nottingham

Friday 13 December

Gaumont Cinema, Southampton

The final date on the long "Autumn Tour" which had started in Cheltenham on 1 November.

Saturday 14 December

Wimbledon Palais, High St Merton, Wimbledon, London

The Beatles' Southern Area Fan Club's equivalent to the Liverpool festivities the previous Saturday. In addition to their mid-afternoon live performance, the Beatles lined up behind the Palais' bar and shook hands with all 3000 ecstatic fans who filed slowly past them, often in less than orderly fashion. Television and cinema news cameras filmed here and there throughout the event.

The management of the Palais, fearing their precious stage might be damaged by an onslaught of rampaging Beatlemaniacs, created a makeshift platform for the Beatles and erected a steel cage around it to keep the hordes at bay. Though safe, the Beatles were not best pleased with this arrangement, although seeing the fans crushed up against the wire prompted John to crack "If they press any harder they'll come through as chips".

Sunday 15 December

Alpha Television Studios, Aston, Birmingham

Following its success with the 29 June all-Liverpool edition of *Lucky Stars (Summer Spin)*, ABC Television this day shot a second such programme for the main series *Thank Your Lucky Stars*. All of the acts were Merseysiders, and Cavern Club compere Bob Wooler appeared as part of the regular "Spin-A-Disc" record review section. Taped in Aston during the afternoon, it was transmitted on Saturday 21 December, from 5.50 to 6.35 pm.

Recording an interview for the globe's far-flung corners with Dibbs Mather of the BBC's Transcription Service, Doncaster, 10 December 1963.

Making their eighth *TYLS* appearance of the year (counting the two *Summer Spin* editions), the Beatles mimed to four songs, the most they had performed on this show to date: 'I Want To Hold Your Hand', 'All My Loving', 'Twist And Shout' and 'She Loves You'. They were also presented, on camera, with two more gold discs to add to their quickly-growing collection.

This edition was selected as ITV's official entry in the next annual International Contest For Television Light Entertainment Programmes, held in Montreux, Switzerland, in April 1964 (see also 20 March 1964), but it did not win.

Tuesday 17 December

Playhouse Theatre, London

Another top-billed appearance on the BBC radio show *Saturday Club*, rehearsed and recorded from 3.00 to 6.30 pm and broadcast in the Christmas edition, transmitted in the Light Programme between 10.00 am and 12.00 noon on 21 December.

The Beatles performed six songs, 'All My Loving', 'This Boy', 'I Want To Hold Your Hand', 'Till There Was You', 'Roll Over Beethoven' and 'She Loves You', and also sang a scat 'All I Want For Christmas Is A Bottle' (a pastiche of Dora Bryan's contemporary chart hit 'All I Want For Christmas Is A Beatle', performed in session in this very programme by Susan Maughan) and a wacky medley – the

'Chrimble Mudley' – comprising 'Love Me Do', 'Please Please Me', 'From Me To You', 'She Loves You', 'I Want To Hold Your Hand' and 'Rudolph The Red-Nosed Reindeer', all crammed into 29 seconds.

The second half-hour section of this programme, 10.31–10.59, was broadcast simultaneously by the BBC's General Overseas Service, including the Beatles' 'All My Loving' and 'This Boy'.

Wednesday 18 December

BBC Paris Studio, London

In the summer the Beatles had enjoyed their own 15-part BBC radio series. This day's recording was for perhaps an even greater honour: their own two-hour special, to be broadcast in the Light Programme on Boxing Day "bank holiday", Thursday 26 December 1963, between 10.00 am and 12.00 noon.

The programme was conceived under the working title *Beatletime*, but this was altered to *From Us To You* before the recording. Since every 1960s pop programme had to have a signature tune, the Beatles' first task at this 7.00–10.30 pm session (inclusive of rehearsal time) was to tape a new, slightly amended version of their former number one hit 'From Me To You', turning it into 'From *Us* To You', with other lyrics altered where appropriate. A 55-second version opened the show, another closed it two hours later.

Taping 'This Boy' for the Christmas Saturday Club, *17 December 1963, at the end of "a really gear year".*

In between, listeners heard the Beatles perform 'She Loves You', 'All My Loving', 'Roll Over Beethoven', 'Till There Was You', 'Boys', 'Money (That's What I Want)', 'I Saw Her Standing There' and 'I Want To Hold Your Hand'. The show was hosted by Australian singer/entertainer Rolf Harris, also set to appear with the Beatles in their forthcoming Christmas stage production, and the Beatles joined Rolf for a humorous, Beatleised version of his 1960 chart hit 'Tie Me Kangaroo Down Sport', Rolf's new lyrics referring to the Beatles' long hair and their Christian names.

From Us To You was the first of five BBC radio "bank holiday" specials over the next 18 months to feature the Beatles, four going under this title. Typically, though, they were never the only act on the show. On this occasion the programme also featured sessions by Susan Maughan, Jeanie Lambe, Kenny Lynch, Joe Brown and the Bruvvers, the Kenny Salmon Seven, Alan Elsdon's Jazzband with Mick Emery, and Rolf Harris.

Note: not wishing to be outdone, the British service of Radio Luxembourg launched *It's The Beatles* on 23 December, a 15-part series of 15-minute programmes broadcast each Monday evening from 9.00 to 9.15 until 30 March, presented by Peter Carver. But the group did not specifically contribute any interviews or music material, the series merely airing their disc releases.

Saturday 21 December

Gaumont Cinema, Bradford

The first of two special northern previews of "The Beatles' Christmas Show", although in concert form only – without the elaborate costumes and inelaborate comedy sketches, and the almost extravagant stage sets, still being assembled in London.

Sunday 22 December

Empire Theatre, Liverpool

The second concert-form-only presentation of "The Beatles' Christmas Show".

Tuesday 24 – Tuesday 31 December

Astoria Cinema, Seven Sisters Rd, Finsbury Park, London

This stage production, "The Beatles' Christmas Show", conceived and presented by Brian Epstein, and typical of the man, encompassed comedy, pantomime and music. It settled in at the Astoria for a 16-night run, two "houses" each except for 24 and 31 December when there was only one. (There were no shows at all on 25 and 29 December and 5 January, and the season ended on Saturday 11 January 1964.) One hundred thousand tickets for the 30 shows went on sale on 21 October. By 16 November they were all sold.

The Beatles' music repertoire for the season comprised 'Roll Over Beethoven', 'All My Loving', 'This Boy', 'I Wanna Be Your Man', 'She Loves You', 'Till There Was You', 'I Want To Hold Your Hand' 'Money (That's What I Want)' and 'Twist And Shout'. They also participated in a number of sketches and routines which proved extremely popular with the audiences.

The Beatles and other northern-based members of the large cast, most of whom were managed by Brian Epstein's NEMS Enterprises, flew home to Liverpool late on 24 December to spend Christmas with their families, returning to London during Boxing Day morning.

O**N 14 JANUARY,** after the final ten nights of "The Beatles' Christmas Show" and a return spot on the live ATV show *Val Parnell's Sunday Night At The London Palladium*, the Beatles – minus Ringo who was fogbound in Liverpool – set out for Paris and a marathon season at the Olympia Theatre. Accompanied by Neil Aspinall, Ringo followed a day later, arriving just in time for the group's first performance in France, a dress-rehearsal for the Olympia held at the Cinéma Cyrano in Versailles.

The night was not a success, however, and the Beatles were far from pleased with not only the French organisation but also their own performance. The opening night at the Olympia, on 16 January, was no better – their amplification equipment broke down three times and George, for one, suspected sabotage. The audience at this opening Olympia show mostly comprised the Paris society set, in full evening regalia, and there was clearly little mutual affection between them and the four Liverpudlians. The Beatles received a cool reception and, as this was also the show attended by representatives of the French press, the reviews were similarly frosty. Brian Somerville, the Beatles' new press officer, even had to create a ham-fisted rumpus backstage in order to generate extra publicity.

Although somewhat slighted by this unexpected hiatus in their overwhelming climb to success, the Beatles actually couldn't much care. For upon returning to their suite at the George V hotel they received a telegram carrying advance news of the following week's singles chart in *Cashbox* (one of two American record-industry journals): 'I Want To Hold Your Hand' had jumped from 43 straight to number one.

This, above all else, was the breakthrough for which Brian Epstein and the Beatles had been waiting; apart from isolated incidents, no British act had ever broken through in the USA. After just three days, 'I Want To Hold Your Hand' had sold 250,000 copies across the States, by 10 January sales had topped one million, by 13 January it was selling 10,000 copies an hour in New York City alone. And the fact that there were two labels other than Capitol – Vee Jay and Swan – both pushing Beatles discs onto the market at the same time (with at least two other labels, Liberty and Laurie, ruing their decision to reject 'Please Please Me' before it got to Vee Jay) meant that all of their 1963 singles and two albums were quickly crashing onto the American charts at an incredible rate.

And all this was happening just days before the Beatles' visit to New York, set up three months previously, to appear on nationwide television via *The Ed Sullivan Show*. The coincidence – for it was nothing more – was truly fantastic.

While the UK press, not untypically, having set 'the Beatles upon a pedestal were now seeking to topple them, the American press was suddenly insatiable for news of the British pop group which had gripped the nation's youth. Top US reporters flocked to Paris to see and interview them.

Brian Epstein had a visitor too: Norman Weiss, a New York theatrical agent. Weiss worked for General Artists Corporation and was in Paris as the manager of Trini Lopez, also on the Beatles' bill at the Olympia. As an independent promoter under his company Theatre Three Productions, Sid Bernstein – Weiss's associate at GAC – had for some time been keen to book the Beatles into New York's Carnegie Hall. He had even tentatively reserved a date, 12 February, but Epstein had been loath to commit the Beatles to the booking until the time was right. Now it was right, and Weiss, on Bernstein's behalf, concluded the arrangements with Epstein in Paris. For a total fee of $7000, the Beatles were booked for two shows, then, under the GAC umbrella, Weiss also signed them for a single appearance in Washington DC on 11 February. On 3 February, shortly before the end of an uneventful three weeks at the Olympia, the Beatles visited the American Embassy in Paris and obtained the visas and permits necessary to visit and work in the United States. On the 5th they returned to England.

Two days later, on Friday 7 February, at 1.20 pm local time, the Pan American Boeing 707, PA 101, carrying among its passengers the four celebrated young men from Liverpool, touched down at the newly re-named John F Kennedy International Airport in New York. The reception that greeted them was startling – even by the exaggerated standards of Beatlemania. Three thousand lusty screams rained down upon the four Beatles, each of whom was pondering why they should be so welcomed. Did not America have all the stars it needed? Had not America created the very music which had inspired and influenced the Beatles in the first place? All they were doing, surely, was giving back to the Americans what they already had.

What the Beatles didn't realise was that America, in her post-Kennedy assassination gloom, was more than ready to embrace this welcome diversion. Virtually the entire

Photographed by United Press International Candid Camera Team. **EXCLUSIVE**

Written by RALPH COSHAM in New York 2/6
Over 60 illustrations

population – as preposterous as it may now seem – succumbed to the Beatles in a typically uncompromising, all-enthusiastic manner.

On 9 February, before an extremely live audience of 728 frantic New York teenagers, the Beatles gave their first live performance on *The Ed Sullivan Show*. The A C Nielsen ratings reported that 23,240,000 households saw the broadcast, something like 73 million people, smashing the previous world record for the largest-ever TV audience. Two days after that, amid scenes of utter pandemonium, the Beatles stepped on stage at the Washington Coliseum and gave their first live concert performance in the United States. Then, 24 hours later, a similarly frenzied reception greeted their two shows at the famous Carnegie Hall, where – to ensure that the Beatles remained physically unscathed – 362 policemen had to be employed.

When the Beatles flew out of America on Friday 21 February they left behind them a nation truly besotted – a fact as inexplicable as it was improbable. But Brian Epstein, who had conceived the visit in his own inimitable fashion – weighing up, as no other manager would, the value of a cut-price television appearance against its great promotional value – moved swiftly to reject the tidal-wave of offers for an immediate return visit. Fearing over-exposure, and cognisant of other demands, the Beatles did not return to North America until August.

If 1963 had been the year in which the Beatles conquered Britain, then in 1964 they conquered the world. With immortality at home already assured, manager Brian Epstein began to look elsewhere. On 9 March, sitting at his desk in NEMS' new London office (situated, not unintentionally, next to the London Palladium), he surveyed bookings from Australasia, the Netherlands, Denmark, Hong Kong and Sweden. British promoter Arthur Howes was anxious for another domestic tour, and Epstein also wanted to stage a second Christmas show. Somehow, the Beatles accomplished all of this, and also recorded two albums, singles, and made a film.

On Monday 2 March, just nine days after their return from the USA, the Beatles began shooting *A Hard Day's Night*. Almost without exception, films starring pop musicians, American as well as British, had an abysmal track record. Ever low-budget but with quick exploitative profits

in mind, they were mostly an insult to intelligence. The Beatles' film, however, was stamped with that hallmark of quality which typified everything that they touched. Though made with that same small budget (£180,000), financed by a company (United Artists) which saw it as just another exploitation piece, and though shot over a mere eight weeks, the *cinéma-vérité*, semi-documentary *A Hard Day's Night* was a classic of its kind, a piece of Art which truly captured its moment.

Just as Brian Epstein was so clearly the best manager the group could have – the perfect blend of style, vision, naivety and devotion – just as George Martin was the perfect producer for the group – creative, keen to experiment, willing to listen, an expert about music but nicely inexperienced in pop and rock, and a veteran of comedy-sound effects records – just as Dick James was the right music publisher for them – an avuncular and protective man hungry for success – so now they happened upon the virtually unknown film director Richard Lester – observant, witty, prone to the surreal and

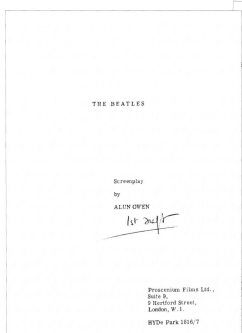

the unexpected and the best man for the job. Lester's direction of A Hard Day's Night was quite superb, as indeed was the script, written – at Brian Epstein's and the Beatles' suggestion – by Alun Owen, a Liverpudlian with numerous TV, radio and stage successes to his credit. Although, years later, John criticised its glib, stereotypical role-casting, the film was, from first to last, immensely watchable, enjoyable, interesting, clever and funny.

Throughout all this time the pace of the Beatles' work – filming, composing, recording, press interviews, live concerts, radio and TV appearances – was awesome, yet never was the quality shown to suffer. On 20 March a new single was released, 'Can't Buy Me Love'. Three days previously EMI announced that, once again, it had received advance orders for more than a million copies in Britain alone. In America the advance sales were 2,100,000. The Beatles were guaranteed another lengthy spell at number one on both sides of the Atlantic; in the States 'Can't Buy Me Love' happily augmented the Beatles' now total domination of the charts which, until so recently, were impenetrable to British artists. The "Hot 100" singles listing for 4 April 1964 published by Billboard (the other US trade journal) showed the Beatles at numbers 1, 2, 3, 4, 5, 31, 41, 46, 58, 65, 68 and 79. A week later two more Beatles singles entered the fray, while in the album charts they held numbers one and two. Furthermore, a number of other British groups were also making headway in the USA, now that the Beatles had made the American audience look to Britain in a new light.

But the Beatles' chart dominance was by no means restricted to the UK or USA. In Australia the group occupied every one of the top six placings on the Sydney singles chart on 3 April 1964, and it was there that the Beatles headed after completing A Hard Day's Night and the album of the same name.

Viewed with hindsight, the Australasian trip was not a particularly happy one for the group. Due to give concerts in Denmark, the Netherlands and Hong Kong en route, Ringo collapsed with tonsillitis and pharyngitis the day before departure, 3 June. It was too late to cancel the tour so there was really only one alternative: to hire a temporary replacement. George, in particular, opposed this idea and said that if Ringo couldn't go then neither would he. Although Epstein and George Martin were able to persuade him otherwise, the Beatles' manager realised that, in what few hours remained, they must recruit a drummer sufficiently inconspicuous and unknown to prevent talk of his employment being anything other than temporary. He and George Martin immediately thought of Jimmy Nicol, who led his own group, the Shubdubs, assigned to the Pye label. Nicol had been around for several years, beginning his career as a drum repairer for Boosey and Hawkes and then playing with, among others, Georgie Fame's Blue Flames. As a session musician he had recently backed Epstein-protégé Tommy Quickly and had also played on an anonymous cover version LP called Beatlemania, released on the budget label Top Six. At least he would be familiar with the Beatles' material.

Later that morning George Martin telephoned Nicol and summoned him to EMI Studios for a 3.00 pm session with the group. They rehearsed six numbers and 18 hours later

John, Paul, George and Jimmy were on their way to Denmark, and from there to the Netherlands, Hong Kong and Down Under.

The Beatles' reception in Australia was, if anything, more riotous than their American welcome four months previously. Manic scenes preceded and then accompanied their every move throughout the tour. Many were hurt in the 24-hour-a-day chaos, and the Beatles, paraded before a seemingly endless procession of mayors, civic dignitaries, airport receptions, press conferences, street receptions and shrieking audiences, were pulled and pushed, shoved, grabbed and screamed at from close proximity throughout the entire trip. Despite the occasional fun moments they were beginning to loathe the whole charade. In Adelaide a crowd estimated at 300,000 congregated outside the Beatles' hotel in the hope of a balcony appearance akin to the royal wave at Buckingham Palace, while in Melbourne there was a gathering of 250,000. The Beatles viewed these scenes as potential Third Reich rallies so John would lead the others into a quick Sieg Heil, using black combs to parody Adolf Hitler's toothbrush moustache.

It was in Melbourne, on 14 June, that Ringo reunited with the Beatles, having left his London hospital on the morning of the 11th temporarily cured of tonsillitis (the tonsils were finally removed on 2 December) and flown out via San Francisco, Honolulu, Fiji and Sydney. His arrival marked the end of Jimmy Nicol's short stint as a Beatle and little was ever heard of him again. Apart from immortality, his short innings with the group brought him a fee of £500 plus expenses, and a gold Eternamatic wrist-watch inscribed "From the Beatles and Brian Epstein to Jimmy – with appreciation and gratitude".

The concerts of the Australasian tour grossed over £200,000, were seen by almost 200,000 people and smashed several concert-attendance records. But the Beatles never went back. They returned to London and the 6 July royal world charity premiere of A Hard Day's Night at the London Pavilion, for which Piccadilly Circus and the surrounding streets were closed by the police in anticipation of the seething 12,000 crowd hoping to see the Beatles arrive. The film drew universally ecstatic reviews, even from the "serious newspapers" whose critics were expecting another dirge-like B-movie. Four days later, on 10 July, the Beatles travelled to

Liverpool for the northern premiere. Prior to the screening they were afforded a civic reception at the Town Hall, and before that were driven into the city centre from Liverpool airport along a pre-arranged route. Some 200,000 people, more than one in four of all Liverpudlians, lined the route while outside the Town Hall 20,000 more were gathered.

And along with the film came the album of the same name, comprising the seven new songs from the soundtrack and six others. During the incessant madness of Beatlemania and touring, Lennon-McCartney had somehow composed 13 new high-quality songs, a truly remarkable achievement. The album, and accompanying single, breezed to the top of the charts all over the world.

'HERE THEY COME
THE FABULOUS'

BEATLES

American Tour 1964

Aug 19 San Francisco Cow Palace	Sept 4 Milwaukee Auditorium
Aug 20 Las Vegas Convention Hall	Sept 5 Chicago International Amphitheater
Aug 21 Seattle Municiple Stadium	Sept 6 Detroit Olympia Stadium
Aug 22 Vancouver Empire Stadium	Sept 7 Toronto Maple Leaf Gardens
Aug 23 Hollywood Bowl	Sept 8 Montreal Forum
Aug 26 Denver Red Rock Stadium	Sept 11 Jacksonville Gaiter Bowl, Florida
Aug 27 Cincinatti Gardens	Sept 12 Boston Gardens
Aug 28 New York Forest Hills Tennis Stadium	Sept 13 Baltimore Civic Center
Aug 29 New York Forest Hills Tennis Stadium	Sept 14 Pittsburgh Civic Arena
Aug 30 Atlantic City Convention Hall N.J.	Sept 15 Cleveland Public Auditorium
Sept 2 Philadelphia Convention Hall	Sept 16 New Orleans City Park Stadium
Sept 3 Indianapolis State Fair Coliseum	Sept 18 Dallas Memorial Coliseum

HEAR THE BEATLES GREATEST HITS ON CAPITAL RECORDS

In August, following some British stage appearances and a second trip to Sweden, the Beatles headed back to the United States for their first nationwide trek, the tour which, for Americans, will be remembered above all others, just as the group's November/December 1963 tour of their home-land will be remembered in Britain. And a trek it certainly was: 32 shows at 26 concerts in 24 cities in 34 days. That sort of itinerary, commonplace in Britain, was absurd in a land the size of America and the Beatles spent almost the entire trip on airplanes, in hotels, in limousines, enduring one-a-city press conferences, and being smuggled in and out of towns and arenas. It earned them a veritable fortune (and, therefore, the close attention of the Internal Revenue Service) but half the time they wouldn't even know which city they were in. So incessant were the scenes of rampaging Beatlemania that to try and detail every incident would be

impossible. There are, however, a few anecdotes which encapsulate the mayhem surrounding the Beatles during those 34 days in America.

They arrived in the USA in San Francisco on 18 August to a frenzied airport reception from 9000 delirious fans. Still on the tarmac, they were herded into a limousine and driven 50 yards into a protective fenced enclosure within which press photographers could take pictures. Suddenly the 9000 fans, pressed all around the fencing, began to push, many fainting in the crush. The Beatles managed to escape split-seconds before the assemblage collapsed under the feet of shrieking fans. From there, visibly shaken, the Beatles were whisked to their 15th-floor luxury suite at the city's Hilton Hotel, under siege not only from fans but also armed police-men and security guards. Still, on the sixth level, a middle-aged woman was slugged unconscious and robbed, her pleas for help ignored in the belief that she was another screaming Beatles fan.

During the course of the Beatles' concert in San Francisco, Brian Epstein was visited by Charles O Finley, the millionaire owner and president of the Kansas City Athletics baseball team. Finley was disappointed that Kansas City hadn't been included in the tour itinerary and had vowed to the city that he would somehow get the Beatles to play there. He offered Brian Epstein first $50,000 and then $100,000 for one concert but was refused both times. It could only be arranged for 17 September but this was designated as a rest day to enable the Beatles to visit New Orleans. But Finley was persistent, and eventually, in Los Angeles, came his breakthrough: in Epstein's face he tore up the $100,000 cheque, tossed it into an ashtray and wrote out another for $150,000, a record fee paid in America for one show. Epstein told Finley to wait a moment while he talked it over with "the boys". The boys were in the middle of another interminable card game when Epstein walked in and showed them the cheque. "What do you want to do about it?" he asked. With the other three nodding in agreement, John – hardly bothering to look up – simply shrugged his shoulders and replied, "We'll do whatever you want". Epstein went back to Finley and accepted. For that one night the Beatles reluctantly earned $4838 per minute. It was, remember, just 13 months after they had last played at the Cavern Club.

After the Beatles left Kansas City the manager of their hotel sold all of their bed linen – 16 sheets and eight pillow-slips – to two Chicago businessmen for $750. Unlaundered, it was then cut into three-inch squares, mounted on a card and sold with a legal affidavit at $10 a time. The towels used by the Beatles to mop their faces immediately after their Hollywood Bowl concert on 23 August were similarly cut into portions and sold. In New York City cans of "Beatle Breath" were on sale and requests were received for the Beatles' bathwater and used shaving foam. Meanwhile, back-stage at several concerts, disabled people were wheeled into the Beatles' dressing rooms to meet the group and receive a Messianic healing touch from the hand of one of the four Liverpudlians. The Beatles were appalled.

On 1 September, after their show in Atlantic City, the Beatles had a clear two-day break before their next engage-ment but were unable to leave their hotel because of the

pandemonium outside. The tension *inside* was electric. Before the second of their two shows at the Convention Center in Las Vegas the management received an anonymous bomb scare so the Beatles had to play in the knowledge that at any second they could be killed. And one proven successful astrologer hit the headlines when she predicted that the Beatles' chartered airplane, hired by Brian Epstein for the tour at a cost of $37,950.50, would crash en route from Philadelphia to Indianapolis with no survivors. (She was nearly right: the airplane crashed in April 1966, killing more than 80 soldiers.)

The tour eventually ended on Sunday 20 September with a charity performance in New York City. Tempers frayed in the audience when elegantly-dressed socialites mingled with screaming teenagers while, on stage, the Beatles were disgusted by probably the worst amplification system they ever had the misfortune to use. They flew home to London the next day having spent over 63 hours travelling 22,621 miles since 18 August (22,441 in the air, 180 on the road). Never again would they undertake such a tour.

Nineteen days later, however, on 9 October, the Beatles were off again – this time on their first and only British tour of 1964. Announced back in April to appease the home-based fans, it consisted of 54 shows at 27 concerts in 25 cities in 33 days. The Beatlemania was, of course, the same – only on a smaller scale than it had been in America. The Beatles' sense of "imprisonment", though, was as great. Once again, the tour visited most major British towns and cities, playing the Gaumont, ABC and Granada cinema circuits. But a cinema rarely held more than 3000 people, often less, and thousands of disappointed fans were unable to obtain tickets.

The tumultuous year of 1964 ended with the Beatles atop the worldwide singles charts with 'I Feel Fine' and at number one in the LP charts with yet another new offering, *Beatles For Sale*, somehow recorded in between one activity or another. (In America, where Capitol contrived to release 18 Beatles albums from 1964 to 1970 in place of the 12 in Britain – without using any extra tracks except singles – it was titled *Beatles '65*.) On stage at the Hammersmith Odeon in London, the Beatles were involved in "Another Beatles' Christmas Show": 132,240 tickets had gone on sale on 7 September and every one was sold.

It had been quite a year, but never, never again.

Fame, touring, and the tiresome, endless meetings with mayors and holding of children. John's face says it all.

1964

Wednesday 1 – Saturday 11 January

Astoria Cinema, Finsbury Park, London

Sunday 5 January

Green Street, London

Tuesday 7 January

Playhouse Theatre, London

The Astoria dates comprised the last ten nights (5 January was a rest day) of "The Beatles' Christmas Show", which had opened on 24 December 1963.

At some point on 5 January (time unknown, the location was either Tony Hall's or George and Ringo's flat, situated on opposite sides of Green Street in central London), George and Ringo made an unusual radio recording for broadcast in the Light Programme magazine series *The Public Ear* on Sunday 12 January (3.00–4.00 pm). It took the form of a letter they had written, recorded onto tape and played in the programme's regular "Air Mail" slot. In the letter, the two Beatles referred to a previous edition of the series (29 December) in which friend Hall had encouraged listeners to appreciate the music that the Beatles themselves preferred, principally American R&B.

This new contribution from George and Ringo echoed Hall's sentiments, and requested a song to be played (the Miracles' 'I've Been Good To You' was chosen). At least two takes were attempted. Listing his favourite artists, George said "...Mary Wells, Miracles, not to mention Marvin Gaye." This was the cue for Ringo to butt in "Marvin Gaye?" and George to reply "I told you not to mention Marvin Gaye!" In the first take, Ringo missed his cue, prompting amusing admonishing at the end; in the second he got it right. (The former was broadcast on 12 January, the second finally made it onto

the air in 1972, in the BBC Radio 1 documentary series *The Beatles Story*.)

On 7 January the Beatles, as a group, made a more conventional BBC radio recording, a music session for *Saturday Club*, broadcast in the Light Programme on 15 February 1964 between 10.00 am and 12.00 noon, while they were in the USA. Inclusive of rehearsal time, recording took place at the Playhouse Theatre between 2.30 and 4.00 pm. They then nipped up to Finsbury Park for their two evening "Christmas Show" performances.

The Beatles taped seven numbers for broadcast: 'All My Loving', 'Money (That's What I Want)', 'The Hippy Hippy Shake', 'I Want To Hold Your Hand', 'Roll Over Beethoven', 'Johnny B Goode' and 'I Wanna Be Your Man'. The first two of these were included in the 10.31–10.59 am section broadcast simultaneously by the BBC's General Overseas Service.

Sunday 12 January

London Palladium, London

A return booking for the Beatles on the live Associated TeleVision show *Val Parnell's Sunday Night At The London Palladium*, following their auspicious début on 13 October 1963. Their fee then was £250, now it was £1000.

The group spent most of the day at the Palladium, taking part in rehearsals. The live broadcast went out from 8.25 to 9.25 pm, the Beatles – as bill-topping act – appearing in a card-carrying skit with compere Bruce Forsyth and, at the end of the show, performing a five-song set comprising 'I Want To Hold Your Hand', 'This Boy', 'All My Loving', 'Money (That's What I Want)' and 'Twist And Shout'.

Other artists on the programme were singer Alma Cogan (with whom the Beatles would enjoy a warm friendship up to her death in 1966) and Irish comedian Dave Allen (who had first met the Beatles when he compered their début package tour, with Helen Shapiro in February 1963). The Beatles joined Forsyth, Cogan and Allen on the revolving podium for the traditional waved finale to the tune of 'Startime'.

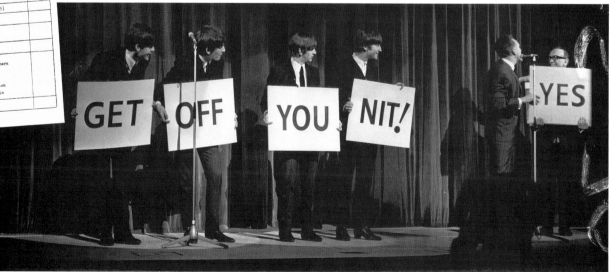

Wednesday 15 January

Cinéma Cyrano, Rue Rameau, Versailles, France

The Beatles' first night in France was a warm-up show for all of the artists participating in the forthcoming three-week season at the Paris Olympia, performed before 2000 people.

The Beatles had enjoyed a rare day off on the 13th. On the night of the 14th John, Paul and George (Ringo followed the next day) flew out of London Airport for Le Bourget, Paris, and a welcome from 60 French teenagers.

Thurs 16 Jan – Tues 4 Feb

Olympia Theatre, Boulevard des Capucines, Paris, France

Wednesday 29 January

Pathé Marconi Studios, Rue de Sevres, Boulogne-sur-Seine, Paris, France

A marathon concert season at the Olympia – 18 days of two, sometimes three (such as on 19 January), shows each, on a nine-act bill. At no time was it made clear who was headlining: the Beatles, French *chanteuse* Sylvie Vartan, or Trini Lopez, the US singer famous for 'If I Had A Hammer', although it was the Beatles who closed each performance, with a repertoire comprising 'From Me To You', 'Roll Over Beethoven', 'She Loves You', 'This Boy', 'Boys', 'I Want To Hold Your Hand', 'Twist And Shout' and 'Long Tall Sally'. (For some matinée performances they delivered a shorter set.) There were only two days of rest in the three-week season – the first two Tuesdays, the 21st and 28th – and on the second of these John and George flew back to London for a few hours.

A part of the matinée performance on Sunday 19 January was broadcast live by the French radio station Europe 1 in its programme *Musicorama*, 1.00–2.00 pm. Listeners heard Trini Lopez, Sylvie Vartan and then five songs by the Beatles: 'From Me To You', 'This Boy', 'I Want To Hold Your Hand', 'She Loves You' and 'Twist And Shout'.

A short interview with the Beatles was broadcast by Europe 1 the following day, Monday 20 January, probably in Robert Marcy's programme (12.00 noon–12.30 pm). (Further details have proven impossible to research.)

The Beatles *nearly* made an appearance on the French television programme *Age Tendre et Tête de Bois*, broadcast from 8.30–9.15 pm on Wednesday 22 January (at this time there was only one TV channel in France). The national listings journal *Télérama* described their booking for this show as provisional, subject to confirmation. In fact, they never appeared.

On Friday 24 January the Beatles went to a Paris studio and recorded a radio interview for AFN (the American Forces Network), broadcast the next day – on a programme entitled *Weekend World* – to US troops stationed in West Germany. (AFN broadcasts could also be received in Britain on 344m, but only from 6.00 pm. This was transmitted earlier in the day.)

From 10.00 to 10.45 am this same Friday the 24th, back at Abbey Road in London, balance engineer Norman Smith made a tape-to-tape copy of the 'I Want To Hold Your Hand' rhythm track, take 17 from 17 October 1963. He and George Martin took it over to France for the group's first and only EMI session outside of England – for, during the late-morning and early-afternoon of 29 January (more precise timings not available), the Beatles could be found in a French recording studio taping their two most famous songs to date in German.

EMI's West German branch, Electrola Gesellschaft, had been making overtures to Brian Epstein and George Martin for the group to record in the vernacular, insisting that they would be unable to sell sizable quantities of Beatles records unless they were sung in the local language. The Beatles needed some persuading that this was so, but eventually relented and recorded 'Sie Liebt Dich' ('She Loves You') and 'Komm, Gib Mir Deine Hand' ('I Want To Hold Your Hand') on this day. Electrola sent over a translator to coach John, Paul and George, although the three were familiar with German having lived in Hamburg for so long during 1960–1962.

'Komm, Gib Mir Deine Hand' was completed in 11 takes, the German-language vocals being added to the copy of the 17 October 1963 rhythm track, and the master being prepared by editing takes five and seven. For 'Sie Liebt Dich' the group recorded the entire song anew, completing it in 14 takes. This work must have been done well within the allotted time for – apart from the fact that a second session, booked for 31 January, could now be cancelled – the Beatles also recorded another song, in English this time, Paul's 'Can't Buy Me Love'. Four takes were taped, completing the recording but for a lead guitar overdub by George and a vocal overdub by Paul effected at Abbey Road on 25 February.

At 1.00 pm on Wednesday 5 February the four Beatles returned to London Airport from Le Bourget to a boisterous reception from 100 schoolgirls, obviously well versed in the art of truancy.

Playing to a not-so-responsive and predominantly male audience at the Paris Olympia, 16 January 1964.

*Top-left, facing page:
Paul, Ringo, Neil and John,
in rehearsal for
The Ed Sullivan Show.*

Friday 7 – Saturday 22 February

various US locations

Right from the moment that their Pan Am flight touched down at John F Kennedy International Airport, the Beatles were subjected to every form of media exposure known in 1964: journalists, photographers, radio stations and TV news crews covered their every single move, many with live reports. Hundreds of people were clamouring, constantly, for their attention if only for a few seconds, in person, by phone, by any means imaginable.

In addition to all of this, and with the express permission of Brian Epstein and the Beatles, film cameras were documenting the group's first US visit from an exclusive vantage point: *inside* their entourage. This was a complicated production, with Granada Television – the north of England ITV franchise – chipping in financially, Epstein's NEMS company retaining some form of editorial control and Albert and David Maysles producing the documentary for their own company Maysles Films. (Five years later they were to direct the Rolling Stones' *Gimme Shelter*.) The Maysles took their cameras virtually everywhere that the Beatles went during these remarkable two weeks in America: not only at Kennedy Airport but inside the group's Plaza suite, inside their limousines, at a photo shoot in Central Park, at New York rehearsals for *The Ed Sullivan Show*, at the Peppermint Lounge night club, on the train down to Washington DC and in Miami Beach. The Maysles also filmed Brian Epstein conducting business, Beatles-mad radio disc-jockey Murray The K broadcasting on New York station 1010 WINS, and a New York family watching the Beatles' début on *The Ed Sullivan Show*.

Granada was quick to capitalise upon its involvement and rushed footage from the first few days back to England for immediate screening. Advertised schedules for the night of Wednesday 12 February were hastily re-arranged by every one of the ITV stations in Britain so that Granada could network *Yeah! Yeah! Yeah! The Beatles In New York* (also known as *Yeah! Yeah! Yeah! New York Meets The Beatles*) from 10.25 to 11.05 pm, a 40-minute slot for a film that lasted 36 mins 25 secs.

Meanwhile, the Maysles continued shooting. Viewers in Britain never got to see any of the remaining footage, but Americans did on Friday 13 November 1964 when CBS broadcast *The Beatles In America* (also known as both *What's Happening! The Beatles In The USA* and *The Beatles In New York*), presented by Carol Burnett as part of the weekly documentary series *The Entertainers*. The 45-minute programme was broadcast, with commercials, from 8.30–9.30 EST (Eastern Standard Time) and it featured footage shot all the way through to the Beatles' arrival back in England on 22 February.

One of the first events filmed by the Maysles occurred at around 6.00 pm on Friday 7 February, when – in their 12th floor suite at the Plaza Hotel – the Beatles received a pre-arranged telephone call from the BBC presenter Brian Matthew. Back in England, at Broadcasting House in London, it was 11.00 pm, and Matthew was due on air a few

hours later with that week's edition of *Saturday Club*. But tiredness mattered not one jot: the Beatles' sensational reception in the United States, unprecedented for a British act, was such hot news at home that he stayed up to record telephone interviews with Paul, John, Ringo and George for inclusion in the next morning's show. Typifying the degree of coverage afforded the Beatles at this time, as well as being taped "down the line" and filmed by the Maysles, the interviews were recorded in the Beatles' hotel suite by another BBC radio correspondent, Malcolm Davis, and then sent over to England again via a later New York-London "circuit", allowing for improved audio signals. Matthew then re-taped his own side of the conversation the following morning, ensuring best quality.

These interviews, and a separate report from Malcolm Davis, were duly broadcast in *Saturday Club* on 8 February. (Davis's report included on-the-spot accounts of the events at Kennedy Airport and the Plaza Hotel, interviews with fans and with Murray The K and brief extracts from Matthew's interviews.) The full interviews were transmitted as the concluding item in the part of the show, up to 11.00 am, simultaneously broadcast by the GOS. Davis's piece then ran at the end of the entire two hours, between 11.50 and 12.00 noon, when an audience of approximately 11 million – one fifth of the United Kingdom population – was listening.

Saturday 8 February

**Studio 50, Broadway and West 53rd St,
New York City, New York, USA**

The first of what would be several studio rehearsals by the Beatles for *The Ed Sullivan Show*, and another opportunity for the hordes of US radio and press reporters to gain access to the group. This one began at 1.30 pm. These rehearsals, plus the two next-day actual performances, took place inside CBS Television's Studio 50 in midtown Manhattan.

Sunday 9 February

Studio 50, New York City, USA

In the morning there was yet another Studio 50 rehearsal for *The Ed Sullivan Show*. George was unwell and did not participate; in his stead, the cameras rehearsed their positioning with a stand-in, the Beatles' assistant Neil Aspinall.

During the afternoon, before their celebrated live *Sullivan* début that evening, the Beatles – with George – taped the appearance, ostensibly their third, that would be screened after their departure from America, on Sunday 23 February (8.00–9.00 pm, EST). For this, before a different audience from that which would attend the evening performance, they played just three numbers: first 'Twist And Shout' and 'Please Please Me' and then, in a different setting for inclusion later in this programme, 'I Want To Hold Your Hand'. Before any of this happened, though, Sullivan claimed the spotlight and delivered one of his haughty pronouncements that summed up US reaction to this first Beatles visit:

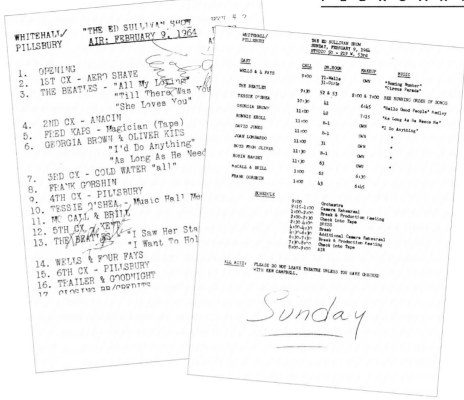

"All of us on the show are so darned sorry, and sincerely sorry, that this is the third and thus our last current show with the Beatles, because these youngsters from Liverpool, England, and their conduct over here, not only as fine professional singers but as a group of fine youngsters, will leave an imprint of everyone over here who's met them…"

Along with the Beatles, this edition featured Cab Calloway and Gordon and Sheila MacRae, and the programme was repeated on Sunday 23 August 1964 (8.00–9.00 pm, EST).

The first and most famous of the Beatles' two live *Sullivan* transmissions was performed in front of a Studio 50 audience of 728, and an estimated 73 million people in 23,240,000 homes across the United States, tuning in from 8.00–9.00 pm, EST. It was easily the highest US TV audience figure amassed to that time.

for your recent request for tickets to THE ED SULLIVAN SHOW & REH. FOR FEB. 9, 1964

We appreciate your interest and are sorry to tell you that so many ticket requests already have been received that we are unable to send you any at this time.

Ticket Bureau, CBS Television Network
485 Madison Avenue, New York 22, New York

The Beatles performed five songs, three at the beginning of the show, 'All My Loving', 'Till There Was You' and 'She Loves You', and two in the second-half in a different setting, 'I Saw Her Standing There' and 'I Want To Hold Your Hand'. It was a daunting yet remarkably confident performance, marred only slightly by an awkward sound balance. During 'Till There Was You', each of the Beatles came in for individual camera attention, at which point his christian name appeared on screen. When it came to John, an additional caption read "Sorry Girls, He's Married".

As it transpired, this edition of *The Ed Sullivan Show* had a pronounced British slant, for apart from the Beatles it also featured singer/banjoist Tessie O' Shea and the New York cast of Lionel Bart's London musical *Oliver*, starring Georgia Brown and – as the Artful Dodger – Davy Jones, the future member of the Monkees. (Another guest act was the

American impressionist Frank Gorshin, later to appear as The Riddler in the *Batman* TV series.)

This celebrated edition of *The Ed Sullivan Show* was repeated on Sunday 12 July 1964 (8.00–9.00 pm, EST), while highlights from the Beatles' sequences went into *The Ed Sullivan Show: The Swinging Soulful Sixties*, a retrospective of musical moments from Sullivan's shows throughout the decade, broadcast by CBS on Sunday 21 December 1969 (again, 8.00–9.00 pm, EST).

Tuesday 11 February

Washington Coliseum, Third and M St North East, Washington DC, USA

Early on this day the Beatles travelled by train from New York to Washington DC, and at 8.31 pm stepped on stage at the 8092-seat Coliseum to give their first concert in North America. For the next half-hour, a manic audience was treated to 'Roll Over Beethoven', 'From Me To You', 'I Saw Her Standing There', 'This Boy', 'All My Loving', 'I Wanna Be Your Man', 'Please Please Me', 'Till There Was You', 'She Loves You', 'I Want To Hold Your Hand', 'Twist And Shout' and 'Long Tall Sally'.

With Brian Epstein's consent, the performance was shot by CBS and shown by National General Corporation – together with unrelated footage of the Beach Boys and Lesley Gore – in cinemas across the USA as a closed-circuit telecast on Saturday 14 and Sunday 15 March, two matinee screenings each day. Though 'Long Tall Sally' was omitted at editing stage, rarely did concert footage of the Beatles capture the excitement so evidently as this, or so humorously highlight the crude stage setting with which the Beatles were content to contend. The film starts with the Beatles having made their entrance but Ringo attempting to re-position his drum kit. George switched his microphone at the end of the first verse of the opening number because it wasn't working, only to find a faulty replacement. After the third song, all the Beatles turned 180 degrees – Mal Evans revolving Ringo's kit – in order to face the audience which had been behind them; this exercise was then repeated at the end of the sixth number while, at the end of the ninth, they all turned again, 45 degrees this time, to face the side audience.

Wednesday 12 February

Carnegie Hall, 7th Ave and West 57th St, New York City, New York, USA

The Beatles returned this day to New York, again travelling by train, and gave two 34-minute shows at the famed Carnegie Hall, at 7.45 and 11.15 pm, with a capacity audience of 2900 at each. Tickets went on sale at the theatre's box-office on 27 January and were sold by the next day. Such was the demand that seating was allocated on stage with the Beatles, on their left and right flanks and behind them.

A plan by Capitol Records to record these two shows was thwarted by the American Federation of Musicians. With greater time to solve the union problems, however, Capitol succeeded in gaining AFM permission to tape their Hollywood Bowl shows on 23 August 1964 and 29/30 August 1965 (see separate entries).

Friday 14 February

Deauville Hotel, Collins Ave, Miami Beach, Florida, USA

Sunday's second live appearance on *The Ed Sullivan Show* was set to be broadcast direct from the Deauville Hotel in Miami Beach, so the Beatles flew from New York to the Florida city on Thursday 13 February, in the hope of catching a few days' rest in between the (surprisingly numerous) TV rehearsals. The first of these took place this day, in the hotel. As for the much-needed rest, Beatlemania ensured that this was well-nigh impossible.

Saturday 15 February

Deauville Hotel, Miami Beach, USA

A full afternoon rehearsal for *The Ed Sullivan Show*.

A telephone interview with the Beatles was broadcast this day on Dick Clark's long-running, influential ABC-TV series *American Bandstand* (12.30–1.00 pm, EST). The Beatles never got to appear in person on this show although another phone interview was broadcast two months later, on Saturday 18 April (also 12.30–1.00 pm, EST), and they filmed an interview for screening on *New American Bandstand* on Saturday 10 October 1964 (1.30–2.30 pm, EST), in what was billed as an "all-Beatle program". Recording dates/locations for these cannot be researched.

Sunday 16 February

Deauville Hotel, Miami Beach, USA

The Beatles' second live appearance on *The Ed Sullivan Show* took place during this evening (8.00–9.00 pm, EST) before a 3500 audience at the Deauville Hotel in Miami Beach. Surprisingly, the Beatles did not top the bill on this occasion, that honour going to Mitzi Gaynor. Nonetheless, an estimated 70 million people viewed, in 22,445,000 homes – and it certainly wasn't because of Gaynormania. Another guest on the show was Myra Cohen.

A full dress-rehearsal beginning at 2.00 pm (also taped, but not broadcast) preceded the live TV transmission; in both this and the broadcast the Beatles performed 'She Loves You', 'This Boy', 'All My Loving', 'I Saw Her Standing There', 'From Me To You' and 'I Want To Hold Your Hand'.

This edition of *The Ed Sullivan Show* was repeated on Sunday 20 September 1964 (8.00–9.00 pm, EST).

Following several more days of "rest", the Beatles flew home to England from Miami, via a short stopover in New York, arriving at London Airport at 8.10 am (half an hour later than scheduled) on Saturday 22 February.

Saturday 22 February

Kingsford-Smith Suite, London Airport, Heathrow, Middlesex

The return of the Beatles to England after such an eventful first trip to the USA was deemed a matter of such national importance that BBC footage of their touchdown at London Airport, and an accompanying interview, was slotted into the Saturday afternoon TV sports programme *Grandstand*, broadcast between 1.00 and 5.15 pm. Correspondingly, the interview was conducted by David Coleman, the BBC's premier sports commentator.

The item – not a brief filler but of 13 mins 23 secs duration – was shown along with horse-racing, Eddie Waring commentating on live rugby league from Hunslet, amateur boxing from Cardiff and the classified football results.

The return was, indeed, covered by most film and TV organisations. Pathé News turned its footage into a special *Beatles Welcome Home* report for cinema distribution, narrator Bob Danvers-Walker piling on the puns in best Pathé style, "Never mind crush-barriers, the Beatles' fans would smash the sound-barrier!" And it was covered by radio, too: the Beatles crowded around a telephone at London Airport shortly after landing and were interviewed by Brian Matthew, 4 mins 20 secs of which went into the last 20-minutes of this morning's edition of *Saturday Club*, broadcast, as usual, by the Light Programme from 10.00 am to 12.00 noon. (The interview was followed, incidentally, by a dedication for George's imminent 21st birthday – 'Shop Around' by the Miracles was requested and played – sent in by George's mother!)

The return was also covered by radio news (such coverage is outside the scope of this *Chronicle*) and a brief extract from one such interview, Neville Barker talking to George Harrison, was repeated in *The Public Ear* on Sunday 8 March (3.00–4.00 pm) as part of a feature titled 'Beatlemania'.

Sunday 23 February

Studio One, Teddington Studio Centre, Teddington

Scarcely did the Beatles have time to overcome any jet-lag before they were thrust back into the hurly-burly of homeland activities. This morning they travelled to the Teddington Studio Centre of ABC Television to tape their second appearance on the variety show *Big Night Out*. Following rehearsals, the programme was shot in front of an audience during the evening – and it wasn't until 10.30 pm that the Beatles were able to leave the premises. The programme was transmitted by most of the ITV network the following Saturday, 29 February, 6.35–7.25 pm, although in the London area it was screened the following Tuesday, 3 March, 8.00–8.55 pm (the duration was the same, more commercials and trailers would have occupied the extra five minutes). Other guests on the show were Billy Dainty, Jackie Trent and Lionel Blair.

Viewers saw the Beatles participate in three comedy skits with show hosts Mike and Bernie Winters. One of these took advantage of the group's famous return from the USA, with them filmed sailing in a boat down the adjacent River Thames, alighting at the studio, driving in an open-top car around the studio lot and entering through a door marked "Customs", with the Winters dressed as customs officers. Naturally, they opted to search the group's luggage, finding each suitcase stuffed with cash.

The Beatles also mimed a music set, playing 'All My Loving', 'I Wanna Be Your Man', 'Till There Was You', 'Please Mister Postman', 'Money (That's What I Want)' and 'I Want To Hold Your Hand' ('Money' was omitted from the programme for overseas sales purposes.)

Note: news cameras from ITN filmed the Beatles' River Thames jaunt for its early-evening bulletin (6.05–6.15 pm), and George volunteered to provide the commentary, parodying the annual Oxford v Cambridge boat race broadcasts by John Snagge.

Tuesday 25 February

Studio Two, EMI Studios, London

The Beatles' first feature-film, to begin shooting the following Monday, necessitated the writing and recording of a crop of new Lennon-McCartney songs. Some (for the soundtrack) were required before the film went into production, others (for the tie-in LP) were to be recorded after the film

Hard work at EMI, 25 February 1964. Below: John instructs his fellow Beatles over the control room-to studio talkback.

was completed. So this day saw the first in a new series of EMI sessions. It was also George's 21st birthday.

But the most pressing duty of the day was to finish off, with vocal and guitar overdubs, what would be their next single, 'Can't Buy Me Love', and then tape its B-side, John's 'You Can't Do That', a nine-take recording completed in one session, 10.00 am–1.30 pm.

Between 2.30 and 5.30 pm two film songs were recorded, although both would be re-made this same week: Paul's 'And I Love Her' (two takes) and John's 'I Should Have Known Better' (three).

Wednesday 26 February

Studio Two, EMI Studios, London

This long day at Abbey Road began with a three-hour mono mixing session, 10.00 am–1.00 pm, preparing British and US masters of the single 'Can't Buy Me Love'/'You Can't Do That'. Issued at home on Friday 20 March and in America the previous Monday, the 16th, it seized upon what was now global Beatlemania and sold in immense quantities, topping the charts everywhere. In the USA Capitol shifted more than two million copies within a week, the single earning a gold disc on its day of issue, an unprecedented achievement. In Britain, advance orders alone passed the million mark.

From 2.30 to 5.30 and 7.00 to 10.15 pm, the Beatles turned their attention to re-makes of 'I Should Have Known Better' (takes 4–22) and 'And I Love Her' (3–19), although they ended up leaving this latter title for yet another time and a second re-make.

Thursday 27 February

Studio Two, EMI Studios, London

Two sessions at Abbey Road, 10.00 am–1.00 pm and 2.30–7.15 pm. In two takes of the second re-make, 'And I Love Her' was finally recorded to everyone's satisfaction, and then two more film songs were started and finished, both composed mostly by John: 'Tell Me Why', done in eight takes, and his stunning ballad 'If I Fell', finished in 15.

Friday 28 February

Studio One, BBC Piccadilly Studios, London

Following the success of their initial "bank holiday" special – *From Us To You*, broadcast on 26 December 1963 – the BBC booked the group to headline a second such programme, taped this day and transmitted in the Light Programme under the same title between 10.00 am and 12.00 noon on Easter Monday, 30 March. Recording took place between 6.30 and 9.00 pm (inclusive of rehearsal time) at the Corporation's studios at 201 Piccadilly, central London. (Other guests in the show, booked by the BBC but supposedly at the invitation of the Beatles, included Acker Bilk, the Swinging Blue Jeans and Vince Hill. They were all taped at a different session.)

The Beatles' contribution was the usual mixture of music and wit, the latter surfacing in the form of light-hearted interviews with the programme's host Alan Freeman. Recordings made especially for the show were 'You Can't Do That', 'Roll Over Beethoven', 'Till There Was You', 'I Wanna Be Your Man', 'Please Mister Postman', 'All My Loving', 'This Boy' and 'Can't Buy Me Love'. Additionally, the show opened and closed with an appropriately adapted 55-second recording, 'From Us To You' – however, this was not the version recorded on 18 December 1963 for the first such "bank holiday" special, but a new rendition taped at this 28 February session. (The two subsequent *From Us To You* shows – taped on 1 May and 17 July 1964 – repeated this new version.)

Reaction to the programme was mixed. A BBC audience research report noted, among others, two widely different opinions from members of the public. A security guard considered the Beatles "vastly over-rated; their performance was decidedly amateur, and their entertainment value nil", while a solicitor, self-described as being "over-20", stated "How can anyone fail to like them? Their music is so gay and uninhibited, and they themselves are full of *joie de vivre*."

Sunday I March

Studio Two, EMI Studios, London

The Beatles' first Sunday session for EMI, recording three songs in three hours, 7.00–10.00 pm. The first was 'I'm Happy Just To Dance With You', written by John for George to sing, and recorded in four takes. They then taped two songs which would end up not as part of *A Hard Day's Night* but on an EP: 'Long Tall Sally' and 'I Call Your Name'. (Surviving paperwork suggests that the latter, if not both, were intended for the film soundtrack at this early stage.)

'Long Tall Sally' was a stupendous recording. Just as John had once captured 'Twist And Shout' to perfection in a single take, so Paul, performing his greatest ever Little Richard impersonation, put his all into 'Long Tall Sally' – and, again, one take was all that was required. The Beatles' backing – including George Martin on piano – was perfect too, so they didn't even bother with a second take.

'I Call Your Name' was also a recording of merit, the Beatles lending a ska beat to the middle-eight section of this Lennon composition. The song had been released before, by Billy J Kramer with the Dakotas as the B-side of their August 1963 number one 'Bad To Me' (also written by John). The Beatles' recording was completed in seven takes, the "best" being take seven but the finest ska solo coming in take five, so this was edited into take seven at mixing stages.

Monday 2 – Friday 6 March

various locations, London to the West Country

On Monday 2 March 1964 the Beatles became film actors for the first time, hurriedly joining the closed-shop actors' union Equity only minutes beforehand, on the platform at Paddington Station. They were proposed and seconded by Wilfrid Brambell and Norman Rossington, the two main support players in the group's début feature-film which, for the moment, was untitled.

They were all gathered at Paddington for a purpose, of course: the first six day's shooting – Monday to Friday of this first week and the Monday of the second week – was to take place on a train. Hire of the train and the track facilities set back Proscenium Films – producer Walter Shenson's company, making the film for United Artists – a tidy £600 per day, but the results were certainly worthwhile.

At 8.30 am this first day, amid scenes of Beatlemania at Paddington Station, the train pulled out from Platform Five and headed for the West Country. The destination for the first three days was Minehead, then it was Taunton and Newton Abbot for the rest of the week. Shooting in the cramped environment of a moving train lent just the right atmosphere to the feeling of fan-inspired claustrophobia which was a hallmark of the film.

No actual shooting was done at Paddington, however – the film's opening sequence, shot at a London station, was done instead at Marylebone (see 5 and 12 April) – indeed, the Beatles decided after this first day that they could board the train more discreetly elsewhere, so for the remaining five days of shooting they embarked at Acton Main Line, in west London. Similarly, they never returned to Paddington in the evenings, jumping out at interim suburban stations like Acton Main Line, West Ealing, Westbourne Park and Hayes & Harlington, where they would be met by their chauffeur-driven car.

Another train-related sequence was shot on 4 March at the station in Crowcombe, Somerset, when the Beatles ran along the platform adjacent to the slowly-moving train, pestering the upper-crust passenger (Richard Vernon) and shouting "Hey mister! Can we have our ball back?"

One of the two schoolgirls cast by director Richard Lester for a train sequence – shot, in fact, on the first day – was Pattie Boyd, with whom he had previously worked in a television commercial for Smith's potato crisps. Right away, George Harrison took a liking to Pattie and they soon began dating, leading to their marriage on 21 January 1966.

In the meantime, work on the Beatles' recordings was being carried out in their absence by George Martin at EMI Studios in Abbey Road. On Tuesday 3 March in studio one (10.00 am–1.45 pm) he produced mono mixes of 'I Should Have Known Better', 'If I Fell', 'Tell Me Why', 'And I Love Her', 'I'm Happy Just To Dance With You' and 'I Call Your Name'. EMI was not the only recipient of the work, for United Artists also required the recordings for the Beatles to mime to during shooting. ('And I Love Her' was later remixed for UK album release – see 22 June 1964.) Then on Wednesday 4 March in studio three (10.00–11.00 am) George Martin produced a mono mix of 'I Call Your Name', released on the US LP *The Beatles' Second Album* and the Canadian LP *Long Tall Sally*.

Off-camera conversation on-board the West Country train, with actors John Junkin and Wilfrid Brambell (both seated), assistant director John Merriman explaining a point to Ringo and Paul, and director Richard Lester talking to John.

Monday 9 March

various locations, London to Newton Abbot

The conclusion of the train filming, travelling this time from London to the Devonshire town of Newton Abbot, 2500 miles having been clocked-up during the past week. A Monday to Friday work schedule, leaving weekends free, was maintained throughout the shooting but for necessary exceptions (see 5 and 12 April).

Tuesday 10 March

The Turks Head, Winchester Rd, St Margaret's, Twickenham, Middlesex
and **Studio Two, EMI Studios, London**

One of the main talking points in what was to be called *A Hard Day's Night* was Ringo's long solo sequence, in which – having been encouraged to desert the group by Paul's "grandfather", Wilfrid Brambell – he embarks upon a series of adventures, most ending in disaster.

The first element to be shot was his trip to a pub, where he complains about the sandwiches, accidentally smashes a beer bottle and then almost maims a parrot positioned uncomfortably close to the dart board. The sequence was filmed on this day at the Turks Head public house in Winchester Road, St Margaret's, close by Twickenham Film Studios where the film production was based and where the studio work would be filmed.

Also this day, at Abbey Road, George Martin produced stereo mixes of 'Can't Buy Me Love', 'Long Tall Sally', 'I Call Your Name' and 'You Can't Do That', and mono mixes of 'Long Tall Sally', 'Komm, Gib Mir Deine Hand' and 'Sie Liebt Dich'. An intriguing document was uncovered at EMI

Waiting for the camera call: the Beatles and actor Norman Rossington with Neil Aspinall and the A Hard Day's Night film crew, Gatwick, 13 March 1964.

in 1991 suggesting that a "drummer" participated in this 10.00 am–1.00 pm session with regard to 'Can't Buy Me Love' – which can only mean that he did some overdubbing. He was paid a Musicians' Union session fee of £5 15s (£5.75) – the Beatles were also paid for their sessions in these early years, quite distinct from their royalty calculations – but his name was not detailed on the document.

This answers one question that has long puzzled some Beatles students: why the drumming on this song's stereo mix differs slightly from the mono. But it also raises a new question re the drummer's identity: Ringo's *A Hard Day's Night* shooting schedule would seem to suggest that he had little, if any, opportunity to visit Abbey Road on this day.

Wednesday 11 March

Twickenham Film Studios, The Barons, St Margaret's, Twickenham, Middlesex

The Beatles' first day of shooting at Twickenham Film Studios, where they would make not only *A Hard Day's Night* but also *Help!* (in 1965), several promotional videos (1965 and 1968), *Get Back/Let It Be* (1969) and where Ringo would shoot the studio scenes in his solo venture *The Magic Christian* (also 1969).

On this day, working from 8.00 am until 10.00 pm (the early starts were maintained throughout the shooting), the group filmed on a set resembling a train guard's van, where they played cards and also mimed to 'I Should Have Known Better', later edited into the film's train sequences.

Thursday 12 March

Twickenham Film Studios, St Margaret's, Twickenham

Shooting of the "hotel room" sequences, in which road managers "Norm" and "Shake" (actors Norman Rossington and John Junkin re-creating the roles of Neil Aspinall and Mal Evans) order the Beatles to remain in their room and answer fan mail, and in which – having sneaked out to a night-club – the group return to discover a hotel waiter, minus his suit, bound and gagged in a wardrobe.

Meanwhile, working at EMI from 10.00 am to 12.00 noon, George Martin made stereo mixes of the two German-language recordings, 'Komm, Gib Mir Deine Hand' and 'Sie Liebt Dich'. Copy tapes were despatched to West Germany, and even to the USA, for record release.

Friday 13 March

Gatwick Airport South, Surrey

Shooting moved 27 miles south of London for two of the film's most important sequences. It meant an early start for the Beatles, who arrived at Gatwick at 10.00 am. The first task of the day was to shoot the film's closing sequence, in which the Beatles ran into view and clambered into a helicopter which then took off into the sky, scattering promotional photographs of the group onto the ground below.

After lunch, the Beatles were filmed larking about on a nearby helicopter launch pad (the helicopter was overhead, with the cameraman on board). Along with footage shot on 22 and 23 April, this formed a part of the 'Can't Buy Me Love' "liberation" sequence.

Monday 16 March

Twickenham Film Studios, St Margaret's, Twickenham

Filming of the "studio canteen" sequence, in which Wilfrid Brambell persuades Ringo to take his nose out of "a boooook" and go "parading" instead, deserting his fellow Beatles in their hour of need.

The other Beatles were not involved in this day's action so George took the opportunity to accompany Brian Epstein at a Cilla Black session for *Saturday Club*.

Tuesday 17 March

Les Ambassadeurs, Hamilton Place, London

The Beatles twice visited this splendid private club, situated just off Park Lane in central London, to film sequences for *A Hard Day's Night*: on this day and again on 17 April.

On this first occasion they filmed the sequence in which they discovered Ringo's father gambling at "Le Circle Club".

Veteran BBC broadcaster Jack de Manio came to Les Ambassadeurs to record an interview with John about his imminent foray into the world of books (*In His Own Write* being due for publication on the 23rd). The interview was broadcast in the Home Service news-magazine programme *Today* (presented by de Manio) the next morning, Wednesday 18 March, between 7.15 and 7.45 am. It was also repeated in the second-half of the programme, on air 8.15–8.40 am.

Wednesday 18 March

Twickenham Film Studios, St Margaret's, Twickenham

Shooting of "dressing-room" sequences for the film.

While waiting around on the set at Twickenham the Beatles recorded a number of items for broadcast in the BBC Light Programme radio series *The Public Ear* on Sunday 22 March (3.00–4.00 pm) and also transmitted simultaneously by the BFBS – British Forces Broadcasting Service – in West Germany. In keeping with the sophisticated nature of the series, they interviewed themselves, rather than be interviewed by a BBC man, so humour was at a premium.

Listeners on the 22nd heard a novel opening to the programme: a reader had written in to *The Public Ear* asking that advance warning be given if ever the Beatles should be set to appear, so that fans could contact other fans and ensure that as many as possible were tuned in. This letter was read out, following which Ringo announced, "We're on today, later on, so don't forget, get on the phone and get all your friends listening!"

When "later on" arrived, George assumed the role of BBC

interviewer, adopting a plum accent and discussing John's book *In His Own Write* first with Ringo and then with the author, who proceeded to read an excerpt, 'Alec Speaking'. George then chatted about the making of *A Hard Day's Night* with Paul and, to round-off the show – joined part-way through by Ringo – he read out the cast and production credits, ascribing themselves joint producer credits along with the real incumbent, John Fawcett Wilson.

Note: extracts from this broadcast, together with extracts from the Beatles' first appearance on *The Public Ear* (see 13 October 1963), an interview given by Brian Epstein to Bill Grundy, an interview given by George Martin to Edward Greenfield, various discs and a linking script written and read by William Mann (music critic on *The Times*) comprised an interesting 30-minute programme, *The Beatles – Who Are They?*, broadcast globally by the BBC's General Overseas Service on Wednesday 24 June 1964 (10.30–11.00 am), 25 June (7.00–7.30 pm) and 26 June (1.30–2.00 am), all times GMT.

Thursday 19 March

Twickenham Film Studios, St Margaret's, Twickenham
and Dorchester Hotel, Park Lane, London
and Twickenham Film Studios, St Margaret's
and Television Theatre, London

During the early morning and mid-to-late afternoon the Beatles filmed at Twickenham, spending the first of two consecutive days shooting TV studio "corridor" scenes. They were also visited on the set by film columnist Peter Noble who interviewed them for the BBC radio Light Programme series *Movie-Go-Round*, broadcast on Sunday 12 April (3.00–4.00 pm). It was followed in the programme by an interview done the next day, with Ringo only.

Around noon they left to attend the 12th annual luncheon of the Variety Club of Great Britain, at the Dorchester Hotel in Park Lane, central London, where leader of the opposition Harold Wilson presented them with the award for "Show Business Personalities Of 1963". The moment was captured on film by several TV and newsreel companies, including the BBC which made a 30-minute programme of the luncheon – *The Variety Club Of Great Britain Awards For 1963* – screened from 10.30 to 11.00 pm on Friday 20 March.

In the evening, between 7.00 and 8.30 (including rehearsal time), the Beatles could be found at the BBC's Television Theatre in Shepherd's Bush, west London, taping (without an audience) their début appearance on Britain's most famous TV pop show, *Top Of The Pops*, the first edition of which had been transmitted on New Year's Day 1964. Though broadcast at this time from Manchester, the Beatles were allowed to pre-tape and to do so in London, miming to both sides of their new single, 'Can't Buy Me Love' and 'You Can't Do That'. Both performances were included in the following Wednesday's edition, 25 March, transmitted from 6.35 to 7.00 pm, while 'Can't Buy Me Love' alone was repeated on 8 April (same times).

Note: in other weeks, before the Beatles had taped an appearance, or if the BBC had used up its contracted number of transmissions of a particular item, *Top Of The Pops* would run either its own commissioned, non-descript film item to accompany a song, or the studio audience would be shown dancing to a spinning disc. This situation applied until the early 1970s.

Friday 20 March

Twickenham Film Studios, St Margaret's, Twickenham
and **Studio Nine, Television House, London**

During the late-morning and afternoon the Beatles shot more "corridor" scenes for *A Hard Day's Night* at Twickenham. Ringo was also interviewed by reporter Lyn Fairhurst for the BBC radio programme *Movie-Go-Round*, broadcast on 12 April, following immediately after a group interview done the day before with Peter Noble. (See that entry for further details.)

During the late-afternoon and early-evening the Beatles went to Television House, the central London HQ/studios of Associated-Rediffusion, where they quickly rehearsed and then appeared live on *Ready, Steady, Go!*, broadcast from 6.15 to 7.00 pm. It was their second live spot on the programme but also their last, for their next and final group appearance was pre-taped (see 23 November 1964).

The Beatles mimed to three disc recordings: 'It Won't Be Long', 'You Can't Do That' and 'Can't Buy Me Love', took part in a humorous fashion parade, were presented by *RSG!* co-host Keith Fordyce with a special award from the US trade magazine *Billboard* to recognise the fact that they held the top three singles chart positions simultaneously (this was

soon extended to four and then five) and were interviewed by the series' other main host, Cathy McGowan.

This performance of 'Can't Buy Me Love' was twice re-shown. The first time was on Friday 24 April 1964 (6.10–7.00 pm) in *Ready, Steady, Go To Montreux!*, a special edition recorded at the Casino in Montreux, Switzerland, during the annual International Contest for Television Light Entertainment Programmes (see also 15 December 1963). The second time was on Thursday 15 July 1965 in *Pick Of The Songs* (see 13 July 1965 for details).

Monday 23 March

Scala Theatre, Charlotte Street, London
and **Lime Grove Studios, London**
and **Empire Ballroom, Leicester Square, London**

Filming of *A Hard Day's Night* switched to the Scala Theatre in central London for seven working days (this day through to 2 April). The main premise of the film was that the Beatles appear on a television show – the Scala was therefore mocked-up as "United TV House". The film's "performance" finale was shot here on 31 March.

To promote his first book, *In His Own Write* – this was the date of publication – John appeared on the live BBC TV programme *Tonight*, broadcast from 7.00 to 7.35 pm from the Corporation's Lime Grove Studios in west London. Following the reading of brief extracts by programme presenter Cliff Michelmore and regulars Derek Hart and Kenneth Allsop, John was interviewed by Allsop for exactly four minutes.

Later the same evening, the Beatles attended the annual Carl-Alan ballroom dancing awards event, at the Empire Ballroom in Leicester Square, central London, where the Duke of Edinburgh (Prince Philip) presented them with two awards for their musical achievements in 1963. The moment was filmed by TV and newsreel companies, including the BBC which broadcast proceedings live from the ballroom – titling its programme *The Carl-Alan Awards* – from 10.25 to 11.15 pm.

Tuesday 24 – Thursday 26 March

Scala Theatre, London

More filming at the Scala. During a break on the 24th, John discussed his new book in an interview given to the British-based Australian broadcaster/actor Dibbs Mather (see 10 December 1963), which was then distributed exclusively to overseas radio stations by the BBC's Transcription Service in its series *Dateline London*. Neither the series nor the interview was heard in Britain.

An extended Easter weekend break followed the Thursday shoot, with John and Cynthia, accompanied by George and girlfriend Pattie Boyd (see 2 March), spending the weekend at the remote Dromolan castle in County Clare, Ireland, Paul staying in London and Ringo and friends spending Easter at the country house Woburn Abbey, in Bedfordshire. Filming resumed the following Tuesday.

Tuesday 31 March

Scala Theatre, London
and **Playhouse Theatre, London**

This was perhaps the most exciting and rewarding day's work on *A Hard Day's Night*: the "TV performance" that was the climax of the film. It was shot this day at the Scala before an audience of 350 screaming fans, film union rules dictating that each person – even though thousands would have gladly done it for nothing – be paid for the pleasure of screaming at the Beatles. (Among these 350 was a 13-year-old child actor named Phil Collins, later to achieve worldwide fame of his own with Genesis and as a solo musician.)

In the finished film the Beatles mime to four songs in this sequence: 'Tell Me Why', 'And I Love Her', 'I Should Have Known Better' and 'She Loves You'. They filmed others too, certainly 'You Can't Do That' was one to be left unused (see 17 April). During 'Tell Me Why' director Richard Lester allowed himself to be briefly visible on camera, appearing – Hitchcock-like – in a shot that looks out from the back of the stage into the Scala auditorium.

This hectic day for the Beatles concluded with a lengthy evening session for BBC radio at the Playhouse, recording an insert for the next edition of the weekly series *Saturday Club*, broadcast in the Light Programme between 10.00 am and 12.00 noon on 4 April. Additionally, during a session break, John recorded an interview for broadcast on the BBC's Home Service radio network.

For the *Saturday Club* session, from 7.00 to 10.30 pm (inclusive of rehearsal time), the Beatles chatted with host Brian Matthew and recorded 'Everybody's Trying To Be My Baby', 'I Call Your Name', 'I Got A Woman', 'You Can't Do That', 'Can't Buy Me Love', 'Sure To Fall (In Love With You)' and 'Long Tall Sally'. The last three songs fell into the final half-hour of the domestic broadcast, simultaneously transmitted by the BBC's General Overseas Service.

Between 9.00 and 9.30 pm, while the other Beatles took a break, John was interviewed again by Brian Matthew, this time for the Home Service series *A Slice Of Life*. The subject of this edition, broadcast from 4.00 to 4.30 pm on Saturday 2 May, was 'Hobbies', and for just under three minutes listeners heard John speak about his writing and best-selling book.

Wednesday 1 and Thursday 2 April

Scala Theatre, London

More shooting at the Scala. On the Thursday the Beatles filmed the "press party" sequence, written by Alun Owen as an approximate re-creation of a reception the Beatles had attended at the British Embassy in Washington DC (after their 11 February concert at the Coliseum), in which they had grown irritated by the condescending and rude line of questioning and had then walked out after someone, without warning, produced a pair of scissors and cut off a lock of Ringo's hair.

Friday 3 April

Twickenham Film Studios, St Margaret's, Twickenham

Among the action filmed this day at Twickenham was a trailer for the film, a bizarre sequence in which John/George and Ringo/Paul sat in two adjacent baby prams, their legs dangling over the sides. John typed, Paul spoke, George mumbled and Ringo twice answered a telephone saying "It's for you, John," to which John twice replied, "Don't be soft." Quite how this promoted *A Hard Day's Night* seems unclear, but it was distributed to cinemas nonetheless.

The Beatles also filmed an unusual engagement with Tyne Tees Television, the ITV franchise for north-east England. Viewers of the area's weekly movie programme *Star Parade* had been invited to send in questions for the Beatles, and the best of these were put to the group by the programme's presenter Adrian Cairns this day at Twickenham. All four Beatles participated, giving their answers straight to camera, then – back in Newcastle – Tyne Tees later filmed the questioners (girls) posing their questions, again straight

At the Scala, 31 March 1964. Where are you, Phil Collins?

"Don't be soft."

to camera, and the two sets of footage were edited together into a Q&A format. But the lack of genuine inter-play, the clearly different settings and the uncomfortable straight-to-camera scenario also resulted in a somewhat stiff six-minute outcome which, together with a brief interview the Beatles gave to Adrian Cairns, was transmitted in *Star Parade* on Thursday 9 April, 10.10–10.40 pm.

Sunday 5 April

Marylebone Station, Great Central St, London

Working, unusually, on a Sunday, the film crew came to Marylebone Station this afternoon (and again the following Sunday) to shoot the first sequences for *A Hard Day's Night*. This usually busy central London terminus was closed to the public on Sundays, so filming could only be done then. By the conclusion of their two Sunday's work, the Beatles had been filmed running across Melcombe Place and into the station, using its public telephones and a photo booth, leaping over a hoarding, Paul sitting in disguise on a concourse bench with his "grandfather" Wilfrid Brambell, and the group running down the length of platform one and jumping onto an already-moving train. (From here, the film cut to the footage shot between 2 and 9 March.) All this time, the group were being chased by more than one hundred screaming fans, each paid £7 10s (£7.50) for the privilege, plus plenty of willing, unpaid extras.

While at Marylebone, John, George and Ringo were also filmed in the station's adjacent street, Boston Place, running towards the camera and being chased by the same frenzied fans. This sequence was used at the very beginning of the film, under the titles.

Monday 6 and Tuesday 7 April

Twickenham Film Studios, St Margaret's, Twickenham

Two days filming at Twickenham. On Monday morning they shot the "make-up room" sequence, on Monday afternoon and all day Tuesday the interior "police station" footage. (The exterior police-station sections were filmed on location on 16 April.)

Shooting at Twickenham on Wednesday 8 April did not require the Beatles, the movie's Strauss operetta scene being filmed.

Thursday 9 April

River Thames towpath, Kew, Surrey

The shooting of Ringo's solo sequence resumed this day with his riverside scene, filmed on the Thames towpath and embankment south of the river and just west of Kew Bridge. The other Beatles were not involved.

Friday 10 April

Twickenham Film Studios, St Margaret's, Twickenham

Back to base for the "production office" sequence.

Sunday 12 April

Marylebone Station, London

A return to Marylebone, without fans this time, for more shooting of the film's opening sequences.

Monday 13 April

Twickenham Film Studios, St Margaret's, Twickenham

Shooting in the morning of George's solo sequence in the film, in which he is taken to the marketing boss of a clothing company and mistaken for the model of their new range of what George describes as "grotty" shirts.

George also featured in the afternoon "bathroom" filming, in which he shaved in front of a mirror while John played submarines in the bath, sang "Rule Britannia" and apparently disappeared down the plug-hole. Paul and Ringo did not attend filming this day – had they done so they would have re-met Roy Orbison, visiting Britain and keen to catch up with the group which had, theoretically, been a support act on his previous British concert tour.

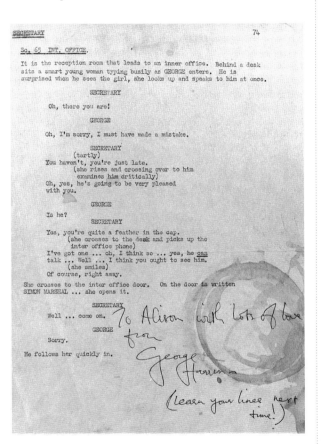

Tuesday 14 April

Twickenham Film Studios, St Margaret's, Twickenham
and Arlington Road, St Margaret's, Twickenham

Studio and also location shooting for a sequence deleted from the finished film, in which the Beatles, stuck in a traffic jam, are cursed at by a passenger in another car. Playing the part of the Beatles' chauffeur was British comedy actor Frank Thornton. The location shooting was done in a road neighbouring the studios, outside the house of one Ken Lewis, a Liberal Party council-election candidate who loaned his campaign bus to the traffic queue.

Wednesday 15 April

Scala Theatre (exterior), London
and Studio 4, Television Centre, Wood Lane, London

A return to the Scala Theatre in central London, although only to the outside of the building, filming scenes in Scala Street, Tottenham Street and also Charlotte Mews.

Paul taped his first solo TV appearance in the evening, being interviewed in a one-off chat/revue show presented by David Frost, the fast-rising young star of British TV. Under the title *A Degree Of Frost*, the programme was transmitted from 10.15 to 11.00 pm on Wednesday 18 May by the BBC1 network (now with the numerical suffix, to differentiate it from BBC2, which had opened on 20 April 1964). It was repeated on Tuesday 1 September, 8.00–8.45 pm.

The show was taped from 8.30 pm in front of an audience at the BBC's Television Centre premises in White City, west London, with rehearsals having begun eight hours earlier, at 10.30 am. (Busy filming at the Scala, Paul would have arrived some time later.) It was produced by Joe McGrath, the first of several occasions that he would be associated with the film and TV work of the Beatles, individually and as a group.

Thursday 16 April

Notting Hill Gate locations, London
and Studio Two, EMI Studios, London

The Beatles spent much of this day on location in Notting Hill Gate filming "chase scenes" with mock-policemen. The "police station" was actually St John's Secondary School at 83 Clarendon Road. (Although the interior sequences were shot on a set at Twickenham – see 6–7 April – the Beatles did spend time inside St John's on this day, mostly using it as a refuge from fans.) They also filmed in a neighbouring cul-de-sac (Heathfield Street) and, in a sequence cut from the finished production, at the Portland Arms public house, running in through an entrance in Portland Road and immediately exiting through another door onto Penzance Place. (Because it was deleted, director Richard Lester was able to use the same idea and location for his next film, *The Knack*.)

Although it was now approaching completion, the Beatles' film remained untitled – until, that is, Ringo emerged somewhere after a long day's work (reputedly 19 March), commented to someone "it's been a hard day" and then, seeing that it was already dark, tacked "'s night" on the end. The phrase captured to perfection the mood of the film and was immediately adopted as its title, announced to the press on 17 April. (Ringo may have previously seen the phrase in John's book, for it appears in the 'Sad Michael' story.)

However the title had come about, though, was immaterial to the problem it now presented John and Paul: they had to write a song "to order", the title already set. And they did not disappoint – within a few days it was ready for recording, and the Beatles came to

THE BEATLES FILM IN WEST LONDON

The crowds loved them, yeah, yeah, yeah

Being chased by the cops outside the Portland Arms pub in Notting Hill Gate, shot on 16 April 1964 but deleted from the film.

Abbey Road this evening to do just that, beginning the session at 7.00 and ending it at 10.00, completing the song in just nine takes.

A *Hard Day's Night* was not only the title of the film: it was also (obviously) the title of the accompanying 13-track album released by EMI on Friday 10 July 1964, all songs composed by Lennon-McCartney, and of the Beatles' next British single, issued on the same date.

Friday 17 April

Les Ambassadeurs, London

A return to Les Ambassadeurs, shooting the film's discotheque sequence in the club's Garrison Room, the Beatles dancing to 'I Wanna Be Your Man' and 'Don't Bother Me'.

Suddenly their biggest American champion, Ed Sullivan flew to England on Wednesday 15 April, ready to interview the Beatles on location the next day. But Thursday had seen the group frantically busy even by their own high standards, so Sullivan's appointment was re-scheduled for today.

For all of his travelling and waiting, one wonders if Ed could have been happy with the result. The interview – conducted in the club's walled-garden – was extremely brief, a mere 1 min 34 secs, for insertion into the Sunday 24 May edition of *The Ed Sullivan Show* (transmitted by the CBS network, 8.00–9.00 pm, EST). A bonus, however, came in the form of a clip from A *Hard Day's Night*, supplied to Sullivan by United Artists to accompany the interview: it was a section from the Scala Theatre "live performance" filming on 31 March, the group miming to 'You Can't Do That'. When final editing was taking place this sequence was cut from the film, so – although he couldn't have known it at the time, being six weeks before the film's world premiere – Sullivan's US broadcast had the footage exclusively.

Saturday 18 April

Twickenham Film Studios, St Margaret's, Twickenham and **Hall Of Remembrance, Flood St, London**

The Beatles spent the morning undertaking post-sync work on A *Hard Day's Night*, adding and re-recording bits of dialogue where necessary. The afternoon, however, was devoted to an entirely different project.

A *Hard Day's Night* had still to be completed when Brian Epstein accepted a proposal from London-area ITV franchise Rediffusion (so re-named on 6 April and no longer Associated-Rediffusion) for the making of a one-hour television special starring the Beatles. Moreover, the two productions overlapped. (Typical of this period's "starring" vehicles, viewers certainly did not see an hour of the Beatles in the one-hour show, for it also featured P J Proby, the Vernons Girls, Long John Baldry, Millie, the Jets [an American dance act], and other NEMS artists Cilla Black and Sounds Incorporated.) At this early stage, the show was provisionally called *John, Paul, George And Ringo* but it was later re-titled *Around The Beatles* to reflect the fact that it showed the acts performing "in the round", rather like an early Shakespeare production.

The group's contract for *Around The Beatles* called for them to attend five days of rehearsals between 17 and 27 April (for some of the other acts, rehearsals had begun on the 13th), to take place up to the 26th at the Hall Of Remembrance in Chelsea, and at Rediffusion's Wembley Studios on the 27th – the same place where video-taping would occur on the 28th (for transmission information, see entry under that date). But owing to the still-busy A *Hard Day's Night* schedule, the Beatles' diary was able to accommodate only three of the five: this afternoon, the 25th and the 27th.

Brian Epstein negotiated a beneficial contract with Rediffusion, which granted him and the Beatles, among other perks, the opportunity to employ their preferred producer and director. Their choice for the former was Jack Good, the maestro behind early British TV pop shows like 6.5 *Special* and *Oh Boy!* As director, they chose Good's longtime associate Rita Gillespie. The Beatles would also work with Good again later in the year (see 2–3 October) when they appeared in his US television show *Shindig*.

Sunday 19 April

IBC Studios, Portland Place, London

Although the acts in *Around The Beatles* would give the *appearance* of a live performance, in that they would not be miming to records, they would, in fact, be miming to a pre-taped soundtrack. Consequently, all of the musical participants in the production assembled today at an independent recording studio – IBC in central London – for a 10.00 am–8.30 pm session. Second engineer/tape op was Glyn Johns, destined to be engineer/producer for the Beatles' *Get Back/Let It Be* album. (Terry Johnson was balance engineer for this IBC session; there was no producer, as such.)

Exercising their right, as stars of the show, to record their session last, the Beatles arrived at IBC in the early evening, by which time the other acts had taped their contributions. The Beatles' session was especially interesting, for apart from recording versions of 'Twist And Shout', 'Roll Over Beethoven', 'I Wanna Be Your Man', 'Long Tall Sally' and 'Can't Buy Me Love', they also, unusually, performed a medley of their hits to date – 'Love Me Do'/'Please Please Me'/'From Me To You'/'She Loves You'/'I Want To Hold Your Hand' – and then finished off with a blistering rendition of 'Shout', the Isley Brothers' 1959 song which the Beatles hadn't performed since the onset of fame.

Although they mimed to these recordings on 28 April, the accompanying audience screams were preserved on the finished television soundtrack, detracting from the performance. An unfettered tape does exist, however.

Monday 20 April

The Jack Billings TV School Of Dancing, Goldhawk Rd, London

The only one of the Beatles not, so far, to have been involved in a solo scene for *A Hard Day's Night* was Paul, and this and the next day balanced that situation with the rehearsing and shooting of a long sequence. Out looking for the missing Ringo, Paul comes across a rehearsal room (actually a west London dance studio), enters and has a long conversation with an actress (Isla Blair) who has been rehearsing lines presuming that she was alone.

Despite the two-day shoot, and some re-writing by Paul and also by Richard Lester of Alun Owen's original script, the sequence was cut from the finished film, so Paul never did appear in a solo sequence.

Meanwhile, back at Abbey Road, 2.00–3.15 pm, George Martin was at work producing mono and stereo mixes of 'A Hard Day's Night', the tapes taken away by United Artists.

Tuesday 21 April

The Jack Billings TV School Of Dancing, London

The second day of Paul's "rehearsal room" shoot with Isla Blair. As with the previous day, the other three Beatles did not attend.

Wednesday 22 April

Odeon Cinema, Queen Caroline St, Hammersmith, London
and other London locations

In the early morning the four Beatles were filmed running down the iron staircase at the rear of the Hammersmith Odeon cinema, footage of which, in editing, was butted-up to the "We're out!" "corridor" scene (shot at Twickenham, 18–19 March) as the opening part of the 'Can't Buy Me Love' sequence (see also 23 April and 13 March). The Beatles would return to the Odeon – inside the venue – for their 1964 Christmas show production (see 22 December and 24 December–16 January 1965).

Left: filming at Hammersmith Odeon. Below: interlude between more "chase" takes at St Luke's Road, providing good entertainment for the workmen demolishing St Luke's Church.

The group switched locations but remained in west London for the afternoon, filming another police chase scene up and down St Luke's Road in Notting Hill Gate (while John Bluthal acted the part of a car thief). Then Ringo alone was filmed in nearby Lancaster Road, as part of his solo sequence: stopping to photograph milk bottles, being chased by two girl fans, diving into a secondhand goods shop (at 20 All Saints Road), emerging partly disguised (the success of which was immediately proven when his attempt to chat up a passing girl led to instant rejection) and then walking up All Saints Road, his progress monitored by a policeman. Finally, Paul was filmed walking along Goldhawk Road in Shepherd's Bush, entering through the door of the Jack Billings TV School Of Dancing, temporarily sign-posted "TV Rehearsal Room".

Thursday 23 April

Thornbury Playing Fields, Bridge Rd, Isleworth, Middlesex
and **Studio Two, EMI Studios, London**

The aerial shots of the Beatles cavorting on a helicopter launch/landing pad to the tune of 'Can't Buy Me Love', filmed at Gatwick Airport South on 13 March, were considered insufficient for this sequence, so Richard Lester had the Beatles congregate early this morning at Thornbury Playing Fields in Isleworth, near London Airport, for some more filming, done at ground-level this time and on a fake helicopter pad constructed in four pieces. The Beatles ran about and played the fool as before, and Lester also had John, Paul and George jump off a ladder, filmed by a cameraman laying on the ground, to give viewers the impression of high-altitude leaping.

Later in the morning John had to leave Isleworth to attend a literary luncheon being held in his honour at the Dorchester Hotel, so the final items of shooting took place without him. (This is why only Paul, George and Ringo appear at the very end of the 'Can't Buy Me Love' sequence, when a groundsman shouts at them "I suppose you know this is private property" and George sarcastically responds, "Sorry we hurt your field, mister".)

Filming at Isleworth ended at 1.00 pm so it's possible that any or even all of the Beatles attended a 4.30–5.45 mix session at Abbey Road, which resulted in another mono version of 'A Hard Day's Night', this one for record release.

Friday 24 April

Edgehill Rd, West Ealing, London

A Hard Day's Night was completed during the morning with the filming of one final section of Ringo's solo sequence: where he obligingly drapes his coat over some puddles for a lady to step on, only to discover, by the worst possible means, that the final puddle was not a puddle at all but a large hole in the road, presently inhabited by a workman. The sequence was shot in a residential street in West Ealing.

During the afternoon the cast (including the four Beatles) and crew met up in a private hall behind the Turks Head public house in St Margaret's (see also 10 March) for an end-of-film party. One of the finest British musical films of all time, certainly the best "pop movie" of all, had been completed from start to finish in a mere eight weeks. Its world premiere, attended by the Beatles, took place at the London Pavilion cinema on Piccadilly Circus, central London, the evening of Monday 6 July.

Note: during the course of shooting A Hard Day's Night United Artists ensured that considerable additional footage was shot, showing the group in candid off-camera moments, being filmed by director Richard Lester's main cameras, and recording some of the soundtrack at EMI Studios in Abbey Road (mute film; no one has yet been able to deduce which song was being taped when the cameras were there, nor on which date it was shot). UA then reached a deal with the BBC for exclusive British television rights to the material, and the Corporation set about compiling an excellent 28-minute documentary, Follow The Beatles, transmitted by BBC1 on Monday 3 August 1964, 7.50 to 8.20 pm. Apart from the opening introduction by critic Robert Robinson, all of the film was supplied by UA – five minutes of 35mm stock and almost 21 of silent 16mm footage – the BBC over-dubbing 11 interviews onto the silent material, with the likes of George Martin, Richard Lester, producer Walter Shenson, writer Alun Owen and actors Wilfrid Brambell, Norman Rossington and Lionel Blair, all of whom described what it was like to work with the Beatles.

(ATV chose a different approach to the subject, producing a documentary – working title The Road To Beatlemania but shown on 29 July as Fans! Fans! Fans! – which traced the history of fan adulation through to the Beatles. The programme did not include any film of the group, however, just of their fans.)

Saturday 25 April

Hall Of Remembrance, London

More rehearsals for Around The Beatles (see 18 April).

Sunday 26 April

Empire Pool, Wembley

A bill-topping return to the concert platform – the Beatles' first live appearance in Britain for 15 weeks – at the New Musical Express 1963–64 Annual Poll-Winners' All-Star Concert, the yearly spring afternoon gala. They performed 'She Loves You', 'You Can't Do That', 'Twist And Shout', 'Long Tall Sally' and 'Can't Buy Me Love' before an audience of 10,000.

The event was taped by ABC Television and networked as a two-part special, Big Beat '64. The Beatles appeared in the second part, transmitted on Sunday 10 May, 4.05–5.35 pm, and repeated (though not in all areas, and not in London) on Sunday 8 November, 3.15–4.40 pm. Viewers of this second part also saw the Beatles receive their poll-winners awards from the actor Roger Moore.

Monday 27 April

Studio 5A/B, Wembley Studios, Wembley

A full evening dress-rehearsal for *Around The Beatles*, with an audience, on the set at Rediffusion's Wembley Studios, just along the road from the Empire Pool.

Tuesday 28 April

Studio 5A/B, Wembley Studios, Wembley

Prior rehearsals and recording session accomplished, the TV special *Around The Beatles* was taped before an audience between 9.00 and 10.15 this evening. The Beatles arrived at the studios at 11.00 am, however, for final rehearsals, and somehow also found the time to record long radio interviews for Swedish radio with visiting presenter Klas Burling.

What with all of their guests, the Beatles actually participated in only two of the show's main items: their music set (see 19 April for details) and a humorous opening spoof of the Interlude section of Shakespeare's *A Midsummer Night's Dream* (Act V Scene I), in which John portrayed the beauteous lady "Thisbe", Paul "Pyramus", George "Moonshine" and Ringo "Lion", all attired in costume. Apart from this, John, Paul and George were seen at the very start of the show, miming a trumpet fanfare, and then Ringo followed by hoisting a flag and setting off a cannon ball. Later, as a group, they introduced P J Proby's performance.

The finished 60-minute production was networked by Rediffusion on Wednesday 6 May (9.45–10.45 pm) and repeated, in slightly edited form – the Beatles' sections remained untouched – on Monday 8 June (only part-networked, 6.08–7.00 pm). NEMS was granted overseas sales rights and so was supplied with a print of the finished programme. For the US market, Brian Epstein sold it to ABC, the first transmission occurring on Sunday 15 November 1964 (7.30–8.30, EST).

Wednesday 29 April

ABC Cinema, Lothian Rd, Edinburgh, Midlothian

The first of two hugely successful nights in Scotland, jointly promoted by Albert Bonici and Brian Epstein.

In their dressing-room at the ABC the Beatles gave an interview to BBC Scotland radio reporter Bill Aitkenhead, broadcast this same evening on the Scottish Home Service bulletin *Scottish News* (6.10–6.32 pm).

Thursday 30 April

Roman Camp hotel, Callander, Perthshire
and **Theatre Royal, Glasgow**
and **Odeon Cinema, Glasgow**

Early in the afternoon the Beatles were visited at their hotel in Callander, Perthshire, by a BBC Scotland camera crew, shooting a 2 min 38 secs interview with reporter Evelyn Elliot for screening this evening in the local BBC1 news-magazine programme *Six Ten* (on air 6.10–6.31 pm).

Then, during the late-afternoon, before the first of the their two evening "houses" at the nearby Glasgow Odeon, the Beatles made a return visit to the Theatre Royal studios of Scottish Television (see also 8 January 1963), to tape a contribution to *Roundup*, transmitted by STV on Tuesday 5 May (5.00–5.55 pm). Though they did not perform, the Beatles participated in the show's "Personality Parade" section by giving lengthy interviews with the programme's two regular hosts: first John and Paul chatted to Morag Hood and then George and Ringo spoke to Paul Young. The four Beatles and two interviewers then came together to discuss group topics and generally act the fool, George at one point humorously attempting to strangle John.

Friday I May

BBC Paris Studio, London

The session for the Beatles' third consecutive "bank holiday" special on BBC radio's Light Programme, again titled *From Us To You* and broadcast this time on Whit Monday, 18 May, 10.00 am to 12.00 noon.

Recording took place at the Paris Studio in central London between 6.30 and 9.30 pm (inclusive of rehearsal time), and the group taped eight numbers: 'I Saw Her Standing There', 'Kansas City'/'Hey-Hey-Hey-Hey!', 'I Forgot To Remember To Forget', 'You Can't Do That', 'Sure To Fall (In Love With You)', 'Can't Buy Me Love', 'Matchbox' and 'Honey Don't' (with John singing the lead vocal, not Ringo who would do so on the EMI recording – see 26 October 1964). Once again, the show opened and closed with title music, the adapted version of 'From Me To You' re-taped on 28 February. The Beatles also engaged in the usual light-hearted banter with the host (Alan Freeman, for the second "special" in succession), read requests, and twice performed an off-the-cuff 'Whit Monday To You', to the tune of 'Happy Birthday'.

Spoofing Shakespeare in the round at Wembley, 28 April, with assistance from Trevor Peacock as Wall. Sounds Incorporated look down from the balcony.

Clearly, the Beatles remained keen to be heard performing the songs that had once been the backbone of their stage act, before fame and the enforced brevity of their concerts ensured that only released material be featured in live performance. Four of those eight numbers were vintage Sun material.

The Beatles set off on holidays on 2 May, John and George returning on the 26th, Paul and Ringo the following day. In their absence, radio listeners could listen not only to this *From Us To You* but also to two editions of Radio Luxembourg's regular Sunday-night series *This Is Their Life* (a radio version, for pop groups, of the TV programme first screened in America in 1952), presented by Peter Aldersley each week from 9.00 to 9.15 pm. The Beatles were featured on 10 and 17 May.

Friday 22 May

The Beatles were still holidaying abroad when George Martin supervised a 10.00–11.00 am EMI studio two overdub session this day, personally adding a piano track to take nine of 'You Can't Do That'. But it was never used.

Sunday 31 May

Prince Of Wales Theatre, London

A return visit to the scene of their Royal Variety Show triumph the previous 4 November. This concert was the fifth in a series of seven consecutive *Pops Alive!* Sunday-night pop shows at this theatre promoted by Brian Epstein. There were six support acts for each of the two "houses" this evening: Kenny Lynch, Cliff Bennett and the Rebel Rousers, the Vernons Girls, the Lorne Gibson Trio, the Chants and the Harlems.

The Beatles' repertoire comprised 'Can't Buy Me Love', 'All My Loving', 'This Boy', 'Roll Over Beethoven', 'Till There Was You', 'Twist And Shout' and 'Long Tall Sally'.

Monday 1 June

Studio Two, EMI Studios, London

The film completed, and holidays taken, the Beatles returned to EMI Studios for three days to record the non-soundtrack side of the LP *A Hard Day's Night,* any surplus songs being set aside for an EP, *Long Tall Sally,* with that title song and 'I Call Your Name' already in the can.

They worked this day from 2.30 to 7.15 and 8.00–11.15 pm, first recording five takes of 'Matchbox' (released on the EP) and then tackling 'I'll Cry Instead' (the LP), taped in two sections with six takes of the first and two of the second recorded for later editing, six takes of 'Slow Down' (for the EP) and 16 of 'I'll Be Back' (LP).

Visiting the afternoon session, and watching the Beatles record a cover of 'Matchbox', his original recording, was Carl Perkins, one of the biggest influences on the group, who was over from America on a promotional tour.

Tuesday 2 June

Studio Two, EMI Studios, London

Two more sessions, each running 15 minutes over the booked times of 10.00 am–1.00 pm and 2.30–5.30 pm. Songs taped this time were John's 'Any Time At All' and 'When I Get Home' (11 takes each) and Paul's 'Things We Said Today' (three takes), all for the second side of the album *A Hard Day's Night*.

Wednesday 3 June

Studio Two, EMI Studios, London

The Beatles' work at EMI Studios on this date can be separated into two distinct sections: 3.00–4.00 pm rehearsing and 5.30–9.30 pm recording.

The afternoon rehearsal, which was not taped, replaced a pre-booked 2.30–5.30 recording session and was swiftly arranged by Brian Epstein to familiarise session drummer Jimmy Nicol with the Beatles and their material. Just a few hours earlier, Nicol had been pottering around his home in Barnes, west London, when a telephone call came through from George Martin, on behalf of Epstein, inviting him to become a temporary Beatle. Ringo had been taken ill during a photo session that morning (in, coincidentally, Barnes, west London) and since he was now in hospital it was clear that he wouldn't be going out on tour with the Beatles the following morning. With some urgency, Nicol was recruited as his temporary replacement.

So Nicol went to EMI where, instead of recording, the three remaining Beatles ran him through a half-dozen songs in their present stage routine – 'I Want To Hold Your Hand', 'She Loves You', 'I Saw Her Standing There', 'This Boy', 'Can't Buy Me Love' and 'Long Tall Sally'. A mere 27 hours later, John, Paul, George and Jimmy were on stage in Copenhagen, giving their first concert.

When Nicol left the studio, John, Paul and George remained behind to do some recording (documentary evidence that this session took place, and its details, only came to light in 1991). In Ringo's absence, each of the three took the opportunity to tape simple demo (demonstration) versions of recent compositions. The resulting tapes were taken away either by the composers or by their music publisher Dick James, for they weren't deposited in the Abbey Road tape library, not then nor at any time since.

George began the 5.30–9.30 pm session, recording a demo of a song entitled 'You'll Know What To Do'. This composition was copyrighted by Jaep Music (a company formed by Dick James and Brian Epstein, to which George was presently contracted) just the previous day, 2 June, but it was never formally recorded by the Beatles nor, indeed, by anyone else, and it remains unissued.

Paul followed, taping a demo of a revised arrangement of 'It's For You' in order that he could give this to Cilla Black for her exclusive release. (The session document called Paul's recording 'You're My World' but this was a Freudian slip on the part of an administrative staff member at EMI, in

Memorandum of Agreement made this 2nd day of June

One thousand nine hundred and sixty-four

BETWEEN Brian Epstein c/o NEMS Enterprises Limited, Sutherland House,
5/6, Argyll Street, London W.1.......for and on behalf of:
                              George Harrison

(hereinafter referred to as "the Writer") of the one part and   JAEP   MUSIC LIMITED
71-5, New Oxford Street, London W.C.1
WHEREBY IT IS AGREED AND DECLARED as follows:—

whose handwriting the title was documented, for Paul neither wrote nor recorded the Cilla Black song of this title which happened to be number one in the British charts at the time of this session.) 'It's For You', certainly a McCartney song, was first recorded by Cilla at EMI on 10 April, however she taped this new arrangement as a re-make on 29 June (and then recorded a second re-make on 2 July, with Paul contributing piano).

Note: in the July 1964 *Beatles Book* magazine, a ghosted "interview" with Paul stated that he had written two songs while on holiday in late-May and recorded both on his return: 'Things We Said Today' and 'Always And Only'. Conclusive session documentation at EMI proves that no recording of the latter title was ever made, neither by the Beatles nor by anyone else; also, no McCartney song of this title was copyrighted, even though – as proven by 'You'll Know What To Do' – Dick James registered all new Beatles compositions whether released or not. So it could be that 'Always And Only' was really the ghost-writer's misinterpretation of 'It's For You'.

The third demo was made by John, of new composition 'No Reply'. This would be issued later in the year on the album *Beatles For Sale* (for which a proper recording was done on 30 September – see that entry), but John made this demo because he donated first use of his song to fellow NEMS artist Tommy Quickly, for release by him as a single. The demo served as Quickly's tutor, but although he did record it, and release was set for 7 August, Quickly's version of 'No Reply' never materialised.

Towards 9.30 pm, John, Paul and George returned to EMI four-track recording, taping (unspecified) overdubs onto 'Any Time At All' and 'Things We Said Today'.

Thursday 4 June

KB Hallen, Peter Bangsvej, Frederiksberg, Copenhagen, Denmark

Two shows (at 6.00 and 9.30 pm), each seen by 4400 people, kicked-off the Beatles' 27-day world tour, which spanned Denmark, the Netherlands, Hong Kong, Australia and New Zealand. For the first five dates, Copenhagen through to Adelaide, Jimmy Nicol replaced Ringo Starr.

For the two Copenhagen "houses", and the following ten dates until they reached Wellington, their repertoire comprised 'I Saw Her Standing There', 'I Want To Hold Your Hand', 'You Can't Do That', 'All My Loving', 'She Loves You', 'Till There Was You', 'Roll Over Beethoven', 'Can't Buy Me Love', 'This Boy' and 'Long Tall Sally'. Occasionally 'Twist And Shout' would replace 'Long Tall Sally' or be inserted before it, while just once – on the first show of this Copenhagen date – the Beatles opened with 'I Want To Hold Your Hand' and switched 'I Saw Her Standing There' to the second song.

With the Beatles out of the country (except for Ringo, that is, who remained behind in a London hospital), George Martin and balance engineer Norman Smith were left with the task of completing the group's batch of recent recordings. Between 2.30 and 7.00 pm this day they mixed into mono 'Long Tall Sally', 'Matchbox' and 'I Call Your Name' and then – after George Martin had overdubbed piano – did likewise for 'Slow Down', completing the four songs for the British EP *Long Tall Sally*, released by EMI on Friday 19 June. Mono mixing for the non-soundtrack side of the album *A Hard Day's Night* then took over, with 'When I Get Home', 'Any Time At All' and 'I'll Cry Instead' all produced by 7.00 pm.

Rehearsing at EMI with the understandably bemused Jimmy Nicol, 3 June 1964. Only a few hours earlier he was known to few, now Nicol was about to become a world famous Beatle.

PRINCESS THEATRE JUNE 9th

THE BEATLES SHOW

ALSO STARRING

THE MAORI HI-FIVE

and

SOUNDS INCORPORATED

the greatest instrumental group

....

TICKETS STILL AVAILABLE

at

HARRY ODELL PRODUCTIONS LTD.

9, ICE HOUSE ST TELS 21832 & 31488

AN ASSOCIATED ARTISTES INTERNATIONAL PRESENTATION.

Friday 5 June

Café-Restaurant Treslong, Vosselaan, Hillegom, The Netherlands

The Beatles' first duty in Holland following their 1.00 pm arrival and press conference at Schiphol airport, Amsterdam, was to tape a performance for VARA-tv – one of the group's best television appearances of all. For this they were driven south, to the town of Hillegom, near Haarlem, arriving around 4.00 pm at this restaurant with theatre facilities often hired by TV companies. Rehearsals began at 5.30 and recording at 8.00.

The programme fell into two distinct sections. In the first part, members of the 150-person audience put some questions to Herman Stok, who was seated among them; Stok then fed the questions by microphone/headphone to Berend Boudewijn, seated in the theatre's bar area with the Beatles, Boudewijn translated them into English and the group responded.

The second part was a music performance – the Beatles miming to EMI recordings but adding new vocals on top if they felt like doing so because the microphones were left open. (Their guitars were also plugged in, but no amplifiers nor new sounds were evident.) They began with 'Twist And Shout' then followed with 'All My Loving' and 'Roll Over Beethoven'. During the next number, 'Long Tall Sally', dancing members of the audience (mostly men) began to encroach onto the stage, they got even closer during 'She Loves You' and by the time John, Paul and George began 'Can't Buy Me Love' they were completely engulfed. Mal Evans, Neil Aspinall and Derek Taylor came on to clear the area but, being unable to do so, Neil directed the three Beatles to leave the stage. Meanwhile, because they were miming, the music continued in their absence, only Jimmy Nicol remaining behind, seemingly determined to fulfil his job as the Beatles' temporary drummer even though the others had left.

Together with news footage shot when the Beatles took an extended canal trip around Amsterdam the next day, VARA broadcast the Hillegom tape as *The Beatles In Nederland* on the TV network Nederland 1 on Monday 8 June (8.30–9.10 pm), and repeated the 40-minute programme on Saturday 18 July (3.50–4.30 pm).

Saturday 6 June

Veilinghal Op Hoop Van Zegen, Veilingweg, Blokker, The Netherlands

Two shows in an auction hall in Blokker, 40 km north of Amsterdam, near Hoorn: a 2.30 matinée attended by only 2000 fans and a 7.00 pm performance for which all of the 7000 tickets were sold. The Beatles appeared on stage at 4.30 and 10.05 pm respectively, following eight support acts, and played for around 25 minutes each time. Typical of so many of the group's latter-day concerts, the evening performance was filmed, in this instance by television news and newsreel cameras.

Tuesday 9 June

Princess Theatre, Un Chau St, Kowloon, Hong Kong

Two "houses" at the 1700-seater Princess Theatre in Kowloon. Beatlemania was evident even here in the Orient, although predominantly among the English-speaking population. Nevertheless, neither performance here was sold out, principally because of the high ticket price, HK $75, set by the local promoter without the knowledge of Brian Epstein. Equivalent to £4 10s (£4.50) at the time, this was then the average working man's weekly wage in Hong Kong.

The Beatles had left Amsterdam during the morning of 7 June and flown back to London where they took a connecting flight, conveniently delayed to allow for their switch-over, and set out for Hong Kong. The plane made scheduled re-fuelling stops at Zurich, Beirut, Karachi, Calcutta and Bangkok and at each airport terminal, at any time of the day or night, and irrespective of whether one or more of the Beatles actually alighted the plane, Beatlemania erupted. Then, when the plane landed at Kaitak Airport in Hong Kong more than a thousand fans were on hand to greet them.

Also on the 9th, back in England (2.00–5.45 pm), George Martin supervised new mono mixes of 'A Hard Day's Night' and 'Things We Said Today' and the copying of two sets of *A Hard Day's Night* mono mixes for dissemination to Capitol Records and United Artists Records in the USA ('I Should Have Known Better', 'If I Fell', 'Tell Me Why', 'And I Love Her', 'I'm Happy Just To Dance With You', 'I'll Cry Instead', 'Can't Buy Me Love' and 'A Hard Day's Night').

Wednesday 10 June

A new mono mix of 'I'll Be Back' was prepared between 10.00 and 11.00 in studio two at Abbey Road this morning – in the Beatles' absence, of course.

Friday 12 and Saturday 13 June

Centennial Hall, Showgrounds, Wayville, Adelaide, South Australia, Australia

The Beatles arrived in Australia on Thursday 11 June, flying direct from Hong Kong, except for a planned stop in Manila to refuel. But this was ruled out by the Philippine airport authorities because of the extreme heat so an unscheduled refuelling stop was made instead at Darwin in the Northern Territory of Australia. Even at 2.35 in the morning, 400 fans materialised at the remote Darwin airstrip – symbolic, by ratio, of the remarkable reception the group would receive on reaching the major Australian cities. From the brief stop in Darwin the Beatles flew on to Sydney, arriving in the midst of a torrential rainstorm, particularly felt by the Beatles who were obliged to parade before the packed airport viewing terraces in an open-top truck, the rain instantly shrinking coats they had excitedly acquired in Amsterdam. Once in Sydney the Beatles, as usual, were unable to leave their hotel because of the massed fans outside.

THE ONLY LIVE RADIO BROADCAST OF THE BEATLES
NEXT MONDAY NIGHT at 8

Every activity of the Beatles Australian tour will be covered by top DJs Don Lunn and Bob Rogers. 3UZ will bring you an on-the-spot picture of their arrival in Melbourne on Sunday next June 14 and from the 3UZ fleet of radio cars and aircraft 3UZ personalities will describe the Beatles every move as they drive from Essendon Airport to the Southern Cross Hotel.

SPONSORED BY *New Rinse Clean* **SURF** ON **3UZ**
THE BEATLE STATION

The Beatles did not play any concerts in Sydney at this point, and the entourage flew on to Adelaide during the morning of the 12th. It was here, at Centennial Hall, that the group gave their first four shows in Australia, over two nights, the repertoire identical to that performed in Denmark, the Netherlands and Hong Kong. Fifty-thousand applications arrived for 12,000 seats here.

In exchange for a handsome fee, NEMS permitted one of the two shows on the 12th to be recorded for radio transmission. The broadcast, titled simply *Beatles Show* and sponsored by the manufacturers of Surf detergent, went out the following Monday evening, 15 June. Transmission times/stations varied according to city: in Adelaide, for example, it went out 8.30–9.30 on 5DN, in Melbourne it was 8.00–9.00 pm on 3UZ.

Monday 15 – Wednesday 17 June

Festival Hall, Dudley St, Melbourne, Victoria, Australia

The Beatles arrived at Essendon Airport, Melbourne, on 14 June and on the 15th began a three-night concert stint, two shows each. Ringo re-joined the group for the first of these and so Jimmy Nicol made his way back to Britain. A total of 45,000 people saw the six performances.

Television cameras from Australian Channel 9 taped the sixth and last concert here and turned the footage into an hour-long programme, *The Beatles Sing For Shell* (Shell, the

petrol company, being sponsors of the broadcast), aired 7.30–8.30 pm on Wednesday 1 July. Of course, Beatles live performances scarcely ran to half of this length, so the TV production also featured a selection of Australian and other international musical acts.

Viewers saw nine of the Beatles' song performances: 'I Saw Her Standing There', 'You Can't Do That', 'All My Loving', 'She Loves You', 'Till There Was You', 'Roll Over Beethoven' (the tape was slightly defective during these two latter songs), 'Can't Buy Me Love', 'Twist And Shout' and the closing number 'Long Tall Sally', during which a man rushed from the audience onto the stage to shake John's hand.

Brian Epstein had originally insisted that only 12 minutes of the Beatles' performance be included in the broadcast. However, one hour after the concert he watched the entire uncut performance on video-tape and was so pleased with the result that he increased this to 20 (actually 22) minutes.

Thursday 18 – Saturday 20 June

Stadium, Rushcutter's Bay, Sydney, New South Wales, Australia

The Beatles returned to Sydney from Melbourne for six clamorous shows over three nights, with 12,000 fans – the biggest pop concert audience in Sydney at that time – packing into the Stadium on each occasion.

Typically, newsreel cameras were allowed to film a part of one of the Sydney performances. Not especially typical, however, was the production of a stand-alone production from this footage, *Beatles At The Stadium*, a "Cinesound exclusive!" which opened on 25 June at Wyngard & State Theatrettes in Sydney. Advertisements for the film boasted "Hear them sing excerpts from their five greatest hits, including 'She Loves You', 'Love Me Do', 'I Want To Hold Your Hand' and more!" The Beatles didn't perform 'Love Me Do' in Sydney nor at any other venue on this tour.

On 20 June, at their Sydney hotel, the Beatles recorded a telephone conversation for broadcast a week later (Saturday 27 June, 5.00–6.30 pm) back in Britain on the BBC Light Programme show *Roundabout*, chatting to the programme's compere Colin Hamilton. The interview was split into three sections for the transmission, totalling five minutes.

Monday 22 and Tuesday 23 June

Town Hall, Cuba St, Wellington, North Island, New Zealand

Four shows in Wellington, two per night, at the 2500-seat Town Hall, kicked-off the Beatles' seven-day visit to New Zealand, to where they had flown from Sydney on the 21st. His cords recovered from tonsillitis, Ringo resumed his one-vocal-per-concert quota with 'Boys' at the first of these Wellington shows, returning the Beatles' performing repertoire to 11 songs.

Meanwhile, back in England, working at EMI on Monday 22 June, producer George Martin, balance engineer Norman Smith and second engineer/tape op Geoff Emerick spent an exhaustive day undertaking mono and stereo mixes of Beatles recordings. Between 10.00 and 11.30 am in studio one the team produced mono mixes of 'Any Time At All', 'When I Get Home', 'I'll Be Back' and 'And I Love Her'. From 11.30 am to 1.00 pm and 2.30 to 5.30 pm stereo mixes were made of 'And I Love Her', 'When I Get Home', 'Any Time At All', 'I'll Be Back', 'If I Fell', 'A Hard Day's Night', 'I Should Have Known Better', 'I'm Happy Just To Dance With You', 'I Call Your Name', 'Can't Buy Me Love', 'You Can't Do That', 'Tell Me Why', 'Things We Said Today', 'Matchbox', 'Slow Down', 'Long Tall Sally' and 'I'll Cry Instead'.

Switching then to studio two, 5.45–9.00 pm, the team completed the long day's work by making copies of the 'Slow Down' and 'Matchbox' mono mixes and 'Things We Said Today' stereo mix.

Wednesday 24 and Thursday 25 June

Town Hall, Queen St, Auckland,
North Island, New Zealand

Four shows over two nights, seen by a total of 10,000 people.

Friday 26 June

Town Hall, Moray Place, Dunedin,
South Island, New Zealand

Two shows in this 4000-seater town hall.

The flight from Auckland to Dunedin had been an anxious one following an anonymous threat that a "germ bomb" had been placed somewhere on board the plane.

Saturday 27 June

Majestic Theatre, Manchester St, Christchurch,
South Island, New Zealand

The day after this concert, on 28 June, the Beatles flew out of Christchurch for Sydney, Australia, switching planes in Auckland. From Sydney they changed planes again, landing in Brisbane just after midnight (29 June).

Monday 29 and Tuesday 30 June

Festival Hall, Charlotte St, Brisbane,
Queensland, Australia

Four shows over two nights, each before 5500 people, closed the Beatles' hectic tour of the Antipodes.

Early in the morning of 1 July they flew out of Brisbane, changing planes again in Sydney. After refuelling stops in Singapore and Frankfurt, their Qantas flight touched down at London Airport at 11.10 am on 2 July.

Tuesday 7 July

Studio E, Lime Grove Studios, London
and **Television House, London**

Release of a new single meant more appearances on *Top Of The Pops*. The Beatles this day taped mimed performances of three songs: the new A- and B-sides, 'A Hard Day's Night' and 'Things We Said Today', and also the title track of their new EP, 'Long Tall Sally'.

Brian Epstein had agreed that the Beatles would tape their contribution in Manchester on 8 July, a few hours ahead of transmission, but then changed his mind. Instead, they were engaged for a 2.00–5.00 pm taping session (without an audience) this day at Lime Grove Studios in west London. (The three hours broke-down into rehearsal from 2.00–4.00; line-up 4.00–4.15 and recording 4.15–5.00.) Following the *A Hard Day's Night* premiere and party the previous evening, however, the Beatles arrived at the BBC late and weary and were not their usual flexible selves.

Both 'A Hard Day's Night' and 'Long Tall Sally' were included in the 8 July transmission (BBC1, 7.35–8.00 pm). The former was then given a second airing on 22 July (7.35–8.00 pm), while 'Things We Said Today' went out on 29 July (7.10–7.35 pm). Additionally, 'A Hard Day's Night' was included in a special year-end edition of the show, *Top Of The Pops '64*, broadcast by BBC1 on Christmas Eve, Thursday 24 December, between 7.25 and 8.25 pm. (This programme also included a repeat of the 'I Feel Fine' performance taped on 16 November, and a new interview with the Beatles filmed on 22 December – see separate entries.)

Immediately after their Lime Grove activity, the Beatles were driven across town to Television House, Rediffusion's central London studio, where – unusually – they taped an interview for transmission a few minutes later in Granada Television's *Scene At 6.30* programme (6.30–7.00 pm), discussing *A Hard Day's Night* (a short clip of which was shown).

Also on this day, probably while he was at Television House, John gave an interview to *New Musical Express* news editor Chris Hutchins, although not for the paper. Hutchins had also been taken on as a freelance contributor to *The Teen Scene*, a new BBC radio series broadcast every Thursday night (9.30–10.00 pm) on the Light Programme. This particular interview – John discussing *A Hard Day's Night* for 3 mins 27 secs – went out on 9 July. (*The Teen Scene* had been on the blocks for some time, a pilot edition – not transmitted – having been compiled on 27 February. This had included an interview that Hutchins did with the Beatles at some point during their 7–21 February US visit, when he travelled with them covering the trip for the *NME*.)

Friday 10 July

Liverpool locations

The Beatles returned triumphant to their home-town for a press conference at Liverpool airport (located in Speke), a remarkable drive through the streets from there into the city

Scenes from the London Pavilion world premiere, 6 July.

centre, cheered and applauded every inch of the way, a civic reception held in their honour at the Town Hall and then, in the evening, the northern premiere of *A Hard Day's Night* at the Odeon Cinema. More than 200,000 Liverpudlians spent at least some part of the day greeting the group, a reception which, naturally, meant more to John, Paul, George and Ringo than any other.

Television cameras whirred for much of the day, with resulting footage going into news bulletins pretty much the world over. Additionally, this evening's BBC1 local news-magazine programme *Look North* (6.10–6.35) featured a report on their airport arrival plus a four-minute piece comprising actuality from the press conference and an exclusive interview with the Beatles by reporter Gerald Harrison. Over on Granada Television, *Scene At 6.30* (6.30–7.00 pm) broadcast film of their arrival at Speke, an exclusive interview done at the airport and footage of the Town Hall balcony parade, John treating the massed crowd below to Sieg Heil signs.

Saturday 11 July

Teddington Studio Centre, Teddington

A rare live appearance on the ABC Television programme *Lucky Stars (Summer Spin)*, rare because performances for this show and its non-summer incarnation *Thank Your Lucky Stars* were usually taped six days ahead of transmission. This appearance would have been, too, were it not for an ITV technicians strike which aborted plans to pre-tape at the Alpha studios in Aston, Birmingham, the previous Sunday, 5 July.

Following their *A Hard Day's Night* northern premiere celebrations, the Beatles had left Liverpool airport at 1.30 am, arriving at London Airport at 3.00 am. After a few hours' sleep, the group re-assembled in central London, boarded a boat and travelled down the River Thames to ABC's Teddington Studio Centre, which has its own mooring plat-form, arriving there at 1.45 pm for afternoon rehearsals and the 5.50 to 6.35 pm live transmission, in which they mimed to 'A Hard Day's Night', 'Long Tall Sally', 'Things We Said Today' and 'You Can't Do That'.

Sunday 12 July

Hippodrome Theatre, Brighton

The Beatles returned to the British stage this evening for the first of five summer Sunday concerts at seaside holiday resorts (plus another performed for TV purposes) – a far cry from the 47 they played in 1963.

One of the support acts this particular evening was temporary Beatles drummer Jimmy Nicol, together with his group the Shubdubs. But despite being on the same bill, the paths of Nicol and the Beatles failed to cross.

Tuesday 14 July

Studios B7/S2, Broadcasting House, London

As teenagers' pop music slowly began its conceptual changeover into young adults' rock music, and with the sudden arrival of brash, appealing pirate pop/rock radio stations broadcasting to Britain from her surrounding seas, so BBC radio executives realised that they must adapt their programming strategy. The first evidence of change was the launch of a weekly, late-night show, *Top Gear*, on Thursday 16 July 1964. Though put together by the familiar *Saturday Club* team of producer Bernie Andrews and presenter Brian Matthew, this new programme went out at the opposite end of the day, from 10.00 pm until (at first) five minutes shy of midnight. *Top Gear* was to remain the flagship of "progressive" music on Radio 1 (1967 successor to the Light Programme) until September 1975.

The Beatles headlined the first edition, and recorded their contribution this day between 7.00 and 11.00 pm (including rehearsal time) in studio S2 inside Broadcasting House, central London. They taped seven songs – 'Long Tall Sally', 'Things We Said Today', 'A Hard Day's Night' (because they had trouble playing the instrumental middle-eight, the EMI disc was dubbed in here), 'And I Love Her', 'I Should Have Known Better', 'If I Fell' and 'You Can't Do That' – and, as usual, conversed with, and ribbed, Brian Matthew.

Showing their keenness for the new series, and through their personal friendship with producer Bernie Andrews, three of the Beatles (all but John) got together to record several spoken trailers for the show, broadcast by the BBC Light Programme in the preceding days and also on 16 July itself. These were taped privately by Andrews, probably at the central London flat he shared with another good friend of the group, and Brian Epstein business associate, Terry Doran, in Shepherd Street, Mayfair.

Prior to the *Top Gear* session, in studio B7 between 6.15 and 7.00 pm, Paul alone recorded an interview (of almost 13 minutes' duration) with Michael Smee for the BBC General Overseas Service programme *Highlight*: 5 mins 45 secs of it was broadcast on Saturday 18 July between 11.15 and 12.00 pm (GMT) and then a longer version (11 mins 11 secs) was broadcast by the GOS as *A Beatle's Eye View* on Tuesday 22 December (7.30–7.45am). The interview was never transmitted by the domestic BBC network.

Mike 'n' Bernie (Mike is on the right) exercise their cutting wit over a prostrate Ringo on Blackpool Night Out.

Friday 17 July

BBC Paris Studio, London

This second BBC radio recording session inside four days – a schedule reminiscent of 1963 – took place at the Paris between 2.15 and 6.15 pm (inclusive of rehearsal time). The object was the recording of the Beatles' fourth consecutive "bank holiday" special *From Us To You*, to be transmitted in the Light Programme from 10.00 am to 12.00 noon on Monday 3 August. The host this time was Don Wardell, more usually heard as a presenter on Radio Luxembourg and now (1991) a prominent US record industry executive.

The programme comprised the usual mix: a chat with the host, the reading of listener's requests, and eight numbers, in this instance 'Long Tall Sally', 'If I Fell', 'I'm Happy Just To Dance With You', 'Things We Said Today', 'I Should Have Known Better', 'Boys', 'Kansas City'/'Hey-Hey-Hey-Hey!' and 'A Hard Day's Night'. The programme also opened and closed with the now-familiar recording of 'From Us To You' – but there was an unfamiliar voice reading the closing credits, that of John Lennon.

Sunday 19 July

ABC Theatre, Blackpool

An appearance on the live variety programme *Blackpool Night Out* – the summer edition of *Big Night Out* – networked to all ITV stations by ABC Television direct from the town's ABC Theatre between 8.25 and 9.25 pm. As usual, the show was hosted by comedian brothers Mike and Bernie Winters. The Beatles headed the list of guest stars, which also included Chita Rivera, Frank Berry, Jimmy Edwards and Lionel Blair.

The Beatles had flown up to Blackpool the previous day and spent all of the Sunday rehearsing inside the ABC Theatre. As well as performing five songs – 'A Hard Day's Night', 'And I Love Her', 'If I Fell', 'Things We Said Today' and 'Long Tall Sally' – they also participated in comedy sketches, including one where John, Paul, George and the Winters performed a medical operation on Ringo. In another, they acted as refuse collectors.

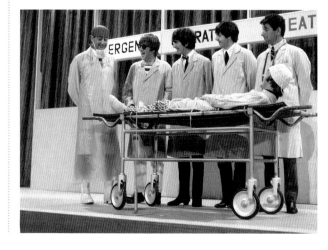

Thursday 23 July

London Palladium, London

A special midnight revue, *The Night Of A Hundred Stars*, in aid of the Combined Theatrical Charities Appeals Council, featuring an array of illustrious names from all walks of show business (Sir Laurence Olivier and Judy Garland, to name but two). Representing "pop music", the Beatles acted out a flying ballet sketch ('I'm Flying') in part one of the show, which necessitated them being winched up high above the stage, and performed a brief musical set in part two.

Saturday 25 July

Studio Four, Television Centre, London

Just as John had done on 22 June 1963, so now George and Ringo appeared individually as members of the panel on *Juke Box Jury*, the record-review programme transmitted by BBC1 early each Saturday evening. (Of course, all four Beatles comprised the panel on 7 December 1963.)

This day's activity first saw George rehearse (4.30 to 5.10 pm), take part in a sound and vision test (5.10 to 5.40) and appear in the 5.40 to 6.05 live broadcast. Then, following a dinner break, Ringo rehearsed (7.30 to 7.45), took part in a sound and vision test (7.45 to 8.15) and appeared in a taped edition (shot 8.15 to 9.00 pm) for transmission seven days later, Saturday 1 August, again between 5.40 and 6.05 pm. Both shows were hosted, as usual, by David Jacobs.

Sharing the panel with George was actress/model Alexandra Bastedo, comic actor Reg Varney and singer Carole Ann Ford, and together they reviewed 'I Should Have Known Better' by the Naturals (a cover of the Beatles' song), 'What Am I To You' by Kenny Lynch, 'Soulful Dress' by Sugar Pie De Santo, 'How Can I Tell Her' by the Fourmost (managed by Brian Epstein), 'Heart' by David Nelson, 'Spanish Harlem' by Sounds Incorporated (another Epstein group), 'All Grown Up' by the Crystals, 'She's Not There' by the Zombies and 'Ain't Love Good, Ain't Love Proud' by Tony Clarke. Of these nine songs, five were voted to "Hit" and four (the Naturals, Kenny Lynch, David Nelson and the Crystals) to "Miss".

Sitting alongside Ringo was TV personality Catherine (Katie) Boyle (who had been on the panel with John a year

previously), actress Judy Cornwell and singer Ray Martine, and they reviewed 'Thinking Of You Baby' by the Dave Clark Five, 'A Summer Song' by Chad Stuart and Jeremy Clyde, 'Don't It Make You Feel Good' by the Overlanders, 'It's For You' by Cilla Black (given to her exclusively by Lennon-McCartney – see 3 June), 'Move It Baby' by Simon Scott, 'I Wouldn't Trade You For The World' by the Bachelors and 'Not For Me' by Sammy Davis Jr. All were voted to "Hit" except for the Stuart/Clyde and Sammy Davis discs. Also reviewed during this recording but omitted from the transmission owing to lack of time were 'Dang Me' by Johnny Duncan and 'The Fever' by Jody Miller.

Sunday 26 July

Opera House, Church St, Blackpool, Lancashire

Tuesday 28 and Wednesday 29 July

Johanneshovs Isstadion, Sandstuvägen, Stockholm, Sweden

The Beatles' second visit to Sweden inside ten months saw them give four performances over two nights at this 8500-seat ice hockey arena, at 6.45 and 10.00 each night. On two occasions they played to less than capacity audiences. During the first show, Paul received a mild electric shock from an unearthed microphone. John, too, suffered a jolt.

The Beatles had flown out of London Airport at 10.10 am on 28 July, and they returned at 3.45 pm on the 30th.

Sunday 2 August

Gaumont Cinema, Bournemouth

Also on the bill with the Beatles were the Kinks, described as a "new and unknown London group", Mike Berry and singer/comedienne Adrienne Poster (later Posta).

Sunday 9 August

Futurist Theatre, Scarborough

Tuesday 11 August

Studio Two, EMI Studios, London

A Hard Day's Night had been out just two months when the Beatles began recording another LP, in keeping with the formula of two albums per year, the second aimed at the Christmas sales market. This one would remain untitled until the release date was in sight, eventually being named *Beatles For Sale*.

Working from 7.00 until 11.00 pm, and as productive as ever, the group began and completed John's 'Baby's In Black' within this time, taping 14 takes and then making 13 separate attempts at perfecting the song's twangy opening guitar notes (none of which was chosen for the finished version).

But before recording began, the Beatles were filmed in

Dylan. It was recorded in eight takes. These and four of Dr Feelgood and the Interns' 'Mr Moonlight' were taped between 7.00 and 9.00 pm.

Between 9.00 and 10.00 pm, mono mixes were made of both titles; presumably, since they were later improved upon, these were for John's personal use – right up to his death in 1980 he liked to take home rough mixes of his day's studio work, usually on a 7½ ips reel.

And that's where the session should have ended. It was 10.00 pm, precisely the time that it had been booked to conclude. Instead, the Beatles wanted to do some more recording, returning to their instruments for five takes of Johnny Preston's 'Leave My Kitten Alone', the "best" being the last, adorned with a number of overdubs. That John did not ask for a rough mix of this title is revealing, for it shows that he could not have been pleased with the result of these 75 minutes, the session ending at 11.15. And the Beatles never again returned to 'Leave My Kitten Alone': it wasn't mixed, and the four-track tape remains, unissued, in the EMI vault, perhaps the most anticipated and discussed unreleased Beatles recording of them all.

performance positions by BBC television cameras for an insert into *Top Of The Pops*. It mattered not what song (if any) they were singing for this was a "wild track" shoot, a collection of mute images onto which a disc recording, in this instance of 'A Hard Day's Night', could be overdubbed for *TOTP* broadcast.

Although the shooting was completed, the film was never screened because the BBC then clashed with Brian Epstein over the size of the group's fee, and the footage was later junked.

Wednesday 12 August

Whaddon House, William Mews, London

During an "At Home" party thrown this evening by Brian Epstein in his home here (Flat 15), Ringo was interviewed by *NME* journalist Chris Hutchins for the BBC Light Programme series *The Teen Scene*, discussing in particular the Beatles' forthcoming North American concert tour. It was broadcast the next night, Thursday 13 August (9.30–10.00 pm).

Friday 14 August

Studio Two, EMI Studios, London

This new LP came too soon after *A Hard Day's Night* for Lennon-McCartney, prodigious composers though they were, to have written a full album's worth of quality new material. They had a few songs, the final quota numbering eight, so for the other cuts the Beatles had to rely on former stage favourites.

Of the three songs tackled during this evening session, only one, 'I'm A Loser', was a Lennon-McCartney number, written mostly by John and showing a definite shift in direction away from the "hand-holding" songs to a more autobiographical and introspective slant, influenced by Bob

Sunday 16 August

Opera House, Blackpool

Shortly to change their name to The Who, one of the support acts on this bill were the High Numbers, billed as "a new R&B group".

Wednesday 19 August

Cow Palace, Geneva Ave, San Francisco, California, USA

The first of 25 dates in "The Beatles' First American Tour" – something of a misnomer since, although it was certainly the group's first jaunt around the continent, it was actually their second concert-playing visit to the USA, and the tour also ventured into Canada for three concerts. (A 26th date, a charity affair, was also added to the itinerary.)

The Beatles performed just 12 songs throughout, usually 'Twist And Shout', 'You Can't Do That', 'All My Loving', 'She Loves You', 'Things We Said Today', 'Roll Over Beethoven', 'Can't Buy Me Love', 'If I Fell', 'I Want To Hold Your Hand', 'Boys', 'A Hard Day's Night' and 'Long Tall Sally'. Occasionally they would drop 'She Loves You', open with 'I Saw Her Standing There' and close with 'Twist And Shout'. The tour's support acts were, in order of appearance, the Bill Black Combo, the Exciters, the Righteous Brothers and Jackie DeShannon.

All 17,130 seats for this one concert in San Francisco were sold, gate receipts totalling $91,670 (then £32,740). The Beatles' gross share of this was $47,600 (£17,000).

The Beatles had left London at noon on 18 August and, after brief stops in Winnipeg and Los Angeles (where 2000 fans gathered to greet them), arrived at San Francisco International Airport at 6.25 pm to a reception from 9000 screaming teenagers.

Thursday 20 August

Convention Center, Paradise Rd, Las Vegas, Nevada, USA

The Beatles flew to Las Vegas immediately after the Cow Palace performance, arriving at 1.00 am. Here they gave two shows, at 4.00 and 9.00 pm, before a combined audience of 16,000. For one of these, 'Till There Was You' was temporarily added to the repertoire.

Friday 21 August

Coliseum, Harrison St, Seattle, Washington, USA

One 29-minute performance watched by 14,720 fans.

Saturday 22 August

Empire Stadium, Exhibition Park, Vancouver, British Columbia, Canada

Attendance at this one show, the Beatles' first in Canada, was 20,261, and it was also broadcast live by local radio station CKNW. Immediately afterwards, the group flew back across the US border to Los Angeles, arriving at 3.55 am.

Sunday 23 August

Hollywood Bowl, North Highland Ave, Los Angeles, California, USA

Capitol Records had planned to tape the Beatles in concert at Carnegie Hall on 12 February, but the American Federation of Musicians refused permission. Instead – six months later, permission received – they recorded the group at the Hollywood Bowl, a concert attended by 18,700 fans. Capitol planned an album for issue to the US record market only, since it was felt then that record buyers in Britain – although obsessed with anything by the Beatles – would not be interested in an LP of songs already in their collections, even if these were different recordings.

The concert was recorded, all 29 minutes of it, the tape

MASTER REEL CONTROL FILE

THE TERM "SCOTCH" AND THE PLAID DESIGN ARE REGISTERED TRADEMARKS OF MINNESOTA MINING AND MANUFACTURING COMPANY, ST. PAUL 19, MINN.

was mixed (see 27 August), it received the thumbs-down from Capitol and the Beatles on the grounds of poor quality and was consigned to the library shelf – until January 1977, that is, when the three-track tapes were exhumed for the release of an historic live album, *The Beatles At The Hollywood Bowl*. This LP was, in fact, a skilful editing job – by George Martin and balance engineer Geoff Emerick – of two concert recordings from the venue, this one from 1964 and another from 30 August 1965, six songs from 1964 and seven from 1965. (Capitol also taped the Beatles' show at the Hollywood Bowl on 29 August 1965 but microphone gremlins prevented any of that material from being usable.) The two-year compilation method was the best way of presenting what were generally erratic stage performances by the Beatles, by now well into their phase of disliking concerts and touring. *The Beatles At The Hollywood Bowl* was issued by EMI in Britain on 6 May 1977 and reached number one on the chart on 18 June, almost 13 years after this first recording was made.

From start to finish, this Hollywood Bowl performance was also captured on film, although quite haphazardly – by an amateur cameraman/woman (inadequate pictures, fairly good sound) and also by a newsreel company (inadequate sound, fairly good pictures).

After the show, and for the next two days, the Beatles rested at a private house in Bel Air, venturing outside only for a private party, held in their honour and in aid of charity, during the afternoon of Monday 24 August.

Wednesday 26 August

Red Rocks Amphitheatre, Lawrence St, Denver, Colorado, USA

Only 7000 fans turned up to see the Beatles' one show in this natural amphitheatre, leaving 2000 seats unoccupied.

Thursday 27 August

Cincinnati Gardens, Seymour Ave, Cincinnati, Ohio, USA

The Beatles gave one performance in Cincinnati, before 14,000 fans, immediately after which they flew to New York City, landing at 2.55 am to a reception from 2000 fans.

Meanwhile, earlier on this day, prior to setting the tapes upon the shelf, Capitol producer Voyle Gilmore and balance engineer Hugh Davies made stereo mixes of the previous Sunday's Hollywood Bowl concert recording, mixed down to two-track, with added equalisation, reverb and limiting. The material, in order, was 'Introduction' (by announcer), 'Twist And Shout', 'You Can't Do That', 'All My Loving', 'She Loves You', 'Things We Said Today', 'Roll Over Beethoven', 'Can't Buy Me Love', 'If I Fell', 'I Want To Hold Your Hand', 'Boys', 'A Hard Day's Night' and 'Long Tall Sally'.

All that could be heard of this material until 1977 was a 48-second extract of 'Twist And Shout' on the US-only album *The Beatles Story* released on 23 November 1964.

Friday 28 and Saturday 29 August

Forest Hills Tennis Stadium, Tennis Place, Forest Hills, New York, USA

One show per night, each performed before 16,000 fans.

Sunday 30 August

Convention Hall, Mississippi Ave and The Boardwalk, Atlantic City, New Jersey, USA

For this one show 18,000 teenagers packed the Convention Hall. The Democratic Party National Convention had taken place here a week earlier and newspapers happily reported that the Beatles received a more boisterous reception than the keynote speech by President Lyndon B Johnson.

Wednesday 2 September

Convention Hall, 34th St and Curie Ave, Philadelphia, Pennsylvania, USA

Following race-riots in the city of Philadelphia a few days prior to this concert, the Beatles – keen Civil Rights supporters, all – were reportedly disgusted to see that their 13,000 audience here was all-white.

The concert was broadcast live by a local radio station (further details untraceable).

Thursday 3 September

Indiana State Fair Coliseum, State Fairgrounds, East 38th St, Indianapolis, Indiana, USA

Two shows, seen by a total of 29,337 people, and netting $85,232 (£30,440) in the process.

Friday 4 September

Milwaukee Arena, West Kilbourn Ave/West State St, Milwaukee, Wisconsin, USA

One performance.

Saturday 5 September

International Amphitheatre, 42nd St/South Halsted St, Chicago, Illinois, USA

One performance.

Sunday 6 September

Olympia Stadium, Grand River Ave/McGraw Ave, Detroit, Michigan, USA

Two shows in the Motor City, famous in popular music as the home of the Tamla Motown record company, responsible for producing some of the Beatles' favourite music at this time.

Monday 7 September

Maple Leaf Gardens, Carlton St, Toronto, Ontario, Canada

Two shows in one evening here in Canada, seen by a total of 35,522 spectators.

Tuesday 8 September

Forum, St Catherine Street, Montreal, Quebec, Canada

Two shows at the Forum, seen by 21,000 fans.

Afterwards, the Beatles' flight to Jacksonville, Florida, was diverted to Key West, on the southern tip of the state, because of "Hurricane Dora" which was heading straight for the Florida city. The plane touched down at Key West airfield, unannounced, at 3.30 in the morning on 9 September to a reception from hundreds of (seemingly prescient) screaming teenagers. "Hurricane Dora" went on to reach Jacksonville as predicted, causing immense damage, so the Beatles didn't fly there until mid-afternoon on 11 September.

Friday 11 September

Gator Bowl, East Adams St, Jacksonville, Florida, USA

The Beatles refused to play this one show until they received an assurance from the local promoter that the audience would not be colour segregated.

Because of extensive damage caused by "Hurricane Dora", 9000 of the 32,000 ticket holders were unable to get to the Gator Bowl.

Saturday 12 September

Boston Garden, Causeway St, Boston, Massachusetts, USA

One performance.

Sunday 13 September

Civic Center, West Baltimore St, Baltimore, Maryland, USA

Two shows, seen by a total 28,000 fans.

Monday 14 September

Civic Arena, Auditorium Place, Pittsburgh, Pennsylvania, USA

One performance, before 12,603 screaming spectators.

Tuesday 15 September

Public Auditorium, East Sixth St, Cleveland, Ohio, USA

During this one performance a gaggle of fans managed to break through the police cordon and clamber onto the stage. Police ordered the Beatles off the stage mid-song and the concert only resumed after a plea over the public-address system from Derek Taylor and a police threat that the rest of the show would be cancelled unless some semblance of order was restored.

Wednesday 16 September

City Park Stadium, City Park, New Orleans, Louisiana, USA

One performance, before a capacity 12,000 audience.

Thursday 17 September

Municipal Stadium, 23rd and Brooklyn, Kansas City, Missouri, USA

The famous "extra" show, the Beatles adding the Little Richard medley 'Kansas City'/'Hey-Hey-Hey-Hey!' to their repertoire, to an especially uproarious reception. Once again, the group had to leave the stage mid-concert, returning only after the audience had calmed down (a little) in the face of a cancellation threat.

Friday 18 September

Dallas Memorial Auditorium, South Akard St, Dallas, Texas, USA

One show. On 19 September the Beatles rested at a remote ranch in Missouri.

"An Evening With The Beatles"

The Committee

Mrs. William C. Langley, *Chairman*
Mrs. George G. Millarøy, *Co-Chairman*
Mrs. Alexander M. Armein
Mr. Lawrence Burnett
Mr. A. Walter Bingham, III
Mrs. Frederica F. Emert
Mr. George M. Gillet, III
Mr. and Mrs. W. French Githens
Mr. and Mrs. Leonard H. Goldenson
Mr. and Mrs. Peter Grimm
Mr. and Mrs. Jack Hausman
Mr. and Mrs. Leo Hausman
Mr. and Mrs. Stanley C. Hope
Mr. and Mrs. Buddy Howe
Mr. and Mrs. Joseph A. Martino
Mr. and Mrs. Henry McE. Matthews
Mr. and Mrs. Charles E. McCarthy
Mr. and Mrs. John Reagan McCrary
Mr. and Mrs. Moore Maxee
Mrs. David Moss
Mrs. Brennan S. Neylack
Mr. and Mrs. Clyde Newhouse
Miss Audrey Palmer
Mr. and Mrs. T. Kirkpatrick Parrish, III
Mr. and Mrs. Gilbert H. Perkins
Miss Mary E. Potter
Mr. and Mrs. Charles Rewson
Mr. and Mrs. Robert I. Rogin
Mr. and Mrs. Francis C. Rooney, Jr.
Mr. and Mrs. Laurence R. Rombach, Jr.
Mr. Herman Rush
Mr. and Mrs. William H. Russell
Mrs. John Barry Ryan
Mr. and Mrs. Donald S. Stralem
Mr. and Mrs. James H. Van Allen
Mr. and Mrs. Clyde E. Weed
Mr. and Mrs. Norman Weist
Miss Audrey Wertheim

(partial listing)

September 20, 1964

Dear Friends:

On behalf of Retarded Infants Services and United Cerebral Palsy, may I extend warm thanks to all of you who have helped make this evening a fabulous success. Your contributions to our organizations will assure continued programs for the coming year.

We are deeply grateful to many people and organizations for their services. First, to Brian Epstein and the Beatles — John, Paul, George and Ringo — who have generously donated their talents to make this evening possible. Then, a special bow to William Zeckendorf, Webb & Knapp and Paramount Pictures who made the facilities of the New York Paramount Theatre available.

We warmly acknowledge the efforts of Buddy Howe, Norman Weiss and the General Artists Corporation for producing this evening's entertainment.

Additionally, United Artists, The American Broadcasting Company, the Newspapers and disc jockeys of New York City, Theatre Authority, Local 802 A. F. of M., I. A. T. S. E. Local 1, Theatre and Amusement Employees Local 54.

Finally, thanks to our "Evening" committee who worked so hard to bring this evening to a successful conclusion.

Sincerely,

Leo Hausman
President
United Cerebral Palsy
of New York City

Sunday 20 September

Paramount Theatre, 7th Ave/Times Square, New York City, New York, USA

Titled "An Evening With The Beatles", this special charity concert, in aid of the United Cerebral Palsy of New York City and Retarded Infants Services, rounded off the Beatles' exhausting North American tour. Paying up to $100 a ticket, 3682 people attended the show, the Beatles and the other artists on the bill giving their services free.

The group flew back to England on 21 September, arriving at London Airport at 9.35 pm.

Sunday 27 September

Prince Of Wales Theatre, London

Along with chairman David Jacobs, Cilla Black, Brian Epstein, Billy Hatton (of the Fourmost), Betty Hale (of *Fabulous* magazine), Alan Freeman and Linda Lewis, Ringo was a member of a jury which judged the final of The National Beat Group Competition, sponsored by the charity Oxfam and held at the Prince of Wales Theatre in central London. As *It's Beat Time*, the second half of the evening, from 9.45 to 10.35, was screened live by BBC2.

Eleven regional heat-winners came together for this final but none of the groups – the Southerns, the Connoisseurs, the Starfires, the Apaches, Formula Five, the Down-Beats, the Vibros, the Countdowns, Roy Stuart and the Cyclones, Danny Clarke and the Jaguars, and the Crusaders – good mid-1960s group names all, achieved any fame beyond this single TV transmission.

Tuesday 29 September

Studio Two, EMI Studios, London

With their remarkable North American jaunt now past but a British concert tour just around the corner, the Beatles quickly returned their attention to recording, and the

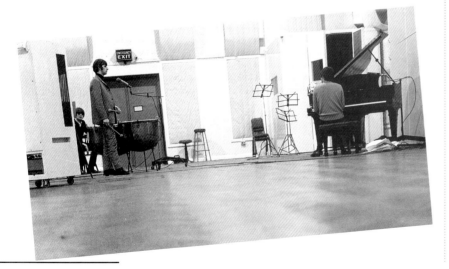

completion of their second album of 1964. They taped three songs this day at Abbey Road, Lennon-McCartney compositions all, recording four takes of 'Every Little Thing' (George arrived late and didn't play on these takes of the song) and the first seven of 'I Don't Want To Spoil The Party' between 2.30 and 6.30 pm. They then resumed at 7.00 to complete the latter song with 12 more takes and begin the recording of 'What You're Doing' – by session's end, 10.45 pm, seven takes of this song's rhythm track had been taped.

Wednesday 30 September

Studio Two, EMI Studios, London

Working between 2.30 and 5.30 pm, the Beatles completed the recording of 'Every Little Thing', taping five more takes to take it through to nine in all. Then, resuming at 6.30, they continued with 'What You're Doing', recording takes eight to 11. (Although the 11th take was marked "best" this was only temporary for the Beatles recorded a re-make on 26 October.)

Before the 10.30 end of session, the ever-productive group also set about, and completed, the recording of 'No Reply', done in a swift eight takes, returning to the song John had first aired in the studio in demo form on 3 June.

Friday 2 October

The Granville Studio, Fulham Broadway, London

TV rehearsals in London with an English producer but for an American show, the ABC network's *Shindig*, one of the two primetime pop series on US TV in the mid-1960s. (The other was NBC's *Hullabaloo* – the Beatles never appeared on this in person, only via a promo clip, although Brian Epstein was the host of a weekly English section during its first season.)

The producer of *Shindig* was Jack Good, the Englishman who had re-located in Hollywood (see 18 April 1964), while the executive producer was Leon Mirell (on behalf of Selmur Productions) who would link again with the Beatles in August 1965, filming "The 5th National Jazz And Blues Festival" for their Subafilms company.

Having just returned from an exhausting North American tour, there was no way that the Beatles would consent to a return for the purposes of shooting their *Shindig* appearance, so Jack Good came back to his homeland to make a special all-British edition of his series, with the Beatles topping a bill ahead of Sandie Shaw, P J Proby (American, but British-based), the Karl Denver Trio, Tommy Quickly, Sounds Incorporated and Lyn Cornell (former member of the Vernons Girls and wife of early Beatles session drummer Andy White). Since this was a US TV production, and BBC and ITV studios were off-limits, an independent London venue was utilised, the Granville Studio, based in the west London premises of the Granville Theatre, formerly a Victorian music-hall.

This day was set aside for rehearsals – actual taping took place the next day.

Saturday 3 October

The Granville Studio, London

Afternoon recording for *Shindig* – a live performance, not mimed, at the Granville Studio, before a specially-invited audience of London-area Beatles Fan Club members. The group sang three songs, 'Kansas City'/'Hey-Hey-Hey-Hey' (which was shown at the beginning of the programme), 'I'm A Loser' and 'Boys' (which came later), and they also joined in the finale which was led by the Karl Denver Trio.

The show was networked on US television by ABC on Wednesday 7 October 1964 (8.30–9.00 pm, EST). It wasn't screened in Britain.

Tuesday 6 October

Studio Two, EMI Studios, London

Recording at Abbey Road from 3.00 to 6.45 and 7.00 to 10.00 pm, taping 13 takes of 'Eight Days A Week' and experimenting all the while with various ways of opening and closing this new song – a novel fade-up at the start and fade-down at the end was decided upon, effected at later mix stages. The recording was completed on this day except for some edit pieces done on Sunday 18 October.

The session tapes reveal that another new song, 'I Feel Fine', was being worked out at this time, John strumming its distinctive guitar riff between takes of 'Eight Days A Week'.

Thursday 8 October

Studio Two, EMI Studios, London

Intended not for the in-the-works LP but for a simultaneous single release, the Beatles recorded Paul's bluesy 'She's A Woman' this day, beginning and completing it in just two sessions, 3.30–5.30 pm for the seven-take basic track and 7.00–10.00 pm for overdubs. The song was indicative of Paul's fast growing awareness of other forms of music, and the ease with which he could slip into those styles.

Friday 9 October

Gaumont Cinema, Bradford

This eagerly awaited British tour, the Beatles' only one in 1964, got underway in Bradford, as had the Helen Shapiro tour in February 1963 and that year's "Christmas Show".

On this tour, earning £850 for two "houses" per date, the Beatles' repertoire comprised 'Twist And Shout', 'Money (That's What I Want)', 'Can't Buy Me Love', 'Things We Said Today', 'I'm Happy Just To Dance With You', 'I Should Have Known Better', 'If I Fell', 'I Wanna Be Your Man', 'A Hard Day's Night' and 'Long Tall Sally'.

Saturday 10 October

De Montfort Hall, Leicester

PROGRAMME

1 THE RUSTIKS

2 MICHAEL HASLAM

3 BOB BAIN

4 SOUNDS INCORPORATED

5 **MARY WELLS**

INTERVAL

6 THE REMO FOUR

7 BOB BAIN

8 TOMMY QUICKLY

9 BOB BAIN

10 **THE BEATLES**

BOB BAIN
Britain's top compere is a great fan of the Beatles and they are great fans of Bob's, as are most of the pop stars. This is easy to understand because Bob, with his warm personality and rapid fire wit is always ready to throw a gag, a line or a joke, not only on but off stage, as well.
Bob has held the star comedy spot in most of the Country's leading night clubs and is no stranger on TV. He has appeared in shows with many of the world's top names.

The management reserve the right to refuse admission, also to make any alteration in the cast which may be rendered necessary by illness or any other unavoidable cause.

In accordance with the requirements of the local authority: 1 All gangways, passages and staircases must be kept entirely free from chairs or any other obstruction 2. The public shall be permitted to leave by all exit and entrance doors after each performance or entertainment 3 No smoking shall be permitted to take place on the stage except as part of a performance or entertainment 4 The safety curtain must be lowered and raised at least once during every performance or entertainment, to ensure its being kept in proper working order.

Photographing in the theatre is forbidden.

Sunday 11 October

Odeon Cinema, New St, Birmingham, Warwickshire

Monday 12 October

Studio Two, EMI Studios, London

Enjoying a day-off from the tour, the Beatles may have attended this mix session at Abbey Road, George Martin and Norman Smith preparing mono and stereo mixes of 'She's A Woman' between 10.00 and 10.30 am and then, in a 2.30–3.00 pm session, producing a mono mix of 'Eight Days A Week'. (At this point, 'Eight Days A Week' was being considered as the A-side of the group's next single.)

Tuesday 13 October

ABC Cinema, Station Rd, Wigan, Lancashire

Wednesday 14 October

Studio Four, Granada TV Centre, Manchester and **ABC Cinema, Ardwick, Manchester**

During the afternoon the Beatles made a rare return visit to the Granada TV Centre in Manchester, taping a mimed performance of 'I Should Have Known Better'. It was slotted into *Scene At 6.30* on Friday 16 October (6.30–7.00 pm), the eve of the second anniversary of their TV début, on Granada's *People And Places*.

Backstage at the ABC the Beatles gave an interview to Manchester-based TV reporter David Tindall, broadcast in this evening's edition of the BBC1 local news-magazine programme *Look North* (6.35–7.00 pm). In sound only, the interview was repeated by the BBC North Home Service radio programme *The Week In The North* on Saturday 17 October (9.30–10.00 am).

Thursday 15 October

Globe Cinema, Stockton-on-Tees

The Beatles' first visit to Stockton-on-Tees had occurred on the same day (22 November 1963) that President Kennedy was assassinated. This second and last visit to the north-east town coincided with a General Election in the United Kingdom, which returned the Labour Party, headed by Harold Wilson, to government after 13 years of Conservative rule. In their Stockton hotel room, the Beatles were visited by an interviewer and camera crew from local ITV station Tyne Tees and asked, among discussion about other subjects, about their voting intentions. The item was held over for a day and then transmitted in the news-magazine programme *North-East Newsview* on 16 October (6.35–7.00 pm).

Friday 16 October

ABC Cinema, Hull

While George Martin was busy in studio one at Abbey Road, 2.30 to 5.30 pm, producing two mono mixes of 'No Reply', the Beatles were about to arrive in Hull for their night's work at the ABC. After this date the tour resumed on the 19th.

Sunday 18 October

Studio Two, EMI Studios, London

Scarcely baulking at the idea of having to record during this break from their concert tour, and a Sunday at that, the Beatles put in a solid nine hours' work at Abbey Road, starting and completing the recording of six new album tracks *and* the A-side of their next single.

Working from 2.30 to 11.30 pm – a late finish by any standard, even more so considering they had to give two performances in Edinburgh the next evening – the Beatles first completed the 6 October recording of 'Eight Days A Week' with two edit pieces, one for the intro (not used) and the other for outro (used), and then set about the new material.

Only two of the six new recordings were Lennon-McCartney songs, and one of these was already several years old. For the others, the Beatles dived into their memories and returned with four songs from their pre-fame stage act. First to be taped (in just two takes but the first was "best") was Little Richard's medley of 'Kansas City'/'Hey-Hey-Hey-Hey!'; next was a re-make of Dr Feelgood and the Interns' 'Mr Moonlight', improving upon the 14 August recording with four more takes; next was the new single, John's 'I Feel

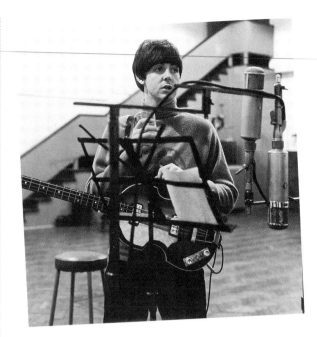

Fine' (nine takes); Paul's late-1950s composition 'I'll Follow The Sun' (eight); Carl Perkins' 'Everybody's Trying To Be My Baby' (just one take); Chuck Berry's 'Rock And Roll Music' (just one take) and Buddy Holly's 'Words Of Love' (three takes).

'I Feel Fine', released as the Beatles' next single on Friday 27 November (backed with 'She's A Woman') gave public warning that recording studio experimentation was afoot, its distinctive opening sound being deliberately-administered amplifier feedback.

Monday 19 October

ABC Cinema, Edinburgh

The first of three consecutive nights in Scotland.

Tuesday 20 October

Caird Hall, Dundee

A camera crew from Grampian Television – the ITV franchise for north-east Scotland – visited the Beatles in their Caird Hall dressing-room before the first of this evening's two "houses", filming an interview they gave to June Shields. The crew also shot some more general footage concerning the concert, including some Beatles stage action. The resulting package, running a little over five minutes, was inserted into *Grampian Week*, introduced by Shields and transmitted on Friday 23 October, 6.10–6.45 pm.

Wednesday 21 October

Odeon Cinema, Glasgow

While the Beatles were in Scotland, George Martin and team worked this day from 2.30 to 5.45 pm at Abbey Road producing mono masters of 'I Feel Fine', 'I'll Follow The Sun', 'She's A Woman' and 'Everybody's Trying To Be My Baby', with tapes of 'I Feel Fine' and 'She's A Woman' being cut out and dispatched to Capitol Records in Hollywood the next day.

Thursday 22 October

Odeon Cinema, Leeds

For George Martin, another mono mix of 'I Feel Fine', made between 11.00 am and 12.00 noon in studio one at EMI. For the Beatles, two more performances in Leeds.

Friday 23 October

Gaumont State Cinema, Kilburn, London

Saturday 24 October

Granada Cinema, Walthamstow, London

Sunday 25 October

Hippodrome Theatre, Brighton

After this date the tour resumed on the 28th.

Monday 26 October

Studio Two, EMI Studios, London

Another "rest day" from the tour in which the Beatles did anything but rest. Between 10.00 am and 12.45 pm they attended a mono mix session for 'I Don't Want To Spoil The Party', 'Rock And Roll Music', 'Words Of Love', 'Baby's In Black', 'I'm A Loser' and 'Kansas City'/'Hey-Hey-Hey-Hey!'.

Then, from 12.45 to 1.05 pm, a mere 20 minutes, they watched George Martin and his team mix 'Kansas City'/'Hey-Hey-Hey-Hey!' into stereo.

After a long break, they began recording more material for *Beatles For Sale*, taping five takes of 'Honey Don't' between 4.30 and 6.30 pm (the lead vocal role now handed to Ringo) and seven takes (numbered 13–19) of a re-make of 'What You're Doing' between 7.30 and 10.00 pm.

This final period of the day also saw the group record all of the material for 'Another Beatles Christmas Record', edited together at the end of the evening from five takes, including one solely of marching feet, and compiled into the finished production to be mailed out in December as a flexidisc to members of the Official Fan Club.

The less common view of EMI studio two, George midway down the 20 steps from the control room.

Tuesday 27 October

Studio Two, EMI Studios, London

Mono mixing, and editing where appropriate, of 'What You're Doing', 'Honey Don't', 'Mr Moonlight', 'Every Little Thing' and 'Eight Days A Week', completed between 10.00 am and 12.30 pm, and stereo mixing/editing of 'Eight Days A Week', 'Every Little Thing', 'What You're Doing' and 'Honey Don't' done from 12.30–1.00pm. (Observing that these four stereo masters for *Beatles For Sale* were made in a mere 30 minutes, it is obvious that mono was considered the important medium in 1964.)

Wednesday 28 October

ABC Cinema, Exeter

Thursday 29 October

ABC Cinema, Plymouth

Friday 30 October

Gaumont Cinema, Bournemouth

Saturday 31 October

Gaumont Cinema, Ipswich

Sunday 1 November

Astoria Cinema, Finsbury Park, London

Monday 2 November

King's Hall, Showgrounds, Balmoral, Belfast

This date had been assigned as a rest-day but promoter Arthur Howes squeezed in a late booking for Northern Ireland. The entourage flew into Aldergrove Airport from London during the afternoon.

Wednesday 4 November

Studio Two, EMI Studios, London
and **Ritz Cinema, Gordon St, Luton, Bedfordshire**

The remaining stereo mixes/edits for the LP, a three-hour session (10.00 am–1.00 pm) – which the Beatles may well have attended before driving up to Luton – producing masters of 'I'll Follow The Sun', 'Everybody's Trying To Be My Baby', 'Rock And Roll Music', 'Words Of Love', 'Mr Moonlight', 'I Don't Want To Spoil The Party', 'I'm A Loser', 'Baby's In Black', 'No Reply' and also, for the library shelf, the new single 'I Feel Fine'.

Beatles For Sale was released by EMI on Friday 4 December, the group's fourth LP in 21 months and yet another number one.

Thursday 5 November

Odeon Cinema, Nottingham

Friday 6 November

Gaumont Cinema, Southampton

Before the first "house" the Beatles were interviewed in their Gaumont dressing-room by Tony Bilbow, presently a reporter for Southern Television (and later a mainstay of the BBC2 arts series *Late Night Line-Up*), screened in the news-magazine programme *Day By Day* this evening, 6.05–6.40 pm.

Saturday 7 November

Capitol Cinema, Cardiff

Sunday 8 November

Empire Theatre, Liverpool

The Beatles' first home-town concert since 22 December 1963.

Monday 9 November

City Hall, Sheffield

Tuesday 10 November

Colston Hall, Bristol

The last night of the tour.

Saturday 14 November

Teddington Studio Centre, Teddington

A 1.00–5.00 pm visit to ABC Television in Teddington to rehearse and then video-tape, without an audience, a show-closing contribution to the following Saturday's edition of *Thank Your Lucky Stars* (21 November, 5.50–6.35 pm). They mimed to four songs: 'I Feel Fine', 'She's A Woman', 'I'm A Loser' and 'Rock And Roll Music'. To have the Beatles back on the show was deemed such a coup by ABC executives that they re-named this edition *Lucky Stars Special* in their honour.

As well as performing, the group participated in a humorous opening skit, in which, after delivering a short speech, Ringo pulled a cord to lift the covering from an adjacent statue. The statue turned out to be the real-life show host Brian Matthew, who promptly introduced the first act. The Beatles then popped up again just before the programme's only commercial break, giving the thumbs-up when Matthew announced that they would play in part two of the programme, following which they draped the cover back over him!

Monday 16 November

Studio Two, Riverside Studios, Crisp Rd, Hammersmith, London

A video-taping session for *Top Of The Pops*, shot at the Riverside Studios in west London (then leased exclusively by the BBC). On hand from 2.00 to 5.00 pm, inclusive of rehearsal time, the group mimed to the A- and B-sides of their new single, 'I Feel Fine' and 'She's A Woman'. Both went into the edition of Thursday 3 December, broadcast by BBC1 from 7.30 to 8.00 pm. 'She's A Woman' was then repeated on Thursday 10 December (again 7.30–8.00 pm) while 'I Feel Fine' was repeated in a special year-end edition of the show, *Top Of The Pops '64*, broadcast by BBC1 on Christmas Eve, Thursday 24 December, between 7.25 and 8.25 pm. (This latter programme also included a repeat of the 'A Hard Day's Night' video-tape shot on 7 July, and a new interview with the Beatles filmed in London on Tuesday 22 December – see separate entries.)

Tuesday 17 November

Playhouse Theatre, London

This session for BBC radio – the Beatles' 50th music programme contribution since 1962 – was another insert into the new series *Top Gear*, for broadcast in the Light Programme on Thursday 26 November, between 10.00 and 12.00 pm. Taping took place from 7.30 to 11.30 pm (including rehearsal time) at the Playhouse.

The group recorded six songs: 'I'm A Loser', 'Honey Don't', 'She's A Woman', 'Everybody's Trying To Be My Baby', 'I'll Follow The Sun' and 'I Feel Fine', and took part once again in a playful interview with show host Brian Matthew.

Friday 20 November

Wimbledon Common, London

John had latterly made the acquaintance of Peter Cook and Dudley Moore; he had also appeared alongside Norman

John with Dudley Moore and Norman Rossington, wombling free for the BBC on Wimbledon Common.

1964

Rossington in *A Hard Day's Night*. So for the first edition of a new Light Entertainment series for BBC Television, in which Moore was set to star and Cook and Rossington to guest, there was a fair chance that John may be involved, too. On 4 November, Rossington and the new series' producer, Joe McGrath, visited John backstage at the Ritz Cinema in Luton and invited him to participate. At this time Moore's series was still untitled; nearer the broadcast it was named *Not Only…But Also*. Cook eventually assumed a co-starring role, and the two continued to make excellent programmes under this title until 1970. This first edition, with John, went out on BBC2 on Saturday 9 January 1965, 9.20–10.00 pm.

John's involvement was two-fold. On this day, 20 November, he, Moore and Rossington shot a surrealistic film sequence to accompany the reading of his *In His Own Write* piece 'Deaf Ted, Danoota, (and me)'. The shoot location was Wimbledon Common, in south-west London; precise times of arrival/departure are not known, but they worked early and had completed the work before mid-morning.

The remainder of his contribution was taped on Sunday 29 November.

Monday 23 November

Wembley Studios, Wembley

Beatlemania, coupled perhaps with the enviable position to dictate terms, now ruled out any possibility that the Beatles might make another live appearance on *Ready, Steady, Go!* So on this Monday afternoon, before a clapping and dancing

audience at Rediffusion's studios in Wembley, north of London, the Beatles taped a four-song performance for insertion into the following Friday's edition of the series (27 November, 6.08–7.00 pm), miming to 'I Feel Fine', 'She's A Woman', 'Baby's In Black' and 'Kansas City'/'Hey-Hey-Hey-Hey!' They also chatted with programme host Keith Fordyce. It was the Beatles' third and final *RSG!* appearance as a group.

Wednesday 25 November

Studio One, Aeolian Hall, London

The Beatles' tenth and last music session for the BBC Light Programme radio show *Saturday Club*. Recording took place between 7.00 and 10.30 pm (including rehearsal time), transmission was on Boxing Day (26 December) between 10.00 am and 12.00 noon.

Six session recordings were broadcast in this programme: 'Rock And Roll Music', 'I'm A Loser' (these were included in the 10.31–10.59 am section transmitted simultaneously by the BBC's General Overseas Service), 'Everybody's Trying To Be My Baby', 'I Feel Fine', 'Kansas City'/'Hey-Hey-Hey-Hey!' and 'She's A Woman', together, as usual, with conversations with host Brian Matthew.

However four of these six – 'I'm A Loser', 'Everybody's Trying To Be My Baby', 'I Feel Fine' and 'She's A Woman' – were actually repeats from the 17 November *Top Gear* session. Whether the BBC felt these to have been more representative performances, or whether the Beatles simply instructed the BBC to re-use the material, to save themselves having to record them over again, is not known. The subterfuge was not announced.

Saturday 28 November

'Kenwood', Wood Lane, St George's Hill, Weybridge, Surrey

The 4 December issue of *New Musical Express* carried a full-page feature about John's new house in Weybridge, written after a visit this day by news editor Chris Hutchins. The *NME* man also took along his portable BBC tape recorder and interviewed John about the property for the Light Programme radio show *The Teen Scene*; the item was broadcast the following evening, Sunday 29 November, between 10.45 and 11.31.

Sunday 29 November

Studio One, Television Centre, London

The second part of John's contribution to the opening edition of *Not Only…But Also* was taped this evening, from 8.30, before an audience at the BBC's Television Centre in west London.

Several items from his book *In His Own Write* were read, mostly straight to camera. John alone read 'About The Awful' – his own biography from the book's back-cover – he and Norman Rossington recited 'Good Dog Nigel' and 'The Wrestling Dog' and then John, Rossington and Dudley Moore delivered 'All Abord Speeching'. Additionally, Rossington and Moore, without John's involvement, read 'Unhappy Frank'. Right at the end of the programme, as the credits were rolling to Moore's signature tune 'Goodbye-ee', John also flitted somewhat maniacally across the screen.

Tuesday 22 December

Odeon Cinema, Hammersmith, London

Although two previously-taped mimed music performances were already slotted into the programme (see 7 July and 16 November) Johnnie Stewart, the producer of *Top Of The Pops '64* – the special year-end edition of the weekly show set for transmission between 7.25 and 8.25 pm on 24 December – was keen to feature something altogether new by the group. When he learnt that one of the four hosts of his programme, Jimmy Savile, would be appearing in the forthcoming "Another Beatles Christmas Show" production, he dispatched cameras to the nearby Hammersmith Odeon to film a brief interview during a rehearsal break on this day. Brief was the word – Savile and the Beatles were seen chatting for all of 1 min 23 secs, the interview coming up into view after a few bars of 'I Want To Hold Your Hand' and fading out again near to the end of the song, neatly obscuring the fact that the Beatles had never filmed/taped this song for the BBC's cameras.

Thurs 24 – Thurs 31 December

Odeon Cinema, Hammersmith, London

Following the previous year's seasonal extravaganza, Brian Epstein now presented "Another Beatles Christmas Show" at the Hammersmith Odeon, across town from Finsbury Park. The venue may have changed but the formula was much the same: music, pantomime, comedy and, of course, a constant barrage of screaming from the youthful audience. The Beatles appeared in two sketches, one with Freddie Garrity (of the Dreamers) and another with disc-jockey Jimmy Savile, and sang 11 songs, 'Twist And Shout', 'I'm A Loser', 'Baby's In Black', 'Everybody's Trying To Be My

Baby', 'Can't Buy Me Love', 'Honey Don't', 'I Feel Fine', 'She's A Woman', 'A Hard Day's Night', 'Rock And Roll Music' and 'Long Tall Sally'.

Rehearsals began on 21 December and the show ran for 20 nights, two "houses" each, until 16 January 1965, except for 24 and 29 December where there was only one – a total of 38 performances. (There were no performances at all on 25 and 27 December, 3 and 10 January.)

At some point during this first week (the precise date was not documented), radio broadcaster/DJ Chris Denning visited the Beatles in their dressing-room at the Odeon and interviewed them, unfortunately while they were eating dinner, for a new series on Radio Luxembourg. Called *The Beatles* it was broadcast for 42 weeks every Sunday night (8.45–9.00 pm) from 3 January to 17 October 1965. The Beatles did not record music sessions for this series, in fact they had little to do with it at all, Radio Luxembourg having to spread thinly what scant interview material the group gave Denning – taped on this date and on 20 March, 29 April and 20 June 1965. Most of each week's 15 minutes was given over to news items and listeners' record requests.

The Beatles also read out listeners' letters during these interviews and dedicated songs to family and friends. This was especially revealing, and showed the group keen to maintain contact with their Liverpool past. In this first interview John dedicated records to Pete Shotton and to Nigel Whalley, Paul to Ivan Vaughan (Shotton, Whalley and Vaughan were ex-Quarry Men) and to the boys at his former school the Liverpool Institute and girls at Blackburne House (across the road from the Institute), George dedicated records to school friends Arthur Kelly and Tony Workman, and Ringo to friend Roy Trafford and also to Ernie and Vi and Al Caldwell (Al Caldwell being Rory Storm, Ernie and Vi his parents).

Bottom-left: the back-cover of the Christmas show programme – a seasonal drawing by John Lennon.

THIS WAS a curious year for the Beatles, one in which they consolidated all the successes and excesses of 1964 by virtually repeating everything already achieved. They made a second feature-film, *Help!*, they toured North America again, where Beatlemania continued to rage on an unparalleled scale, and then they toured Britain again, though only briefly. John even had a second book published.

But it was a transitional year, too, with an important shift in attitude. As the Beatles became ever more suffocated by the adulation around them they began to concentrate on pleasing themselves rather than pleasing the public. The most obvious result of this directional switch was a significant leap forward in their always innovative recordings, culminating this year with the album *Rubber Soul*. They also wound down their radio and television appearances, as if suddenly cognisant of the fact that they didn't have to wear themselves out, rushing around from one studio to another, in a hopeless attempt at satisfying demand. They were now more successful, popular and famous than any group or singer had ever been, bigger even than Elvis. Let the world come to them, and let them decide if the offer was or wasn't suitable. (And usually it wasn't.)

Help! was different from *A Hard Day's Night* in oh so many ways. It had to be different: no one could see any point in producing another semi-documentary, least of all the Beatles who, as their recording output showed, never stood still or did the same thing twice. *A Hard Day's Night* had been an almost-believable fictionalised account of real-life; *Help!* was

fiction pure and simple. *A Hard Day's Night* had been realistic, *Help!* was unadulterated fantasy. *A Hard Day's Night* had been shot in black and white and in equally colourless locations, *Help!* was shot in colour, in London, in the beautiful Bahamas and amid stunning Austrian snowscapes.

Help! certainly had its moments, and was an enjoyable, if implausible, film, but it was no match for the innovative and artful *A Hard Day's Night*. And the Beatles knew it, too. Paul and John, in particular, later declared that they had ended up, in effect, guest stars in their own movie, victims of an overwhelming plot and an arguably too-strong supporting cast. And this dissatisfaction was never forgotten: despite scores of rumours, despite talk of this title or that title, of this or that writing commission, despite numerous meetings and suggestions over the next two years, the Beatles never again as a group made any fiction feature-films.

On 12 June, seven weeks before *Help!* was premiered, Buckingham Palace announced that the four Beatles had each been awarded Membership of the Most Excellent Order of the British Empire in the Queen's Birthday Honours list. While it crowned the group's acceptance by the Establishment, a great many previous recipients of this and other awards were upset to see their own honour "cheapened" by the granting of MBEs to four Liverpudlian pop stars. For their part, the Beatles were also bemused by the award, but accepted it nonetheless. (John, who never felt easy about the decoration, returned his medal – though the award itself cannot be revoked – to Buckingham Palace in November 1969.)

With the controversy still raging, the Beatles set off for Paris on 20 June to begin their first concert tour of the year, a quick two-week saunter around France, Italy and Spain. Mostly the tour was remarkable for what it *didn't* produce – sold-out concert venues. Maybe once or twice over the previous two years a Beatles show hadn't been seen by a capacity house, but here it was a regular occurrence. Fewer people, too, were now at airports to welcome or bid farewell to the group. Certainly there remained huge numbers of fans following the Beatles' every move, and causing chaos at every juncture, but Beatlemania had noticeably diminished since 1963. Perhaps the fans were at last realising the futility of paying money to see the group give an inaudible 25-minute performance. The Beatles themselves had realised it long ago.

They realised, too, that touring was unlikely ever to return to the sanity of pre-1963, when they could enjoy a performance as much as their audience. The Beatles began to hanker for those days of lunchtime Cavern Club sessions, where their musicianship could progress and not be stifled by enveloping screams, where no one would make a grab for them except to thrust forward a piece of paper carrying a song request. The very antithesis of this lamented era was a 1965 Beatles concert tour of North America.

INTRODUCTION 1965 AND DIARY

With George Martin and Brian Epstein, receiving awards from EMI chairman Sir Joseph Lockwood (whom the group called "Sir Joe") at EMI's London HQ during the morning of 16 February.

Off on tour again *the Beatles – with Maureen Starkey and Cynthia Lennon – receive another enthusiastic send-off from British fans.*

Brian Epstein had flown to the USA as early as 19 January to fix the dates for their August American shows. It was to be a hit-and-run tour, typified by the selection of large and still-larger stadia capable of satisfying the biggest of ticket demands, by the Beatles' arrival in these stadiums in armoured cars, by a swift sub-30-minutes on stage and by a quick escape to an airport or besieged hotel, usually in the same armoured vehicle, the engine of which would be left running throughout the concert, by the stage, in case of a pitch invasion by fans. It was a military-style operation that attempted to mix spectacle with safety but which, on occasions, lost on both counts.

The tour certainly opened in fine style with the *pièce de resistance*, a concert before a world record-breaking, screaming and swooning crowd of 55,600 fans at Shea Stadium in New York. Perhaps the most famous of all Beatles concerts, it remains the apogee of their live career and, pleasingly, was filmed for television screening. It being the first date on the tour and a momentous occasion, the Beatles at least injected extra effort into their playing. But during the rest of the tour this sparkle disappeared: the group's musicianship at some of these concerts was little short of abysmal, certainly not

the calibre one would expect from the world's undisputed number-one group.

Not that the Beatles were entirely to blame; two years of playing to audiences which could scarcely hear a single note, and which would not have cared even if they *had* heard sloppy instrumentation and off-key singing, had made the Beatles lazy on stage. They had, by now, all but ceased rehearsals before a show or even, incredibly, before an entire tour. Ringo has since said that, on occasions, all four of them might suddenly stop playing a song and no-one in the audience would notice. John, who had long been shouting at the screaming fans to "Shurrup!", now began to scream off-mike obscenities at concert audiences.

For the Beatles' American fans, just plain glad to have the group back on US soil, the tour was as exciting and as memorable as the previous year's visit. Like the rest of the world, they had no inkling of the growing unhappiness within the Beatles' camp, of their reluctance to perform inaudible music to a sea of far-off Beatlemaniacs. Existing tapes of the group's concerts from this 1965 tour, and of their one-a-city press conferences (consistently ruined by the staggering inanity of the proffered questions) portray a noticeably irritable, bored

Tony Barrow directing yet
another press conference.

PRESS CONFERENCE
ADMIT ONE
BEATLE CONCERT
SAM HOUSTON COLISEUM
AUGUST 19, 1965

Signature

Radio Station KILT
Presents
The Sixth Annual Back-To-School Show
Sponsored By
THE VARIETY BOYS CLUB OF HOUSTON
STARRING THE BEATLES
(IN PERSON)
AND ALL-STAR SUPPORTING CAST
Master of Ceremonies: RUSS KNIGHT—The Weird Beard
GENERAL ADMISSION TICKET: $5.00
SAM HOUSTON COLISEUM — 8:00 P.M.
THURSDAY, AUGUST 19, 1965 • HOUSTON

KILT Nº 603 KILT

and frustrated group, no longer the "happy-go-lucky Fab Four".

The Beatles flew back to England on 1 September, collectively one million dollars the richer but with the embryo of a plan in their minds: the touring had to stop. They had already said as much to Brian Epstein when he had proposed an autumn/winter concert tour of Britain, a second appearance in the Royal Variety Show and a third successive Christmas show. Both of the latter suggestions were unanimously vetoed by the group, now beginning to flex strong collective muscle over their manager's wishes.

But Epstein's persistence about a British tour paid off, although it certainly took some time for the Beatles to change their mind. On 2 August NEMS announced "the Beatles will not be undertaking a tour of Britain this year". On 1 September a reverse statement was issued, saying that the group would tour Britain after all. Six weeks of protracted logistical haggling then took place between the Beatles, Brian Epstein and tour promoter Arthur Howes, the group remaining adamant that if they were to tour at all it would

be a very brief one. Eventually, a token nine-night December itinerary was drawn up and announced to the press on 11 October.

These nine concerts – for which, for the first time in Britain, the Beatles earned £1000 per night – constituted the last tour the group played in their home country. It wasn't announced as such, of course, because at this time it was a secret shared by just four people. Viewed with hindsight, however, the fact that something was amiss in the Beatles' attitude is obvious. The first date on the tour, Glasgow on Friday 3 December, coincided to the day with the release of their superb new album *Rubber Soul*. In the becalmed confines of the recording studio, despite being under severe deadline pressure, the Beatles had invested all of the energy they once devoted to daily live performances into making better music and experimentation with sound. This was their new escape and future direction. *Rubber Soul* comprised 14 new songs, lyrically and instrumentally the group's most ambitious project to date. Yet, on the tour, the Beatles performed just two numbers from the album, 'Nowhere Man' and 'If I Needed Someone'.

Granted, it would have been difficult for them, in those days of primitive concerts and equipment, to reproduce on stage the increasingly unusual and multi-tracked sounds they were now concocting inside the recording studio. Difficult, but not impossible.

The Beatles didn't bother – after all, what was the point? No one wanted to listen, they only wanted to scream.

Friday 1 – Saturday 16 January

Odeon Cinema, Hammersmith, London

The final 14 nights (excluding 3 and 10 January) of the production "Another Beatles Christmas Show", which had opened on 24 December 1964.

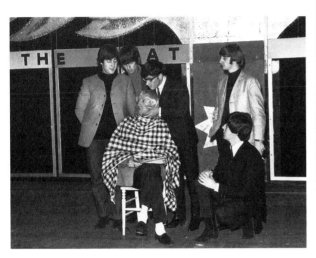

Monday 15 February

Studio Two, EMI Studios, London

Another year, another film, another set of recording sessions, and yet more furious industry. Work this day began at 2.30 pm with the recording of two takes of John's 'Ticket To Ride', and the song was completed and ready for mixing by 5.45. Released as the A-side of the Beatles' next single on

Friday 9 April, as well as on the soundtrack album for the yet-to-be-started film, 'Ticket To Ride' was the result of much more work than the two-take figure would suggest, with – from this year – overdubs onto the multi-track tape not being given separate numbers as before. Here, the Beatles twice taped a rhythm track (the first was a false-start, the second was "best") and then recorded any amount of overdubs – numbers were never specified on recording documents – onto vacant tracks of the tape, perfecting vocals and anything else that they felt needed more attention.

Between 7.00 and 10.30 pm the Beatles recorded Paul's 'Another Girl' (one take, plus ten edit pieces) and George's 'I Need You' (five takes), both of which were completed with overdubs the next day.

Tuesday 16 February

Studio Two, EMI Studios, London

This second of six consecutive days at EMI began with a 2.30–5.00 pm session that saw 'I Need You' and then 'Another Girl' completed with the overdubbing of George's vocal, cowbell and tone-pedal guitar onto 'I Need You' and guitar onto 'Another Girl'.

The Beatles spent the remainder of the session, from 5.00 until 10.00 pm, recording and perfecting in 14 takes 'Yes It Is', an exquisite three-part harmony ballad written by John and sung by John, Paul and George in a style reminiscent of 'This Boy'. 'Yes It Is' was not selected for the film soundtrack, nor was it included on the non-soundtrack side of what was to become the *Help!* album. Instead it appeared merely as the B-side of the Beatles' next single, such was their songwriting wealth.

Wednesday 17 February

Studio Two, EMI Studios, London

The recording of two more songs for the film soundtrack, Paul's 'The Night Before' and George's 'You Like Me Too Much', although the latter was later relegated to the non-soundtrack side of the *Help!* album. 'The Night Before' was taped and completed in two takes from 2.00 until 7.00 pm, 'You Like Me Too Much' was done to a finish in eight takes from 7.00 until 11.00 pm.

Thursday 18 February

Studio Two, EMI Studios, London

This full day's work at Abbey Road began quietly with a 10.00 am–1.00 pm mono mix session for 'Ticket To Ride', 'Another Girl', 'I Need You' and 'Yes It Is'. (Later, in between the two recording sessions, 5.15–6.00 pm, more mono mixes were produced, of 'The Night Before' and 'You Like Me Too Much'.)

Between 3.30 and 5.15 pm the Beatles began and completed, in nine all-acoustic takes, John's Bob Dylan-influenced ballad 'You've Got To Hide Your Love Away'.

With Jimmy Savile.

1965

RECORDING SHEET

From a recording point of view, this song is especially noteworthy in that it marked the first time the Beatles called in a session musician to augment their line-up. (Andy White, who drummed on 'Love Me Do' and 'PS I Love You', was called in to *replace* Ringo for those early recordings, not complement his contribution – see 11 September 1962.) The musician was musical arranger and flautist Johnnie Scott, and in return for his £6 session fee (but no sleeve credit) he contributed tenor flute and alto flute parts.

Ringo had secured a lead vocal on all Beatles albums to date excepting *A Hard Day's Night*. But since he had yet to provide a self-composition for his outings a suitable "vehicle" was always provided. For *Please Please Me* it was the Shirelles' song 'Boys'. For *With The Beatles* John and Paul gave him 'I Wanna Be Your Man'. On *Beatles For Sale* he had sung Carl Perkins' 'Honey Don't', and he had sung another Perkins song, 'Matchbox', on the EP *Long Tall Sally*. But what would be his contribution to this new LP? Written especially for the

occasion by John and Paul, the answer was a rocker entitled 'If You've Got Trouble'. To this day the song remains unreleased, locked in the EMI vault – and it's not difficult to see why. It wasn't one of the better Lennon-McCartney numbers by any stretch of the imagination, nor was it brilliantly performed in the one and only take (with overdubs) recorded in the early part of a 6.30–10.30 session this evening.

In the latter part of the same session, Paul's 'Tell Me What You See' was started and completed in four takes. As with George's 'You Like Me Too Much', this was submitted, but not selected, for the new film, so it ended up on the non-soundtrack side of the associated album.

Friday 19 February

Studio Two, EMI Studios, London

John's 'You're Going To Lose That Girl' was recorded from start to finish in a single afternoon session, 3.30–6.20 pm, with two basic takes and overdubs. A later attempt to improve the song (see 30 March) was abandoned and never used, and the *Help!* soundtrack album featured this 19 February recording.

Saturday 20 February

Studio Two, EMI Studios, London

There being so few Beatles/EMI recordings remaining unreleased, it's somewhat bizarre that inside three days the group should tape two songs destined for such a fate, for with 'If You've Got Trouble' scarcely yet a painful memory, another Lennon-McCartney song begun this day, 'That Means A Lot', suffered the same ending. Written for the new film, the Beatles made two separate attempts at recording it – in two takes between 12.00 noon and 5.15 pm this day, and again on 30 March, before giving up and, instead, donating it to P J Proby for his exclusive use. (Proby recorded his version at EMI on 7 April 1965, produced by Ron Richards.)

Five more mono mixes were done on this day too – of 'If You've Got Trouble', 'Tell Me What You See' and 'You're Going To Lose That Girl' between 11.00 am and 12.00 noon, and of 'That Means A Lot' and 'You've Got To Hide Your Love Away' between 5.15 and 6.00 pm – thereby completing a full mixed set of all 11 songs recorded by the Beatles during the week of 15–20 February. Stereo mixes of all 11 new songs were made in studio one at EMI between 10.00 am and 1.00 pm on Tuesday 23 February under the supervision of balance engineer Norman Smith.

Tues 23 February – Tues 9 March

various locations, New Providence, Bahamas

In its quest to be, above all else, different from *A Hard Day's Night*, the Beatles' new film began shooting in the Bahamas. That first film had been shot in black-and-white, under dull skies and in drab London-area locations like Gatwick,

Notting Hill Gate, Hammersmith and West Ealing. *Help!* (though it didn't have this title yet) was filmed in colour on bright Bahamanian beaches, glittering Austrian mountains and, even in the London area, at more affluent locations such as Asprey's and the beautiful country house at Cliveden.

There was another reason why *Help!* was part-filmed in the Bahamas, however: the Beatles' financial adviser, Dr Walter Strach, had recently established there a tax shelter for the group. This obliged him to live on the island for a year and led to the suggestion that, to show goodwill, the Beatles should film in this British crown colony. And there were no ifs and buts about it: director Richard Lester and producer Walter Shenson – the same team that was behind *A Hard Day's Night* – were *told* that this was where shooting would begin. Anyway, few would argue with the prospect of filming in the North West Indies in February, so the Beatles flew into the Bahamas on the 22nd and set up residence in a house at the luxurious Balmoral Club, near Cable Beach.

All of the shooting here took place on the 21-mile-long island of New Providence, amid great numbers of sightseers. And it wasn't only Bahamanians eager to spectate – several foreign journalists also made the trip, the Beatles recording a number of interviews for US radio and press while here.

Although designated for unpacking and as an opportunity for the crew to recce locations, filming began during the first clear afternoon, **Tuesday 23 February**, first with Ringo listening to conch shells at a dock-side location near Mackey Street (this was one of numerous filmed scenes which did not feature in the finished print) and then all four Beatles being filmed while swimming, fully clothed, in the pool at the Nassau Beach Hotel in the West Bay area.

On Wednesday the **24th** the Beatles had their first full day of shooting, adhering to an 8.30 am–5.30 pm schedule which, approximately, was maintained each day. They were filmed for the first of several occasions cycling around on Interfield Road, near to the airport.

On the **25th** the four filmed again on Interfield Road; Ringo and John were filmed at the nearby stadium of the Bahamas Softball Association; and Paul only was filmed at some lime quarry caves.

Friday 26 February was an especially busy day, Ringo filming at the yacht basin and in front of the Post Office on Bay Street, George and Ringo at the kapok tree-house in the gardens of the Royal Victoria Hotel, and John running out of the public library shouting "Ringo!" (Non-Beatles action also took place this day at the swampland at Lake Cunningham, where the prison-camp sequences were filmed.)

Saturday the **27th** (the Beatles worked both days of both weekends while in the Bahamas) was spent shooting on Balmoral Island, including a sequence miming to 'Another Girl'.

On **Sunday 28 February** they filmed on Cabbage Beach on Paradise Island, returning there the next day (**1 March**) to shoot at a French gourmet restaurant called Café Martinique. Also on Monday 1 March Ringo was filmed with Professor Foot (Victor Spinetti), Algernon (Roy Kinnear) and Ahme (Eleanor Bron) on a schooner moored offshore.

Tuesday to Thursday, 2 to 4 March, the Beatles continued filming on both Cabbage Beach and Victoria Beach, shooting in particular (on the 3rd) the final sequence in the film, where Ringo is staked out on the sand.

On **5 March** the Beatles filmed sequences at a number of locations on the island and at some cloisters, concentrating in particular on the scenes where John, Paul and George scour the island calling out "Ringo!".

On the **6th** they filmed at Nassau International Airport, descending airplane steps and madly taking photographs of each other.

On the **7th and 8th** they filmed at what, in the movie, they assumed to be a temple, and what, in real life, they assumed to be a disused army camp. (In fact, it was a ramshackle hospital for handicapped children and old people, the state of which disgusted the Beatles.)

"Help!" Director Richard Lester humorously exasperated as the Beatles film on Interfield Road, New Providence, 24 February 1965.

Finally, on the 9th, the Beatles returned to Paradise Island for some pick-up shots.

The Beatles left the Bahamas on Wednesday 10 March and returned to England, arriving at London Airport at 7.05 in the morning of the 11th.

Sunday 14 – Saturday 20 March

Obertauern, Austria

On Saturday 13 March, two days after returning from the Bahamas, the Beatles and their film crew once again departed England for foreign climes: this time to the snow-capped mountains of Austria. They flew out of London Airport on the 11.00 am flight for Salzburg, where they were greeted by some 4000 fans and scores of Austrian journalists. After a press conference at a nearby hotel – filmed, typically, by newsreel and TV cameras – the Beatles were taken to the Hotel Edelweiss in Obertauern, where they were based until departure on the 22nd. All of the filming took place in Obertauern.

Shooting began on **Sunday 14 March** in front of the hotel, where they filmed a "toboggan hire" sequence not used in the finished print. They then moved elsewhere in the locality and were filmed falling backwards together into snow. Beatles "doubles" were also in action this first day, filmed riding on a horse-drawn sleigh. (The doubles were Cliff Diggins, Mick Dillon, Peter Cheevers and Joe Dunne, Londoners all.)

Beatles and "doubles" filmed on **Monday 15 March** on a ski-lift and on the slopes. The ski-lift sequence was then completed on the **16th**.

On the **17th** the Beatles filmed a sequence at the curling rink and then ended this extended day by filming amid some

bushes. It was on this day that the film's title was announced as *Eight Arms To Hold You*, and so it would remain for almost another month.

The **18th** was another busy day, filming at an Olympic jump location, on the mountainside and in an après-ski cellar, while on **Friday the 19th** pick-up shots were filmed on a terrace and in the snow.

The **20th** was the last day of shooting, with the Beatles and their "doubles" back out on the slopes, miming to part of 'Ticket To Ride' and generally being silly. The filming was then completed with an outdoor restaurant sequence involving Ringo and his "double" (not in the finished film).

Although the Beatles stayed behind, the film unit left Obertauern on the 21st, shooting a scene at Radstadt station with the "doubles" and another in a tunnel en route to Salzburg, where they stayed for the night. The Beatles left Obertauern on the 22nd and flew back to London from Salzburg, arriving in the early evening.

The group undertook at least two telephone interviews while in Obertauern. The first was on Friday 19 March, with the BBC. It was now almost three months since Brian Epstein had allowed BBC radio any exclusives concerning the Beatles: no music sessions, not even an interview, and the Corporation's executives were growing increasingly concerned at the paucity of appearances of the country's peak attraction on the country's national broadcasting network. Finally, under pressure, Epstein agreed to the group's recording a telephone interview from their suite at the Hotel Edelweiss.

The call came through from London at 8.00 pm local time (7.00 pm British time) and, once again, Brian Matthew was on the other end of the phone. The ensuing conversation was slotted into the next morning's (20 March) *Saturday Club* at just after 11.00 am. (As usual, the show was broadcast in the Light Programme between 10.00 am and 12.00 noon. This morning's section of the programme to be simultaneously broadcast by the General Overseas Service was 10.31 to 10.59.)

At around the same time the following evening, 20 March, John and Ringo were interviewed by telephone by Chris Denning, back in London, for his weekly Radio Luxembourg series *The Beatles* (see 24 December 1964). George and Paul did not participate in this brief exchange.

Recording-related note: on Monday 15 March, back at EMI in London (studio two, 10.00–11.00 am) a new mono mix of 'Ticket To Ride' was made by balance engineer Norman Smith for use by Capitol Records as the master for the imminent new Beatles single, and also by film company United Artists.

Wednesday 24 – Friday 26 March

Twickenham Film Studios, St Margaret's, Twickenham

At last, shooting began on home territory, and familiar territory at that: Twickenham Film Studios in the west of London suburb of St Margaret's, where *A Hard Day's Night* had been shot at this same time in 1964. Working a similar schedule – something like 8.30 am–5.30 pm daily – the

Beatles filmed here and hereabouts on location until Sunday 9 May. Including the Bahamanian and Austrian sections, but discounting occasional days off, this second Beatles film was shot in 11 weeks, three more than for *A Hard Day's Night*.

Sequences filmed during these first few days included the interior temple sequences (set in the Bahamas section of the film) – including a part where John, Paul and George dive through a hollow sacrificial altar and into water (surfacing at the Nassau Beach Hotel on 23 February).

Sunday 28 March

Alpha Television Studios, Aston, Birmingham

Taping of the Beatles' final personal appearance on ABC Television's weekly pop series *Thank Your Lucky Stars*, the show which had launched them on national TV in January 1963 but which was now in steady decline. (It ended on 25 June 1966, by which time it was no longer screened by all of the ITV regions.)

On this occasion, while it was still fully networked, the Beatles returned to the scene of that début, Alpha Television Studios in Birmingham, and mimed performances of three songs, 'Eight Days A Week', 'Yes It Is' and 'Ticket To Ride', before an extremely enthusiastic studio audience. Paul and Ringo were also interviewed by the show's host, Brian Matthew, and the programme was broadcast on Saturday 3 April (5.50–6.35 pm).

Monday 29 March

Twickenham Film Studios, St Margaret's, Twickenham

The first day of the second week of studio shooting at Twickenham. Sequences such as the long laboratory scene with Professor Foot and Algernon, and the interior railway station scene, were filmed during this week.

Tuesday 30 March

Twickenham Film Studios, St Margaret's, Twickenham and Studio Two, EMI Studios, London

After today's filming the Beatles returned to London for an unsuccessful evening's recording at Abbey Road. Booked for 7.00 until 9.00 pm but running over until 10.00, they first attempted a re-make of 'That Means A Lot' but abandoned the song again after five more uninspired takes (numbered 20–24). They then recorded some overdubs – of which instrument(s) is not specified on the EMI session documentation – onto the existing "best" take of 'You're Going To Lose That Girl', although none was used for the released version.

Wed 31 March and Thurs 1 April

Twickenham Film Studios, St Margaret's, Twickenham

More shooting for *Eight Arms To Hold You*.

Friday 2 April

Twickenham Film Studios, St Margaret's, Twickenham

While the Beatles were filming at Twickenham George Martin was working at Abbey Road (10.00–11.00 am) producing a stereo mix of 'You're Going To Lose That Girl' that incorporated the 30 March overdub. It was never used.

Monday 5 – Friday 9 April

Twickenham Film Studios, St Margaret's, Twickenham

The first two days of this week were spent shooting the interior dining-area and kitchen sections of the "Rajahama" restaurant sequence, all on a set built at Twickenham. During a break in filming on the 6th the Beatles received a "Bell" award from Radio Caroline, presented to them by disc-jockey Simon Dee and filmed by newsreel cameras, and Dee also took the opportunity to interview the Beatles for a broadcast on the pirate airwaves. (Date unknown, but around this time here at Twickenham, the Beatles also recorded an interview with the other leading British pirate station, Radio London.)

On Wednesday 7 April the four Beatles filmed the "pub cellar" sequence, in which Ringo, having fallen through a trap door, is confronted by "Raja, the famous Bengal man-eater".

On the 8th four sequences were filmed, only two involving the Beatles: all four of the group took part in a washroom sequence, in which havoc was wreaked by an excessive hot-air hand-drier and then Ringo shot a solo sequence in a bathroom, not in the finished film.

Another unused scene was shot on Friday 9 April, set in a warehouse interior with the four Beatles, Superintendent Gluck (Patrick Cargill), seven of his policemen and 12 "thugs" belonging to Clang (Leo McKern).

Saturday 10 April

Studio Two, Riverside Studios, London

With a new single out, another *Top Of The Pops* television appearance was necessary, and for the last time the group went into BBC studios and shot a mimed performance exclusively for *TOTP* screening. Video-taping (including rehearsals) took place from 1.30 pm and two songs were shot, the usual A- and B-side formula: 'Ticket To Ride' and 'Yes It Is'. For the first time, the Beatles wore the fawn-colour jackets which they would don again the next day at the *NME* concert and then wear for their famous Shea Stadium concert (see 15 August).

Both song performances were included in *Top Of The Pops* on Thursday 15 April, transmitted from 7.30 to 8.00 pm. 'Yes It Is' was then repeated the following week (22 April) and 'Ticket To Ride' on 29 April and again on 6 May (all 7.30–8.00 pm).

Note: another broadcast of this 'Ticket To Ride' tape, albeit a brief one (25 seconds), occurred, of all places, in an edition of the weekly children's sci-fi drama *Dr Who*. ('The Executioners', the first episode of a six-part Dalek story which carried the overall title 'The Chase', transmitted by BBC1 on Saturday 22 May 1965, 5.40–6.05 pm.) This came about when Vicki (Maureen O'Brien), the good Doctor's main assistant, was describing the workings of his "time and space visualiser" machine. "Anything that ever happens anywhere in the universe is recorded in light neutrons," she explains, pointing out that the Doctor's machine "converts the energy from light neutrons into electrical impulses… that means that you can just tune in and see every event in history!" By way of a demonstration, the Doctor (William Hartnell) switches it on and a random image flickers onto the screen: the Beatles, each standing on a small round podium, performing 'Ticket To Ride'.

Receiving their poll-winners awards on stage at the New Musical Express concert with (L to R) NME editor Andy Gray, American singer Tony Bennett and NME owner/executive director Maurice Kinn.

Sunday 11 April

Empire Pool, Wembley
and **Studio One, Teddington Studio Centre, Teddington**

An appearance in the *New Musical Express* 1964–65 Annual Poll-Winners' All-Star Concert, the Beatles' third consecutive contribution to this afternoon show presented by the weekly pop paper. In front of a 10,000 audience they performed 'I Feel Fine', 'She's A Woman', 'Baby's In Black', 'Ticket To Ride' and 'Long Tall Sally'.

Highlights of the concert were broadcast in two 85-minute ABC Television specials titled *Poll Winners Concert*, the first of these, the one including the Beatles' appearance, transmitted on 18 April (Easter Sunday), 3.15–4.40 pm in most of Britain, 4.10–5.35 pm in the London area. Viewers also saw the group collect their poll awards from American singer Tony Bennett.

Immediately after the *NME* performance, the Beatles left Wembley and drove to ABC's Teddington studios, arriving at 6.30 pm. After dinner and a change of clothes, they participated in a rehearsal/camera run-through (7.30–8.30), dress rehearsal (8.45–9.30) and, finally, live transmission (11.05–11.50 pm) of the weekly series *The Eamonn Andrews Show*.

Their involvement spanned three sections. First, with John joining Eamonn at the presenter's desk, Ringo and George sitting on the settee and Paul in the swivel-chair, they participated in the opening ten-minute chat segment, discussing, among other topics, the making of their new feature-film, whether they had tried to analyse their success, and the likelihood of them assuming individual careers after a group split. After the first commercial break they performed (miming) 'Ticket To Ride' and 'Yes It Is', then, finally, they took part in Andrews' main discussion forum, running 18 mins 35 secs, in which two additional guests participated, in this instance newspaper columnist Katharine Whitehorn and the author/critic Wolf Mankowitz. (For this section of the programme Paul joined John at the desk, Mankowitz joined Ringo and George on the settee and Whitehorn bagged ABC's prized swivel-chair.)

Monday 12 April

Twickenham Film Studios, St Margaret's, Twickenham

Shooting of the scene, supposedly set inside Buckingham Palace, in which the Beatles, running along a corridor, are triggered into slow-motion by Professor Foot's "Relativity Cadenza".

Tuesday 13 April

Twickenham Film Studios, St Margaret's, Twickenham
and **Studio Two, EMI Studios, London**

In the morning the Beatles completed shooting the "Relativity Cadenza" scene begun the previous day. They weren't required at Twickenham for the rest of the day, however, with studio and location shots involving Professor Foot, Algernon, Clang, Bhuta (John Bluthal) and their "thugs" being filmed here and on location through the afternoon and evening. But the group remained at the film studios long enough to give a live interview for BBC radio.

BBC executives had been expecting the Beatles to make another "bank holiday" radio special for broadcast on Easter Monday (19 April), albeit one with a different structure to the four previous editions, perhaps with each of the group choosing and introducing his favourite records. But their hopes were dashed; instead, Brian Epstein could offer only a brief group interview for the Light Programme's daily lunchtime record and chat show *Pop Inn*. It was broadcast between 1.00 and 1.55 pm this day and included a live interview beamed direct from Twickenham Film Studios, the Beatles sitting in the BBC's "radio car", parked on the studio lot. Accompanied by the playing of 'Ticket To Ride', they appeared just after 1.45 pm.

Director Richard Lester had wanted the Beatles' second feature-film to be called *Beatles 2*. Then Ringo had suggested *Eight Arms To Hold You*, but after a couple of days nobody seemed to care for this very much either, especially John and Paul who didn't fancy the prospect of writing a song with such a laboured title. Now, in mid-April, *Help!* was conceived (most probably by Lester) – and, once again, John and Paul had to go away and compose a title song. In the end, it was written almost exclusively by John, and in later years he would look back upon the lyric as being one of his first real "message" numbers, the author pleading for help from somebody, anybody, to relieve his insecurity. Recording of the song was started and finished in a single evening session this day at EMI, 7.00–11.15 pm, with 12 takes and numerous distinctive overdubs onto the last of these.

Being the film title, 'Help!' was also the title of the soundtrack album, issued in Britain by EMI on Friday 6 August, and of the Beatles' next single, released two weeks previously, on Friday 23 July.

Wednesday 14 April

Ailsa Ave, St Margaret's, Twickenham, Middlesex

The first time the Beatles are seen in *Help!* is when their Rolls-Royce pulls up in a suburban residential street, they get out and proceed to enter four adjacent terraced houses here in Ailsa Avenue (located not far from the studio) – Ringo in number 5, John 7, Paul 9 and George 11, while, across the road, two women bystanders (Dandy Nichols, later to star in the BBC sitcom *Till Death Us Do Part*, and Gretchen Franklin), ponder on the boys' remarkable normality and whether or not they would appreciate a wave.

What neither they nor the world could see was that, on the inside, the four houses had been knocked into one enormous communal area – although this, of course, was shot on a set at Twickenham. While in Ailsa Avenue this day the Beatles also shot some street scenes.

The group were not involved in shooting on the 15th and then they and the crew enjoyed a long Easter weekend break, re-convening at the studio on Tuesday 20 April.

What it's like when the Beatles come down your road

AILSA AVENUE, Twickenham, is a quiet suburban street. The mornings are quiet except for the occasional clink of a milk bottle or call by the baker or laundry man.

But during the past few weeks Ailsa Avenue has been a hive of activity and sometimes bedlam, for it is here that United Artists were filming part of the Beatles' new film, "Help." It's not a long film—only about one-and-a-half hours—but it is a film that must be a box office winner. Judging

Twickenham and Teddington

from the popularity of their first film, "A Hard Day's Night," United Artists will rake it in again with this story of intrigue centred upon the famous quartet.

Ailsa Avenue plays a big part in the film, which involves a plot by an Eastern cult to obtain Ringo for their next feast—not as a guest but as a meal. A fan sends Ringo a ring (he collects them) and a note which tells him he is about to become a meal. Ringo doesn't fancy this at all and is helped to evade capture by John, Paul and George.

Ailsa Avenue is their London home in the film.

The front doors of No. 7 and three adjoining houses are used for the film. The inside of the house is all one, but there is a separate front door for each Beatle. The inside of the home is a stage set.

Occupier of No. 7 is Mrs. Beatrice Pennington, who made tea for the Beatles during the filming.

"I loved the whole thing," she said. "I had them all in to tea and they gave me an autographed picture to put in the sitting room. It was no trouble, we even got the front door and windows painted into the bargain.

"It is very quiet around here but this certainly broke the monotony."

Break the monotony it did—it also helped break the silence, with dozens of screaming fans on school holidays, surging up and down the street.

Police were on hand to take control, but they couldn't stop the noise. During filming the crowds were kept well back so there would be no interference.

Funniest of all was Leo McKern, Australian-born actor who lives in Hampton. Mr.

McKern, high priest of the Eastern cult, could be seen dressed in cult regalia moving industriously up and down the street chatting occasionally with members of the film crew.

One scene shows him emerging slowly from under a manhole cover, and he was watched with much amusement from nearby homes. The Beatles themselves enjoyed the whole thing immensely.

For the girls it was a day of organising. The fans were really on the ball. They started an elaborate warning system to tell them when the Beatles were coming. At the Chertsey Road roundabout a girl was posted to tell them when the Beatles' car was arriving.

The warning girl in turn would signal a friend at the corner of Ailsa Avenue and they were all prepared when they arrived.

Girls not taking part in this system were sometimes caught napping and missed a chance to get near.

Most of those waiting for the Beatles were girls who brought packed lunches and sometimes little picnic chairs to help them in their wait.

Sometimes the Beatles didn't turn up at all, but when they did it was screams and struggles all round.

The filming is finished now. Ailsa Avenue is quiet again, and Mrs. Pennington and other people in the street await anxiously the first showing of the film.

John Lennon talks to actor Leo McKern outside a house in Ailsa Avenue, Twickenham.

Friday 16 April

Studio One, Wembley Studios, Wembley

An appearance on Rediffusion's *Ready, Steady, Go!* was still one of the best ways for an artist/group to promote the release of a new single. The problem was, the Beatles would no longer appear live on the programme and they would no longer pre-tape (as they had done on 23 November 1964). A partial solution was effected this evening, when John and George (only) went along to Rediffusion's Wembley Studios to plug 'Ticket To Ride' and be interviewed by show host Cathy McGowan in this live Good Friday broadcast, 6.08–7.00 pm. Among the other guests appearing in this edition were Adam Faith, Doris Troy, the Kinks and Herman's Hermits.

Actually, it wasn't *Ready, Steady, Go!* anymore: the title had changed to *Ready Steady Goes Live!* on 2 April when the programme adopted a live-music policy and switched location from Studio Nine at Kingsway to the bigger Studio One at Wembley. (The change was also intended to breathe new life into this 18-month-old series which, despite the golden glow it enjoys among 1990s nostalgic memories, was certainly floundering by this time. Rumours of its imminent death were many throughout 1965 and 1966, the title reverted to *Ready, Steady, Go!* on 4 June 1965 and it remained like this until the final edition, on 23 December 1966, which was called *Ready, Steady, Goes!*)

Sunday 18 April

Room 65, EMI Studios, London

An early mono mix of 'Help!' and stereo mixes of this and also 'The Night Before', made between 10.00 am and 12.30 pm. ('Help!' would be done again in both mono and stereo on 18 June.)

Tuesday 20 April

Twickenham Film Studios, St Margaret's, Twickenham

The resumption of shooting after the Easter break. Among the scenes shot today was the one in which a "thug" attempts to remove Ringo's "Sacrificial Ring" as he puts his hand into a mail-box to post a letter. (The location element of this sequence was filmed on 9 May.)

Wednesday 21 April

Twickenham Film Studios, St Margaret's, Twickenham

Filming of the scene, supposedly set inside Scotland Yard, in which the Beatles visit the office of Superintendent Gluck.

Thursday 22 April

Twickenham Film Studios, St Margaret's, Twickenham

One of the first sequences in *Help!* has the Beatles performing the title song in what is supposed to be a television appearance (hence the black-and-white footage: British TV did not begin colour transmissions until December 1967). It was also shown being projected onto a home-movie screen at which Clang, filmed in colour, threw darts. The scene was shot this day at Twickenham.

The untouched B&W footage (that is, without McKern and his darts), as supplied to them by United Artists, was distributed to TV companies by NEMS to promote 'Help!' when it was released as a single on 23 July. BBC1's *Top Of The Pops*, for example, showed the clip in the programmes of 29 July (7.30–8.00 pm) and 19 August (7.25–8.00 pm). (This latter edition also included UA-supplied movie

footage of 'Another Girl'.) On commercial television, what has come to be known as the "dartless" clip was included in the 200th edition of *Thank Your Lucky Stars*, this time titled *Lucky Stars Anniversary Show*, networked by ABC on

Titter ye not. The Beatles with the great Frankie Howerd shooting Help! *at Twickenham.*

Saturday 17 July (5.50–6.30 pm), and on TWW's *Discs A Gogo* on Monday 26 July (5.00–5.25 pm).

Later in the day, the Beatles began shooting a long scene which did not make the finished print, in which they were joined by British comedian Frankie Howerd, playing the part of Sam Ahab, teacher of dramatic art, and – as Lady Macbeth, one of Ahab's pupils – the then unknown actress Wendy Richard (later to play Miss Brahms in the BBC sitcom *Are You Being Served?* and more recently appearing as Pauline Fowler in the BBC soap *EastEnders*).

Friday 23 April

Twickenham Film Studios, St Margaret's, Twickenham

More filming of the drama-school sequence with Frankie Howerd and Wendy Richard. Clang and Ahme joined the sequence this time.

Saturday 24 April

City Barge, Strand-on-the-Green, Chiswick, London

The Beatles went out on location this day, shooting the sequence that precedes the one in which Ringo is trapped in a cellar with a man-eating tiger (shot 7 April). They filmed in the tiny Chiswick hamlet of Strand-on-the-Green, walking down the narrow Post Office Alley and out onto the River Thames towpath. Then, as they realise their life is in danger (from marauding "thugs" dressed as bagpipe players), they seek shelter inside the City Barge public house (interior City Barge footage was shot on a set at Twickenham – see 28 April). They then re-emerged onto the towpath without Ringo (trapped in the cellar) by diving straight through the pub's glass window frontage.

John and Paul weren't needed after this filming. George and Ringo went elsewhere (not used in the finished film, and location not documented) to shoot a street and telephone-box scene, and then an additional item was filmed, without any of the Beatles, inside the food department at Harrods in Knightsbridge. (Again, not used in the finished film.) There was no shooting on Monday, filming commencing again on Tuesday 27 April.

Tuesday 27 April

Twickenham Film Studios, St Margaret's, Twickenham

One of the most remarkable scenes in *Help!* was that in which, heavily disguised, the Beatles are seen at an airport terminal (actually a film set, shot this day), prior to flying out to the Bahamas. It was remarkable because, as the years passed, so three of the Beatles assumed his make-believe disguise in real life. With his long flowing beard and granny glasses, John was anticipating his summer-1969 look. Bewhiskered George looked this way again in spring 1967 (*Sgt Pepper* sleeve era) and Ringo's tight-cropped hair and chin beard was his mid-1970 image.

Also shot on this day, preceding the imminent visit to

Salisbury Plain, the Beatles filmed a scene with Ahme atop a tank turret.

Wednesday 28 April

Twickenham Film Studios, St Margaret's, Twickenham

Filming of the drama-school sequence with the Beatles, Frankie Howerd, Wendy Richard, Leo McKern and Eleanor Bron was completed during the morning, the best part of two working days having been spent on a scene which ended up on the cutting-room floor.

Shot in the afternoon was the interior pub scene that follows on from the City Barge location shooting the previous Saturday, concluding with Ringo falling through a trap-door.

While on the "pub" set, filming for a different purpose also took place: Peter Sellers arrived at Twickenham to present the Beatles with a prestigious Grammy Award (he called it a "Grandma Award") on behalf of the US National Academy of Recording Arts and Sciences, 'A Hard Day's Night' having won the "Best Performance by a Vocal Group" category for 1964. In a brief though amusing (and certainly pre-arranged) item, John began speaking nonsense French, something like "Izza longois", the others joined in with "ta tipe, à réri" and then all five put the words together, singing a verse from 'It's A Long Way To Tipperary'.

The item was networked on US television by NBC on Tuesday 18 May 1965 (8.30–9.30 pm, EST) in the Grammy Awards programme *The Best On Record*, and was followed in the show by a clip from *A Hard Day's Night*, of 'I'm Happy Just To Dance With You'.

Braving the blustery conditions to film Help! *on Salisbury Plain, with Mal and Neil keeping close company as always.*

Thursday 29 April

Twickenham Film Studios, St Margaret's, Twickenham

A re-shooting of the night-club bathroom scene, in which a hot-air hand-drier sucks rather than blows, tampered-with by Clang's "thugs" no doubt, in yet another attempt to wrest the sacrificial ring from Ringo's finger. It was first filmed on 8 April but a re-shoot was obviously necessary.

Another scene shot this day had Ringo restrained on a table in a storeroom underneath the Beatles' recording studio (see 30 April), with Clang powering up a chainsaw to remove his entire finger, and thus free the ring. Ringo is rescued by the temptress Ahme, however, and she quickly effects his escape along a neighbouring corridor.

Radio Luxembourg DJ Chris Denning, host of the weekly Sunday-night series *The Beatles* (see 24 December 1964), came to Twickenham this day to record new interviews with the Beatles, taping John, Paul and George together (while Ringo was filming the above scene), and Ringo separately (when he had finished). None of the interviews was very noteworthy, however, the Beatles sounding distracted and distanced, as if they rather regretted any involvement in a series which was more appropriate, perhaps, to 1963 than 1965.

Friday 30 April

Twickenham Film Studios, St Margaret's, Twickenham

Shooting of the scene with the Asprey's jeweller (Peter Copley), who examines and then unsuccessfully attempts to remove Ringo's ring. Also filmed this day was the "Attempt Number One" to rid Ringo of his ring, he and John riding in a lift which suddenly becomes magnetised, attracting all metal objects (except for the ring, of course) to the walls and ceiling.

Most of the day, however, was spent filming "Attempt Number Five", in which the Beatles, in a film-set re-creation of EMI Studios, are supposedly recording 'You're Going To Lose That Girl', Ringo working quite oblivious to the fact that the floor area around his drum kit is being cut, following which he tumbles through the hole to an underneath storeroom (filmed the previous day).

Monday 3 – Wednesday 5 May

Knighton Down, Larkhill, Wiltshire

For three days filming switched to this location on cold and windswept Salisbury Plain, the Beatles arriving at their local hotel – the Antrobus Arms in Amesbury – at 11.20 pm on Sunday night and departing during the afternoon of Thursday the 6th. Considerable filming was done here, including an open-air (mimed) performance of 'I Need You', shot amid troops from the real-life 3 Division (which uses

Salisbury Plain for exercises), gunners, machine-gunners and even a troop of horse-artillery.

Friday 7 May

Twickenham Film Studios, St Margaret's, Twickenham

Back to Twickenham for the filming of Paul's main solo scene in *Help!*, when he has been accidentally injected with reducing fluid and enjoys "exciting adventures" on the floor amid everyday but seemingly giant-sized objects.

Sunday 9 May

London and St Margaret's locations

Out and about in London, Sunday certainly being the best day of the week for location-hopping with the minimum of fuss and bother. The first stop was New Bond Street where the Beatles were filmed walking past a Watches of Switzerland jewellers shop and then dashing into Asprey's directly over the road. (The interior footage was shot on 30 April on a set at Twickenham.)

Next on the agenda was the exterior of the "Rajahama" Indian restaurant, actually the Dolphin Restaurant in Blandford Street, close by EMI Records' headquarters at 20 Manchester Square. (Interior scenes shot at Twickenham on 5–6 April.)

John and Ringo then travelled to the familiar St Margaret's area, near to Twickenham Film Studios and just yards from the Turks Head public house, scene of *A Hard Day's Night* shooting. Together they were filmed walking along South Western Road, Ringo posting a letter in a mail-box (cut to 20 April), and then Ringo alone filming "Attempt Number Three" on a weighing scale, almost getting his hand chopped off while waiting for a print-out of his weight. This scene was shot outside a grocery store in Winchester Road.

Monday 10 May

Cliveden House, Cliveden, Maidenhead, Berkshire and **Studio Two, EMI Studios, London**

The outside view of Buckingham Palace was seen in *Help!* (filmed on 12 May) but there was, of course, no way that permission could be obtained for the Beatles to film inside the real edifice. Instead, the Beatles went to the sumptuous Cliveden House, situated by the River Thames in leafy Berkshire, built in 1850–51 and presently owned and preserved by the National Trust.

The Beatles filmed here over two days, looking out of a window on the east side of the house, playing cards in the "French" dining room, and also shooting the brief but fascinating "Intermission" sequence in Bluebell Wood, a section of the extensive Cliveden grounds.

During this evening the Beatles returned to London for a recording session at EMI, where – taping especially for the US record market – John steered the group through two of his favourite songs by the American rocker Larry Williams: 'Dizzy Miss Lizzy' and 'Bad Boy'. Both were completed between 8.00 and 11.30 pm, and then mixed into mono and stereo between 11.30 pm and 1.15 in the morning. George Martin took away the mix tapes and dispatched them by air-freight the next day to Hollywood, and within five weeks they were in the record stores, on the Capitol-compiled LP *Beatles VI*.

Being well versed at performing such material from their pre-fame stage days, the Beatles played both songs live in the studio, with minimal overdubbing. 'Dizzy Miss Lizzy' was perfected in seven takes, using only three of the available four tracks. 'Bad Boy' was recorded in just four takes.

At best, so the music press reported at the time, the songs might turn up on a British EP later in the year. In fact, 'Dizzy Miss Lizzy' was included on the upcoming *Help!* album but 'Bad Boy' wasn't issued in the UK until the December 1966 compilation *A Collection Of Beatles Oldies*.

Tuesday 11 May

Cliveden House, Cliveden, Maidenhead

Not only the conclusion of filming at Cliveden but also the last shooting done by the Beatles for their second film. The unit concluded filming the following day, 12 May, with location shots all over London for which the Beatles' presence was not required.

At one point during their two days at Cliveden, the Beatles were challenged to a relay running-race around part of the splendid gardens. The contest was filmed with an 8mm home-movie camera by a member of the *Help!* film crew and the footage still exists. They competed against three other teams from the unit – the electricians, the carpenters and the camera operators – and each team had six runners, the Beatles being augmented by Neil Aspinall and their chauffeur Alf Bicknell. (To the surprise of many, because they were considered unfit, the Beatles' team won the race.)

Beatles film at Cliveden

WHILE Lord Astor rested in his bedroom after an illness, the Beatles filmed below his window this week. The group was at Cliveden on Monday and Tuesday filming scenes for their new film—HELP!

Lady Astor watched the filming from her bedroom window on the second floor.

Outside the estate, carloads of girls waited patiently for the boys to leave.

In between filming, George Harrison, wearing a corduroy suit, played softball on the immaculately mown lawn, Ringo Starr slept in a chair, Paul Macartney sat on the balustrade talking to the ADVERTISER, and John Lennon stood quietly waiting for his next scene.

The film, the group's second, is in colour and is due to be released on July 27. It also stars Patrick Cargill, who was filming with the boys on Monday, and Roy Kinnear.

Most of the filming was done inside the house. But short scenes took place on the terrace outside.

RECORDING

George told the ADVERTISER that in the evening the group had to travel to London to record tracks for a new LP. "We may not get through until the morning," he said.

Which would he rather do, record or film? In true Beatle fashion, George replied: "Both!"

Paul, sitting astride the balustrade, regarded the scenery from the terrace. "It's really beautiful," he said. "We've picked the right day, haven't we."

And from veteran film star Patrick Cargill who plays a police superintendent in the film, what it is like acting with the Beatles?

"Marvellous," he replied.

Tuesday 18 May

Twickenham Film Studios, St Margaret's, Twickenham

A great deal of post-sync work was required of the Beatles during post-production of *Help!*, overdubbing speech (clear as well as plenty of incoherent muttering and "ho-hos"). For the sequence (shot 9 May) in which John and Ringo were filmed on their way to a post-box they even overdubbed an extract from 'I Sat Belonely', one of the pieces in John's first book *In His Own Write*.

Tuesday 25 May

Cannes, France

At some point during this day John gave a brief interview to US television reporter Martin Ogronsky, screened a week later – Tuesday 1 June – on the CBS programme *The Merv Griffin Show* (11.00 pm–12.30 am, EST). The interview was filmed close to the sea-front in Cannes during a short and scarcely publicised visit that John and his wife Cynthia made to the town's annual film festival. In fact, this was their last day on the Riviera and they returned to England during the afternoon.

Wednesday 26 May

Studio One, BBC Piccadilly Studios, London

In a little over three years since their initial broadcast, the Beatles had outgrown the desire or need to record music sessions exclusively for broadcast on BBC radio, and this – their 52nd music programme contribution – was also the last. Transmitted in the Light Programme as a "bank holiday" special on Whit Monday, 7 June (10.00 am–12.15 pm, 15 minutes longer than usual), it went under the new title *The Beatles (Invite You To Take A Ticket To Ride)*. *From Us*

Giving a radio interview about the MBEs on a set at Twickenham, 12 June 1965.

To You was no longer an appropriate name considering the progression of the group's music since spring 1963, and the Beatles had offered to think of a replacement. Their final, unimaginative decision indicates the degree of importance they now attached to this type of engagement.

The session took place between 2.30 and 6.00 pm (inclusive of rehearsal time) during which they taped seven numbers: 'Ticket To Ride' (used twice in the programme, faded out after 37 seconds at the start and then played in full at the end), 'Everybody's Trying To Be My Baby', 'I'm A Loser', 'The Night Before', 'Honey Don't', 'Dizzy Miss Lizzy' and 'She's A Woman'. They also engaged in idle jocularity with the host, musician and broadcaster Denny Piercy, but the general feeling among listeners when surveyed later by the BBC was that the Beatles had featured far too seldom in what was, after all, their own show. (As usual, there were a host of guest artists to pad out the 135 minutes.)

During a meeting with BBC radio executives on 12 March 1965 Brian Epstein promised that the group would record more "bank holiday" specials during 1965, principally for 30 August and 26 December (Boxing Day). However, despite an announcement to this effect over BBC airwaves, Epstein failed to meet his promise – listeners on 30 August did still hear an exclusive Beatles programme, however (see 15 August).

Tuesday 8 June

A new stereo mix of 'I Want To Hold Your Hand' was produced by Norman Smith between 10.00 and 10.30 this morning at Abbey Road, destined for Beatles albums being compiled this year by EMI affiliates in Australia and the Netherlands.

Saturday 12 June

Twickenham Film Studios, St Margaret's, Twickenham

The embargo restricting publication of the Queen's Birthday Honours list was lifted during the night of Friday 11 June, so news of the Beatles' MBE awards was splashed across all of the British daily newspapers this morning. The Beatles were at Twickenham Film Studios to view a rough cut of *Help!* for the first time when they were besieged by representatives of the world's press, radio and TV and so convened a press conference. Radio and television interviews went into bulletins across the globe during the afternoon and evening.

One such interview, with George Yateman, was packaged together with film and performance clips and screened in New York on the educational channel WNDT (channel 13) on Wednesday 30 June (8.15–8.30 pm, EST), in the programme *British Calendar: News*.

During the evening of the 11th, as the embargo was lifted, Paul was interviewed, by telephone, by BBC staff reporter Ronald Burns, 1 min 40 secs of which was broadcast in *Late Night Extra* (on air 10.35–11.30 pm). Another phone interview, Peter Haigh chatting to Brian Epstein, was included earlier in the same programme.

Monday 14 June

Studio Two, EMI Studios, London

A remarkable day's work at Abbey Road, dominated by Paul and perfectly illustrating this young man's mastery of three different styles of musical composition and singing. It was on this day that he began recording 'Yesterday', the song which, by public acclaim, will always rank among his best.

But it was more than just a great tune. It was also a trend-setting recording, the (17 June) employment of a string quartet for the first time on a Beatles record introducing a new era: the group would continue to utilise strings and orchestras on a regular basis to the end. Typifying their working relationship, Paul assisted George Martin with his score, adding little touches here and there.

Two takes of 'Yesterday' were recorded by Paul alone, acoustic guitar and vocal, between 7.00 and 10.30 pm and then the four-track tape was set aside for completion on the 17th. (Newspapers of the time made a fuss of the fact that none of the other Beatles played on the recording, and that they weren't even present in the studio, but the session tape reveals that George, if not John and Ringo, was certainly there.)

What makes Paul's recording of 'Yesterday', the supreme melodic ballad, all the more remarkable, is that it directly followed the taping of 'I'm Down', a quasi-soul/rock and roll song delivered by Paul in the most larynx-tearing, cord-shredding style. This was started and completed in seven takes during a 2.30–5.30 afternoon session along with the first song to be taped this day, Paul's folk-rock 'I've Just Seen A Face', begun and finished in six takes.

Tuesday 15 June

Studio Two, EMI Studios, London

The second of three mid-June recording sessions at Abbey Road, completing the non-soundtrack side of the forthcoming Help! album. On this day, working a 2.30–6.15 afternoon session, the Beatles began and completed (in six takes) John's mainly acoustic ballad 'It's Only Love'.

Wednesday 16 June

Twickenham Film Studios, St Margaret's, Twickenham and NEMS Enterprises, Sutherland House, Argyll St, London

More post-sync work at Twickenham for the Help! soundtrack. (See also 18 May.) With this, the Beatles' contribution to their second feature-film was complete. Like its predecessor, Help! was given a royal world premiere at the London Pavilion cinema on Piccadilly Circus, in central London, on Thursday 29 July 1965. (Unlike its predecessor, the Beatles did not film a special trailer for Help!, which merely comprised extracts from the full-length film – albeit one not seen in the finished print, shot in the Bahamas, of George sheltering inside a plastic-bubble car which is being pounded by natives.)

With his second book of prose and verse, A Spaniard In The Works, set for publication on 24 June, it was also time for John to do the publicity rounds once again. Between 8.00 and 8.30 this evening in the NEMS office in central London he was interviewed by Wilfred De'Ath for an insert into the Saturday 3 July (10.10–10.40 pm) edition of the somewhat austere weekly BBC Home Service programme The World Of Books.

It was a particularly interesting interview, and unusually long – 15 minutes were recorded, more than 12 broadcast, including a reading by John of 'The Fat Budgie'. An extract lasting more than five minutes was also broadcast in the Light Programme series *The Teen Scene* on Monday 5 July (10.35–11.15 pm) (a programme produced by De'Ath) and another, of 3 mins 30 secs duration, was transmitted by the Home Service in *Pick Of The Week* on Saturday 10 July (3.15–4.00 pm). Additionally, the BBC's Transcription Service distributed the interview on disc as the self-contained programme *John Lennon – Bookbeatle*.

Also during this evening, John recorded an interview with BBC contributor Tim Matthews – reading, too, two verses of 'The National Health Cow' – for broadcast in the Home Service news-magazine programme *Today*. It was aired twice on Monday 21 June: as the first item in the 7.15–7.45 edition, and also in the 8.15–8.40 am edition.

Thursday 17 June

Studio Two, EMI Studios, London

'Yesterday' was completed this day with a 2.00–4.00 pm session that saw the overdubbing, onto take two from 14 June, of an additional vocal track by Paul and an ad hoc string quartet: Tony Gilbert (first violin), Sidney Sax (second violin), Francisco Gabarro (cello) and Kenneth Essex (viola). Complete now in its stunning simplicity, the song was mixed into mono.

The rejection of 'If You've Got Trouble', recorded on 18 February, meant that Ringo had still to record a lead vocal for the now almost completed *Help!* album. A fan of country and western music, he plumped for a cover of Buck Owens' 'Act Naturally' and the Beatles recorded it in 13 rhythm track takes between 4.00 and 5.30 pm, George playing the distinctive acoustic guitar. With harmony provided by Paul, Ringo overdubbed his vocal onto the 13th take.

From 7.00 until 9.30 pm (ending the session 30 minutes ahead of schedule) the Beatles recorded a new Lennon-McCartney song called 'Wait', taping guitars, drums, bass and John and Paul's shared lead vocal in four takes. But it was left unissued until, on 11 November 1965, in urgent need of one more song, the Beatles pulled the tape from the library shelf, polished it up and included it on *Rubber Soul*.

Friday 18 June

Studio Two, EMI Studios, London
and NEMS Enterprises, London
and Lime Grove Studios, London

Mono mixes of 'I've Just Seen A Face', 'I'm Down', 'It's Only Love', 'Act Naturally', 'Wait' and 'Help!' were prepared between 10.00 am and 12.30 pm at EMI. Stereo mixes of 'I've Just Seen A Face', 'I'm Down', 'Yesterday', 'It's Only Love' and 'Act Naturally' were made from 12.30–1.30 pm. Problems with preparing satisfactory mixes of 'Help!' meant that a separate afternoon session (2.30–3.30) was devoted to this one title. The end result was that its mono and stereo

mixes *appear* to have been produced from a different take. But this is not so – both the mono (used for the single and the monaural album) and the stereo (heard on the stereo album) do come from the same take 12, the apparent differences in John's lead vocal being the result of deft George Martin/Norman Smith editing.

Set to appear in Italy for the first time a few days hence, the Beatles consented to record a 15-minute interview with the BBC's Italian language service, part of the Corporation's European Service. It was taped this day from 3.30 pm in the NEMS office and broadcast to Italy from Bush House in London in *Londra Ultima Ora* on 23 June (11.00–11.30 pm, GMT), the eve of the Beatles' arrival in the country.

After the Italian Service interview, John travelled across London to the BBC's Lime Grove Studios for rehearsals and a live appearance on the last-ever edition of the television programme *Tonight* (BBC1, 7.00–7.35 pm). In an interview with Kenneth Allsop he promoted the publication of *A Spaniard In The Works*, and also read extracts from two pieces, 'We Must Not Forget The General Erection' and 'The Wumberlog (Or The Magic Dog)'.

Sunday 20 June

Palais des Sports, Place de la Portes de Versailles,
Paris, France

Two shows at the Palais des Sports, at 3.00 and 9.00 pm, got a short European concert tour underway. Six thousand people saw each of these two performances, and the relationship between the Parisian audience and the Beatles was now far warmer than in January 1964.

The Beatles' repertoire throughout this 14-day European tour comprised 'Twist And Shout' (truncated version), 'She's A Woman', 'I'm A Loser', 'Can't Buy Me Love', 'Baby's In Black', 'I Wanna Be Your Man', 'A Hard Day's Night', 'Everybody's Trying To Be My Baby', 'Rock And Roll Music', 'I Feel Fine', 'Ticket To Ride' and 'Long Tall Sally'.

The afternoon performance here in Paris was recorded by the French radio station Europe 1, and broadcast on 27 June (1.00–2.00 pm) in the series *Musicorama*. Additionally, the evening performance was broadcast live by Europe 1 (9.00–11.00 pm), titled *Les Beatles (en direct du Palais des Sports)*.

This same evening performance was also taped by the French television channel 2 and screened on Sunday 31 October (7.30–8.00 pm) in a programme simply titled *Les Beatles*. Viewers saw 11 of the 12 songs, although in a different order: 'Twist And Shout', 'She's A Woman', 'Ticket To Ride', 'Can't Buy Me Love', 'I'm A Loser', 'I Wanna Be Your Man', 'A Hard Day's Night', 'Baby's In Black', 'Rock And Roll Music', 'Everybody's Trying To Be My Baby' and 'Long Tall Sally' – this final song being performed as an encore, a great rarity for a Beatles concert. 'I Feel Fine' was taped too, but appears not to have been included in the broadcast.

The Beatles had arrived at Orly airport, Paris, at 9.55 am on 20 June and they stayed in the city until 1.15 pm on the 22nd, when they flew on to Lyon. While in Paris, resident again at the George V hotel, the Beatles gave their final interviews to Chris Denning for Radio Luxembourg's weekly series *The Beatles*. As he had done the previous December, Denning also invited the group to concoct some song dedications of their own, John doing so for Harold Wilson, Paul for critics Bernard Levin, Donald Zec and Wolf Mankowitz, and also for his family, Ringo doing so for newspaper pop writers Don Short and Judith Simons, for fan club secretary Freda Kelly and for all of the dockers in Liverpool, and George, retaliating, dedicating a song to "all of the miners in Scunthorpe". Even Neil Aspinall was pressurised into being interviewed, the Beatles suggesting he dedicate a song to Mal Evans!

Tuesday 22 June

Palais d'Hiver de Lyon, Rue Louis Guerin, Villeurbanne, Lyon, France

Two "maisons", at 8.00 and 10.00 pm, each seen by 3500 people. The Beatles travelled by rail from here to Milan during the evening of the 23rd.

Thursday 24 June

Velodromo Vigorelli, Via Arona, Milan, Italy

The Beatles' only visit to Italy saw them play in three cities, beginning with two shows in Milan at the Velodromo Vigorelli, a 22,000-seat open-air arena, at 4.30 and 9.30 pm. Neither was a sell-out, the afternoon show attracting just 7000 spectators while the evening concert was seen by 20,000. At both shows 700 policemen, 400 civilian guards and 30 firemen were on hand to quell any overt Beatlemania.

This concert may have been recorded for Italian radio but no details can be traced.

Friday 25 June

Palazzo dello Sport, Piazza Kennedy, Genoa, Italy

Two performances in this 25,000-capacity arena, at 4.30 and 9.30 pm. The show in the afternoon was seen by just 5000 spectators.

The Beatles spent little time in Genoa, arriving from Milan in the morning by road and then flying off to Rome in a chartered airplane immediately after the second show.

Sunday 27 and Monday 28 June

Teatro Adriano, Piazza Cavour, Rome, Italy

A total of four shows in Rome, at 4.30 and 9.30 pm on each of these two days. The Sunday shows alone were originally scheduled, Monday's two being added later – an odd decision since the Adriano was never more than half-full for any of the four performances. The Beatles flew on to Nice at 11.35 am on 29 June.

No Full Houses Yet For The Beatles
Heat Wave's Effect On Italian Tour

Rome newspapers to-day showed mixed reactions to the Beatles' concert there last night. Il Messaggero said they sang well and had good rhythm. It went on: "No more than four ugly faces, four long heads of hair, four sublime idiots, four barefoot bums—but they succeeded in creating a spectacle that one can only admire."

Il Tempo said: "The real show was by the fans, and for this reason it was not a good show."

ELEMENT OF TRIUMPH

Some Italian newspapers said the Beatles' visit had the elements of a triumph, even without the capacity audiences the organisers had predicted.

Paese Sera, pro-Communist Rome daily, noted that the Adriano Cinema was not air-conditioned and said: "Who-ever succeeds in half-filling a cinema in mid-afternoon with the temperature at 37 (98 Fahrenheit) can well be satisfied."

The Beatles are coming to the end of their Italian tour with something of a record for them—they have not played to a full house yet.

Making their Italian debut in Milan last week in the 22,000-seat Vigorelli Velodrome, they attracted 7,000

fans. A second performance was better, with 20,000.

Two Genoa performances failed to fill the 25,000-seat Lido Sports Palace there. At one show the audience barely reached 5,000, including 1,000 police on hand to keep order. They proved unnecessary.

TO SPAIN NEXT

In Rome yesterday, at two performances in the Adriano Cinema, there were empty seats in the 2,000-seat theatre. The organisers had claimed that all the seats had been sold. The Adriano Cinema advertised that seats were available for the two final performances to-day.

From here the Beatles go on to Spain.

Rome newspapers suggested that high prices was one reason for the lack of spectators. Seats for the Rome performances ranged from 11s 6d to £4. The cheapest and most expensive seats were selling best—the cheapest to teenagers, the expensive ones to such Beatle fans as actor Marcello Mastroianni and actress Ursula Andress, who attended last night's show.

The heat wave may have kept the crowds down.—Associated Press.

Wednesday 30 June

Palais des Expositions, Esplanade Maréchal de Lattre de Tassigny, Nice, France

One show, at 9.00 pm. The group flew to Madrid at 3.45 pm on 1 July.

Friday 2 July

Plaza de Toros de Las Ventas, Plaza Las Ventas, Madrid, Spain

One show in the bullring, at 8.30 pm. The Beatles flew on to Barcelona at 2.45 the following afternoon.

Saturday 3 July

Plaza de Toros Monumental, Avenue de les Corts Catalanes, Barcelona, Spain

Another bullring concert, at 10.45 pm, and the last date on the European tour. The Beatles' two-hour Iberia flight from

Barcelona to London Airport on 4 July touched down at 12.00 noon.

Tuesday 13 July

Savoy Hotel, The Strand, London

Paul went this lunchtime to the Savoy Hotel in central London to collect, from Sir Billy Butlin, five Ivor Novello Awards on behalf of the Beatles. He arrived late, however, having forgotten about the event, while John – also supposed to attend – failed to show at all. The entire luncheon, including Paul's acceptance of the awards and his thank-you speech, was filmed by Rediffusion TV cameras and broadcast from 10.33 to 11.05 pm on Thursday 15 July as *Pick Of The Songs*. Clips from the *Ready, Steady, Go!* archive were used to illustrate the various winners – for the Beatles it was the 20 March 1964 (mimed) performance of 'Can't Buy Me Love'.

Friday 30 July

Saville Theatre, Shaftesbury Avenue, London

Set to perform live on British television on 1 August, their first such appearance in more than a year, the Beatles spent part of this day in private rehearsal on stage at the Saville Theatre, a central London venue leased by Brian Epstein's NEMS Enterprises from 1 April 1965 until after his death.

While there, the group also gave two interviews for BBC radio, principally discussing *Help!*, premiered in London just the night before, 29 July. The first interview was with Dibbs Mather (see also 10 December 1963 and 24 March 1964), a long and witty conversation which was, most unusually, distributed by the BBC's Transcription Service to the British Information Service (BIS), a division of the British Council which promoted British culture in foreign countries. Along with disc material, it was packaged into a programme simply

titled *The Beatles*, sent to the British Council in New York and dispatched from there to specified US radio stations for local broadcast.

The second interview was with British entertainer/comic actor Lance Percival, two minutes of which was broadcast the next day, between 12.00 noon and 12.29 pm, in his Light Programme records show *Lance A Gogo*. (In 1967, Percival was recruited by the producers of the feature-film *Yellow Submarine* to provide character voice-overs.)

Sunday 1 August

ABC Theatre, Blackpool

The Beatles' only British television appearance to promote 'Help!' – all of the other shows had to make do with a clip from the movie (see 22 April) – was a return booking on the ABC Television variety show *Blackpool Night Out*, networked live to all but one ITV company direct from the town's ABC Theatre between 9.10 and 10.05 pm. As usual, the show was compered by Mike and Bernie Winters, and the Beatles topped a bill that comprised Teddy Johnson and Pearl Carr, Johnny Hart and Lionel Blair. They also took part in stage rehearsals throughout the afternoon.

The Beatles played six songs: 'I Feel Fine', 'I'm Down', 'Act Naturally', 'Ticket To Ride', 'Yesterday' (a solo performance by Paul, the others having left the stage; on their return John announced "Thank you Ringo, that was wonderful") and 'Help!' They did not participate in any comedy routines on this occasion.

Saturday 14 August

Studio 50, New York City, USA

And so the Beatles travelled to North America for the third time, and their second full concert tour, departing from London Airport with a lusty *au revoir* from one thousand fans at noon on 13 August, arriving in New York at 2.30 pm local time and setting up residence at the Warwick Hotel on Manhattan until the morning of the 17th.

Their first engagement – after the obligatory press conference, that is – was the taping of an insert for *The Ed Sullivan Show*. The Beatles didn't perform any TV duties during their August/September 1964 tour and it was now 18 months since those three February 1964 top-rated spots on Sullivan's Sunday night variety series.

During this morning the Beatles returned to the scene of their triumphant *Sullivan* début, CBS-TV's Studio 50, located at Broadway and West 53rd Street, rehearsing from 11.00 am to 2.00 pm, playing a dress rehearsal before an audience of 700 from 2.30 pm and then taping from 8.30 pm, also before an audience. They performed six songs live (the same six in same order that they had played on *Blackpool Night Out* a fortnight previously): 'I Feel Fine', 'I'm Down', 'Act Naturally', 'Ticket To Ride' (with a long instrumental intro, so that profile shots of each of the Beatles could be shown on screen), 'Yesterday' (sung by Paul accompanied only by a pre-taped track of three violins; when it was over John

Another premiere: Help! *this time.*

returned to the stage and commented "Thank you Paul, that was just like him") and 'Help!' There was a clear break after 'Act Naturally', the Beatles returning for the final three songs amid a different stage-setting.

The segment was used as the main attraction in *The Ed Sullivan Show* on 12 September, the first programme in his new fall season, broadcast from 8.00 to 9.00 pm, EST. Other acts in this edition were Cilla Black (taped along with the Beatles this day), Soupy Sales, Allen and Rossi, and Fantasio the Magician.

Sunday 15 August

William A Shea Municipal Stadium
[Shea Stadium], 126th St and Roosevelt Ave,
Queens, New York City, USA

The Beatles' first and most momentous concert at Shea Stadium, home of the New York Mets baseball team. Seen by 55,600 fans, it created a new world record for a pop concert in terms of attendance and gross revenue. The Beatles' share of the $304,000 box-office takings was also a record – $160,000 (then just over £57,000).

A planned spectacular entry into the stadium by helicopter, landing on the baseball playing area, was vetoed by the New York City authorities. Instead, the group travelled by limousine from the Warwick Hotel to a waterfront heliport, flew from there over New York City to the roof of the World's Fair building and made the final 100-yard journey into Shea Stadium in a Wells Fargo armoured truck. They sprinted through a tunnel, out into a deafening wall of screams and onto the stage (positioned at second base) at 9.16 pm.

The Beatles' repertoire for this concert, and for the remainder of the tour, comprised 'Twist And Shout' (truncated version), 'She's A Woman', 'I Feel Fine', 'Dizzy Miss Lizzy', 'Ticket To Ride', 'Everybody's Trying To Be My Baby', 'Can't Buy Me Love', 'Baby's In Black', 'Act Naturally' (some other shows had 'I Wanna Be Your Man' here instead), 'A Hard Day's Night', 'Help!' and 'I'm Down'. The tour's support acts were, in order of appearance, Brenda Holloway and the King Curtis Band, Cannibal & The

Headhunters, and Sounds Incorporated, and at this Shea concert the Young Rascals were added to the bill, too.

Together with the helicopter ride and backstage sequences, the show was filmed by Sullivan Productions (Ed Sullivan's company) in association with NEMS Enterprises (Brian Epstein's) and Subafilms (directors: Brian Epstein, John Lennon, Paul McCartney, George Harrison and Richard Starkey) for a colour television special one-hour long for US TV (which meant 48 minutes if shown without commercials). Its world premiere occurred on Tuesday 1 March 1966 (BBC1, 8.00–8.50 pm) and it was repeated by the same network on Saturday 27 August 1966 (6.15–7.05), both transmissions screened in monochrome. It was first shown on US television, and in colour, at a surprisingly late date, on Tuesday 10 January 1967 (7.30–8.30 pm, EST), networked by ABC. (There were two other 1960s extract screenings on the BBC: the first was on Monday 28 February 1966 in the BBC2 arts programme *Late Night Line-Up* (11.00–11.45 pm), which included 1 min 50 secs of 'Ticket To Ride' followed by a ten-minute interview with Brian Epstein by host Denis Tuohy. The other was on Wednesday 31 December 1969 when BBC1 marked the end of a remarkable musical decade by transmitting *Pop Go The 60s* (10.35–11.50 pm), a compilation programme for which Apple Corps permitted the use of seven minutes of Shea footage: 'I Feel Fine', 'Help!' and 'Can't Buy Me Love'.)

The Beatles At Shea Stadium is certainly a remarkable film, capturing not only the intense excitement of this record-breaking concert, but also a degree of fan hysteria so fantastic it has to be seen to be believed. Imaginatively filmed utilising 12 cameras, it also shows well the non-performing side of the group, craning to look out of their helicopter as it flies over New York landmarks and idling away time backstage.

The film opens, unusually, with the Beatles' closing number from the concert, 'I'm Down'. Then, apart from the helicopter sequences and views of the stadium being prepared for the event, there is a barrage of non-Beatles stage footage: New York disc-jockey Murray The K acting peculiarly; the Discotheque Dancers prancing to music played by the King Curtis Band; Brenda Holloway; a frantic set by Sounds Incorporated and then, introducing the Beatles onto the stage, Ed Sullivan.

Not all of the Beatles' Shea set is in the film – 'She's A

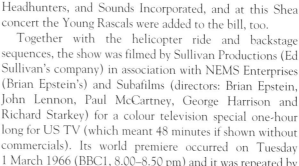

In rehearsal for a return spot on The Ed Sullivan Show, *New York City, 14 August 1965. Despite the colour photograph, the show was recorded in black-and-white.*

at 11.25 am in this 10.00 am–12.00 noon broadcast, concluding just before the final half-hour section simultaneously beamed across the globe by the BBC World Service (so re-named on 1 May 1965, no longer the General Overseas Service).

But the main thrust of Matthew's material – especially his exclusive interviews with the Beatles backstage and in their hotel rooms – was packaged together into a 45-minute documentary *The Beatles Abroad*, broadcast by the Light Programme on "bank holiday" Monday 30 August, from 10.00 to 10.45 am. The music included was taken from discs, not from the live concerts or a BBC session, however. (Because Scotland did not then share the same "bank holiday" dates as England, Wales, Northern Ireland and the Channel Islands, listeners there did not hear *The Beatles Abroad* until Monday 3 January 1966 (11.00–11.45am). The Scottish audience also missed entirely the Beatles' five 1963–65 "bank holiday" music programmes, none of which was broadcast north of the border.)

Note: although Matthew returned to England on 21 August, the remainder of the tour was covered for the BBC Transcription Service by US broadcaster Jay Peeples, who continued to file reports back to London for inclusion in *Top Of The Pops* and a specially compiled programme *The Beatles In New York*.

Tuesday 17 August

Maple Leaf Gardens, Toronto, Canada

Two 27-minute performances at this indoor arena, each watched by 18,000 people. The Beatles flew into Toronto from New York during the morning having spent the previous days entertaining a succession of visitors to their hotel suite, including Bob Dylan and the Supremes. (Mick Jagger and Keith Richard of the Rolling Stones were also among the 55,600 crowd at Shea.) They also met representatives of the North American chapter of their official fan club, Beatles (USA) Limited.

Wednesday 18 August

Atlanta Stadium, Capitol Avenue South West, Atlanta, Georgia, USA

One show, seen by 30,000 fans in this new 55,000-seat baseball park.

Thursday 19 August

Sam Houston Coliseum, Bagby Street, Houston, Texas, USA

Two shows at this 12,000-capacity arena, netting the Beatles $85,000. The group had arrived in Houston at 2.00 am to find Beatlemania at possibly its most acute level yet witnessed. (It is likely that both performances here were broadcast by a local radio station but further details cannot be traced.)

Woman' and 'Everybody's Trying To Be My Baby' are both omitted – and what is included was subjected to audio sweetening back in London (see 5 January 1966). Additionally, throughout the film, the Beatles are heard via voice-overs, recorded by the US broadcaster Larry Kane (taping date not known).

Although this was not the Beatles' first North American tour, interest in it remained very high back home in Britain and, indeed, around the world. And the promise of a world-record audience at Shea Stadium added extra glitter to the package. The BBC Transcription Service therefore negotiated with Brian Epstein that its regular programme host Brian Matthew – also, incidentally, a business associate of Epstein's – should be allowed to join the group's entourage for a part of the tour, until 20 August, recording interviews with the Beatles, compiling a documentary of the momentous events and filing a number of reports back to the BBC in London. (Matthew's other task during the trip was to plug the Transcription Service's weekly radio show *Top Of The Pops* – not to be confused with the entirely different BBC TV series of the same name – and he made many personal appearances on US radio doing just this.)

Matthew's first report, an on-the-spot account of the Shea concert, went into both editions of the next-morning's (16 August) edition of the Home Service news-magazine programme *Today* (7.15–7.45 and 8.15–8.40), and another went into the Light Programme's *Roundabout '65* during the same afternoon (5.31–6.45). Immediately upon his return on 21 August, Matthew went to the BBC so that he could play some of his tapes and discuss the events on *Saturday Club* (otherwise hosted this day by Simon Dee), appearing on air

Friday 20 August

White Sox Park, 35th and Shields, Chicago, Illinois, USA

Two shows in Chicago, at 3.00 and 8.00 pm, with 25,000 fans attending the first performance and 37,000 the second.

The Beatles' share of the overall gate receipts was $155,000.

Saturday 21 August

Metropolitan Stadium, Cedar Ave, Bloomington, Minneapolis, Minnesota, USA

One show, seen by around 25,000 people in this 45,000-capacity stadium.

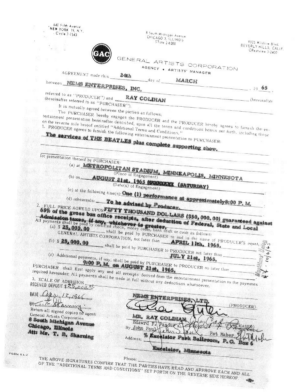

Sunday 22 August

Memorial Coliseum, North Wheeler Ave, Portland, Oregon, USA

Two shows, before a total of 20,000 fans. In between performances the Beatles were visited in their dressing-room by Carl Wilson and Mike Love of the Beach Boys.

Saturday 28 August

Balboa Stadium, Russ Boulevard, San Diego, California, USA

Between the morning of 23 August (when they flew into Los Angeles) and this concert, the Beatles enjoyed a clear break, resting in a massive house, amid tight security, in Benedict Canyon, Hollywood.

Late in the evening of 27 August, the group drove across to Perugia Way, Beverly Hills, to meet their one-time idol Elvis Presley, a summit conference arranged by Presley's manager, "Colonel" Tom Parker, and greatly anticipated by the Beatles and Brian Epstein. But the meeting was not a great success, although Elvis and the Beatles did have a brief jam session, a poor-quality tape of which has long been rumoured to exist, although this has never been confirmed and must be considered unlikely.

Paul had already spoken with Presley – and perceived his now decidedly unmagnetic personality – during a telephone conversation from the group's Atlantic City hotel to Memphis on 31 August 1964.

Sunday 29 and Monday 30 August

Hollywood Bowl, Los Angeles, USA

Two concerts, one each evening, at this splendid outdoor arena set against the Hollywood Hills. The Beatles' share of the total $156,000 gate receipts was $90,000.

Although the previous year's concert recording from the same venue was gathering dust in a vault this did not prevent Capitol from trying again, taping the Beatles' performance on both nights for possible release on record.

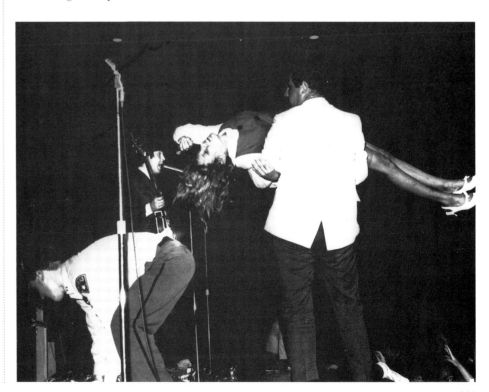

Nothing from the Sunday performance could be used owing to technical problems, a fault with Paul's vocal microphone in particular, which obliterated his singing and introductions on the first four songs. Capitol accomplished a better recording on Monday evening, however, albeit one dominated by audience screaming rather than stage-craft. From this, 'Twist And Shout', 'She's A Woman', 'Dizzy Miss Lizzy', 'Ticket To Ride', 'Can't Buy Me Love', 'A Hard Day's Night' and 'Help!' made it onto *The Beatles At The Hollywood Bowl* in 1977. 'I Feel Fine', 'Everybody's Trying To Be My Baby', 'Baby's In Black', 'I Wanna Be Your Man' and 'I'm Down' did not. These 1965 recordings also had a more immediate use (see 5 January 1966).

Tuesday 31 August

Cow Palace, San Francisco, USA

The tenth and final concert of the 1965 North American tour, at the venue which had opened the 1964 itinerary. There were two shows – a matinée seen by 11,700 and an evening performance seen by 17,000. The Beatles flew home during the evening of 1 September, landing at London Airport the morning of the 2nd, and then enjoyed almost six weeks' break without work.

Tuesday 12 October

Studio Two, EMI Studios, London

The Beatles had released two albums in 1963 and 1964, and now in 1965 they were compelled to do the same again. The problem was, they had little new material to work with and time was getting on. John and Paul had to force themselves to come up with more than a dozen new songs and then, with George and Ringo, zip through a crash series of recording sessions in order to have the LP in the stores by early December. These did not even begin until 12 October.

How very ironic, therefore, that the resulting LP, *Rubber Soul*, was acclaimed then and now, and quite rightly so too, as both a high quality product and a major turning point in the Beatles' career, in terms of musical composition and recording technique. *Rubber Soul* has proven a durable and very necessary platform between the class pop music of *Help!* and the experimental ideas of *Revolver*.

John later admitted that in having to write and record quickly he would sometimes rely on other records for his ideas. Certainly he did so for 'Run For Your Life', the first song taped in these new sessions, lifting two lines from 'Baby Let's Play House' (Elvis Presley, 1955). The recording was begun and completed in five takes, 2.30 to 7.00 pm.

Rather than break for dinner, the Beatles immediately began to tape another new John Lennon song, and one of which he was, justifiably, more than a little proud. At this stage it was called 'This Bird Has Flown', although it became 'Norwegian Wood (This Bird Has Flown)' when it was re-made nine days after this first attempt. The term re-make can often imply that the initial recording has imperfections – not so for 'This Bird Has Flown', however, for while it may not

have been an exact realisation of what John, as its composer, wanted, it was still a superb recording, quite different but arguably as dazzling as the version which ended up on the LP.

Just one take of this, with a number of overdubs, was recorded between 7.00 and 11.30 pm, with George's sitar contribution (double-tracked) marking the first appearance of this Indian instrument on a pop record. This version remained "best" until the re-make (see 21 October).

Wednesday 13 October

Studio Two, EMI Studios, London

This session was to prove a landmark in the Beatles' recording career, extending past midnight for the first time. The 10 May 1965 session had also run into the following morning but that was only for mixing. There would soon come a time when a session *not* running into the next day would prove the exception.

The song which took the Beatles past midnight, to 12.15 am to be exact, was 'Drive My Car', eventually chosen to open *Rubber Soul*. Work began at 7.00 pm and in the following 315 minutes the group taped four takes, the last of which was marked "best" and seen through to completion.

Saturday 16 October

Studio Two, EMI Studios, London

Interviewed in 1966, John and Paul admitted that 'Day Tripper' was a "forced" composition, written under the pressure of having to come up with a single. Well, other composers would have been proud to have come up with a song like this. It formed one of the two A-sides of the Beatles' next single, issued on the same day as *Rubber Soul*, Friday 3 December, yet independently of that album.

The group worked from 2.30 to 7.00 pm rehearsing and recording the rhythm track, with only the final take, the third, making it through to the end. They began the 7.00–12.00 pm session overdubbing the vocals onto this, John and Paul sharing lead and backing roles. Once again, the Beatles had started and completed a classy, influential recording within a matter of hours.

With the clock heading towards midnight, the group then recorded one take of a basic rhythm track for George's new composition 'If I Needed Someone', leaving vocals and additional instruments to be overdubbed the next day.

Monday 18 October

Studio Two, EMI Studios, London

'If I Needed Someone' was the first priority of this one afternoon session, 2.30–5.45, George's lead vocal, John and Paul's backing vocal and Ringo's tambourine being overdubbed onto the previous night's take one rhythm track.

The remainder of the afternoon was spent taping another marvellous new John Lennon song, the autobiographical 'In My Life'. The "best" was take three, completed but for a gap left in the middle-eight section which was plugged with an imaginative overdub on 22 October.

Wednesday 20 October

Studio Two, EMI Studios, London

The song which shared with 'Day Tripper' the A-side of the next single, 'We Can Work It Out', was begun and virtually completed (but for a little overdubbing on 29 October) during two Abbey Road sessions this day, 2.30–6.30 and 7.00–11.45 pm. Once again, it displayed Lennon-McCartney's absolute mastery of the two-minute pop song and is another example of typically 1965 Beatles fare: excellent musicianship allied with a new lyrical direction.

The basic track was captured in just two takes, onto which innumerable overdubs were applied, including the song's distinctive harmonium part played by John.

Thursday 21 October

Studio Two, EMI Studios, London

'This Bird Has Flown', now 'Norwegian Wood (This Bird Has Flown)', was re-made from start to finish during the afternoon, 2.30–7.00 pm, in just three more takes. Without breaking for dinner, the Beatles then began to tackle John's 'Nowhere Man'. Two takes were attempted but the recording was incomplete when the session concluded at midnight; a re-make commenced the following evening.

Friday 22 October

Studio Two, EMI Studios, London

The day began with a 10.30–11.30 morning session – probably without the Beatles in attendance – during which George Martin filled the hole in the middle of the otherwise complete 'In My Life' with a beautiful baroque-style piano solo. To achieve the desired texture he played the piece at half-speed for playback at double-speed.

The Beatles were certainly around for one continuous 2.30–11.30 pm session which saw them start afresh with a re-make of 'Nowhere Man' and conclude the recording in only three more takes.

Sunday 24 October

Studio Two, EMI Studios, London

Though stacked with potential, Paul's new song 'I'm Looking Through You' wasn't easy to realise on tape. The Beatles spent the first half of this nine-hour session, 2.30–7.00 pm, recording one take of the song's rhythm track and overdubbing onto this, then spent the second half, until 11.00 pm, adding vocals. By the end of the night they had what most would recognise as a classy recording – most, that is, but not the Beatles, who were to tape a re-make on 6 November and a second re-make on the 10th–11th.

Monday 25 October

Studio One, EMI Studios, London

Mono mixes of 'Drive My Car', 'In My Life', 'If I Needed Someone', 'Day Tripper', 'Norwegian Wood (This Bird Has Flown)' and 'Nowhere Man', produced by George Martin from 10.00 am to 1.00 pm, probably without the Beatles in attendance.

Tuesday 26 October

Stereo mixes of 'Drive My Car', 'Day Tripper' (used on Australian and US albums), 'In My Life', 'If I Needed Someone', 'Norwegian Wood (This Bird Has Flown)' and 'Nowhere Man', were prepared by George Martin between 10.00 am and 12.30 pm this day in studio one at EMI.

Although the Beatles were beginning to attend mix sessions they certainly missed this one, instead collecting their MBEs from the Queen at Buckingham Palace and hosting a subsequent press conference at the Saville Theatre. There was, naturally, considerable newsreel, TV and radio news coverage of these events. (As an example, even the BBC Home Service's somewhat august news and current affairs programme *The World At One*, anchored by William Hardcastle, had four consecutive reports about the morning's activities: two from outside the Palace, one from inside and another commentating on the Beatles' arrival at the Saville.)

Thursday 28 October

Studio One, EMI Studios, London

A rough mono mix of 'We Can Work It Out', made between 5.00 and 5.30 pm, not for record release but for the Beatles to mime to during the video-taping of *The Music Of Lennon & McCartney* (see 1–2 November).

It was only when they heard a playback of this mix-for-TV that the Beatles realised the song's vocal tracks required an overhaul. They were overdubbed again the next day, 29 October, instantly rendering this mix unusable.

Friday 29 October

Studio Two, EMI Studios, London

Vocal repair work was effected onto take two of 'We Can Work It Out' between 2.00 and 4.00 pm, and from then until 5.00 both this song and also 'Day Tripper' were mixed twice into mono – once for record release and once for TV playback on 1–2 November.

Monday 1 and Tuesday 2 November

Studio Six, Granada TV Centre, Manchester

Quite apart from the Beatles' remarkable success as a group, considerable public interest was maintained in them through the songwriting endeavours of Lennon-McCartney, it

remaining something of a novelty at this time for two young British pop singers/musicians to compose and perform such high-quality material. In the summer of 1965, Granada Television proposed to Brian Epstein a TV special about John and Paul's music, a big-budget production that would feature top international stars singing their songs, with the Beatles themselves topping the bill.

The idea was an attractive one so planning went ahead and the resulting 50-minute "special", *The Music Of Lennon & McCartney*, was rehearsed and taped on a specially-constructed set at Granada over these two days. It was broadcast all over Britain, except in the London area, on Friday 17 December (9.40–10.35 pm). In London, it went out the previous evening (same times).

As a group, the Beatles performed (mimed) to two songs, first 'Day Tripper' and then 'We Can Work It Out', this being an ideal opportunity to plug the new single, after all. For the latter song, John forsook his guitar in favour of Granada's studio harmonium, the very same instrument played by Ena Sharples in *Coronation Street*! As well as miming, the Beatles (along with all of the other acts) pretended to be playing to a studio audience, nodding and acknowledging applause. In fact, there was no audience, a laughter and clapping track being overdubbed by Granada in post-production. (Indeed, one of the items, Peter Sellers' hilarious performance of 'A Hard Day's Night' in mock-Shakespearean/Sir Laurence Olivier style, had been pre-taped in London.)

John and Paul popped up throughout the production, clambering around the scaffold-like set, introducing many of the artists, discussing foreign-language versions of their songs (part of the Beatles' own 'Sie Liebt Dich' was played) and having fun with Cilla Black. Alone, Paul also performed 'Yesterday' for 22 seconds, sound-and-vision then cutting to Marianne Faithfull for the remainder of the song.

The full line-up of songs (artists) was: song medley (the George Martin Orchestra), 'A World Without Love' (Peter and Gordon), 'I Saw Him Standing There' (Lulu), 'From Me To You' (Alan Haven and Tony Crombie), 'She Loves You'/song medley (Fritz Spiegl's Ensemble), 'Day Tripper' (the Beatles), 'Yesterday' (Paul McCartney, then Marianne Faithfull), 'She Loves You' (Antonio Vargas), 'Things We Said Today' (in French; Dick Rivers), 'Bad To Me' (Billy J Kramer with the Dakotas), 'It's For You' (Cilla Black), 'Ringo's Theme (This Boy)' (the George Martin Orchestra), 'If I Fell' (Henry Mancini), 'And I Love Him' (Esther Phillips), 'A Hard Day's Night' (Peter Sellers) and, finally, 'We Can Work It Out' (the Beatles).

The Music Of Lennon & McCartney was ITV's official entry for the Golden Rose Of Montreux Award, decided at the 1966 Montreux Festival (22–30 April), but it did not win.

Wednesday 3 November

Studio Two, EMI Studios, London

Nine hours, 2.30–11.30 pm, spent recording and completing Paul's new ballad 'Michelle'. From 2.30–7.00 the Beatles perfected the rhythm track in one take. At 7.00 this was reduced ("bounced down") into take two to vacate a track on the four-track tape, and from then until 11.30 they filled this with vocal and guitar overdubs.

Thursday 4 November

Studio Two, EMI Studios, London

It was now less than a month before the desired release date for the new LP, yet only half of the songs had been completed. Several had still to be written.

This prompted two actions. Late-night sessions became not just something the group casually drifted into but a deliberate plan. The session on this day, for example, was booked in advance to end at 3.00 am (it actually finished at 3.30). The second action, shown this day and again on 11 November, was for the Beatles to revive previously discarded songs.

It was on 5 March 1963 that they had first hoped to record 'What Goes On', although lack of time ruled this out. It was, even then, quite an old Lennon-McCartney song. Now it was revived and handed to Ringo for his statutory one-vocal-per-LP (he ended up with a joint composing credit too). The song was recorded in one take, with overdubs of Ringo's rockabilly lead vocal and John and Paul's backing.

Sometime after midnight the Beatles undertook a curious exercise, recording – presumably for possible LP inclusion – their first attempt at an instrumental number, '12-Bar Original'. This was a rather unoriginal – though absolutely accurate – title for what was essentially just a rambling 12-bar blues, typical of Booker T and the MG's but certainly untypical of anything the Beatles had attempted before. Moreover, this was no mere improvisation, the final take, the second, being identical to what the group was trying in take one before that broke down. Take two was in fact complete – running to an uncommonly long 6 mins 36 secs – and was recorded live, without overdubs, with George's tone-pedal lead guitar work and George Martin's harmonium to the fore, augmented by John's lead guitar, Paul's bass and Ringo's drums.

Saturday 6 November

Studio Two, EMI Studios, London

The first of two re-makes of 'I'm Looking Through You'. Between 7.00 pm and 1.00 am the Beatles taped two takes (numbered two and three to follow the 24 October version), overdubbing all required sounds onto the second of these. By the end they were considerably nearer to the desired end result – but not near enough.

Monday 8 November

Studio Two, EMI Studios, London

Time was running out not just for the new LP but also for the Beatles' annual Christmas disc for their fan club members.

For this purpose – that is, in case they said anything particularly witty – George Martin deliberately recorded the Beatles rehearsing George Harrison's 'Think For Yourself' during the early part of this 9.00 pm–3.00 am session. In the end, nothing was suitable for the Christmas disc but, just to ensure the tape was not scrapped, the words "This will eventually be issued" were scrawled onto the box. And it was, for in 1967 the tape was loaned to the producer of the animated film *Yellow Submarine* and when that film finally appeared it included a six-second snatch of John, Paul and George practising their 'Think For Yourself' vocal harmonies.

Actually, it wasn't quite 'Think For Yourself' yet – that title was cooked up later in the evening. At first it laboured under the working title 'Won't Be There With You', recorded – with overdubs – in one take, its most distinctive instrument being a fuzz bass.

The Beatles were tired towards the 3.00 am end of the session, when they came to record their Christmas message. They stumbled through three takes of unrehearsed banter, a wild, off-key rendition of 'Yesterday' and vaguely witty chat, at one point joking that George Martin had the (obviously unenviable) task of making sense of it all. As usual, he did just that, editing and mixing the tapes 12 hours later.

Tuesday 9 November

Room 65, EMI Studios, London

More mixing, probably in the Beatles' absence, 2.30–5.30 pm, with mono masters being prepared for 'Michelle', 'What Goes On', 'Run For Your Life', 'Think For Yourself' and 'The Beatles' Third Christmas Record' (also edited), and stereo masters being made for 'Think For Yourself', 'Michelle' and 'What Goes On'.

Wednesday 10 November

Room 65/Studio Two, EMI Studios, London

A 2.30–5.30 pm mix session in Room 65 yielded stereo masters of 'Run For Your Life' and 'We Can Work It Out' (not on *Rubber Soul*, this mix was destined for Australian and US albums). The Beatles did not attend – they arrived at Abbey Road for a 9.00 pm–3.00 am studio two session (which over-ran to 4.00), the first product of which was the recording from start to finish, in three takes, of John's song 'The Word', the lyric of which was a prototype 'All You Need Is Love', two years ahead of that world anthem. Then the group set about the second re-make of Paul's 'I'm Looking Through You', taping in one take (numbered four) a new "best" rhythm track by session's end.

Thursday 11 November

Room 65/Studio Two, EMI Studios, London

Mono and stereo mixes of 'The Word' were produced in Room 65, probably in the Beatles' absence, between 4.00 and 5.30 pm. The Beatles began recording at 6.00 pm, one hour ahead of time, in this final *Rubber Soul* session, and they also worked four hours beyond its 3.00 am scheduled end, clocking up 13 uninterrupted hours in studio two. They knew that the deadline had come, that their new album had to be finished this night. They also knew that they needed three more songs. Paul came up with one, John another, and for the third they pulled off the shelf 'Wait', the discarded *Help!* track, added various bits and pieces and pronounced it fit for inclusion on the new LP. Balance was everything in 1965: a 14-song album meant seven songs per side and everything hunky-dory. (Still, despite the pressure, no one considered including on the album either or both songs on the new single, 'We Can Work It Out'/'Day Tripper'.)

Paul's song, 'You Won't See Me', was recorded from start to finish in two takes, as was John's song, 'Girl'; then the Beatles added tone-pedal guitar, tambourine, maraca and more vocals onto take four of the five-month-old 'Wait', overdubbed vocals onto the previous night's 'I'm Looking Through You' rhythm track and, suddenly, to the accompaniment of the St John's Wood dawn chorus, they knew that the new album was complete.

Right: a colour still from the never-seen B&W promotional video for 'I Feel Fine'.

Monday 15 November

Studio One, EMI Studios, London

Final production for *Rubber Soul* was effected from 2.30 to 5.30 pm, with 'I'm Looking Through You', 'You Won't See Me', 'Girl', 'Wait' and 'Michelle' being mixed into mono, and 'Wait', 'I'm Looking Through You', 'You Won't See Me', 'Girl' and 'The Word' (improving upon the 11 November edition) mixed into stereo.

On 16 November George Martin worked out the LP running order and telephoned it over to Abbey Road. On 17, 19 and 23 November discs were cut, lacquers were rushed to the pressing plant, the sleeve was quickly printed, and finished copies of the LP were in the shops by Friday 3 December.

Considering the rush, and how it must have clashed with the Beatles' desire to inject ever-greater care into their work, it should be no surprise to note that 1965 marked the last time they issued two separate albums of wholly new material within a calendar year.

Tuesday 23 November

Twickenham Film Studios, St Margaret's, Twickenham

Increasingly reluctant to do the rounds of television shows every time they issued a new single, the Beatles decided to self-produce and video-tape their own promotional clips and distribute them to TV stations, thereby heralding the dawn of pop's promo-video age.

With the same old demands to perform arriving every few months from British and foreign television companies, it's perhaps odd that they hadn't thought of this before, and it took the Granada taping of *The Music of Lennon & McCartney* to awaken the Beatles to the possibilities. Now they could be seen not only on *Top Of The Pops* and *Thank Your Lucky Stars* with the minimum of fuss and effort but also appear on TV shows in America, in Australia, in Japan, in fact anywhere, and make a tidy profit too.

This shooting was financed by NEMS Enterprises (which therefore owned the resulting clips), appointing Joe McGrath as director and InterTel (VTR Services), reputedly the first independent video facilities company in Europe, to provide the production crew. Nicholas Ferguson, from *Ready, Steady, Go!*, designed the sets, there were four cameramen – Harry Storey, Terry Heath and two others (who, because they were moonlighting from the BBC, wish to remain nameless), there was a lighting man, a sound-man and a "runner" (David Mallet, later a prominent director). Also on the set, representing NEMS, were Tony Bramwell and Vyvienne Moynihan (the latter formerly employed at Associated-Rediffusion).

A Hard Day's Night and *Help!* had been filmed all over the Twickenham complex, on each of the three stages, but these promos were taped only on Stage Three, set-construction having been completed in the two previous days. The

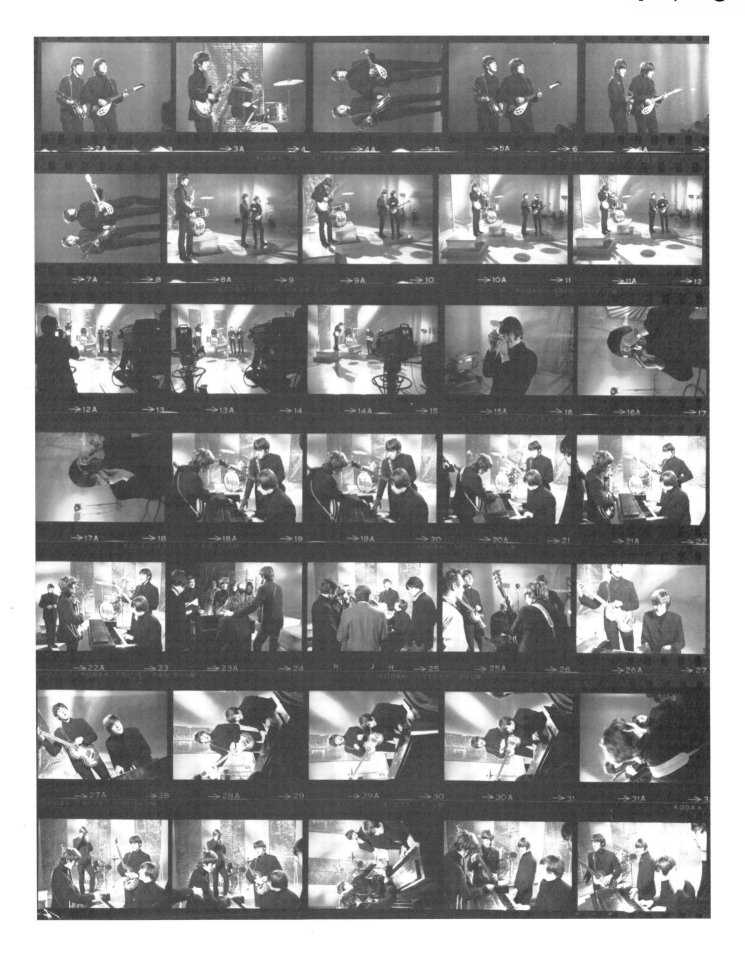

Beatles arrived during the late-afternoon and worked through until the early hours of the 24th – and, as productive here as they were in the recording studio, ten clips were shot in this time, nine of which have been seen on TV. (Certain programmes, especially those in Britain, were sold clips different from those sold to rivals, enabling presenters to boast exclusivity.) Clearly miming, and shooting onto two-inch black-and-white video tape (although some clips were later transferred onto 16mm for TV distribution), these were the ten:

'**We Can Work It Out**' – three versions. John sat at an organ for all three, but there were clear enough differences in the group's actions, especially towards the end of each clip, to distinguish one from another. One opened with a photo still of John with a sunflower over his eye, in another they wore their "Shea Stadium" suits.

'**Day Tripper**' – three versions. The first, in which the Beatles again wore their Shea suits, had George and Ringo standing behind a prop railway-carriage frontage (Ringo soon disposed of his drumsticks, took out a saw and began to dismantle it) and John and Paul standing a few feet away behind a 1920s-style airplane façade. The other two were largely identical to each other but with minor differences in Ringo's actions near to the start and the end. For these clips the Beatles stood in typical group formation, three guitars and drums.

'**Help!**' – one version. The Beatles sat astride a work-bench, swaying from side to side and bobbing up and down as they mimed to playback. Unable to balance drums on the workbench Ringo held aloft a white umbrella, especially useful towards the end of the clip when a heavy fall of fake snow descended upon the group.

'**Ticket To Ride**' – one version, shot before a backdrop comprising enlarged bus and train tickets.

'**I Feel Fine**' – two versions. In the first, George, John and Paul walked onto the set a few seconds after the song had begun, George then sang into a punch-ball while John and Paul (not using gym equipment but with a chest-expander and bar-bell at their feet) sang straight to camera. Ringo arrived on the set 38-seconds into the clip and proceeded to ride an exercise-bike. In the second version, shot on the same "set" (the gym equipment was unused this time except for when, near to the end, George sat on the exercise-bike), the Beatles spent the duration of the song eating newspaper-wrapped fish and chips with their fingers, scarcely making any attempt at vocal miming. (Of the ten videos produced from this Twickenham shoot this was the only one not sold to TV, reportedly because Brian Epstein was unhappy with the result.)

Distribution of the promos was immediate. On payment to NEMS of a £1750 fee (the entire set of ten had cost Epstein's company only around £750 to produce), the BBC broadcast certain clips several times in *Top Of The Pops* (all BBC1). On Thursday 2 December (7.30–8.00 pm), it showed 'We Can Work It Out' and 'Day Tripper'; on the 9th (also 7.30–8.00 pm) it showed 'We Can Work It Out'; in *Top Of The Pops '65* on Christmas Day (10.35–11.50 pm) – repeated Boxing Day, 26 December (12.15–1.30 pm) – it featured 'I Feel Fine', 'Help!', 'Ticket To Ride' and 'Day

Tripper'; on Thursday 30 December (7.30–8.00 pm) it included 'We Can Work It Out'; and then, a whole year on, on Monday 26 December 1966 (6.15–7.00 pm), in *Top Of The Pops '66 – Part 1* – a programme featuring the number one records of the January to June period – it screened 'Day Tripper' and 'We Can Work It Out'.

Another early British transmission of 'We Can Work It Out' and 'Day Tripper' occurred in ABC Television's *Thank Your Lucky Stars* on Saturday 4 December 1965 (5.15–5.55 pm), while the first broadcast of the promos on US television occurred in NBC's networked *Hullabaloo* on Monday 3 January 1966 (7.30–8.00 pm, EST), which showed 'Day Tripper' and 'We Can Work It Out'.

Monday 29 November
Studio One, Aeolian Hall, London

An interview with Brian Matthew, taped between 2.15 and 2.45 pm at the BBC's Aeolian Hall premises in central London for inclusion, in three parts, in the Christmas Day edition of *Saturday Club*, broadcast in the Light Programme between 10.00 and 11.30 am.

As well as indulging in typically humorous badinage with Matthew, the Beatles also decided to ham-up a quick, vocalised version of the programme's instrumental signature tune 'Saturday Jump', usually performed by either Ted Heath and his Orchestra or Tony Osborne and his Jazz Group. Listeners on Christmas morning duly heard 15 seconds of the Beatles' scat rendition segued into Heath's disc version at the start of the show.

Tuesday 30 November
NEMS Enterprises, London

George and John went to the NEMS office in Argyll Street during the afternoon to be interviewed, separately, by Brian Matthew for *Pop Profile*, a programme produced by the BBC's Transcription Service expressly for overseas sale (and, therefore, with no specific broadcast date). They were not aired in Britain. Paul and Ringo recorded interviews for this series on 2 May 1966.

George's was the first to be taped, a 15-minute interview that started at 4.30 pm. Then it was the turn of John, his interview beginning at 5.00. Each tape was later edited down to eight minutes, which – with the *Pop Profile* signature tune – made for nine-minute programmes distributed by mail in March 1966 as custom-pressed Transcription Service seven-inch discs.

Although it did not figure on the imminent *Rubber Soul*, nor indeed on any other release, '12-Bar Original' was mixed into mono between 4.45 and 5.00 this afternoon at EMI in order that the Beatles could have acetate discs cut for their private collections. These 15 minutes saw the end of balance engineer Norman Smith's association with the group. He had been with them since their first visit to Abbey Road on 6 June 1962 but in February 1966 was promoted to the rank of producer, working out of the A&R department at EMI's

November 16th. 1965.

Mr. G.N. Bridge.   Mr. I. Middleton.
Mr. R.N. White.
Mr. R. Oldfield.   Mr. D. Woodward.
Mr. R. Featherstone.   Mr. F. Chalmers.
Mr. J. Florey.   Mr. A. Dewdney.
Mr. R. Dockerill.   Miss P. Britt.
Mr. G. Freshwater.   Mr. E. Fowler.
Mr. R. Dunton.

PARLOPHONE L.P. 'RUBBER SOUL'.

Artist:	THE BEATLES.
Recorded:	October/November, 1965. Job. No. 3003.
Release:	December 1965.
Cover:	Robert Freeman.

Recording produced by George Martin.

Side 1.	DRIVE MY CAR.	Paul and John. (with George) (Paul on piano)
	NORWEGIAN WOOD. (This Bird has flown)	John (with Paul) (George on Sitar)
	YOU WON'T SEE ME.	Paul (with John and George) (Paul on piano: Mal "organ" Evans on Hammond)
	NOWHERE MAN.	John and Paul and George.
	THINK FOR YOURSELF.	George (with John and Paul) (Paul on...)
	THE WORD.	John and Paul and George. fuzz Bass (Paul on piano; George Martin on harmonium.)
	MICHELLE.	Paul (with John and George)
Side 2.	WHAT GOES ON.	Ringo (With Paul and John)
	GIRL.	John (with Paul and George)
	I'M LOOKING THROUGH YOU.	Paul (with John) (Ringo on Hammond Organ)
	IN MY LIFE.	John and Paul. (George Martin on piano)
	WAIT.	John and Paul.
	IF I NEEDED SOMEONE.	George (with John and Paul)
	RUN FOR YOUR LIFE.	John (with Paul and George)

All titles composed Lennon-McCartney except:-
    THINK FOR YOURSELF and IF I NEEDED SOMEONE.
                                (George Harrison)
All titles published - Northern Songs Ltd.

George Martin.
A.I.R. London.

Manchester Square headquarters. When, in 1972, under the name of Hurricane Smith, Norman scored a number one single himself in America (*Cashbox* chart) with 'Oh, Babe, What Would You Say?' John and Yoko were the first to send a congratulatory telegram.

Smith's promotion to the rank of EMI staff producer followed the August 1965 defection of three of the company's main men, George Martin, Ron Richards and John Burgess, all of whom – along with Decca's Peter Sullivan – quit to form an independent production company, Associated Independent Recordings (London) Limited, better known as AIR. With Martin no longer on the staff EMI could have allotted another producer to work with the Beatles but this did not happen. The partnership was too successful to break and neither Brian Epstein nor the Beatles would have stood for such an action. The change was especially good news for Martin – he could now reap personal reward in the form of an EMI royalty from all future Beatles productions, rather than draw a fairly unsubstantial salary from a company growing ever richer as a result of his and the Beatles' work.

Friday 3 December

Odeon Cinema, Glasgow

The Beatles' last homeland tour, and their only one in 1965, was a brief affair compared to previous British excursions – visiting only nine venues (eight cities) in ten days, with two "houses" each date. Their repertoire throughout comprised

a mere 11 songs: 'I Feel Fine', 'She's A Woman', 'If I Needed Someone', 'Act Naturally', 'Nowhere Man', 'Baby's In Black', 'Help!', 'We Can Work It Out', 'Yesterday' (with Paul accompanying himself on an electric organ), 'Day Tripper' and 'I'm Down'.

In their dressing-room here in Glasgow the Beatles recorded a message of welcome for a new pirate station, Radio Scotland; at some other point during this month – dates not known – the group also taped a Christmas Day greetings message for the listeners of Radio Caroline and Paul gave an interview for the same station's *Pop's Happening* programme, broadcast on Boxing Day.

The Beatles' only, scant rehearsal for their final tour of Britain: a quick busk at Neil and Mal's London flat.

Saturday 4 December

City Hall, Newcastle-upon-Tyne

Sunday 5 December

Empire Theatre, Liverpool

The Beatles' last Liverpool concert. Forty thousand ticket applications were received for the two "houses", although the Empire could accommodate only 2550 for each.

During the second show Paul briefly joined one of the support acts, the Koobas, playing drums during their version of 'Dizzy Miss Lizzy'.

Tuesday 7 December

ABC Cinema, Ardwick, Manchester

Wednesday 8 December

Gaumont Cinema, Barker's Pool, Sheffield, Yorkshire

Thursday 9 December

Odeon Cinema, Birmingham

Friday 10 December

Odeon Cinema, Hammersmith, London

Saturday 11 December

Astoria Cinema, Finsbury Park, London

Sunday 12 December

Capitol Cinema, Cardiff

The final night of what turned out to be the Beatles' last British concert tour.

"I **RECKON** we could send out four waxwork dummies of ourselves and that would satisfy the crowds. Beatles concerts are nothing to do with music any more. They're just bloody tribal rites." So said John Lennon in 1966. The concerts really had to end. The Beatles knew so after their British tour of December 1965; by August 1966 any lingering vestige of doubt had been eradicated, following the fantastic sequence of events which accompanied their overseas concerts during the summer.

The Beatles didn't play live at all until 1 May – easily their longest break between stage engagements since Quarry Men days – and even this was only a 15-minute set at the annual *New Musical Express* Poll-Winners' Concert. It was also the group's final British concert of all, for although NEMS issued a press statement in February announcing "The Beatles will tour Japan, the USA and West Germany in the summer and Britain at the end of the year", the winter UK tour was put on ice, permanently, after the summer's events.

On 6 April, after three months of glorious inactivity, the Beatles began recording a new album, untitled until after completion and released as *Revolver*. The vital plateau between their "touring years" and "studio years", *Revolver* is the album which, by common consent, shows the Beatles at the peak of their creativity, welding strong, economical but lyrically incisive

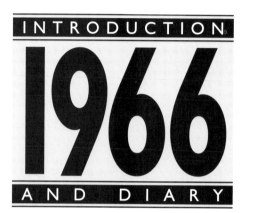

song material with brave studio experimentation. It remains today one of those rare albums which is able to retain its original freshness and vitality. Quite simply, *Revolver* is a masterpiece, born out of a sudden artistic and creative freedom, and the remarkable maturation – despite all the chaos surrounding them – of these four young men. Recording was now their prime interest and motivation, what was the point of going back out on the road and suffering all that touring nonsense?

Although eager to ditch live performances, the Beatles had commitments to fulfil. The first leg of a brief tour that later visited Japan and the Philippines found the group making a return visit to West Germany, and to Hamburg, for the first time since 1962. This part of the tour, at least, proved uneventful, except that is for the usual screaming mayhem and mania, some street riots, police arrests for ticket forgery, with a dose of nostalgia thrown in for good measure. And it wasn't even as if the Beatles were worth listening to any more, for the standard of their live musicianship reached its absolute nadir during these final months on the road. Their repertoire numbered a mere 11 songs, and they murdered each in turn with off-key, out-of-time singing and playing.

The Beatles' only visit to Japan caused a real flap, however. Local promoter Tatsuji Nagashima had booked the group to give five shows over three days at the Nippon Budokan Hall, deemed by many to be sacred, suitable only for the presentation of Japanese martial arts. Even the selection of the Nippon Budokan for judo during the 1964 Olympic Games had caused upset, and now it was to be used as a venue for amplified Western pop music with its attendant wild audiences. Opposition to the Beatles' concerts was considerable and there were public demonstrations – consequently, police presence was intensely heavy throughout their four-day stay on Japanese soil with, incredibly, a total of 35,000 security men employed. At Haneda airport on 29 June, despite landing at 3.40 am, 1500 fans crowded the terminal to catch a glimpse of the group, only to be unnecessarily manhandled by a phalanx of riot police. During each of the Beatles' five shows at the Nippon Budokan the police numbered 3000 among the 10,000 audience, standing two abreast at strategic places in every aisle to quell any pandemonium.

In their over-zealous protection of the group, eager to ensure their safety, the Japanese security forces imprisoned the Beatles at the Tokyo Hilton Hotel from arrival to departure, the group leaving there only to zoom to and from the Nippon Budokan in 70 mph escorted motorcades. They were installed in suites on the 18th floor so all lifts stopped on the 17th, there were armed guards outside all lift-shafts and stairwells and police stationed in every other bedroom. As the Beatles couldn't go out, merchants were invited in, selling the group goods in their suite. The Beatles attempted an

escape, were caught and returned to their rooms like naughty children, and when John alone finally managed to break out at 7.00 one morning the police seriously threatened to withdraw.

From Tokyo the Beatles flew on to their next stop, the Philippines. Criticism here of the Beatles was stoked up just three hours after they had landed, when the group held their obligatory press conference. The local media took a dislike to their flippant answers to questions – always the same old queries like "When are you getting married, Paul?" and "When did you last have a haircut, George?" – and were upset over the group's ignorance of the Philippines itself. In fact, the Beatles had long ceased to be interested in the history or topography of the country in which they were touring. It didn't matter where they were for they only saw airports, screaming crowds, limousines, screaming crowds, hotel rooms, screaming crowds, concert halls, screaming crowds, more limousines, more screaming crowds and finally another airport.

The *Manila Sunday Times* on 3 July, the day before the Beatles' two live shows there, sowed the seeds of the story which would soon break into a giant-sized rumpus. Its article ran:

"President Marcos, the First Lady, and the three young Beatles fans in the family, have been invited as guests of honour at the concerts. The Beatles plan to personally follow up the invitation during a courtesy call on Mrs Imelda Marcos at Malacañang Palace tomorrow morning at 11 o'clock."

The Beatles, in fact, planned no such thing. All they were aware of was a vague mention of a swift afternoon (3.00 pm) Palace drop-in, printed on their Philippine schedule drawn up by local concert promoter Ramon Ramos, and they had already rejected this because their first show was scheduled to start at 4.00 pm and they wanted to arrive at the stadium at least two hours earlier. Anxious to offend neither the Palace nor the Beatles, Ramos let matters rest there and when, the next morning, a Palace official came to collect the Beatles they were still in bed. Brian Epstein refused to rouse them.

After the group had failed to show at the Palace all hell

was unleashed, the *Manila Times* the next morning, under a bold-type headline screaming, "Imelda Stood Up", accusing the Beatles of "snubbing the First Lady and the three Marcos children…[keeping them] and a crowd of 400, all friends of the First Family, waiting". The ramifications were serious. The promoter refused to pay the Beatles their substantial share of the gate receipts from the two shows. Bomb and death threats were telephoned through to the British Embassy and to the Beatles' hotel suite.

Brian Epstein was so stricken with worry and guilt that he arranged for a TV camera crew to visit the hotel and tape a press statement he had written with Tony Barrow. But when the recording was transmitted an unfortunate surge of static blighted every TV screen in the Philippines just as he began speaking. It obliterated his every word until the speech finished, when the static vanished.

The next day proved a watershed in the Beatles' career. A tax commissioner insisted that the Beatles couldn't leave the country until they had paid income tax on their concert receipts (which Ramon Ramos was still withholding). A furious row developed until Brian Epstein, although correct in his insistence that Ramos was responsible for the tax levy, filed a bond for Pesos 74,450 (£6840) to settle the matter. Arguing about contractual logistics was pointless. Paying the

Taping the 'Paperback Writer' and 'Rain' performance videos at Abbey Road, with director Michael Lindsay-Hogg. As well as working again with the Beatles he went on to make the remarkable Brideshead Revisited *TV series.*

35,000 Police Being Mobilized To Protect Beatles

A total of 35,000 police officers will be mobilized to protect the Beatles from possible teenage mobs during the popular British quartet stay in Tokyo from June 28 through July 3, it was decided Monday.

A special police meeting also decided to keep the Beatles' course from Tokyo International Airport to Tokyo a top secret. A special police headquarters will be set up during the Beatles' stay in an attempt to minimize the confusion.

When the Beatles land at Tokyo International Airport on June 28 at 5.15 p.m. the airport will be guarded by 3,000 officers, including unarmed riot policemen, plainclothes men and woman officers. The airport will be closed to the public several hours prior to their arrival.

Another 2,000-man force will stand guard around Tokyo Hilton Hotel, where the British teenage idols will stay. Roadblocks will be set up on all 11 roads leading to the hotel to forestall any onslaught by fans of the entertainers.

During the three-day performance at the Budokan Hall, starting June 30, the mammoth building will be surrounded by 2,200 policemen every day. In front of the stage will be 250 plainclothes men to seperate the Beatles from their fans.

1966

Furor Over Beatles 'Snub' Mars Show

The Beatles belch out a popular song before 50,000 fans at the Rizal Stadium last night. Fans, like those shown above, screamed and yelled.

Thousands of teenagers among an estimated crowd of 50,000 shrieked, screamed, cried and moaned as the Beatles — Britain's mop-haired exponents of pop music — let out a succession of 10 hit tunes during their matinee show yesterday afternoon at the Rizal Football Stadium.

A sour note, however,

By ROBERTO D. CUEVAS
Chronicle Reporter

toned down an otherwise enthusiastic response when the quartet failed to show up for an 11 a.m. appointment and luncheon with the First Lady and her three children at Malacañang yesterday.

Paul McCartney, one of the foursome, was later reported to have

offered his apologies, saying they didn't know about the engagement.

MIX-UP

Later in the day, their local promoters and their managers called at the Malacañang Press Office and blamed each other for the schedule mix-up.

Four hundred other
To page 9, col. 6

Furor Over Beatles
Snub Dampens Show

From page 1
children and their mothers also waited for more than half an hour at the Palace grounds.

Hours after the furor erupted, McCartney, Ringo Starr, George Harrison, and John Lennon were at the Coliseum to sing songs before hysterical fans.

Every number was accompanied by screams and shrieks from the "Beatle-maniacs" so much so that people could hardly hear the songs above the din.

WORRIED PARENTS

If the Beatles show was a hit among the young, it didn't seem so among countless parents.

"This is pure madness," said one middle-aged woman. "There's nothing spectacular about the Beatles anyway. I am worried for my daughter who might go crazy about them."

Even at the show was going on, people were still jostling for vantage positions for a clearer view of the Beatles. But tight security measures thrown by about 750 uniformed Manila policemen and 300 security guards put the huge throng in check.

The security detail of the Beatles was so tight that one was heard to say: "It's just like getting in a shipment of gold bars to Fort Knox."

CAN'T HEAR.

CAN'T SEE

But songs were hardly audible to those whose P2 tickets consigned them to the far-end stand. About 20,000 of them could only get a glimpse of the Beatles from 300 meters away.

Even people with P5 deckets and seated at the rear side of the stand could only get a glimpse of the Beatles' back.

But most of them didn't seem to mind at all. "It's different when you see them in persons," they said.

NOT ANY BETTER

Nevertheless, many of those near the stage were one in saying that any local group could give the Beatles a run for their money. "They are not any better than any of our finest Beatle imitators," a wag commented.

The two-hour matinee show, which featured numbers from local performers, started at 4 p.m. But the crowd started milling outside the stadium as early as 11 a.m. The games were thrown open at 1:30 p.m. Another show was held at 8:30 last night.

SPECIAL GUESTS

The 2,000-strong Philippine contingent to South Viet Nam were special guests in the matinee show.

Pepsi Cola Bottling Company of the Philippines, sponsor of the Beatles' one-day stand here, said that the Liverpool quartet collected a cool

$100,000 for their two performances yesterday.

The Beatles will emplane at 5 o'clock today, ending a three-month tour that brought them half-way around the world.

WHO DID IT?

Their local promoters and their managers last night blamed each other for the snub on the First Lady.

Led by Ramon Ramos Jr., officials of Cavalcade Promotions blamed Brian Epstein, manager of the Beatles, for refusing to send the British singing group to Malacañang and have lunch with the First Lady and other guests even if they were already late.

On the other hand, Vic Lewis, a director of the NEMS, the company running the Beatles, blamed the local promoters for the snafu in the arrangement of schedules.

NO COMMENT

On the part of Malacañang, Press Secretary Jose D. Aspiras would not say anything beyond, "We will not dignify the Beatles with a statement.

Aspiras refused to meet the promoters and the director of the Beatles and assigned the chore to Assistant Press Secretary Jacobo Clave.

Clave explained that it was not the First Lady but the Beatles, through their local promoters, who had asked for the appointment.

---

money just seemed the simplest way to get out of the country.

But could they do so? All of the security forces protecting them had been withdrawn. Kicked and jostled as they left their hotel, the Beatles and their entourage arrived at Manila International Airport in a harassed state. The airport manager ordered that they be rendered no assistance, even shutting down power to the escalators so that the Beatles had to climb several flights of stairs with their luggage. An angry crowd of 200 Filipinos finally caught up with their prey on the second floor of the airport and, amid much scuffling, the Beatles were manhandled. According to the *Manila Times*

"Drummer Ringo Starr was floored by an uppercut. As he crawled away the mob kicked him. George Harrison and John Lennon received kicks and blows as they ran to the customs zone. Paul McCartney was relatively unhurt as he sprinted ahead. Manager Brian Epstein received the brunt of the mob's fury. He was kicked and thrown to the floor. As a result he suffered a sprained ankle and had to be helped to the customs area."

In reality, the *Manila Times* was guilty of some exaggeration because all four Beatles actually remained unscathed, although they were certainly pushed and shoved. But Brian Epstein was indeed injured, as was Mal Evans who received several hefty kicks to his ribs after being felled to the floor. Alf Bicknell, the Beatles' chauffeur, suffered a fractured rib in addition to a spinal injury. And they were not out of danger yet. As the Beatles' haggard party proceeded through immigration they were greeted by a barrage of cat-calls and boos, and an angry mob baying "*Beatles Alis Diyan!*" ("Beatles Go Home!") Acutely conscious of the possibility of sniper fire, the Beatles' and entourage sprinted across the tarmac and up the steps to the shelter of their airplane.

The Filipinos still had two more carefully orchestrated ploys to play. Shortly before takeoff the pilot of the airplane received an instruction that Mal Evans and Tony Barrow were to return to the terminal. Both nervously made their way back across the tarmac, Barrow certain that they were going to be detained. Instead they were told that no one could leave: owing to a convenient bureaucratic bungle, there was no record of the Beatles' arrival in the Philippines two days previously. Since, technically, they hadn't arrived, they couldn't leave either, being – in effect – illegal immigrants. The Beatles spent 44 anxious minutes on board the plane, unaware of the reason for the delay, before Evans and Barrow returned with the necessary paperwork and the plane took off.

The second move was a press statement issued by

President Marcos which read "There was no intention on the part of the Beatles to slight the First Lady or the Government of the Republic of the Philippines." In a remarkable feat of good timing, the statement was issued minutes after the Beatles' departure from Philippine soil.

On board their plane the Beatles were livid about the whole ghastly affair, and with Brian Epstein specifically and concert tours generally.

What was intended as a peaceful post-Philippines rest in New Delhi was all but ruined too by – amazingly – vast screaming crowds of Indian Beatlemaniacs. The Beatles were rapidly approaching the end of their tether. After two days the group flew home to England, still angry. At London Airport on 8 July a reporter asked George what was next on the Beatles' schedule. His acidic reply, although he could hardly have known it then, was a painfully accurate prediction: "We're going to have a couple of weeks to recuperate before we go and get beaten up by the Americans." Portentous words indeed.

*

High up on the 27th floor of the Astor Towers Hotel, in lakeside Chicago, John faced the worst experience of his 25-year life. It was 11 August, five months and seven days after an interview had been published in the London *Evening Standard* in which he had told trusted friend and writer Maureen Cleave that he was reading extensively about religion (although he didn't actually say it, paying particular attention to Hugh J Schonfield's best-seller *The Passover Plot*) adding, "Christianity will go. It will vanish and shrink. I needn't argue with that; I'm right and I will be proved right. We're more popular than Jesus now." Tucked midway through the full-page interview, John's quote went unnoticed. People were used to his caustic remarks and, besides, it was valid comment.

Then, on 29 July, long after the article had been forgotten, the US teen magazine *Datebook* reproduced the interview under a syndication arrangement, announcing the item with a front-page banner which quoted John saying "I don't know which will go first – rock 'n' roll or Christianity!" Uproar. Ignominiously led by a station in Birmingham, Alabama, 22 radio stations banned the Beatles' music indefinitely from their airwaves (some never broadcast it anyway but were keen to jump on the pro-Jesus anti-Beatles bandwagon). Several even went so far as to organise, and broadcast live, public burning of Beatles memorabilia, where people were invited to toss records, books and Beatles merchandise onto a blazing bonfire while smiling at conveniently placed press and television cameramen.

The situation was so nasty that Brian Epstein considered cancelling the Beatles' impending US tour – due to start on 12 August. His worst fear of all was that one of the Beatles might be shot, so on 6 August he flew to New York and held a press conference in an attempt to stem the rising anti-Beatles tide and, at the same time, qualify John's remarks. He was only partially successful. The tour, however, was to go ahead.

The Beatles' opening press conference, at the Astor

Epstein checks on U.S. "holy war" against Beatles

The Beatles' manager, Mr. Brian Epstein, to-day weighed the prospects of a U.S. tour by his mop-haired quartet in the face of a 'holy war" against them in America.

The furore was caused by Beatle John Lennon's reported remark that the Beatles are more popular than Jesus Christ.

As a result, fans in several U.S. cities have been urged to make bonfires of their Beatle records, and radio stations across the nation have banned Beatles records.

Mr. Epstein, who cut short a holiday to fly to New York last night from London, said he hoped that the Beatles' four-week tour would go ahead. It was to start on August 12.

He said no decision would be made until he had talked with the General Artists' Corporation, the agency which booked the Beatles for their 14-city tour.

"MISINTERPRETED"

The "holy war" against the Beatles started in America's "Bible Belt" and quickly spread across the nation. In Mississippi an imperial wizard of a Ku Klux Klan group said he believed the Beatles had been "brain-washed" by the Communist Party."

On arrival in New York Mr.

Epstein was asked whether he thought the Beatles were more popular than Christianity. "Of course not," he said.

He said: "John Lennon's views have been misinterpreted," but he declined to say whether he meant that he had been misreported. "The whole thing," he added, "is a typical Beatles furore."

Mr. Epstein, who has managed the Beatles since their earliest days, will be keeping a close watch on the pop record charts for any reaction by the buying public.

A radio station which has never before played a Beatles record started playing one every 30 minutes last night, preceding the records with a statement denouncing the "hypocrisy" of banning the group's music.

Station W.S.A.C. said in a commentary: "his is the best way we can think of to show our contempt for hypocrisy personified."

Some of the stations which have banned the Beatles records play other songs that are "the most pornographic melodies since Elizabethan times," the station said.

"Perhaps the Beatles could become more popular than Jesus," as Beatle John Lennon allegedly said.

"Perhaps that is what is wrong with society, and there they are, dear friend. You made them so, not Jesus, not John Lennon, and not the Beatles."

W.S.A.C. plans to continue broadcasting the commentary and playing a Beatles record indefinitely, a spokesman said.

baseball stadium was interrupted for half an hour while 2500 screaming fans invaded the pitch. Before the Beatles' 15 August concert in Washington DC five members of Prince George's County Ku Klux Klan, led by the Imperial Wizard of the Maryland clan, and dressed in red, white and green robes, paraded outside the venue. On 19 August the Beatles received an anonymous phone call that one or all of them would be assassinated at some point during the group's two shows that day in Memphis. Midway through the second show somebody threw a firecracker onto the stage which exploded. Each of the Beatles looked to the others to see who had been shot. On 20 August the promoter of the Beatles' concert in Cincinnati failed to provide a canopy cover for the open-air performance. A downpour just as they were due on stage promised certain electrocution if they played so with 35,000 fans already inside the stadium the show was cancelled and re-scheduled for lunchtime the following day. The Beatles' planned armoured-truck departure from the stage in Los Angeles was thwarted when the driver found the main gate locked. They had to wait more than two hours inside the truck, surrounded by fans, until an alternative means of escape was effected.

The Beatles were playing these huge open-air stadiums in order to satisfy as many fans as possible with the minimum of effort and maximum income. In Los Angeles, instead of playing one or two shows at the 18,700-capacity Hollywood Bowl, as they had done in 1964 and 1965, they played one concert at the Dodger Stadium before 45,000 fans. Unfortunately, the Beatles could no longer sell out this type of venue and few of their concerts in this final tour played to capacity audiences. The show-business newspaper *Variety* wrote that the box-office success of the tour was "solid, if not as spectacular or hysterical as in previous years". It certainly wasn't. The 55,600-capacity Shea Stadium in New York was left with 11,000 unsold tickets for the Beatles' 23 August concert. The previous year it had sold out within hours.

Towers in Chicago, was dominated by the "Jesus incident". For once – well, not for a few minutes anyway – there were no shallow "teen" questions, and no false bonhomie from ingratiating local disc-jockeys. John was placed firmly under the spotlight and grilled by American news reporters over his so-called "blasphemous remarks". He reasoned, he qualified, he explained once and then a second time what he had really meant. But would he apologise? To please them, though he expressed puzzlement at what he was apologising for, he did and the whole trumped-up, unnecessary incident was over. The Beatles had "learned their lesson". (Later on in the tour John gave vent to his true feelings. "In England they take what we say with a pinch of salt," he said, caustically adding that the anti-Beatles protesters were "middle-aged DJs and 12-year-olds burning a pile of LP covers".)

The entire episode seemed ridiculous then, now it's almost impossible to comprehend how so many people could have become so agitated over the purely personal opinion of a pop star. But then, the Beatles always were considered by others to be more than mere musicians.

The tour that followed was a chronicle of ineptitude and bad experiences. On 14 August their concert at a Cleveland

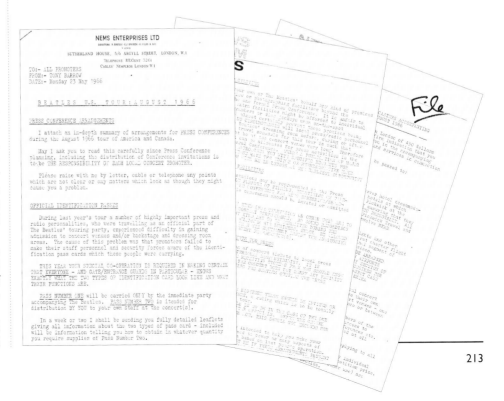

1966

Paul with George Martin at EMI Studios, composing themes for The Family Way, November–December 1966.

If box-office business wasn't, as *Variety* reported, "hysterical", the fans certainly were, still. The Beatles had matured very quickly between 1963 and 1966 and their fans just couldn't match the pace. They still screamed and sobbed and demanded "She loves you, yeah yeah yeah" which, to the Beatles in 1966, was little more than a children's nursery rhyme. Forget 'She Loves You'! The Beatles had recorded the jangling and mysterious, experimental and innovative *Revolver*. Now was the time for the lyrical 'Eleanor Rigby', for the ruthless wit of 'Taxman', for the primitive psychedelia of 'Tomorrow Never Knows', for backwards tapes and for Eastern musical instruments. The Beatles didn't perform a single song from *Revolver* at any time during their US tour. It was almost as if two entirely separate personalities had evolved – the Beatles as recording artists and the Beatles as concert performers.

Amid the never-ending Beatlemania, the group churning out songs they did better not to hear, even if it was possible, and running humourlessly through infuriatingly brief 33-minute concerts, they came to 29 August and the last show. On a bracing San Francisco night, the wind whipping in off the Pacific, the Beatles stood at second base in the airy open spaces of Candlestick Park, on a stage elevated five foot above the ground. They were fully encaged by a six-foot-high wire fence, around which gathered private and city policemen. An armoured truck stood by, its engine running. They played from 9.27 pm until precisely 10.00 pm when, after closing with 'Long Tall Sally', they stepped off the stage for ever. After nine years and more than 1400 live appearances the Beatles had given their last show.

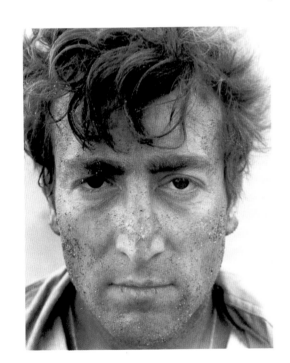

Reclining in his seat as the Beatles' airplane flew out of San Francisco that night, George commented, "Well, that's it, I'm not a Beatle anymore". Certainly, if being a Beatle meant being an active live musician then he would no longer be a Beatle.

With each of the group keen to pursue individual freedom and interests, an extended period of collective inactivity followed. They were temporarily between recording contracts with EMI (a new one was signed on 27 January 1967) and no one could pressure them into recording or releasing new material until they felt like it. It was, in essence, a time to take stock, to consider what life held in store for them if they didn't tour again. In fact, did the Beatles have any future at all? Odd though it seems now, where it scarcely matters if rock acts tour or don't tour, or do so only every few years, live performance was the essential backbone of the scene in the 1960s. Was it possible for the Beatles to remain united without playing live? How would they fill their days, weeks, months and years?

These were the questions that occupied their minds in the autumn of 1966, as John filmed without the other Beatles in Richard Lester's *How I Won The War*, as Paul – eager for something to do – had NEMS find him a film score to write (*The Family Way*), and as Ringo pottered around with his family as the Surrey country squire. Only George seemed certain of his future, spending a month in India quietly immersing himself in its music, culture and religion, suddenly aware, at the age of just 23, of the Beatles' unimportance in the great scheme of life itself.

Seeing the four Beatles exploring individual freedoms, the world concluded that the group had split. *The Sunday Times* in Britain published a heavyweight obituary-style piece, examining the reasons for the break-up and pondering the future without them. Even the BBC speculated on the group's dissolution in its news bulletins. The Beatles weren't around to deny the stories, were not completely certain of their own future and, besides, no longer felt compelled to play the media game. Brian Epstein issued denials as best he could but even he was unable to do more, being hospitalised for much of the time, suffering from fits of depression that had led to a suicide attempt.

It was only in late November that the Beatles reunited in London and decided to resume recording together. On the 24th they had their first EMI session in five months, taping the remarkable 'Strawberry Fields Forever'. Other songs followed, and as the weeks and months passed it became obvious that the group *could* remain a unit without playing concerts, that recording activities *could* bond the group and yet also leave time for the vital exploration and expression of individual interests.

To accompany this significant new phase, the Beatles ditched the "Mop Tops" image that had plagued them for too long. In fact, though they scarcely knew or desired it, they were at the epicentre of an imminent artistic earthquake, of music, of drugs, of fashion, of counter-culture. Having (unintentionally even then) caused one cultural revolution in 1963, the Beatles were about to do the same in 1967.

Wednesday 5 January

CTS Studios, Kensington Gardens Square, London

Just as it would be naive to believe that the sound on live-concert rock music albums is ever truly live and undoctored, so the same is true for live-concert films (and, these days, videos). Stage performances can sound not merely all right but distinctly amazing on the night, amid the heady atmosphere of an excited auditorium or stadium, but a close listen to the tapes some weeks or months later in a cold recording studio or cutting-room can prove decidedly disappointing.

In the case of the Beatles' momentous 15 August 1965 Shea Stadium concert, the audio tapes specifically revealed not only musical flaws on the Beatles' part but also technical imperfections caused by the sheer size of the venue, the high-decibel screaming and the less than state-of-the-art mobile recording equipment around in 1965. To have screened unaltered such a high-profile film on peak-time television would have done the group a disservice.

So it was that, amid some secrecy, the Beatles came to CTS Studios in central London this day, to "sweeten" the soundtrack, by whatever means necessary, of their in-production television film *The Beatles At Shea Stadium*.

The session began with Paul only, overdubbing new bass tracks onto 'Dizzy Miss Lizzy', 'Can't Buy Me Love', 'Baby's In Black' and 'I'm Down'. Onto this latter song John also overdubbed a new organ track.

More drastic repair work was then effected by the group as a whole, with entirely new recordings completed for two songs: 'I Feel Fine' (done at George Martin's specific request) and 'Help!' The Beatles strove to re-create a live-concert sound with these recordings rather than their more typical EMI studio feel, and they also had to match carefully their singing and playing with the on-screen images, hence the use of CTS, the premier audio-to-film dubbing studio in London. (CTS is an abbreviation for Cine Tele Sound.)

To fix 'Act Naturally' the Beatles did nothing: the film's post-production team merely replaced the Shea recording with the Beatles' disc version (recorded 17 June 1965), syncing it to the picture by means of audience cutaways and even, in places, cuts in the music. (Intentionally or otherwise, one moment – where Ringo's vocal is evident but his mouth is closed – was left in the film uncorrected.)

Documentation also suggests that John wished to record a new version of 'Ticket To Ride', and that it was done during this CTS session, but close study of the film indicates that the original Shea version was used (although perhaps a little instrumental overdubbing was effected).

Additionally, George Martin desired a new recording of 'Twist And Shout', but there wasn't time to do this. Instead, the post-production team used the unreleased 30 August 1965 Hollywood Bowl concert recording to bolster the sound, causing – in one place – John's live vocal to be double-tracked. In fact, the Bowl recording was used extensively during the film's post-production processes for recordings of the screaming audience, especially on the two all-new London recordings.

No doctoring appears to have been done to either 'She's

A Woman' or 'Everybody's Trying To Be Baby', suggesting that, by this time, they had already been excluded from the film. They were, however, included in an early print which Epstein received from Sullivan Productions around 5 November 1965, which then ran to 54 minutes. By January, as it would be for the transmission, the film's duration had been cut to just under 48 minutes. (For broadcast and all other details, see 15 August 1965.)

Friday 25 March

The Vale, London

Since forming NEMS Enterprises in June 1962, Brian Epstein had launched or acquired a number of other business ventures, leasing the central London venue Saville Theatre, for example (see 30 July 1965). In September 1964 he had bought a controlling stake in the Liverpool pop paper *Mersey Beat*, renaming it *Music Echo* and giving it a national perspective and distribution. *Music Echo* then merged with IPC's well-established *Disc*, landing Epstein a 50 per cent stake in the newly-named *Disc And Music Echo*, unveiled on 23 April 1966. One of the promotions devised to push the re-launch was free distribution of a flexi-disc single containing interviews with top singers and groups, made available to readers on submission of a number of completed coupons. The disc was called *Sound Of The Stars* and, probably because of the Epstein connection, the Beatles contributed.

They were recorded between 3.00 and 3.30 this afternoon, interviewed by Radio Caroline disc-jockey Tom Lodge at a photographic studio at 1 The Vale, in the Chelsea area of west London (following which the Beatles got down to the main business of the afternoon, a photo shoot with Robert Whitaker which produced, among other shots, the famous "Butcher" photographs – see also 19 May 1966). Devised and produced by NEMS' Tony Barrow, *Sound Of The Stars* also featured Cilla Black, Cliff Richard, the Hollies, Pete Townshend, Spencer Davis, the Walker

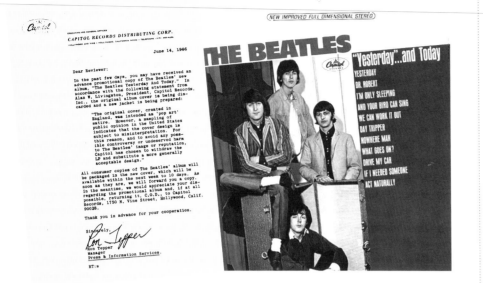

NEW IMPROVED FULL DIMENSIONAL STEREO

CAPITOL RECORDS DISTRIBUTING CORP.

June 14, 1966

Dear Reviewer:

In the past few days, you may have received an advance promotional copy of The Beatles' new album, "The Beatles Yesterday And Today." In accordance with the following statement from Alan W. Livingston, President, Capitol Records, Inc., the original album cover is being discarded and a new jacket is being prepared:

"The original cover, created in England, was intended as 'pop art' satire. However, a sampling of public opinion in the United States indicates that the cover design is subject to misinterpretation. For this reason, and to avoid any possible controversy or undeserved harm to The Beatles' image or reputation, Capitol has chosen to withdraw the LP and substitute a more generally acceptable design."

All consumer copies of The Beatles' album will be packaged in the new cover, which will be available within the next week to 10 days. As soon as they are, we will forward you a copy. In the meantime, we would appreciate your discarding the promotional album and, if at all possible, returning it, C.O.D., to Capitol Records, 1750 N. Vine Street, Hollywood, Calif. 90028.

Thank you in advance for your cooperation.

Sincerely,

Ron Tepper
Manager
Press & Information Services.

RT:s

quite nicely, but here was a quantum jump into not merely tomorrow but sometime next week, 'Tomorrow Never Knows' displaying an unrivalled musical progression and the Beatles' willingness first to observe the boundaries and then smash right through them.

It would be wrong, however, to assume that the Beatles alone were responsible for this remarkable recording, or for the progressiveness which would be the hallmark of much of their future output. George Martin was, as ever, a vital ingredient in the process, always innovative himself, a tireless seeker of new sounds and willing translator of the Beatles' frequently vague requirements. Now he was joined by balance engineer Geoff Emerick, promoted to replace Norman Smith. Though he'd been an occasional second engineer/ tape op on Beatles sessions since 1963, Emerick was only 20-years-old and as willing and eager to experiment with new recording techniques as were the Beatles. The Beatles-Martin-Emerick triumvirate immediately gelled, producing some of the most stunning of all rock music recordings over the next three years.

Revolver also heralded the first use of Artificial Double Tracking, invented by Abbey Road technical engineer Ken Townsend directly at the Beatles' request and now in use at studios worldwide. ADT saved the Beatles the chore of having to manually double-track their voices or instruments, an effect they so frequently sought. But 'Tomorrow Never Knows' didn't only feature ADT – it also boasted tape loops and voices put through a Leslie speaker.

Perhaps the most striking sounds on 'Tomorrow Never Knows' are the tape loops – an effect achieved by tape saturation, by removing the erase head of a machine and then recording over and over onto the same piece of tape. All of the Beatles owned Brennell tape machines and toyed with them in this fashion during leisure time – which, with far fewer tours and other engagements to fulfil, they now had more of than ever before. The seagull-like noise on 'Tomorrow Never Knows' is actually a distorted guitar while other scarcely recognisable sounds include a speeded-up guitar and a wine glass, all played simultaneously into the mixing console from tape machines commandeered all over EMI Studios.

Brothers, Sandie Shaw and others. The Beatles were briefly heard at the start of side one and then ended the second side of the disc with 1 min 37 secs of silly answers to silly questions.

Wednesday 6 April

Studio Three, EMI Studios, London

The first session for what was to become the significant album *Revolver*. Here was a set of recordings destined to rock the rock world, and change forever the course of popular music. And its momentous closing song 'Tomorrow Never Knows' was the first to be taped. What a start! It took just three takes – one of them a breakdown – to tape 'Tomorrow Never Knows' (which carried the working title 'Mark I' at this point in time), although by its very essence the recording was also the result of innumerable overdubs. The Beatles spent this 8.00 pm–1.15 am session recording in three takes the song's stunning rhythm track.

In 1965 the Beatles' recordings had been progressing

MONO/STEREO 4T				RECORDING SHEET							
Sheet : 1 of :	Class : PoP	Overall Title					Date of Session 6th April 66		Job No : 3009		
ARTISTIC INFORMATION					COSTING INFORMATION						
ARTISTE(S) AND/OR CAST	THE BEATLES.	CONDUCTOR			MATERIALS USED	2 × 7"	ORDER NUMBER				
		ORCHESTRA			SESSION BOOKED TIME	7 - 10	COMPANY	PARLOPHONE			
		ACCOMPANIMENT			SESSION ACTUAL	8.00 - 1.15	STUDIO/CONTROL ROOM	103-1 A.			
		ART. DEPT. REP.	MR P, H MARTIN		SET-UP/PLAYBACK		ENGINEERS	GE PMc			
TITLES and MATRIX Nos.		AUTHOR/COMPOSER/ PUBLISHER	REEL NUMBERS	*ALSE STARTS	TAKE No.	TAKE DETAILS FROM	TO	DUR.	M	REMARKS	
MARK I			59734	2B 3		COMPLETE		2·46		BEST.	

'Tomorrow Never Knows' featured, too, a John Lennon vocal that sounded like no other before, having been fed through the electronic circuitry of a revolving Leslie speaker (so named after its inventor, Donald J Leslie) inside a Hammond organ – a technical innovation conceived by the Beatles, Martin and Emerick team based upon composer Lennon's vision of 4000 monks chanting in the background of his song while he sang as if perched on the highest mountain-top.

And all of this less than three years after 'She Loves You'.

Thursday 7 April

Studio Three, EMI Studios, London

While the afternoon, 2.30–7.15, was spent overlaying many of the aforementioned effects onto take three of 'Tomorrow Never Knows', the evening session, 8.15 pm–1.30 am, saw the Beatles start work on Paul's superb Tamla Motown-inspired 'Got To Get You Into My Life', recording five takes. The song was to chop and change a great deal before it ended up on *Revolver* with recording taking place sporadically until 17 June.

Friday 8 April

Studio Two, EMI Studios, London

Working from 2.30–9.00 pm, the Beatles recorded three more takes of 'Got To Get You Into My Life', perfecting the rhythm track. The eighth was deemed "best", later to be overdubbed with vocals, guitar and the song's distinctive brass passages.

Monday 11 April

Studio Two, EMI Studios, London

After overdubbing guitars onto 'Got To Get You Into My Life', the initial session of the day, 2.30–7.00 pm, saw George begin the recording of 'Love You To', his first Indian-flavoured composition. (It was untitled at first and then assumed the working title 'Granny Smith', after the apple, only becoming 'Love You To' near to the album's release date.)

The recording grew progressively more complex with each of the six takes, the first three being taped during the afternoon, the next three from 8.00 pm to 12.45 am. The sixth was marked "best" and included George's acoustic guitar and guide vocal, Paul's bass, and overdubs of sitar and tabla. Anil Bhagwat was credited on the *Revolver* sleeve as the tabla player, but there was no credit for the sitar player. This may have been George himself, although newly discovered session documentation suggests that, like Bhagwat, someone from the Asian Music Circle in north London – founded by a friend of George's, Ayana Deva Angadi – was recruited for the part.

A rough mono mix of the recording was made between 12.45 and 1.00 am for George to take away.

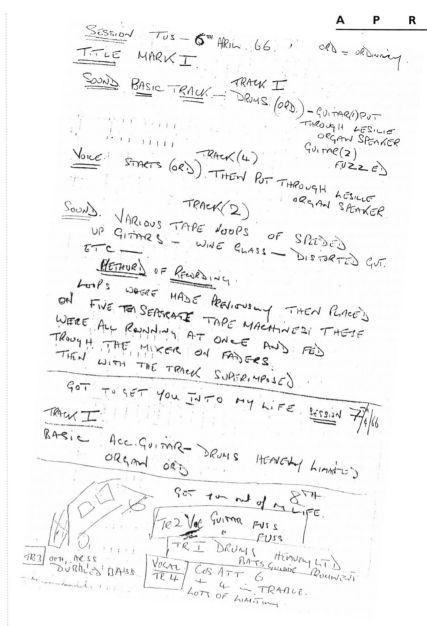

Wednesday 13 April

Studio Three, EMI Studios, London

Two distinct sessions this day. From 2.30 to 6.30 pm George's 'Granny Smith' ('Love You To') was completed with the reduction of take six into take seven and subsequent overdubs of a new Harrison lead vocal, Ringo's tambourine and an occasional harmony vocal from Paul (omitted during mixing). Deemed complete, three mono mixes and various edits were made before the 6.30 pm conclusion.

Independent of the album *Revolver*, which would be issued in August, the Beatles released a new single on Friday 10 June, with two songs from these current sessions. Recording of the A-side, Paul's 'Paperback Writer', began at 8.00 pm this evening, concluding, for the present, at 2.30 am. In this time, two takes of the rhythm track were made, only the second being complete. Marked "best" it served as the platform onto which 14 April overdubs were recorded.

Tape op Phil McDonald's hurriedly handwritten but important notes about the Beatles' first three days' revolutionary work on Revolver.

Thursday 14 April

Studio Three, EMI Studios, London

'Paperback Writer' was completed between 2.30 and 7.30 pm, with numerous overdubs onto the previous night's take two, including Paul's lead and John and George's novel 'Frère Jacques' backing vocal, evoking schoolboy memories of French lessons. The finished recording was mixed into mono between 7.30 and 8.00 pm.

At 8.30 pm, after a 30-minute pause, recording began of 'Rain', to be the B-side of 'Paperback Writer' when issued in June. Like many of the *Revolver*-era recordings, 'Rain' was full of all of the latest technological advancements: limiters, compressors, jangle boxes, Leslie speakers, ADT, tapes played backwards, machines deliberately running faster or slower than usual, and vari-speed vocals.

By the end of the session, at 1.30 am, the Beatles had made five passes at completing a rhythm and vocal track. The song would be taken through to completion in the next session.

Saturday 16 April

Studio Two, EMI Studios, London

Eleven uninterrupted hours, 2.30 pm–1.30 am, completing 'Rain', overdubbing tambourine, bass and more vocals, then doing tape-to-tape reductions to add yet more overdubs. Four mono mixes, the third marked "best", were produced at the end of the session. ('Rain' was first mixed into stereo on 2 December 1969.)

Sunday 17 April

Studio Two, EMI Studios, London

A 2.30–10.30 pm session, the Beatles recording in seven takes the basic track of John's new composition 'Doctor Robert', written about a certain New York doctor who, allegedly, administered hallucinogenic drugs to friends from his Manhattan practise.

Tuesday 19 April

Studio Two, EMI Studios, London

'Doctor Robert' was completed with vocal overdubs onto take seven and, at the end of the 2.30–12.00 pm session, rough mono mixes.

Wednesday 20 April

Studio Two, EMI Studios, London

Two new songs were begun in this 2.30 pm–2.30 am session, although both would be re-made for record release. The lion's share of the 12 hours was devoted to John's 'And Your Bird Can Sing', taping two takes and then, considering it complete, producing mono mixes of the "best", take two. However, a re-make was recorded on 26 April.

Four rehearsal rhythm track takes of George's 'Taxman' were taped towards the end of the session but recording started afresh the next day.

Thursday 21 April

Studio Two, EMI Studios, London

George's wonderfully sardonic 'Taxman' was virtually completed during a 2.30 pm–12.50 am session, in which the Beatles recorded 11 takes of the rhythm track and then set about overdubbing onto the last of these.

By the end, the song lacked only the final version's spoken count-in, the "Mister Wilson, Mister Heath" refrain which extended the fame of Britain's two most prominent politicians right around the world, a cowbell and the distinctive guitar solo outro. (This solo was in fact a copy of the middle-eight piece, edited onto the end of the song during the final mono and stereo mix stage on Tuesday 21 June.)

Friday 22 April

Studio Two, EMI Studios, London

A 2.30–11.30 pm session at Abbey Road which resulted in more overdubs onto 'Taxman', a cowbell and the "Mister Wilson, Mister Heath" parts, and also a sitar and vocal overdub onto 'Tomorrow Never Knows', still titled 'Mark I' at this time.

Monday 25 April

Two rough mono mixes of 'Got To Get You Into My Life', without echo or the Beatles' attendance, were made this day at EMI, 10.00–11.00 am, for the purpose of cutting acetates.

Tuesday 26 April

Studio Two, EMI Studios, London

Booked for 2.30–5.30 and 7.00–10.00 pm, the Beatles got thoroughly stuck into this day's re-make of John's 'And Your Bird Can Sing', working uninterrupted from 2.30 pm until 2.45 the following morning. They recorded 11 more takes of the song's rhythm track and overdubbed onto what they considered to have been the "best" of these, take ten. (An interesting blend of lead guitar vamping and Paul's bass guitar notes ended the song, and the best version of this section came in take six, so future mixes combined the two elements.)

Wednesday 27 April

Studio Three, EMI Studios, London

That the Beatles were beginning not only to attend mix sessions but also to make their presence felt is clear from this day's studio documentation. One mix of 'Taxman', one of 'And Your Bird Can Sing' and nine of 'Tomorrow Never Knows' were produced between 6.00 and 11.30 pm, yet none was used for the finished album.

Between 11.30 pm and 3.00 am the Beatles started work on a new song, John's dreamy 'I'm Only Sleeping', taping 11 takes of a mostly acoustic basic track. Overdubs were added on 29 April and 5, 6 May.

Thursday 28 April

Studio Two, EMI Studios, London

It too was inspired and beautiful. It too (excepting backing vocals) featured just Paul and outside session musicians, no other Beatles. It too was arranged by George Martin (for which he received a £15 fee). But that was where the comparisons ended. 'Eleanor Rigby' was certainly no mere re-hash of 'Yesterday'.

During this long session, 5.00 pm–2.00 am, the bedrock of the song – its string section – was recorded. Paul and John sat in the studio two control room, conducting their conversations with George Martin via the talkback system, George being down on the studio floor conducting the musicians. There were eight this time – a double string quartet. Tony Gilbert was first violinist, leading Sidney Sax, John Sharpe and Jurgen Hess, the violas were played by Stephen Shingles and John Underwood and the cellists were Derek Simpson and Norman Jones.

The eight instruments were recorded across all four tracks of the tape, two per track, so the last job of the day was to bounce-down the "best" and final take, 14, into take 15, vacating space for an overdub of Paul's lead and John and George's occasional harmony vocal.

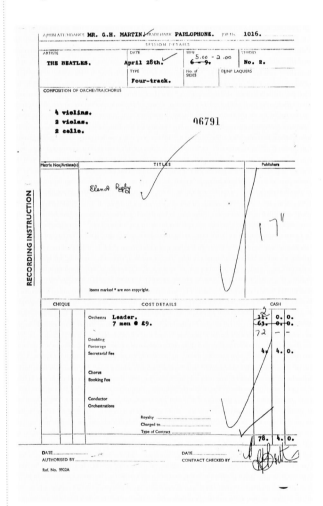

Friday 29 April

Studio Three, EMI Studios, London

Vocal overdubbing onto 'Eleanor Rigby' was the main task in this 5.00 pm–1.00 am session, after which the recording was considered complete and mixed into mono. (A further overdub on 6 June rendered this mix redundant, though, and a new one was made on 22 June for inclusion on the LP.)

Following this work, John added his lead vocal onto the previously recorded 'I'm Only Sleeping', the first of three overdub sessions for the song.

Sunday 1 May

Empire Pool, Wembley

A fourth and final appearance at the *New Musical Express* Annual Poll-Winners' All-Star Concert, this time the 1965–66 version, performed before an audience of 10,000 during this Sunday afternoon. It was also the Beatles' last live concert in Britain, a short set in which they delivered 'I Feel Fine', 'Nowhere Man', 'Day Tripper', 'If I Needed Someone' and 'I'm Down'.

As in 1964/1965, the proceedings were video-taped by ABC Television, but the cameras were switched off for the Beatles' and also the Rolling Stones' performances because of contractual disagreements between ABC and the respective managements. The cameras did tape the Beatles receiving their poll-awards, however, and John receiving an individual award, and this footage was included in the second of ABC's two 70-minute *Poll Winners Concert* programmes, shown by some ITV companies on Sunday 15 May, 3.50–5.00 pm. Owing to the Beatles' and, to a lesser extent, Rolling Stones' omission, a number of ITV regions – including London – did not screen the programmes.

MAURICE KINN
The organiser of today's concert

WATCH THIS CONCERT ON YOUR
ITV SCREENS
ON SUNDAY AFTERNOONS
MAY 8th and 15th
Presented by
ABC TELEVISION

Monday 2 May

Playhouse Theatre, London

Speech recordings for BBC radio. The first item on the agenda was a group interview with Brian Matthew for inclusion in the celebratory 400th edition of *Saturday Club*, broadcast 10.00 am–12.00 noon on 4 June by the BBC Light Programme. Taped at the Playhouse Theatre from 5.00 pm, the group discussed their in-the-works album, the North American concert tour to begin in August, and dodged questions about their lower public profile. A 32-second excerpt opened the programme, a much longer (3 mins 34 secs) section appeared between 10.30 and 11.00 am and then two more extracts appeared from 11.31 to 11.59 am in the section broadcast simultaneously by the BBC World Service: a 1 min 24 secs piece and a 35-second farewell in which the group dum-dummed the show's theme tune 'Saturday Jump', segued into Tony Osborne and his Jazz Group's disc version. (In the Christmas Day 1965 edition the Beatles had "sung" this theme, too – see 29 November 1965.)

When the group activity was over, Paul and Ringo stayed behind to be interviewed again by Matthew, but individually this time and for the programme *Pop Profile*, produced by the BBC Transcription Service solely for overseas sale – the same series for which George and John had been interviewed

on 30 November 1965. Ringo's interview began at 5.00, Paul's at 5.30 pm. (They had originally been booked to do these at EMI Studios during the afternoon of 29 April.)

Both interviews ran to about 15 minutes but were later edited down to eight, which – with the *Pop Profile* signature tune – made for nine-minute programmes mailed worldwide to subscribing stations later this month as seven-inch discs.

Thursday 5 May

Studio Three, EMI Studios, London

Typically, when the Beatles decided to adorn take 11 of 'I'm Only Sleeping' with the sound of backwards guitars, they chose to do it the hard way, working out a pleasing sequence of notes and then playing them in reverse order so that although the sound still had the aural attraction of a backwards tape the result was a melodic, forward-sounding run. George Harrison spent this 9.30 pm to 3.00 am session undertaking the exercise, and not once but twice, the two solos being superimposed one on top of the other.

Friday 6 May

Studio Two, EMI Studios, London

More vocal overdubbing onto 'I'm Only Sleeping' and then a reduction mix of take 11 into take 13 (creating space for yet further sounds) occupied this 2.30 pm–1.00 am session. From then until 2.15 am, the recording was mixed into mono.

Monday 9 May

Studio Two, EMI Studios, London

Ten piano/drum takes of another superbly crafted Paul McCartney ballad, 'For No One', formed the basis of this 7.00–11.00 pm session, Paul then overdubbed a clavichord track (the instrument hired, at a cost of five guineas, from George Martin's AIR company) and Ringo added cymbals and maraca onto take ten. There was no role for either John or George in the recording of 'For No One'.

Paul added his lead vocal as an overdub on 16 May and the song's fine French horn solo was taped three days after that.

Thursday 12 May

Studio Three, EMI Studios, London

By making *Help!* a seven-song Beatles album and reducing *Rubber Soul* to 12 songs (two of those refugees from the British *Help!* LP) Capitol Records had, by 1966, almost enough material to compile a new album of songs unissued in the US to that time. There were eight available, three more would be ideal, so an application was made for three of the new *Revolver* recordings to be sent across for release a few months earlier than planned. The answer was positive and mono mixes and edits made between 1.45 and 3.30 pm this day, of 'Doctor Robert', 'I'm Only Sleeping' and 'And Your Bird Can Sing', were done for just such a purpose. (The stereo mixes were prepared on 20 May.)

"Yesterday"…And Today was issued by Capitol on Monday 20 June but these three songs were later mixed again for the British *Revolver* LP, causing some slight differences between the two sets.

Monday 16 May

Studio Two, EMI Studios, London

A long (2.30 pm–1.30 am) day of overdubs, mixing and, for the purposes of assembling a master reel, copying some of the best mixes to date. 'Taxman' received its final ingredient (the "One, two, three, four" intro) and was then mixed into mono, and Paul overdubbed his lead vocal onto 'For No One'.

Wednesday 18 May

Studio Two, EMI Studios, London

Twelve solid hours, 2.30 pm–2.30 am, that took 'Got To Get You Into My Life', begun on 7 April, to completion (but for a final, minor overdub on 17 June). It was during this session that the recording received its distinctive brass sound, over-dubbed onto take eight by Eddie Thornton (Super-olds trumpet) and Peter Coe (tenor sax), both being members of Georgie Fame's Blue Flames, and three freelancers, Ian Hamer and Les Condon (trumpets) and Alan Branscombe (tenor sax). Each man received £18 for his contribution and, because details of the session were published in the weekly music press, a fair amount of extra work from other artists.

The four-track tape was now full but the vocals previously recorded were thought no longer suitable so they were removed during a tape-to-tape reduction that created take nine. Onto this Paul overdubbed a fresh lead vocal, backed by John and George, and guitars were also superimposed. Two mono mixes were made at the end of the session.

Thursday 19 May

Studios One/Three, EMI Studios, London

With the odd exception of 16 June 1966 (see that entry), the Beatles would no longer appear on television to promote their new singles. Shooting promotional clips the previous 23 November at Twickenham had established a pattern that would continue through to 1969. So with 'Paperback Writer' due out on 30 May in the USA and 10 June in Britain it was time to go before the cameras again.

As they had done in November, the Beatles shot a number of different clips for distribution to US, British and other TV stations and programmes. This was the first of a two-day shoot that saw them produce, in total, four promos for 'Paperback Writer' (two colour, two black-and-white) and three for its B-side 'Rain' (two colour, one black-and-white).

On this first day they worked in the familiar territory of studio one at EMI in Abbey Road, shooting straightforward mimed performance clips onto video tape. (The next day they worked on location and shot on film.)

As before, InterTel (VTR Services) provided the crew and equipment, while the director on both days was Michael Lindsay-Hogg, known to the group through his imaginative direction of *Ready, Steady, Go!* The Beatles and Lindsay-Hogg would team up again for the 'Hey Jude' and 'Revolution' promo clips (see 4 September 1968) and the *Get Back* project that became the feature-film *Let It Be* (see 2 January 1969 and onwards).

Work began at 10.00 am with a camera rehearsal, and at 10.40 the first colour take of 'Rain' was taped, following which (a definite plus for video-taping) the Beatles were able to watch a playback and check how it had turned out. Between 1.10 and 2.00 pm they then taped a colour performance clip of 'Paperback Writer'. Both of these were destined for US television (British TV remained

Paul perusing the so-called "Butcher" transparencies from 25 March during the 'Paperback Writer' shoot on 19 May.

monochrome for another 18 months) and they were broadcast exclusively by CBS's *The Ed Sullivan Show* on Sunday 5 June (8.00–9.00 pm, EST), together with a special sequence taped between 6.15 and 6.30 pm this day in which the Beatles sent greetings to Ed and his TV viewers. This short item, inserted before 'Paperback Writer', began with the Beatles holding over their faces sheets of colour transparencies from their "Butcher" photo session with Robert Whitaker on 25 March. (The 'Paperback Writer' clip also began with Paul perusing the transparencies. And it's worth noting, too, that Paul looked facially different in all of the promos shot over these two days: he had a chipped front-top tooth, the result of a moped accident.)

After a break for lunch, the Beatles returned to studio one to tape black-and-white promo clips between 3.30 and 6.15, two for 'Paperback Writer' and one for 'Rain'. The first B&W 'Paperback Writer' was screened by ABC Television (though not all ITV regions took the show) on Saturday 25 June (5.50–6.35pm) in *Goodbye Lucky Stars*, the final edition of the long-running *Thank Your Lucky Stars*. The second B&W 'Paperback Writer' and the monochrome 'Rain' were shown by Rediffusion in *Ready, Steady, Go!* on Friday 3 June (6.07–6.35 pm), the series breaking for the first time its long-standing policy of only screening material from its own studio.

Having spent all day in studio one, Paul (if not the other Beatles, too) then moved into studio three for the evening, 7.00–11.00 pm, to watch and supervise the overdubbing of a majestic French horn solo onto 'For No One'.

The musician brought in by George Martin to undertake this work was Alan Civil, principal horn player in the Philharmonia, and he made several passes at the solo, each wiping out the previous attempt, until Paul and George Martin agreed that it could not be bettered. Civil was paid what, for the time, was a generous session fee indeed of 50 guineas (£52.50) and also received a credit on the *Revolver* sleeve, which, he was to realise with irony in the years that followed, meant more to most people than his distinguished career in the classical field.

Chiswick House, Burlington Lane, Chiswick, London

The Beatles, director Michael Lindsay-Hogg and their retinues went out on location this day, descending upon the beautiful early 18th-century gardens of Chiswick House in west London. Their object was to film (not tape) two more promo clips, one each for 'Paperback Writer' and 'Rain'. These were only partially performance films, with some of the footage showing the group walking and relaxing in the expansive gardens.

For 'Rain' the Beatles were filmed inside the walled garden and the conservatory, and then miming in some bushes and also sitting on a low horizontal branch of a cedar tree (for this sequence, Ringo sat on a marble plinth in place of an absent statue). For 'Paperback Writer' the Beatles were filmed sitting on a bench in front of the conservatory and miming to playback in the statue garden.

Although both clips were shot in colour, on 35mm film, these and not the more appropriate black-and-white promos taped the previous day were screened in monochrome by BBC1 on *Top Of The Pops*. 'Paperback Writer' was shown on 2 June and 23 June, 'Rain' on 9 June (all programmes Thursdays, 7.30–8.00 pm).

Meanwhile, back at EMI, working between 11.00 am and 12.30 pm, George Martin prepared the first set of stereo mixes and edits since sessions for *Revolver* began. Following the production of three monaural mixes for Capitol on 12 May, for its *"Yesterday"...And Today* collection, Martin now made two sets of stereos of the same three songs ('And Your Bird Can Sing', 'Doctor Robert' and 'I'm Only Sleeping'), one for Capitol, the other for the domestic *Revolver* master. (Strangely, however, Capitol did not use these George Martin mixes for the first pressing of *"Yesterday"...And Today* – they may have arrived too late – instead producing fake-stereo versions processed from the mono masters.)

Earlier on this day, Dylan and John Lennon were filmed riding in the back of a chauffeured limousine, driving into central London – to the May Fair Hotel in Stratton Street – from John's house in Weybridge, Surrey. Without a script and no apparent direction other than to be themselves, the piece was long, incoherent and incomprehensible, made worse by the fact that Dylan (and possibly John, too, though not as much) was clearly well under the influence of drugs. After muttering a lot of stoned gibberish Dylan suddenly announced that he felt ill and needed to puke. The car had reached Park Lane by this time and, presumably, he was able to perform this function in the privacy of his hotel suite.

The sequence was intended to form part of *Eat The Document*, a chronicle of Dylan's latest European concert tour which he had hired D A Pennebaker to direct. The US TV network ABC advanced Dylan money but he maintained artistic control, overseeing the film-editing back in America with assistance from Robbie Robertson of The Band. But one bad experience led to another, ABC rejected the rough-cut and then Dylan had his infamous motor-cycle accident, as a result of which *Eat The Document* bit the dust. Outside of a one-week screening at a small New York cinema in 1969, and a single showing on WNDT-TV, the educational channel in New York, it remains unseen to this day. In the "finished" film, the long Lennon/Dylan sequence is thought to have been edited down to only two or three minutes.

Strictly for his private use, D A Pennebaker turned some of the same European footage into a film entitled *You Know Something Is Happening*, which included around six minutes of the car footage, but this has never been seen publicly.

Thursday 26 May

Studio Three, EMI Studios, London

Written mostly by Paul as a song to please children of all ages, 'Yellow Submarine' ranks among the most famous of all Beatles recordings, issued not only on *Revolver* but as a simultaneous number one single. Taping of the basic track, plus Ringo's lead and John, Paul and George's backing vocals, was effected during this 7.00 pm–1.00 am session which took the song from take one through to take five.

Recovering elsewhere from a bout of food poisoning, George Martin missed the session, which was overseen in his absence by engineer Geoff Emerick (although George did send along his fiancée Judy Lockhart-Smith to minister to the Beatles' studio needs).

Friday 27 May

Weybridge to London

The transition from the "innocent" era of pop music into savvy artist-controlled rock music was well illustrated by a long sequence filmed this day involving Bob Dylan and John Lennon.

Dylan was in Britain on a memorable concert tour, the one in which he spurned his folk image, and folk following, by performing an electric set backed by The Band. In fact it was on this evening that the tour reached the Royal Albert Hall in London, John and George cheering Dylan amid a jeering audience.

Wednesday 1 June

Studio Two, EMI Studios, London

Recording sessions don't come much more unusual than this one – the sound effects overdubs for 'Yellow Submarine'. Working from 2.30 pm to 2.30 am, the Beatles and a host of assistants had a glorious time, mucking in and making all manner of noises that, on the multi-track tape, ran throughout the duration of the song (whereas, for record release, the effects were audible only in certain places).

John blew bubbles in a bucket and shouted out things like "Full speed ahead Mister Captain" from inside the echo chamber adjoining studio two, and Brian Jones, Marianne Faithfull, George's wife Pattie, George Martin, Beatles assistants Neil Aspinall and Mal Evans, the other Beatles, and Abbey Road staff members John Skinner and Terry Condon, all joined in the fun, making noises and lending their voices to the song's increasingly raucous choruses. After the recording was over, Mal Evans marched around the studio wearing a huge bass drum on his chest, with everyone else in line behind him, conga-style, singing "We all live in a yellow submarine".

Ironically, one of the most remarkable overdubs – the one which took the most time to plan and record – never made it onto the finished record. It was a spoken passage by Ringo for the beginning of the song, faded up into the acoustic guitar intro and lasting a long 31 seconds. It consisted of at least four separate recordings, dominated by Ringo's speaking voice but with George, Paul and John all talking likewise, mixed into one *mélange*, the theme of the lesson being the walk from Land's End to John O' Groats (the south-west foot of England to the north-east tip of Scotland) – "And we will march to free the day to see them gathered there, from Land O' Groats to John O' Green, from Stepney to Utrecht, to see a yellow submarine." Running under Ringo's voice while he repeated these words was the sound of marching feet (made by putting coal in a cardboard box and sliding it from side to side). It was a fascinating overdub, and the result of considerable effort, but the Beatles chose to discard it.

Thursday 2 June

Studio Two, EMI Studios, London

In securing an unprecedented three compositions on a 14-song Beatles album, George was having problems with his titles. What was in the end to become 'Love You To', itself a title not mentioned in the lyric, had the working name 'Granny Smith', after the brand of apple. Now, for the song 'I Want To Tell You', the problem arose again. George Martin asked George Harrison for the title, the latter replied "I don't know" (because of which, it was actually called this for a brief time) and it was left to Geoff Emerick to dub the new song 'Laxton's Superb', another type of British apple. Only later did it become 'I Want To Tell You'.

Apart from the production of a rough mono mix of 'Yellow Submarine', all of this 7.00 pm–3.30 am session was spent recording 'Laxton's Superb', taping the rhythm track in five takes, overdubbing onto the third of these and then making a reduction mixdown, called take four, to facilitate more overdubbing the next night.

Friday 3 June

Studio Two, EMI Studios, London

The final overdub onto what would be titled 'I Want To Tell You' was of Paul's bass guitar. (Recording the bass separately onto a vacant track of the four-track tape allowed greater manipulation of its sound during mixing.) Four mono mixes of this song and five of 'Yellow Submarine' concluded this 7.00 pm–2.30 am session.

Monday 6 June

Studio Three, EMI Studios, London

Tape copying and mono mixing of 'And Your Bird Can Sing', 'For No One', 'I'm Only Sleeping' and 'Tomorrow Never Knows', done from 7.00–12.00 pm, and one final vocal overdub by Paul onto 'Eleanor Rigby', midnight to 1.30 am.

Wednesday 8 June

Studio Two, EMI Studios, London

One of the quickest recordings on *Revolver* was Paul's 'Good Day Sunshine' in that the released version was take one – although it had numerous overdubs and could in no way be compared with the truly-live one-take recordings of 1963 and 1964. Actually, the group recorded three takes of the rhythm track during this 2.30 pm–2.30 am session but returned to the first to overdub Paul's lead and John and George's backing vocal. More overdubs would also be taped on 9 June.

Work this day had begun when Geoff Emerick edited

together two of Monday's mono mixes of 'And Your Bird Can Sing', done from 1.00 to 2.00 pm.

Thursday 9 June

Studio Two, EMI Studios, London

A 2.30–8.00 pm session that brought completion to 'Good Day Sunshine' with such overdubs as George Martin's honky-tonk piano solo. Six mono mixes concluded the evening, two hours ahead of the scheduled 10.00 pm end-time.

Tuesday 14 June

Studio Two, EMI Studios, London

Paul had already shown himself adept at writing beautiful ballads, and they rarely come any better than this gorgeous song, 'Here, There And Everywhere', the recording of which was spread over three days.

Four rhythm track takes were recorded during this first session, 7.00 pm–2.00 am, only the last of which was complete, and initial vocal overdubs were then applied.

Thursday 16 June

Studio Two, Television Centre, London
and Studio Two, EMI Studios, London

Top Of The Pops producer Johnnie Stewart had been a patient man. Throughout the two-and-a-half years that the programme had been on the air, in which time it had easily attained premier status among Britain's TV pop shows, and despite all of their visitations to the studios of *Thank Your Lucky Stars* and *Ready, Steady, Go!*, not to mention *The Ed Sullivan Show* in the USA, the Beatles had never made a live appearance. True, in the early days, *TOTP* cameras had taped exclusive performances by the group in BBC studios, but latterly, with each new single, the programme had been seemingly fobbed off with an independently produced clip. So, on Monday 13 June, Stewart wrote to Brian Epstein, beseeching him to persuade the Beatles to make a personal appearance on the coming Thursday's edition. For reasons unknown, when Epstein put the proposal to them during Tuesday's 'Here, There And Everywhere' session, the Beatles said yes.

Ironically, it was not just the group's first personal appearance on the show, nor just their first before any TV audience in ten months, it was also (excepting the unique worldwide transmission of 'All You Need Is Love' on 25 June 1967) their last live musical television appearance of all, and certainly their last on a recognised "pop show". Johnnie Stewart could never have played a better winning hand.

The Beatles arrived at the BBC's Television Centre in White City, west London, in time for a 2.30 pm camera rehearsal, publicity photographs and press interviews. Further camera rehearsals ran from 4.15 to 5.30 and again from 6.30 to 7.00 before live transmission on BBC1 began at

Beatles 11th-hour Yes to live 'Top Pops' TV

THE Beatles were last night (Thursday) making a surprise live TV appearance on BBC-1's "Top Of The Pops"! They were singing both sides of their new single which enters this week's NME Chart at No. 2. It was the first time they have appeared live on TV since they were in ABC's "Blackpool Night Out" in July, 1965.

Brian Epstein explained to the NME on Wednesday: "On Monday, 'Top Of The Pops' producer Johnnie Stewart wrote me a letter saying that although he had scheduled a Beatles film clip for the programme, there had been an unprecedented demand for them to appear live in the show and would they reconsider their decision not to.

"I put it to the boys late on Tuesday and they said 'yes'."

On Wednesday the Beatles had completed 13 of the 14 tracks for their next British LP, and by this weekend the album will be finished for late-summer release.

A new Beatles LP has been issued in America featuring three tracks from their latest recording sessions; some others previously issued in Britain but not in America; and the remainder from past singles.

Following complaints, a colour sleeve in which the album was issued showing the Beatles draped with raw meat (as featured in their NME advertisement on June 3) was withdrawn and a new cover hurriedly prepared.

7.30, finishing at 8.00. The Beatles appeared as the final act, miming to both 'Rain' and 'Paperback Writer' (in that order), and host Pete Murray couldn't disguise his absolute Autocued pleasure as he introduced the two numbers.

The performance of 'Paperback Writer' was repeated in the edition of Thursday 30 June (BBC1, 7.30–8.00 pm) and again in *Top Of The Pops '66 – Part 1* (BBC1, Monday 26 December, 6.15–7.00 pm), while a 1 min 22 secs extract went into the BBC2 programme *Line-Up Review* the night after this initial *TOTP* transmission, Friday 17 June 1966, screened from 11.05 to 11.37 pm.

But such good fortune, like lightning, rarely strikes twice. For the Beatles' next single, the double-A-sided 'Yellow Submarine'/'Eleanor Rigby', not only would the group make no personal appearances but they didn't produce promotional clips either. *Top Of The Pops* was forced to put its own images to the recordings – for the former, filming 11 members of the British Sub Aqua Club in action at a London swimming pool, while for the latter stringing together a sequence of stills of a BBC scene-shifter (who also happened to be a former actor), dressed as a priest and posing with props in a Manchester cemetery.

Immediately after the television broadcast the Beatles headed for St John's Wood and a recording session at EMI. Arranged to begin at 7.00 pm, they couldn't have

arrived much before 8.30, working through until 3.30 am perfecting 'Here, There And Everywhere' with nine more takes and a fresh set of overdubs onto the "best" rhythm track, take 13. A 14th take was created by reduction, onto which Paul superimposed his lead vocal, slowed down on the tape to sound speeded up on playback.

Friday 17 June

Studio Two, EMI Studios, London

A 7.00 pm–1.30 am session during which 'Here, There And Everywhere' received an additional Paul McCartney vocal overdub, backing his own lead, and an extra guitar passage was added onto 'Got To Get You Into My Life'. The evening ended with five new mono mixes of the latter recording and one of the former.

Monday 20 June

Studio One, EMI Studios, London

A new mono mix of 'Got To Get You Into My Life' doubling the brass sound of previous versions, prepared between 6.00 and 8.30 pm.

Tuesday 21 June

Studio Three, EMI Studios, London

An exceptionally hectic day, with the taping of the album's 14th and final song plus mono and stereo mixing galore.

The new number, John's 'She Said She Said', was recorded from start to completion in four takes between 7.00 pm and 3.45 am. Untitled at the beginning of the session but

titled by the end, the lyric recounted John's unusual conversation with film actor Peter Fonda, who was experiencing an LSD trip, in Los Angeles during the Beatles' most recent North American tour (see 28 August 1965). Three mono mixes were made at the end of the session.

Earlier (10.00 am–1.00 pm, 2.30–6.30 pm) stereo mixes and edits were produced for 'Love You To', 'I Want To Tell You', 'Here, There And Everywhere', 'For No One' and 'Taxman', and mono for 'Here, There And Everywhere', 'For No One', 'Doctor Robert' and 'Taxman'.

Wednesday 22 June

Studio Three, EMI Studios, London

The final mono and stereo mixing for *Revolver*, the late session time, 7.00 pm–1.30 am, indicating the direct involvement of the Beatles. 'Eleanor Rigby', 'She Said She Said' and 'Good Day Sunshine' were mixed into mono, 'Eleanor Rigby', 'She Said She Said', 'Good Day Sunshine', 'Yellow Submarine', 'Tomorrow Never Knows' and 'Got To Get You Into My Life' into stereo. The album was issued in Britain on Friday 5 August.

Revolver was just one of a number of potential album titles the Beatles toyed with before they cabled EMI with their final decision from Japan on 2 July. It could have been *Abracadabra* but that had already been used by someone else. *Magic Circles* and *Beatles On Safari* were among the other alternatives.

Friday 24 June

Circus-Krone-Bau, Marsstrasse, Munich, West Germany

The Beatles flew into Munich on 23 June and, the next day, performed two shows here, at 5.15 and 9.00 pm, commencing a brief international concert tour (the West German part of which was dubbed the "Bravo Blitztournee", sponsored by the country's entertainments magazine *Bravo*). Their repertoire for the tour comprised 'Rock And Roll Music', 'She's A Woman', 'If I Needed Someone', 'Day Tripper', 'Baby's In Black', 'I Feel Fine', 'Yesterday', 'I Wanna Be Your Man', 'Nowhere Man', 'Paperback Writer' and 'I'm Down'.

The second of the two concerts here was filmed by a five-man camera crew from the national West German broadcasting network Zweites Deutsches Fernsehen (ZDF) and transmitted as *Die Beatles* by channel 2 on Tuesday 5 July (8.00–8.45 pm). The 45-minute programme began with footage of the support acts – Cliff Bennett and the Rebel Rousers, the Rattles and then Peter and Gordon – before screening seven of the Beatles' 11 songs (omitting 'If I Needed Someone', 'Day Tripper', 'I Wanna Be Your Man' and 'Paperback Writer').

The Beatles' complete lack of pre-tour rehearsal was proven before 'I'm Down', John, Paul and George having to confer on-stage about the lyric in the first verse. In spite of this, though, Paul still managed to make a hash of it, and also messed up the next two verses. George even introduced

'Yesterday' (performed this time by all four Beatles, with electric guitars and drums) as a track from *Beatles For Sale*.

Saturday 25 June

Grugahalle, Norbertstrasse, Essen, Nordrhein-Westfalen, West Germany

The Beatles travelled from Munich to Essen in a special train which, a year previously, had been utilised by Queen Elizabeth II during her royal visit to West Germany. The four Beatles, plus entourage of five, each had their own suite of rooms on board.

They gave two shows at the Grugahalle and then returned immediately to the station to continue their railway journey across the country. Next stop: Hamburg.

Sunday 26 June

Ernst Merck Halle, Jungtusstrasse, Hamburg, West Germany

The Beatles' train pulled into the central station in Hamburg a little after 6.00 am on 26 June. It was the first time any member of the group had set foot in the city since 1 January 1963, when – as relative nobodies – they had completed their fortnight's Christmas stint at the Star-Club.

On hand at the station, and backstage before their two shows at the Ernst Merck Halle, were many faces from the past, ranging from Astrid Kirchherr to Bert Kaempfert and even Bettina Derlien, the buxom, blonde barmaid from the Star-Club.

After the two shows, each performed before a 5600 audience, 44 Hamburg youths were arrested for rioting inside and outside the concert venue. Then John and Paul managed to take a nostalgic midnight stroll down the Reeperbahn, visiting old haunts and friends.

The Beatles flew back to London Airport on 27 June and a few hours later flew out again for Japan. Because of a typhoon warning, however, their airplane was forced to make an unscheduled nine-hour stop in Anchorage, Alaska. The Beatles discreetly took over an entire floor of a local hotel but within 30 minutes word got around that they were in town, soon after which a local radio station parked a caravan outside the hotel and broadcast live up-to-the-minute reports until they departed, arriving at Haneda airport, Tokyo, at 3.40 am on 30 June.

Thurs 30 June – Sat 2 July

Nippon Budokan Hall, Daikan-cho, Chiyoda-ku, Tokyo, Japan

Five shows in the Nippon Budokan Hall, one on 30 June and two each on 1 and 2 July, before 10,000 fans on each occasion.

The opening show (on 30 June) and the first on 1 July were video-taped in colour by Nippon Television (NTV), both performances still existing today in their entirety, best

distinguished by the group's apparel: in the first they wore black suits, in the second white ones. Highlights from the two performances were put together and shown in the second half of a one-hour programme *The Beatles Recital, From Nippon Budokan, Tokyo* screened by NTV Channel 4 on Friday 1 July, 9.00–10.00 pm. The first half of the programme presented Japanese singers Yuya Uchida and Isao Bitoh plus colour footage of the Beatles' arrival at Haneda airport and a press conference they later gave at the Hilton Hotel in Tokyo.

The Beatles departed for the Philippines at 10.40 am on 3 July, landing there after a 70-minute stop-over in the VIP lounge at Kaitak airport, Hong Kong.

Monday 4 July

Rizal Memorial Football Stadium, Vito Cruz St, Manila, Luzon, The Philippines

The calm before the storm – that is, if two performances before a total of 80,000 fans, 30,000 at the afternoon show and 50,000 in the evening, could be called calm.

The Beatles finally left Manila International Airport at 4.45 pm on 5 July and headed for New Delhi, India (via a brief refuelling stop in Bangkok). Anticipating a few days of peaceful rest and exploration of Indian music, the four harassed musicians found that 600 fans were on hand to greet them at the airport and besiege their hotel. Eventually, the group returned to England, touching down at London Airport at 6.00 am on 8 July. A brief press meeting followed, during which George and Ringo were interviewed by BBC staff reporter Tom Mangold, 2 mins 45 secs of which was broadcast in this morning's Home Service news-magazine radio programme *Today* (7.15–7.45, also repeated in the 8.15–8.40 edition).

Monday 1 August

Studio B15, Broadcasting House, London

Just as Paul had once agreed to a solo appearance on a David Frost TV show (*A Degree Of Frost*, see 15 April 1964), so he now agreed to participate with him, and without the other Beatles, in a BBC Light Programme radio show, *David Frost At The Phonograph*, a series in which Frost interviewed "a personality" and commented on everyday matters in between playing records new and old. The entire programme, including Paul's "live" personal appearance, was recorded from 8.30 this evening in a basement studio at Broadcasting House; it was transmitted from 12.00 noon to 1.30 pm on Saturday 6 August.

Saturday 6 August

Cavendish Ave, London

The Granada Television documentary *The Music Of Lennon & McCartney* (see 1–2 November 1965) had been a celebration of the pair's songwriting, a number of their compositions being performed by a range of artists in the TV studio. Now, nine months later, John and Paul were involved in a similar production for BBC radio, a one-hour programme entitled *The Lennon And McCartney Songbook*, the only difference between this and the TV show being that the two Beatles cast their critical eye over 15 recorded and already released versions of their handiwork, by such artists as Peggy Lee, Ella Fitzgerald, the Mamas and the Papas and, remarkably, the Band of the Irish Guards (which had issued 'She Loves You').

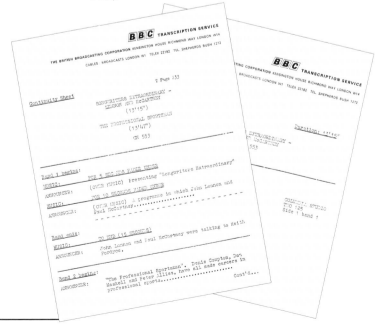

Although set to have been recorded at John's house in Weybridge, Surrey, the location was switched beforehand to Paul's in St John's Wood, north London, to where BBC producer Derek Chinnery and the interviewer Keith Fordyce travelled. Taping took place from 4.00 to 6.00 pm, interrupted only by the arrival of tea and the whining of Paul's newly acquired sheepdog puppy Martha. The production was broadcast by the Light Programme between 4.30 and 5.30 pm on "bank holiday" Monday 29 August, while the Beatles were in America about to give their last concert performance.

The programme was also pressed onto disc and distributed to subscribing overseas radio stations by the BBC's Transcription Service. Here, without the music, it lasted just 13 mins and was renamed *Songwriters Extraordinary – Lennon And McCartney*.

Friday 12 August

International Amphitheatre, Chicago, USA

The start of the Beatles' final concert tour. Not bothering to rehearse any new songs, even though they had a new album just released, they performed the same repertoire used in West Germany, Japan and the Philippines, albeit with one exception: the occasional playing of 'Long Tall Sally'. The tour's supports acts, in order of appearance, were the Remains, Bobby Hebb, the Cyrkle and the Ronettes, and there were two shows on this first date, 3.00 and 7.30 pm, each seen by an audience of 13,000 (a little short of full capacity).

The Beatles flew into the United States from London Airport on 11 August, landing at Boston and switching planes there within minutes for Chicago, arriving at 4.55 pm. That evening they hosted their usual one-a-city press conference, this one relieved of its usual monotony by a resolution of the "We're more popular than Jesus" row, in which John, supported by the three other Beatles, tried to placate the American public about his famous statement. Naturally, the Beatles' press conferences were usually filmed and recorded by local radio and TV stations, but this one carried additional worldwide interest so extracts were screened in news programmes around the globe. In the USA, the three TV networks, NBC, CBS and ABC, all screened special programmes this evening. In Britain, Independent Television News used this and other US footage to compile a *Reporting '66* programme devoted entirely to the Beatles' current concert tour, shown on Thursday 25 August (in the London area from 6.07 to 6.35 pm).

Saturday 13 August

Olympia Stadium, Detroit, USA

Two shows, 2.00 and 7.00 pm, before a total of 28,000 fans at this indoor arena, although neither concert was sold out. The Beatles had arrived in Detroit at 11.00 am; they left for Cleveland by Greyhound bus immediately after the second show, arriving there at 2.30 am.

Sunday 14 August

Cleveland Stadium, West 3rd St, Cleveland, Ohio, USA

This one Cleveland concert, at 7.30 pm, like the Public Auditorium show there on 15 September 1964, was held up for 30 minutes when – during the fourth song, 'Day Tripper' – 2500 of the 20,000 fans invaded the Cleveland Indians' baseball field, on which the Beatles were playing. The entourage stayed in the city until Monday afternoon and then flew on to Washington DC.

Monday 15 August

DC Stadium, East Capitol St, Washington DC, USA

One show, at 8.00 pm, seen by 32,164 fans, after which the Beatles and their entourage moved straight on to Philadelphia by bus.

Tuesday 16 August

John F Kennedy Stadium, Broad St and Patterson Ave, Philadelphia, Pennsylvania, USA

The Beatles' one show here, at 8.00 pm, seen by 21,000 people in this 60,000-seat open-air stadium, was marred by almost constant lightning. But the potentially lethal rain held off until ten minutes after the concert had ended, by which time the Greyhound bus carrying the entourage was en route for the airport and a flight to Canada.

Wednesday 17 August

Maple Leaf Gardens, Toronto, Canada

Two shows at this 18,000-capacity arena, at 4.00 and 8.00 pm. The first was seen by 15,000, the second by 17,000. The Beatles flew back to the USA on the Thursday afternoon.

Thursday 18 August

Suffolk Downs Racetrack, Waldemar Ave, East Boston, Massachusetts, USA

Twenty-five thousand people saw this one show, held at 8.00 pm in one of the most unlikely Beatles concert venues of all: mid-centre green on a horse-racing course. The group left Boston at 11.30 the next morning, flying south to Memphis.

Friday 19 August

Mid-South Coliseum, South Fairgrounds, Early Maxwell Boulevard, Memphis, Tennessee, USA

Two shows at this 13,300-seat venue, 4.00 and 8.30 pm, 10,000 attending the afternoon performance and 12,500 the evening. (It was during the latter that the infamous fire-cracker episode took place – see Introduction.) The Beatles

effected their escape from the Coliseum back to Metropolitan Airport in the Greyhound bus while their limousine was sent out as a decoy. They flew directly from here to Ohio, arriving at 1.35 am.

Saturday 20 August

Crosley Field, Findlay St at Western Ave, Cincinnati, Ohio, USA (postponed)

This 3.30 pm open-air show, which would have been the Beatles' 13th performance in nine consecutive days, was cancelled because of heavy rain and re-scheduled for Sunday midday.

Sunday 21 August

Crosley Field, Cincinnati, USA
and Busch Stadium, Stadium Plaza, St Louis, Missouri, USA

The re-arrangement of the Cincinnati show meant that the Beatles had to give two concerts this day in cities 341 miles apart, a schedule reminiscent of 1962 and 1963. The 8.30 pm open-air St Louis show, seen by 23,000 customers, took place during heavy rain, the Beatles playing under a tarpaulin cover.

The group flew to New York immediately afterwards, arriving at 3.50 am and spending the best part of two days inside the Warwick Hotel, giving two press conferences on the Monday.

Tuesday 23 August

William A Shea Municipal Stadium [Shea Stadium], New York City, USA

Although 2000 fans had been in the queue here on 31 May, before the box-office for this one 7.30 pm performance had even opened, the concert failed to sell out, with 11,000 of the 55,600 seats remaining empty. This only partly explained the lack of excitement in the stadium compared to the heady atmosphere of the record-breaking 1965 show. Still, the concert grossed $292,000 (£104,600) – of which the Beatles received 65 per cent, $189,000 (£67,700), greater than their 1965 take.

Immediately after the show the Beatles flew to Los Angeles, arriving early in the morning on 24 August, for a 24-hour rest in Beverly Hills. At 10.00 am on the 25th they flew north to Seattle.

Thursday 25 August

Coliseum, Seattle, USA

Two shows in this 15,000-seat arena, 3.00 and 8.00 pm. Only 8000 tickets sold for the afternoon performance while the evening show was fully subscribed. The Beatles returned to Los Angeles on an 11.00 pm flight.

Beatles 'escape' in an armoured car

The Beatles fled in an armoured car from thousands of screaming fans after their concert in the Dodgers baseball stadium at Los Angeles last night.

As the quartet tried to leave by the main gates scores of delirious teenagers climbed all over the limousine and it was forced to turn back.

The Beatles then fled to offices under the grandstand as crowds charged the 151 foot high entrance gates.

Time and again, police were forced to hit out with their clubs to keep the fans' off the gates.

Youths then charged the gates with wooden barricades which had been set up to keep the crowds back.

They hurled sticks and bottles at police until they were finally turned away with a shoulder-to-shoulder charge by officers who cleared a sort of no-man's-land between the crowds and the exit gates.

DOZENS HURT

Meanwhile, the Beatles, virtually imprisoned beneath the grandstand by fans stampeding from one spot to another in the vast outdoor stadium, made good their escape by armoured car at the opposite end of the field.

Police said dozens of people among the 45,000 attending suffered minor injuries in the clashes between fans and police and in the crush of the stampeding crowds.

Debris littered the area around the exit gates and crowds milled around for about an hour after the performance ended.

The Beatles tour ends in San Francisco to-night and the quartet then return to the Hollywood hills hideaway where they have been based during the west coast part of the tour. They leave to-morrow for London.

Mr. S. W. Combs, chief of the 102-man private security force hired for the concert, said about 25 people were detained by his police. It had not been decided whether to make formal charges against them.

Two of the Beatles, Paul McCartney and George Harrison, are planning to present and promote modern plays and other theatrical productions such as musicals.

With the Beatles in the scheme are pop singers Donovan and Eric Burdon, of the Animals group.

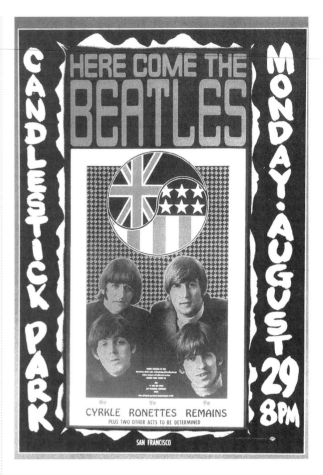

Sunday 28 August

Dodger Stadium, Elysian Park Ave, Los Angeles, California, USA

After three more days of rest in Beverly Hills the Beatles returned to the concert stage with this one show, seen by 45,000 largely uncontrollable fans. The group flew to San Francisco at 4.00 pm on the 29th, arriving there at 5.45.

Monday 29 August

Candlestick Park, Jamestown and Harney Way, San Francisco, California, USA

A crowd of 25,000 saw the Beatles' final concert, which began at 8.00 pm. Recognising its significance, John carried a camera up on stage and took photographs of the other Beatles between songs, as well as of himself from arms-length; Paul did the same and also asked NEMS Enterprises press officer Tony Barrow to make an audio cassette recording of the performance. (Without being flipped, though, Barrow's cassette, 30 minutes per side, could not accommodate all of the group's 33-minute set, so it ran out before the final song, 'Long Tall Sally'.)

After the show, at 11.00 pm, the Beatles flew back down the California coast to Los Angeles, arriving at 12.50 am. They left the USA on Tuesday, arriving back at London Airport during the morning of Wednesday 31 August.

Tuesday 6 – Wednesday 14 September

various locations, Celle, West Germany

When *A Hard Day's Night* and *Help!* director Richard Lester was casting for his next film, *How I Won The War*, he invited John to play his first (and only, as it turned out) acting role outside of the Beatles, portraying the kleptomaniac musketeer Pvt Gripweed. The screenplay was written by Charles Wood (who did likewise for *Help!* as well as other Lester films *The Knack*, *The Bed-Sitting Room* and *Cuba*) based upon Patrick Ryan's bitter 1963 novel about the obscene glorification of war. Lester also produced the film, his first, for distributors United Artists.

It was not a major role for John Lennon so he was happy to accept the invitation, news of which was announced on 3 August. Their at-times exasperating US concert tour over, the Beatles had nothing scheduled for some months, allowing each member time to expand and explore individual interests.

Set in World War Two, shooting of *How I Won The War* took place in two main locations: in a NATO tank range in Celle – a town in northern West Germany, not far from Hanover – and then, to simulate the North Africa desert, in Carboneras, southern Spain, just across the Mediterranean from Algeria.

John flew out to Hanover on 5 September and the next day, in a moment that, amazingly, made headlines around the world, was given an army regulation haircut and handed a pair of National Health spectacles to wear for the part of Pvt Gripweed. Off-camera the "granny glasses" quickly became a part of the John Lennon image, remaining so for the rest of his life.

John wasn't involved in all of the filming, and on one day (date unknown) he went to Hamburg with accompanying assistant Neil Aspinall, shopping at many of the stores frequented by the Beatles at the start of the decade. Then, during the evening of Thursday 15 September, they left Germany, travelling by train to Paris for a weekend's rendezvous with Paul and Brian Epstein. On Sunday the 18th John and Neil moved on to the second, main film location, in Spain.

Mon 19 September – Sun 6 November

various locations, Carboneras, Spain

The main bulk of *How I Won The War* was filmed here in hot and dusty southern Spain, in complete contrast to damp and cold northern Germany. John later admitted that he became bored by all of the hanging around: spending seven weeks in a desert for what was, after all, only a minor role, is hardly scintillating fun – but then, that's war. Filming began early each day and there was nothing to do in the evenings but sit around in an uncomfortable rented house in Santa Isabel, near Almeria, conversing, playing games and songwriting (John wrote 'Strawberry Fields Forever' while here).

Eventually, location shooting was complete, and although some later filming was done in and around London, John was not involved in these scenes. (He did, however, participate in post-production audio dubbing – see 11 February 1967.) He returned home to England, flying in from Madrid, on 7 November – and two nights later met Yoko Ono for the first time.

Tuesday 20 September

Taj Mahal Hotel, Apollo Bunder, Bombay, India

While Ringo pottered about in Surrey with his family, John filmed *How I Won The War* in West Germany and Spain, and Paul remained in London, immersing himself in the burgeoning "underground" movement and composing his first feature-film score, for *The Family Way*, George flew to India to study the sitar, Yoga, Indian philosophy and its culture. He intended to keep the visit quiet, checking in at the Taj Mahal Hotel in Bombay under the pseudonym Sam Wells, but it didn't take long for his cover to be blown.

George recognised that the only chance he had of regaining some solitude was to hold a press conference, answer everybody's questions and then escape to a new location. The press conference was held in the hotel on 19 September.

A day later, before he left Bombay, George was happy to grant an exclusive interview about his Indian interests and Eastern beliefs to the BBC's radio correspondent there, Donald Milner, doubtless pleased to have the opportunity to speak about more worldly and philosophical matters than "the hit parade". Milner and George chatted about weighty

John in southern Spain, biding time during a filming break for How I Won The War. *He quickly became bored by the long periods of inactivity and eight-week shooting schedule.*

topics for about ten minutes, more than seven of which were broadcast on the BBC Home Service, back in Britain, on Sunday 11 December (4.00–4.30 pm) in the series *The Lively Arts*. It was considered such an interesting interview that a 2 mins 25 secs extract was also transmitted in the Home Service series *Pick Of The Week*, featuring highlights from the previous seven days' radio and TV broadcasting (Friday 16 December, 12.10–12.55 pm; repeated Sunday 18 December, 11.30 am–12.10 pm).

Monday 31 October

When Brian Epstein let it be known to EMI that there would be no new Beatles album available for the Christmas market, and probably not even a single, the record company took the opportunity to release the first British "greatest hits" compilation. (It wasn't issued in the US.) The title was *A Collection Of Beatles Oldies*, the back cover adding the phrase "But Goldies!"

The LP was issued in both mono and stereo formats but since some of the songs had never been mixed into stereo – principally singles, which were released in mono until 1969 – a series of mix sessions was set up. None was attended by so much as a solitary Beatle. This day saw the first such session, George Martin mixing 'Paperback Writer' between 2.30 and 4.30 pm in EMI studio one.

On Monday 7 November (also studio one, 2.30–5.30 pm) a new stereo mix of 'I Want To Hold Your Hand' was made; on Tuesday 8 November (Room 53, 4.00–5.30 pm) Geoff Emerick produced a mock-stereo mix of 'She Loves You' (a true-stereo version was impossible to produce because the original two-track session tapes had long been destroyed and the best existing source was the master tape of the mono single); and on Thursday 10 November (Room 65, 2.00–4.30 pm), new stereo mixes of 'Day Tripper' and 'We Can Work It Out' were made by balance engineer Peter Bown. Owing to an administrative error, the 1963 B-side 'This Boy' was also mixed into stereo, but it wasn't required for the LP.

The 16-song *A Collection Of Beatles Oldies* was released on Friday 9 December, the only new track for British listeners being 'Bad Boy', first issued in the USA on 14 June 1965. But its inclusion on this otherwise hit-packed collection ensured that – excepting their two German-language songs – all Beatles recordings, 1962 to date, were available on both sides of the Atlantic, neatly wrapping up the first momentous phase of the group's studio life.

Thursday 24 November

Studio Two, EMI Studios, London

And so the Beatles entered the new phase of their career. No longer the tidy, smiling "Fab Four", singing boy/girl pop songs on stage. Now they were the casually dressed, sometimes mustachioed, not always smiling Beatles who would make the greatest ever batch of rock recordings at and for their merest whim, strictly not for performing on stage.

John, Paul, George and Ringo had scarcely spent a day together since early September. Now they had decided to reunite and begin recording a new album. 'Strawberry Fields Forever' was the first song to be taped although it was whipped away for a February 1967 single and never appeared on a Beatles LP apart from compilations put together outside of the group's direct control.

'Strawberry Fields Forever' captured in one song much of what the Beatles had learned in the four years spent inside recording studios, and especially 1966, with its backwards

tapes, vari-speeds and uncommon musical instruments. And it could only have been born of a mind (John Lennon's) under the influence of outlawed chemicals. Strawberry Field is a Salvation Army home in Liverpool, around the corner from where John was brought up. He went there for summer fêtes and had called the surrounding wooded area Strawberry Fields. 'Strawberry Fields Forever' evoked those childhood memories through a dreamy, hallucinogenic haze. It was, and remains, one of the greatest pop songs of all time.

It is also known, correctly, for being among the most complicated of all Beatles recordings, changing shape not once but several times. Take one, recorded from 7.00 pm to 2.30 am in this first session, was certainly far removed from the final version, the only similarity being a mellotron introduction. (The precursor of the synthesiser, this instrument contained tapes which could be "programmed" to imitate another instrument, in this instance a flute.) By 2.30 am take one sounded like this: simultaneous with the mellotron, played by Paul, was John's first lead vocal, followed by George's guitar, Ringo's distinctive drums (with dominant use of tomtoms), maracas, a slide guitar piece, John's double-tracked voice and scat harmonies by John, Paul and George. The song came to a full-ending with the mellotron. The entire take was recorded at 53 cycles per second so that it sped up on replay, but still it lasted only 2 mins 34 secs.

Friday 25 November

Dick James House, New Oxford St, London

An immediate but temporary departure from serious work to record 'Pantomime: Everywhere It's Christmas' – the Beatles' fourth annual gift to their fan club members – in the tiny first-floor demo studio at the London office of publisher Dick James Music.

It took place in the evening, but precise details of the session no longer exist. The disc features ten separate items including the title song, sung (briefly) by all four Beatles, with Paul on piano.

Sunday 27 November

Broadwick Street, London

For the second time, John agreed to appear without the other Beatles in *Not Only…But Also*, now established as a popular BBC2 series for Peter Cook and Dudley Moore.

But viewers had to watch carefully to catch him, for John popped up for all of 51 seconds, acting the role of Dan, a smartly-outfitted doorman at trendy London night-club the "Ad Lav" (a spoof on the Ad Lib Club, formerly much visited by the Beatles) who succeeded in wangling a £5 backhander admission fee from American TV presenter Hiram J Pipesucker Jr (Cook). Bizarrely, the "club" was situated in an underground men's lavatory (although all interior footage was shot, without Lennon, at Television Centre a few days later, on 9 December), John's brief role being to stand at the top of the steps for this outdoor sequence.

The chosen location was the underground gents' toilet in

Broadwick Street (close by the junction with Berwick Street) in the Soho area of central London. Filming took place during this Sunday morning, when the area is at its quietest, and the sketch was included in the Boxing Day edition of the series (Monday 26 December, 9.00–9.50 pm). The programme was then repeated on Tuesday 7 February 1967 (BBC1, 9.05–9.50 pm).

Note: earlier in this same sketch, Peter Cook joined the Dudley Moore Trio and an orchestra in a performance of their new composition 'The LS Bumble Bee', a thinly disguised song about the drug LSD, later issued as a single. Over the following years, a myth took hold that John had either written or performed this song, or both, but he had not.

Monday 28 November

Studio Two, EMI Studios, London

Back to 'Strawberry Fields Forever'. For the first time there was no real pressure on the Beatles to deliver product to a pre-set deadline. They would work on a song until they and only they were satisfied with it. At EMI this evening between 7.00 pm and 1.30 am, the group recorded three more takes, numbered two to four, with take four roughly mixed into mono at the end of the session.

Tuesday 29 November

Studio Two, EMI Studios, London

A 2.30–8.00 pm session, recording takes five and six of 'Strawberry Fields Forever'. John overdubbed a vocal onto the latter before it was reduced into take seven and more overdubs were applied. This was then marked "best" – with rough mono mixes immediately made – and so it remained for nine more days.

Friday 2 December

Mono mixing and editing of 'Pantomime – Everywhere It's Christmas', overseen by Tony Barrow between 9.00 am and 12.00 noon. The finished production was rushed to Lyntone Records for the pressing of the flexi-discs.

Tuesday 6 December

Studio Two, EMI Studios, London

The Beatles remained public champions of the "pirate" radio stations which operated from ships moored off the British coastline. A disc-jockey from each of the two major pirates, Caroline and London, was even invited to accompany the Beatles during their final North American tour in August 1966, interviewing them and filing reports back home by telephone. (For Caroline Jerry Leighton made the trip, for London it was the zany Liverpudlian Kenny Everett.)

To mark further their appreciation of the pirates' efforts, the Beatles this evening taped Christmas and New Year goodwill greetings for the staff of the two stations and their listeners. ("Hello, this is John Lennon. All good wishes to everyone everywhere and best of luck for '67!") These greetings were initially spoken unaccompanied but some later ones were announced above station identification tunes and, later still, some featured three Beatles tinkering on studio instruments – any note, any key – behind the fourth doing the speaking.

With 'Strawberry Fields Forever' thought complete, the Beatles next turned their attention to the second song for the new album, Paul's vaudeville-style charmer 'When I'm Sixty-Four'. This was not a new song: the Beatles had performed a variation of it back in their Cavern Club days whenever the amplifiers broke down. What remained of this 7.45 pm–1.00 am session was spent rehearsing and then recording two takes of the rhythm track.

Thursday 8 December

Studios One/Two, EMI Studios, London

The other Beatles were not present when Paul overdubbed his lead vocal onto 'When I'm Sixty-Four' during a 2.30–5.30 afternoon session in EMI studio one. However, all four were around for the long evening session in studio two, 7.00 pm–3.40 am. It was during this night that the group set about what is best described as the "orchestral re-make" of 'Strawberry Fields Forever', recording rhythm track takes nine through to 24 (there was, for some reason, no take numbered 19, nor was there an eight) and then, at the end, watching as balance engineer Geoff Emerick edited together the first three-quarters of take 15 with the last quarter of take 24. An attempt to reduce the resulting edit into take 25 was started but aborted, to be continued the next day.

Emerick and producer George Martin did not attend the entire session, spending the early part of the evening at the premiere of Cliff Richard's feature-film *Finders Keepers*. In their place, although he shouldn't really have been so

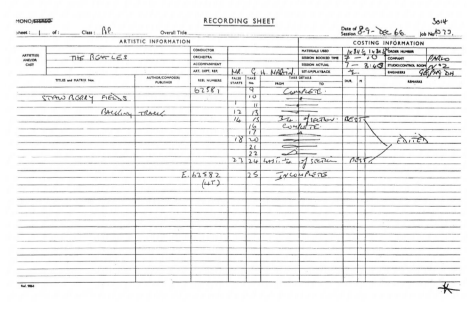

involved, technical engineer Dave Harries temporarily produced/engineered the Beatles, diving out of the control room when he heard Martin and Emerick returning.

Friday 9 December

Studio Two, EMI Studios, London

With much overdubbing still to be done to 'Strawberry Fields Forever', the previous night's edit of takes 15 and 24 was reduced to just one track on the four-track tape and called take 25 at the start of this 2.30–10.00 pm session. All manner of overdubs were then applied onto this, everything from backwards cymbals to a swordmandel (an Indian instrument, not unlike a table harp). For the purpose of cutting more acetates a quick mono mix was prepared halfway through the session.

Thursday 15 December

Studio Two, EMI Studios, London

Four trumpets and three cellos, brilliantly scored by George Martin, provided the distinctive brass and string sound which he and John had decided was necessary for the re-make of 'Strawberry Fields Forever'. (The trumpeters were Tony Fisher, Greg Bowen, Derek Watkins and Stanley Roderick, the cellists John Hall, Derek Simpson and Norman Jones.) The instruments were recorded onto take 25, which was then reduced again into take 26; onto this was then added two separate Lennon lead vocals.

By the end of the 2.30–12.00 pm session 'Strawberry Fields Forever' had taken on an intensity of almost frightening proportion. With its frantic strings, blaring trumpets, heavy drum sound and two manic, exceptionally fast John Lennon vocals it was now but a distant relative of the original, acoustic take one. Would John be satisfied with it? For the time being, at least, it was labelled "best" and so was subjected to more rough mono mixing.

c.c. Mr. George Martin's office

Our ref: 27821/PJB/DMJ

4th January, 1967.

George Martin Music Limited,
c/o A.I.R. (Record Productions) London Ltd.,
101 Baker Street,
London, N.W.1.

Dear Sirs,

We have pleasure in enclosing herewith a cheque for £36. 0. 0. in respect of the Arrangements of the titles recorded by the Beatles on the 24th November and 6th December, 1966.

Also enclosed is the usual form of receipt which we shall be glad if you will have signed and returned. Stamped addressed envelope herewith.

Yours faithfully,
E.M.I. RECORDS

Receipt returned
7-1-67

Pamela J. Britt
A. & R. Contracts Administration

Encs.
Job No. 1033

Tuesday 20 December

Studio Two, EMI Studios, London

A 7.00 pm–1.00 am session in which Paul, George and John overdubbed backing vocals onto 'When I'm Sixty-Four', with Ringo adding the sound of bells. This was followed by another reduction mix, take two becoming takes three and four (the latter marked "best").

Keen to put an end to the nonsense that proliferated in the world's media about the group breaking-up, each of the Beatles consented to give an interview to Independent Television News (ITN) reporter John Edwards for inclusion in the 25-minute weekly series *Reporting '66* ("reporting in depth on key stories of the week"). This edition was at first subtitled 'Beatles Breaking-Up Special' but then became, more correctly, 'End Of Beatlemania', and each member of the group was filmed outside EMI Studios upon arriving for this session, all sporting moustaches and George, additionally, a beard. Each one chatted about how the four were remaining together and working on new song material.

Reporting '66 was seen all over Britain, although screened by the various ITV regions on different days and times. This edition went out on Wednesday 28 and Thursday 29 December (in London, Rediffusion screened it at 6.08–6.35 pm on the Thursday), the remainder of the 25-minute programme comprising library footage of the group – especially from their recent North American tour – and interviews with fans.

Wednesday 21 December

Studio Two, EMI Studios, London

Originally planned for 15 December (but there was no time to do it that day), 'When I'm Sixty-Four' was adorned with the sound of three clarinets between 7.00 and 9.00 pm: two

RECORDING SHEET

ordinary and one a bass clarinet, played by Robert Burns, Henry MacKenzie and Frank Reidy. The recording was then mixed into mono, for acetate-cutting purposes, between 9.00 and 10.00 pm.

Between 10.00 and session's end at 11.45 pm John's added yet more vocals and another piano track to take 26 of 'Strawberry Fields Forever'.

Thursday 22 December

Studio Two, EMI Studios, London

John's problem with the two markedly different recordings of 'Strawberry Fields Forever' was that he liked both the first minute of the lighter, original version, and the remainder of the more intense, scored version. Could not George Martin cut them together? As Martin pointed out, this was unlikely: they were in different keys and tempos. "Well," John replied, "you can fix it!" So George Martin and Geoff Emerick came into EMI this evening, 7.00–11.30 pm, to see if John's wish could be fulfilled.

And it could – by speeding up a new mix of take seven and slowing down a new mix of take 26, a miracle occurred: keys and tempos matched and a master take could be cut. The join, for those who wish to know, occurs 60 seconds into the released version.

'Strawberry Fields Forever', which had taken life in the studio on 24 November, was finally and gloriously complete.

Thursday 29 December

Studios Three/Two, EMI Studios, London

Working in studio three between 2.30 and 5.45 pm, George Martin prepared mono mixes of 'When I'm Sixty-Four' and mono and stereo mixes of 'Strawberry Fields Forever'.

Speaking at Granada TV Centre in Manchester on 1 November 1965, during a break from taping *The Music Of Lennon & McCartney*, Paul mentioned to an interviewer that he'd been toying with the idea of writing a song called 'Penny Lane' because he liked the poetry of the name. (Penny Lane was, and still is, the name of a road in the suburb south of Liverpool city centre, close to where the Beatles grew up.) It took another year for Paul actually to write the song but with its description of the shops and the people and the "blue suburban skies" his 'Penny Lane' was a fine counterpoint to John's 'Strawberry Fields Forever'.

The basic track of 'Penny Lane' was taped this evening by Paul alone, working from 7.00 pm to 2.15 am in studio two. Special care was taken over the various keyboard tracks that would underpin the song. These and various strange percussive effects were recorded in six takes, with two rough mono mixes made at the end of the night.

Friday 30 December

Studio Two, EMI Studios, London

The mono mixes of 'When I'm Sixty-Four' done on 29 December and marked "best" for the UK and US did not satisfy Paul. He suggested that they scrap all previous mixes and begin again, speeding up the new mix by as much as a semitone, a big difference. Such work began this 7.00 pm–3.00 am session, and was followed by the making of simple tape-to-tape copies of the "best" mono mix of 'Strawberry Fields Forever' from the previous afternoon.

The remainder of the session was devoted to 'Penny Lane', with a reduction of take six into take seven and an overdub of Paul's lead vocal, backed by John. It was well into the wee hours by the time these had been taped, so the other overdubs planned for the song had to wait until the next session and another year – 1967. All that was left to do in 1966 was mix into mono 'Penny Lane', as it presently stood, so that an acetate disc could be cut.

As much as 1963 had been, 1967 was a truly remarkable year for the Beatles. At the apex of their collective creative ability, finally liberated from the shackles of touring, with monumental popularity assured and Beatlemania in welcome decline, they were now four self-possessed and financially secure young men, and they spoke for youth because they were a part of youth themselves – in January, as they set about continuing the recording of their next album, John and Ringo were still only 26, Paul 24 and George 23.

Baffling the British music business with their seemingly peculiar desire for peace, privacy and as few public appearances as they could manage, the Beatles worked through the winter and into the spring of 1967 at EMI Studios, slowly piecing together the record with which they would revolutionise the role of the album in rock music. Their already vibrant creative senses fired even further by mind-expanding drugs – with which they dabbled more seriously this year than any other – the Beatles were on the crest of an artistic wave that assumed mountainous proportions.

The long silence since *Revolver*, punctuated only by the February 1967 release of 'Strawberry Fields Forever'/'Penny Lane', surely the greatest pop/rock single of all time, was finally broken on 1 June when the

dawn of that most famous of all post-war summers, clichéd now as "the summer of love", was heralded by *Sgt Pepper's Lonely Hearts Club Band*, the Beatles' eighth album. It was issued just a few days short of five years since their first EMI recording session.

Millions of words have been written about this LP, almost every one fulsome in its praise, but what surely stands out most of all is the Beatles' sheer *progression* to this point in time. Here were four musicians, raw and inexperienced in June 1962, changing popular music right-about-face by June 1967. With their astonishing fame, respect and talent the Beatles made *Sgt Pepper* amid a heady atmosphere in which they they could do virtually *anything* and succeed. Paul McCartney conducting a 40-piece orchestra? No problem!

With *Sgt Pepper* it was as if the Beatles were suddenly stepping out of black-and-white and into full-blown, glorious colour. Think of 1963, '64, '65, and even '66, and think of monochrome, think of 1967 and think of colour: brilliant, dazzling, kaleidoscopic ideas, imagery, clothes, films and music. The record itself was housed in what was then a novel, de-luxe colour sleeve, with free cardboard cut-outs and (for the first time on a pop/rock LP) the song lyrics printed in full. More money was invested in the cover than had previously been

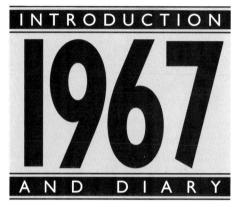

INTRODUCTION
1967
AND DIARY

It was a proposition which would have gone to no other group, an unprecedented opportunity for the global plugging of a new song, not repeated until Live Aid in 1985.

In what has since been described, with some justification, as the greatest single moment in the history of popular music, the Beatles, now at their absolute zenith, performed 'All You Need Is Love' with the apparent nonchalance of a private rehearsal session. From playing skiffle music in an abattoir workers' social club in 1957 to instructing 350 million people, live across the globe ten years later (and only 15 days after the Israeli-Arab six-day war) that "love is all you need" is a leap in scale so colossal that it's still hard to comprehend.

*

Throughout the previous two or three years, especially now that they had abandoned live appearances, the Beatles had grown less and less reliant upon Brian Epstein. They were no

spent recording entire albums. And the Beatles' new contract with EMI, effective for nine years from 27 January, also ensured that *Sgt Pepper* was issued identically all over the world, even in the USA where Capitol Records fell into corporate line with Britain on a Beatles album for the first time.

It is likely, however, that *Sgt Pepper's Lonely Hearts Club Band* represented the Beatles' last real *united* push behind a project. Certainly, after the LP had been completed, their immediate batch of recordings – throughout the remainder of April, all of May and early June – did display a lack of cohesion and enthusiasm, as though they had injected their all into *Sgt Pepper* and now wanted to take things easy. And when they came to make their next album (*The Beatles*, 1968), the creative environment and driving sense of purpose that had distinguished *Sgt Pepper* had completely disappeared.

Here in the summer of 1967, though, minds were re-focused when the BBC invited the Beatles to appear in the world's first global television programme, in which five continents would be linked simultaneously by new-fangled satellites orbiting the Earth. It would mean having TV cameras inside EMI Studios and performing there live before an audience of 350 million people.

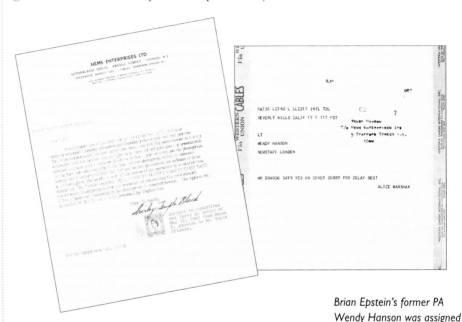

Brian Epstein's former PA Wendy Hanson was assigned the task of securing personal approval from each of the people to be depicted on the Sgt Pepper sleeve.

longer youngsters whose unruly spirit and appearance needed marshalling to impress some A&R man or north-west ballroom promoter; they were no longer the fingers-crossed aspirants hopeful of a package tour booking; they were no longer in need of tailoring appointments, schedules and itineraries, television and radio bookings.

Not that Brian hadn't matured too. Still creative, still a visionary, he was as keen as the Beatles to embrace drugs and the so-called "pop culture" of 1967 – "love, flowers, bells, be happy and look forward to the future" is how he concluded one personal letter that summer. But it was to be a future without Brian himself, for on 27 August, while the Beatles were in Wales sitting at the feet of a new leader, Maharishi Mahesh Yogi, teacher of Transcendental Meditation and giver of spiritual guidance, he was found dead in his London house. Older than the Beatles but still ridiculously young to have achieved so much, he was 32.

Suicide was firmly ruled out by a coroner's report: Epstein's death was accidental and was due to an incautious, gradual accumulation of drugs in his body. A pill-popper who

and that they could probably get along independently. Now, with his death, they would see if this was so – quite pointedly, they did not appoint a new manager; they would handle their career themselves.

Following Brian's death, the Beatles immediately threw themselves into the making of their own television film, *Magical Mystery Tour*, conceived in April but on ice through the summer. Like so many of the ideas and projects that arose between now and the Beatles' split, this was Paul's baby. John, George and Ringo never cowered from the prospect of hard work – one glance through this book will prove that beyond any doubt – but, nonetheless, given the choice, and it was a choice they felt they *could* now give themselves, they would rather not work *too* hard. Paul, conversely, thrives on industry. Without presuming to usurp Brian Epstein when he was alive, or take over from him after his death, Paul naturally became the one to corral the others into some activity or other.

Epstein's missing presence was obvious immediately the Beatles began to film *Magical Mystery Tour*, which was an administrative nightmare throughout. Believing that they could do anything, and do it extremely well, they devised, wrote, acted in, composed, produced, directed and edited *MMT*, determined to carry it off without outside guidance or advice.

There were two key flaws in this thinking. One was that the Beatles were artists and not administrators and had little knowledge of how to plan and organise. The second was that, despite their immense abilities, they were forgetting that they had always had a vital crutch on which to lean while they learnt. Yes, they could now record music in the studio without George Martin if they wished, but they could not have done so in 1962. And without someone in a similar role underpinning their unformed, beginners' film ideas, *Magical Mystery Tour* naturally became self-indulgent and amateurish.

There was no shooting script nor any of the other finely detailed paperwork *de rigeur* for film productions. The Beatles merely recruited a loose cast from *Spotlight* (the pictorial A-Z parade of jobbing actors and actresses, published annually), they hired a coach, employed three cameramen and hit the road. The plan was to spend a week shooting in Devon and Cornwall (an area selected merely because Paul hadn't been there since a 1959 hitch-hiking holiday with George), a week shooting at Shepperton Studios and then wrap up the project with a further week in an editing room, following which they would go off to India to study meditation.

But filming in the West Country quickly developed into a tiresome, troublesome mess; they couldn't get into Shepperton because – not realising that they needed to book a stage weeks if not months in advance – it was already occupied, and the paring down of ten hours of film into a finished, synchronised 52 minutes took not one week but 11, causing a postponement of the India visit until February 1968. From start to finish, *MMT* underlined how inexperienced the Beatles were in matters of business and organisation – much greater evidence of which would become apparent in 1968 when Apple Corps was launched.

would as often as not choose a tablet because of its attractive colouring rather than for its recognised purpose, Brian had long succumbed to addiction, which, allied with his violent mood swings, caused his final year to be a deeply unhappy one.

As it happened, his five-year management contract with the Beatles was set to expire on 1 October, and Epstein died not knowing with guaranteed certainty if this same relationship would continue. One can only speculate now that it would have done, but on terms quite different from before, for although they loved and trusted Brian like no one else, the Beatles knew that 1967 was a very long way from 1962,

BEATLE MAGIC TV SHOW
Mystery coach to Devon and Cornwall

A 60-SEATER yellow and blue coach carrying the Beatles and a film crew—and with the words "Magical Mystery Tour" emblazoned on the side—will leave London on Monday heading for Devon and Cornwall. The Beatles plan unscheduled stops on the route to gather location material for a one-hour colour TV special. The programme would be completed by November, and there is a possibility that it could be a Christmas highlight of the new BBC-2 colour service. A follow-up single to "All You Need Is Love" is expected in November while the Beatles are in India—it may be "Magical Mystery Tour," which will be the title and theme number of the spectacular. Next month marks the fifth anniversary of the Beatles first hit "Love Me Do."

RADIO TIMES *December 21 1967*

BOXING DAY

tv BBC 1

6.10 p.m.
THE NEWS
with Michael Aspel
and THE WEATHER

6.15
BRIGADOON
The famous
Lerner and Loewe Musical
The classic fantasy of an enchanted
Scottish village which comes to life
only once every century.
starring
ROBERT GOULET
as Tommy
SALLY ANN HOWES
as Fiona
PETER FALK
as Jeff
with
Finlay Currie
as Mr Lundie
Marlyn Mason
as Meg
Edward Villella
as Harry Beaton
Thomas Carlisle
as Charles Dalrimple
Linda Howe
as Jeannie McLaren
Rhys Williams
as Andrew McLaren
Book and lyrics by Alan Jay Lerner
Music by Frederick Loewe
Choreography by Peter Gennaro
Produced and directed by
Fielder Cook

7.30
FROST OVER CHRISTMAS

8.35
THE BEATLES
present their own film
Magical Mystery Tour
with songs and music from
PAUL McCARTNEY
JOHN LENNON
GEORGE HARRISON
RINGO STARR
starring
THE BEATLES
with
Ivor Cutler
Jessie Robins
Mandy Weet
Nat Jackley
Victor Spinetti
Devised, written, and directed by
THE BEATLES
See page 33

9.25
THE NEWS
with Michael Aspel
followed by
THE WEATHER

9.35
NORMAN WISDOM
In the film comedy
The Square Peg
with
HONOR BLACKMAN
EDWARD CHAPMAN
Screenplay by
Jack Davies and Henry Blyth
Norman Wisdom and Eddie Leslie
Produced by Hugh Stewart
Directed by John Paddy Carstairs
Norman Pitkin NORMAN WISDOM
Gen'l Schreiber
Lesley Cartland HONOR BLACKMAN
Mr Grimsdale EDWARD CHAPMAN
Sergeant Loder CAMPBELL SINGER
Gretchen HATTIE JACQUES
Henri Le Blanc BRIAN WORTH

Badly scheduled (it went out in Britain at peak-time on Boxing Day, traditionally a slot for family films or cabaret entertainment), and shown first in monochrome when colour was so important to the production, *Magical Mystery Tour* was massacred by the British press and viewers alike, the first time that the Beatles had so demonstrably boobed. The film has its great moments, some fine humour and ideas, and stands up better today than it did in 1967, but that doesn't mean that it was, as has been so often claimed, ahead of its time. It could just be that the public has grown accustomed to seeing self-gratifying, half-completed ideas on its television screens.

The year that began so positively ended on this decidedly negative note. *Magical Mystery Tour* proved that the Beatles were fallible, human even; Brian Epstein was dead, personal interests were tugging John, Paul, George and Ringo in separate directions and internecine differences were taking root.

Certainly the Beatles were a group with an unrivalled bond of loyalty and inner strength, and yet, as the world was to witness, even a bond as strong as this could come unstuck.

Wednesday 4 January

Studio Two, EMI Studios, London

The Beatles began the year with a resumption of the 'Penny Lane' recording, overdubbing yet another piano part (John), lead guitar (George) and a vocal (Paul) onto take seven in a 7.00 pm–2.45 am session.

The previous day, 3 January, tape-to-tape copies of 'When I'm Sixty-Four' and 'Strawberry Fields Forever' had been made for dispatch to the USA.

Thursday 5 January

Studio Two, EMI Studios, London

After Paul had overdubbed another vocal onto 'Penny Lane', replacing the one from the previous evening, the Beatles set to work on the main objective of this 7.00 pm–12.15 am session: preparing an effects tape for the "underground" movement's *Carnival Of Light Rave*, due to be held at the Roundhouse in London during the Saturday evenings of 28 January and 4 February. Posters for the event, billboarded around the capital, promised "music composed by Paul McCartney and Delta Music Plus". (The latter name, seemingly, was a different group or person, not a pseudonym for Paul or the Beatles.)

As composer, Paul took charge of the creation on tape this evening of a bizarre collection of loops and distortions. (Or, as it was described in the press at the time, "a tape of electronic noises".) The Beatles had never made a recording quite like this before, although John was to repeat the exercise again, culminating in 'Revolution 9' on the November 1968 double-album *The Beatles*. This day's attempt lasted 13 mins 48 secs, the longest uninterrupted Beatles recording to date, and it was the combination of a one-take basic track plus numerous overdubs, so that by its end it included distorted, hypnotic drum and organ sounds, a distorted lead guitar, the sound of a church organ, various effects (water-gargling was one) and, perhaps most intimidating of all, John and Paul screaming dementedly and bawling aloud random phrases like "Are you alright?" and "Barcelona!"

Paul terminated the proceedings after almost 14 minutes with one final shout up to the control room: "Can we hear it back now?" They did just that, a rough mono mix was made and Paul took away the tape to hand over to the *Carnival Of Light Rave* organisers, who were doubtless thrilled that the Beatles had produced such an *avant-garde* recording just for them.

Friday 6 January

Studio Two, EMI Studios, London

Still more overdubbing onto 'Penny Lane': Paul on bass, John on rhythm guitar and Ringo on drums. John also overdubbed conga drums. With all four tracks on the tape full again, another reduction mix was made, take seven becoming take eight with two vacant tracks. Onto this was over-

dubbed handclaps, John and George Martin playing pianos and John, Paul and George (Harrison) scat-singing at the points where brass instruments would later be added. A further reduction, take eight into nine, was made before the end of the 7.00 pm–1.00 am session, vacating two more tracks.

Monday 9 January

Studio Two, EMI Studios, London

'Penny Lane' overdubbing of four flutes and two trumpets and – with three of the six musicians playing second instruments – two piccolos and a flügelhorn. The four flautists were Ray Swinfield, P Goody, Manny Winters and Dennis Walton and the trumpeters were Leon Calvert and Freddy Clayton. At the same time, unbeknown to all, John was taping the musicians' between-takes conversations for his private collection.

Two more rough mono mixes were made before the 7.00 pm–1.45 am session ended.

Tuesday 10 January

Studio Three, EMI Studios, London

Sound effects experiments for 'Penny Lane', with scat harmonies and a hand-bell overdubbed onto take nine during this 7.00 pm–1.40 am session.

Thursday 12 January

Studio Three, EMI Studios, London

The second set of classical instrument overdubs onto 'Penny Lane': two trumpets, two oboes, two cor anglais and a double-bass. The trumpeters were Bert Courtley and Duncan Campbell, the oboists, who also doubled with cor anglais, were Dick Morgan and Mike Winfield, and the bassist was Frank Clarke. Two more rough mono mixes brought the 2.30–11.00 pm session to an end.

Tuesday 17 January

Studio Two, EMI Studios, London

Paul still felt that 'Penny Lane' needed a finishing touch and while watching the BBC2 series *Masterworks* during the evening of Wednesday 11 January, he saw David Mason, a member of the New Philharmonia, playing Bach's *Brandenburg Concerto No 2 in F Major* with the English Chamber Orchestra from Guildford Cathedral. Mason was playing a piccolo trumpet.

The musician was telephoned the next morning and invited along to Abbey Road for this Tuesday night session, 7.00 pm–12.30 am. He took with him nine trumpets and, by a process of consultation with Paul and George Martin, settled on the B-flat piccolo trumpet. Typically, there was no notation for Mason to follow, Paul instead singing the parts he wanted and George Martin writing them out. He taped two separate overdubs – a solo in the middle-eight section and a flourish towards the end of the song – and was paid a special fee of £27 10s (£27.50) for his trouble.

'Penny Lane' was now complete, close on three weeks after it had been started. Three more mono mixes were then made, with the "best", numbered RM11, copied for dispatch to the USA.

Wednesday 18 January

Granada Television, Upper James St, London

In a rare interview for the period, Paul went this afternoon to a small ground-floor studio in one of the central London offices (3 Upper James Street) of the north of England-based Granada Television, to discuss for inclusion in a special documentary the "underground" (or "counter-culture") movement presently thriving in the capital, and in which he was a key participant.

Paul was interviewed by Jo Durden-Smith, who conceived and produced this excellent 29-minute film for Granada's late-night *Scene Special* slot (an off-shoot of the early-evening *Scene At 6.30* news-magazine programme). The subtitle of Durden-Smith's film was 'It's So Far Out It's Straight Down', and the director was John Sheppard – who, in 1987, was to embrace the same topic, using *Sgt Pepper's Lonely Hearts Club Band* as the centre-piece, for a two-hour documentary *It Was Twenty Years Ago Today*.

'It's So Far Out It's Straight Down' was screened by Granada, in the north only, on Tuesday 7 March (10.25–10.55 pm), and one can but wonder how the northern viewers reacted to this sympathetic portrait of what was, even to most Londoners, a vexatious social curiosity. Paul appeared right at the beginning and then here and there throughout the film, smartly dressed, mustachioed and seated, with legs crossed, politely doing his best to explain the movement's aims. ("The straights should welcome the 'underground' because it stands for freedom…it's not strange it's just new, it's not weird it's just what's going on around.")

Durden-Smith also filmed the editorial board of *International Times*, the interior of the Indica Bookshop, Pink Floyd playing 'Interstellar Overdrive' at the UFO Club, a "performance" at the Roundhouse and a "happening" at Piccadilly Circus, and the documentary also included footage of a poetry gathering at the Royal Albert Hall with Allen Ginsberg, Adrian Mitchell and Lawrence Ferlinghetti. In a sense, Paul's interview was used to add weight, credibility and an approvable dimension to balance the occasionally unusual visual scenes.

Thursday 19 January

Studio Two, EMI Studios, London

The start of 'A Day In The Life', the song which was to become the stunning finale of the Beatles' next album. The first four takes were recorded in this 7.30 pm to 2.30 am session.

At this stage the Beatles only knew that something would

'A Day In The Life' periphery: the Daily Mail item that prompted perhaps the song's most memorable verse, and the alarm-clock sounded on the finished recording.

The holes in our roads

THERE are 4,000 holes in the road in Blackburn, Lancashire, or one twenty-sixth of a hole per person, according to a council survey.

If Blackburn is typical there are two million holes in Britain's roads and 300,000 in London.

later be taped for the song's middle section. Precisely *what* they were uncertain, but to mark out the place where the item would go they had Mal Evans count out the bars, one to 24, his voice plastered with tape echo and backed by a tinkling piano, and to flag the end of this section an alarm clock was sounded.

Friday 20 January

Studio Two, EMI Studios, London

Reduction mixdowns of 'A Day In The Life', vacating tracks for more overdubbing, began this 7.00 pm–1.10 am session. Take six was marked "best" and so was adorned with another John Lennon lead vocal, Paul's bass and Ringo's drums. Paul's vocal also appeared for the first time. Here was a prime example of how the Lennon-McCartney songwriting partnership had evolved: John's song had a beginning and an end but no middle; Paul's had a middle but no beginning or end. But the two pieces came naturally together, creating a complete picture and the impression that they were *intended* as one. The illusion was compounded by the fact that Paul's vocal, the first line of which was "Woke up, fell out of bed", occurred immediately after the alarm clock had been sounded on the original recording to mark the end of the first 24-count gap. Making good use of the happy coincidence, the alarm clock was kept on the track permanently.

Paul re-recorded his vocal on 3 February, instantly wiping out this 20 January version, which served only as a rough guide, ending on an expletive after he had made an error.

The Beatles at their most creative, Sgt Pepper time, with Neil and Mal in a unique position to witness a 20th century Meisterwork in the making.

Famous signatures on a contract that bound the Beatles – mostly individually, as it turned out – to EMI until January 1976, a nine-year recording agreement effective from 27 January 1967.

Wednesday 25 January

Studio One, EMI Studios, London

A copy of master mono mix RM11 of 'Penny Lane' had been sent to Capitol Records on 23 January for American pressing. But Paul felt it could be bettered, so three more mono mixes were made between 6.30 and 8.30 this evening, the new master being RM14. The main difference between this and RM11 was the omission of some David Mason trumpet figures from the very end of the song. A copy of RM14 was made for America between 9.00 and 10.00 pm. While it was not too late to substitute new for old in Britain, however, a few singles using RM11 had already been pressed and distributed to US radio stations as advance promotion/broadcast copies – although for the commercial release Capitol used the correct mix.

The single 'Strawberry Fields Forever'/'Penny Lane' was issued in Britain on Friday 17 February, the Beatles' third double-A sided 45 in four releases, and both songs thus dropped out of the running for the album currently in the making.

Monday 30 January

Knole Park, Sevenoaks, Kent

With another single due – 'Strawberry Fields Forever'/'Penny Lane' – more promotional clips were required. At least this time, with the demise of *Thank Your Lucky Stars* and *Ready, Steady, Go!*, each requiring a different clip from, say, that sold to *Top Of The Pops*, the Beatles needed to produce only one promo for each new song.

They were produced by Tony Bramwell for Subafilms, one of the Beatles' two film production companies, and shot on colour 35mm film (for showing on US television in colour, on British TV in black-and-white) using a crew from the London-based company Don Long Productions.

The director – following in the footsteps of Joe McGrath (see 23 November 1965) and Michael Lindsay-Hogg (19–20 May 1966) – was Peter Goldmann, a director of TV pop shows in his native Sweden. He was recommended to the Beatles by mutual good friend Klaus Voormann, the German who had first met the Beatles in Hamburg in 1960, became a musician and was signed by Brian Epstein, became an artist and designed the Beatles' *Revolver* sleeve and who, presently, was bass player with Manfred Mann.

At the Beatles' request, Goldmann arrived in England during the early part of January and spent time surveying suitable shoot locations in and around London as well as watching the group record at Abbey Road. He chose two locations, and Knole Park – near Sevenoaks, Kent, around 20 miles south-east of London – was the first to be used. This enormous area, where deer roam freely, is owned and maintained by the National Trust and contains a 15th-century house and golf course. The Beatles came to Knole Park on three occasions: the first two to shoot sequences for 'Strawberry Fields Forever' (see also 31 January) and the third to film for 'Penny Lane' (see 7 February).

Typically, the films broke new ground, for having already helped to pioneer rock-era promo films in the first place – with their self-produced, relatively straightforward performance clips – the Beatles now forged ahead with storyboard films in which there was no performance element at all, just a succession of sequences which directly or indirectly explored the meaning and feeling of the music.

This first shoot in Knole Park took place in the evening darkness, the group filming a number of sequences for 'Strawberry Fields Forever' around a large, dead oak tree behind the Birdhouse.

While they were filming, George Martin was working at EMI Studios (7.00–8.30 pm), producing a rough mono mix of 'A Day In The Life' so that acetate discs could be cut.

Tuesday 31 January

Knole Park, Sevenoaks

The Beatles returned to Sevenoaks during this afternoon, staying through to the evening and completing in that time the 'Strawberry Fields Forever' clip. Among the scenes shot this day was the one where Paul dropped down from a high branch in the dead oak tree and ran backwards to a piano – a sequence which, when played in reverse, showed Paul running towards the tree and jumping *up* onto the branch. All clever stuff – inspired, no doubt, by the Beatles' present fascination with backwards recordings.

Wednesday 1 February

Studio Two, EMI Studios, London

It wasn't going to be *Sgt Pepper's Lonely Hearts Club Band* until 'Sgt Pepper's Lonely Hearts Club Band' came along. That is, the album was not "The Sgt Pepper Project" until the recording of this Paul McCartney song and Paul's realisation soon afterwards that the Beatles could pretend they were actually Sgt Pepper's band, the remaining songs on the LP forming part of a show given by the fictitious combo.

Takes one to nine of the title song's rhythm track were recorded during this 7.00 pm–2.30 am session.

Thursday 2 February

Studio Two, EMI Studios, London

Overdubbing of Paul's lead and the group's backing vocal onto 'Sgt Pepper's Lonely Hearts Club Band', followed by a reduction mixdown of take nine into take ten, ready for future overdubs. A rough mono mix, for acetate-cutting purposes, was made at the end of the 7.00 pm–1.45 am session.

Friday 3 February

Studio Two, EMI Studios, London

More overdubs onto take six of 'A Day In The Life'. Paul re-recorded his vocal track, and also bass, and Ringo wiped his original drum track in favour of a new and distinctive tom-tom sound. The session took place from 7.00 pm to 1.15 am.

Sunday 5 February

Angel Lane, Stratford, London

With the shooting of the 'Strawberry Fields Forever' clip now complete, the Beatles and film director Peter Goldmann turned their attentions to 'Penny Lane'. Keen to capture the flavour of the Liverpool suburban lane, yet unwilling or unable to travel to the actual area itself, the Beatles went to Stratford, in the East End of London, where they were filmed riding white horses and walking in and around Angel Lane between 12.00 noon and 4.00 pm.

To further the illusion that the Beatles were walking in Penny Lane, Goldmann and his crew from Don Long Productions went there without the group (date unknown) and shot footage of some of the local landmarks mentioned in the song: the barber's shop and the bus shelter in the middle of the roundabout, as well as the famous green Liverpool buses. This footage was then inter-cut with the Beatles' sequences.

Tuesday 7 February

Knole Park, Sevenoaks

To complete the 'Penny Lane' clip, the Beatles returned to Knole Park during the late morning and filmed two final sequences: one in which they rode their white horses out through an archway in a ruined wall, and around the wall to their right; the other in which, despite the bitterly cold weather, they sat at a dinner table by the furthest of two nearby ponds and were served with their instruments by two bewigged men (one of whom was Mal Evans).

Following final editing, the superb promotional clips for 'Strawberry Fields Forever' and 'Penny Lane' were quickly distributed/sold to important television stations around the world.

In Britain they were screened mostly by the BBC – a 1 min 10 secs extract from 'Penny Lane' was shown on *Juke*

Box Jury on Saturday 11 February (BBC1, 5.15–5.40 pm); both 'Penny Lane' and 'Strawberry Fields Forever' were screened on *Top Of The Pops* on 16 February (BBC1, 7.30–8.00 pm); 'Penny Lane' was on *TOTP* a week later (23 February, same times) and 'Strawberry Fields Forever' a week after that (2 March, same times). (They were not included in the year-end *TOTP* compilations of number one hits because, according to the BBC chart, the single climbed only to number two.) One ITV showing for 'Penny Lane' was in the first edition of a locally screened Southern Television series *As You Like It*, directed by Mike Mansfield and presented by Pete Murray (Saturday 11 March, 5.15–5.40 pm).

In America the clips were screened on ABC's *The Hollywood Palace* (Saturday 25 February, 9.30–10.00 pm, EST), *Clay Cole's Diskotek* (Saturday 11 March, 6.00–7.30 pm, EST), an edition of *American Bandstand* this same day and *Where The Action Is* (Tuesday 14 March, 4.30–5.00 pm, EST).

THE BEATLES

(handwritten acetate disc cutting sheet)

Aware of mounting and perhaps unnecessary costs, EMI formally noted the number of acetate discs – 47 – cut during the making of 'Strawberry Fields Forever' and 'Penny Lane', showing where, when and who did the cutting, and for whom.

Wednesday 8 February

Studio Two, EMI Studios, London

A 7.00 pm–2.15 am session in which the Beatles taped eight fairly straightforward rhythm track takes of a new song, John's 'Good Morning Good Morning', its title inspired by a British TV commercial for Kellogg's cornflakes.

Thursday 9 February

Regent Sound Studio, Tottenham Court Rd, London

The Beatles' first EMI session at a British studio other than Abbey Road. Regent Sound was one of the few independently owned facilities in London at this time.

No longer a member of EMI staff, George Martin was free to travel with the Beatles, but balance engineer Geoff Emerick and the usual crew of Abbey Road tape ops were all EMI employees so they couldn't go along. Adrian Ibbetson, chief engineer at Regent Sound, filled Emerick's role for this session, in which three takes of Paul's new song 'Fixing A Hole' were recorded, the second being "best". (Start and finish times for the session weren't noted down.)

Friday 10 February

Studio One, EMI Studios, London

There can be no doubt that 1967 was a heady year for the Beatles, and 10 February must rank as one of the highlights.

It was Paul who had decided upon the best way of filling the 24-bar gap in 'A Day In The Life': an orchestral build-up, with perhaps 90 musicians playing from a pre-selected low note to the highest their respective instrument could play. As usual, the task of making this vision a reality fell to George Martin, paid £18 for his arrangement in which the instruction to each musician was (a) start very quietly and end very loud, (b) start very low in pitch and end up very high, and (c) make your own way up the scales, independent of your neighbour.

Although only 40 musicians were used instead of 90 (still the cost came to £367 10s, quite an investment), Paul got more than he had requested because the orchestra was recorded four times, onto all the tracks of a four-track tape (it was later mixed down to one) so, in essence, there was the equivalent of 160 musicians. They were: *violin*: Erich Gruenberg (leader), Granville Jones, Bill Monro, Jurgen Hess, Hans Geiger, D Bradley, Lionel Bentley, David McCallum, Donald Weekes, Henry Datyner, Sidney Sax, Ernest Scott; *viola*: John Underwood, Gwynne Edwards, Bernard Davis, John Meek; *cello*: Francisco Gabarro, Dennis Vigay, Alan Dalziel, Alex Nifosi; *double-bass*: Cyril MacArther, Gordon Pearce; *harp*: John Marson; *oboe*: Roger Lord; *flute*: Clifford Seville, David Sandeman; *trumpet*: David Mason, Monty Montgomery, Harold Jackson; *trombone*: Raymond Brown, Raymond Premru, T Moore; *tuba*: Michael Barnes; *clarinet*: Basil Tschaikov, Jack Brymer; *bassoon*: N Fawcett, Alfred Waters; *horn*: Alan Civil, Neil Sanders; *percussion (including timpani)*: Tristan Fry.

George Martin and Paul McCartney took turns in conducting the orchestra, leaving Geoff Emerick in the control room to carefully manipulate the faders to capture the crescendo. The recording was made using the unique "ambiophonics" system of the massive EMI studio one, whereby 100 loudspeakers, fitted symmetrically to all four walls, artificially tailor the acoustics by feeding signals delayed at different intervals, the resulting sound being called "ambiophony".

But the technical aspects of the recording tell only half the story. The 8.00 pm–1.00 am session was, more than anything else, *an event*. The Beatles asked the musicians to wear full evening dress but then, additionally, don novelties. Violinist David McCallum wore a red clown's nose, lead violinist Erich Gruenberg a gorilla's paw on his bow hand. Everyone wore funny hats or some other sort of carnival novelty. The two bassoons had balloons tied to their ends which inflated and deflated as the instruments were played.

When the orchestra had gone home the Beatles and some friends stayed behind and attempted to record the song's coda – later a crashing piano chord – which at this stage was going to be a long "hummmmmm". Three such takes dissolved into laughter, but the next was good enough for the ensemble to add overdubs, filling the four-track tape. This was to remain the best idea of ending 'A Day In The Life' until the famous piano chord was taped on 22 February.

The orchestral element of the session was filmed by NEMS Enterprises, with Tony Bramwell producing, exercising as much control as he could over the seven hand-held cameras utilised for shooting this most chaotic of events. The film was later edited, along with some stock (that is, non-Beatles) footage, into a finished clip for 'A Day In The Life' but it was never screened at the time – neither in Britain (where, anyway, the song was banned by the BBC, see 20 May 1967) nor elsewhere – which is a pity because the footage captured the essence of the evening, making for a compelling, if chaotic, little film, with all of the musicians in evening dress, many wearing silly novelties like upside down spectacles, plastic stick-on nipples, red noses, false eyes, fake cigars and, on heads, imitation bald pates and knotted handkerchiefs. It also showed George's wife Pattie and the many friends especially invited along by the Beatles – among them Mick Jagger, Marianne Faithfull, Keith Richard, Mike Nesmith, Donovan and Simon and Marijke of designer group the Fool. (Marijke played a tambourine during the orchestral overdub which remained in the final mixes.) It showed girl fans being ejected by Neil Aspinall and bubbles floating around the expanse of EMI studio one.

The principal reason why 'A Day In The Life' wasn't shown is that it was held back for a full-length *Sgt Pepper's Lonely Hearts Club Band* TV special, which remained very much a possibility throughout 1967. (Had the production gone ahead it would have presaged the era of video-albums, otherwise brought into prominence by Blondie in 1979 with *Eat To The Beat*.) Though ultimately abandoned, the Beatles nurtured hopes for the film from the spring right through to the autumn of 1967, for although talk of the film ceased in the weekly music newspapers by the early summer, giving the impression that the Beatles had abandoned the idea, a complete filming schedule was put together, at their request and for their approval, on 26 September by Peacock Productions Ltd – right in the midst of *Magical Mystery Tour* production.

Although these plans were dropped – indeed, the filming never even started – the schedule makes for fascinating reading. It detailed a £34,000 budget, a one-month principal photography period (21 October to 21 November) and a final running length of 52 minutes – 'A Day In The Life' alone (obviously utilising much more of the 10 February session footage than the song clip) running to 19 mins 15 secs. The film was to have been shot in colour, with a screenplay written by Ian Dallas, it would have been directed by Keith Green and co-produced by Vic Singh and Tommy Weber; it would have used two cameramen (one of whom, Aubrey Dewar, shot *Magical Mystery Tour*) and, at a cost of £2200, employed 115 extras (including 24 children, 24 office workers, 12 "rockers" on motor-bikes, 12 "Model Rita Maids", eight morris dancers, one milkman, one meditator, one "loon" and one Arab sheik).

Saturday 11 February

Twickenham Film Studios, St Margaret's, Twickenham

In marked contrast to the films *A Hard Day's Night* and *Help!*, which had been finished and released a few short months after going into production, *How I Won The War* was a much slower affair. Although shot through the autumn of 1966 – John completing his role on 6 November – its world premiere did not occur until 18 October 1967 (at the London Pavilion, with all four Beatles in attendance).

During this long interlude, the film's post-production processes were undertaken, with post-sync dubbing of voices and music being done in the Recording Theatre here at Twickenham from this date through to 3 March. John attended at least once – though a precise record of date(s) no longer exists – overdubbing his voice onto the soundtrack.

In an opportunistic, if not downright cheeky, attempt to promote the film, the United Artists record company released as a British single on 13 October 1967, a few days before the premiere, a "song" called 'How I Won The War', attributed to Musketeer Gripweed and the Third Troop – Gripweed being the name of John's film character. The clear inference was that this was, in effect, a John Lennon single, issued without the other Beatles. In fact, it was almost without John Lennon too, for the "song" combined the film's theme music written by Ken Thorne (who'd done likewise for *Help!*) with a *mélange* of effects and dialogue extracted from the soundtrack, and John was evident for less than two seconds.

Monday 13 February

Studio Two, EMI Studios, London

This 7.00 pm–3.30 am session began with the preparation of four new mono mixes of 'A Day In The Life' and then turned to the recording of a new number, George's 'Only A Northern Song'. (In keeping with George's frequent shortage of song titles, it started out this night as 'Not Known'.)

A wry comment on the fact that it would be published by Northern Songs, 'Only A Northern Song' was going to be George's chief contribution to *Sgt Pepper's Lonely Hearts Club Band*. As it transpired, though, the song didn't see commercial release until January 1969, on the *Yellow Submarine* film soundtrack album.

1967

Geoff Emerick's studio plan for 13 February, detailing equipment and layout requirements. Such forms went to the Abbey Road technical engineers who would ensure that everything was provided as requested.

This evening, the Beatles recorded nine takes of the song's rhythm track, the third marked "best".

Tuesday 14 February

Studio Two, EMI Studios, London

More work on 'Only A Northern Song', George overdubbing two lead vocals onto take 12, which was a reduction of take three made at the start of this 7.00 pm–12.30 am session. Rough mono mixes were then made so that acetate discs could be cut.

Thursday 16 February

Studio Three, EMI Studios, London

A 7.00 pm–1.45 am session which began with the overdubbing of vocals and bass onto the best 8 February basic track recording of 'Good Morning Good Morning'. A rough mono mix was done before take eight was reduced into takes nine and ten. Overdubs onto the latter would begin on 13 March.

Friday 17 February

Studio Two, EMI Studios, London

The day that their single 'Strawberry Fields Forever'/'Penny Lane' was released in Britain saw the Beatles engaged in a 7.00 pm–3.00 am session at EMI, beginning the recording of 'Being For The Benefit Of Mr Kite!' John's lyric for this song derived almost entirely from a poster advertising a circus near Rochdale, Lancashire, in February 1843, which he had bought in a Sevenoaks antique shop on 31 January, while there for the shooting of the 'Strawberry Fields Forever' promotional film.

The first seven takes were rhythm track recordings only (with George Martin playing harmonium); John then overdubbed a vocal onto the last of these, the four-track tape was reduced into takes eight and nine and John recorded another vocal onto the latter. A rough mono mix was made at the end of the session.

Monday 20 February

Studio Three, EMI Studios, London

When the Beatles started work on 'Being For The Benefit Of Mr Kite!' John had told George Martin, in effect, that he wanted the recording bathed in a circus atmosphere. Unable to trace an authentic hand-operated steam organ for the part, George realised that the required sound would have to be self-created inside Abbey Road using other means. So he got hold of some old calliope tapes of Sousa marches and had Geoff Emerick chop them up into small sections, throw them in the air and re-assemble the pieces at random.

The work was done in this 7.00 pm–2.15 am session (although the effects were not superimposed onto the Beatles' recording until 29 March), along with a rough mono mix of 'Good Morning Good Morning' for acetate-cutting purposes.

Tuesday 21 February

Studio Two, EMI Studios, London

'Fixing A Hole', one of the least complicated recordings on *Sgt Pepper*, was completed during this 7.00 pm–12.45 am session by means of overdubs onto a reduction mixdown of the second take from the Regent Sound session of 9 February. The song was then mixed into mono several times, with an edit of mixes numbered three and six serving as the master.

Wednesday 22 February

Studio Two, EMI Studios, London

The question remained of how to end 'A Day In The Life', how to follow the staggering orchestral crescendo after John's last vocal line. The so-described "choir" of voices taped at the end of the 10 February session was along the right lines, but perhaps wasn't powerful enough. So in the first part of this 7.00 pm–3.45 am session John, Paul, Ringo and Mal Evans, sharing three pianos, recorded the sound of the simultaneous striking of one note (E major). This alone took nine takes to perfect because the four players were rarely able to hit the keys at precisely the same moment. The ninth take was considered "best" so this was overdubbed three more times, with George Martin compounding the sound further on a harmonium, until all four tracks of a tape were full. The resultant wall of sound, which lasted for 53 seconds (it was faded a little early on the record), was the perfect ending, not only to 'A Day In The Life' but to *Sgt Pepper* as a whole.

The Beatles were especially keen to sit in on the various mono and stereo mixes and edits of this song which followed, and even found the energy to record another of their experimental numbers before the session ended. Ringo was to the fore in this one, titled 'Anything' and comprising 22 mins 10 secs of drum beat, augmented by tambourine and congas. Quite what it was meant for is not clear. It was certainly never used, nor, apparently, was it even mixed.

Thursday 23 February

Studio Two, EMI Studios, London

This 7.00 pm–3.45 am session began with Geoff Emerick preparing the stereo master of 'A Day In The Life'. When completed, the Beatles set to work on a new song, Paul's 'Lovely Rita', recording eight rhythm track takes and reducing the eighth into take nine, onto which Paul overdubbed bass.

Friday 24 February

Studio Two, EMI Studios, London

A 7.00 pm–1.15 am session, the essence of which was Paul's overdubbing of his lead vocal onto 'Lovely Rita'. This was followed by a reduction mixdown that took take nine into ten and 11, ready for more embellishments on 7 and 21 March.

Tuesday 28 February

Studio Two, EMI Studios, London

It was, by 1967, customary procedure for the Beatles to spend unlimited time rehearsing in the studio before recording "takes". This may seem extravagant today, with studio costs being so high, but with EMI recording the Beatles at its own facility studio time was merely an internal cost, and certainly not one deducted from the group's royalties.

Rehearsals during this 7.00 pm–3.00 am session, of John's new song 'Lucy In The Sky With Diamonds', took so long that no proper recordings were made at all – these began the next night instead. The song's title had come about when John's three-year-old son Julian returned home from nursery school with a painting of a girl in his group. John asked him what it was called and Julian replied "It's Lucy, in the sky, with diamonds".

So it was mere coincidence that the song's initial letters spelt LSD, although there can be little doubt that it was this very substance which caused, for the song's lyrics, such colourful word imagery to spill from John's head onto paper.

Wednesday I March

Studio Two, EMI Studios, London

Seven takes of 'Lucy In The Sky With Diamonds' were recorded in this 7.00 pm–2.15 am session and then the seventh was reduced into take eight, ready for overdubbing. The first task of this session, though, was to add a new piano track onto take six of 'A Day In The Life', an odd move considering that the master mono and stereo mixes had already been made. Whatever the purpose, this additional overdub went unused.

Thursday 2 March

Studio Two, EMI Studios, London

'Lucy In The Sky With Diamonds' was one of the quickest *Sgt Pepper* recordings: one night for the rhythm track, another for overdubs. This 7.00 pm–3.30 am session took care of the latter, with a succession of vari-speeded vocal and instrument recordings being added to take eight. Eleven mono mixes completed the night's work, the last being considered "best", albeit only until the next session.

Friday 3 March

Studio Two, EMI Studios, London

Since the Beatles were pretending that Sgt Pepper's Lonely Hearts Club Band was a real band, four musicians were recruited to play French horns on the title track – James Buck, Neil Sanders, Tony Randall and John Burden. Paul hummed the phrases he wanted, George Martin and the musicians translated them onto paper and the recording was overdubbed onto take ten. At the same time, as he had done on 9 January, John surreptitiously taped the musicians' conversations for his personal archive.

After the horn players had secured Beatles' autographs (a common practice) and gone home, George Harrison became the focus of attention, overdubbing a much-distorted lead guitar solo onto the same track. This 7.00 pm–2.15 am session then ended with four more mono mixes of 'Lucy In The Sky With Diamonds'.

1 9 6 7

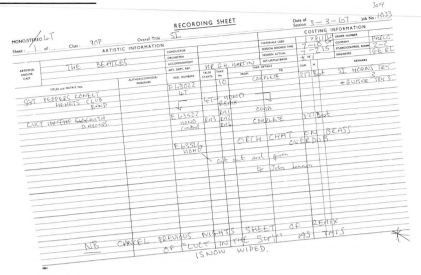

Thursday 9 March

Studio Two, EMI Studios, London

A 7.00 pm–3.30 am session which saw the start of Paul's 'Getting Better', with seven rhythm track takes recorded and then take seven being reduced five times, into takes eight through 12 (the last marked "best"), ready for overdubbing on 10, 21 and 23 March.

Friday 10 March

Studio Two, EMI Studios, London

A 7.00 pm–4.00 am session in which George overdubbed a droning tamboura, Paul bass guitar and Ringo drums onto take 12 of 'Getting Better'.

Monday 13 March

Studio Two, EMI Studios, London

The overdubbing of brass onto take ten of 'Good Morning Good Morning', played by six members of Sounds Inc: three saxophones (Barrie Cameron, David Glyde and Alan Holmes), two trombones (John Lee and one other) and a French horn (Tom someone – no one can recall his surname). Previously Sounds Incorporated, Sounds Inc were a top instrumental group who had a long history of backing American stars in Europe, had first met the Beatles at the Star-Club in April 1962, were signed to a NEMS management contract by Brian Epstein in March 1964 and had then played on some of the Beatles tours, including the August 1965 US visit that resulted in the TV film *The Beatles At Shea Stadium*. The six were paid £201, via NEMS Enterprises, for this 7.00 pm–3.30 am session.

Wednesday 15 March

Studio Two, EMI Studios, London

As well as 'Only A Northern Song', George came up with another composition for *Sgt Pepper*: 'Within You Without You'. Typically untitled at this earliest stage, it was the most Indian-sounding song ever to appear on a Beatles album, although George was to write and record others later for his *Wonderwall* film soundtrack (see 28 November 1967 and also 12 January 1968).

The basic track of 'Within You Without You', take one, was taped during this 7.00 pm–1.30 am session. Contributing tabla was Natver Soni from the north London-based Eastern (not Asian) Music Circle, Amrat Gajjar played dilruba, P D Joshi played the swordmandel while one other man, his name not documented by EMI, played a droning tamboura along with George and also Neil Aspinall. At no time did any of the other Beatles participate in the recording of this song. A rough mono mix of the night's work was made between 1.30 and 2.00 am and taken home to Esher by George.

Monday 6 March

Studio Two, EMI Studios, London

To further the pretence that Sgt Pepper's was a real band, Paul decided that the album's title track should additionally include typical sounds from one of the band's fictitious concerts: the musicians warming up, the audience settling down and then clapping and laughing. During this 7.00 pm–12.30 am session such effects were overdubbed onto the song's tenth take.

A recording of a band readying itself for a performance was easy to find: during the 10 February orchestral session for 'A Day In The Life' four tapes had been made of such miscellaneous effects. The remaining sounds for 'Sgt Pepper's Lonely Hearts Club Band' came courtesy of an invaluable archive kept in an old storeroom at Abbey Road; extracts from 'Volume 28: Audience Applause And Atmosphere, Royal Albert Hall And Queen Elizabeth Hall' were used for the audience murmuring, while the applause and laughter was taken, appropriately, from 'Volume 6: Applause And Laughter', a tape made in 1961 during the London live recording of the revue *Beyond The Fringe*. (Later, when the LP title track was segued into 'With A Little Help From My Friends', the edit was masked by one further sound effect: audience screaming from one of the at-this-time unreleased recordings of the Beatles in concert at the Hollywood Bowl.)

Master mono and stereo mixes of 'Sgt Pepper's Lonely Hearts Club Band' were made before the session ended.

Tuesday 7 March

Studio Two, EMI Studios, London

Harmony vocals/effects and miscellaneous overdubbing onto 'Lovely Rita', including – once the correct tensile strength had been ascertained from a suitable selection – the percussive sound of a piece of toilet paper (each sheet marked 'The Gramophone Company Ltd !' being blown through a hair-comb. The session began at 7.00 pm and ended at 2.30 am.

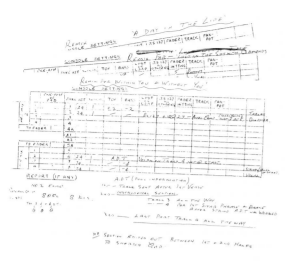

A selection of Geoff Emerick's original notes showing his console settings for the mixing of Sgt Pepper.

Friday 17 March

Studio Two, EMI Studios, London

A 7.00 pm–12.45 am session during which, in six takes, the orchestral score for another new Paul McCartney song, 'She's Leaving Home', was recorded. Unusually, the score was not by George Martin but by a different freelance producer and arranger, Mike Leander, paid £18 for all rights to his work. George had been busy with one of his several other artists and Paul, reluctant to wait, had gone to Leander, a decision which stung Martin.

Showing good grace nonetheless, George was prepared to conduct the musicians in the studio, and admit that Leander's arrangement was effective. There were ten players: Erich Gruenberg (the leader), Derek Jacobs, Trevor Williams and Jose Luis Garcia (violins), John Underwood and Stephen Shingles (violas), Dennis Vigay and Alan Dalziel (cellos), Gordon Pearce (double-bass) and Sheila Bromberg (harp), the latter being the first woman especially recruited to play on a Beatles recording.

Monday 20 March

Studio Two, EMI Studios, London

The Beatles deliberately kept themselves very much to themselves during the recording of *Sgt Pepper*, so an interview given by John and Paul to their old mate Brian Matthew this evening was certainly an important coup for BBC radio.

Underlining the Beatles' new "workshop" use of Abbey Road, Brian Matthew had to interview them there – the first time any of the Beatles (and, indeed, EMI) had consented to this – the session recording sheet logging the interview as 'Beatle Talk' and showing that it was taped at the start of the 7.00 pm session.

Matthew's purpose was two-fold. Most importantly, he recorded John and Paul's acceptance speeches for three 1966 Ivor Novello Awards – for 'Yellow Submarine' (winner of the long-winded category "The 'A' Side of the Record Issued in 1966 Which Achieved the Highest Certified British Sales

in the Period 1st January 1966 to 31st December 1966", for 'Michelle' ("The Most Performed Work of the Year") and for "Yesterday" ("Runner-Up to the Most Performed Work of the Year"). These speeches (2 mins, 1 min 25 secs and 1 min 35 secs respectively) were broadcast by the BBC Light Programme on 27 March (Easter Monday), 2.00–3.00 pm, in *The Ivor Novello Awards For 1966*. The event was otherwise recorded live, before a music industry audience, at the Playhouse Theatre in London on 23 March; John and Paul had no wish to attend so their three statuettes were received on their behalf by NEMS' Tony Barrow and by Ron White, the general manager of marketing services at EMI Records. After each presentation the relevant "thank you" speech by John and Paul was played over the PA (and dropped into the programme), following which the song was performed live at the Playhouse by Joe Loss and his Orchestra. (The lead vocal on 'Michelle' was sung by Ross MacManus, father of Declan, aka Elvis Costello.)

Up to 1970, John and Paul won several other Ivor Novello Awards too, in presentation ceremonies also broadcast by BBC radio, but they never again recorded a special interview, nor did they receive the awards in person. George Martin and Dick James accepted them on their behalf and made short speeches.

The secondary purpose of Brian Matthew's visit to EMI Studios this evening was to record a brief additional interview with John and Paul for exclusive use by the BBC's Transcription Service in its weekly show *Top Of The Pops*, sold by subscription to overseas stations. (So it wasn't broadcast on the domestic network.) It was only a brief interview, from which precisely four minutes were used, although John and Paul still had ample time to explain the Beatles' change in direction towards recording and away from touring – John in particular being emphatic about there being no more concert tours, succinctly saying that there would be "no more 'She Loves You's".

After the interview, Paul and John devoted the remainder of the session to 'She's Leaving Home', overdubbing vocals onto take nine (a reduction of the previous night's take one). This lovely song was now complete because there were no overdubs of any of the Beatles playing any musical instrument: the only music playing on 'She's Leaving Home' was the strings. The recording was then mixed into mono before the close of play at 3.30 am.

Tuesday 21 March

Studio Two, EMI Studios, London

Rather an infamous Beatles recording session. There with Paul and George to overdub vocals onto a newly made reduction mixdown of 'Getting Better', John was simultaneously experiencing an LSD trip. Feeling unwell, he excused himself and went up the stairs to the control room to see George Martin.

Realising that he was sick – though innocent of the reason why – and cognisant of the fact that the entrance/exit of EMI Studios was, as ever, patrolled by Beatles fans, George took John onto the roof of studio two for some fresh spring air, left him there and returned to the session. When Paul and George – who knew John had taken LSD – found out where he was, knowing too that this particular roof had no rails or barriers, just a 30-foot drop to the ground below, they quickly fetched him back.

Hardly surprisingly, the 'Getting Better' vocals had to be recorded again another time (23 March).

Also recorded in this 7.00 pm–2.45 am session was the piano solo in 'Lovely Rita', taped as an overdub onto take 11, following which the song was mixed into mono.

Wednesday 22 March

Studio Two, EMI Studios, London

A note, in Geoff Emerick's hand, illustrating the care injected into compiling the animal sound effects collage for 'Good Morning Good Morning'.

Overdubbing of two more dilruba parts and another sword-mandel part onto George's 'Within You Without You', played by the same musicians as on 15 March: Amrat Gajjar, P D Joshi and Natver Soni respectively. A reduction mixdown then took take one into take two and a rough mono mix was made for acetate-cutting purposes.

While George's 7.00 pm–2.15 am session was taking place in studio two, any other Beatle interested in listening to the thus far completed masters for *Sgt Pepper* did so in the control room of studio one between 11.00 pm and 12.30 am.

Thursday 23 March

Studio Two, EMI Studios, London

Another attempt at recording the vocals for 'Getting Better', overdubbed onto take 14. A reduction mixdown into take 15 and overdubbing of bongos onto this completed the recording, which was then mixed into mono before the end of this 7.00 pm–3.45 am session. But it wasn't the usual team of George Martin and Geoff Emerick doing the recording and mixing – they were otherwise engaged this night so another EMI Studios balance engineer, Peter Vince, fulfilled both these roles.

Tuesday 28 March

Studio Two, EMI Studios, London

John's lead vocal for 'Good Morning Good Morning' was recorded for the first time in this 7.00 pm–4.45 am session. Take ten was then reduced into take 11 onto which a lead guitar solo (played by Paul) and John and Paul's backing vocal were overdubbed.

Between its last session and this, John had decided that he would like to end his song with animal sound effects, and asked that they be compiled in such a way that each successive animal was capable of frightening or devouring its predecessor. The effects were made during the middle part of

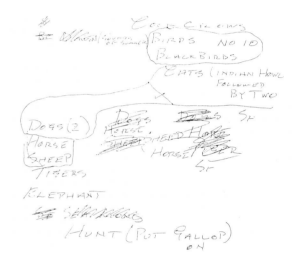

this session by recourse to the Abbey Road collection – with two tapes being particularly useful, 'Volume 35: Animals And Bees' and 'Volume 57: Fox-hunt' – although they were not spun into the four-track tape until the following evening.

Before the end of this session 'Being For The Benefit Of Mr Kite!' received some more overdubs: George, Ringo, Mal Evans and Neil Aspinall all playing harmonica, John an organ and Paul adding a guitar solo.

Wednesday 29 March

Studio Two, EMI Studios, London

With the overdub of the animal effects, 'Good Morning Good Morning' was now complete. The next task in this 7.00 pm–5.45 am session was to add more tracks to 'Being For The Benefit Of Mr Kite!' – the elaborate sound effects compiled on 20 February went onto the four-track along with a swirling organ piece played by George Martin and some harmonica effects played by George and John.

As of yet, there was no Ringo vocal vehicle on *Sgt Pepper*, but John and Paul rectified this with a song written especially for him, 'With A Little Help From My Friends', initially – but only very briefly – titled 'Bad Finger Boogie'. It had been decided that this would be joined to its preceding cut on the album, the title song, so, in each and every

take, recording began where the "Billy Shears" vocal line would go. Ten takes of rhythm track were recorded, this was then reduced into take 11 and Ringo overdubbed his lead vocal onto two of the three newly vacated tracks.

Thursday 30 March

Studio Two, EMI Studios, London

Before this 11.00 pm–7.30 am session – hence its very late start/finish times – the Beatles went to Chelsea Manor [photographic] Studios in Flood Street, Chelsea, to pose for the splendid Michael Cooper shots which would adorn Peter Blake's sleeve design, and also the inside gatefold display, of *Sgt Pepper's Lonely Hearts Club Band*. A trend-setting photo session indeed.

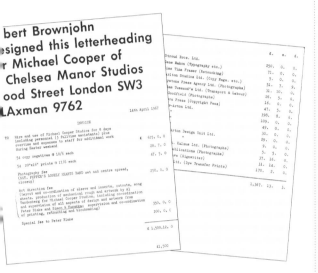

On reaching EMI, the group settled straight back into 'With A Little Help From My Friends', completing the recording by overdubbing guitars, bass, tambourine and backing vocals.

Friday 31 March

Studio Two, EMI Studios, London

'With A Little Help From My Friends' and 'Being For The Benefit Of Mr Kite!' were mixed into mono during this 7.00 pm–3.00 am session – the latter only after overdubbing of another organ part and a glockenspiel.

Saturday 1 April

Studio One, EMI Studios, London

Now more than four months in the making, *Sgt Pepper* was getting very near the end – albeit an enforced one, for Paul was flying out to the USA on 3 April – staying until the 12th – and delivery of the mono master tape had been promised to EMI in between. Except for a special item dropped in on 21 April, this was Paul's last chance to contribute vocals or instruments to the LP.

With *Sgt Pepper's Lonely Hearts Club Band* assuming the concept of a show, Paul came up with the idea of reprising the title song as the penultimate item, just before the rousing end performance which, it had already been decided (since it was certainly impossible to follow), would be 'A Day In The Life'.

'Sgt Pepper's Lonely Hearts Club Band (Reprise)' was an upbeat, abbreviated version of its parent, recorded from start to finish in this one 7.00 pm–6.00 am session on a single four-track tape, without any reduction mixes. There was neither the time nor the necessity for frills. It was completed in nine rhythm track takes, with overdubbing onto the ninth of the shared lead vocals, various bits of percussion and more audience sounds from the Abbey Road effects collection, and was then mixed into mono.

Monday 3 April

Studio One, EMI Studios, London

The completion of 'Within You Without You'. No other Beatle was in the studio for this marathon session which began when, between 7.30 and 10.30 pm, George Martin conducted eight violinists and three cellists through overdubs of a score he had written (and for which he was paid £33) based upon George Harrison's requirements. The violinists were Erich Gruenberg (leader), Alan Loveday, Julien Gaillard, Paul Scherman, Ralph Elman, David Wolfsthal, Jack Rothstein and Jack Greene; the cellists Reginald Kilbey, Allen Ford and Peter Beavan. (Kilbey also stayed behind for an additional half-session in case an additional cello part was required.)

From 10.30 pm to 3.00 am George taped his lead vocal, a sitar part and an occasional dash of acoustic guitar. Then, from 3.00 until the session ended at 6.30 am, the song was mixed into mono – although not yet conclusively.

Tuesday 4 April

Studio Two, EMI Studios, London

Final mono and stereo mixing and editing of 'Within You Without You', from 7.00 pm to 12.45 am. At George Harrison's request, a few seconds of laughter were added to the end of both mixes, courtesy of the Abbey Road effects tape 'Volume 6: Applause And Laughter'.

Thursday 6 April

Studio Two, EMI Studios, London

A 7.00 pm–1.00 am session that produced mono and stereo mixes of 'Good Morning Good Morning' and crossfades (a method of overlapping the end of one song with the start of the next) for the mono LP. There were two crossfades on *Sgt Pepper*: the title song into 'With A Little Help From My Friends' and the reprised title song into 'A Day In The Life'.

A prototype album master tape was compiled this day utilising the Beatles' specification unique for a pop album –

Peter Blake's original rough sketch for the Sgt Pepper sleeve design.

1967

A P R I L

The first, rejected Sgt Pepper master reel, with a different running order on side one, compiled by Malcolm Davies per George Martin's instructions.

it was to have no "rills" (gaps) between songs. Interestingly, at this stage, side one of the album had a running order different to that finally chosen, the last five songs being 'Being For The Benefit Of Mr Kite!', 'Fixing A Hole', 'Lucy In The Sky With Diamonds', 'Getting Better' and 'She's Leaving Home'.

Friday 7 April

Studio Two, EMI Studios, London

The Beatles were mostly absent when the stereo mixes of *Sgt Pepper* were prepared – they considered mono of paramount importance and so were always around for these, but were generally content to leave the stereos to George Martin and Geoff Emerick. Working this day from 7.00 pm to 1.00 am, they produced stereo masters of 'With A Little Help From My Friends' (with its preceding crossfade into the title song), 'Being For The Benefit Of Mr Kite!', 'Fixing A Hole' and 'Lucy In The Sky With Diamonds'.

Though he wasn't aware that he'd won until some days after the event, Geoff Emerick was awarded a Grammy for his engineering work on Sgt Pepper, presented to him by Ringo at EMI in March 1968.

Monday 17 April

Studio Two, EMI Studios, London

Stereo mixing of 'Getting Better', 'She's Leaving Home', 'When I'm Sixty-Four' and 'Lovely Rita', done from 7.00 to 10.30 pm. 'She's Leaving Home' was mixed into stereo without reference to the speeded-up mono, for this ran 3 mins 26 secs while the stereo, noticeably slower, lasts 3 mins 34 secs.

Wednesday 19 April

Studio Two, EMI Studios, London

Although a 6 April mono mix of 'Good Morning Good Morning' had been inserted into the master reel, it did not fit snugly up to the 'Sgt Pepper' reprise. So the former was mixed again in this 7.00 pm–12.30 am session, RM23 solving the problem by means of merging the final cluck of the sound effect hen at the end of 'Good Morning Good

Morning' into the similar first guitar note at the beginning of 'Sgt Pepper's Lonely Hearts Club Band (Reprise)'.

With Paul now back from the USA, the Beatles had a recording session booked for the next night, picking up 'Only A Northern Song' for the first time since 14 February. To remind them of the work done so far, another rough mono mix was made.

Thursday 20 April

Studio Two, EMI Studios, London

'Sgt Pepper's Lonely Hearts Club Band (Reprise)' was mixed into stereo in studio three between 5.00 and 6.15 pm, then the Beatles arrived at 7.00 for a session in studio two which ended at 2.15 am, recording overdubs onto 'Only A Northern Song'.

First they returned to take three from 13 February, wiping some existing material and overdubbing bass, a trumpet and a glockenspiel. Then they advanced to take 11 – itself a reduction mixdown of take three – and added vocals. On 21 April the two versions were mixed together in sync to give one complete recording.

Friday 21 April

Studio Two, EMI Studios, London

How does an artist know when – or how – to apply the final brush stroke to a masterpiece? With 'A Day In The Life' *Sgt Pepper* was already set to end with an orchestral crescendo

followed by a tremendous, crashing piano chord lasting more than 40 seconds. But as no silence had been left between the songs it would be a pity, the Beatles thought, if there was silence *after* the final chord. Why not put something in the record's concentric run-out groove? People with automatic players would hear a quick burst of it before the pick-up arm lifted, people without would find the noise playing on and on *ad infinitum*.

So, after some discussion, the Beatles ran down to the studio floor and recorded twice, onto each track of a two-track tape, funny noises and nonsense gibberish. Geoff Emerick then chopped up the tape, re-assembled it at random and edited it backwards into the mono and (by making a copy) stereo master reels.

And still the Beatles were not finished, for across the spiral of the run-out groove – after the piano chord but before the concentric nonsense – John suggested that they insert into the master tape a high-pitch 15 kilocycle whistle especially for dogs.

With this done, *Sgt Pepper's Lonely Hearts Club Band* was finally finished. Geoff Emerick later totted up the number of hours spent by the Beatles in making the LP and came up with 700, 318 times greater than the time spent making *Please Please Me*, a difference that was clear for all the world to hear when the album was officially unveiled on 1 June.

Also done in this 7.00 pm–1.30 am session was the rather complicated mono mixing of 'Only A Northern Song', for future – but as yet unspecified – release.

Tuesday 25 April

Studio Three, EMI Studios, London

On 7 April, during his trip to the USA, Paul hit upon the idea for a Beatles TV film about a mystery tour on a coach, a sort of British seaside version of Ken Kesey's Merry Pranksters, who were happily driving the highways of California in their multi-coloured school bus, spreading the LSD gospel.

Flying home to England from Los Angeles during the night of 11 April, Paul borrowed a scrap pad from a stewardess and jotted down lyrics for the title song and some ideas for the film itself, drawing a circle to represent 60 minutes and dividing it into sections representing songs and sketches. A few days later he showed his ideas to the other Beatles and,

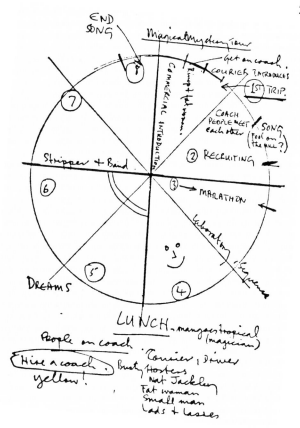

after some discussion, the film was approved: *Magical Mystery Tour*. Though shooting did not begin until 11 September, and the film length ultimately came down from 60 to 52 minutes, the first *MMT* recording session, which began the taping of Paul's title song, took place this night, beginning at 7.00 and ending at 3.45 am.

The initial task of this first session was to prepare a tape loop of coach and traffic noises for dropping into the song whenever needed. 'Volume 36: Traffic Noise Stereo' from the Abbey Road effects collection provided this. Then the Beatles recorded three takes of a basic rhythm track and reduced take three into takes four through eight (the latter marked "best basic").

Wednesday 26 April

Studio Three, EMI Studios, London

Overdubbing of bass, maracas, cowbell, tambourines and backing vocal shouts onto 'Magical Mystery Tour' took up the lion's share of this 7.00 pm–2.00 am session. Another reduction mixdown then took take eight into take nine.

Thursday 27 April

Studio Three, EMI Studios, London

A 7.00 pm–12.45 am session that saw vocal overdubbing onto 'Magical Mystery Tour' followed by rough mono mixes of the recording in order that acetate discs could be cut.

Saturday 29 April

Alexandra Palace, Alexandra Park, London

Some months behind Granada Television (see 18 January) the BBC also decided to document the still-flowering "underground" scene in London, in a BBC2 *Man Alive* film (subtitled 'What Is A Happening?'). It was broadcast on Wednesday 17 May (8.05–8.35 pm) and included much the same cast of characters and formula as Granada's *Scene Special* 'It's So Far Out It's Straight Down'. Paul had appeared in an exclusive interview in Granada's documentary, in *Man Alive* it was John – albeit not in conversation: he was filmed attending the *14-Hour Technicolor Dream* event at Alexandra Palace this night, at which – probably coincidentally – Yoko Ono was one of the performers.

Wednesday 3 May

Studio Three, EMI Studios, London

The overdub of trumpets onto 'Magical Mystery Tour', played by David Mason (his third Beatles session in as many months), Elgar Howarth, Roy Copestake and John Wilbraham. Each musician was paid £30: £15 for the basic session and an additional £15 because it ran over time, starting at 7.00 pm but not finishing until 12.15 am.

Thursday 4 May

Studio Three, EMI Studios, London

Seven mono mixes of 'Magical Mystery Tour', made from 7.00 to 11.15 pm.

Tuesday 9 May

Studio Two, EMI Studios, London

A long (11.00 pm–6.15 am) but decidedly unproductive session in which the Beatles committed to tape a mere 16 minutes of an out-of-tune untitled instrumental jam comprising two guitars (one with vibrato effect), drums and a harmonium.

Thursday 11 May

Olympic Sound Studios, Church Rd, Barnes, London

Another session outside of Abbey Road – Olympic being one of the top independent studios in Britain – and certainly a productive one, for in six hours, 9.00 pm–3.00 am, the Beatles began, completed and mixed into mono 'Baby, You're A Rich Man' with producer George Martin, balance engineer Keith Grant (also the Olympic studio manager) and tape op Eddie Kramer, soon to forge a brilliant artist/engineer-producer working relationship with Jimi Hendrix. This was the first song to be recorded especially for the animated feature-film *Yellow Submarine*. Yet another new project, the movie was to be announced to the press on 7 June 1967, a statement adding that the Beatles would provide at least three new recordings exclusively for the soundtrack. But although it was used in the film, 'Baby, You're A Rich Man' was released first as the B-side of the Beatles' next single and hence never made it onto the soundtrack LP.

The group recorded the basic track in 12 takes, overdubbed onto a reduction of this, and then reduced it again for yet more work. Showing the words "+ Mick Jagger?", one of the session's two tape boxes suggests that the Rolling Stone may also have joined in the recording, perhaps adding backing vocals in the free-for-all choruses near the end of the song. He certainly attended the session.

Friday 12 May

Studio Two, EMI Studios, London

Perhaps it was a hangover from the Olympic session for, once again, this time back at EMI, the Beatles started, finished and mixed into mono another new song in a solitary session, and this time in less than six hours, 7.00 pm–12.30 am. George Martin was absent, Geoff Emerick taking charge of the control room.

The song was 'All Together Now', for the *Yellow Submarine* soundtrack, and it was recorded in nine rhythm track takes with overdubs onto the last of these.

Wednesday 17 May

Studio Two, EMI Studios, London

The Beatles released no more peculiar song than John's quirky 'You Know My Name (Look Up The Number)', nor was any Beatles recording held for so long "in the can", for it was to remain unissued until March 1970. (To be fair, though, the master was not completed until 26 November 1969.)

That master was a composite of five different parts, each recorded separately, and the first was tackled in this 7.00 pm–2.30 am session, again with Geoff Emerick as producer/engineer. Out of 14 takes, the tenth was marked "best", featuring guitars, drums, bass, handclaps, bongos and a little vocal work.

Saturday 20 May

Typical of the new *laissez-faire* environment, Beatles appearances on BBC radio were no longer the highly organised everything-in-triplicate affairs of old. In this day's edition of the Light Programme show *Where It's At*, hosted by Chris Denning, there was a self-contained and pre-produced feature by Kenny Everett (see also 6 December 1966) about *Sgt Pepper's Lonely Hearts Club Band*, including his privately-

recorded interviews with John, Paul and Ringo. (Hence there is no record of where or when they were taped.)

Introduced by Everett in his characteristic delivery – all funny voices, mixed tapes and sound effects put through heavy echo, phasing and compression – the feature was divided into two parts, for transmission at the beginning and end of this 90-minute programme (4.00–5.30 pm). John was heard introducing the album's title track and also 'Lucy In The Sky With Diamonds' and discussing the merits of ADT ("double-flanging we call it"), Ringo talked about the past year and Paul chatted about why the album had taken so long to complete before saying some nice things about Everett and signing off at the end of the show.

Every song bar one from the album was broadcast – the exception being 'A Day In The Life' which had been banned by the BBC the previous day, 19 May, on the grounds that it could encourage a permissive attitude toward drug-taking. (The Beatles and drugs were much in the news again exactly

a month later, on 19 June, when Paul was interviewed by a reporter from ITN about his *Life* magazine revelation that he had taken LSD. An interview lasting 2 mins 14 secs was included in that night's 8.55 pm ITN bulletin, following which there was widespread condemnation.)

Thursday 25 May

De Lane Lea Recording Studios, Kingsway, London

Again in George Martin's absence, the Beatles had their first session in another new London location this evening (7.00 pm–2.30 am): De Lane Lea's studio in the basement of an office building opposite Holborn tube station. Engineer Dave Siddle ran the control room, assisted by tape op Mike Weighell.

The purpose was to record another *Yellow Submarine* number, George's somewhat chaotic 'It's All Too Much' (known at this stage as 'Too Much'). After much limbering up, the Beatles taped four rhythm track takes.

Wednesday 31 May

De Lane Lea Recording Studios, London

Back to Kingsway for a 7.00–12.00 pm session (George Martin still absent; the 26 May team operative again) in which George's lead vocal, John and Paul's backing vocal, additional percussion and handclaps were overdubbed onto a new reduction mixdown of 'It's All Too Much'. (This session was incorrectly reported in the *Recording Sessions* book as 26 May.)

Thursday 1 June

De Lane Lea Recording Studios, London

On this day, perhaps the most celebrated in their career, when *Sgt Pepper's Lonely Hearts Club Band* was issued in their home country, the Beatles returned to the Kingsway studio of the De Lane Lea company, again without the supervision of George Martin, and recorded untitled, unplanned, and amateurish instrumental jams in a 10.30 pm–3.30 am session. The single-minded channelling of their great talent so evident on *Sgt Pepper* did seem, for the moment at least, to have disappeared.

Friday 2 June

De Lane Lea Recording Studios, London

George Martin returned for this 7.00 pm–2.15 am session at Kingsway, ostensibly for 'It's All Too Much' although the Beatles also found time to fill two more tapes with the kind of rambling, untitled instrumental jamming they had played the previous night. The session was booked for 8.00–11.00 pm, with Paul Harvey recruited to play bass clarinet and contra bass clarinet during those three hours and four trumpeters (one of whom, again, was David Mason) set to record from

8.30 to 11.00. In fact, the musicians worked until 2.00 am trying to capture the desired but largely unspecified sounds.

Wednesday 7 June

Studio Two, EMI Studios, London

More crazy 'You Know My Name (Look Up The Number)' recordings, developing into more crazy untitled, unstructured instrumental jams, with numerous takes of an amateurish flute track (played, presumably, by a Beatle), electric guitar, drums, organ and tambourine. George Harrison took home a rough mono mix of take 24, comprising 20 minutes of just such sounds, at the end of this 7.00 pm–2.00 am session.

Thursday 8 June

Studio Two, EMI Studios, London

Numerous takes of the various distinct parts of 'You Know My Name (Look Up The Number)' were recorded during this 7.00 pm–1.00 am session. In addition to the Beatles' own piano, drums, lead guitar, bass and vibraphone tracks, Brian Jones of the Rolling Stones contributed at the invitation of Paul McCartney, playing alto saxophone.

Friday 9 June

Studio Two, EMI Studios, London

'You Know My Name (Look Up The Number)' was first collated into something resembling its final form during this 7.00–11.00 pm session, with the editing and mono mixing of its various parts into one whole. This mix was then copied across to one track of a four-track tape ready for vocal overdubbing. (Not done until 30 April 1969.)

Wednesday 14 June

Olympic Sound Studios, London

Never a group to shirk from a tricky challenge, it was announced on 18 May (news was strictly embargoed until

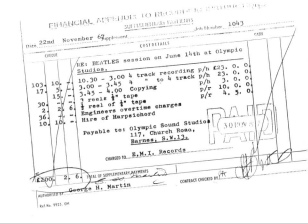

Monday 19 June

Studio Three, EMI Studios, London

A 7.00 pm–1.45 am session in which the Beatles overdubbed lead and backing vocals, drums, piano and banjo onto a newly made copy of the 'All You Need Is Love' take ten.

Note: a studio two session booked for the evening of 20 June did not take place.

Wednesday 21 June

Studio Three, EMI Studios, London

From 4.30–5.00 pm in Room 53, without the Beatles in attendance, 'All You Need Is Love' was mixed into mono. Then, between 7.00 and 11.30 pm, the job was done again, this time with the Beatles on hand. An acetate pressing of this latter mix was given to Derek Burrell-Davis, director of the BBC outside broadcast team for 25 June.

Note: a studio two session booked for the evening of 22 June did not take place.

Friday 23 June

Studio Three, EMI Studios, London

Enter the orchestra for the first time in the 'All You Need Is Love' story, recording a number of takes as overdubs onto a reduction of take ten in this 8.00–11.00 pm session. (See 25 June for the full list of the 13 musicians plus conductor.)

then) that the Beatles had agreed to be one of two British representatives in a television programme set for live worldwide broadcast during the evening (UK time) of Sunday 25 June, the first-ever global satellite link-up. They had agreed to be shown in the studio, recording a song composed especially for the occasion.

John and Paul each wrote one for this purpose (it is not known for sure but Paul's may have been 'Your Mother Should Know' – see 22 August) and the two then decided whose was the more suitable. They opted for John's composition, 'All You Need Is Love', *the* perfect embodiment of the summer of 1967. It also fitted the one and only brief given the Beatles by the BBC: keep it simple so that viewers across the globe will understand. Right from the beginning of take one 'La Marseillaise' (the French national anthem) was a vital part of the song, emphasising the international flavour of the historic broadcast.

The first 33 takes of 'All You Need Is Love' – the basic rhythm track and a little vocal work – were taped between 10.30 pm and 3.00 am this night at Olympic Sound Studios in Barnes, with George Martin producing, Eddie Kramer as balance engineer and the Beatles playing instruments normally associated with session musicians: John on harpsichord (hired from Olympic at a cost of ten guineas), Paul the double-bass and George dabbling on a violin. (Drums were as important as ever so Ringo assumed his familiar role.) Between 3.00 and 3.45 pm the "best" basic track recording, take ten, was given a reduction mixdown, then this was treated to a rough mono mix between 3.45 and 4.00 am.

Saturday 24 June

Studio One, EMI Studios, London

Now just one day from The Big Event, the Beatles and EMI threw open the usually closed Abbey Road studio doors to more than a hundred journalists and photographers for a press-call that took up most of the late-morning. Between 2.00 and 4.00 pm there was a BBC camera rehearsal for the Beatles and their 13 musicians plus conductor, and then between 5.00 and 8.00 pm everyone settled down to tape overdubs onto the 'All You Need Is Love' rhythm track, made especially important by a new decision to swiftly issue 'All You Need Is Love' as a single after the worldwide television broadcast.

Sunday 25 June

Studio One, EMI Studios, London

To quote BBC publicity, *Our World* was "for the first time ever, linking five continents and bringing man face to face with mankind, in places as far apart as Canberra and Cape Kennedy, Moscow and Montreal, Samarkand and Söderfors, Takamatsu and Tunis". Clearly, this was going to be one remarkable Beatles recording session.

The programme was the brainchild of the BBC, which took its idea to the European Broadcasting Union in 1966 and then, under project editor Aubrey Singer (a BBC executive), continued to play the leading role in bringing about this most ambitious, indeed historic, of television programmes. National broadcasting networks from 18 countries agreed to provide material for the live 125-minute (black-and-white) transmission: Australia (ABC), Austria (ORF), Canada (CBC), France (ORTF), Italy (RAI), Japan (NHK), Mexico (TS Mexicana), Spain (TVE), Sweden (SRT), Tunisia (RTT), United Kingdom (BBC), USA (NET), West Germany (ARD) and the state networks in the Soviet Union, Poland, East Germany, Czechoslovakia and Hungary.

Additionally, 13 countries agreed to broadcast the programme without themselves making a contribution: Belgium, Bulgaria, Denmark, Eire, Finland, Luxembourg, Monaco, the Netherlands, Norway, Portugal, Romania, Switzerland and Yugoslavia.

All told, the potential viewing audience was estimated in advance to be around 500 million. Not untypically in those Cold War days, however, all seven of the Iron Curtain countries dropped out *en bloc* only days before transmission, meaning not only that a possible 150 million viewers were lost but that the contributions from the Soviet Union, Poland, East Germany, Czechoslovakia and Hungary were lost too. Quickly, Denmark (DZR) was invited to contribute; indeed the first item in *Our World* came from there, broadcast from a hospital in Århus.

In Britain, *Our World* was screened by BBC1 between 7.55 and 10.00 pm (actually 7.57–9.59), but, of course, transmission times varied greatly around the globe. In Japan and Australia, for example, the programme began on Monday 26 June, and people there watched the Beatles at around breakfast time. Conversely, in some parts of the USA, where NET (National Educational Television) broadcast the show on its network of 113 affiliate stations, it was still Sunday lunchtime.

The programme was divided into a number of sub-sections ('This Moment's World', 'The Hungry World', 'The Crowded World', 'Physical Excellence', 'Artistic Excellence' and 'The World Beyond') and each was linked and narrated in the local language for ease of understanding: Cliff Michelmore was the anchorman for the BBC.

The Beatles appeared twice in *Our World*, the first time for five seconds right at the beginning, when viewers saw a fleeting visual "menu" of the programme's content, and then at 9.36 pm (local time) as the concluding item in 'Artistic Excellence'. Their appearance lasted for 6 mins 11 secs, with Derek Burrell Davis directing and Steve Race reporting direct from EMI Studios.

It was, as one might well imagine, a hectic, unforgettable day for all concerned. The Beatles arrived at EMI at 2.00 pm and spent much of it perfecting 'All You Need Is Love' and rehearsing (3.00–5.00 pm) for the BBC cameras set up in studio one. These were linked with cables by the score to an outside-broadcast van squeezed into the tiny Abbey Road car park. From there the sound and pictures would traverse the globe via the Early Bird "space booster" and Lani Bird and ATS/B satellites.

Take 58 was the all important broadcast version, although George Martin greatly decreased the dreaded possibility of an on-air foul-up by having the Beatles play to their own pre-recorded rhythm track of take ten. The vocals, Paul's bass guitar, the lead guitar solo in the middle-eight section, Ringo's drums and the orchestra were actually live, however. An instantaneous mono mix by George Martin and Geoff Emerick was fed directly to the BBC van and thence to the world.

The televised sequence of events seem a little corny now and studio tapes reveal the considerable rehearsal time which went into this "spontaneous" performance. Using material taped from 5.00 pm up to the actual live sequence, Steve Race introduced the Beatles playing and singing the basic song, the cameras then cut to the control room where George Martin suggested it was time to bring in the orchestra, the musicians filed in, and Mal Evans got into the picture by collecting empty tea cups. This was shown from 9.36 to 9.38. From 9.38 to 9.42 pm it was back to the studio floor for the all-important live sequence: orchestra and Beatles –

all except for Ringo sitting on high stools and surrounded by a large group of friends – playing 'All You Need Is Love' in its entirety.

The broadcast took the form of a party. The orchestral musicians wore formal evening dress while the many friends sitting cross-legged on the studio floor – among them Mick Jagger, Marianne Faithfull, Keith Richard, Keith Moon, Eric Clapton, Pattie Harrison, Jane Asher, Mike McCartney, Graham Nash and his wife, Gary Leeds and Hunter Davies wore more typical, colourful clothes of the day. There were plenty of streamers, balloons and humorous placards too, and much singing along. At the song's end some of the friends danced the conga around the studio.

With George Martin – looking especially dapper in a white suit – busy in the studio control room, the task of conducting the 13-man ad hoc orchestra was given to former Manfred Mann saxophonist and multi-instrumentalist Mike Vickers. This same ensemble had also been employed on 23

and 24 June for recording and rehearsals. There were four violinists – Sidney Sax (leader), Patrick Halling, Eric Bowie and John Ronayne; two cellists – Lionel Ross and Jack Holmes; two tenor saxophonists – Rex Morris and Don Honeywill; two trombonists – Evan Watkins and Harry Spain; one accordionist – Jack Emblow; and two trumpeters – Stanley Woods (also doubling on flügelhorn) and David Mason, playing the same piccolo trumpet he used for 'Penny Lane'.

After the excitement was over, the TV cameras switched off and the guests departed, John re-recorded some of his vocal track, the session ending at 1.00 am.

At the suggestion, ironically, of the Soviet Union, a

16mm print of the full *Our World* broadcast was deposited with the United Nations for posterity, and there it remains still. The programme was also preserved by many of the participating broadcasting companies and corporations, although none is allowed to repeat the Beatles' sequence without prior permission. In Britain, the BBC paid the group extra fees to repeat the core (3 mins 40 secs) of their appearance, singing 'All You Need Is Love'. It was shown again on *Top Of The Pops* on Thursdays 6 July (BBC1, 7.40–8.00 pm) and 3 August (BBC1, 7.30–8.00 pm) and in *Top Of The Pops '67 – Part Two* on Tuesday 26 December (BBC1, 5.10–6.10 pm). Additionally, a 16-second extract was included in *Points Of View* on Wednesday 5 July (BBC1, 7.55–8.00 pm). (On three other occasions, *Top Of The Pops* screened stock – ie, non-Beatles – footage to accompany the record.)

Monday 26 June

Studio Two, EMI Studios, London

A 4.00–8.00 pm session which saw the overdubbing of a snare drum roll by Ringo for the opening of 'All You Need Is Love' followed by final mono mixing. Backed with 'Baby, You're A Rich Man', the song was issued as a single in Britain on Friday 7 July. Here, and elsewhere, it cruised effortlessly to number one. With the *Our World* promotion it could hardly have failed.

The release of 'All You Need Is Love' occurred just five weeks after the issue of the LP *Sgt Pepper* and yet the single did not appear on the album. Nor were any of the album's songs issued as singles. Such a quality and quantity of output was the understandable envy of all of the Beatles' contemporaries.

Saturday 1 July

This day's edition of the BBC Light Programme show *Where It's At* (4.00–5.30 pm), hosted by Chris Denning, included a pre-recorded interview by Kenny Everett with Paul McCartney, in which Paul discussed 'All You Need Is Love'. It was taped at some point during the preceding week, Monday to Friday, after the *Our World* transmission, but more precise date/location information is not known. 'All You Need Is Love' was played twice in the 90-minute show, with B-side 'Baby, You're A Rich Man' played once.

Monday 31 July

Radio London, Curzon Street, London

The Beatles' support for pirate radio didn't waver right to the end – the end, that is, of the golden era. Radio London closed for ever on Saturday 5 August 1967. On 31 July, six days earlier, Ringo popped along to the station's central London office, at 17 Curzon Street, and recorded a brief (11-second) farewell message, on behalf of all the Beatles, with the company's managing director Philip Birch. It was broadcast on London's last day.

Tuesday 22 August

Chappell Recording Studios, Maddox St, London

The first of two consecutive evenings at Chappell, a central London facility owned by the musical instrument and publishing company. They interrupted what would otherwise have been a 72-day interlude between Beatles recording sessions.

Work on both evenings began at 7.00 pm, the Beatles recording Paul's 'Your Mother Should Know', and, although it was later re-made at EMI, it was this Chappell version (with 29 September EMI overdubs) which made it onto the *Magical Mystery Tour* EP. (End of session times were not noted, although for 22 August Chappell invoiced EMI for more than twice as much studio time as it did for the 23rd, suggesting that the first session was quite long and the second quite short.)

Wednesday 23 August

Chappell Recording Studios, London

The Beatles' second and last session at Chappell, recording overdubs onto take nine of 'Your Mother Should Know', a reduction made earlier this evening of the previous night's take eight.

This was the Beatles' last recording session before the death of Brian Epstein, who passed away on 27 August. Although he had been an increasingly infrequent visitor to the group's sessions, Epstein happened to attend this second night at Chappell.

On Friday 25 August the Beatles travelled to Bangor, north Wales, to spend the weekend studying Transcendental Meditation under Maharishi Mahesh Yogi, whom they had met only the previous evening, 24 August, in London. Proof that the Bangor visit was hurriedly arranged is clear from the fact that the Beatles had booked a London recording session for 7.00 pm on 25 August, at De Lane Lea. EMI picked up the £45 cancellation charge.

Tuesday 5 September

Studio One, EMI Studios, London

The Beatles met up at Paul's house on Friday 1 September, four days after the death of Brian Epstein, and decided many things, one being to press on with *Magical Mystery Tour*, temporarily postponing a planned visit to India to further study Transcendental Meditation. Recording sessions for MMT began in earnest on 5 September; filming started on the 11th.

With two songs – 'Magical Mystery Tour' and 'Your Mother Should Know' – already earmarked for the project, the Beatles now set about completing the remaining numbers for the soundtrack and any associated record releases. Recording of the first new song, John's glorious 'I Am The Walrus', began in this 7.00 pm–1.00 am session, the group taping 16 takes of the rhythm track and then overseeing a rough mono mix for acetate-cutting purposes. The many

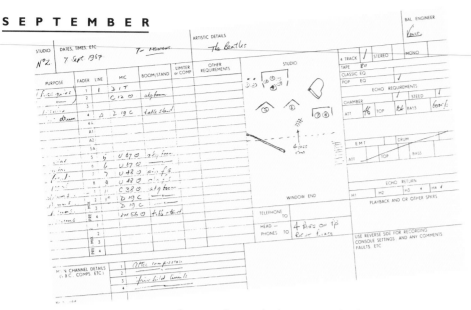

other ingredients which were to make this one of the Beatles' most remarkable recordings were added in later overdubs.

Wednesday 6 September

Studio Two, EMI Studios, London

A reduction mixdown of 'I Am The Walrus', take 16 into 17, was the first task of this 7.00 pm–3.00 am session. Paul then overdubbed bass, Ringo drums and John his memorable lead vocal before the recording was mixed into mono in order that more acetate discs be cut.

If 'I Am The Walrus' was John's classic contribution to *Magical Mystery Tour*, Paul's was 'The Fool On The Hill'. Recording proper of this song would not begin until 25 September but during this evening he taped a one-man demo version, sitting alone at the piano.

The Beatles then set about recording the first rhythm track take of George's 'Blue Jay Way', which would be their sole focus the following evening.

Thursday 7 September

Studio Two, EMI Studios, London

A 7.00 pm–3.15 am session devoted entirely to 'Blue Jay Way', with overdubbing of vocals onto take two (a reduction of take one), a reduction of take two into take three and more vocals added to this.

Friday 8 September

Studio Three, EMI Studios, London

Right: Gadding about the West Country on board the magic bus, John and George with the youngest passenger, Little Nicola.

'Flying' – which went under the working title 'Aerial Tour Instrumental' until into November – was more than just the Beatles' first instrumental released by EMI, it was also the first song to be composed jointly by all four members of the group: Harrison-Lennon-McCartney-Starkey as the record label alphabetically detailed them.

But the version on record was quite different from these early takes. The six recorded during the early part of this 7.00 pm–2.45 am session included, for example, a jazzy saxophone recording at the end of the song, seemingly copied straight from an unidentifiable modern jazz record. Take six saw the introduction of three separate organs, recorded and then played backwards on separate tracks, and this take was then reduced into takes seven and eight (the latter marked "best") onto which John added a mellotron track and the four Beatles overdubbed a scat chant. Four rough mono mixes concluded the session.

Mon 11 – Fri 15 September

various locations in Hampshire, Devonshire, Cornwall and Somerset

The first of a two-week core shooting period for *Magical Mystery Tour*, the Beatles boarding their coach this Monday morning and heading for five days of location work in the West Country.

Pop package tours, of the kind played by the Beatles in the spring of 1963, usually began in Allsop Place, adjacent to Baker Street underground station in central London, where all of the artists would board a coach, piling equipment into the hold. Paul decided that *MMT* should start from the same place – especially as his St John's Wood house was nearby – and arrived, along with the other chosen coach passengers (relations, friends, friends' relations, relations' friends, fan club secretaries, etc), in time for a 10.45 am departure. But

the coach was nowhere to be seen; still being hastily decorated in its technicolour *Magical Mystery Tour* livery, it eventually arrived two hours late, evidence right from the beginning of the slapdash nature of the project.

As Neil Aspinall handed each of the 33 non-crew passengers a £5 note to cover meal expenditure for the week, the coach headed out of London on the principal south-west route, the A30 (there were no motorways in this part of England in 1967), making its first stop in Virginia Water, Surrey, where John, George and Ringo boarded. As the coach set off again, the three new passengers piled into the back of the vehicle and changed into the clothes they wished to wear for the filming, and would have to wear throughout the next five-days.

Shooting then began straight away, ad lib scenes on the coach and inside the Pied Piper restaurant in Winchester Road, Basingstoke, Hampshire, where they stopped for lunch, and it wasn't until late in the evening that the MMT crusade arrived at its first stop for the night, the three-star Royal Hotel in The Den, Teignmouth, Devon, 183 miles from London. Four hundred local teenagers, privy to the supposedly secret news of the Beatles' booking – arranged only the previous Friday and confirmed during this Monday morning – were waiting in the rain to greet the group as they pulled up in a car (they'd swapped vehicles outside of town) and dashed into the hotel.

Paul later held an impromptu press conference to vaguely announce the Beatles' (equally vague) shooting plans, and then slipped away to join Neil Aspinall in sorting out a typically unexpected but important MMT problem: the room arrangements for the huge numbers of cast and crew, so-and-so not wishing to share with so-and-so, and so on. Following this, he and John got together with technical director Peter

Theobalds to roughly shape the next day's work, something they did each evening while in the West Country.

No filming was done here in Teignmouth and after breakfast on **Tuesday 12 September** everyone boarded the coach and set off again, heading for the picturesque Dartmoor village of Widecombe in the Moor. Its annual fair was being held and the Beatles decided to film there, but in an attempt to beat considerable traffic queues on the most direct roads, MMT coach driver Alf Manders took an alternative route and the coach became stuck attempting to negotiate a narrow bridge that occurred on a sharp bend. As traffic snarled up behind them, tempers inside were equally as snarly. Amid shouting and film-shooting (none of the footage was used), the coach had to reverse for half a mile before turning around, the Beatles abandoning plans to go to the fair, and disappointing (though they did not know so) many local fans who had heard rumours about their visit and had turned up in Widecombe to see them.

Instead, the coach rejoined a trunk road, the A38, and headed 24 miles south-west for Plymouth, the party descending on the Grand Hotel for lunch, situated on the famous Hoe – where, in 1588, Sir Francis Drake had played bowls when receiving news of the Spanish armada. Afterwards, in an attempt to appease a posse of London press reporters and photographers, which had been following the MMT coach in a 20-car convoy since leaving Allsop Place, the Beatles posed for photographs sitting on the Hoe. John and Paul also gave an interview here to BBC TV reporter Hugh Scully for inclusion in the next evening's (13 September, 5.55–6.15 pm) edition of the BBC1 local news-magazine programme *Spotlight South West*. It ran for four minutes as the first item.

Back onto the A38, the coach made three more stops before reaching the Cornish resort of Newquay, over on the opposite (Atlantic) coast. The first was in Liskeard (no filming done here, it would seem) and then it made two separate stops in the Cornish moor town of Bodmin, famous as the setting for Daphne Du Maurier novels. Filming took place here in two locations – the first was outside West End Dairy in Higher Bore Street where owner Mr D G Medland sold ice-creams, fruit and lollipops to the Beatles and other coach passengers. (This sequence was deleted during editing.) The second location was in Paull Road, where Jolly Jimmy Johnson The Courier (Derek Royle) boarded the coach, rubbed his hands with glee and welcomed everybody to the Magical Mystery Tour (this part seen at the beginning of the film after Ringo and his Aunt Jessie (Jessie Robbins) had climbed on board – see 29 October).

Then it was on to Newquay and the three-star Atlantic Hotel in Dane Road. The Beatles intended to stop here for just one night but after considerable private discussion, in which they weighed up the merits of either moving on to a new hotel each day or staying put in one location and using it as a base, they opted for the latter alternative and decided to remain at the Atlantic for three nights, Tuesday to Thursday, staying in four holiday flats.

Much filming was done on **Wednesday 13 September**, beginning in the late-morning when the Beatles and some of the actors (but not the full complement of passengers) set out in the coach, north along the B3276, to nearby Watergate Bay. Here, after John, Paul, George and Ringo had each been filmed looking through a telescope (another deleted scene), Aunt Jessie was filmed enjoying a romantic sojourn with Mr Buster Bloodvessel (Ivor Cutler) on Tregurrian Beach, a strangely charming sequence which, for some equally strange reason, the BBC decided was unsuitable for its viewers and cut from both its initial screenings of *Magical Mystery Tour* (although when the BBC showed the film again in 1979, the sequence was included).

The Beatles and cameramen then returned to the Atlantic Hotel and split into two groups for the afternoon's work, John remaining at the hotel and also filming in Holywell (just south of Newquay), George watching the hotel shooting but then staying put (not going on to Holywell) and Paul and Ringo taking the coach and most of the passengers back along the road to Watergate Bay, stopping this time to film in Porth.

John took charge of directing a sequence that he had conceived: Happy Nat The Rubber Man (veteran comic actor Nat Jackley) chasing young women, first around the Atlantic Hotel's outdoor swimming pool – where, despite the cold weather, the women had to wear bikinis – and then up on the cliffs at Holywell. (For all of the effort, however, the sequence wasn't included in the finished print.)

Paul and Ringo, meanwhile, headed for Porth, filming en route a humorous ad lib sequence in which Ringo and his Aunt Jessie had a storming argument. Once at Porth, in the late afternoon, Paul filmed on the beach with Little George The Photographer (George Claydon), cycling together on a tandem, trudging along the sand and gesturing out to sea.

George remained at the Atlantic for the afternoon, recording a long radio interview with Miranda Ward for inclusion in a new programme, *Scene And Heard*, broadcast on the BBC's equally new national pop network, Radio 1. In fact, part one of the interview, lasting 6 mins 22 secs, went into the series' premiere edition, transmitted on the opening day of the station, Saturday 30 September, between 6.32 and 7.29 pm. (It was on this date that the BBC revolutionised its domestic radio output, dissolving the Light Programme into two networks, Radio 1, for pop, and Radio 2, for easy listen-

ing, and changing the classical Third Programme into Radio 3 and the spoken-word Home Service into Radio 4.) The second-half of Ward's interview with George, a further 6 mins 50 secs, was broadcast in the following week's programme, Saturday 7 October, again 6.32 to 7.29 pm.

Ward ended up staying in Newquay with the Beatles until their Friday departure and at some point on **Thursday 14 September** interviewed Ringo for another edition of *Scene And Heard*, 3 mins 53 secs of which was broadcast by Radio 1 on Saturday 14 October (6.32–7.29 pm) and a 19-second extract going into the programme on Saturday 23 December (same times).

During the Thursday morning the Beatles and their coach-load of passengers set off looking for a suitably quiet and private field in which to film, although when they did find one (not far from Newquay), and set up the cameras, scores of onlookers were soon crowding around and police had to deal with an ensuing traffic jam. Two sequences were shot here: one showing George, wearing an outsize blue jacket, sitting meditating in the cornfield (not included in the finished film), the other showing the Beatles and all of

the passengers crowding into a tiny tent, which – because the Mystery Tour was Magical, and thanks to editing trickery – led into a small theatre in which the 'Blue Jay Way' sequence (shot in West Malling during the second week) was shown.

When the field filming was completed cast and crew returned to the Atlantic Hotel for a 4.00 pm late lunch, everybody sitting at a huge T-shaped table in the otherwise-closed dining room, with music provided by the "strict tempo" band which played the hotel's ballroom every evening. The lunch was filmed for *Magical Mystery Tour* but, again, it didn't appear in the finished print.

During this evening, Paul, Ringo, Neil Aspinall and others (including the BBC's Miranda Ward) went to a pub in the nearby coastal town of Perranporth where they met up with Spencer Davis (leader of the Spencer Davis Group) and his family, who were on holiday there. Sadly, this was one time the cameras were idle, for Paul happily led a sing-song around the pub piano until past 2.00 am, performing, as Miranda Ward later noted, "every pub standard bar 'Yellow Submarine', which he refused to play". (On Wednesday evening Davis had met up with the Beatles at the Atlantic Hotel in Newquay.)

Following breakfast on **Friday 15 September**, and the filming of a brief scene in front of the coach and the hotel – in which the Beatles, actors, actresses, coach passengers and assorted gatecrashers cheered and waved at the camera – the entourage left Newquay and headed back to London. Again they shot en route: the first filming took place at lunchtime (in yet another sequence left out of the finished production) when everyone crowded into a tiny fish and chip shop in Roman Road, Taunton, Somerset, owned by James and Amy Smedley. The Beatles were filmed first from behind the counter, queueing up to be served, and then in the main part of the shop, tucking into their takeaway lunch.

Other filming during the homebound trip took place in a country pub somewhere (a Hall & Woodhouse hostelry, location not known, footage unused) and on board the coach, accordionist Shirley Evans (see also 12 October) entertaining the beer-swilling travellers with a selection of singalong numbers like 'Toot Toot Tootsie', 'When Irish Eyes Are Smiling', 'When The Red, Red Robin Comes Bob, Bob, Bobbin' Along' and the 'Can Can' dance from Offenbach's *Orpheus In The Underworld*.

On Friday evening, four days after joining it, John, George and Ringo got off the coach in Virginia Water, Paul remaining on board with the rest of the passengers until it reached Allsop Place in central London.

Saturday 16 September

Studio Three, EMI Studios, London

A re-make of 'Your Mother Should Know', with 11 more takes numbered 20–30, began this 7.00 pm–3.45 am session, the Beatles creating a more forceful sound than the earlier Chappell version. The recording was then left for Paul to ruminate further on what exactly should be done with it.

A rough mono mix of 'Blue Jay Way' was made next and then tape copies of this and also 'I Am The Walrus' were

THE BEATLES SAMPLE OUR FISH AND CHIPS

MRS. AMY SMEDLEY, who, with her husband, James, runs a fish and chip shop in Roman Road, Taunton, served four V.I.C.s (Very Important Customers) last Friday.

For that was the day that the Beatles popped in for a meal. And it all came about as a result of a chat Mrs. Smedley had with the famous four, in Newquay. Mrs. Smedley was on holiday there when she took part as an extra in the television film the Beatles are making.

In the course of chatting with them, she mentioned that she and her husband had a fish and chip shop in Taunton. On Friday morning, she had a telephone call to say that the Beatles would be arriving later.

Film shots

"They got here at lunch time and shot some film outside our shop," said Mrs. Smedley. "Then all four of them came inside to have some fish and chips, which they ate in the shop.

"It was marvellous. The Beatles are really very nice people. They chated away to my husband and I like old friends," she added.

"I still can't really believe that they actually ate my fish and chips."

John taking his turn at directing the Peggy Spencer formation dancers in the huge hangar at West Malling, 24 September 1967.

taken away by a member of the *Magical Mystery Tour* film production team for the Beatles to mime to during shooting of these sequences. (For the finished film print, the mono disc mixes were used.)

Monday 18 September

Raymond Revuebar, Walkers' Court, London

Filming of *Magical Mystery Tour* switched to this Soho striptease club for one day, shooting the sequence in which the Beatles and the other male coach passengers watch Jan Carson strip topless to the accompaniment of the then-unknown Bonzo Dog Doo-Dah Band performing 'Death Cab For Cutie'.

The word CENSORED covered Carson's bare breasts in the finished film, placed there during the editing process by the Beatles in the certain knowledge that, otherwise, the entire scene would be cut by the BBC and other broadcasting organisations.

Tuesday 19 – Sunday 24 September

West Malling Air Station, West Malling, Maidstone, Kent
and High Street, West Malling, Maidstone, Kent

Unable to book a stage at Shepperton or any of the other London-area film studios at such short notice, NEMS Enterprises hired West Malling Air Station for a week to complete (or so it was thought) *Magical Mystery Tour*. Situated 28 miles south-east of London, West Malling was used in World War II as a base for the United States Army Air Force, and the airfield is architecturally distinguished by 32 enormous concrete walls, built to absorb the impact from enemy bombs and so preserve the US planes for their own raids. The Beatles filmed both interior and exterior footage at West Malling, working there for six days from 9.00 am each day, and staying overnight in a nearby hotel.

With one exception, the interior scenes were shot in an enormous empty hangar, these being the "Magicians' Laboratory" sequence, in which the four Beatles and Mal Evans cast wonderful magical spells on the destiny and direction of the coach; "Aunt Jessie's Dream" (see also 12 October) in which John – whose idea the scene was – shovelled mountains of spaghetti onto Jessie's dining table while Buster Bloodvessel offered her endless handkerchiefs from his pocket; and George's 'Blue Jay Way' sequence, in which he sat cross-legged on the floor amid swirling fog, playing a "keyboard" roughly chalked in front of him.

On the last day, Sunday 24 September, a huge ballroom set was erected in the hangar for the film's 'Your Mother Should Know' finale. After considerable rehearsals, the Beatles were filmed wearing all-white suits and shoes, sweeping majestically down a glittery staircase while all around them twirled 160 members of Peggy Spencer's formation-dancing team, the rest of the cast and even 24 cadets from the West Malling-based Women's Royal Air Force. Also shot this day was the sequence in which a large crowd (including Mal Evans but not the Beatles) cheered and waved, and the film's very last sequence, in which everyone (including the Beatles in their magicians costumes) shuffled forward towards and past the camera.

The one interior sequence at West Malling which wasn't shot in the hangar was filmed inside one of the adjacent huts, dressed up as an army recruiting office. With Paul appearing as Major McCartney, it starred Victor Spinetti (veteran of *A Hard Day's Night* and *Help!*; see also 28 November) as a bombastic Recruiting Sergeant, aurally bombarding Ringo, Aunt Jessie and other coach passengers with his army-doubletalk. This sequence ended up on the airfield outside with (for some unknown reason) the Sergeant barking orders to a papier-mâché cow.

Other exterior scenes shot at West Malling during this week were the "Marathon", filmed on the main runway and perimeter road; a sequence in which a group of people (including Neil Aspinall and Mal Evans but not the Beatles) had their picture taken by Little George The Photographer; a "Tug of War" involving 12 children and assorted blindfolded vicars; an unused sequence (shot on the 24th) in

which the inimitable Ivor Cutler performed a vocal number at a white organ, supported by the four Beatles and the coach passengers; and, most memorably of all, the terrific 'I Am The Walrus' sequence, in which the Beatles mimed to the song at two airfield locations, making superb visual use of the concrete anti-blast walls, with four hand-holding "policemen" and then later the Beatles themselves swaying on the narrow ledge atop one particular wall.

One additional scene – for the very beginning of the film – was shot in West Malling during this week, but in the local High Street, not at the Air Station. On Friday 22 September (one of two consecutive days in which George – confined to his bed with flu – did not participate), Ringo was filmed entering a shop and buying (from John) tickets for the Mystery Tour. The shop was Town Newsagency, at 90 High Street in the town centre.

Monday 25 September

Norman's Film Productions, Old Compton St, London and **Studio Two, EMI Studios, London**

Reckoning on a week for the editing of *Magical Mystery Tour*, the Beatles booked time at this Soho cutting-room and engaged Roy Benson to do the job, supervised at all times by one, two, three or occasionally all four of the group, Paul the only one who was ever-present. Allegedly, while Paul would insist that a certain scene be cut a certain way, John would then order a re-cut the way that he preferred it, and so on until, what with one thing and another, the editing took 11 weeks, typically from around 10.00 am to 6.00 pm each day (following which the Beatles would occasionally go on to EMI for a recording session). During these 11 weeks approximately ten hours of film were cut down to 52 minutes, losing along the way entire scenes and such unusual ideas as an unrelated film insert showing Traffic performing contemporary hit single 'Here We Go Round The Mulberry Bush'.

Some recording was done here in Old Compton Street too, John dubbing an occasional commentary narrative over the pictures. (Exact taping date(s) not known, but no earlier than the beginning of November.)

The Beatles worked this night at EMI, a 7.00 pm–3.00 am session which resulted in the first proper recording of 'The Fool On The Hill', following Paul's 6 September demo. Three takes of the basic rhythm track were taped, including harmonicas played by John and George; overdubs of a recorder (played by Paul), drums and Paul's lead vocal were then added onto take four (a reduction mixdown of take three). A rough mono mix ended the session.

In an effort to get through the *MMT* recordings quickly, the Beatles booked studio time Monday through Friday this week, afternoon and evening sessions both, and on the final three days simultaneously reserved not one but two studios. As it happened, they under-used this allotted time – but, then again, they didn't have to worry about footing the bill.

Tuesday 26 September

Studio Two, EMI Studios, London

A re-make of 'The Fool On The Hill', with a basic track recording numbered take five, onto which a host of instruments were overdubbed. This was then reduced into take six with vocals and bass superimposed.

Producer George Martin was absent for this 7.00 pm–4.15 am session, the Beatles' new balance engineer Ken Scott having to fulfil double duties.

Wednesday 27 September

Studios One/Three, EMI Studios, London

Two separate overdubs for 'I Am The Walrus': a 2.30–5.30 pm orchestral session in studio one and a 7.00 pm–3.30 am vocal session in studio three, during which John's song became one of the Beatles' most fascinating numbers.

The orchestral overdub went onto simultaneous reduction mixdowns of take 17, with 16 musicians playing George Martin's marvellous score – *violins*: Sidney Sax (leader), Jack Rothstein, Ralph Elman, Andrew McGee, Jack Greene, Louis Stevens, John Jezzard, Jack Richards; *cellos*: Lionel Ross, Eldon Fox, Bram Martin, Terry Weil; *clarinet*: Gordon Lewin; *horns*: Neil Sanders, Tony Tunstall, Mo (Morris) Miller.

Moving across to studio three, the Beatles entertained 16 members of the Mike Sammes Singers from 7.00 until around 10.00 pm, these highly experienced MOR vocalists, eight male and eight female, being asked to sing things like "Ho-ho-ho, hee-hee-hee, ha-ha-ha", "Oompah, oompah, stick it up your jumper!", "Got one, got one, everybody's got one" and make a series of shrill whooping noises, all as overdubs onto take 25 (a reduction of take 20, the "best" with the orchestra). The eight female singers were Peggie Allen, Wendy Horan, Pat Whitmore, Jill Utting, June Day, Sylvia King, Irene King and G Mallen, the eight males were Fred Lucas, Mike Redway, John O' Neill, F Dachtler, Allan Grant, D Griffiths, J Smith and J Fraser. (This Mike Sammes overdub was originally booked for 15 September, but no session took place that day.)

Before the 3.30 am end of session Paul added another vocal onto 'The Fool On The Hill' and the recording was then mixed again into mono.

Thursday 28 September

Studio Two, EMI Studios, London

This hectic day began with a 4.00–5.30 pm session in studio two in which, first, tape copies of 'Magical Mystery Tour' and 'Flying' were made for reference by the film company (as previously stated, the later "best" mixes were used in the final print of the film) and then, more vitally, the four-track tape of 'I Am The Walrus' was completed when a reduction mixdown of take 25 was overdubbed back onto the take from which it had been borne, take 17. Working from 7.00 pm to 3.00 am, this was mixed into mono, edited and marked "best", albeit for only 24 hours.

'Flying' – still titled 'Aerial Tour Instrumental' – was next on the evening's agenda, with overdubs onto take eight and the creation by John and Ringo of various effects and backwards tapes, also overdubbed onto the same recording. This was then mixed roughly into mono and edited before the session ended.

Friday 29 September

Studio One, Wembley Studios, Wembley
and Studio Two, EMI Studios, London

The Beatles were no longer the "happy-go-lucky pop stars" they had been long perceived by the public. With their embracement of drugs and now Transcendental Meditation, there was ample scope for one or more of the group to feature not just in teenage pop shows but in intelligent discussion programmes.

Between 10.30 and 11.15 this evening John and George were seen doing just this, chatting with David Frost about TM for the entire second-half of this, the third edition in his new thrice-weekly late-night series *The Frost Programme*, made and networked by Rediffusion and taped before an audience in studio one between 6.00 and 7.00 pm at the company's Wembley facility, from where the Beatles had previously appeared on such programmes as the children's series *Tuesday Rendezvous* in what now seemed like a distant, previous era. (The first section of this 45-minute programme, up to the commercial break, focused on the same subject: an interview with Maharishi Mahesh Yogi. This was taped by Frost earlier in the day, at London Airport, before the Maharishi flew out of the country.)

Immediately after the Rediffusion taping, John (and maybe George too) drove south, to Abbey Road, for a long night's work at EMI Studios behind the mixing desk, arriving at around 7.30 pm.

In fact, no other Beatles mix session was as unusual or inventive as this one – but then, it wasn't every occasion in which John took so active a role. Although 17 mono mixes of 'I Am The Walrus' were prepared during the session, only two were complete, the master being an edit of these. The first part, up to the lyric "Sitting in an English garden", was from RM10. The other half, from RM22, was made with a live feed from a radio, making that unique night-time sound of being flicked through foreign stations.

IN THE THIRD PROGRAMME AT 7.30

THE TRAGEDY OF KING LEAR

by

William Shakespeare

John Gielgud

AS KING LEAR

WITH

Virginia McKenna as Cordelia
Barbara Jefford as Goneril
Timothy Bateson as the Fool
Derek Godfrey as Edmund
Michael Goodliffe as Albany
Howard Marion-Crawford as Kent
Barbara Bolton as Regan
Mark Digham as Gloucester
Philip Guard as Edgar
Roger Delgado cs Cornwall

Osw. Let go, slave, or thou diest!
Edg. Good gentleman, go your gait, and let poor volk pass. And chud ha' been zwaggered out of my life, 'twould not ha' been zo long as 'tis by a vortnight. Nay, come not near the old man; keep out, che vor ye, or ise try whether your costard or my bat be the harder: chill be plain with you.
Osw. Out, dunghill!
Edg. Chill pick your teeth, zir: come; no matter vor your foins.
 [*They fight, and* EDGAR *knocks him down.*
Osw. Slave, thou hast slain me:—villain, take my purse.
If ever thou wilt thrive, bury my body; [me
And give the letters which thou find'st about
To Edmund Earl of Gloster; seek him out
Upon the British party:—O, untimely death!
 [*Dies.*
Edg. I know thee well: a serviceable villain;
As duteous to the vices of thy mistress
As badness would desire.
Glo.　　　　 What, is he dead?
Edg. Sit you down, father; rest you.—
Let's see these pockets: the letters that he speaks of 　　　　　 [sorry
May be my friends.—He's dead; I am only
He had no other death's-man.—Let us see:—
Leave, gentle wax; and, manners, blame us

At around 10.30 pm, the tuning dial came to rest on the BBC Third Programme during a 190-minute production (recorded on 24 August) of Shakespeare's *The Tragedy Of King Lear*, starring John Gielgud. Parts of Act IV, Scene VI can be clearly heard on the record, commencing with the lines, spoken by Gloucester and Edgar respectively, "Now, good sir, what are you?" and "A most poor man, made tame by fortune's blows". The Shakespeare broadcast is particularly evident at the end of the mix, from Oswald's "take my purse" through to Edgar's "Sit you down, father; rest you." It is not known whether the actors – Mark Dignam (Gloucester), Philip Guard (Edgar) and John Bryning (Oswald) – ever discovered their appearance on a multi-million-selling Beatles record.

Paul's 'Your Mother Should Know' had now been around for more than two months in an unfinished state, so he and John got together this night to complete it. Ignoring the remake attempted on 16 September, they delved back to take nine from 22–23 August, gave it three reduction mixdowns and then overdubbed organ (John) and bass (Paul). In this brisk manner the song was finished, and it was treated to its first mono mix before the session ended at 5.00 am.

Sunday 1 October

West Malling Air Station, West Malling, Maidstone

A one-day return to West Malling to film miscellaneous *Magical Mystery Tour* pick-up shots with the coach.

Monday 2 October

Studio Two, EMI Studios, London

A 10.00 pm–2.30 am session, the first task of which – successfully achieved – was to perfect a mono mix of 'Your Mother Should Know'. They then set about a new song, Paul's 'Hello, Goodbye' (working title 'Hello Hello') which was not to be a part of the forthcoming *Magical Mystery Tour* package but their next single, typically released concurrent with a major work while remaining separate. Fourteen takes of the basic rhythm track were recorded this evening, with two reduction mixdowns taking 14 into 15 and 16 (the latter marked "best").

Note: a 7.00 to 12.00 pm recording session booked for 4 October was cancelled.

Wednesday 4 October

Studio One, Wembley Studios, Wembley

Public interest in the previous Friday's appearance was such that, to continue the conversation, John and George made a return visit to Rediffusion this evening to appear in what was the following edition of *The Frost Programme* (it was shown on Wednesdays, Thursdays and Fridays each week).

Once again, the entire 45-minute show was devoted to the subject of Transcendental Meditation, John and George answering questions from David Frost, from viewers (by

letter) and from the studio audience, and participating in a lively discussion with a group of prominent pro- and anti-meditation intellectuals (writer John Mortimer, for one, who was anti) sitting in the front row.

As on the previous occasion, the show was taped between 6.00 and 7.00 pm and screened from 10.30 to 11.15 this same evening.

Friday 6 October

Studio Two, EMI Studios, London

A 7.00 pm–2.00 am cello and tambourine overdub onto take three of 'Blue Jay Way', completing the recording. (The identity of the cellist was not documented, but he/she was paid £27.)

Thursday 12 October

De Lane Lea Recording Studios, London
and Studio Three, EMI Studios, London

Two distinct sessions. From 2.30 to 4.30 pm, at the studio where it had been recorded – De Lane Lea, in Holborn – 'It's All Too Much' was mixed into mono.

Then, from 6.30 pm to 2.00 am, back at EMI (although originally booked for Olympic Sound Studios in Barnes), John assumed the role of producer for the first time, supervising a session for *Magical Mystery Tour*. The first part saw 'Blue Jay Way' mixed into mono and edited. Then the fun

Shirley Evans and her wild accordion, with producer John Lennon.

began, with accordionist Shirley Evans and her musical partner/percussionist Reg Wale recording a Lennon-McCartney instrumental composition, 'Shirley's Wild Accordion', arranged by Mike Leander (the second time in seven months that he had been employed by the Beatles). Fifteen takes were taped, with Ringo and Paul contributing a little musical assistance. The tenth was marked "best" so this was then overdubbed with more accordion tracks courtesy of Shirley Evans and, finally, it was mixed into mono.

The idea was to include 'Shirley's Wild Accordion' as incidental music in the soundtrack of the film – it wasn't used, however, even though Shirley Evans appears in *MMT*, playing accordion in the coach singalong sequence near to the end (see 15 September). *Magical Mystery Tour* did include another piece of incidental music though: the quirky 'Jessie's Dream', copyrighted to McCartney-Starkey-Harrison-Lennon, performed by one or more of the Beatles and heard in the sequence where John Lennon, the greasy restaurant waiter, serves Aunt Jessie with spadefuls of spaghetti. This item was recorded privately, not at EMI or under George Martin's supervision, date/place unknown.

Thursday 19 October

Studio One, EMI Studios, London

Overdubbing of two guitar parts, Paul's vocal and John and George's backing vocal onto take 16 of 'Hello, Goodbye', then reduced into take 17 before the end of this 7.00 pm–3.30 am session.

Friday 20 October

Studio Three, EMI Studios, London

The Beatles did not play in this 7.00 pm–3.45 am session, though all four attended. Between 8.00 and 11.00 pm three flautists – brothers Christopher and Richard Taylor, and Jack Ellory – added the final touches to 'The Fool On The Hill'. Then from 11.00 until 2.30 am Ken Essex and Leo Birnbaum overdubbed viola onto 'Hello, Goodbye', George Martin having instantaneously scored string ideas which came to Paul while doodling at a piano.

Wednesday 25 October

Studio Two, EMI Studios, London

A 7.00 pm–3.00 am session in which 'The Fool On The Hill', now complete, was mixed into mono and edited, and then Paul overdubbed bass onto simultaneous reduction mixdowns of 'Hello, Goodbye', the "best" being take 21.

Sunday 29 October

Acanthus Rd/Lavender Hill, London

Four weeks spent editing *Magical Mystery Tour* showed that the film required some additional scenes to help weave the "plot" together. So three sequences were filmed over the next six days, completing the shooting.

The first was done early this Sunday morning in the Battersea district of south London, with Ringo and Aunt Jessie argumentatively puffing their way up Acanthus Road and then turning right into Lavender Hill where they are greeted by Jolly Jimmy Johnson The Courier and Miss Wendy Winters The Hostess (Mandy Weet) and then board the coach. (The film then cut to Jolly Jimmy's scene shot on 12 September.)

Monday 30 and Tuesday 31 October

Nice, France

With recording of the song completed on 20 October it was obvious that 'The Fool On The Hill' would be an important part of *Magical Mystery Tour*, and yet, to date, no filming had been done to accompany the number.

To rectify the situation, Paul (without the other Beatles) flew to France on 30 October with film cameraman Aubrey Dewar to shoot a number of random scenes – shown in *MMT* in a daydream sequence – at various locations around Nice, most notably on a mountainous rocky outcrop. They returned to England on Wednesday 1 November.

Wednesday 1 November

Studio Three, EMI Studios, London

Between 10.00 am and 1.00 pm, in Room 53, 'All You Need Is Love' and 'Lucy In The Sky With Diamonds' were mixed again into mono for the soundtrack of the feature-film *Yellow Submarine*. Work on this project then carried over to a 2.30–6.00 pm session in studio three, with the assembling of applause sound effects for the film (utilising the Abbey Road collection), before switching to more immediate Beatles matters: more reduction mixdowns of 'Hello, Goodbye' and stereo mixes of 'The Fool On The Hill'.

Thursday 2 November

Studio Three, EMI Studios, London

A 2.30–6.00 pm session for a final overdub onto 'Hello, Goodbye': a second bass line, played by Paul, following which the recording was mixed into mono for the last time. Backed with 'I Am The Walrus', it was released on Friday 24 November as the A-side of the Beatles' third 1967 single.

Friday 3 November

'Sunny Heights', South Rd, St George's Hill, Weybridge, Surrey

The filming of *Magical Mystery Tour* was completed this day with inserts for George's 'Blue Jay Way' sequence (otherwise shot at West Malling) done at Ringo's country house in Weybridge, 19 miles south-west of London.

Principally, the Beatles filmed in Ringo's spacious back garden, each of them pretending to play a lovely white cello. (When the West Malling filming was done, 19–24 September, the recording did not feature cello; the instrument was overdubbed at EMI on 6 October hence the need for additional shooting now.) When it was John's turn, the other three rushed into the picture fooling around with a football. George was also filmed running down some garden steps, and the cello – without a player – was filmed in front of plopping and fizzing fireworks (easily obtained at this time of year, with Guy Fawkes night only 48 hours away). A number of children were also filmed playing around in the garden.

Moving inside the house, a topless Mal Evans was filmed with George's West Malling 'Blue Jay Way' sequence projected onto his chest, and then various Beatles were filmed watching 'Blue Jay Way' on a screen, John doing so while bobbing to and fro on a rocking-horse (presumably the possession of Ringo's two-year-old son Zak).

BBC Television bought *Magical Mystery Tour* for two screenings, the first in black-and-white on BBC1 (Tuesday 26 December 1967 – Boxing Day – 8.35–9.25 pm), the second on the colour channel BBC2, not yet available to all Britons (Friday 5 January 1968, 9.55–10.45 pm).

Additionally, *Top Of The Pops* twice broadcast short *MMT* extracts to accompany music performances: 'The Fool On The Hill' on Thursday 28 December (7.30–8.00 pm) and then mute footage to accompany the playing of 'Hello, Goodbye' on Thursday 11 January 1968 (also 7.30–8.00 pm).

Monday 6 November

Studio Three, EMI Studios, London

Stereo mixing between 2.30 and 6.00 pm of 'Hello, Goodbye', 'I Am The Walrus', 'Your Mother Should Know' and 'Magical Mystery Tour'. 'I Am The Walrus' was the most difficult because it had to incorporate the live radio feed found only in the 29 September mono mix, hence the final two minutes of the stereo version – from the line "Sitting in an English garden" onwards – had to be in mono too.

Tuesday 7 November

Studio One, EMI Studios, London

A long day's work at EMI. Employed in studio two, 2.30–5.45 pm, George Martin produced and edited stereo

Filming 'Hello, Goodbye' at the Saville Theatre on 10 November.

mixes of 'Blue Jay Way' and 'Flying'. 'Blue Jay Way' was then re-done, and in both mono and stereo, at the start of a 9.00 pm–4.30 am session in studio one which also saw Paul simultaneously overdub a new vocal and more sound effects onto mono and stereo mixes of 'Magical Mystery Tour'. Then copies of a batch of mixes – some mono, some stereo, some both – were made and taken away by Voyle Gilmore, visiting from Capitol Records: 'I Am The Walrus', 'Your Mother Should Know', 'Flying', 'Magical Mystery Tour', 'Blue Jay Way', 'The Fool On The Hill' and 'Strawberry Fields Forever'.

Magical Mystery Tour posed a problem for the Beatles and EMI. Six songs were too many for an EP, but too few for an LP. One idea, to have an EP playing at LP speed, was considered but rejected because it would have suffered from loss of volume and fidelity. The problem was solved at the beginning of November: it would be packaged as a hitherto untried double-EP set, in a heavy-duty gatefold sleeve with a 28-page booklet, some pages in colour, including all of the song lyrics. The price of this superb package was 19s 6d (97½ p) and it was issued in Britain on Friday 8 December.

Capitol Records, however, decided that the US market would not accept this unusual format, and opted instead for an album, filled out with the Beatles' five other 1967 song releases outside of *Sgt Pepper*: 'Hello, Goodbye', 'Strawberry Fields Forever', 'Penny Lane', 'Baby, You're A Rich Man' and 'All You Need Is Love'. (The latter three were issued in "duophonic" form – that is, mock stereo – since true stereo mixes had not yet been prepared. 'All You Need Is Love' was first mixed into stereo on 29 October 1968 while 'Penny Lane' and 'Baby, You're A Rich Man' first went into stereo, for a West German MMT LP, on 30 September 1971 and 22 October 1971 respectively. Additionally, 'Strawberry Fields Forever' was remixed for this album on 26 October 1971.)

But whatever the shape and size of the vinyl, *Magical Mystery Tour*, the record, was everything the associated 52-minute television film was not – a runaway success, selling more than half a million copies in the UK and a million in the USA before Christmas 1967 and capping a memorable year for the Beatles.

Friday 10 November

Saville Theatre, London

Though, to most people, *Magical Mystery Tour* contained everything but the proverbial kitchen-sink, it certainly didn't include a performance, or any other visual material, for the Beatles' forthcoming single 'Hello, Goodbye' (although the song's so-called "Maori Finale" was heard over the closing credits). So on 10 November the Beatles took to the stage at the Saville Theatre – still leased by NEMS Enterprises, despite Brian Epstein's death – where, without an audience, they filmed promo clips for the song. Emboldened by the *MMT* experience, Paul took personal charge as director.

Three colour 35mm clips were produced from this day's shooting, with different costumes, antics and backcloths to distinguish one from another. In clip number one – for the

first time since the cover was photographed on 29 March – the Beatles wore their *Sgt Pepper* uniforms, Paul playing electric bass guitar, George playing electric lead guitar, John (not wearing his glasses) an acoustic guitar, and Ringo playing the drums (without a name on the front). This was filmed in front of what could be called a "psychedelic" backcloth. This clip also contained cutaways to all four Beatles wearing their 1963 collarless suits and waving to the camera, and featured a number of local dancing girls dressed Hawaii-style (grass skirts, flower-garlands) who came on to jig around the Beatles and jollify the "Maori Finale" section.

In the second clip, with the same instrumental line-up (although Ringo's bass-drum now showed the Beatles' usual logo), the group were filmed wearing their everyday clothes, performing in front of a pastoral backcloth. Again, the Hawaiian-style dancers came on for the coda.

The third clip was a combination of outtakes from the first two films and footage from what was clearly a third shoot, the Beatles – especially John – frantically and hilariously doing the twist in front of a backcloth comprising red and yellow diamond/square shapes. (The remaining footage from this third clip wasn't used.)

Later, incidentally, acting on his own initiative, *MMT* film editor Roy Benson (who also cut these three promo films) made a fourth clip for 'Hello, Goodbye' comprising a montage of unused footage from *Magical Mystery Tour*. This clip has never been screened, but does still exist in its original 16mm form.

Neil Aspinall flew to the USA carrying copies of the different promos on 17 November, and the first transmission of a clip there (version one) was included in the Sunday 26 November edition of CBS-TV's *The Ed Sullivan Show* (8.00–9.00 pm, EST), Sullivan reading out a short telegram sent to him by the Beatles just before the screening. The clip then showed up again on the following night's edition of ABC's *The Hollywood Palace* (10.00–11.00 pm, EST).

In Britain, however, there was trouble in store. In June 1966 the Musicians' Union, which operated a closed-shop policy, instigated a miming ban for all television appearances made by singers and musicians. Whereas TV companies could screen without problems such promo films as 'Penny Lane' and 'Strawberry Fields Forever', because they were conceptual rather than performance-orientated, 'Hello, Goodbye' fell firmly into the performance category. And, despite the clear presence of guitar leads and Vox amplifiers, the Beatles *had* been miming when they shot the three clips at the Saville. As a consequence, none of the three was screened in Britain, neither by the BBC nor ITV. (See 21 November for further information.)

In an effort to circumvent anticipated Musicians' Union problems, a new mono mix of 'Hello, Goodbye', eliminating the violas, was prepared by George Martin between 10.30 and 11.00 am on Wednesday 15 November. Since the viola players were not in the films – making the miming transparently obvious – this mix was dubbed onto the print given to the BBC. It was a wasted task however, for the Beatles' own miming couldn't be masked nor the ban evaded so easily.

Note: mono tape copies of 'It's All Too Much', 'All Together Now' and 'Only A Northern Song' were made between 11.00 am and 12.00 noon this same day, 15 November, by Geoff Emerick for the producers of the *Yellow Submarine* film. For the same purpose, Emerick made copies of 'Sgt Pepper's Lonely Hearts Club Band', the reprise version of same, and 'Nowhere Man' on 22 November (2.30–3.30 pm, studio two), while on 23 November (for five hours in Room 13) Malcolm Davies made copies of 'Yellow Submarine', 'All You Need Is Love', 'Eleanor Rigby', 'A Day In The Life', 'With A Little Help From My Friends', 'Yesterday', 'Strawberry Fields Forever', 'All Together Now', 'Michelle', 'When I'm Sixty-Four', 'Nowhere Man', 'Lucy In The Sky With Diamonds', 'It's All Too Much', 'You Know My Name (Look Up The Number)' (rhythm track only), 'Help!' and 'Love You To'. Some, though not all, of these were used in the film soundtrack.

Friday 17 November

Room 53, EMI Studios, London

A new stereo mix of the first half of 'I Am The Walrus', for editing into the stereo master, prepared from 10.00 am to 1.15 pm. (There were now a number of variations between this and the mono master, the most obvious being the mellotron bars in the song's intro: the mono had four, the stereo six.)

Tuesday 21 November

Norman's Film Productions, London

Top Of The Pops planned to transmit one of the Saville Theatre 'Hello, Goodbye' promo films (in monochrome) on Thursday 23 November (7.30–8.00 pm) but earlier that week producer Johnnie Stewart realised that the Musicians' Union miming ban ruled this impossible. Instead, much to the Beatles' annoyance, *TOTP* played 'Hello, Goodbye' over mute footage from *A Hard Day's Night*, supplied to them by United Artists.

Quite apart from the Beatles' objection to a 1964 "mop top" sequence being juxtaposed with a late-1967 recording, they were angry because, during this evening (21 November), they permitted the BBC to film them at work with Roy Benson in the *MMT* cutting-room, a sequence directed by one Michael Goodwin. The idea was that the resulting footage would smother the most obvious miming sections in the 'Hello, Goodbye' clip, allowing the remainder to be shown untouched. NEMS also supplied the BBC with up-to-date stills of the Beatles to perform the same function. Defending the fact that it hadn't used the cutting-room footage, the BBC claimed that there had been insufficient time to develop and edit it before transmission.

'Hello, Goodbye' did not feature in *Top Of The Pops* on 30 November; then, on 7 December (7.30–8.00 pm) *TOTP* screened the cutting-room footage for the first time, with stills supplied by NEMS comprising the remainder of the single's duration. Clearly, now that the Beatles' Saville Theatre miming was public knowledge, none of the official promo material could be screened at all. The film/stills combination

was also used in *Top Of The Pops* on Thursdays 14 December, 21 December and 4 January 1968 (all 7.30–8.00 pm) and in *Top Of The Pops '67 – Part One* on Christmas Day (2.05–3.00 pm). However, on 11 January 1968 a clip from *Magical Mystery Tour* was played to accompany 'Hello, Goodbye' and on Christmas Day 1968, in *Top Of The Pops '68 – Part One* (1.25–2.10 pm), the music was accompanied by stock BBC footage of the London to Brighton train journey, which had no Beatles connection at all.

Saturday 25 November

In this day's edition of the Radio 1 programme *Where It's At* (2.00–3.00 pm), co-hosted by Kenny Everett and Chris Denning, there was a self-contained feature about the new *Magical Mystery Tour* double-EP set, including a privately-taped piano/vocal jingle for the two DJs performed solely by Paul (untitled but best described as 'All Together On The Wireless Machine') and an interview the pair had conducted with John. As with the 20 May 1967 feature about *Sgt Pepper*, produced in the same fashion, there is no precise record of where these items were taped (although Paul probably recorded his jingle at home and John's interview was probably done at EMI Abbey Road) or when they were taped (although both were probably circa mid-November).

The John Lennon conversation was scarcely what one might term an interview anyway: constantly encouraged by the wacky and unpredictable Everett, John's comments rarely rose above meaningless gibberish, and the two seemed to have made a pact to gang together against Denning whenever he gave them the opportunity (which was frequently). During the interview, which lasted just over 18 minutes, both Everett and Denning had John tape trailers for their respective solo series.

All six tracks from the *Magical Mystery Tour* EP were broadcast, although soon afterwards the BBC quietly agreed to block any future radio use of 'I Am The Walrus' because of the line "you let your knickers down", which the Corporation considered its listeners would find offensive. Though essentially the same as a "ban", such as that which had earlier befallen 'A Day In The Life', use of this contentious word was now carefully avoided.

Tuesday 28 November

Studio Three, EMI Studios, London

The making of the Beatles' fifth fan club Christmas record, taped 6.00 pm–2.45 am. As in 1966, the Beatles injected considerable time and skill into the disc, preparing a skit-full script and recording a song written especially for the purpose, 'Christmas Time (Is Here Again)' (also the name of the overall disc), copyrighted to Lennon-McCartney-Harrison-Starkey. Short extracts of this song were used on the disc but the full uncut version lasted 6 mins 37 secs and featured the four Beatles assisted by George Martin and visiting actor/friend Victor Spinetti. The recordings were mixed into mono up to 2.45 am.

This was the Beatles' last Christmas fan club disc to be recorded collectively and at EMI. In 1968 and again in 1969 – the final edition – the four Beatles taped their items individually, in their homes or wherever they happened to be, in Britain or abroad. Both discs were edited (there was no "producer", as such) by Kenny Everett, the 1969 edition under his real name, Maurice Cole.

Note: although the Christmas disc was completed by 2.45 this session continued until 4.30 am because John stayed behind to compile sound effects tapes for the forthcoming stage production *The Lennon Play: In His Own Write*, based primarily on his two books *In His Own Write* and *A Spaniard In The Works*. It would be directed by Victor Spinetti, hence his attendance at the session. This was, in fact, John's third such session at EMI, producing the compilation of effects tapes, some from pre-made records and tapes, others concocted especially by him and others. The first was on 24 November (7.00 pm–12.30 am; studio two), the second earlier on the 28th (2.00–5.00 pm; studio three).

And John was not the only Beatle presently using EMI Studios for a solo project. George had just begun to produce the recordings for his soundtrack for the film *Wonderwall*. On Wednesday 22 November (7.00 pm–2.00 am; studio two) he produced tracks for two numbers that went under the working titles 'India' and 'Swordfencing', employing two flautists (Richard Adeney and Jack Ellory) and one tabla player (name not documented). On the 23rd (2.30–5.45 pm and 8.00 pm–1.00 am; studio three) he continued this work with two oboists (J Crackston and G Morgan), one trumpeter (D Clift) and two flautists (Jack Ellory with N Knight in the first session and Clifford Seville in the second). George was also recording concurrently at De Lane Lea in Kingsway and on 7 January 1968 he flew to India to continue the good work at the EMI studio in Bombay. George did not play on any of the *Wonderwall* sessions.

Wednesday 29 November

A 2.30–5.30 pm session in EMI studio one in which George Martin and Geoff Emerick edited the 1967 Christmas disc mono mixes into a finished master and copied this onto a reel for the pressing of flexi-disc singles at Lyntone Records.

Tuesday 5 December

Apple, Baker Street, London

With Ringo in Italy (see 7 December) and Paul holidaying in Scotland for 17 days, it was left to John and George to represent the Beatles at the party marking the opening of their Apple shop, at 94 Baker Street in central London. All manner of friends and celebrities came to Apple this evening to socialise, drink apple juice and toast the future of the Beatles as retailers. (The shop opened to the public on the 7th.)

Early on during the party, John and also Cilla Black were interviewed for the BBC by freelance radio reporter Brian Cullingford, who sped the tape back to nearby Broadcasting House for transmission in this evening's edition of the Radio 1/Radio 2 programme *Late Night Extra* (10.00–12.00 pm). A total of 2 mins 42 secs was broadcast, John appearing on air for 1 min 46 secs, leading, somewhat inappropriately, into the record of 'A Hard Day's Night'.

Thursday 7 – Saturday 16 December

various locations, Rome, Italy

Keen to add a solo project to *his* CV, following John's role in *How I Won The War*, Paul's soundtrack for *The Family Way* and now George's for *Wonderwall*, Ringo asked NEMS to look out for a solo acting vehicle. *A Hard Day's Night* and *Help!* had clearly proven that, of the four Beatles, Ringo had the most acting promise, so the cinema was his natural solo direction.

The first such film in which he appeared was *Candy*, written by Buck Henry (involved in *Get Smart*, one of Ringo's favourite television shows of the 1960s) and based on the very successful novel by Terry Southern and Mason Hoffenberg. Ringo particularly enjoyed Southern's work and would later co-star in his *The Magic Christian* (see 3 February 1969). His appearance in *Candy*, however, was very much in the form of a cameo rather than a starring role, playing the part of Emmanuel, a Mexican gardener who works for Candy's father every Saturday and, like everyone else, lusts after her body.

Southern and Hoffenberg's somewhat crude and subversive novel was faithfully transferred to the big screen in this French/Italian co-production directed by Christian Marquand, and the result was disappointing – despite a fabulous cast that included, as well as Ringo, Marlon Brando, Richard Burton, John Huston, James Coburn, Walter Matthau, John Astin, Charles Aznavour, Elsa Martinelli and even the boxer Sugar Ray Robinson. All, including Ringo, failed to shine in what was, essentially, an X-certificate romp in which Candy (played by Ewa Aulin, the former Miss Teen Sweden) shed her clothes and had sex with pretty much everyone, everywhere. The too-long 119-minute film drew appalling reviews when it was released (17 December 1968 in New York, 20 February 1969 in London) and has scarcely been seen since. One critic recommended it as an emetic.

Ringo flew to Rome from London Airport on Sunday 3 December to shoot his role, and his two-week schedule there went like this: no filming on 3, 4, 5, 6, 8 and 10 December (although, on the 4th, he was fitted for his costume, had his hair dyed jet-black and was coached in the Mexican dialect).

From 8.30 am on **Thursday 7 December** he filmed in the garden of a house just down the road from Incom Film Studios, where the production was based.

During the afternoon of **Saturday 9 December** he filmed on a sound-stage at Incom, mocked up as the basement of Candy's house, with Candy (Aulin) and Professor McPhisto (Burton).

During the afternoons of **Monday 11 December** and **Tuesday 12 December**: more filming at Incom for the same sequence.

All day on **Wednesday 13 December**, until 8.30 pm:

filming of the scene in which Emmanuel attempts to have sex with Candy on a pool table.

During **Thursday 14 December**: filming of the conclusion of the previous day's scene, in which Candy's father (Astin) bursts in on the coupling couple and throws Emmanuel out of the house. Also shot this day: a scene in which Ringo rode a motor-bike with Candy's sister (Italian actress Marilu-Tolo).

Friday 15 December: during the day Ringo was filmed with 80 hippies in a field for a "love-in" scene, then during the evening (until past midnight) he was filmed pursuing Candy and her father to Rome airport, where she boarded a plane and departed.

Saturday 16 December was Ringo's last day of shooting. He spent the afternoon and evening completing the previous day's scene on location at Rome airport.

Ringo flew back to London on Sunday 17 December, his first solo acting role completed. He was not involved in any of the film's post-production processes.

Wednesday 27 December

Studio One, Wembley Studios, Wembley

A solo appearance by Paul on Rediffusion's *The Frost Programme*, taped before a studio audience at Wembley between 6.00 and 7.00 pm for transmission this same evening, 10.30–11.15. Other guests in this edition included the singer Blossom Dearie.

Paul occupied the first half of the show, up to the commercial break, much of David Frost's interview concen-

RINGO SOLO FILM
Beatles "Mystery" discs

BEATLE Ringo Starr is to have a solo acting role in a big-budget movie to be made by a major Hollywood company. Titled "Candy" and adapted from the best-selling satire of that name, it goes into production in the late autumn. Ringo will have the cameo role of a Mexican gardener, with other parts in the picture played by Richard Burton and Marlon Brando—but the title role has not yet been cast. The director is Christian Marquand.

The location of the film has still to be announced, but it is possible that Ringo will fly to America to film his contribution. It is also probable that he will have to curtail his meditation visit to India in order to meet filming schedules.

In accepting this solo part, Ringo is following in the footsteps of fellow Beatle John Lennon, who made his solo debut in "How I Won The War".

The Beatles' TV spectacular "Magical Mystery Tour" will include up to seven brand new compositions by the group. It is probable that two of the songs will be issued as the Beatles' next single, with the remainder forming a special EP release. The score includes an instrumental number—the first non-vocal composed by the group since it rose to stardom five years ago. Another track is "Blue Jay Way," written by George Harrison during his visit to Los Angeles in August.

WRITING SCORE

Throughout this week, the Beatles have been engaged in extensive soundtrack recordings for the TV show. They will also be writing and recording all the incidental music for the spectacular but work on this cannot begin until editing has been completed, and the group is able to see exactly what is required.

The final decision on the exact number of new songs in the show has not yet been taken by the Beatles. An official statement from NEMS Enterprises says: "Apart from the title number, there will be four—perhaps six—new songs." As previously reported, the Traffic appear in a guest spot in the show.

The complicated process of preparing the incidental score is likely to take some weeks. This will probably mean that the Beatles' meditation visit to India is even further delayed, and may not now take place until November.

● The Beatles have rejected an offer of a million dollars to play two concerts at New York's Shea Stadium. It was submitted by U.S. promoter Sidney Bernstein, who presented the

group's previous appearances at this venue. A spokesman for the Beatles commented: "The reason is that they cannot perform on stage the kind of music they are recording now".

● The title song from the film "How I Won The War", recorded by Musketeer Gripweed and the Third Troop, is released as a United Artists single next Friday (13th). Although it is largely instrumental, the voice of John Lennon—who plays Gripweed in the picture—is heard on the disc.

trating on the lambasting that British TV critics had given *Magical Mystery Tour* in the morning newspapers, with Paul doing his best to explain the Beatles' motives, ideals and current direction. He also answered questions from the audience and discussed broader topics such as war, humans, responsibility and money.

THE TRANQUILLITY and new dimension of peace and perception engendered by the Beatles' spring 1968 sojourn to Rishikesh, India, sadly failed to produce much in the way of harmony and understanding between the group when it was needed most. Although the Beatles split officially in 1970 and unofficially in 1969, it was in 1968 that the rot well and truly set in.

In fact, the visit to India didn't go as well as expected. Ringo stayed just 11 days, Paul a little over a month, and then, after two months, John and George left with some haste, having become disillusioned with Maharishi Mahesh Yogi. It wasn't Transcendental Meditation that they were abandoning, just the Maharishi personally, but neither subject was mentioned much again. As ever, the Beatles had had to endure public comment, mocking and intrusive scrutiny of hobbies and interests which, for anyone else, would have been strictly a private affair.

The traditional image of the Beatles as happy-go-lucky mop-tops was maintained rather against the run of play in the summer of 1968 with the release of the feature-film *Yellow Submarine*. It was a magnificent work of animation, achieving the aim detailed right from the very first screenplay outline: "The goal should be nothing less than to take animation beyond anything seen before in style, class and tone, but avoiding the precious

and pretentious." That outline, dated November 1966, was prepared by writer Lee Minoff with direct co-operation from Paul, so it's clear that the Beatles, at some stage, were prepared to be involved in the production. But as it swung into action through 1967 *Yellow Submarine* became something of an irritation to them, irrelevant to their present-day lives

and output, like a relic from the days of Beatlemania. (Which, in a sense, it was, since the film followed on from a US TV series of Beatles cartoon adventures launched on 25 September 1965, made by the same company, King Features, a division of the Hearst Corporation.)

Although they consented to appear in a live-action sequence for the end of the film, attended the premiere and gave King Features four otherwise unissued songs, the Beatles were not as closely associated with *Yellow Submarine* as the public imagined when the film reached the cinema screens in July 1968. Even if one subscribes to the notion that the Beatles never released *any* sub-standard musical material, it has to be admitted that the four songs they donated to the project were scarcely up to their usual impeccable quality – though good, 'All Together Now' from 1967 and 'Hey Bulldog' from 1968 were both one-session throw-away recordings, 'Only A Northern Song' was a *Sgt Pepper* reject and 'It's All Too Much' a less than wonderful piece of work from the Beatles' creative dip in the late-spring of 1967.

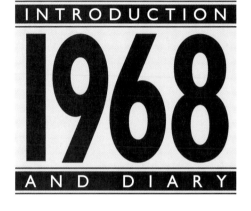

The world premiere of *Yellow Submarine* was one of the first occasions that John was seen in public with Yoko Ono, his partner since mid-May. An examination of the Beatles' private relationships is beyond the scope of this book and has been explored in several biographies, but their coming together had an undeniably negative bearing on the functioning of the Beatles as a unit, even if it only accentuated the disharmony which had already taken hold.

In particular, Yoko alerted John to the seemingly infinite means by which he could expand and explore his career, leading him to realise that being a member of the Beatles was restrictive, blocking his wider aspirations and functions as an

artist. Yoko strongly encouraged John to branch out, and in particular to liberate the *avant-garde* leanings he had hitherto kept private.

The other Beatles soon grew resentful of John and Yoko's fanatical degree of togetherness. As John so succinctly put it, they considered themselves johnandyoko, an inseparable unit. What upset Paul, George and Ringo was that this unity extended even to those areas which had always been the exclusive domain of the four – work activities in particular. Yoko attended every Beatles recording session and would encourage hostility by whispering conspiratorially into John's ear, by sitting on his amplifier and appearing to preside over the session, by openly criticising and suggesting changes to the music being recorded and, perhaps more than anything else, by simply inhibiting the others and making them feel uncomfortable and ill at ease in what had always been their ideal environment and refuge away from the madness outside. Coupled with the group's own self-disintegration, ongoing since they ceased touring, sessions became unbearable, with victimisation, shouting and lost tempers a common occurrence.

In fact, recording sessions became so tense that, on 22 August, Ringo actually quit the Beatles and went on holiday while they carried on without him. Claiming that he "wasn't getting through" to the others anymore, he intended not to return, but did so after a two-week absence had repaired some of the damage. For the steady, easy-going and reliable Ringo to have stormed out, though, was a clear indication that things were now going badly awry. News of his departure was suppressed.

The sessions that ran on and on through the late-spring, summer and into the autumn were for *The Beatles*, the double-LP set which has since become known as the 'White Album' because of its famous stark-white cover – the perfect minimalist antidote to the scores of increasingly garish *Sgt Pepper* imitations flooding the market in 1968.

This was a massive out-pouring of Beatles recordings, 30 in total. It was what the Beatles themselves wanted – and they were now in charge – but producer George Martin told them that he considered some unworthy of release, and that they ought to separate the wheat from the chaff and issue, instead, one dynamite collection of, say, 14 songs. The Beatles chose to ignore his advice.

It has long been recognised that *The Beatles* is more a collection of four men's solo recordings than a united group effort. Certainly, apart from the basic tracks for each song, most – though even then not all – of which were made with all four Beatles present, much of the overdubbing was done solely by the composer of the song. And with John and Paul as prodigious as ever, with George now getting firmly into songwriting mode, and even Ringo starting to compose, there was much material to be pooled. The crux of the problem was that group interests, for the first time, were no longer the prime objective: none of the four seemed prepared to sacrifice his own material. George Martin even thinks that in releasing 30 songs in one batch, the Beatles may have been attempting partly to fulfil, in as quick a manner as possible, a pre-set song quota in their 1967–76 EMI recording contract.

But whether *The Beatles* is viewed merely as the group's

ninth album, or as a collection of solo material, it must be by the music that it is finally judged, and in that respect it was a winner, a very enjoyable set and an *enormous* seller all around the world – nearly two million copies were shifted in the USA in the first week alone. Typically, too, as well as issuing a 30-song album, the Beatles had on their hands enough quality material to release a separate single, 'Hey Jude' backed with 'Revolution', another of the all-time great

MEMO

FROM	TO
George Harrison	Everybody at Apple

OUR REFERENCE	YOUR REFERENCE	4th December 196[8]

Hells Angels will be in London within the next week, on the way to straighten out Czechoslovakia. There will be twelve in number complete with black leather jackets and motor cycles. They will undoubtedly arrive at Apple and I have heard they may try to make full use of Apple's facilities. They may look as though they are going to do you in but are very straight and do good things, so don't fear them or up-tight them. Try to assist them without neglecting your Apple business and without letting them take control of Savile Row.

45rpm couplings, rivalling the previous year's 'Penny Lane'/ 'Strawberry Fields Forever' in terms of sheer musical brilliance and variety.

The Beatles was also the group's first album to appear on their own Apple Records label (although, for the Beatles themselves, including almost all of their solo output, this was a façade because their recordings continued to be owned exclusively by EMI). Paul and George played a vital role in shaping some of Apple's exclusive acts, especially in the summer of 1968, when, concurrent with sessions for *The Beatles*, Paul produced Mary Hopkin, George produced Jackie Lomax, they both played on James Taylor's Apple album, and they both, and with Ringo too, played on Lomax's album. Such sessions usually took place at EMI or at Trident Studios, a new London facility which had opened on 8 March. This all resulted in an additional burden on Beatles time, blurring their collective concerns when a period of sharp focusing was so important.

Apple, as a whole, is another single subject capable of filling entire books – which, indeed, it has done. Its importance to the Beatles as a united group, however, was of paramount importance, especially in 1969 when troubles within the company led directly to an irreparable rift within the four.

By the time *The Beatles* was finished and ready for release, when socialising and liaison within the group had greatly diminished, and when John and Yoko were convicted for possession of cannabis, Paul made a clear attempt to provide the necessary focus by suggesting that, after what had been a two-year gap, the Beatles return to live performances. His reasoning was clear: it was music, not business, which had brought the group together, and it was music which would keep them together and re-ignite their creative, cohesive spirit. The announcement went out – the Beatles would give three concerts in mid-December at the Roundhouse in London.

As the first date approached, however, the plans were put on hold. Away from the headlines, Paul was having trouble persuading John, George and Ringo to see things his way. But while unable to agree on the form or venue for their live return, the Beatles at least agreed to begin rehearsals, and to film them, commencing the second day of 1969.

INTERNAL MEMO

DATE   18TH JUNE 1968.

FROM   THE BEATLES

TO   EVERYONE

RE: SUGGESTIONS.

TRY TO THINK OF SUGGESTIONS FOR A SUBSIDIARY LABEL FOR APPLE WHICH WOULD PUT OUT MORE FREAKY SOUNDS.

SUGGESTIONS SO FAR HAVE BEEN:

MAGIC EYE (BUT THAT'S NO GOOD BECAUSE IT WAS LAST SUMMER).

I RECORDS (THAT WASN'T GOOD ENOUGH EITHER).

ANYWAY, YOU GET THE PICTURE. SO THINK OF AS MANY IDEAS AS YOU CAN AND STICK THEM IN THE SUGGESTION BOX.

Friday 12 January

EMI Recording Studio, Phirozeshah Mehta Rd, Fort, Bombay, India

In order to continue producing the *Wonderwall* music soundtrack, George flew to India on 7 January for a five-day series of sessions at EMI's Bombay studio. (On 5 January, before leaving, George produced another session in Abbey Road's studio two, 7.00 pm–3.00 am, and he completed the soundtrack recording there on 30 January.) The sessions in Bombay, using local musicians, started on 9 January and ended on the 13th, each day's work beginning around 10.00 am and finishing around 7.00 pm.

By 12 January *Wonderwall* was all but completed and so, wishing neither to waste studio time nor under-use the musicians, George produced a number of ragas (traditional Hindu musical pieces) for possible use on Beatles records. One of these, to become 'The Inner Light', had quite an exquisite melody and was indeed released by the Beatles after overdubs had been taped back at Abbey Road on 6 and 8 February.

Only the instrumental track of 'The Inner Light' was recorded at this point, in five takes. The *precise* line-up of musicians is not known although it would have been a selection of the following, all employed by George here in Bombay: Ashish Khan (sarod), Mahapurush Misra (tabla and pakavaj), Sharad Jadev and Hanuman Jadev (shanhais), Shambu-Das, Indril Bhattacharya and Shankar Ghosh (sitars), Chandra Shakher (sur-bahar), Shiv Kumar Sharmar (santorr), S R Kenkare and Hari Prasad Chaurasia (flutes), Vinayak Vohra (taar shehnai) and Rijram Desad (dholak, harmonium and tabla-tarang).

Note: George did not himself play on any of the *Wonderwall* recordings, even though the finished album *Wonderwall Music* was attributed to him. It was the first LP released on the Beatles' Apple label, issued in Britain on Friday 1 November 1968. The film itself was unveiled at the Cannes Film Festival, France, on Friday 17 May, with George, and also Ringo, present.

Thursday 25 January

Twickenham Film Studios, St Margaret's, Twickenham

Although *Yellow Submarine* was, is and always will be regarded as an animated feature, the Beatles were cajoled into making a personal appearance on camera for the very end of what was, after all, meant to be their own film. One could surmise a number of reasons for this: perhaps, though, it was simply a way of convincing audiences that the Beatles had been closely involved in the production – even if this was not the case.

The shooting of their carefully scripted cameo appearance took place during this afternoon at Twickenham, following the obligatory run-throughs and camera rehearsals. The world premiere of *Yellow Submarine*, which the Beatles attended, took place at the London Pavilion cinema in central London on Wednesday 17 July 1968, and it opened in the USA in New York on Wednesday 13 November.

Note: *Yellow Submarine* was mostly assembled at the studios of TVC (TV Cartoons), a company run by the feature-film's director George Dunning and situated in Dean Street, in the Soho area of central London. When the Beatles visited TVC on one occasion at the beginning of November 1967 (exact date not documented), they were filmed, perusing the celluloids, for inclusion in a seven-minute promotional short titled *A Mod Odyssey*, made on behalf of United Artists by an American company, Tarot Associates. The film also included offbeat footage of the Beatles at Twickenham this day (25 January 1968). *A Mod Odyssey* was networked on US television by NBC on Saturday 12 October 1968, immediately after the screening of *Help!* in the 9.00–11.00 pm (EST) slot.

Yet more footage of the Beatles at TVC, albeit very brief, was included in a cinema-distributed trailer for the feature-film: this showed the Beatles sitting on a sofa, supposedly watching (and greatly enjoying) the film being projected onto a screen situated behind the camera.

Saturday 27 January

'Kenwood', Weybridge

Kenny Everett visited John's house in Surrey this day to record an interview for his Sunday morning BBC Radio 1 series *The Kenny Everett Show*. It was broadcast eight days later, on 4 February, between 10.00 am and 12.00 noon.

Thursday 1 February

Television Rehearsal Rooms, Victoria Rd, North Acton, London

Off-camera daytime rehearsals for Ringo at the BBC's specially designated premises in North Acton, west London, running through with Cilla Black his guest appearance in her TV series, set for live broadcast the following Tuesday evening. (See 6 February for full details.)

Friday 2 February

Television Rehearsal Rooms, London

While Ringo was engaged in more daytime rehearsals for *Cilla*, George Martin was working at Abbey Road, 12.00 noon–1.00 pm, making a copy of the 'Only A Northern Song' vocal track, presumably to aid his incidental soundtrack contribution to *Yellow Submarine*, now approaching completion.

Saturday 3 February

Studio Three, EMI Studios, London

The Beatles' oft-postponed visit to India to study under Maharishi Mahesh Yogi was imminent, John and George flying out on 15 February, Paul and Ringo four days later. As they weren't due to return until late-April, they decided to record a new single for release *in absentia* in mid-March. As it happened, this concentrated series of sessions, ending on 11 February, was more productive than expected and realised four new songs, all mixed and ready for issue.

The first of these was Paul's 'Lady Madonna'. Three piano/drum takes were recorded between 2.30 and 6.00 pm, then from 7.00 until 12.00 the Beatles overdubbed bass, fuzz guitars, drums and lead and backing vocals.

Sunday 4 February

Studio Three, EMI Studios, London

John's offering for the new single was the philosophical 'Across The Universe', begun this day and completed on the 8th. Six takes were recorded (there was no take three, so these were numbered one to seven) between 2.30 and 5.30, then – with John considering himself best pleased with take seven – the Beatles began an 8.00 pm–2.00 am session overdubbing onto this.

But after John had taped his vocal contribution, recorded with the machine running slow to play back fast, he and Paul realised that the song lacked falsetto harmonies. Finding two female singers on a Sunday evening without prior arrangement would usually have been impossible, but for the Beatles all they had to do was step outside the front of EMI Studios and invite inside two of the many fans who congregated there whenever the Beatles were recording. Paul did just this, selecting Lizzie Bravo, a 16-year-old from Brazil temporarily living close to Abbey Road, and Gayleen Pease, 17, a Londoner, who were naturally thrilled at being the only fans ever invited to contribute to a Beatles recording.

Once the girls had taped their "nothing's gonna change our world" high harmonies they left the studio so that the Beatles could record more overdubs. These included three unusual effects: the first was 'Hums Wild' – a 15-second take

of humming, recorded and overdubbed three more times to fill the four-track tape, the second was a guitar piece, the third a harp-like sound, the tape box denoting that these latter two were "to be played backwards". At least two of these, 'Hums Wild' and the guitar played backwards, were temporarily inserted into 'Across The Universe' long enough for John to make a 7½ ips copy for taking home.

Monday 5 February

Television Theatre, London

Following the North Acton run-throughs the previous Thursday and Friday, preparations for *Cilla*, with guest Ringo Starr, switched to the BBC's Television Theatre on Shepherd's Bush Green in west London – for 1.30–5.30 and 6.30–10.00 pm camera rehearsals.

Tuesday 6 February

Television Theatre, London
and Studio One, EMI Studios, London

In less than six years, Ringo had come a long way from playing with Rory Storm and the Hurricanes at Butlin's, Skegness. In the 50 minutes of this television appearance, as a guest of Cilla Black in the second edition of her new live series *Cilla*, he showed a multi-faceted talent as an all-round show business entertainer. (Cilla, too, groomed by Brian Epstein – he arranged this series shortly before his death – had clearly come a long way from the Cavern Club and St John's Hall, Tuebrook.)

Following 10.30 am–1.00 pm and 2.00–6.30 pm rehearsals, Ringo popped up several times in the live show,

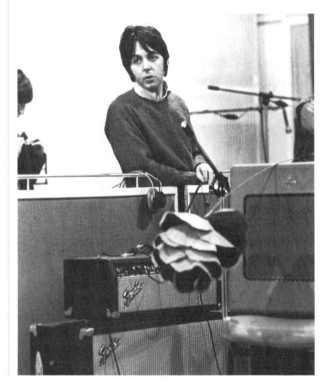

broadcast by BBC1 8.00–8.50 pm from the Television Theatre. He was seen at the very beginning, when the camera panned to the week's guest stars (Spike Milligan and ventriloquist Peter Brough – with his puppet "Educating" Archie Andrews – were among the others) and then he participated in two sketches, first acting as a ventriloquist, with Cilla – dressed in gymslip and pigtails, and called Ariadne – his dummy, joining together for a version of 'Nellie Dean'; then he duetted with Cilla on 'Do You Like Me?', Ringo tap dancing towards the end of the number. ('Nellie Dean', written in 1905 by H W Armstrong, was a between-wars standard; 'Do You Like Me?', written by Herbert Darnley, was from the 1917 revue *The Bing Girls Are There*, sung then by Violet Loraine and Joseph Coyne.)

The signature tune for *Cilla* was 'Step Inside Love', written especially for her, for this purpose, by Paul McCartney. Though apparently never screened in Britain, the BBC produced something akin to a promotional film for 'Step Inside Love'. Paul was in camera during most of the two-minute clip, which was shot in a recording studio while Cilla rehearsed it to his acoustic guitar accompaniment. The shoot date for this is not known; it may have been 21 November 1967 (during that evening, the Beatles were also filmed for *Top Of The Pops*), when Cilla first recorded the song, at Chappell Studios in central London. (The version on the single was a re-make, however, taped at EMI on 28 February 1968 when Paul was in India.)

While Ringo was busy with *Cilla* at the BBC, the three other Beatles spent virtually 12 hours at EMI, although a clear break in the session – they worked from 2.30–8.00 pm and then 9.00 pm–2.00 am – indicates that they took time out to watch his live TV appearance, probably at Paul's house nearby.

'The Inner Light' was all but completed during the first session, George adding vocals to a copy of the Bombay backing track and then mixing the recording into mono. The 9.00 pm session saw the completion of 'Lady Madonna', with the overdubbing of a second lead vocal by Paul, a second piano piece, handclaps, backing vocals by Paul, John and George, a vocalised brass imitation for the middle-eight section and, finally, in a late decision, a real four-man sax section, hurriedly recruited to EMI by session fixer Laurie Gold. Harry Klein and Bill Jackman contributed baritone sax, Ronnie Scott (the London night-club owner) and Bill Povey played tenor.

Now finished, 'Lady Madonna' was mixed into mono before the session ended.

Thursday 8 February

Studio Two, EMI Studios, London

Apart from a brief John and Paul vocal overdub onto 'The Inner Light' and that song's final mono mixing, this 2.30–9.00 pm session was spent completing 'Across The Universe', the Beatles trying out a variety of sounds and instruments. Despite their labours, however, John remained dissatisfied with the work, which obviously hadn't captured the feel that only he, as its author, could recognise – and

during a 10.00 pm–12.15 am mono mix session he could not disagree with a group decision to select 'Lady Madonna' as the A-side of the planned single and 'The Inner Light' as the B-side, relegating 'Across The Universe', unused, to the library shelf.

Spike Milligan, who happened to be attending the session as a guest of George Martin, requested permission to include 'Across The Universe' on a charity album to benefit the World Wildlife Fund, a project he had conceived in December 1967. The Beatles agreed. But the LP – *No One's Gonna Change Our World*, the title based on the lyric of 'Across The Universe' – wasn't released until December 1969, and for that purpose the song was adorned with wildlife sound effects during a stereo mix session at EMI on 2 October 1969. This February 1968 recording *was* released

"Gottle of geer…"
Ringo with Archie Andrews and Peter Brough, long-established stars of British radio, TV and music-hall, backstage at the BBC for Cilla.

BBC1: in *Top Of The Pops* on Thursdays 14 March and 4 April (both editions 7.30–8.00 pm), in *All Systems Freeman* on Friday 15 March (6.40–7.05 pm) and in the Christmas Day part one edition of *Top Of The Pops '68* (1.25–2.10 pm). The first US TV transmission of 'Lady Madonna', in colour, was in ABC's *The Hollywood Palace* on Saturday 30 March (9.30–10.30 pm, EST).

Thursday 15 February

Studio Three, EMI Studios, London

A 4.30–6.00 pm session that produced the mono singles master of 'Lady Madonna'. (Its first stereo mix was prepared on 2 December 1969.) The single was issued in Britain on Friday 15 March.

Tuesday 14 May

WNDT, East 46th St, New York City, New York, USA

and Studio 6B, Rockefeller Center, New York City, New York, USA

On Saturday 11 May John and Paul flew together to the USA for the first time since the Beatles' final concert tour in August 1966. Their purpose this time, though, was quite different. Staying in New York and wearing their businessmen hats, they went to officially unveil the group's Apple Corps venture via a series of interviews with the "serious" press (all day at the St Regis Hotel on Monday the 13th), a press conference (1.30 pm at the Americana Hotel on Tuesday the 14th) and an appearance on NBC-TV's *The Tonight Show* (later this same day). They also had an Apple business meeting aboard a Chinese "Junk" sailing around the Statue of Liberty (the afternoon of Sunday the 12th).

All these events went according to plan; additionally, once in New York, John and Paul agreed to tape a lengthy interview with reporter Mitchell Krause for broadcast on the local educational TV station WNDT – channel 13 in New York City. It was recorded during Tuesday afternoon (probably at the station's East 46th Street facility; if not then at another WNDT studio, at West 55th and 9th Avenue) and was screened on the programme *Newsfront* the following evening, Wednesday 15 May, 10.00–11.00 pm local time (EST). Owing to demand from viewers it was also repeated the following week, most likely on Friday 24 May.

John and Paul's appearance on *The Tonight Show* was taped in studio 6B at the Rockefeller Center early on the Tuesday evening for screening a few hours later. In New York it went out from 12.00 pm (midnight) to 1.00 am, and the two Beatles watched it back at their residence for these few days in New York: the apartment of lawyer Nat Weiss, Brian Epstein's principal business partner in the United States, at 181 East 73rd Street.

In the absence of Johnny Carson, the regular presenter of *The Tonight Show*, this edition was hosted by the major-league baseball player Joe Garagiola, who was somewhat surprisingly at a loss for questions to put to the two Beatles in what was, after all, the first appearance either had made on a

---

without these effects, however – though with many others added – on the *Let It Be* album, after much additional work had been carried out by Phil Spector (see 23 March 1970 and 1 April 1970).

Sunday 11 February

Studio Three, EMI Studios, London

The Beatles were certainly very productive at this time. They had recorded three songs so quickly, in just four sessions, that a 2.30–12.00 pm studio two session booked for Saturday 10 February was cancelled. Now, on the 11th, they came to EMI to shoot a promotional film clip for 'Lady Madonna', showing them at work in the studio. But why pretend? Instead of mocking-up a 'Lady Madonna' session they instead began, completed and mixed an altogether new song, John's 'Hey Bulldog', submitted for *Yellow Submarine* in place of the still to be completed 'You Know My Name (Look Up The Number)'. (While it's on that film's soundtrack album, the 'Hey Bulldog' sequence was included only in British prints of the film. US viewers did not see it.)

While the cameras whirred, the Beatles recorded ten rhythm track takes of 'Hey Bulldog' and completed it with overdubs. Then, at the conclusion of this 4.00 pm–2.00 am session, after the filming had ended, they watched as it was mixed into mono.

On behalf of brand new enterprise Apple Films, the shooting was overseen by Tony Bramwell, also the director in the absence of any recognised appointee to this position. Not one but two 35mm colour clips were later edited from the session footage, basically similar but with definite shot-by-shot differences.

NEMS Enterprises distributed the clips to British and US television stations. One of the two was screened on four occasions in the UK, each time in black-and-white and on

US television chat show. And the situation wasn't exactly helped along by the shared presence on the *Tonight* sofa of Tallulah Bankhead, the 66-year-old gravel-voiced actress who didn't seem too kindly disposed to being upstaged by the young men at her side. (She was the show's first guest, before John and Paul came on.) All in all, it was a somewhat disappointing appearance, reportedly watched in stony silence by John and Paul a few hours later back in the comfort of Nat Weiss's apartment.

Sometime over these few days – the date not known but probably this same Tuesday – John and Paul filmed another TV interview, this one with Larry Kane, the Miami-based disc-jockey who had been among the keenest and most likeable of the Beatles' media supporters since their arrival in the USA in February 1964. No transmission information is known for this interview, and it may indeed still be unbroadcast.

John and Paul flew back to London during the night of Wednesday 15 May, arriving early morning on Thursday the 16th.

Sunday 19 May
'Kenwood', Weybridge

The *probable* date (though it's long proven impossible to corroborate) of the union of John Lennon and Yoko Ono. Having met on 9 November 1966 and subsequently maintained occasional contact, it was now that they became a couple. Or, to précis the well-worn story, this is the night that John invited Yoko to his house in Surrey (wife Cynthia being abroad on holiday), when they made some sound-collage recordings together and then consummated their new-found love at dawn. Less than six months later John and Cynthia were divorced, less than nine months later Yoko was divorced from her husband (film-maker Tony Cox) and less than ten months later, on 20 March 1969, John and Yoko were married.

The night warrants an entry in this book strictly because of those recordings, which were issued as an album entitled *Unfinished Music No 1: Two Virgins* on Friday 29 November, credited to John Lennon and Yoko Ono. It comprised an uninterrupted wash of *avant-garde* sound effects, beyond the ken of pretty much everyone, and was housed, as the whole world surely knows, inside a sleeve which featured, on the front side, the front view of John and Yoko naked, and on the other the naked view of John and Yoko's backside. Banned, mercilessly criticised and attacked, it made number 124 in *Billboard* and failed to chart at all in Britain, not that chart positions were relevant.

Two Virgins was but the start of a huge number of privately made John and Yoko works, both audio and visual, much of which cannot be pinpointed to a specific date (for the purposes of this book) and not all of which, anyway, was made available for the ever-unwilling consumption of the public at large. Such projects in 1968 (some not issued until 1969) included the films *Smile*, *Two Virgins* and *Rape* and recordings for the album *Unfinished Music No 2: Life With The Lions*.

Thursday 23 May
EMI Studios, London

Proving that pop/rock music was now being taken every bit as seriously as it had once been considered trivial, documentaries began to appear around this time attempting to penetrate the veneer and examine this still-young phenomenon. British producer/director Tony Palmer was the first to undertake such a project with his BBC film *All My Loving*, first shown on BBC1 in black-and-white as part of the *Omnibus* arts series on Sunday 3 November 1968 (10.40–11.35 pm) and repeated in colour by BBC2 on Sunday 18 May 1969 (9.30–10.25 pm). Nine years later, Palmer was even more ambitious, making a series of 17 x 50-minute films for London Weekend Television about the history of popular music, again titled after a Beatles song, *All You Need Is Love*.

Paul and Ringo made personal, individual contributions to *All My Loving* in the form of exclusive interviews filmed inside an unidentified control room at Abbey Road on this day. Also interviewed, at different times and locations, were George Martin, the new Apple press officer Derek Taylor, and George Harrison's mother Louise, while small snippets of archive material that made their way into the finished production included news footage of the Beatles in Rishikesh, an interview with the Maharishi, Beatlemania scenes circa 1964, John and Paul on *The Tonight Show* on 14 May, and a few mute extracts from the 'Lady Madonna' promo filming on 11 February.

Thursday 30 May
Studio Two, EMI Studios, London

The relaxing weeks in India yielded a bumper crop of new compositions. Around the third week of May, the Beatles congregated at 'Kinfauns', George's bungalow in Esher, Surrey, and taped 23 demo recordings using George's Ampex four-track machine. Most, though not all, ended up on the Beatles' next LP, the double-set commonly called the 'White Album' but actually titled, simply, *The Beatles*. In probable order of recording, these were those 23 demos, the main composer and any other pertinent information noted in parentheses:

'Cry Baby Cry' (John)
'Child Of Nature' (John; never recorded professionally by the Beatles, he put a new lyric to this melody in 1971 and released it then as 'Jealous Guy')
'The Continuing Story Of Bungalow Bill' (John)
'I'm So Tired' (John)
'Yer Blues' (John)
'Everybody's Got Something To Hide Except Me And My Monkey' (John)
'What's The New Mary Jane' (John; recorded at EMI 14 August 1968 to 26 November 1969 but unreleased)
'Revolution' (John)
'While My Guitar Gently Weeps' (George)

'Circles' (George; never recorded professionally by the Beatles, he first released this song in 1982)

'Sour Milk Sea' (George; never recorded professionally by the Beatles, he donated this song to Jackie Lomax in summer 1968 – see 25 June entry)

'Not Guilty' (George; recorded by the Beatles at EMI 7–12 August 1968 but not released by them. He issued a solo version in 1979)

'Piggies' (George)

'Julia' (John)

'Blackbird' (Paul)

'Rocky Raccoon' (Paul)

'Back In The USSR' (Paul)

'Honey Pie' (Paul)

'Mother Nature's Son' (Paul)

'Ob-La-Di, Ob-La-Da' (Paul)

'Junk' (Paul; never recorded professionally by the Beatles, he first released this song in 1970 on his initial solo album)

'Dear Prudence' (John)

'Sexy Sadie' (John)

On 14 May, Beatles sessions at EMI were booked Mondays through Fridays for a ten-week period, 20 May to 26 July, 2.30–12.00 pm each day. However, it was only in July that the group began to adhere to this schedule, and the opening session actually took place ten days late, on this day (30 May).

The first song recorded for *The Beatles* was 'Revolution', although it appeared on the LP under the title 'Revolution 1' because by that time a re-make version had been issued as 'Revolution' (on the B-side of 'Hey Jude'). The album also included a sound effects collage titled 'Revolution 9' which was born directly out of this initial session, 2.30 pm–2.40 am, when rhythm track recordings, up to take 18, were made. That 18th take ran to a remarkable 10 mins 17 secs and would receive equally remarkable overdubs the next day.

Friday 31 May

Studio Three, EMI Studios, London

This 2.30–12.00 pm session saw the overdubbing of Paul's bass and two separate John Lennon vocals onto take 18 of 'Revolution 1', a reduction mixdown of this into take 19, more overdubbing (of Paul and George's backing vocals), and a rough mono mix of the work so far.

By the end of the session, the last six minutes of this 10 mins 17 secs recording was the sound of pure chaos – the sound of a 'Revolution', if you will – with discordant instrumental jamming, feedback, John repeatedly screaming "alright" and then, simply, repeatedly screaming, with lots of on-microphone moaning by John and Yoko Ono, with Yoko talking and saying such off-the-wall phrases as "you become naked", and with the overlaying of miscellaneous, home-made sound effects tapes. (This session was Yoko's first with the Beatles and she attended virtually every one from this point onwards, remaining by John's side in spite of occasionally subtle – and occasionally blatant – adverse comments from the others.)

So 'Revolution' was certainly riveting stuff, but not the stuff of singles, which is how John was considering it at this point. Before very long the last six minutes would be hived off to form the basis of 'Revolution 9'.

Tuesday 4 June

Studio Three, EMI Studios, London

A session of unusual overdubs and experiments for 'Revolution 1', 2.30 pm–1.00 am. John re-taped his lead vocal – enigmatically volunteering to be counted both "in" and "out" if there was to be talk of destruction as a form of revolution – and, attempting to alter his voice in some way, he lay flat out on the floor of studio three while doing so. Paul and George added a persistent backing vocal that went along the lines of "Mama Dada Mama Dada Mama Dada"

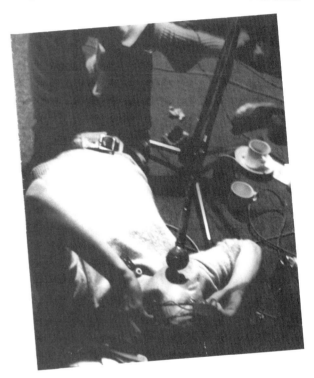

towards the end of the ten-minute recording, Ringo added some percussive clicks, John a tone-pedal guitar part, Paul an organ part and the group then spent some time creating two tape loops, neither of which was used.

A rough mono mix of take 20 (which was a reduction of 19) and an additional copy of this were made at the end of the session for taking away by John and one other person (unnamed on studio documents).

Wednesday 5 June

Studio Three, EMI Studios, London

An especially noteworthy day, for it marked the start of the recording of Ringo's début solo composition, 'Don't Pass Me By'. Strangely, it began the 2.30 pm–1.30 am session as 'Ringo's Tune (Untitled)' and then became, equally

1968

JUNE

temporarily, 'This Is Some Friendly'. Strange because, as early as 1963, it was reported in the press and revealed in a BBC radio interview that Ringo was halfway through the writing of his own song, and even then it he was calling it 'Don't Pass Me By'.

A basic track of piano (Paul) and drums (Ringo) was recorded in three takes. Another piano piece and, oddly, a Christmassy sleigh-bell were then overdubbed, filling the four-track tape. Two reduction mixdowns followed, take five being "best", onto which more bass overdubs were applied; then this became take six via yet another reduction.

Thursday 6 June

Studio Two, EMI Studios, London

More work by Ringo and Paul on 'Don't Pass Me By', beginning at 2.45 pm. During this day they returned first to take five, wiping the two bass tracks in favour of two Ringo lead vocals; this was then reduced into take seven, onto which Paul overdubbed a new bass part. This left one track free, and so it would remain until 12 July. In the meantime, a rough mono mix was prepared and three copies were made for taking away.

At some point during the session, the Beatles were visited in the studio by Kenny Everett, who was granted a group interview for broadcast in the last edition (for now) of his weekly BBC Radio 1 series *The Kenny Everett Show*, on Sunday 9 June (10.00 am–12.00 noon). Even more bizarre than his previous encounters with them on a individual basis, this "interview" was utterly chaotic from the first second to the last. Like Everett himself, the Beatles were anarchically unruly, barely uttering anything of any value and happily dropping into perverse, brief ad-lib parodies of the Beach Boys' 'Cotton Fields' and Nilsson's 'River Deep, Mountain High' (John) and Ray Noble's 1931 dance-band shuffler 'Goodnight Sweetheart' (Ringo). Paul and John together, and then Paul and Ringo together, also recorded jingles for Everett's show.

George wasn't heard in the Radio 1 transmission but he was evident, along with much more of the recording, when the "interview" was pressed as a seven-inch disc by Apple and distributed, for some peculiar reason, as a promotional item in Italy (*Una Sensazionale Intervista Dei Beatles*). The disc was more listenable than Everett's Radio 1 broadcast because that had suffered from his typical surfeit of echo and effects.

While Ringo and Paul returned to 'Don't Pass Me By' in studio two John went elsewhere within EMI Studios to be interviewed, with Victor Spinetti, for an insert into the Saturday 22 June edition of the BBC2 arts programme *Release* (broadcast 10.05–10.45 pm). Filming, in colour, took place from 5.00 pm, John and Victor discussing with Peter Lewis the forthcoming (it opened on 18 June) National Theatre production of *In His Own Write*, which Victor was directing. In the context of the programme, the interview, after editing, was divided into four parts (lasting 7 mins 41 secs, 4 mins 14 secs, 1 min 35 secs and 18 secs), which ran between extracts from the production shot in a BBC studio

on 21 June (John wasn't involved). John also used the interview as an opportunity to candidly vent his latest, radical, political views.

Indeed, the last few hours of this day's session, which ended at 2.45 am, were devoted to *In His Own Write*. Continuing the work of the previous year (see 28 November 1967) John here supervised the making of 12 more sound effects for use in the production, copied them onto a 7½ ips reel and took it away at the end of the session.

Monday 10 June

Studio Three, EMI Studios, London
and **Big Sur, California, USA**

Never before had any of the Beatles left the country while group recordings were in progress. Yet – although some sessions were cancelled (7 and also 12–14 June) – when George and Ringo went to the USA from 7 to 18 June, work continued. John compiled sound effects for 'Revolution 9' on 10 and 11 June, while also on this latter date, when John was employed elsewhere in the building, Paul alone taped 'Blackbird' and mixed the mono master. Then Paul himself flew to the USA on 20 June, on Apple business, missing sessions that day and on the 21st and 25th.

'Revolution 9' began to take shape in this 2.30–5.45 pm session. It was credited on the LP to the Beatles, of course, but in reality it was John's conception from the outset, assembled (rather than "recorded") almost exclusively by him and by Yoko Ono, excepting a little later assistance from George. John spent much of the next few days preparing tapes and loops of sound effects, some of his own making, others culled from his own and the EMI collections.

285

The main purpose of George's US visit was to appear in a feature-film documenting the life of sitar maestro Ravi Shankar, shot under the working title *East Meets West* and, later, *Messenger Out Of The East*. In fact, it wasn't released until three years later – the world premiere was at the Carnegie Hall cinema in New York City on 23 November 1971 – by which time the title had become *Raga*, with the film accompanied by an Apple soundtrack album produced by George.

George only had a brief role in the 96-minute film and shot his contribution on 10–11 June at a country location overlooking the Pacific Ocean, in the Big Sur area south of San Francisco, a 45-minute drive from Monterey where he and Ringo (who went along for the ride) stayed during the early part of their US trip.

On this first day George was filmed being taught a new raga by Ravi, sitting on the grass overlooking the Pacific. There was neither planned dialogue nor prior rehearsal: George and Ravi just played and spoke while the cameras filmed – for about 30 minutes in all, a little section of which went into the finished production.

Tuesday 11 June

Studios Two/Three, EMI Studios, London
and Big Sur, California, USA

Two simultaneous sessions at Abbey Road: a telling first. While John was in studio three (7.00–10.15 pm), experimenting with tape loops for 'Revolution 9', Paul was in studio two (3.30 pm–12.15 am), starting, completing in 32 acoustic guitar/vocal takes, and mixing into mono his new ballad 'Blackbird'.

Also at EMI Studios this day Paul was filmed with Apple's new discovery Mary Hopkin, listening to a playback of one of her first recordings. Directed by Tony Bramwell and shot on 16mm, it was done not for public broadcasting but for inclusion in a short colour film being assembled by Bramwell to promote Apple Records. The film also included footage of the Beatles having a business meeting with Dick James in the Apple office at 95 Wigmore Street, of Alexis Mardas (head of Apple Electronics), and of Paul performing 'Blackbird' live with his acoustic guitar here at EMI Studios and, at one brief point, dropping into 'Helter Skelter' (see also 18 July and 9 September). No shoot date is documented for either of these three last items, although Bramwell remembers that the 'Blackbird' sequence was filmed about two days after it was recorded (circa 13 June).

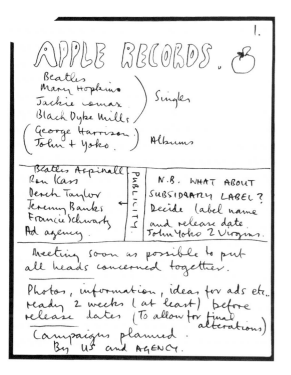

The completed film, untitled, was shown on only three occasions: the first time privately to Capitol Records executives on Friday 21 June; the second time later that same day when Paul and Tony Bramwell attended a Capitol sales convention at the Century Plaza hotel in Los Angeles; the third in Britain, on 26 August, when Derek Taylor showed it at an EMI sales conference.

Meanwhile, back in California this Tuesday 11 June, George and Ravi Shankar returned to the previous Big Sur location and were filmed participating in a teach-in and chatting as they walked together along the cliff-top.

Sunday 16 June

Stonebridge House, Wycombe Rd, Wembley, Middx

An appearance by Paul in a TV programme made for exclusive screening in the USA, taped in England with an English audience by the English TV host David Frost and with entirely British guests (Frankie Howerd, Paul, Mary Hopkin). An independent studio was used: the Stonebridge Park premises, just north of London, of InterTel (VTR Services), the facilities company which had previously been involved in Beatles promo film productions. (See also 10–11 December 1968 and 14 June 1969.)

Originally scheduled to have been recorded on 2 June, the programme was, in effect, a Frost showcase for British talent, and this edition was transmitted, in colour, on Sunday 23 February 1969 (6.00–7.00 pm, EST) as *David Frost Presents...Frankie Howerd*, the stand-up comedian/actor (who was very nearly in *Help!*) being presented to a large US audience for probably the first time. Paul was briefly and semi-humorously interviewed by Howerd (the questions were written for him by Frost), discussing the Beatles' fan following, his (Paul's) young image and the various Apple projects, and this then allowed Paul to introduce the label's young protégée Mary Hopkin, who sang two songs to her own acoustic guitar accompaniment.

Thursday 20 June

Studios Two/Three/One, EMI Studios, London

Paul's absence – he flew to Los Angeles an hour before this 7.00 pm–3.30 am session began – did not affect the work in hand: assembling the ingredients for the master version of 'Revolution 9'.

This was a hectic session, John commandeering all three EMI studios for the spinning in and recording of his assembled myriad tape loops. Just like the 'Tomorrow Never Knows' session two years earlier, there were people all over the premises spooling loops onto tape machines with pencils. But instead of Geoff Emerick sitting at the console, fading them in and out in a live mix, now it was John himself, with Yoko closely by his side.

The most famous of all the 'Revolution 9' sound effects made its bow during this session: the faceless voice which utters "number nine, number nine, number nine". This came from a Royal Academy of Music examination tape in the EMI archive; John had it made into a never-ending loop and faded it up into the multi-track whenever he felt like it. He also overdubbed a mellotron track and – joined by George and Yoko – a number of spoken-word items.

The resulting master recording was the culmination of probably a hundred effects, tape loops, overdubs and more, and all these years later a close listen can still reveal hitherto undiscovered sounds.

Friday 21 June

Studio Two, EMI Studios, London

'Revolution 1' – now with that title – was completed in a 2.30–9.00 pm session with a brass overdub, a reduction mixdown and the addition of a lead guitar part. The brass musicians were Derek Watkins and Freddy Clayton (trumpets), Don Lang (of 6.5 *Special* fame), Rex Morris, J Power and Bill Povey (trombones).

'Revolution 1' and 'Revolution 9' were mixed into stereo between 10.00 pm and 3.30 am, although both were improved upon on 25 June. John had a fine time mixing 'Revolution 9', pushing different images through the separate channels and panning the words "number nine" across the stereo in fractions of a second.

Tuesday 25 June

Studio Two, EMI Studios, London

A 2.00–8.00 pm session that saw final mono and stereo mixing of 'Revolution 1' and editing of the 'Revolution 9' stereo master, cutting its length by almost a minute.

Once again, Paul missed this session, returning from the USA while it was in progress. And George, although he was inside EMI Studios, missed it too – for the second day in succession he was working in studio three with Jackie Lomax, producing and playing guitar on 'Sour Milk Sea' (see 30 May).

Wednesday 26 June

Studio Two, EMI Studios, London

A 7.00 pm–3.30 am session in which the Beatles ran through numerous (but unnumbered) rhythm track rehearsal/recording takes of John's 'Everybody's Got Something To Hide Except Me And My Monkey'. They started again the next night, 27 June, simultaneously wiping all of this session's endeavours.

Thursday 27 June

Studio Two, EMI Studios, London

Seven rhythm track takes (this time numbered) of 'Everybody's Got Something To Hide Except Me And My Monkey', described, for the time being, as 'Untitled' on the recording sheet and tape box. A reduction mixdown of take seven into take eight concluded this 5.00 pm–3.45 am session.

Friday 28 June

Studio Two, EMI Studios, London

There were two sides to John Lennon. On the one he was the composer of raucous rockers like 'Revolution' and 'Everybody's Got Something To Hide Except Me And My Monkey'. On the other he was the writer of tender ballads like 'Good Night' and 'Julia'.

'Good Night' was a children's lullaby, pure and simple, written for his five-year-young son Julian, and it was clear from the start of this first session, which began at 7.00 pm and ended at 4.30 am, that John had handed the lead vocal role to Ringo, whose doleful, plaintive voice suited the song's mood to perfection.

With John accompanying Ringo on an acoustic guitar, several unnumbered rehearsals were taped before five proper takes were made.

Sunday 30 June

Exhibition Rd, Saltaire, Yorkshire

Working in Saltaire, about five miles north of Bradford, producing for the Apple label recordings by the Black Dyke Mills Band (of two of his compositions, the new 'Thingumybob' – written as the theme music for a forthcoming LWT situation comedy series – and the old 'Yellow Submarine'), Paul McCartney consented to film a TV interview with BBC reporter Tony Cliff. It was shot in Exhibition Road, location of Victoria Hall, where – both inside and outside the building – the recordings were taped during this morning.

The interview, duration 4 mins 22 secs, was screened the following evening, Monday 1 July, in the Yorkshire edition of the local news-magazine programme *Look North* (BBC1, 5.55–6.15 pm).

first to take seven and then, after more consideration, back onto take four.

The EMI Studios recording schedule for four days in July 1968. The rich variety of artists – everyone from Adge Cutler to Yehudi Menuhin, via the Shadows, Kathy Kirby, Cliff Richard, Sammy Davis Jr and Paul Jones – made for a creative, workshop environment at Abbey Road which benefited everyone, the Beatles included. Of the abbreviations among the Beatles' schedule entries, "4.T." indicates four-track recording, "GE/RL" the control room team of Geoff Emerick and Richard Lush, and "KNT" and "DH" technical engineers Ken Townsend and Dave Harries.

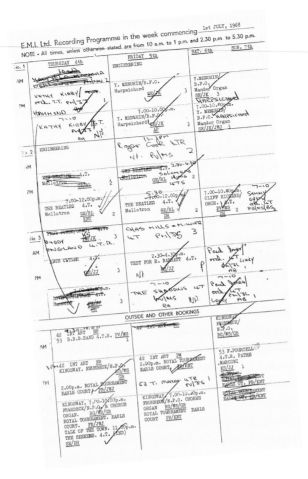

Monday 1 July

Studio Two, EMI Studios, London

The overdubbing of bass followed by two reduction mix-downs and recording of John's lead vocal onto 'Everybody's Got Something To Hide Except Me And My Monkey' occupied this ten-hour session, 5.00 pm–3.00 am.

Tuesday 2 July

Studio Two, EMI Studios, London

A new overdub of Ringo's lead and backing vocals onto 'Good Night', seeing the song through to take 15. George Martin took away two copies of the 15th at the end of this 6.00 pm–12.15 am session so that he could arrange the recording for an orchestra and choir.

Wednesday 3 July

Studio Two, EMI Studios, London

Paul's 'Ob-La-Di, Ob-La-Da' proved to be a somewhat difficult recording, spanning an original version and two re-makes, and taping took place during most sessions from now until mid-July. In this one, 8.00 pm–3.15 am, he and Ringo taped seven rhythm track takes, with overdubs being added

Thursday 4 July

Studio Two, EMI Studios, London

An overdub of Paul's lead and John and George's high-register backing harmonies onto take four of 'Ob-La-Di, Ob-La-Da' began this 7.00 pm–2.15 am session. Take four was then reduced into a new take five onto which Paul added another lead vocal.

Friday 5 July

Studio Two, EMI Studios, London

A 5.00 pm–1.30 am session that produced numerous over-dubs onto 'Ob-La-Di, Ob-La-Da'. Three saxes and one set of conga drums were added between 6.00 and 10.30 (James Gray, Rex Morris and Cyril Reuben on saxes, Jimmy Scott the congas); then from 10.30–11.45 someone (whose name was not noted down) overdubbed a piccolo. This last instrument was quickly deemed surplus to requirements, however, for Paul replaced it with another bass track taped between 11.45 pm and 1.00 am. A rough mono mix, taken away by Paul, occupied the final 30 minutes.

Monday 8 July

Studio Two, EMI Studios, London

In undertaking a re-make of 'Ob-La-Di, Ob-La-Da', the Beatles were for the first time rejecting a recording for which they had recruited outside musicians. This new version occupied all of this 5.00 pm–3.00 am session, the group taping 12 rhythm track takes, including John's distinctive piano intro. Take 12 was then reduced into 13, onto which was over-dubbed lead and backing vocals and percussion. A rough mono mix was then made for Paul to take away.

Tuesday 9 July

Studio Three, EMI Studios, London

Paul couldn't have been completely satisfied with the previous day's re-make of 'Ob-La-Di, Ob-La-Da' either, because between 4.00 and 9.00 pm he set about a second re-make. However, he completed just two takes of this before concluding that the first re-make was not to be improved upon after all. The early part of a second session, 10.00 pm–3.30 am, was then spent overdubbing a new set of lead and backing vocals plus handclaps and vocal percussion onto take 13 and also onto a reduction of this, take 22.

The remainder of the time was devoted to rehearsing 'Revolution'. Paul and George hadn't wanted 'Revolution 1' as the Beatles' next single, fearing that it was not upbeat enough, so John set about a faster and louder re-make while maintaining the same sentiment and – but for one word – the same lyric. This 'Revolution' did indeed appear on the Beatles' next single, albeit as the B-side, and it was every inch the tremendous recording that John had envisaged, ranking with earlier songs like 'This Boy' as the sort of B-side which could have easily been an A-side.

Wednesday 10 July

Studio Three, EMI Studios, London

There were few more exciting, hard-rocking Beatles recordings than the B-side version of 'Revolution', most of which was taped in this 7.00 pm–1.30 am session. A blistering rhythm track was completed in ten takes, vocals were overdubbed onto take 13 (a reduction of take ten) and then 13 was further reduced into takes 14 and 15. John took home rough mono mixes of these and returned the next day declaring take 15 to be "best", ready for more superimpositions.

Thursday 11 July

Studio Three, EMI Studios, London

A reduction mixdown and overdub session, 4.00 pm–3.45 am, by the end of which 'Revolution' also included electric piano and bass while 'Ob-La-Di, Ob-La-Da' had three saxophones and bass. The 'Revolution' piano track was played by rock session player supremo Nicky Hopkins, paid £6 10s (£6.50) for his excellent contribution, while two of the three saxophonists playing on 'Ob-La-Di, Ob-La-Da' are likely to have been Rex Morris and Ronnie Scott. (The identity of the third is not known.) A rough mono mix of this latter song was made before the end of the session.

Friday 12 July

Studio Two, EMI Studios, London

But for an edit piece taped on 22 July, 'Don't Pass Me By' was completed today with the 3.00–6.40 pm overdubbing of a violin followed by bass and piano overdubs and four mono mixes, the best of which was copied for Ringo to take away. The violinist was Jack Fallon, a musician-cum-agent who had engaged the Beatles for their first professionally organised live performance in the south of England, in Stroud on 31 March 1962, and had later booked them for a return visit

there as well as for further dances in Swindon, Lydney and Salisbury.

Two new mono mixes of 'Ob-La-Di, Ob-La-Da', the best being copied for both John and Paul, concluded this particular part of the session at 11.00 pm.

Even allowing for the Beatles' nocturnal habits, it was uncommon for them to *begin* recording at midnight, but that's what happened with the final overdub session for 'Revolution'. Working up to 4.00 am, John added another lead guitar and Paul another bass and then the recording was mixed into mono, again with copy tapes of the best mix being made for both John and Paul to take away.

Monday 15 July

Studio Two, EMI Studios, London

Listening over the weekend to their tape copies of 'Ob-La-Di, Ob-La-Da' and 'Revolution', John and Paul evidently felt that both recordings could be improved still further. So between 3.30 and 8.00 pm this day 'Revolution' was given two new mono mixes and Paul overdubbed a new lead vocal onto 'Ob-La-Di, Ob-La-Da' before mixing for mono anew.

From 9.00 pm to 3.00 am the Beatles rehearsed 'Cry Baby Cry', filling four 30-minute tapes with unnumbered and unusable takes.

Tuesday 16 July

Studio Two, EMI Studios, London

Concentrated work on 'Cry Baby Cry': from 4.00–9.00 pm the Beatles recorded ten takes, a reduction took ten into take 12 and then from 10.00 pm until 2.00 am they overdubbed a harmonium (played by George Martin) and piano (John) onto this.

Loyal balance engineer Geoff Emerick quit working with the Beatles during this session, unable to withstand the rapidly worsening atmosphere and tension within the group. Observers frequently point to these sessions for *The Beatles* when tracing the break-up of the group and many certainly took place in a fraught atmosphere, with lost tempers and open swearing commonplace – essentially the way things would continue until the break-up.

Thursday 18 July

Studio Two, EMI Studios, London

There was no session on 17 July: the Beatles attended the world premiere of *Yellow Submarine* at the London Pavilion and went from there to a party. But work resumed on this day with 'Cry Baby Cry', brought to a conclusion in a 2.30–9.30 pm session by overdubs of a new lead vocal by John, backing vocals, a new harmonium track, a tambourine and sound effects.

From 10.30 pm until 3.30 am the Beatles taped three extended rehearsal versions of Paul's 'Helter Skelter'. The recording on *The Beatles* was a re-make begun on

9 September and so these 18 July versions remain unreleased. Take one lasted 10 mins 40 secs, take two 12 mins 35 secs and take three an epic 27 mins 11 secs, the longest of all Beatles recordings. Each consisted of live drums, bass, lead and rhythm guitars, with vocals by Paul, and each developed into a tight and concisely played jam with long instrumental passages.

Friday 19 July

Studio Two, EMI Studios, London

The original title of John's 'Sexy Sadie' was 'Maharishi', and the lyric would have left no one in any doubt of John's disillusionment with his Yogi. But John replaced 'Maharishi' with 'Sexy Sadie' (also four syllables) to avoid any upset. It was certainly 'Sexy Sadie' from the first EMI recording session, indeed it was already 'Sexy Sadie' when the Beatles had routined a demo at Esher in late-May (see 30 May).

Recording of the song began in this 7.30 pm–4.00 am session with plenty of jamming and 21 rehearsal takes, some up to eight minutes long. More structured recordings, in the form of a re-make, began on 24 July.

Monday 22 July

Studio One, EMI Studios, London

The completion of the album's two Ringo songs: his own 'Don't Pass Me By' and John's 'Good Night'. The larger studio one was necessary to accommodate the 26 musicians

brought in to play a lush orchestral and vocal arrangement for the latter, scored and also conducted by George Martin for a £36 fee. The orchestra (documentation of the musicians' names is lost) comprised the following instruments: 12 violins, three violas, three cellos, one harp, three flutes, one clarinet, one horn, one vibraphone and one string bass. A celeste and a piano were also made available for use by George Martin.

All previous takes of 'Good Night' were overlooked and the song was recorded anew, from start to finish, during this 7.00 pm–1.40 am session. The orchestra was taped first, in 12 takes. Then, from 10.30 to 11.50 pm, eight of the Mike Sammes Singers taped a choral overdub; these were Ingrid Thomas, Pat Whitmore, Val Stockwell, Irene King, Ross Gilmour, Mike Redway, Ken Barrie and Fred Lucas. From 11.50 pm until 1.40 am Ringo recorded his lead vocal, with live backing from the Sammes troupe.

'Don't Pass Me By' had been completed at the start of the session with a tinkling piano intro. Four such edit pieces were recorded, the best being the fourth.

Tuesday 23 July

Studio Two, EMI Studios, London

'Everybody's Got Something To Hide Except Me And My Monkey' was completed during this 7.00 pm–2.30 am session, 22 days after take ten had been marked "best" and the recording thought finished, with a new John Lennon lead vocal and then the overdubbing of backing vocals and handclaps onto a fresh reduction mixdown. Both this and 'Good Night' were then mixed into mono, with copies of the best mixes being taken away by John and Ringo.

Wednesday 24 July

Studio Two, EMI Studios, London

Despite recording 23 more takes of 'Sexy Sadie' (commencing with number 25) in this 7.00 pm–2.30 am session, and the labelling of take 47 as "best", a second re-make would begin on 13 August. The Beatles ended the session taping some sound effects, untitled and unidentified on the recording documents, and then took away the only tape.

Thursday 25 July

Studio Two, EMI Studios, London

George had been patiently suppressing his new material since sessions for *The Beatles* began on 30 May. Almost two months on, he unveiled 'While My Guitar Gently Weeps', the first of four compositions he would snatch for the finished double-album.

This was actually more of a rehearsal session than an attempt to capture the perfect take, and George took away two reels of outtakes for home listening. But he left behind the 7.00 pm–3.15 am session's one and only numbered take, an exquisitely simple solo vocal and acoustic guitar job –

including an extra, final verse not included in the released version – in which he was joined only near the end by an overdubbed organ.

Monday 29 July

Studio Two, EMI Studios, London

There hadn't been a session on Friday 26 July because John was at Paul's house helping him to put the finishing touches to 'Hey Jude'. The song wasn't meant for *The Beatles*, it was to be issued as a single, the group's first since March.

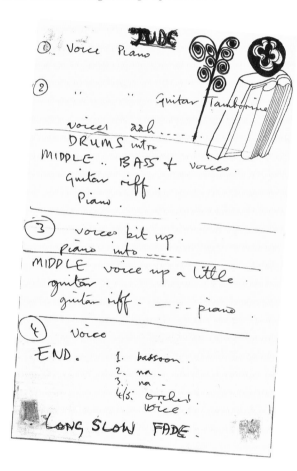

Time and time again the Beatles had shown that they would not stand loitering around musical barriers, but would smash through them. One "rule" was that pop music singles had to last no longer than three minutes. In 1963 it had been more like two. Richard Harris, with 'MacArthur Park', was the first to break the mould and the Beatles swiftly compounded it with 'Hey Jude', the single lasting 7 mins 11 secs. (Had 12-inch singles existed then, 'Hey Jude' would probably have been a regular three-minute single, with the full 7 mins 11 secs version being saved exclusively for the 12-inch.)

Without George Martin in the control room, marshalled for this 8.30 pm–4.00 am session by the Beatles' new regular balance engineer Ken Scott, the Beatles rehearsed/recorded six takes of vocals and piano (Paul), acoustic guitar (John), electric guitar (George) and drums (Ringo).

Tuesday 30 July

Studio Two, EMI Studios, London

'Hey Jude' rehearsals/recordings continued in this 7.30 pm–3.30 am session, moving the song through to take 23 with a reduction mixdown into 25. But it was not the Beatles' intention to capture the perfect recording yet. Sessions over the next few days at Trident Studios had been booked for that purpose, and a large orchestra engaged for a session there on 1 August. (George Martin took away a rough stereo mix of take 25 at the end of this EMI session, enabling him to finalise the song's orchestral score.)

Instead, this session took place primarily to fulfil a promise given by the Beatles to the National Music Council of Great Britain, that they could be filmed for a documentary about the various forms of British music, being produced by James Archibald. The resulting colour feature-film – *Music!* – included two sections of interesting Beatles footage, 2 mins 32 secs and then 3 mins 5 secs compiled from several hours of shooting during this long session (the used bits came mostly from take nine of the song, though), showing the Beatles busking, chatting and rehearsing. They were also seen again, momentarily, at the very end of the film. The musical takes recorded during this session featured just piano, drums and acoustic guitar – so there was no role for George. *Music!* showed him in the control room of studio two sitting between George Martin and balance engineer Ken Scott.

Music! was screened in cinemas in Britain, distributed as the support feature to Mel Brooks' *The Producers* in October 1969. In the USA, however, it was shown on television, introduced by Alistair Cooke in the regular series *NBC Experiment In Television* on Sunday 22 February 1970 (4.30–6.00 pm, EST).

Wednesday 31 July

Trident Studios, St Anne's Court, off Dean Street/ Wardour St, London

Working with Apple artists had introduced Paul and George to Trident, a new studio in central London. Now the Beatles came here for the first time, attracted by its eight-track facil-

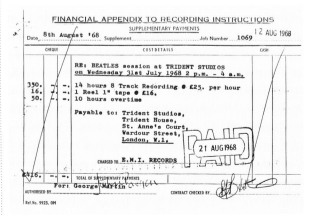

Paul's constructive thoughts about the recording of 'Hey Jude'.

ities. EMI still used four-track; it had an eight-track recorder but the Beatles weren't aware of this because it hadn't been installed.

Assisted by Trident balance engineer and co-owner Barry Sheffield, George Martin produced this 14-hour session, 2.00 pm–4.00 am, in which – utilising the eight-track tape facility economically – the Beatles set about a re-make of 'Hey Jude' with a basic rhythm track captured in four takes, the best of which was the first.

Thursday 1 August

Trident Studios, London

A 5.00 pm–3.00 am session at Trident. From 5.00 until 8.00 Paul overdubbed bass and lead vocal onto 'Hey Jude' while the other Beatles contributed backing vocals. Then from 8.00 until 11.00 pm a 36-piece orchestra overdubbed the arrangement written by George Martin and for which he requested, and received, a precedent-setting £25 fee. There were ten violins, three violas, three cellos, two flutes, one contra bassoon, one bassoon, two clarinets, one contra bass clarinet, four trumpets, four trombones, two horns, one timpanist and two string basses. The musicians' names are no longer on file but it is known that Bobby Kok was one of the three cellists and Bill Jackman – tenor saxophonist on 'Lady Madonna' – played flute.

The musicians were also asked to contribute handclaps and backing vocals ("nah, nah nah nah nah nah nah, nah nah nah nah, Hey Jude") for the powerful build-up in the refrain. Most were happy to oblige but there was one dissenter who reportedly walked out saying "I'm not going to clap my hands and sing Paul McCartney's bloody song!"

Friday 2 August

Trident Studios, London

The completion of 'Hey Jude' with more overdubbing and perfecting from 2.00–11.30 pm, and stereo mixing from then until the session ended at 1.30 am.

Tuesday 6 August

Trident Studios, London
and Revolution, Bruton Place, London

Working, unusually, from the best available stereo mix rather than the original eight-track session tape, 'Hey Jude' was mixed into mono during this 5.30–7.30 pm session at Trident. It was then remixed in the more conventional manner back at EMI on 7–8 August.

Upon leaving Trident Studios (if indeed he was there), John went to a fashion show held at a Mayfair discotheque, the Revolution, where – together with Pattie Harrison and fashion editor Suzy Menkes – he was interviewed by freelance BBC radio reporter Matthew Robinson. The tape was then rushed back to the BBC for inclusion at the end of this day's edition of *Late Night Extra*, broadcast by Radio 1 and 2 from 10.00 to 12.00 pm.

Wednesday 7 August

Studio Two, EMI Studios, London

The Beatles returned to Abbey Road this day for two distinct sessions. From what was noted as 3.00 to 7.45 pm (though it surely couldn't have taken so long), a tape-to-tape copy of the Trident 'Hey Jude' mono mix was made. Then, from 8.45 pm until 5.30 am, they began recording George's 'Not Guilty'. This was to become something of a marathon task, for rehearsal/recording takes exceeded 100 for the first time on a Beatles song and still it would be left unreleased. Not all were complete, however: of the 46 rhythm track takes recorded in this first session only five were worked through to the end of the song.

Thursday 8 August

Studio Two, EMI Studios, London

'Hey Jude' was remixed into mono at the start of this 6.40 pm–6.30 am session, and George Martin took away copies of both this and the mono master for 'Revolution' at the end of the session. As A- and B-sides respectively, the two were issued in Britain as the Beatles' next single on Friday 30 August, the first to bear their Apple record label. It went on to sell more than eight million copies worldwide.

The continuation of 'Not Guilty' occupied the lion's share of this 12-hour session, takes proceeding through to the 101st. Take 99 was marked "best".

Friday 9 August

Studio Two, EMI Studios, London

'Not Guilty' was given a reduction mixdown at the start of this 7.30 pm–2.00 am session, developing take 99 into take 102 onto which overdubbing then began: a second drum track, a second lead guitar and a second bass track. More work would be done on 12 August.

The second song was 'Yer Blues'. The rhythm track was recorded in 14 takes before take six was reduced into take 15 and a part of take 14 was reduced into take 17. Then, for the first time on a Beatles session, the four-track tape itself was edited (editing was otherwise always done at the two-track quarter-inch tape stage), tacking the beginning of take 17 onto the end of take 16. On the finished record the edit is quite clear: it occurs at 3 mins 17 secs and runs through to the fade-out.

Wednesday 14 August

Studio Two, EMI Studios, London

'Yer Blues' was completed at the beginning of this 7.00 pm–4.30 am session (but for a short edit piece taped on 20 August) with the overdub of a second lead vocal by John. The recording was then mixed into mono.

Yoko's influence over John's musical ideas was now clearly evident. Quite apart from their already-taped and soon-to-be-issued audio collage album *Two Virgins*, there was 'Revolution 9', typical of the work John had long been compiling at home but which now, with Yoko's encouragement, he was keen to thrust into the public ear for the first time. In this session, again with Yoko in evidence, John set about the recording of the bizarre 'What's The New Mary Jane', which he later claimed to have written with Alexis Mardas but which was copyrighted to Lennon-McCartney. This wacky "song" nearly made it onto *The Beatles* but was left off at the last minute and remains unreleased – even though John later made a second attempt at putting it out (see 11 September 1969 and 26 November 1969).

John and George were the only Beatles playing on 'What's The New Mary Jane' and John the only singer. But Yoko and Mal Evans also participated in the four takes recorded during this session, the "best" [*sic*] of which, the fourth, was mixed into mono, the tape being taken away by John along with the best mix of 'Yer Blues'.

After the other Beatles had gone home Paul stayed behind to record, alone, his new acoustic ballad 'Mother Nature's Son'. Although it was later to receive a brass overdub, the song was to feature no other Beatles, like the already-taped 'Blackbird' and one other double-album song to follow (see 20 August). On this night Paul recorded 25 takes, the 24th being marked "best" ready for overdubbing another time.

Monday 12 August

Studio Two, EMI Studios, London

George's lead vocal was the final overdub onto take 102 of 'Not Guilty', taped, unusually, in the studio control room rather than in the studio itself. (Even more unusually, this prompted John to decide that the Beatles' next recording session would be held in the tiny annexe to the studio two control room.)

'Not Guilty' was mixed into mono following George's overdubbing, and Mal Evans took away the tape at the end of this 7.00 pm–4.15 am session to have acetate discs cut. And that was that: the song was never mixed again, was left off *The Beatles* and it didn't re-surface until George's 1978 re-recording for his eponymous 1979 album. The Beatles' version remains unissued.

Tuesday 13 August

Studio Two/annexe, EMI Studios, London

Working from 7.00 pm to 5.00 am in the cramped annexe to the studio two control room, the Beatles recorded two John Lennon songs. The session began with the second re-make of 'Sexy Sadie', the best rhythm track being take 107 (take numbers began at 100), which was then given four reduction mixdowns, through to take 111.

Breaking EMI's "staff shalt not take photographs of recording artists" rule, technical engineer Richard Hale poked his camera through a venetian blind and took these snaps of Paul, George and Ringo arriving at Abbey Road for a 'White Album' session.

Thursday 15 August

Studio Two, EMI Studios, London

A 7.00 pm–3.00 am session that saw the recording of Paul's new song 'Rocky Raccoon'. George remained in the control room while the three other Beatles taped the basic track in nine takes. This was then reduced into take ten onto which John overdubbed harmonica, George Martin a honky-tonk piano solo and John, Paul and also George, now down from the control room, backing vocals. John and Paul took away copies of a rough mono mix done at the end of the session while George and Ringo took away copies of the previous night's 'Yer Blues' mix.

Friday 16 August

Studio Two, EMI Studios, London

George returned to 'While My Guitar Gently Weeps' with this session, embarking upon an electric version much different from the gentle acoustic take one recorded on 25 July.

Fourteen takes of the rhythm track were taped during this 7.00 pm–5.00 am session, with the last of these then reduced into take 15 to vacate space for overdubbing.

Tuesday 20 August

Studios Three/Two, EMI Studios, London

With George having suddenly decided on a visit to Greece – he left Britain on 17 August and returned on the 21st – Monday's session was cancelled. But two sessions went ahead on this day, despite his absence. John and Ringo were involved in the first, 5.00–5.30 pm in studio three, completing 'Yer Blues' with Ringo's "two, three…" count-in, edited onto the previous "best" mono mix to make the finished master. Then they watched as Ken Scott (George Martin was absent) prepared the mono master of 'Revolution 9' by making a copy of the best stereo mix.

Only Paul was involved in the second session, which took place in studio two from 8.00 pm until 4.00 am. The first task was to complete 'Mother Nature's Son' by overdubbing timpani, a second acoustic guitar track, drums (positioned in the corridor to alter the timbre) and then – courtesy of George Martin's arrangement, for which, by special dispensation, he again received a £25 fee – two trumpets and two trombones. (Their players' names are no longer on file.)

As a stiff reminder that all was not well within the Beatles' ranks, the session's balance engineer Ken Scott has recalled that the creative, good humoured atmosphere of the 'Mother Nature's Son' brass overdub session was shattered when John and Ringo happened to walk in, but that the sudden tension evaporated immediately they left.

So John and Ringo weren't around to witness two other recordings made by Paul this same night. The first was a demo of a song called 'Etcetera', the only tape of which was taken away and has never been heard since. The second was a 53-second ditty called 'Wild Honey Pie' which was included on *The Beatles*, the result of several solo overdubs (vocals, guitars and a thumping bass drum) onto a single basic track recording. Spontaneity was the key, and the finished mono master was in the can by session's end.

Wednesday 21 August

Studio Two, EMI Studios, London

'Sexy Sadie' was completed during this long 7.30 pm–7.15 am session by way of two reduction mixdowns and various overdubs: another lead vocal by John, an organ, bass, two sets of backing vocals and a tambourine. It is not clear whether George participated in any of this since he returned from Greece only a little earlier in the day. The recording was mixed into mono at the end of the session.

Thursday 22 August

Studio Two, EMI Studios, London

Tensions within the Beatles came to a head at the start of this session and Ringo quit the group. Everyone privy to his decision was sworn to secrecy, however, so news didn't reach the press.

But while Ringo left the country for a chance to think over his future, work did continue in his absence. On this first night without their drummer the three remaining Beatles began the recording of Paul's 'Back In The USSR', taping five takes of a basic rhythm track: drums (Paul), lead guitar (George) and bass (John).

Note: for reasons unknown, a copy of the 'Baby, You're A Rich Man' mono master was made at the end of this 7.00 pm–4.45 am session and was taken away by George Martin.

Friday 23 August

Studio Two, EMI Studios, London

Ironically, Ringo's absence spurred the remaining Beatles into the fast and efficient recording of 'Back In The USSR', completed in this 7.00 pm–3.00 am session. By the time they'd overdubbed once and then overdubbed again onto a reduction mixdown, the finished multi-track featured two more drum tracks (probably by John and George), two more bass parts (probably by Paul and George), two more lead guitar parts (probably by John and Paul), a piano, lead vocals (Paul), fine Beach Boys-style backing vocals (John and George) and handclaps. The final touch was added when the recording was mixed into mono this same evening: the sound of airplanes taking off and landing, which appear at the beginning of the song, here and there as the number progresses and then come to the forefront again at the end. These sounds were taken from the Abbey Road effects collection, 'Volume 17: Jet And Piston Engine Aeroplane'.

Also, four sets of copy mixes were made of 'Back In The USSR', 'Rocky Raccoon', 'Wild Honey Pie', 'Mother Nature's Son' and 'Sexy Sadie', all taken away by Mal Evans.

Saturday 24 August

Studio One, Wembley Studios, Wembley

For much of the British viewing public, John and Yoko nailed their true colours to the mast during this remarkable TV appearance, an interview with David Frost on the fourth edition of his latest series, *Frost On Saturday*, networked live from Wembley Studios by the capital's new ITV station London Weekend Television (LWT) between 6.45 and 7.30 pm. (Other guests in this edition were the singer Blossom Dearie and satirist Stan Freberg.)

The word "Beatles" scarcely came into the conversation: John and Yoko were there to explain to Frost and his studio/viewing audience their views about "vibrations" and about Art, in its manifest forms, demonstrating their beliefs via participation pieces typical of their recent exhibitions. Whether playing devil's advocate or otherwise, Frost was generally cautious, causing John and Yoko to enliven and heat up the discussion a few notches. The resulting interview was so novel that it merited a repeat in a highlights series, *The Best Of Frost*, transmitted by LWT (though only in some regions) on Sunday 18 May 1969 (11.20 pm–12.05 am).

Note: the London-area ITV franchises had latterly undergone radical transformation. Weekday programming was now in the hands of a new company, Thames, with former incumbent Rediffusion bowing out of TV production, while responsibility for the weekends switched from ATV (which did remain in business, though, providing every-day programming for the Midlands area) to new company London Weekend Television. Another casualty of the franchise-switching was ABC Television, once responsible for *Thank Your Lucky Stars*, *Big Night Out*, *Blackpool Night Out* and other series, which was subsumed into Thames. Initially, Thames and LWT utilised the studios of their predecessors: Thames – on-air from 30 July 1968 – broadcast from Rediffusion's Television House in central London, and also from ABC's Teddington complex; LWT broadcast from Wembley, beginning 2 August.

Monday 26 August

Ringo's absence provided an opportunity for tidying up loose ends. In a 4.00–5.00 pm EMI studio two session this day Ken Scott made an improved mono master of 'Revolution 9' by copying straight from the stereo. On the 27th (4.30–5.00 pm) Scott prepared tape copies of 'Ob-La-Di, Ob-La-Da', 'Blackbird' and 'Not Guilty' (all mono) and 'Revolution 9' (stereo).

Wednesday 28 August

Trident Studios, London

Back to Trident, Ringo still absent. The recording of John's 'Dear Prudence' began in this 5.00 pm–7.00 am session, the Beatles creatively using the eight-track facility, piecing together the song instrument by instrument onto a one-take basic track of guitars (George and John) and drums (Paul).

It's worth noting the fiscal generosity – albeit perhaps of a gritted-teeth variety – now being accorded the Beatles by EMI. When they recorded at Abbey Road the studio cost was merely an in-house accounting procedure; this one session at Trident cost EMI £431 in real money, representing studio hire charges, engineer's overtime and blank tape.

Thursday 29 August

Trident Studios, London

A 7.00 pm–6.00 am session which saw overdubbing onto 'Dear Prudence' of bass (Paul), a manually double-tracked lead vocal (John) plus backing vocals, handclaps and tambourines (Paul, George, Mal Evans, Jackie Lomax and John McCartney – Paul's visiting cousin), piano (Paul) and flügelhorn (Paul).

Friday 30 August

Trident Studios, London

On the day that 'Hey Jude' was released, the Beatles returned to Trident, mixing 'Dear Prudence' into mono and stereo in a 5.00–11.00 pm session. (Both would be remixed back at EMI for the finished LP, however.)

Tuesday 3 September

Studio Two, EMI Studios, London

His drum kit smothered in flowers, arranged there by Mal Evans, Ringo rejoined the Beatles with this session – although, ironically, there was nothing for him to do. And though *he* was back, George Martin was absent – now away on holiday, he wouldn't work with the group again until Tuesday 1 October. Balance engineer Ken Scott ran the control room this night.

Recording at Trident had whetted the Beatles' appetite:

they now wanted all of their recordings to be eight-track. So when they got to hear that EMI Studios did have a 3M eight-track recorder but that it was still in the office of technical expert Francis Thompson, they decided to "liberate" it – an action which, although the Beatles themselves were considered beyond reproach, almost resulted in the dismissal of technical engineer Dave Harries, who did the dirty work for them.

Working alone in this 7.00 pm–3.30 am session, George Harrison made first use of the new expanded facilities with a painstaking backwards guitar solo for track five of the tape, the first duty of the session having been to copy the existing four-track tape across to another for eight-track use.

George's final task before leaving at 3.30 am was to oversee a tape-to-tape copy of the basic track of 'Revolution' (from take 16), done so that the Beatles could add a new vocal track – and thereby escape the Musicians' Union ban on miming – during the taping of promotional videos a few hours later at Twickenham.

Wednesday 4 September

Twickenham Film Studios, St Margaret's, Twickenham

Needing to shoot promo clips for both sides of new single 'Hey Jude'/'Revolution' the Beatles came to Twickenham, arriving at 1.30 pm and working through the afternoon and evening in stage one, on a set built over the previous three days.

Michael Lindsay-Hogg was the director, having previously worked with the Beatles on the 'Paperback Writer' and 'Rain' clips (see 19–20 May 1966), this being the first time the group had used a recognised director for a promo shoot since February 1967.

Two finished clips were made for each of the two songs, all four being video-taped in colour. 'Hey Jude' was done first, with Paul sitting at an upright piano, John and George sitting on an adjacent podium playing guitars, and Ringo sitting at the drums up and behind them. The Beatles were also augmented by a 36-piece orchestra decked out in white tuxedos and, for the extended refrain, by 300 extras, from teenager to pensioner, recruited after 20 students had distributed leaflets in the area, and Mal Evans had invited along fans congregated outside EMI Studios during a recent recording session.

At least three takes of 'Hey Jude' were taped, the most regularly seen clip being an edit of two of these, the first half from take one, the last half from take three. The camera and action differences between them were minor, but definite. In all three, Paul sang live to his own pre-recorded vocal during the body of the song and then sang entirely live in the long refrain. (Despite the presence of the orchestra and the Beatles' guitar amps, only the vocals were live, fooling the Musicians' Union into believing that no miming had been perpetrated.)

The two clips for 'Revolution' were largely identical to each other but had some lighting differences. These were very exciting versions, the Beatles – in more typical three guitars and drums set-up – adding a new vocal track to the pre-recorded EMI backing track, blending the fast style of vocals from the B-side version with the lyrics from the slow 'White Album' recording ('Revolution 1'), at this time unissued.

The world premiere of 'Hey Jude' in visual form occurred (in monochrome) during the sixth edition of the London Weekend Television series *Frost On Sunday* on 8 September (9.00–10.00 pm). To fake the illusion that the Beatles were appearing exclusively on his programme, live in the LWT studio, David Frost came to Twickenham this afternoon and was taped on the 'Hey Jude' set introducing the Beatles. First they scooted through a version of Frost's long-established theme music (composed by George Martin and titled 'By George! It's The David Frost Theme') and then Frost spoke into the camera, as only he can, saying "Magnificent! A perfect rendition! Ladies and Gentlemen, there you see the greatest tea-room orchestra in the world. It's my pleasure to introduce now, in their first live appearance for goodness knows how long in front of an audience, the Beatles." (There was, of course, no audience.) At this point, the Beatles dropped into a shocking parody of Elvis Presley's 'It's Now Or Never' but viewers of *Frost On Sunday* did not see this: they saw instead a seamless edit into 'Hey Jude'.

All other British screenings of 'Hey Jude' occurred (also in monochrome) on BBC1, in *Top Of The Pops* on Thursdays 12 and 26 September (both 7.30–8.00 pm), and in the second part of *Top Of The Pops '68* on Boxing Day, Thursday 26 December (6.35–7.15 pm). The one and only British television transmission of a 'Revolution' promotional clip was on *Top Of The Pops* on Thursday 19 September (7.30–8.00 pm).

In the USA, 'Hey Jude' and 'Revolution' were screened, in colour, on successive editions of the CBS series *The Smothers Brothers Comedy Hour*. The former was shown on Sunday 6 October (9.00–10.00 pm, EST), the latter on 13 October (9.00–9.55 pm, EST).

The decision to shoot these relatively straightforward performance clips only came about after an imaginative 38-scene storyboard idea for a 'Hey Jude' promo had been completed by film editor Roy Benson (with whom the Beatles had worked on the 'Hello, Goodbye' clips and *Magical Mystery Tour*). Initially, the Beatles were keen to participate in Benson's production, but they changed their minds upon learning that it would take up to three days to shoot. Consequently, it was not until the evening of 29 August that they decided to video-tape instead at Twickenham.

Another idea around this time which came to nothing was for Apple Corps to buy 90 seconds of peak-time commercial space on network ITV, at around 9.20 pm (just after the main evening ITN news bulletin) on Sunday 17 November, with which to advertise the release of *The Beatles*. The commercial would have featured snatches of music and a personal (pre-filmed) appearance by either Paul or Ringo, and it got as far as an almost-finalised script before being dropped. While television advertising of albums is common practice these days, it would have been a precedent-setting move for the Beatles had they gone ahead with the plan.

Thursday 5 September

Studio Two, EMI Studios, London

The greatest tea-room orchestra in the world, video-taping 'Revolution' and, with David Frost, 'Hey Jude'.

Overdubbing onto take 16 of 'While My Guitar Gently Weeps' continued in the early part of this 7.00 pm–3.45 am session, George adding two separate lead vocals and another lead guitar part, and Ringo adding maracas and drums. But that was as far as it went: George heard a playback, didn't like what he heard and immediately set about a substantially different re-make, recording takes 17–44 of a new basic track comprising drums (Ringo), acoustic guitar and guide vocal

(George), lead guitar (John) and, alternately, piano or organ (Paul). An end-of-session review revealed that take 25 had been "best", so all overdubbing would be applied to this.

Balance engineer Ken Scott again manned the control room this night.

Friday 6 September

Apple Corps, Savile Row, London
and Studio Two, EMI Studios, London

Accompanying her at a piano, Paul briefly participated in a film made this day about Mary Hopkin, shot at the Apple HQ in Savile Row by a camera crew from Thames Television. All told, Mary's filming here and at other locations (without Paul) took place from 11.00 am until 4.30 pm.

Edited down to 3 mins 45 secs, the film was included as the centre-piece of a six-minute feature about Mary in the following Tuesday's (10 September, 5.10–5.50 pm) edition of Thames' new children's series *Magpie*, networked across all ITV stations. Pete Brady, one of the programme's three hosts, anchored the item. (Mary also appeared live on the show, immediately following the filmed insert, broadcast from studio three at Teddington.)

The most famous instance of an outside musician playing on a Beatles studio recording was Eric Clapton's appearance on 'While My Guitar Gently Weeps'. Clapton's superb solo, played on his Les Paul guitar, was just one of a number of overdubs recorded this evening at EMI, 7.00 pm–2.00 am,

Paul at the Apple piano with Pete Brady and Mary Hopkin, filming for the ITV children's series Magpie.

which brought 'While My Guitar Gently Weeps' to a conclusion. Paul played a fuzz bass guitar, George threw in a few high-pitch organ notes, Ringo added percussion, and George – with Paul adding harmonies – taped his lead vocal. Again, Ken Scott ran the control room.

Monday 9 September

Studio Two, EMI Studios, London

Sitting alongside George Martin through many of the summer sessions for *The Beatles* was Chris Thomas, taken on by AIR as Martin's assistant. The 21-year-old ran errands but also watched and studied Martin at work, hoping himself to become a famous producer one day. (And he succeeded.) But Thomas was quite unprepared for the sight of a note from his mentor when he returned from a break on this Monday morning: "Chris: Hope you had a nice holiday; I'm off on mine now. Make yourself available to the Beatles. Neil and Mal know you're coming down."

Effective from this session, then, Chris Thomas became producer of the Beatles, remaining so until George Martin resumed duties on 1 October – although, as Thomas has since acknowledged, it not only took a while for the Beatles to accept him but, in a sense, they scarcely required a producer at this time anyway, being fully cognisant of all aspects of recording. Nonetheless, it was as "producer" that Chris Thomas was described on the relevant recording sheets and tape boxes.

If the guiding and tempering hand of George Martin was ever missed during a Beatles session it was on this night, 7.00 pm–2.30 am, when the group set about a re-make of 'Helter Skelter'. Paul's desire to create a rock music cacophony was fulfilled with 21 quite extraordinary takes: John played bass and a decidedly unskilled saxophone, Mal Evans played an equally amateurish trumpet, there were two lead guitars, heavy drums, a piano, built-in distortion and feedback, backing vocals from John and George, various mutterings and then a raucous lead vocal by Paul, taped while George was running around the studio with a flaming ashtray held above his head, *à là* Arthur Brown.

Tuesday 10 September

Studio Two, EMI Studios, London

A 7.00 pm–3.00 am session that saw the last overdubs applied to 'Helter Skelter'.

Wednesday 11 September

Studio Two, EMI Studios, London

John's song for those wretches who dissected his lyrics for hidden – but *almost* always unintended – revelations and conundrums, 'Glass Onion' is peppered with references to the Beatles' recent output: 'Strawberry Fields Forever', 'I Am The Walrus', 'Lady Madonna', 'The Fool On The Hill' and 'Fixing A Hole'. Recording began in this 7.00 pm–3.30 am session with 34 takes of the basic track, the 33rd being marked "best".

Thursday 12 September

Studio Two, EMI Studios, London

Overdubbing of John's lead vocal and a tambourine onto 'Glass Onion' occupied this 8.30 pm–1.30 am session.

Friday 13 September

Studio Two, EMI Studios, London

An 8.00 pm–1.45 am session that saw the overdubbing of an additional drum track and a piano onto 'Glass Onion'.

Monday 16 September

Studio Two, EMI Studios, London

George was not involved in this 7.00 pm–3.00 am session for Paul's new ballad 'I Will'. The other three Beatles taped 67 takes of the song, Paul singing and playing acoustic guitar, Ringo playing maraca and cymbals and John tapping out a beat with wood on metal. Paul also slipped in several ad-lib numbers between takes, one of which was included on *The Beatles*: an untitled ditty along the lines of "Can you take me back where I came from, can you take me back?" It lasted 2 mins 21 secs, and a 28-second section was cut out later for inclusion in the master, slotted between 'Cry Baby Cry' and 'Revolution 9'. (Also used to usher in 'Revolution 9' was a piece of studio control room chatter which had Alistair Taylor, office manager at Apple, apologising to George Martin and beseeching forgiveness for not bringing him a bottle of claret. The recording date of this item was never documented.)

As for 'I Will', the four-track of take 67 was copied into an eight-track take 68 to facilitate overdubbing another time.

With the eight-track running, 'Glass Onion' received two overdubs of a recorder before this session ended, dropped in at the point where the lyric mentioned 'The Fool On The Hill' as a parody of that original.

Note: between 2.30 and 5.30 pm this day in studio two the first of two "title line" tapes was compiled, whereby the mono masters for all of the Beatles' recorded output, 1962-present, were borrowed from the tape library and, when the title of each song occurred, this little section alone was copied across onto another tape. Studio documentation does not reveal why this curious project was undertaken. It may, for example, have been done for copyright reasons. Interestingly, however, it was given the same "Job Number", for accounting purposes, as the double-album currently in preparation, so it's possible to speculate that a sharply-edited barrage of the Beatles singing their own song titles might well have been considered for inclusion on the 'White Album'.

In seemingly random order, 20 song titles were copied this

day, 27 more on 17 September, 30 more on the 23rd and 22 more on the 24th. There's no evidence that any of the Beatles attended these laborious sessions, the onerous duty of constant tape threading, spooling, searching and copying falling to engineer Ken Scott and tape op Mike Sheady, under the occasional supervision of Chris Thomas.

Tuesday 17 September

Studio Two, EMI Studios, London

'I Will' was completed during this 7.00 pm–5.00 am session with Paul's solo overdubbing of a backing vocal, a baritone dum-dum-dum bass impersonation and a second acoustic guitar track. Also done was a mono mix of 'Helter Skelter' (it lasted 3 mins 36 secs whereas the 12 October stereo mix would run the full length 4 mins 29 secs) and a four-track to eight-track copy of 'Cry Baby Cry' – made, presumably, to facilitate more overdubs although none ever took place.

Wednesday 18 September

Apple Corps, London
and Studio Two, EMI Studios, London

At some time during Apple office hours today, George gave an interview to the *NME* journalist Alan Smith – who, in 1962, had been among the first London-based writers to meet the Beatles (and whose wife worked at Apple). As well as being published in the *NME*, the interview was broadcast in the BBC Radio 1 series *Scene And Heard* on Saturday 28 September, between 6.32 and 7.30 pm, cut down to 5 mins 26 secs. The entire programme was then repeated by Radio 1 on Monday the 30th (7.45–8.44 pm) and also broadcast on three occasions in edited form by the BBC World Service (11.15–11.45 pm on the 28th, 5.15–5.45 am and 1.30–2.00 pm on the 29th, all times GMT).

1968

Although this day's EMI session was logged on the recording sheet as having started at 5.00 pm and finished at 5.00 am, there was nonetheless a clear break in the middle, for all four Beatles, Yoko Ono, Pattie Harrison and Chris Thomas, and probably others too, left the studio to pop around the corner to Paul's house to watch the classic rock and roll film *The Girl Can't Help It* on BBC2, 9.05–10.40 pm.

Earlier, the first to arrive, Paul had concocted a new song right there in studio two, developing a catchy riff into a full-blown rock number called 'Birthday'. Then the others arrived and by 8.30 they'd recorded 20 four-track takes, completing the backing track. Returning to the studio around 11.00 pm – energised after watching Eddie Cochran, Little Richard, Gene Vincent, Fats Domino and other heroes – 'Birthday' was finished off with a four-track to eight-track copy and a host of overdubs onto this: tambourine, piano, handclaps (helped out by Mal Evans), backing vocals (helped out by Yoko and Pattie) and Paul's lead vocal with occasional contributions from John. The completed recording was mixed into mono from 4.30 to 5.00 am.

Thursday 19 September

Studios Two/One, EMI Studios, London

Basic track recordings for 'Piggies', a splendidly acerbic social comment song written by George. The session spanned two studios because, while the Beatles were recording the rhythm track in studio two, Chris Thomas wandered into studio one and spotted a harpsichord that had been set up for a classical session the next morning. His idea to move the instrument into studio two was vetoed by Ken Scott, so, instead, the Beatles shifted their session into studio one.

George suggested that Thomas play the harpsichord part (as a child, he had studied part-time at the Royal Academy of Music), which he did, and for which he later received a £9 fee, and by the end of this 7.15 pm to 5.30 am session 11 takes of 'Piggies' had been recorded, the last marked "best basic".

While busily working on 'Piggies' George played to Chris Thomas another song he had just written, 'Something'. Thomas's enthusiastic response prompted George to consider offering it exclusively to Jackie Lomax; instead he later gave first use to Joe Cocker, helping him to record it in the early spring of 1969. The Beatles taped their version later for *Abbey Road* but Cocker's release, much delayed, came out two months after the Beatles'. Other 1969 tracks surfacing during the recording of *The Beatles* were Paul's 'Let It Be' and 'The Long And Winding Road'.

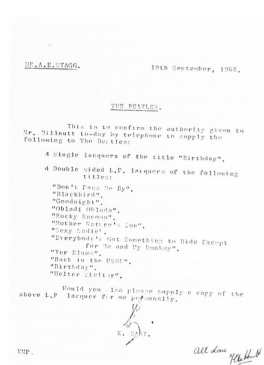

MR.A.E.STAGG.   19th September, 1968.

                    THE BEATLES.

        This is to confirm the authority given to
Mr. Dillnutt to-day by telephone to supply the
following to The Beatles:

        4 Single lacquers of the title "Birthday".

        4 Double sided L.P. lacquers of the following
                    titles:

        "Don't Pass Me By".
        "Blackbird".
        "Goodnight".
        "Obladi Oblada".
        "Rocky Racoon".
        "Mother Nature's Son".
        "Sexy Sadie".
        "Everybody's Got Something to Hide Except
                    for Me and My Monkey".
        "Yer Blues".
        "Back in the USSR".
        "Birthday".
        "Helter Skelter".

        Would you also please supply a copy of the
above L.P lacquer for me personally.

                    K. HART.

VMP.
                    all done

Friday 20 September

Studio Two, EMI Studios, London

'Piggies' was completed in this 7.00–11.00 pm session with overdubbing (onto an eight-track copy of take 11, called take 12) of George's lead vocal and a tape loop of pigs grunting and snorting, created by John with recourse to the Abbey Road sounds effects tape 'Volume 35: Animals And Bees', augmented by real pig-like grunting.

Monday 23 September

Studio Two, EMI Studios, London

Recording of John's 'Happiness Is A Warm Gun In Your Hand', the title soon shortened to 'Happiness Is A Warm Gun'. John later revealed that the song had been drawn together from three distinct parts, but this was done before it reached the studio. The first 45 takes of the rhythm track were taped in this 7.00 pm–3.00 am session: bass, drums, John's lead guitar, his guide vocal and George's fuzzed lead guitar.

Tuesday 24 September

Studio Two, EMI Studios, London

The recording of rhythm track takes 46–70 for 'Happiness Is A Warm Gun' occupied this entire 7.00 pm–2.00 am session. The first half of 53 and the second of 65 were preferred so the actual eight-track tape was cut and spliced together to form a composite "best" take.

Wednesday 25 September

Studio Two, EMI Studios, London

'Happiness Is A Warm Gun' was completed between 7.30 pm and 5.00 am with the overdubbing of John's lead vocal, splendid "bang bang, shoot shoot" backing vocals by John, Paul and George, organ and piano parts, a tuba (virtually deleted in the mixes), a snare drum beat, bass and a tambourine. The recording was mixed into mono between 5.00 and 6.15 am.

Thursday 26 September

Studio Two, EMI Studios, London

Mono mixing of 'Happiness Is A Warm Gun', 'What's The New Mary Jane', 'Glass Onion' and 'I Will', done so that acetates could be cut. A set of such discs was given to George Martin on his return from holiday.

John evidently found the mono mix of 'Glass Onion' lacking and spent the remainder of this 7.00 pm–1.30 am session compiling a bizarre four-track tape of sound effects: a ringing telephone, one note of an organ, BBC TV soccer commentator Kenneth Wolstenholme shouting "It's a goal!"

over a roaring crowd, and the sound of a window being smashed. Despite the considerable effort that he injected into this 2 mins 35 secs tape, nothing from it was ever used because, on his return, George Martin suggested that the song be overdubbed with strings instead.

Tuesday 1 October

Trident Studios, London

The Beatles returned to Trident Studios for no other reason than a week's change of scenery, now that EMI also had eight-track. This first session, 4.00 pm–3.30 am, comprised recordings for Paul's 'Honey Pie', beginning and completing the basic track of piano (Paul), bass (George), drums (Ringo) and electric guitar (John). Two reels of tape were filled but the "best" was called take one, and a rough mono mix of this was taken away by George Martin – now back from his holiday – so that he could arrange a brass and woodwind score.

Wednesday 2 October

Trident Studios, London

A 4.00 pm–3.30 am session of Paul's lead vocal and lead guitar overdubs onto 'Honey Pie'.

Thursday 3 October

Trident Studios, London

The first session for 'Savoy Truffle', a new song written by George and inspired by Eric Clapton's fondness for chocolates – in particular for Mackintosh's Good News boxed selection. Working between 4.00 pm and 2.30 am, George, Paul and Ringo taped a one-take basic track of drums, bass and lead guitar.

Friday 4 October

Trident Studios, London

Paul's 'Martha My Dear' was begun and almost completed in this 4.00 pm–4.30 am session. Apart from a string and horns overdub, it's likely that the master recording featured only Paul, no other Beatles. Piano, drums and a guide vocal were taped first as the basic track for the 14 recruited musicians to follow in their 9.00–12.00 pm overdub: Bernard Miller, Dennis McConnell, Lou Sofier and Les Maddox (violins), Leo Birnbaum and Henry Myerscough (violas), Reginald Kilbey and Frederick Alexander (cellos), Leon Calvert, Stanley Reynolds and Ronnie Hughes (trumpets), Tony Tunstall (French horn), Ted Barker (trombone) and Alf Reece (tuba). Leon Calvert also contributed a flügelhorn part.

Earlier, between 6.00 and 9.00 pm, seven musicians had overdubbed onto 'Honey Pie' – Dennis Walton, Ronald Chamberlain, Jim Chester, Rex Morris and Harry Klein (saxophones) and Raymond Newman and David Smith (clarinets).

Between midnight and 4.30 am Paul recorded his lead vocal and handclaps onto 'Martha My Dear' and then added the quaint "now she's hit the big time!" vocal line to 'Honey Pie'.

Note: as George Martin had prepared a score and booked musicians for this first recording of 'Martha My Dear', Paul must have first given him a privately-taped demo upon which to devise his arrangement.

Saturday 5 October

Trident Studios, London

Overdubbing of George's lead vocal onto 'Savoy Truffle' and bass and electric guitars – both played by Paul – onto 'Martha My Dear'. This latter song, along with 'Honey Pie' and 'Dear Prudence', was then mixed into mono, while 'Honey Pie' and 'Martha My Dear' were mixed into stereo at the end of this 6.00 pm–1.00 am session.

Monday 7 October

Studio Two, EMI Studios, London

Most of this remarkably long session – Monday 2.30 pm to Tuesday 7.00 am – was spent recording the basic track of another new song by George, 'Long Long Long' (at this early stage it was called 'It's Been A Long Long Long Time'). In

Universally bought and loved they may have been, but Beatles albums were usually put together amid the unglamorous clutter of a cramped EMI control room. This 'White Album' picture shows deputy producer Chris Thomas with George Harrison, taken when George Martin was on holiday and away from Abbey Road for four weeks.

what was becoming a familiar pattern with George's songs, John was not present for the session, nor for any of the overdubs, so the line-up was acoustic guitar and vocal (George), organ (Paul) and drums (Ringo). The "best" take, the 67th and last, also featured the sound of a vibrating wine bottle, which rattled on top of a Leslie speaker cabinet when Paul hit a certain organ note. To compound the sound, Ringo recorded an extra spurt of fast drumming for the same passage near to the end of the song.

The earlier part of the session was spent making tape-to-tape copies of the Trident mono and stereo mixes for 'Honey Pie' and 'Martha My Dear', and preparing mono/stereo mixes for 'While My Guitar Gently Weeps'.

Tuesday 8 October

Studio Two, EMI Studios, London

Though it spanned 16 hours – Tuesday 4.00 pm to Wednesday 8.00 am – it was rare for a 1968 Beatles session to be so productive, for two new John Lennon songs, 'I'm So Tired' and 'The Continuing Story Of Bungalow Bill', were started and completed in this time, and George's 'Long Long Long' also received overdubs.

'Long Long Long' began the session, George adding a second acoustic guitar track and a manually double-tracked lead vocal and Paul adding a bass track. Then 'I'm So Tired' was recorded in 14 takes and overdubs.

The basic track of 'The Continuing Story Of Bungalow Bill' was taped in a mere three takes and although it was then crowded with overdubs, it showed the Beatles far removed from the days of *Sgt Pepper*, with a slap-happy, slapdash recording, preserving imperfections in an effort to capture the right atmosphere. 'Bungalow Bill' was a free-for-all, with everyone in the studio shouting out the choruses,

applauding, whistling and backing John's lead vocal. Yoko sang one line solo – "not when he looked so fierce" – the first and only female lead vocal on a Beatles recording, and Maureen Starkey, Ringo's wife, was also one of the assembled chorale. Adding mellotron to the song and gaining another £9 fee was Chris Thomas.

Wednesday 9 October

Studios Two/One, EMI Studios, London

This 7.00 pm–5.30 am session began with stereo and mono mixing of 'The Continuing Story Of Bungalow Bill' and then moved on to 'Long Long Long', Paul adding a sporadic backing vocal and Chris Thomas overdubbing piano, completing the recording. A mono copy of the 27-minute 'Helter Skelter' from 18 July was also made, taken away by Paul for his personal, private collection.

While Chris Thomas was making his piano contribution, Paul beckoned Ken Townsend to join him in studio one, where the technical engineer did a spot of balance engineering and tape operating while Paul quickly recorded the basic track of his short and *risqué* 'Why Don't We Do It In The Road'. Excepting a drum part overdubbed by Ringo the next night, this was another McCartney solo recording, taped on a four-track machine. Five takes of lead vocal and acoustic guitar were recorded and he then added a piano overdub onto the last of these.

Thursday 10 October

Studios Two/Three, EMI Studios, London

Recording of the double-album approaching an end, three songs were finished during this 7.00 pm–7.15 am session: 'Piggies', 'Glass Onion' and 'Why Don't We Do It In The Road'. The first two were completed with 7.00–10.30 pm strings overdubs, played by the same eight musicians: Henry Datyner, Eric Bowie, Norman Lederman and Ronald Thomas (violins), Eldon Fox and Reginald Kilbey (cellos), John Underwood and Keith Cummings (violas). 'Glass Onion' was then mixed into mono and stereo and 'Rocky Raccoon' and 'Long Long Long' into stereo only.

While these activities were in progress in studio two, Paul once again invited Ken Townsend to man the control room elsewhere, in studio three this time, as he added the finishing touches to his 1 min 40 secs rocker 'Why Don't We Do It In The Road'. More vocals, handclaps, bass and also drums (Ringo's sole role) were added to take five; this was then reduced into six onto which Paul added an electric guitar track.

Friday 11 October

Studio Two, EMI Studios, London

'Savoy Truffle' still needed some finishing touches. One was a saxophone overdub, scored by Chris Thomas, recorded between 3.00 and 6.00 pm and simultaneously distorted up

in the control room by George Harrison. The six saxophonists were Ronnie Ross and Bernard George (baritone), Art
Ellefson, Danny Moss, Harry Klein and Derek Collins
(tenor).

The session then continued for another 12 hours, to 6.00
am, with mono and stereo mixing of 'Piggies', 'Don't Pass Me
By' and 'Good Night'.

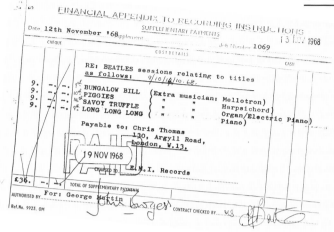

Saturday 12 October
Studio Two, EMI Studios, London

Saturday night mixing, from 7.00 pm to 5.45 am, with mono
and stereo mixes of 'Everybody's Got Something To Hide
Except Me And My Monkey', 'Mother Nature's Son' and
'Ob-La-Di, Ob-La-Da', stereo only of 'Helter Skelter' and
mono only of 'Long Long Long'.

Sunday 13 October
Studio Two, EMI Studios, London

A delivery deadline bearing down upon them, this was the
Beatles' first Sunday session since recording 'Hey Bulldog'
on 11 February, and it saw John start and complete the
album's 32nd and final song, his touching ballad 'Julia'. He
taped it alone – the only solo Lennon recording in the
Beatles' canon – by twice singing along to his acoustic guitar
accompaniment.

A spot of mixing completed this 7.00 pm–6.00 am
session: 'Julia', 'Dear Prudence' and 'Blackbird' were mixed
into mono and stereo, 'Wild Honey Pie' and 'Back In The
USSR' into stereo only.

Monday 14 October
Studio Two, EMI Studios, London

Ringo flew out to Sardinia for a two-week holiday this
Monday morning leaving final mixing and judgement on the
double-album's running order to the three remaining Beatles
and the production team.

This was the last recording session for *The Beatles*, 'Savoy
Truffle' being completed with overdubs of an organ and an
electric piano (both played by Chris Thomas), a second elec-
tric guitar part, tambourine and bongos. The remainder of
this 7.00 pm–7.30 am session was devoted to mixing: 'I Will',
'Birthday', 'Yer Blues', 'Sexy Sadie' and 'What's The New
Mary Jane' going into stereo, 'Savoy Truffle' and 'While My
Guitar Gently Weeps' into mono and stereo, 'Long Long
Long' only into mono.

Tuesday 15 October
Studio Two, EMI Studios, London

A 6.00 pm–8.00 am session mixing 'Happiness Is A Warm
Gun' into stereo and 'I'm So Tired' and 'Cry Baby Cry' into
mono and stereo.

Wed 16 and Thurs 17 October
Rooms 41/42 & Studios One/Two/Three,
EMI Studios, London

The Beatles' first and only 24-hour session – Wednesday
5.00 pm to Thursday 5.00 pm – and it took place without
George, who flew out to Los Angeles Wednesday daytime
leaving John, Paul and George Martin, with balance engineer Ken Scott and tape op John Smith, the problematic
task of working out the running order for *The Beatles* from
the 31 available songs and compiling/editing the mono/
stereo masters. (As 'Not Guilty' was never mixed into stereo
one can assume that it wasn't a final contender for a place on
the double-album.) It was imperative that they finally finished the job in this long session so at some point or other
during the 24 hours every studio and listening room at
Abbey Road was commandeered.

In the end, after dropping 'What's The New Mary Jane'
to leave a total of 30 numbers, there was an *approximate*
structure: the heavier rock songs ('Birthday', 'Yer Blues',
'Everybody's Got Something To Hide Except Me And
My Monkey', 'Helter Skelter') mostly ended up on side C,
three songs with an animal in the title ('Blackbird', 'Piggies',
'Rocky Raccoon') were placed together, in succession,
on side B, George's four songs were
spread out one per side, no composer
had more than two songs in succession and each side lasted between 20
and 25 minutes.

As well as the crossfading and editing (*The Beatles*, like *Sgt Pepper*, had
none of the customary "rills" between
songs), 'Why Don't We Do It In the
Road' was mixed into mono and
stereo. (As, too, was the 1967 recording 'It's All Too Much' for release not
here but on the impending *Yellow
Submarine* soundtrack album.)

The next day, 18 October, John
Smith (working alone, 12.00 noon to
1.00 pm in studio one), ironed out

*The downside of bureaucracy.
Despite the umpteen millions
of Beatles discs sold, and vast
profits generated, EMI Records
managing director Ken East had
to memo Abbey Road studio
manager Allen Stagg, and copy
the memo to Ron White and
George Martin, before John and
Paul could be given early
pressings of the 'White Album'.*

lingering master tape imperfections by re-copying the "best" mono mixes of 'Yer Blues' and 'Don't Pass Me By'.

The Beatles was issued in Britain on Friday 22 November, 30 new songs in one remarkable batch. And still there was more: in its November 1968 issue, *The Beatles Monthly Book* magazine reported that two new songs, 'Polythene Pam' and 'Maxwell's Silver Hammer' had been written just too late for *The Beatles*. Both would be recorded in 1969 – along with two more album's worth of material.

Tuesday 29 October

Between 10.00 am and 1.00 pm in EMI studio three Geoff Emerick prepared the remaining stereo mixes for the *Yellow Submarine* soundtrack album: 'Hey Bulldog', 'All Together Now', 'All You Need Is Love' and 'Only A Northern Song'. This latter title was a "mock stereo" mix, worked from the mono master rather than the original four-track.

Some seven months after the film it was supposed to accompany (although the movie didn't open in the USA until mid-November), the *Yellow Submarine* soundtrack album was released in Britain on Friday 17 January 1969, one side comprising the Beatles' music – and only four "new" songs, at that – the other containing George Martin's orchestrated film soundtrack, recorded on 22–23 October 1968 at EMI. (He had originally recorded this for the film itself at Olympic Sound Studios.) The principal reason for the delay was the Beatles' desire to have the 'White Album' issued first, with a clear interval of not less than three weeks following.

The Beatles were mildly criticised over the *Yellow Submarine* LP for giving less than their usually excellent value-for-money. They evidently took the criticism to heart, for there remains in the EMI archive a master tape for a seven-inch mono EP, to run at LP speed, 33⅓ rpm, compiled and banded on 13 March 1969, with the following line-up: Side A) 'Only A Northern Song'; 'Hey Bulldog'; 'Across The Universe'. Side B) 'All Together Now'; 'It's All Too Much'. (Note the bonus inclusion of 'Across The Universe', long finished and mixed but, as of March 1969, still awaiting issue on the World Wildlife Fund charity album.) But despite these labours the EP was never issued. Never exactly rhapsodic with the *Yellow Submarine* project, perhaps the Beatles felt that they were better off consigning it entirely to the past.

Friday 15 November

CBS TV Studio, Sunset Boulevard, Hollywood, California, USA

George's trip to Los Angeles on 16 October was the start of a near seven-week visit, most of this time being spent producing numbers for *Is This What You Want?*, the début album by Apple Records artist Jackie Lomax.

George also appeared once on US television, making an unannounced cameo walk-on in *The Smothers Brothers Comedy Hour*, taped on Fridays in front of an audience at the

CBS TV studio in Hollywood and broadcast primetime two nights later. This particular edition went out on Sunday 17 November (9.00–10.00 pm, EST) and guest-starred Dion and George's good friend Donovan.

During this same visit to California, George was introduced to the electronic music expert Bernie Krause, and Krause, in turn, introduced George to the newly-invented but still largely undiscovered Moog synthesiser. (See also 5 August 1969.) Krause was responsible for some of the effects on Lomax's album and also got together with George at some point in November to record a long (25-minute) instrumental piece – titled 'No Time Or Space' – that comprised the entire second side of an album, *Electronic Sounds*, issued by George on 9 May 1969. (George bought a synthesiser and took it home to England, the other side of his LP – the 19-minute instrumental 'Under The Mersey Wall' – being recorded in Esher some time in February 1969, the precise date not documented.)

Wednesday 20 November

Cavendish Avenue, London

To promote the release of *The Beatles* Paul gave an interview this day to the new programme director of Radio Luxembourg, former Australian radio DJ Tony Macarthur. It was recorded at Paul's house in St John's Wood and aired the following evening (21 November, 7.30–9.30 pm) as part of a special two-hour Luxembourg programme devoted exclusively to the 'White Album', broadcast literally on the eve of its release. The programme also included separately-taped comments by Judith Simons, pop correspondent for the *Daily Express*.

Around this date (20 November) John and Yoko gave a frank, revealing and long (40-minute) TV interview to the respected Dutch sociologist/writer Bram de Swaan. Shot, of all places, in a dentist's waiting-room in Knightsbridge, central London, the first half of the interview featured Yoko only because John was in another room receiving treatment. Acquired by the VARA-tv network, the film was broadcast in the youth interest series *Rood Wit Blauw* by the channel Nederland 2 on Wednesday 15 January 1969 (9.25–10.05 pm).

Tues 10 and Wed 11 December

Stonebridge House, Wembley

Wednesday 11 December

Broadcasting House, London

Inspired, perhaps, by the Beatles' *Magical Mystery Tour*, the Rolling Stones conceived and financed to the tune of about £50,000 their own colour TV special, rehearsed and part-taped on 10 December at the Stonebridge Park studios of InterTel (VTR Services) and taped to completion the next day, Wednesday 11 December. The title was *The Rolling Stones' Rock And Roll Circus* and it remains publicly unseen

at the time of writing (1991) – although the former Stones'
and Beatles' business manager Allen Klein, who owns the
rights, has discussed plans to issue it on home-video. This
remarkable 50-minute film included a noteworthy musical
guest appearance by John Lennon.

As the title suggests, the show mixed music with all the
atmosphere and fun of a circus, with acrobats swinging over
the musicians' heads, midgets, a fire-eater, a trained tiger and
a plate-spinner all borrowed from Sir Robert Fossett's Circus,
and with many of the musical participants wearing circus
costumes (Mick Jagger, for example, wore a ringmaster's outfit). The director was Michael Lindsay-Hogg, well-known to
the Beatles story by now, and the cameraman was Tony
Richmond – within a month the two would team up again
for the Beatles' *Get Back* project (see 2 January 1969).

John was one of a number of guest musicians in the show,
the others including Eric Clapton (Cream were invited to
participate but had just broken up), Jethro Tull, Marianne
Faithfull, The Who and Mitch Mitchell (from the Jimi
Hendrix Experience), while the Rolling Stones topped the
bill, performing a set that didn't begin until 2.00 am on
Thursday, by which time the invited audience, also
bedecked in fancy dress, had mostly left. Playing under a
marquee canopy and joined on bass by Keith Richard (as he
was still calling himself at this point), on lead guitar by Eric
Clapton and on drums by Mitch Mitchell, John first sang
(while playing rhythm) a scintillating live version of 'Yer
Blues', just issued on *The Beatles*. Then he stepped aside to
let Yoko take over, she and the band – joined by "perpetual

violinist" Ivry Gitlis – performing an electric jam which was
later called 'Her Blues'. Other off-stage, ad-lib footage
involving John and Mick Jagger was taped by Michael
Lindsay-Hogg over these two days, as was a
sequence in which everyone lined up in their
circus costumes, John dressed as a juggler,
Yoko as a witch.

In addition to being video-taped, the
entire shoot for *The Rolling Stones' Rock And
Roll Circus* was recorded on a mobile four-
track machine, with Glyn Johns and Jimmy
Miller engineering, the Stones planning to
issue a soundtrack album with the proceeds
going to charity. Like the film itself, this
never reached fruition.

After the *Rock And Roll Circus* taping,
John, with Yoko, headed into central
London to participate in the BBC Radio 1/2
programme *Night Ride*, transmitted live from
Broadcasting House from 12.05 to 2.00 am.
He and Yoko discussed their new album *Two
Virgins* with host of the first hour John Peel
(so they would have been on the air between
12.05 and 1.00 am) and, since it was in the
twilight hours, when few would have been
listening, the BBC dared to play a 3 mins 20
secs extract from the album, which must
have been among its most extensive broadcasts ever.

RECORDING SESSIONS for *The Beatles* had proven to the group that they had entered a tense and difficult period. As their natural motivating force, Paul could think of only one solution: to have them "get back" to what had united them best before inconceivable fame and fortune had clouded the issue – live performances.

The plan which garnered the most approval, even if it was sanctioned only grudgingly in some quarters, was for the Beatles either to broadcast live or video-tape an eight-song/one-hour television show in front of an audience – perhaps along the lines of the September 1968 'Hey Jude' promotional video shoot which everyone had enjoyed so much.

Ideas were tossed around, intoxicating suggestions so typical of the late 1960s: it needn't be at the Roundhouse in north London – they could play in a disused Thames-side flour mill, on board a ship, or from a stage in the middle of the Sahara desert. The most seriously considered suggestion was that they perform in a Roman amphitheatre in North Africa, starting at dawn in an empty venue and finishing with the arena filled with peoples of all races, colours and creeds.

But the vital unanimity which would have propelled the plan into reality could not be achieved, for despite the pitching in of big ideas, none of the other Beatles was *wholly* enthusiastic about Paul's scheme. In a particularly dark mood one day John even suggested that the group simply call it quits and break up. George half-heartedly agreed to the TV performance if it would please the others, and though Ringo was content to go along with the majority decision he

reminded everyone that in February and through the spring he'd be shooting a film, *The Magic Christian*, for which he had been contracted the previous October.

Although they remained unable to agree on a venue, the man appointed as producer of the TV show, Denis O' Dell, suggested that they at least begin rehearsing, and do so at Twickenham Film Studios up to 3 February, when *The Magic Christian* (for which he was also the producer) would go into production there. O' Dell suggested too that the rehearsals themselves be filmed on 16mm, for perhaps a half-hour "Beatles At Work" TV documentary, which would either accompany the concert performance or be shown a few days before or after.

Straight away, however, at Twickenham, the old hostilities returned: Yoko encroaching upon the Beatles' line-up, Paul "bossing" the group around and allegedly "preaching" to George about his playing.

Clearly, it was sensible that the Beatles should have got together soon to paper over, and perhaps even seal, the cracks which had yawned wide open in 1968, yet to be doing so only 11 weeks after concluding the seemingly interminable 'White Album' sessions was asking for trouble. Those wounds hadn't yet healed, now salt was being applied.

What's more, putting 30 songs onto *The Beatles* had fairly exhausted John, Paul and George's cache of unrecorded compositions. They had a few but the onset of a new project so soon forced some into the open before they could be honed and polished as would usually have been the case.

The TV show idea came to a grinding halt in the Twickenham canteen at lunchtime on Friday 10 January. Having bickered, on film, with Paul, and – according to press reports which followed – had a bitter argument with John, and having finally relinquished any vestige of interest in the

Beatles performing an audience TV show, George walked quietly up to the others, said "See you 'round the clubs" and left. No one tried to stop him as he got into his car and drove to his home in Esher and then, according to published reports, journeyed north to see his parents for a few days.

After lunch, John, Paul and Ringo (it was still only five months since he himself had quit) returned to the sound-stage and carried on. As the cameras filmed, but without speaking among themselves, Yoko sat on George's blue cushion, a symbolic moment, and proceeded to scream a long, typically-Yoko jam, a powerful, angry blast in which the Beatles turned *avant-garde*, forcing feedback from their instruments. After it was over, still without speaking, the group left and went home.

A weekend break followed and, although no one expected George to return, the other three Beatles assembled at Twickenham the following Monday morning and spent most of the next three days sitting around on the set, talking meanly and playing only a little music. (No footage from this period made the finished film.)

George eventually returned to London on Wednesday 15 January for a long – reportedly five-hour – meeting with the others in which he announced that he was prepared to leave the group. Provided, however, that they met certain conditions he would acquiesce: the Beatles must abandon all talk of live performances and, instead, make an album, using the songs intended for the TV special with a few more thrown in. So they could cease the Twickenham rehearsals and switch location to Apple, to their own brand-new basement recording studio.

It was at this point, and this point only, that the footage shot at Twickenham for a "Beatles At Work" TV production turned instead into the start of a feature-film idea, to be called – like the album they'd now be making – *Get Back*.

Although the first Apple Studios shoot/recording session was set for Monday 20 January it didn't take place until Wednesday the 22nd. The delay was caused by the fact that Apple Corps had a subsidiary company called Apple Electronics, run by a trusted friend of the Beatles, Alexis Mardas. They named him "Magic Alex" and asked him to install their recording studio in Savile Row. Mardas promised miracles: EMI (Abbey Road) had only just expanded to eight-track recording, Apple would have 72-track. And there would be no need to use those awkward studio "baffles" around Ringo to prevent leakage of his drum sound into the other microphones. Magic Alex would install an invisible sonic force-field which would do the work unobtrusively.

Hardly surprisingly, it all worked out very differently – and the Beatles lost two days work. Those around at the time recall that Alex's mixing console was made of bits of wood and an old oscilloscope and looked not unlike the control panel of a B-52 bomber. The Beatles did a sample recording but when they played back the tape it was patently unusable. George Martin had to call EMI and ask for a temporary loan of two four-track consoles to go with Apple's eight-track recorder. Even prior to this, George Harrison had realised the Heath Robinson nature of Apple's studio when he saw Mardas wandering around in a white coat, with a clipboard,

muttering and trying to place box-loads of tiny loudspeakers around the studio, one for each track.

The Apple recording sessions were slightly less unhappy than the Twickenham rehearsals, and this was mostly due to the presence of Billy Preston on electric piano/organ, who was seized upon by George as someone whose involvement was likely to lift sagging spirits and also improve behaviour: a group of people who know each other intimately well, and have begun to pick away at faults and foibles, will usually be mollified when an outsider is in their midst, and this is exactly what happened.

The chief concern of Michael Lindsay-Hogg, the *Get Back* director, was that now that the hoped-for TV show was no longer on the blocks, how would the project reach a recognisable conclusion? Beatles albums had been known to take five months to record, and he hadn't intended to be shooting for that long. During a *Get Back* meeting at Apple on Sunday 26 January the idea was raised that the group give an unannounced live performance the following Thursday on the roof of their own office building. They hoped to blast out that area of central London and, since it was planned for lunchtime, provide free entertainment for the nearby office and shop workers. A number of people claim to have originated the rooftop idea, which suggests that it was warmly received by all. In fact, though, as the clock ticked past noon that Thursday 30 January, George was still only lukewarm towards the idea and Ringo emphatic that he wouldn't participate. It was only the combined force of John and Paul which made it happen.

John Lennon May 19.

Though he liked to think of himself and Yoko as being blissfully above it all, as shown in this rare drawing, complex business problems plagued John just as much as the other Beatles in 1969, destroying group unity in the process.

So it all worked out in the end: it wasn't the Sahara desert, it wasn't a Roman amphitheatre, and they weren't even visible to the crowds which quickly gathered in the street below, but the Beatles got to play live one last time, and the event was filmed, providing Lindsay-Hogg with a perfect climax to *Get Back*.

The shooting of *Get Back* duly ended the next day, but the project was still far from over, dragging on for more than a year and proving a considerable millstone around the Beatles' neck. As for the album they'd supposedly completed, neither the original *Get Back* LP nor even a revised edition was released, both being rejected by the Beatles who – even though they'd intended to be recorded with rough edges – were dismayed at just how ragged and dispirited they had become. That all this was happening less than two years after *Sgt Pepper's Lonely Hearts Club Band* speaks volumes for the apathy within the group at this time.

Get Back should have finished the Beatles. It certainly led to an artistic parting of ways which, for some time, they looked incapable of bridging. As spring turned into summer, untold business problems and disagreements plagued the group too, and irreconcilable differences of opinion over who should manage their affairs led to the most fundamental schism of all. Hitherto, the Beatles had always discussed problems between themselves and then reached a unanimous decision. But when Paul bitterly rejected the suggestion of John, George and Ringo, that they entrust Apple and 20 per cent of their income to Allen Klein, here was a conflict destined never to be resolved.

Paul's proposition that the New York law firm Eastman and Eastman, his new father- and brother-in-law respectively, manage their affairs instead was rebuffed with equal force by the others. Henceforth the Beatles were split into opposing camps, fighting each other instead of working for the common good in this year when, crucially, Brian Epstein's NEMS Enterprises was taken over by a City investment trust, the Beatles lost a vital battle to take control of their Northern Songs publishing copyrights and a new recording agreement with Capitol was engineered.

It was in July, amid this very fraught atmosphere, that, casting their differences aside, the Beatles came together one last time to record a new album. Untitled at the start (as were most of their albums when in progress), they decided to call it *Abbey Road*, after the leafy north London street where they'd recorded almost all of their music since 1962.

And, miracle upon miracle, it was a magnificent parting shot, an astonishingly good piece of work, quite possibly the best album they had made together. It was astonishing because the

animosity within the group was *mostly* submerged during the sessions and prevented from interfering with what, in the end, the Beatles were all about – music. All four Beatles shone on *Abbey Road*: John's compositions and vocal work, Paul's supreme musical craft in the long medley, George's skilful musicianship and two marvellous songs, and Ringo's truly excellent drumming. Even if, as the recording studio engineers have since stated, the four Beatles really only got together for the recording of the basic tracks, with overdubs being applied in a mostly solo fashion, somehow the sum of those four parts did still make a whole unit, which was the vital ingredient missing from *The Beatles*, recorded in much the same way in 1968.

But although the bad feelings were *mostly* submerged during the sessions, there were still some heavy moments. Any one of the group might perhaps bang down his instrument, not turn up on time, keep the others waiting three or four hours or blame another member for not having rehearsed or played his bit right. In his 1970 plaintiff's affidavit citing reasons why the Beatles' legal partnership should be dissolved, Paul stated "Musical differences became more marked, particularly between myself and John. By the time that *Abbey Road* was recorded we were openly critical of each other's music, and he was no longer interested in the performance of songs which he had not written himself."

With *Abbey Road* the Beatles touched glory for the last time together. Solo projects took over the rest of the year, and all of 1970, and ever thereafter, with John using the Plastic Ono Band as his new creative outlet, even performing two concerts with them this year; in November of 1969 Ringo became the first member of the group to record a genuinely musical solo album (discounting, that is, earlier projects such as George's *Electronic Sounds* and John and Yoko's "experimental" LPs); George went out on the road as the low-key member of Delaney & Bonnie's backing band; and Paul retreated to his Scottish farm to contemplate his future. Come Christmas he, too, had begun recording a solo album, certain now that the Beatles had reached the end of the road.

All that lay ahead, in 1970 and beyond, was the potentially – and real, as it transpired – nightmarish problem of untangling the ties that bound them.

Thursday 2 – Wednesday 15 January

Excluding 4, 5, 11 and 12 January
Twickenham Film Studios, St Margaret's, Twickenham

The start of the *Get Back* enterprise, probably the most confusing and certainly the most frustrating period in the Beatles' career.

Uncertain still of what would be the exact end purpose of their activities, the group came to Twickenham on Thursday 2 January to begin rehearsing new songs for a television show. And they arranged for the rehearsals to be filmed too, for transmission at some unforeseen time, with Michael Lindsay-Hogg recruited as director for both the concert and documentary filming, the Beatles themselves as executive producers (putting up the money), Tony Richmond as director of photography and Glyn Johns invited by Paul to oversee all of the sound aspects.

Though he wasn't given a title, as such, Johns was, in effect, the sound producer. Here at Twickenham it was his task to solve any technical problems, ensure that the right sound balance was achieved and get the music and conversation down on tape – not multi-track tape as used in a recording studio but quarter-inch two-track. (It is important to recognise that none of these Twickenham film sessions was taped in the customary recording studio manner. These were strictly rehearsals, not sessions, and only one tiny speech ad-lib from these two weeks at Twickenham was issued on record.)

Shooting began first thing on the first day, Mal Evans and his assistant being filmed by Michael Lindsay-Hogg carrying the Beatles' musical equipment onto the cold and otherwise empty stage one. The Beatles were due to arrive at 11.00 am, and all did so except for Paul who, presently favouring public transport as a means of travelling around London, finally showed up at 12.30.

Working a Monday to Friday to schedule, typically starting between 11.00 am and 1.00 pm each day, the Beatles made a fairly torrid time of their days at Twickenham. It certainly wasn't all doom and gloom, but much of it *was* unsatisfactory. Working without any clear musical direction, with a cauldron of resentment and anger simmering just below the surface, and often surfacing, and working in the cold and otherwise empty soundstage, the Beatles now were just a tired, jaded rock group going through the motions.

The most digestible of the Twickenham material was included in the *Let It Be* film; much of the remainder was just too awful to be screened, showing the Beatles jamming more than one hundred songs, sometimes just a line sometimes an entire number, dire performances which were mostly out of tune and time and rarely played with any conviction, ranging from children's nursery rhymes ('Baa Baa Black Sheep') to rock standards ('All Shook Up'), to Beatles oldies ('Help!') to future solo titles ('All Things Must Pass', 'Back Seat Of My Car', 'Child Of Nature' ['Jealous Guy'], 'Every Night', 'Give Me Some Truth', 'Maybe I'm Amazed', 'That Would Be Something'), to made-up-on-the-spot tunes which, because of the film, had to be copyrighted ('Suzy Parker', ascribed to Lennon-Starkey-Harrison-McCartney,

'Paul Piano Intro', Lennon-McCartney, and 'Jazz Piano Song', McCartney-Starkey), to nonsense ('Chopsticks') and to childhood radio memories ('When Irish Eyes Are Smiling'). As a two-week exercise in sheer sloppiness it was a good job.

After George quit the rehearsals, and the group, on 10 January the project changed direction, with plans for the television show going the same way as vague plans for concerts – even unannounced and impromptu ones – into the bin. The cameras could remain, but they would be used instead to film the making of an album, to be recorded at the Beatles' own brand new studio at Apple.

Tuesday 21 January

Elstead to London

The first of a number of BBC radio interviews with an individual member of the Beatles by *Daily Express* pop reporter David Wigg, each for broadcast in the weekly Radio 1 news/review programme *Scene And Heard*. This interview with Ringo, from which 6 mins 30 secs was included in the Saturday 25 January edition (1.00–2.00 pm), was recorded in the back of his Mercedes-Benz car, en route from his Surrey home into London. (The entire programme was repeated on Tuesday 28 January, 7.45–8.44 pm.)

In 1976 Wigg collected together extracts from some of his BBC interviews with John, Paul, George and Ringo and released them as an album, *The Beatles Tapes*, which the four by then ex-Beatles attempted but failed to injunct.

Wednesday 22 January

Apple Studios, Savile Row, London

The *Get Back* recording sessions, to use the Beatles' own words in a later advertisement for the 'Get Back' single, saw the group "as nature intended…as live as can be in this electronic age…[with] no electronic watchamacallit". In other words, having pioneered perfectionist multi-track rock recordings, the Beatles were returning to basics, forsaking technical trickery, ADT, tape loops, overdubbing and all. They wanted every song on this new album to be strictly live – even with live mistakes.

As explained earlier, Glyn Johns – called Glynis Johns by John Lennon, after the British actress – was, in a sense, not merely the *Get Back* balance engineer, he was also its uncredited producer, for George Martin's precise involvement in *Get Back* remains unclear. His voice is evident on only some of the Apple session tapes; for the others – with the Beatles addressing their chat, enquiries, requests and musical instructions directly to Johns – one must assume that Martin was absent. Similarly, for the mixing, a question mark remains over Martin's precise role, although Johns was in attendance at every session. Matters became so confused that the 'Get Back' single was issued without any producer's credit at all. To cap it all, when Johns twice compiled a *Get Back* album at the Beatles' specific request – in May 1969 and January 1970 – they rejected his efforts on both occasions.

And Johns' was not the only new face on these Beatles sessions. Billy Preston, a fine American organist, happened to be in the 3 Savile Row reception area on 22 January and was literally grabbed by George Harrison and cajoled into joining the Beatles' basement sessions, to alleviate the tense atmosphere and – since overdubbing was out – add a vital fifth instrument to the live sound. (John, Paul and George had known Preston since 1962, when he was a teenage member of Little Richard's backing group, sharing a two-week bill with the Beatles at the Star-Club in Hamburg.) Preston sat in on almost all of the *Get Back* recording sessions, for which he was paid £500, and was signed to Apple Records in his own right on 31 January. His first Apple album, the recording of which began on 5 May at Olympic Sound Studios, was largely produced by George Harrison and wholly mixed by Glyn Johns.

It is vital to recognise that these *Get Back* sessions – later described by George as "the low of all-time" and as "hell... the most miserable sessions on earth" by John – were, by their very nature, largely unplanned and impromptu. The Beatles would drift in and out of songs and jam almost incessantly, leaving little in the way of finished items in their wake. They would chat, tell jokes and have arguments while the tapes were running. It was then, and remains so today, quite impossible to catalogue the recorded "takes". In some instances, take numbers announced for the film crew were also used on the Apple tape boxes, so the first take of a song might be announced as "take 32". Some sessions were difficult to catalogue at all, even briefly, and many tape boxes were left blank – until Paul found the time and resolve to plough through them, writing brief notes on the labels.

On this first day, 22 January, the tapes captured the Beatles running through John's 'All I Want Is You' (the working title of 'Dig A Pony'), Paul and John's 'I've Got A Feeling', John's 'Don't Let Me Down', a group instrumental that Paul titled 'Rocker' on the tape box, his 'Bathroom Window' (the working title of 'She Came In Through The Bathroom Window') plus covers of the Drifters' 'Save The

No hiding it – the Beatles, and Yoko, listen to an obviously uninspiring Get Back *tape playback at Apple. Boredom, despair, anger, resentment and tiredness show clearly in the once always-smiling faces.*

Last Dance For Me' and, to illustrate something Paul was saying about the group, Canned Heat's 'Going Up The Country'. Billy Preston made his début with the Beatles on electric piano when they were working out the chord structure for Paul's 'Bathroom Window', recorded properly later in the year for *Abbey Road*.

Note: insufficient documentation is available to detail the precise start/finish times of the Savile Row sessions, but it is known that the Beatles returned not only to pre-1965 recording methods but to pre-1965 time routines too, possibly because of the film crew's requirements. Most sessions began in the late-morning, between 10.00 and 11.00 am, and ended in the late-afternoon, around 5.00 pm. One or two ran through until 10.00 pm.

Thursday 23 January

Apple Studios, London

Making his début as the Beatles' tape op on this session was Alan Parsons, later a top producer and creator of the highly successful Alan Parsons Project. Onto his tapes went ten takes of Paul's new song 'Get Back', now the *raison d'être* for the project, plus a one-minute instrumental jam, led by Billy Preston on electric piano, suitably named 'Blues' on the tape box.

Friday 24 January

Apple Studios, London

The tapes rolled for Paul's 'On Our Way Home' (the working title of 'Two Of Us'), Paul's 'Teddy Boy', 'Maggie Mae', John's 'Dig It' and 'Dig A Pony' and Paul and John's 'I've Got A Feeling'.

It was between takes of 'On Our Way Home' that the Beatles burst into a 38-second, hammed-up version of 'Maggie Mae', the traditional Liverpool song about a celebrated local lady of the night. This was released on *Let It Be* with a "Trad arr Lennon-McCartney-Harrison-Starkey" composer credit.

The Beatles' version of 'Teddy Boy' was included on the first of the two unissued *Get Back* albums and remains unissued to the time of writing. However the song was re-recorded alone by Paul and released in April 1970 on his first solo album *McCartney* (see 21 February 1970).

The Beatles recorded two versions of 'Dig It', an impromptu number created by John though released on *Let It Be* as a Lennon-McCartney-Starkey-Harrison composition. The first version, on this day, was never issued, although John's childlike spoken message at the end of the recording – "That was 'Can You Dig It' by Georgie Wood, now we'd like to do 'Hark The Angels Come' " – was tacked onto the end of the other version on the *Get Back* and *Let It Be* albums.

Basic studio documentation shows that certain (unspecified) titles were roughly mixed into stereo by Glyn Johns during a 90-minute session this evening at Olympic Sound Studios in Barnes, without the Beatles in attendance.

Saturday 25 January

Apple Studios, London

Recording of 'Untitled Jamming' (a very brief and entirely instrumental piece), a speedy jam of the 1957 Everly Brothers hit 'Bye Bye Love', and of two new songs: Paul's 'Let It Be' and 'George's Blues', which was the working title of 'For You Blue' (see also 8 January 1970).

Sunday 26 January

Apple Studios, London

The second version of 'Dig It' began this session. Substantially abbreviated, it appeared on the *Get Back* and *Let It Be* albums, for although this recording was 12 mins 25 secs in duration, the *Get Back* version faded-in at 8 mins 27 secs and *Let It Be* used only the part from 8 mins 52 secs to 9 mins 41 secs. Heather Eastman, six-years-old and six weeks away from becoming Paul's step-daughter, contributed amusing backing vocals during the early part of the song and George Martin shook a percussive shaker.

A long rock and roll medley followed: 'Shake Rattle And Roll' (Joe Turner, 1954), 'Kansas City' (Wilbur Harrison, 1959, not at all like the Little Richard cover which the Beatles recorded for *Beatles For Sale*), 'Miss Ann' (Little Richard, 1956), 'Lawdy Miss Clawdy' (Lloyd Price, 1952), 'Blue Suede Shoes' (Carl Perkins, 1956) and 'You Really Got A Hold On Me' (the Miracles with Smokey Robinson, 1962, as covered on *With The Beatles*). George then led the Beatles into a mostly instrumental version of the same group's 'Tracks Of My Tears' (1965 but not a hit until 1969).

Two other songs were taped on this day: Paul's ballad 'The Long And Winding Road', which would be returned to, and a George Harrison demo, untitled, recorded solo with vocal and lightly strummed lead guitar, which would not. When titled, this became 'Isn't It A Pity' but it was never recorded by the Beatles as a group, and it didn't surface publicly until 30 November 1970, when it was one of the outstanding songs on George's solo triple-album *All Things Must Pass*.

Again, basic studio documentation shows that certain (unspecified) titles were mixed into stereo by Glyn Johns during a private 90-minute session this evening at Olympic.

Monday 27 January

Apple Studios, London

Recording of 'Untitled Jamming', 'Get Back', 'Oh! Darling', 'I've Got A Feeling' and 'The Walk'.

'Untitled Jamming' was precisely that: 10 mins 54 secs in duration, heavy, unstructured – and barely listenable. Most of the session was devoted to 'Get Back' but none of the versions was issued, only John busking a parody, "Sweet Loretta Fart she thought she was a cleaner but she was a frying pan", which ended up on the *Let It Be* album. Paul's 'Oh! Darling', to be recorded properly for *Abbey Road*, was given a rehearsal

run-through, and the Beatles also jammed a cover of 'The Walk', a major US hit for Jimmy McCracklin in March 1958.

Tuesday 28 January

Apple Studios, London

A surprisingly productive session, with both sides of the next single – 'Get Back' and 'Don't Let Me Down' – being recorded. It was an interesting session too because the Beatles also resurrected two of their earliest songs, 'Love Me Do' and 'The One After 909' (as well as taping more versions of 'Dig A Pony', 'I've Got A Feeling' and 'Teddy Boy').

The Beatles and Billy Preston suddenly became a cohesive unit for the recording of 'Get Back' and 'Don't Let Me Down', and both were excellent versions. 'Get Back' was faded-out for the single because it ran on for some considerable time, ending with forced "ho-ho-hos" from Paul. This little section was included as the final item on the unreleased *Get Back* LPs and was also used over the end titles of the *Let It Be* film.)

A 1969 Beatles re-recording of 'Love Me Do' – the song which started it all – sounds inviting. Unfortunately, the sound itself was quite the reverse. As with most *Get Back* recordings, it was little more than an impromptu jam – slow and somewhat bluesy – rather than a serious attempt at a modern re-make. Paul handled the vocal with John supporting, and although complete at 2 mins 20 secs, and although the *Get Back* project was supposed to be capturing the Beatles' rough edges, this recording was just too rough to be considered for release.

Several jammed versions of 'The One After 909',

1969

Paul, Ringo, Michael Lindsay-Hogg (in black), Mal Evans and others recce the rooftop a few days before the Get Back live performance. Note the working cameraman – as with so many other entire sequences, the resulting footage never made the finished film.

unissued from the 5 March 1963 session at EMI, were taped during this session, and, additionally, two Billy Preston demos were recorded – 'Billy's Song (1)' and 'Billy's Song (2)' being their only titles – Preston making good use of the four musicians around him. As far as can be ascertained, neither song, both of which were "southern" style blues, was issued even in finished form.

At the end of the session the tape caught a good deal of conversation between the Beatles about whether they should be rehearsing or recording. Or maybe they shouldn't be bothering at all? And filming – when would it end, and what songs would they do? All four contributed opinions and ideas, although it was patently obvious by the questions, answers and attitudes that the *Get Back* project was not going at all well.

Wednesday 29 January

Apple Studios, London

Recording of 'Teddy Boy', 'The One After 909', John's 'I Want You' (re-recorded for *Abbey Road* as 'I Want You (She's So Heavy)' – see 22 February 1969 for first entry) and jams of Buddy Holly's 'Not Fade Away' and 'Mailman, Bring Me No More Blues' and also the Cavern Club crowd-pleaser 'Besame Mucho', one of the four numbers performed by the Beatles during their first visit to EMI on 6 June 1962.

Thursday 30 January

Apple Corps (Roof), London

The Beatles' celebrated rooftop show. An idea conceived during a meeting on 26 January, it was the first of two consecutive Beatles/Billy Preston "performances" which concluded the *Get Back* project, for on 31 January they ran through numbers inside the basement studio.

This day's work has passed into history as the Beatles' last live performance, even if it couldn't be classified as a concert. The 42-minute show (about half of which comprises the sensational close to the *Let It Be* film) was a lunchtime blast into the cold wind – imagine a high London rooftop in January – that brought part of the capital to a standstill, until the police, in turn, brought the show to an enforced conclusion.

Much was commercially used from the 42 minutes on the roof, in the *Let It Be* film and on the *Get Back* (unissued) and *Let It Be* albums. What follows is a detailed description of the full rooftop repertoire, as preserved on EMI's eight-track tapes, with a guide to how it was made available.

1. Setting-up. Michael Lindsay-Hogg shouts, "All cameras, take one!" The first song is a rehearsal of 'Get Back', the end of which is greeted with fairly polite applause which clearly reminds Paul of a cricket match, so he steps back to the microphone and mutters something about Ted Dexter (Sussex and England player of the time). John says, "We've had a request from Martin Luther."

2. Another version of 'Get Back'. (The *Let It Be* film has a well-matched edit of these first two 'Get Back' versions.)

At the end of the song John says "Had a request for Daisy, Morris and Tommy."

3. 'Don't Let Me Down' (*Let It Be* film), straight into…

4. 'I've Got A Feeling' (*Let It Be* film and LP), with John saying at the end, "Oh, my soul…[applause]…so hard". (George sings a little on 'I've Got A Feeling'; he is otherwise vocally silent during the rooftop performance.)

5. 'The One After 909', ending with John sarcastically reciting a line of the 1913 standard 'Danny Boy'. (*Let It Be* film and LP, and *Get Back* LP.)

6. 'Dig A Pony', with a false start ("one, two, three, hold it [John blows nose] one, two, three"). Ends with John saying "Thank you brothers…hands too cold to play the chords." (*Let It Be* film and LP, although for the latter producer Phil Spector edited out the song's opening and closing "All I want is" vocal lines.) The eight-track tape also has a brief rehearsal of the song before it began, and John asking for the words. In the film an assistant can be seen kneeling before him with the lyrics attached to a clipboard.

7. Second engineer Alan Parsons has changed tapes, the first one being full. While waiting, the Beatles and Billy Preston have strummed through a quick version of the national anthem, 'God Save The Queen'. The new tape catches a few seconds of this, but it is neither released on record nor seen in the film.

8. 'I've Got A Feeling', second rooftop version. (Not released on record or seen in the film.)

9. 'Don't Let Me Down', second rooftop version. (Not released on record or seen in the film), straight into…

10. 'Get Back', the third rooftop version, somewhat distracted owing to police presence, seeking to bring the show to a close. The song almost breaks down but lurches to a finish, with Paul ad-libbing "You've been playing on the roofs again, and you know your Momma doesn't like it, she's gonna have you arrested!" At the end Paul acknowledges the fervent applause and cheering from Ringo's wife Maureen with "Thanks, Mo" and then John, having stepped away from the microphone, returns to add, somewhat hammily, "I'd like to say 'thank you' on behalf of the group and ourselves and I hope we passed the audition!" (Paul and John's comments, but not this 'Get Back' song, were included on the unreleased *Get Back* LP. The *Let It Be* LP employs a skilful crossfade from the 28 January "single" version of 'Get Back' to these rooftop ad-libs, implying that the song itself was from the roof performance. The *Let It Be* film is the only publicly available true recording, with the lurching version of 'Get Back' and the closing ad-libs.)

Basic studio documentation shows that certain (unspecified) titles were mixed into stereo by Glyn Johns during a 7.30–10.00 session this evening at Olympic Sound Studios in Barnes. Acting on his own volition, Johns then had acetate discs cut from his mixes and presented them to the Beatles.

When 'Get Back' was issued as a single, with 'Don't Let Me Down' on the B-side, Apple distributed to TV stations 16mm colour promotional clips utilising Michael Lindsay-Hogg's film work. Although neither contained any footage from the actual 28 January studio recordings, both were synchronised to those versions, and both presented material different from that included in *Let It Be* when the film finally surfaced in May 1970. 'Get Back' featured footage from the rooftop performance this day, 'Don't Let Me Down' a combination of Twickenham filming and the rooftop performance.

Only 'Get Back' was screened in Britain, on four editions of *Top Of The Pops* (all monochrome, BBC1, 7.30–8.00 pm) – Thursdays 24 April, 8 May, 15 May and 22 May 1969 – and then, in colour, in part one of *Top Of The Pops* '69, shown on Christmas Day, 2.15–3.00 pm. Both 'Get Back' and 'Don't Let Me Down' were shown in the USA on the CBS-TV programme *The Glen Campbell Goodtime Hour*, on Wednesday 30 April 1969 (7.30–8.30 pm, EST).

Friday 31 January

Apple Studios, London

The "Apple Studio Performance", in other words the final recording of those numbers unsuitable for the rooftop show: two piano songs ('The Long And Winding Road' and 'Let It Be') and one acoustic ('Two Of Us'). The Beatles also ventured into a jam of 'Lady Madonna' which, although later mixed by Glyn Johns as a potential LP track, was barely worthy of release. For these recordings the Beatles and Billy Preston arranged themselves into stage formation on and around a platform. As can be seen in the *Let It Be* film, Paul was the focus of attention throughout because these were all his songs.

With this session, the shooting of *Get Back* was completed, but the finished production would be a long time coming…

To promote 'Let It Be' when it was issued as a single, Apple distributed to TV stations a 16mm colour promotional clip showing one of the nine takes of this song recorded/filmed this day (but different from the one seen in the *Let It Be* movie) combined also with footage from 'Two Of Us' and 'The Long And Winding Road' performances. Synchronised to the "single" version – which included a later overdub (see 30 April 1969) – the 'Let It Be' clip was twice screened in Britain, on *Top Of The Pops* on Thursdays 5 and 19 March 1970 (both times in colour, BBC1, 7.15–8.00 pm). In the USA it was shown on *The Ed Sullivan*

Bottom-left: Paul McCartney's tape-box annotations for the first of the two reels of Apple rooftop recordings.

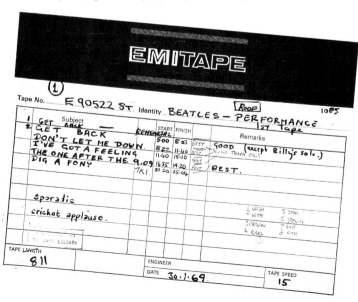

Show (CBS) on Sunday 1 March 1970, as part of an hour-long – 8.00–9.00 pm (EST) – salute to the Beatles, subtitled 'The Beatles Songbook', otherwise featuring acts performing cover versions of their material.

Monday 3 February – Friday 2 May

Twickenham Film Studios, St Margaret's, Twickenham and **London-area locations**

Less than four years after receiving his MBE medal there, Ringo returns to Buckingham Palace, looking rather different, as the hapless dosser in The Magic Christian.

With *Candy* still awaiting its British opening 14 months after being shot (the London premiere was on 20 February 1969), Ringo embarked upon his second film acting role outside of the Beatles. It was a more sizable part this time, playing support to main star Peter Sellers in *The Magic Christian*, the film of Terry Southern's satirical 1959 novel about man's greed and lust for money.

The film is essentially a series of sketches, in which eccentric millionaire Sir Guy Grand (Sellers) tempts and tests people to see if they're prepared to undertake certain tasks in exchange for a money handout. Ringo played the role of Youngman Grand, Sir Guy Grand's adopted son, who accompanies his father as he goes through the film proving that "everyone has a price". This role was especially created for Ringo and does not appear in the original book, although Southern was involved in the production and approved of the amendment. Another key change was the switching of location from the USA, as it appears in the book, to Britain, with filming clearly based in London. It was directed by Joseph (Joe) McGrath – it was he and Peter Sellers who cast Ringo for the Youngman Grand role – and produced for Grand Films by Denis O' Dell (he also worked for Apple) on behalf of the American financiers Commonwealth United.

Despite Southern's involvement and his original novel, he did not write the screenplay alone: Joe McGrath shared the credit with him while Peter Sellers and two young and not yet famous British comedy writers, John Cleese and Graham Chapman, supplied some additional material (and also appeared before the cameras). In fact, the casting was strong throughout: apart from Sellers, Starr, Cleese and Chapman there was Richard Attenborough, Yul Brynner, Roman Polanski, Laurence Harvey, Christopher Lee, Dennis Price, Spike Milligan, Raquel Welch, Wilfrid Hyde White, Patrick Cargill (from *Help!*) and many faces especially recognisable to British viewers.

Shooting took place over a 13-week period (Mondays to Fridays only), based on all of the three stages at Twickenham Film Studios. Documentation proving the precise dates for Ringo's day-by-day action no longer exists, but he was active for almost all of this period, including several location shoots. Among these were a grouse-shooting scene, filmed on Chobham Common in Surrey, south-west of London, on Thursday 13 March; a very funny sequence with Spike Milligan as a traffic warden, filmed on Tuesday 18 March outside the Star & Garter public house in Lower Richmond Road, Putney, on the Thames embankment; a Hamlet striptease scene with Laurence Harvey, filmed at the Theatre Royal in Stratford, east London, on Tuesday 1 April (the Beatles are seen standing outside this theatre in their 'Penny Lane' promotional film); a "boat race" scene (footage from this was intercut with real action from the Oxford v Cambridge race) filmed on Wednesday 9 April at the Barclays Bank rowing club on The Embankment, just along the road from the Star & Garter; and various location scenes for which dates cannot be traced – in Hyde Park, outside Buckingham Palace, in the Quadrangle and in an office at Westminster School, in a field near Elstree, in the car park at Barnes railway station, and at Sotheby's auction room in New Bond Street.

The climax of the film was also shot adjacent to the River Thames, close by the National Film Theatre on the South Bank. In this, Sir Guy Grand has prepared a vast vat full of

slaughterhouse ordure, stirring hundreds of bank notes into it with an enormous paddle. This is the final test, and he is not disappointed: besuited city gents display their hunger for lucre by wading and diving into the vat to extract the sodden money. The original intention was for this scene to be shot on Wall Street in New York but the film's American financiers refused to allow this. In fact, they were unhappy about filming this sequence at all, and it was only when Peter Sellers – who felt strongly that it was a vitally important scene – offered to put up his own money to pay for the shoot that Commonwealth United agreed to back it. This sequence was filmed long after all of the other location material, probably between 23 and 26 June, when final shooting at Twickenham also took place.

Because the production came in on time, and under budget, Ringo, Peter Sellers, Joe McGrath, Denis O' Dell and their respective partners were treated by Commonwealth to a free trip to New York on the *Queen Elizabeth II*, soon after her maiden voyage, leaving Southampton on 16 May and arriving in New York on the 22nd. No shooting for *The Magic Christian* was done in the USA, however, and everyone flew down to the Bahamas for a two-week holiday.

On their return, Ringo and Peter Sellers went back to Twickenham for post-production work, including an audio recording dubbed over the film's trailer. The royal world charity premiere of *The Magic Christian* took place at the Odeon Cinema, Kensington, west London, on Thursday 11 December. Ringo and his wife Maureen attended, as did John and Yoko.

Ringo and Peter Sellers both undertook their fair share of media promotion for *The Magic Christian* upon its December 1969 release. (For Ringo's details, see relevant entries at that point.) Of special note, Sellers was subjected to a full documentary, produced by Denis O' Dell, directed by Tony Palmer (see also *All My Loving*, 23 May 1968) and transmitted as *Will The Real Mr Sellers…* on Thursday 18 December, 9.10–10.00 pm. In addition to a few short extracts from the feature-film, this 50-minute programme included behind-the-scenes footage of Sellers and Starr, and of Paul and John at an end-of-shoot party on 4 May (see that entry). Paul was involved in *The Magic Christian* in one small but vital way: he wrote the main theme song 'Come And Get It', released by Apple group Badfinger (see 24 July 1969).

Wednesday 5 February

Apple Studios, London

Stereo mixes, ending with a tape compilation, of the 30 January rooftop recordings: 'I've Got A Feeling' (two versions), 'Don't Let Me Down', 'Get Back' (two versions), 'The One After 909' and 'Dig A Pony'.

Tuesday 11 February

Room 53, EMI Studios, London

The production of mock-stereo tapes from original mono masters of some of John and Yoko's *avant-garde* recordings.

Precisely which recordings was not detailed on the EMI documentation, and John took away all of the original and newly produced tapes at the end of this 3.00–5.30 pm session.

Saturday 22 February

Trident Studios, London

There was, at most, only a fine dividing line between the end of sessions for *Get Back* and the beginning of sessions for what was to become *Abbey Road*. Although work on the latter did not begin in earnest until July, a number of that album's songs were well under way by then. (*Get Back* filming certainly ended on 31 January, however.)

One such song was John's 'I Want You' – released as 'I Want You (She's So Heavy)' – first rehearsed at Apple on 29 January and now recorded properly in this 8.00 pm–5.00 am session at Trident with 35 takes of the basic track plus guide vocal. But why Trident, and why the three-week gap since 31 January? Trident because – with filming now complete – Apple Studios was undergoing a re-build and technological re-think, but the Beatles remained keen to work in an independent studio. And the delay because of the 7–15 February hospitalisation of George Harrison for the removal of tonsils, and early-February visits to the USA by Glyn Johns and Billy Preston, both back in London to contribute to this session.

Sunday 23 February

Trident Studios, London

A 6.30–12.00 pm session editing takes nine, 20 and 32 of 'I Want You' into one master take, making an eight-track safety copy of this and preparing a rough mono mix for John to take away.

Tuesday 25 February

EMI Studios, London

Perhaps as a 26th birthday present to himself, George went into EMI alone on this day and, with only Ken Scott in the control room, recorded elaborate vocal, guitar and piano demos of three of his latest compositions: two takes of 'Old Brown Shoe' (to become the Beatles' next B-side), one take of 'Something' (to be issued on *Abbey Road* and as the A-side of a single) and two takes of 'All Things Must Pass' (never recorded by the Beatles other than in *Get Back* rehearsal form at Twickenham; the title track of George's triple-album issued on 30 November 1970).

Which studio he used, and the session's start/finish times, were not documented; the recordings were also mixed, so that acetate discs could be cut.

Saturday 1 March

Morgan Studios, High Rd Willesden, London

The successor to Mary Hopkin's multi-million selling début single 'Those Were The Days' was recorded this day at Morgan Studios, a new facility in north London where, in 1970, both Paul and Ringo would work on respective solo albums.

The new song was 'Goodbye', written especially for her by Paul (although copyrighted to Lennon-McCartney), and he produced its recording along with the B-side, Gallagher and Lyle's 'Sparrow'. Tony Bramwell of Apple attended the session, filming some of it on 16mm colour stock for the production of a promo clip. But while one was made – showing Paul and Mary talking and working, not miming – it wasn't shown on any British TV programmes. Nor, it seems, was a second clip, a colour film of Mary (alone) performing the song amid buttercups, shot in the back garden of Paul's house in St John's Wood.

Sunday 2 March

Lady Mitchell Hall, Sidgwick Ave, Cambridge, Cambs

The first concert appearance of a Beatle outside of the group, before a Cambridge University audience of 500. It was not, however, quite the auspicious event it might seem, for this John Lennon stage appearance was far-removed from any recognisable pop/rock performance. While Yoko contorted her larynx into screams, groans and cackles for the front-of-stage microphone, John provided the only suitable

accompaniment: remaining in the half-shadows at the back of the stage, he spent the entire performance producing howling, ear-splitting feedback from his electric guitar and amplifier. Only at the very end of this commotion were they joined by anyone else: a saxophonist and a percussionist. Then, finally, Yoko's unique contribution to this concert of "experimental music" was over.

John and Yoko, naturally, not only recorded the performance but considered it worthy of public issue, it filling one entire side of the album *Unfinished Music No 2: Life With The Lions*, released in Britain on 9 May.

Tuesday 4 March

Apple Corps, London

It was now almost five weeks since the *Get Back* recording sessions, in which time, it seems, the Beatles had decided to all but wash their hands of the entire project. One day in early March John and Paul called Glyn Johns into EMI, pointed to a pile of eight-track tapes – the result of those ten January days at Apple – and offered Johns free rein in preparing a finished album. Glyn duly booked time at his favourite venue, Olympic Sound Studios, and set to work.

Note: accounts/administration department documentation uncovered at EMI in 1991 contains dates for Johns' *Get Back* Olympic mix sessions which differ from (and seem more reliable than) those detailed in the 1988 book *The Complete Beatles Recording Sessions*, so the latest information is used here. However, data about which songs Johns mixed on which dates can no longer be ascertained with absolute accuracy, other than to say that after working on this date (times not known), 3 April, 4 April, 7 April, 2 May, 7 May, 9 May, 15 May and 28 May, the following mixes were eventually delivered back to EMI: 'Get Back' (two versions), 'Teddy Boy', 'Two Of Us' (two versions), 'Dig A Pony', 'I've Got A Feeling' (two versions), 'The Long And Winding Road' (three versions), 'Let It Be' (two versions), 'Rocker', 'Save The Last Dance For Me', 'Don't Let Me Down', 'For

You Blue', 'The Walk', 'Lady Madonna', 'Dig It' (both versions), 'Maggie Mae' and the medley 'Shake Rattle And Roll'/'Kansas City'/'Miss Ann'/'Lawdy Miss Clawdy'/'Blue Suede Shoes'/'You Really Got A Hold On Me'. (Such vague documentation leaves one feeling grateful for EMI's so-called "bureaucratic" admin system which meant that all Beatles sessions 1962–1970 at Abbey Road were fully noted.)

Also on 4 March, George was interviewed in his office at Apple by David Wigg for the weekly BBC Radio 1 programme *Scene And Heard*. It was broadcast over two editions of the series, 5 mins 13 secs on Saturday 8 March, 1.00–2.00 pm (repeated Tuesday 11 March, 7.45–8.44 pm), and a further 4 mins 30 secs on Saturday 12 April, 1.00–2.00 pm (repeated Tuesday 15 April, 7.45–8.44 pm).

Wednesday 12 March

Studio Three, EMI Studios, London

While Paul was down the road at Marylebone Register Office getting married to Linda Eastman, and the police were busy busting George and Pattie for possession of cannabis, John and Yoko were at Abbey Road this day listening to a playback of a privately recorded tape which was named 'Peace Song' on the EMI log sheet. A copy of the tape was made at the end of this 3.30–5.30 pm session and John took away both the original and the copy.

Thursday 13 March

Chobham Common, Surrey

Location filming for the grouse-shooting scene in *The Magic Christian*, with Ringo involved. (See 3 February.)

Tuesday 18 March

Lower Richmond Road, London

Location filming with Ringo for *The Magic Christian*, shooting outside the Star & Garter public house, by the River Thames in Putney, with Spike Milligan acting the part of a ticket-eating traffic warden. (See 3 February.)

Tues 25 – Mon 31 March

Room 902, Amsterdam Hilton,
Apollolaan, Amsterdam, The Netherlands

In the words of the forthcoming single 'The Ballad Of John And Yoko', having married in "Gibraltar, near Spain" on 20 March and spent a few days "honeymooning down by the Seine", the Lennons "drove from Paris to the Amsterdam Hilton" to continue their honeymoon by "talking in our beds for a week…trying to get us some peace". For as the world watched, boggle-eyed, the newly-weds set up, sat up and spoke up in the ninth-floor presidential suite of the Hilton Hotel, Amsterdam, espousing the peace message to the hundreds of press journalists and radio, TV and newsreel reporters who flocked to share their mattress for a few minutes. It was their first "bed-in".

For about ten months John and Yoko had been parading ideas in public about Art in its manifest forms. Now, with a sudden focusing of their beliefs and ideals, world peace became the cornerstone of a remarkable campaign, a subject the couple were to hammer home relentlessly – for the next year particularly – in all manner of public events, showing admirable fortitude in the face of open hostility.

The bed-in was the archetypal coming together of John and Yoko's different ideas and directions, combining Yoko's *avant-garde* sense of the conceptual Event, challenging and almost threatening her audience, with John's engaging humour, magnetic personality and, above all, name. Realising that whatever they did would make front-page news anyway, the Lennons capitalised on this by ensuring that such space was devoted to peace.

The very essence of the bed-in was media saturation, 18-hours-a-day for seven days, so to chronicle each and every radio, TV and filmed interview would be impossible, not least because nothing was noted down at the time. This was conveyor-belt publicity, like a week-long press conference in which John and Yoko spoke to anyone from anywhere who cared to visit their bedroom with a tape recorder, notebook or camera.

In keeping with their own drive to record, film or in some way conserve their activities for posterity, the Lennons also arranged for assistants to film the week-long event, footage they later edited into a 60-minute film titled *Honeymoon*. Selected audio highlights from the week also comprised one side of John and Yoko's third "experimental" LP *The Wedding Album*, issued in Britain on 7 November 1969.

Hand in hand with the peace message was the concept of "bagism", so when they left Amsterdam on 31 March and "made a lightning trip to Vienna" to promote that night's world premiere on Austrian television of their film *Rape*, they held a press conference at the Hotel Sacher fully encased in a white sheet-bag. On the morning of Tuesday 1 April John and Yoko "caught the early plane back to London" and held a press conference at the airport where they were amazed to find the usually hostile British press welcoming them home. (Most interviews done here went into the day's news bulletins; one which didn't was a two-minute conversation with Ian Ross, broadcast this evening, 10.00–12.00 pm, in the BBC Radio 1/2 programme *Late Night Extra*.)

Wednesday 26 March

Four mono mixes of 'Get Back' – supervised by George Martin assisted by balance engineer Jeff Jarratt – were made this day in Room Four at EMI, the intention being to release the "best" as a single. Acetates were cut for the group to listen to.

Tuesday 1 April

Studio Four, Television House, London
and **Theatre Royal, Angel Lane, Stratford, London**

Just a few hours after returning home, John and Yoko journeyed into central London, to Television House in Kingsway, to appear on Thames' live local news-magazine programme *Today*, hosted by Eamonn Andrews and screened from 6.04 to 6.30 pm.

The Lennons several times admitted that they were "willing to be the world's clowns" in order to promote their peace message, and with this being April Fool's Day they were especially happy to act out the role. Their "bagism" concept was the main subject of Andrews' fun-poking interview, John and Yoko appearing from inside a white bag and then, remarkably, tempting Andrews himself to join them there.

This same day, Ringo was involved in a location shoot in Stratford, east London, for *The Magic Christian*, in which an actor (Laurence Harvey) performs a striptease while on stage delivering his Hamlet soliloquy. (See 3 February.)

Thursday 3 April

Studio 3B, Broadcasting House, London
and **Café Royal, Regent Street, London**

George recorded an interview at the BBC during the morning for inclusion in this lunchtime's edition of the BBC Radio 4 current affairs programme *The World At One* (broadcast 1.00–1.30). In a conversation with Sue MacGregor he discussed the work of his great friend Ravi Shankar; Yehudi Menuhin also contributed, and together the two interviews ran to 3 mins 25 secs.

At night, John and Yoko took part in another live Thames Television programme, and again with Eamonn Andrews, but this time for an edition of his own weekly series *The Eamonn Andrews Show* (the Beatles had appeared on this programme on 11 April 1965). Though it had an audience, this edition was broadcast, unusually, not from a TV studio but from the Café Royal restaurant in central London, John and Yoko arriving there at 10.00 pm to join other guests Rolf Harris, Jack Benny, Yehudi Menuhin (a busy day for him) and the singer Gaynor Jones in the 11.00–11.45 pm live transmission. The Lennons participated in an interview and general discussion lasting just under 17 minutes.

Also this evening, 8.30 pm–3.30 am at Olympic Sound Studios in Barnes, Glyn Johns continued his production work on the *Get Back* tapes.

Friday 4 April

New mono mixing of 'Get Back' and its B-side to be, 'Don't Let Me Down', supervised by Glyn Johns. Stereo mixes were also done in this 7.30 to 11.30 pm session at Olympic Sound Studios in Barnes, primarily for issue as the Beatles' first stereo US single; the Beatles' British singles remained monaural until the follow-up, 'The Ballad Of John And Yoko'.

Monday 7 April

Olympic Sound Studios, London

On Sunday 6 April BBC Radio 1 disc-jockeys John Peel and Alan Freeman broadcast 'Get Back' from acetate copies and announced its rush-release as a single on Friday 11 April, the Beatles' first since 'Hey Jude' nearly eight months earlier. But Paul still wasn't entirely happy with this mono mix so he and Glyn Johns booked studio time at Olympic 4.00–8.00 pm this day, Easter Monday, and set about improving it.

'Get Back'/'Don't Let Me Down' was officially issued in Britain on the 11th, although this late mix session meant that copies didn't reach the stores until several days later. Neither A- nor B-side carried a producer's credit, no surprise considering the confused roles of George Martin and Glyn Johns, but the disc label for both sides did bear one new name, the two recordings being accredited to "The Beatles With Billy Preston".

Wednesday 9 April

The Boathouse, The Embankment, Putney, London

More location filming for Ringo in *The Magic Christian*, situated inside and outside Barclays Bank's rowing club on the River Thames at Putney, in south-west London. In this scene, Sir Guy Grand bribes the Oxford University crew to lose their annual boat race against Cambridge University. (See 3 February.)

Monday 14 April

Studio Three, EMI Studios, London

An important Beatles session yet with only John and Paul's participation. Ringo was elsewhere, filming *The Magic Christian*; George, so it was said, was out of the country. Both, anyway, were kept unaware of this session until after it had taken place. The song being recorded was John's 'The Ballad Of John And Yoko (They're Gonna Crucify Me)' – the subtitle in parentheses was dropped before release – a chronicle of the newly married Lennons' recent weeks. Later in the year John recorded these sort of songs with his alternative outlet, the Plastic Ono Band, and had the band existed at this time 'The Ballad Of John And Yoko' would probably have been theirs. For the present, John's sole musical vehicle was the Beatles.

With not only producer George Martin back in the control room but also balance engineer Geoff Emerick, John and Paul enjoyed a highly productive day, completing the recording from 2.30 to 9.00 pm and mixing it into stereo from 9.00 to 11.00 pm, ending the session one hour ahead of schedule. (It thus became the Beatles' first stereo single in Britain and, consequently, their first recording not mixed into mono.)

Despite the wrangling, arguments and bitter business squabbles so widely reported of them in 1969, John and Paul's great musical understanding and togetherness shone through from start to finish. First they set about perfecting a basic track of acoustic guitar/vocal (John) and drums (Paul), done in 11 takes, and then overdubbed onto take ten: bass (Paul), lead guitar (John), second lead guitar (John), piano (Paul), backing vocal (Paul), maracas (Paul) and, finally, percussive thumps on the reverse-side of an acoustic guitar (John).

Backed with George's 'Old Brown Shoe' (see 16–18 April), 'The Ballad Of John And Yoko' was issued as a single in Britain on Friday 30 May, while 'Get Back' was still number one. To promote it on television, Apple distributed two (essentially similar) 16mm colour films, in which the 'Ballad' was transferred into visual glimpses of John and Yoko in Paris, Amsterdam, Vienna, at their London Airport press conference (1 April) and travelling the British roads in their Rolls-Royce. The only Beatles footage to be included – this was, after all, a group single – showed brief, mute extracts from one of the January rehearsal sessions at Twickenham, with a Krishna disciple sitting on the floor behind them.

As well as entering the canon of John and Yoko's private films for screening at cinema clubs, one of the two clips was shown three times in monochrome on BBC1's *Top Of The Pops*, on Thursdays 5, 12 and 26 June 1969 (all 7.30–8.00 pm) and once in colour, in part two of *Top Of The Pops '69* on Friday 26 December (6.20–7.00 pm). A US screening occurred in the premiere edition of the ABC-TV series *Music Scene*, on 22 September 1969 (7.30–8.15 pm, EST).

Keeping Grand company: Ringo alongside Peter Sellers and Richard Attenborough, filming The Magic Christian *at Barclays Bank's boathouse, 9 April 1969.*

Well aware of potential upset over its lyric, John wrote this note to Apple plugger Tony Bramwell instructing him to keep 'The Ballad Of John And Yoko' under wraps until release. Some radio stations outside Britain did subsequently ban it or bleep the word "Christ" during airplay.

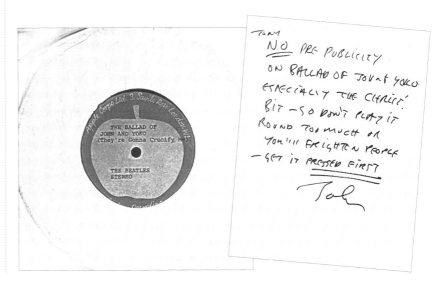

Wednesday 16 April

Studio Three, EMI Studios, London

Proper, group recordings of 'Old Brown Shoe' and 'Something', both taped in demo form by composer George on 25 February. Actually, George recorded a second demo of 'Old Brown Shoe' during this afternoon, 2.30–5.00, before the other Beatles arrived for the evening session which was booked for 7.00–10.00 but ran over until 2.45 am.

The first objective of the group session was to record 'Old Brown Shoe', with a basic track of drums (Ringo), lead guitar and guide vocal (George), jangle piano (Paul) and rhythm guitar (John) perfected in four takes. Onto the fourth was overdubbed bass and lead guitars, backing vocals by John and Paul and a new lead vocal by George. The song was mixed into stereo at the very end of the session (although additional overdubs on 18 April rendered even the "best" of these unusable).

The first 13 takes of 'Something' occupied the time in between, with a basic track of bass (Paul), drums (Ringo), guitar (George) and piano (George Martin). John did not participate. A re-make would begin on 2 May.

Friday 18 April

Studios Three/Two, EMI Studios, London

Under the production supervision of Chris Thomas, not George Martin, 'Old Brown Shoe' was completed between 2.30 and 10.30 pm with overdubs of an organ (wiping, in the process, John's rhythm guitar track) and an additional lead guitar track put through a Leslie speaker, both played by George. The song was then mixed into stereo between 10.30 pm and 1.00 am.

Until now, work had taken place in studio three. But at 1.00 am the session moved into studio two, John and George overdubbing multi-tracked guitars onto the 23 February Trident master of 'I Want You' and then adding yet more to a reduction mixdown of this, called take one. A rough stereo mix was made before the session ended at 4.30 am.

Sunday 20 April

Studio Three, EMI Studios, London

Another session produced by Chris Thomas, working on two songs which had surfaced during the *Get Back* project. The first was 'I Want You', the recording of which continued with 7.00–9.15 pm overdubs of Hammond organ and conga drums. The second was 'Oh! Darling (I'll Never Do You No Harm)' – released on *Abbey Road* without the bracketed sub-title – the recording of which began with 26 rhythm track takes and a Hammond organ overdub onto the 26th, 9.15–12.00 pm. A rough stereo mix was then made between midnight and 12.45 am.

Tuesday 22 April

Studio Two, EMI Studios, London

Recording of John and Yoko's heartbeats, John shouting out "Yoko" and Yoko shouting out "John", for issue as one entire side of their third "experimental" LP, *The Wedding Album*, on 7 November 1969. John produced the session, recording from 11.00 pm–3.45 am and mixing the 22-minute tape into stereo until 4.30 am. Earlier this day, in a similar show of togetherness, John added Ono to his middle-name in a ceremony on the roof of Apple's HQ in Savile Row.

Friday 25 April

A rough mono mix of 'Two Of Us' (still titled 'On Our Way Home' at this point) was produced this day at EMI by Peter Mew so that acetate discs could be cut and given to a potential Apple label act, a New York trio called Mortimer, to whom Paul planned to donate his song. (Their recording was never released, however.)

Saturday 26 April

Studio Two, EMI Studios, London

Apart from an overdub of Paul's lead vocal onto 'Oh! Darling' – the first of several such recordings – this 4.30 pm–4.15 am session was spent perfecting the basic track for Ringo's new composition 'Octopus's Garden'. He didn't have a lead vocal on *Get Back* although he did compose 'Octopus's Garden' during that period, as can be seen in a sequence in the *Let It Be* film, shot on 26 January.

Working without a producer, the group taped 32 takes of the song's rhythm track, the last being marked "best" ready for future overdubbing.

Before this Beatles session, from 2.30 to 4.30, John remixed his and Yoko's 22 April heartbeat/shouting recordings into stereo.

Sunday 27 April

Studio Three, EMI Studios, London

A re-make of the 'John And Yoko' heartbeats recording, taped between 3.00 and 6.00 pm, with John as producer. It was mixed into stereo from 6.00 to 8.00 pm.

Tuesday 29 April

Studio Three, EMI Studios, London

A 7.30 pm to 1.00 am session in which Ringo overdubbed his lead vocal onto 'Octopus's Garden', with Chris Thomas acting producer. Further overdubs were recorded on 17 and 18 July; in the meantime, this session ended with stereo mixes.

Before this session, from 2.30 to 6.30, there was a playback of recently recorded multi-tracks, also overseen by Chris Thomas.

Wednesday 30 April

Studio Three, EMI Studios, London

A most interesting session, produced by Chris Thomas, which began with a lead guitar overdub onto the "best" 31 January recording of 'Let It Be'. Glyn Johns used this overdubbed version for his unissued *Get Back* album, his only deviation from the original live premise. (It was this solo which featured on the single release, too.)

The remainder of this 7.15 pm to 2.00 am session saw the revival of 'You Know My Name (Look Up the Number)', recorded in May–June 1967 but left unfinished after a master edit had been compiled of its constituent parts. Working alone, John and Paul overdubbed vocals and sound effects (assisted in the latter task by Mal Evans) onto the original four-track tape, although much of their work was later edited out, because, when the song was finally released, in March 1970, it was 4 mins 19 secs in duration. These recordings ran on to 6 mins 8 secs. The preparation of mono mixes ended the session.

Before this session, 2.30–6.15, Chris Thomas supervised another playback of recently-recorded titles, for any Beatle who wished to attend.

Thursday 1 May

Studio Three, EMI Studios, London

A 2.30 to 7.00 pm stereo mix session for 'Oh! Darling', produced by Chris Thomas, followed by a 7.00 to 10.45 pm stereo mix session for 'John And Yoko', produced by John and utilising both the 22 April original and 27 April re-make recordings.

Friday 2 May

Studio G, Lime Grove Studios, London
and **Studio Three, EMI Studios, London**

While Glyn Johns toiled again this day on the *Get Back* tapes over at Olympic, the Beatles worked at EMI, recording 36 basic track takes of a 'Something' re-make: bass (Paul), drums (Ringo), guitar (John), piano (Billy Preston) and guitar (George). The main difference between these early versions and the master completed on 15 August was one of duration, take 36 – marked "best" – being 7 mins 48 secs compared to the final timing of 3 minutes owing to an extended piano-led four-note instrumental ending. There was a two-hour break in the middle of this session, the Beatles working from 7.00–11.00 pm and 1.00–3.40 am, with Chris Thomas producing.

Earlier this day, between 12.30 and 1.00 pm, at the BBC's Lime Grove television facility in west London, John and Yoko taped an interview for the seventh edition of a new BBC1 arts/sketch series *How Late It Is*, discussing with Michael Wale their film *Rape*. The programme was broadcast from 10.55 to 11.35 this evening and included, as well as the interview, a 3 mins 31 secs extract from *Rape* loaned by Apple.

Sunday 4 May

Les Ambassadeurs, London

Returning this evening to the venue of some *A Hard Day's Night* filming (see 17 March and 17 April 1964), Ringo, John and Paul attended a private party to celebrate the completion of principal photography for *The Magic Christian* – although, actually, some shooting took place after this date.

The party was filmed by the producers of the movie and a few feet of footage – including a brief interview with Paul and Linda, and sight of John – was included in the BBC1 documentary *Will The Real Mr Sellers...* (see 3 February postscript for details).

Monday 5 May

Olympic Sound Studios, London

The first night of a four-night booking at Olympic, with Glyn Johns manning the control room throughout. In this 7.30 pm–4.00 am session the Beatles recorded overdubs for 'Something', with Paul and George re-taping their bass and guitar tracks respectively.

Tuesday 6 May

Olympic Sound Studios, London

All of the post-January recordings destined for the LP *Abbey Road* were placed on one side of that album. There was a reason for this: much of the other side was to form a medley. Though it's difficult to pin a precise date on the conception of any idea, the *Abbey Road* medley must have been born right around this time for much of this 3.00 pm–4.00 am Olympic session saw its first recording: Paul's upbeat ballad 'You Never Give Me Your Money', the title and lyric directly inspired by the escalating business problems at Apple. Certainly recorded with the medley in mind, the Beatles taped 36 basic track takes (the 30th being "best"): piano and guide vocal (Paul), drums (Ringo), distorted electric guitar (John) and chiming electric guitar (George).

The session broke down in this way: 3.00–3.30 pm mono mix of the previous night's 'Something'; 3.30–5.00 rehearsal of 'You Never Give Me Your Money'; 5.00–5.45 another mono mix of 'Something'; 5.45–6.00 playback of this mix; 6.30 pm–3.15 am recording of 'You Never Give Me Your Money'; 3.15–3.30 editing; 3.30–4.00 am overdubbing onto 'You Never Give Me Your Money'.

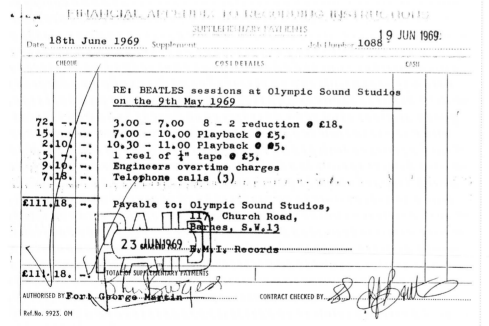

Wednesday 7 May

Olympic Sound Studios, London

More of Glyn Johns' *Get Back* work: stereo mixing (8.00 pm–6.30 am) and playback (6.30–7.30 am), with the Beatles in attendance.

Thursday 8 May

Apple Corps, London

A long interview given by John, with Yoko, to David Wigg for the weekly Radio 1 programme *Scene And Heard*. Extracts were broadcast over two editions of the series, 4 mins 53 secs on Sunday 11 May, 3.00–4.00 pm (repeated Tuesday 13 May, 7.45–8.45 pm), and a further 4 mins 32 secs the following week, 18 May, 3.00–4.00 pm (repeated Tuesday 20 May, 7.45–8.45 pm)

Friday 9 May

Olympic Sound Studios, London

More of Glyn Johns' *Get Back* work: stereo mixing (3.00–7.00 pm) and playback (7.00–10.00 and 10.30–11.00 pm), with the Beatles in attendance.

This was one of several sessions around this period to dissolve into a fractious business meeting between the four Beatles, with, on this occasion, Allen Klein attending too. Under considerable pressure to accept then and there Klein's ABKCO company as Apple's business manager, an agreement signed the previous day by the other three – meaning, in effect, that Klein himself would become the Beatles' personal manager – Paul relieved the tension by remaining behind at Olympic after the others had left and recording a song through the night with Steve Miller, titled, not inappropriately, 'My Dark Hour'.

Paul contributed drums, bass and backing vocals while Miller sang lead and played all the other instruments. Crediting Paul as Paul Ramon – the pseudonym he'd used on the Johnny Gentle tour in 1960 – the recording was released as a US single by the Steve Miller Band on 16 June.

Thursday 15 May

'Rembrandt', Heswall, Cheshire

The day before he and Linda went abroad for a holiday, Paul was back in Liverpool, visiting his family. At some point this day, at his father's house in Heswall, he gave a long interview to former Liverpool Institute contemporary Roy Corlett, now on the staff at the BBC's new local station Radio Merseyside. It was broadcast in the following day's edition of the programme *Light And Local* (Friday 16 May, 12.31–1.00 pm) – or, as Paul called it, "a light at the local".

This same day, down at Olympic Sound Studios in southwest London, Glyn Johns continued his work producing the Beatles' *Get Back* album.

Mon 26 May – Mon 2 June 📺 🎞 ⏭ ✏

Room 1742, Hôtel Reine-Elizabeth, Dorchester Boulevard West, Montreal, Quebec, Canada

John and Yoko's second and last "bed-in" for peace. Unable, as they had hoped, to host the event in New York – because US authorities withheld the granting of John's visa citing his November 1968 drug conviction – and unwilling to hold it in the Bahamas (to where they had flown on 24 May) owing to the extreme heat, the Lennons chose Montreal because of its close proximity to the US border, which meant that their peace messages could be easily relayed back across the border to the desired audience. Not that Canada itself held no attractions for the couple: this was the first of three visits they would make there this year (see also 13 September and 20 December).

The intent of this bed-in was identical to that held in Amsterdam: to stay under the sheets and welcome into their suite as many radio and TV broadcasters, journalists and other visitors as they possibly could during the week. John laid particular emphasis on speaking to US radio stations by telephone, asking assistants and friendly Montreal disc-jockeys to dial stations at random and ask if they'd be interested in having John urge their listeners to adopt peace.

The week-long event was filmed for a full-length feature titled *The Way It Is*, never shown; some of the Montreal footage was included by Yoko in the 1988 film *Imagine: John Lennon* and then, in 1990, she issued the core of the material on home-video as *John And Yoko: The Bed-In*. The highlight of these productions was the footage from the evening of Sunday 1 June when, in five minutes flat, John led the recording of the world's most endurable peace anthem and slogan, 'Give Peace A Chance'. Although credited on the record to Lennon-McCartney, it was John's song alone, the quintessential Lennon in fact: putting the essence of his and Yoko's peace proclamations into a simple but nonetheless rhythmic and catchy song. It was taped on borrowed professional equipment and featured John on acoustic guitar/vocal and a suite chock-full of friends and visitors singing along in the choruses.

It is said that, back in England a few days later, John had Ringo overdub drums to accentuate a rather muddled and wayward beat, and overdubbed a choir of voices to smoothen the ragged chorale, but no documentation exists to prove this or supply a date and location. 'Give Peace A Chance', backed with a privately-taped recording of Yoko's wistful 'Remember Love', was issued as a worldwide single soon afterwards (in Britain on Friday 4 July), credited to the Plastic Ono Band, the first solo single by one of the Beatles.

The Plastic Ono Band was a typical 1969 John and Yoko idea: a conceptual band with no fixed members. ("*You Are The Plastic Ono Band*" read an advertisement for the new single, showing a picture of recording equipment superimposed over a page from the London telephone directory.) This was the extramural creative outlet for which John had long been yearning. Over the next few years virtually all of his musical activities came under this moniker, his fellow Band-mates fluctuating with every occasion.

To promote the 'Give Peace A Chance' single Apple distributed to TV stations a 16mm colour clip of the bed-in recording session. It was twice shown (in monochrome) on *Top Of The Pops*, on Thursdays 10 and 24 July 1969 (both BBC1, 7.30–8.00 pm). It was also screened by John and Yoko in some of their private cinema club evenings.

Wednesday 28 May 🎚

Olympic Sound Studios, London

The conclusion, for now, of Glyn Johns' work on *Get Back*: a completed and banded album master tape, even though George was the only one of the Beatles around to hear and approve it. The other three were all abroad, John and Yoko three days into their Montreal bed-in (see previous entry).

The line-up of this unreleased LP, with recording dates in parentheses, was as follows. Side A: 'The One After 909' (30 January); 'Rocker' (22 January); 'Save The Last Dance For Me' (22 January); 'Don't Let Me Down' (22 January); 'Dig A Pony' (24 January); 'I've Got A Feeling' (24 January); 'Get Back' (28 January, the single release version). Side B: 'For You Blue' (25 January); 'Teddy Boy' (24 January); 'Two Of Us' (24 January); 'Maggie Mae' (24 January); 'Dig It' (26 January); 'Let It Be' (31 January and 30 April overdub); 'The Long And Winding Road' (31 January); 'Get Back (reprise)' (28 January).

The Beatles tried to come full circle with *Get Back*, returning not merely to early recording techniques but even arranging to shoot a re-creation of their first LP cover, *Please Please Me*, using the same photographer, Angus McBean. The Beatles, John especially, were very keen to strike precisely the same pose that they had done in 1963; and they were equally keen to word the *Get Back* cover in a fashion identical to *Please Please Me*, adding the legend "with Let It Be and 11 other songs" under the title.

Although *Get Back* wasn't issued, the photograph session wasn't wasted. A subtly different but otherwise identical shot, placed side by side with one of its 1963 counterparts, was used in 1973 by EMI for its two "best of" Beatles compilation albums, *1962–1966* and *1967–1970*, giving a marvellous visual example of just how much the group had changed from one end of the 1960s to the other. And to think, in 1963/64, that the Beatles were accused of having too long hair…

An early proof slick of the Let It Be *album sleeve, March 1970. The title had already changed from* Get Back *but the cover design had survived, if only temporarily.*

Saturday 14 June

Stonebridge House, Wembley

Establishing himself as a talk-show host of some repute outside as well as inside his native Britain, David Frost launched a weekly US television series in 1969, produced by the Westinghouse group for syndication to stations across the country. Frost flew back and forth across the Atlantic every week, holding down this series and his weekend shows for LWT in Britain.

The edition of *The David Frost Show* seen in most US cities on Thursday 10 July (8.30–10.00 pm, EST) featured as guests three American actors and one actress – John Cassavetes, Peter Falk, Ben Gazzara and Julie London – and, additionally, in a pre-taped sequence shot in England, John and Yoko. Their contribution was recorded the evening of 14 June, before a studio audience, at the Stonebridge Park studios of InterTel (VTR Services) – where, the previous December, they had participated in *The Rolling Stones' Rock And Roll Circus*.

Around this time, unconnected with the above, John and Yoko recorded an interview for broadcast on the British service of Radio Luxembourg. It was transmitted during the evening of Sunday 22 June, probably on *The David Christian Show*, 7.00–10.00 pm.

Tuesday 1 July

Studio Two, EMI Studios, London

The session that began a new, if short-lived, recording era for the Beatles, back to EMI Abbey Road, back as something resembling a cohesive unit and back under the supervision of producer George Martin. Post-*Get Back* material had been taped irregularly and with no specific project in mind. All sessions now had an end objective: a new album (though it didn't yet have this title) called *Abbey Road*. Twenty-two days this month saw Beatles studio action and the group block-booked the 2.30–10.00 pm slot in studio two every weekday from 1 July until 29 August.

Paul was the only Beatle in the studio on this day, overdubbing a lead vocal onto the Olympic recording of 'You Never Give Me Your Money' between 3.00 and 7.30 pm. John couldn't have attended even had he wanted to: along with Yoko, his son Julian and her daughter Kyoko, he was involved in a motor accident while on holiday in Scotland and was hospitalised there until 6 July.

Wednesday 2 July

Studio Two, EMI Studios, London

A 3.00–9.30 pm session. Living so close to Abbey Road, Paul invariably arrived first at EMI and so was often the first to start work. On this day, before the arrival of George and Ringo (John was still in hospital), Paul used the solo studio time to record another of his spontaneous link-tracks: the 23-second 'Her Majesty', singing live to his own acoustic guitar accompaniment and completing it in three takes. It promptly joined the list of songs for medley consideration.

After George and Ringo arrived the three Beatles began recording another of Paul's new numbers, 'Golden Slumbers' – Thomas Dekker's late 16th-century prose set to music by Paul – taping 15 takes of the basic rhythm track: piano and guide vocal (Paul), drums (Ringo) and bass (George). Each take included what the *Abbey Road* sleeve detailed as 'Golden Slumbers' and 'Carry That Weight'. These two were not segued; they were recorded as one continuous piece.

Thursday 3 July

Studio Two, EMI Studios, London

Editing of takes 13 and 15 of 'Golden Slumbers'/'Carry That Weight' and overdubbing onto this of rhythm guitar (Paul), lead guitar (George), two lead vocals by Paul and then, in unison, Paul, George and Ringo chanting the 'Carry That Weight' vocals. A reduction mixdown at the end of this 3.00–8.30 pm session took the song into take 17.

Friday 4 July

Studio Two, EMI Studios, London

The first overdubs onto the newly reduced 'Golden Slumbers'/'Carry That Weight' tape, 2.45–5.30 pm (although much of this time was spent listening to the live BBC Radio 2 broadcast of Britain's Ann Jones beating Billie-Jean King to win the Wimbledon Ladies' tennis championship!).

Monday 7 July

Studio Two, EMI Studios, London

The first session for 'Here Comes The Sun', another *Abbey Road* triumph for composer George Harrison. With John still absent through injury, only three Beatles took part in the session, taping 13 takes of the basic track: bass (Paul), drums (Ringo) and acoustic guitar/guide vocal (George) between 2.30 and 10.45 pm. From then until 11.45 George overdubbed a replacement acoustic guitar track.

Tuesday 8 July

Studio Two, EMI Studios, London

Overdubbing of George's lead vocal and his and Paul's manually double-tracked backing vocals onto 'Here Comes The Sun'. Take 13 was then reduced into 15, of which a rough mono mix was made during the last half-hour of this 2.30–10.45 pm session.

Wednesday 9 July

Studio Two, EMI Studios, London

John's first session after recuperating from his car crash was for Paul's 'Maxwell's Silver Hammer', the song almost recorded in October 1968 as a last-minute addition to *The Beatles* and then rehearsed (but not recorded) at Twickenham Film Studios in January during the shooting of *Get Back/Let It Be*. As inseparable as ever, Yoko returned to EMI Studios with John, although – because she was injured more seriously than he, and because she was pregnant – she rested in a double-bed especially brought into Abbey Road, causing considerable sniggering and whispering around the building.

The basic track of 'Maxwell's Silver Hammer' was recorded in 21 takes from 2.30–8.00 pm. From then until 10.15 pm guitars were overdubbed.

Thursday 10 July

Studio Two, EMI Studios, London

Overdubs onto 'Maxwell's Silver Hammer' of piano (Paul), organ (George Martin), anvil (Ringo), guitar (George) and vocals (Paul lead; Paul, George and Ringo backing), all taped between 2.30 and 9.30 pm. The recording was mixed into stereo between 9.30 and 11.30.

Friday 11 July

Studio Two, EMI Studios, London

Overdubbing by Paul of a further guitar and vocal onto 'Maxwell's Silver Hammer'; by George of the lead vocal onto 'Something'; and – ending the 2.30–12.00 pm session – by Paul of bass onto 'You Never Give Me Your Money'. 'Something' was also roughly mixed into stereo and then given a proper reduction mix, take 36 into 37, at which point its length was cut to 5 mins 32 secs.

Tuesday 15 July

Studios Three/Two, EMI Studios, London

A two-location session – 2.30–6.00 in studio three, 6.00–11.00 pm in studio two – overdubbing vocals and chimes onto 'You Never Give Me Your Money' and roughly mixing this into stereo.

Wednesday 16 July

Studios Three/Two, EMI Studios, London

Another two-location session – 2.30 to 7.00 pm in studio three, 7.00 pm to 12.30 am in studio two – overdubbing handclaps and harmonium onto 'Here Comes The Sun' and then a new lead vocal (George), backing vocals (Paul) and handclapping (George, Paul and Ringo) onto take 36 of 'Something', even though a reduction of this take had previously been made. Now adorned with these new overdubs, the reduction was done again, into take 39.

Thursday 17 July

Studios Three/Two, EMI Studios, London

A third consecutive two-location session – 2.30–6.30 in studio three, 6.30–11.15 pm in studio two. Paul arrived on time at 2.30 to work alone on 'Oh! Darling', overdubbing his lead vocal. Determined to capture a certain vocal feel, Paul made four attempts at this, one each day on 17, 18, 22 and 23 July, until he was happy with the result.

The remainder of this day's work was devoted to 'Octopus's Garden', with the overdubbing of backing vocals (Paul and George), a piano (Paul) and sound effects (all).

Friday 18 July
Studios Three/Two, EMI Studios, London

Working in two locations – 2.30–8.00 in studio three, 8.00–10.30 pm in studio two – Paul tried again with his 'Oh! Darling' lead vocal and Ringo added vocals and percussion onto 'Octopus's Garden'. This latter title was then treated to final mono and stereo mixing, although the mono mixes were never used because *Abbey Road* was the Beatles' first stereo-only album.

Monday 21 July

Studios Three/Two, EMI Studios, London

John had maintained a low profile during recent sessions and hadn't offered the group a new song since 'The Ballad Of John And Yoko' on 14 April. But he corrected matters on this day – working in studio three 2.30–9.30 and studio two 9.30–10.00 pm – recording eight memorable basic-track takes of 'Come Together' onto four-track – handclaps/vocal (John), lead guitar (George), bass (Paul) and drums (Ringo) – and then copying this into an eight-track take nine for later overdubbing.

This day saw the full-time return of Geoff Emerick to the Beatles' recording console. Now chief balance engineer at Apple Studios, Emerick returned to EMI as the first free-lancer to work a board at Abbey Road, his erstwhile friendly colleagues according him a frosty reception.

Tuesday 22 July

Studio Three, EMI Studios, London

A 2.30–9.30 pm session which saw another attempt by Paul at the 'Oh! Darling' lead vocal, plus overdubs of a new lead vocal, electric piano, rhythm guitar and maraca onto 'Come Together'.

Wednesday 23 July

Studios Three/Two, EMI Studios, London

Three weeks after the recording of 'Golden Slumbers'/'Carry That Weight', with its open ending to facilitate the following song in the medley, that next number began. At this point it had no title other than 'Ending' but it would become 'The End'. Never was a title so apt: aside from the 23-second 'Her Majesty', tacked right on the very end of the LP, almost into the run-out groove, 'The End' was the last song on the last-recorded Beatles album.

A good deal of rehearsal must have preceded the rolling of tapes during this studio three 2.30–11.30 pm session, for right from take one it was a tight recording, picking up with

some lead guitar notes and paving the way for Ringo's one and only drum solo on a Beatles song. The group made seven attempts at the recording and the style of his solo changed with each, the last being almost 16 seconds in duration and the song itself 1 min 20 secs. (Later overdubs took it to 2 mins 41 secs, although editing of the "best" mix brought it back down to 2 mins 5 secs.)

At 11.30 pm the Beatles and production staff moved into the control room of studio two for a playback, ending at 12.30 am. Two other recordings they would have heard were Paul's best attempt at the 'Oh! Darling' lead vocal, taped at the beginning of this session, and 'Come Together' with more vocal overdubs, also done this day.

Thursday 24 July

Studio Two, EMI Studios, London

If a composer planned on giving a song exclusively to someone else it was customary for him/her to provide the artist with a demo – usually roughly recorded with either an acoustic guitar or piano. In the case of Lennon and McCartney, demos tended to be recorded privately, with acetate discs usually cut by music publisher Dick James. Paul planned on giving new song 'Come And Get It' to Apple group the Iveys so he taped a demo at EMI between 2.30 and 3.30 this afternoon, before the Beatles' session. John was in the control room but Paul did the recording alone, first singing and playing piano and then overdubbing a double-tracked vocal with maracas, then drums, then bass. The song was mixed into stereo, a copy of the mix was made for Paul to give to the Iveys, and the job was done, all in one hour. (Paul also produced the Iveys' virtual note-for-note copy of his demo, taped at EMI on 2 August. He encouraged the group to change their name – they became Badfinger, arranged for 'Come And Get It' to become the main theme tune for *The Magic Christian* and for Badfinger to snag the soundtrack album, and watched the song, issued as a single, climb to number four on the British chart.)

Between 3.30 and 10.30 pm the Beatles recorded a double-song contribution to the *Abbey Road* medley, John's 'Sun King'/'Mean Mr Mustard' – the two were not segued, they were taped as one straight recording although for a few days it masqueraded under the confusing working title 'Here Comes The Sun-King', although unrelated to George's 'Here Comes The Sun'. The basic track of this double-recording was taped in 35 takes along with jams of Gene Vincent's 'Ain't She Sweet', 'Who Slapped John?' and 'Be-Bop-A-Lula'. These would have been strong contenders for *Get Back* had they been recorded in January and not July 1969.

Friday 25 July

Studio Two, EMI Studios, London

The early part of this 2.30 pm–2.30 am session was devoted to overdubs for 'Sun King'/'Mean Mr Mustard' (vocals, piano and organ) and 'Come Together' (vocal harmonies). Then the Beatles settled down to begin a new recording: John's

'Polythene Pam' and Paul's 'She Came In Through The Bathroom Window' (the latter having first been rehearsed at Apple on 22 January), recorded as one continuous piece. Clearly, whatever their business and personal squabbles, they were still capable of making great music together, as 'The Ballad Of John And Yoko' had already shown.

Encompassing both songs, 39 basic track takes were recorded – acoustic guitar (John), bass (Paul), lead guitar (George) and drums (Ringo) – and then the last four hours of the session were spent overdubbing bass, drums and lead vocals onto take 39.

Monday 28 July

Studios Three/Two, EMI Studios, London

Working from 2.30 to 8.00 pm in studio three the Beatles overdubbed another lead vocal, acoustic and electric guitars, electric piano and an ordinary piano, tambourine and other bits of percussion onto 'Polythene Pam'/'She Came In Through The Bathroom Window'. Moving into studio two from 8.00 to 8.30, take 39 was reduced into take 40.

Tuesday 29 July

Studio Three, EMI Studios, London

A 2.30–10.45 pm session that saw a guitar overdub onto 'Come Together' and vocal, piano, organ and percussion overdubs onto 'Sun King'/'Mean Mr Mustard'.

Wednesday 30 July

Studios Two/Three, EMI Studios, London

This long day began in studio two with a mixdown of 'You Never Give Me Your Money', 2.00–3.30 pm, reducing take 30 into a new "best" take 40. This overlapped with action in studio three, where, between 2.30 and 10.30 pm, a host of overdubs were recorded: guitars onto 'Come Together'; vocals, percussion and guitar onto 'Polythene Pam'/'She Came In Through The Bathroom Window'; vocals onto 'You Never Give Me Your Money'; and vocals onto 'Golden Slumbers'/'Carry That Weight'. And still there was no going home…

The time had come to piece together the constituent songs of the proposed medley, to see how they slotted together and which required additional work. Few were yet in a finished state – 'The End', for example, did not have any vocals yet – but this trial edit was designed to highlight any major faults in the *theory* of the medley, or 'The Long One'/'Huge Medley', as it was presently called by the Beatles and the production staff. Stereo mixing of all the songs, followed by crossfading and editing, took place in studio three from 10.30 pm to 2.30 am so that the medley took this form: 'You Never Give Me Your Money', 'Sun King'/'Mean Mr Mustard', 'Her Majesty', 'Polythene Pam'/'She Came In Through The Bathroom Window', 'Golden Slumbers'/'Carry That Weight', 'The End'.

The total duration was 15 mins 30 secs and all fitted well except for 'Her Majesty', which Paul instructed tape op John Kurlander to cut out and throw away. Kurlander's EMI training was such that he couldn't bring himself to do the latter, so after Paul left he tacked it onto the end of the tape, about 20 seconds after 'The End'. The next day the medley was cut onto acetate discs at Apple, with 'Her Majesty' still on the

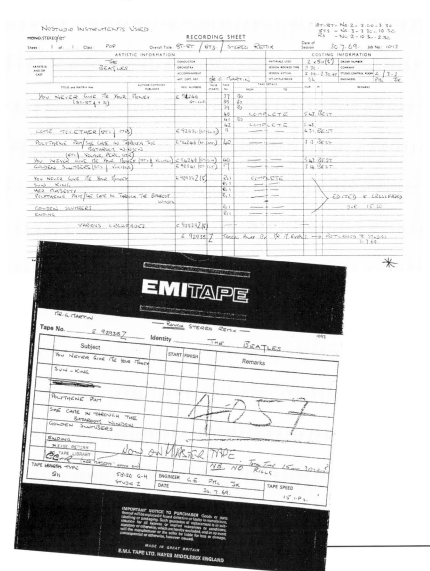

end. Hearing it in this way Paul liked it after all: it was saved from extinction and kept in the same place – which explains why such a long silence precedes it on the finished *Abbey Road* LP.

Thursday 31 July

Studio Two, EMI Studios, London

Overdubbing by Paul of bass and piano onto take 30 of 'You Never Give Me Your Money' (not the previous day's reduction of this), completing the recording. Also taped in this 2.30 pm–1.15 am session were drums, timpani and vocal overdubs onto 'Golden Slumbers'/'Carry That Weight'.

Friday 1 August

Studio Two, EMI Studios, London

One of the most beautiful of all Beatles recordings was John's 'Because', an exquisite exercise in three-part harmony by the writer plus Paul and George. Recording of the rhythm track took place from 2.30 to 7.30 pm this day, comprising an electric Baldwin spinet harpsichord (George Martin), electric guitar (John) and bass (Paul). Ringo provided a gentle hi-hat beat but this was for the musicians' headphones only, it wasn't recorded. Take 16 was "best" so from 7.30–10.30 John, Paul and George began recording the harmony vocals. The finished recording would feature three sets of these three voices; the first set only was taped in this session.

Monday 4 August

Studio Two, EMI Studios, London

Recording of the 'Because' three-part harmonies was completed in studio two between 2.30 and 9.00 pm. Meanwhile, from 7.15–8.45, when his vocal duties had been discharged, George Harrison moved into studio three and produced rough stereo mixes of 'Something' and 'Here Comes The Sun'. These revealed to him that both required more work; an acetate of 'Something' was given to George Martin so that he could arrange an orchestral score.

Tuesday 5 August

Studios Three/Two/Room 43, EMI Studios, London

Home experimentation with tape loops hadn't ended with *Revolver*. On this day Paul brought into EMI a plastic bag containing a dozen loose strands of mono tape, spending the afternoon in studio three transferring the best of these onto four-track. Sounding like bells, birds, bubbles and chirping crickets, the effects allowed for a perfect crossfade (effected on 14 August) from 'You Never Give Me Your Money' into 'Sun King', solving a problem first brought to light on 30 July. (Inside the plastic bag was another tape loop intended for George's 'Here Comes The Sun', but never used.)

The Beatles were among the first popular musicians to make use of an astonishing new musical instrument, Dr Robert Moog's synthesiser. George expressed particular interest in the invention and had bought one in America (see 15 November 1968), recording *Electronic Sounds*, an album full of its strange noises, released on 9 May 1969 by Apple's short-lived "experimental" label, Zapple. Now George had his Moog transported into EMI for the *Abbey Road* sessions and, with Mike Vickers recruited as programmer for a £25 fee, the Beatles began to use it in the closing weeks of the *Abbey Road* sessions. The instrument, with a huge bank of wires and a large two-tiered keyboard, was set up in Room 43 at Abbey Road and its output was fed from there by cable to any studio the Beatles were working in.

'Because' received the Beatles' first Moog overdubs, played by George from Room 43 and taped twice in a 6.30–10.45 pm studio two session, completing the recording. Following this, the Beatles overdubbed the first vocals onto 'The End'.

Concurrent with these activities, 8.00–9.30 pm in studio three, balance engineer Tony Clark and tape op Alan Parsons were making a stereo quarter-inch tape copy from an ordinary cassette of some of John and Yoko's latest privately-recorded sounds. The tape was taken away by the Lennons' assistant, Anthony Fawcett.

Wednesday 6 August

Studios Three/Two/Room 43, EMI Studios, London

With all basic tracks taped and only overdubs left to record, the Beatles were scarcely seen as a foursome at EMI from here on in. On this day two simultaneous sessions took place: George overdubbed acoustic guitar onto 'Here Comes The Sun' in studio three from 2.30 to 11.00 pm, while in Room 43 (the sound fed into studio two), at precisely the same times, Paul added synthesiser onto simultaneous mixdowns of 'Maxwell's Silver Hammer', reducing take 21 into a final "best" of take 27. This was then mixed into stereo from 11.00 pm to 1.00 am.

Thursday 7 August

Studios Two/Three, EMI Studios, London

Stereo mixing of 'Come Together' was done from 2.30 to 6.00 pm in studio two. Then, moving into studio three, 6.00 to 12.00 pm, vocals and, of particular note, a sensational guitar track were overdubbed onto 'The End', with Paul, George and John trading solos in turn.

Friday 8 August

Studios Two/Three/Room 43, EMI Studios, London

Recording this day began at 2.30 pm but the Beatles gathered at EMI Studios for a quite different purpose three hours earlier. At 11.35, with photographer Iain Macmillan balanced up a step-ladder in the middle of Abbey Road, John, Ringo, Paul and George strode across the zebra (pedestrian) crossing just outside the studio gates while Macmillan snapped away. The Beatles crossed the road several times while he took six quick shots, a friendly policeman obligingly holding up traffic. A while later, Paul studied the transparencies with a magnifying glass and picked the best of the six for the sleeve of *Abbey Road*.

Inside EMI, between 2.30 and 9.00 pm in studio two, drums and bass were overdubbed onto 'The End'. Then Ringo added drums and John an overdub of the synthesiser in conjunction with a white-noise generator (to produce a swirling, gale-force wind effect) onto 'I Want You'. From 5.30 to 9.45, while 'I Want You' was being recorded, Paul went into studio three and overdubbed lead guitar and tambourine onto 'Oh! Darling'.

Monday 11 August

Studios Three/Two/Room 43, EMI Studios, London

'I Want You' became 'I Want You (She's So Heavy)' during the early part of a 2.30 to 11.30 pm overdub session in studio two, John, Paul and George adding "she's so heavy" harmony vocals onto the 18 April take one reduction mixdown of 'I Want You'. Undecided about which version to release – the original Trident master with subsequent overdubs, or the 18 April reduction of same with different overdubs – John had these new vocals edited into both versions. Overdubbing of vocal harmonies onto 'Oh! Darling' and of guitars onto 'Here Comes The Sun' ended the session 30 minutes shy of midnight.

Earlier, between 1.00 and 2.00 pm in studio three, balance engineer Phil McDonald had made mono tape copies of two stereo mixes, 'Dig It' (from the unreleased *Get Back*) and 'Maxwell's Silver Hammer', for the purpose of cutting acetate discs.

Tuesday 12 August

Studio Two, EMI Studios, London

Stereo mixing of 'Oh! Darling', 'Because' and 'Maxwell's Silver Hammer', 7.00 pm–2.00 am.

Wednesday 13 August

Studio Two, EMI Studios, London

Stereo mixing of 'You Never Give Me Your Money', 2.30–9.15 pm.

Thursday 14 August

Studio Two, EMI Studios, London

Stereo mixing, crossfading and editing of finished songs for the medley: 'Sun King'/'Mean Mr Mustard', 'Polythene Pam'/'She Came In Through The Bathroom Window' and 'You Never Give Me Your Money' into 'Sun King'/'Mean Mr Mustard', all done between 2.30 pm and 2.30 am together with the stereo mix of an edit piece for 'Maxwell's Silver Hammer'.

The only break from mixing occurred when disc-jockey Kenny Everett visited the control room of studio two to interview John, utilising studio equipment and a studio tape. The interview was broadcast in two parts by BBC Radio 1 in *Everett Is Here*, on Saturdays 20 and 27 September, both 10.00 am–12.00 noon.

Friday 15 August

Studios One/Two, EMI Studios, London

During this long session orchestral tracks were taped for all of the *Abbey Road* songs that required them: 'Golden Slumbers'/'Carry That Weight', 'The End', 'Something' and 'Here Comes The Sun'. While George Martin was in studio

Left: a rare signed copy of Abbey Road. Obtaining all four Beatles' signatures in late-1969 was a far more difficult task than it had been up until then.

Paul working the board at Abbey Road, watched by George Martin and Ringo and photographed by Linda, 1969. The idea of a recording artist performing such a production role would have been out of the question a few years earlier.

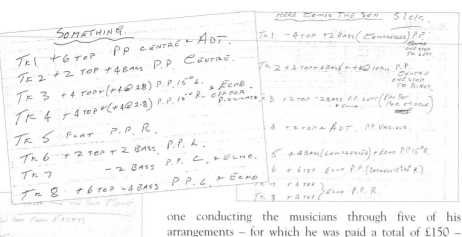

A Linda McCartney photograph of George experimenting for Abbey Road *with his new Fender 'Jazz Bass'.*

one conducting the musicians through five of his arrangements – for which he was paid a total of £150 – balance engineers Geoff Emerick and Phil McDonald and tape op Alan Parsons recorded the proceedings in the control room of studio two, the two rooms linked not only by cable but, for the first time, by closed-circuit TV. (The vision was not recorded, however.) For 'Something' George Harrison shuttled between studio one, where he shared Martin's conductor's podium, and studio two – where, in the control room, he essentially "produced" the recording and, on the studio floor, taped a new lead guitar solo for the song's middle section. The total cost of the musicians – whose names are no longer on file – was £697 2s (£697.10). This was the instrumentation:

For 'Golden Slumbers'/'Carry That Weight' and 'The End' (recorded between 2.30 and 5.30 pm): 12 violins, four violas, four cellos, one string bass, four horns, three trumpets, one trombone and one bass trombone.

For 'Something' (this and 'Here Comes The Sun' were recorded between 7.00 pm and 1.15 am): 12 violins, four violas, four cellos and one string bass.

For 'Here Comes The Sun': four violas, four cellos, one string bass, two clarinets, two alto flutes, two flutes and two piccolos. (Oddly, EMI documentation has preserved one of

the names from this particular part of the session, W G Smith, who played flute, alto flute and the string bass.)

Monday 18 August

Studio Two, EMI Studios, London

A 2.30–10.30 pm session producing stereo mixes of 'Golden Slumbers'/'Carry That Weight' and, after Paul had overdubbed piano, of 'The End'.

Tuesday 19 August

Studio Two/Room 43, EMI Studios, London

George's two songs were completed during this 2.00 pm–4.00 am session, 'Here Comes The Sun' receiving his synthesiser overdub, and then both this song and 'Something' being mixed into stereo. 'The End' was also mixed into stereo and a new crossfade into this from 'Golden Slumbers'/'Carry That Weight' was produced.

Wednesday 20 August

Studios Three/Two, EMI Studios, London

One of the most complex of all Beatles recordings, John's 'I Want You (She's So Heavy)' was completed and mixed between 2.00 and 6.00 pm in studio three, by editing together the 22–23 February recording (with later overdubs) and the 18 April reduction (also with later overdubs). The finished master has the reduction for the first 4 mins 37 secs and the original Trident tape for the remaining 3 mins 7 secs, ending at 7 mins 44 secs with a sudden, full-volume slash in the tape, the inference being that it could have run on forever. (Actually, the tape would have expired 20 seconds later.)

Moving into studio two, 6.00 pm–1.15 am, a prototype of the final *Abbey Road* master tape was compiled. At this point it had two variations from the finished version: the two sides of the album were reversed, so that the LP ended on the slashed guitar chord of 'I Want You (She's So Heavy)', and the placing of 'Octopus's Garden' and 'Oh! Darling' was transposed.

All four Beatles attended this decisive *Abbey Road* session. It was the last time that they were together inside the EMI building from where they had changed the face of popular music.

Thursday 21 August

Room Four/Studio Two, EMI Studios, London

Master tape perfections – a new edit of 'The End', done in Room Four from 1.00 until 2.00 pm; a new crossfade from 'You Never Give Me Your Money' into 'Sun King'/'Mean Mr Mustard' and a new stereo mix of 'The End', studio two 2.30 to 12.00 pm.

Monday 25 August

Studio Two, EMI Studios, London

Final editing of 'Maxwell's Silver Hammer' and 'The End'. Sound effects for the start of 'Maxwell's Silver Hammer' were also made during this 2.30–8.00 pm session but were not used. A safety copy of the final *Abbey Road* master was then made and both this and the original were taken to Apple by Geoff Emerick for disc-cutting by another former EMI Studios employee, Malcolm Davies.

Bestowing instant world fame upon the studio in which they had recorded almost all their output, *Abbey Road* was released at the end of September (in Britain on Friday the 26th). Five weeks later, on 31 October, the single 'Something'/'Come Together' was issued, the first time in Britain that a Beatles single had been pulled from an already-issued album.

Being that, by October, the Beatles would no longer get together even for a few hours of filming, Apple had to come up with some other method of promoting 'Something' on television. The answer was a composite clip produced by Neil Aspinall, showing each member walking around in a beautiful country garden with his wife. It's a charming, poignant 16mm film, full of tenderness, cleverly softening the most obvious blow that it delivers: at no time are even two of the Beatles seen together. No dates are known for the filming, but the late-October period would seem the most likely.

Locations are not identified in the promo, but it's clear that John and Yoko were filmed at their new home, 'Tittenhurst', near Ascot; presumably, George and Pattie were filmed at theirs, in Esher, and Ringo and Maureen in Elstead. Paul and Linda had retreated to their Scottish farm, staying there almost until Christmas, but Paul obligingly tied a camera to the back of a tractor, stepped back to get into the picture with his wife and then sent the film to Neil.

The clip was shown once in Britain, in *Top Of The Pops* on Thursday 13 November (on the still-monochrome BBC1, 7.05–7.50 pm).

Note: the BBC2 arts series *Late Night Line-Up* afforded *Abbey Road* unprecedented television publicity for a pop/rock album. One week ahead of its release, on Friday 19 September (BBC2, 10.55–11.30 pm), and then again on Saturday 10 October in a full repeat (11.25–12.00 pm), the

entire programme was devoted to the album, with, for the most part, non-Beatles footage used to illustrate the music, of which everything but three numbers ('Oh! Darling', 'I Want You' and 'She Came In Through The Bathroom Window') was included. None of the Beatles participated in the programme, however, although Apple did supply photo stills and a little over four minutes of 16mm Beatles footage for screening. The content of this footage is not known, but it may have been amateur home-movie film shot when the four Beatles last came together, for a photo session in John's 'Tittenhurst' house and grounds on Friday 22 August.

Thursday 11 September

As the Beatles had left 'What's The New Mary Jane' unreleased, John was considering issuing it as a Plastic Ono Band single. To refresh his memory, he asked Malcolm Davies to prepare new stereo mixes of the 14 August 1968 recording, made in EMI studio three between 2.30 and 5.30 pm this day. Three were put onto a 7½ ips spool and taken back to Apple for John's listening pleasure.

Saturday 13 September

Varsity Stadium, University of Toronto, Toronto, Ontario, Canada

The concert début of the Plastic Ono Band – proof, if any were still needed, that the good old Beatles days had changed for ever.

The event was a rock and roll revival concert, promoted by local company Brower Walker, for which Chuck Berry, Little Richard, Jerry Lee Lewis, Fats Domino, Bo Diddley and Gene Vincent had been booked, along with more

From the Beatles' final photo session together, at John's 'Tittenhurst' home, 22 August 1969. The dream was over.

modern acts the Doors, Chicago and Alice Cooper. John didn't figure in the original plans, and it was only when inadequate ticket sales were on the verge of causing embarrassment and financial loss that co-promoter John Brower called John in London and asked for his participation. He didn't ask for a performance, just for John to come over and compere the event, but John said that if he'd come over at all, it would be to play. And he wasn't thinking Beatles here – those days were over and he had already announced to the others his intention for "a divorce", an announcement kept publicly silent because of delicate contractual negotiations between Allen Klein and EMI/Capitol.

Instead, John rounded up a suitable Plastic Ono Band: on this occasion himself (rhythm guitar), Yoko (voice), Eric Clapton (lead guitar), Klaus Voormann (bass) and Alan White (drums), and they set off for Toronto the day before the show, their only chance to choose and rehearse material being on the airplane, on unamplified electric guitars.

The Plastic Ono Band went on stage late in the day to a capacity audience of 27,000 – Brower Walker had no trouble shifting tickets once John's involvement was announced, only difficulty in persuading people that it was true – and they performed an understandably unpolished but gritty 40-minute set divided into two distinct sections. In the first, following their introduction and tuning-up, they delivered six songs: the first three from John's Liverpool and Hamburg days – 'Blue Suede Shoes', 'Money (That's What I Want)' and 'Dizzy Miss Lizzy' – the second three from his own considerable catalogue: 'Yer Blues', brand new song 'Cold Turkey' and 'Give Peace A Chance'.

Keen to link the appearance to their peace campaign, John announced before this final number "This is what we came for, really"; and, when, three months later, he and Yoko issued the entire performance as an Apple album they titled it *Live Peace In Toronto 1969*. (See also 25 September and 20 October.)

The remainder of the POB's set saw John step back from the microphone and let Yoko take over (previously she'd been on stage inside a large white bag), treating the audience to an anguished 'Don't Worry Kyoko (Mummy's Only Looking For Her Hand In The Snow)' and the 13-minute 'John John (Let's Hope For Peace)', neither of which went down particularly well. The performance then ended in a style similar to the 2 March concert in Cambridge – with wailing feedback, John and the others propping their guitars against their amps before leaving the stage.

As well as recording the set for album release, John and Yoko gave D A Pennebaker permission to film their appearance for the feature-documentary he was already planning to make about the concert. However, in September 1970, when the edited print was ready for release (as *Sweet Toronto*), business entanglements got in the way. After a few limited screenings the Plastic Ono Band section was excised and the film went back into post-production, emerging without them some time later as *Keep On Rockin'*. The world then had to wait until 1989 to see the Lennons' performance, shown on television and issued on home-video.

Friday 19 September

Apple Corps, London

An interview given by Paul to David Wigg for the BBC Radio 1 series *Scene And Heard*, principally to promote *Abbey Road*. Extracts were broadcast over two editions: 2 mins 45 secs on Sunday 21 September and a further 4 mins 55 secs the following week, 28 September. Both programmes were transmitted from 3.00–4.00 pm.

Note: Ringo and John both gave long interviews to Radio Luxembourg disc-jockey Kid Jensen to plug *Abbey Road*. Ringo's was broadcast from 12.30 to 2.05 am on Friday 26 September, John's 24 hours later, 12.30 to 2.05 am on Saturday the 27th. Both were taped at Apple, dates and times not documented.

Thursday 25 September

Studio Three, EMI Studios, London

On the eve of the release of *Abbey Road*, John returned to EMI Studios for two Plastic Ono Band sessions. First, from 10.00 am to 1.45 pm, he produced stereo mixes of their entire Toronto concert performance: the introduction of the band by announcer Kim Fowley, 'Blue Suede Shoes', 'Money (That's What I Want)', 'Dizzy Miss Lizzy', 'Yer Blues', 'Cold Turkey', 'Give Peace A Chance', 'Don't Worry Kyoko (Mummy's Only Looking For Her Hand In The Snow)' and 'John, John (Let's Hope For Peace)'. The mix tapes were taken to Apple by Geoff Emerick.

Then, returning for a 7.00 pm–1.30 am session, the band – on this occasion comprising John (guitar/vocal), Eric Clapton (guitar), Klaus Voormann (bass), Ringo (drums) and Yoko (unspecified) – recorded the first studio version of 'Cold Turkey', taping 26 takes of the basic track and a simultaneous lead vocal, with John producing.

Sunday 28 September

Trident Studios, London

A re-make of 'Cold Turkey', this time at Trident Studios, the Plastic Ono Band line-up the same as the previous Thursday. (Session start/finish times were not documented.)

Monday 29 September

Room Four, EMI Studios, London

Stereo mixes of the 'Cold Turkey' re-make, produced by John between 8.00 and 12.00 pm.

Thursday 2 October

The World Wildlife Fund charity album was at last about to reach fruition; because it would include the Beatles' 'Across The Universe', recorded 4–8 February 1968, the song was mixed into stereo by George Martin in this 9.30–11.00 am session at EMI.

As the opening track on a wildlife charity album – and the song which gave the LP its *No One's Gonna Change Our World* title – George felt that 'Across The Universe' should begin and end with wildlife sound effects. Tapes of birds twittering, birds flying and, oddly, children in a playground, were copied from the Abbey Road effects collection, 20-seconds being used to open the song and a short burst added near to its close. George also greatly speeded up the Beatles' original recording, clipping ten seconds off the running time.

The finished album was compiled by George Martin at EMI on 3 October and released in Britain on Friday 12 December.

Friday 3 October

Studio A, Lansdowne Studios, Lansdowne Rd, London

Recording of the Plastic Ono Band's studio version of Yoko's 'Don't Worry Kyoko (Mummy's Only Looking For Her Hand In The Snow)', for release as the B-side of 'Cold Turkey'. The band this time featured Yoko (vocal), John (guitar), Ringo (drums), Eric Clapton (guitar) and Klaus Voormann (bass).

Sunday 5 October

Studio Two, EMI Studios, London

A 10.00 am–10.00 pm Plastic Ono Band session, overdubbing onto the Trident re-make of 'Cold Turkey' and mixing it again into stereo, produced by Geoff Emerick. 'Don't Worry Kyoko' was also mixed in this session and the resulting single – John's 'Cold Turkey' on the A-side, Yoko's song on the reverse, was issued in Britain by Apple on Friday 24 October.

A hectic, *cinéma-vérité* 35mm colour film was distributed by Apple to television stations to promote 'Cold Turkey', with a succession of seemingly random images inserted between rough footage of the Montreal bed-in and the 13 September Toronto concert performance. It was screened once (in monochrome) on the BBC1 programme *Top Of The Pops*, on Thursday 6 November (7.05–7.30 pm), and later cropped up in John and Yoko's selected cinema club screenings of their films.

Wednesday 8 October

Apple Corps, London

An interview given by George to David Wigg for the weekly Radio 1 series *Scene And Heard*. He discussed a number of current topics, not just *Abbey Road* but also his production for Apple of the Radha Krishna Temple single 'Hare Krishna Mantra', a surprise Top 20 hit at this time. Extracts were broadcast in two consecutive editions, 5 mins 5 secs on Sunday 12 October and a further 7 mins 40 secs on the 19th, both programmes on air 3.00–4.00 pm.

Monday 20 October

Studio Three, EMI Studios, London

A new stereo mix of the Toronto version of 'Don't Worry Kyoko' began this 2.30–11.30 pm Plastic Ono Band session, replacing the 25 September "best". Various crossfades were then made for the proposed album, and John also used the time to make two copies of a tape loop he'd brought into the studio. Now completed, the LP master tapes were taken back to Apple for cutting and the album was issued in Britain on 12 December.

Tuesday 21 October

Apple Corps, London

An interview given by John to David Wigg for *Scene And Heard*. An extract lasting 5½ minutes was broadcast in the BBC Radio 1 series on Sunday 26 October, between 3.00 and 4.00 pm.

Friday 24 October

Campbeltown, Argyllshire

Keen to determine the truth behind the ridiculous but nonetheless quickly spreading rumour in America that Paul McCartney was dead, and had died in 1966, BBC staff journalist Chris Drake made his way to Paul's remote farm on the Mull of Kintyre in north-west Scotland this day. In an exclusive interview with him, Paul confirmed that he was very much alive, and Drake rushed back to London with his tape to convince Britons, at least, of this. A one-minute extract from the interview was broadcast on the Radio 4 programme *The World This Weekend* on Sunday 26 October (1.00–2.00 pm), 3 mins 30 secs went into the next day's edition of *The*

World At One (27 October, 1.00–1.30 pm, Radio 4) and 3 mins 20 secs was transmitted in *Late Night Extra* a few hours later (Radio 2, 10.00–12.00 pm).

Monday 27 October

Studio Three, EMI Studios, London

With George Martin producing, Ringo became the first Beatle to undertake a solo studio album, beginning work on what was to become *Sentimental Journey* on this day, with 2.30–5.00 and 7.00–10.45 pm sessions in studio three.

The idea for the album was that Ringo would sing a dozen old standards, newly-arranged by some of the biggest names in the world of popular and orchestral music: Elmer Bernstein, Quincy Jones and others. On this first day a 17-piece orchestra recorded 'Night And Day' (the 1937 hit for Tommy Dorsey; newly arranged by Chico O'Farrill) during the afternoon, Ringo overdubbing his vocal in the evening. The song was mixed into stereo 9.30–10.45 pm.

Thursday 6 November

Wessex Sound Studios, Highbury New Park, London

A *Sentimental Journey* session: recording 'Stormy Weather' (the 1943 hit for Lena Horne; the identity of the new arranger not documented) with 18 musicians (7.00–9.00 pm) and Ringo's vocal overdub (9.00–10.00 pm). The song was not included on the album and remains unreleased.

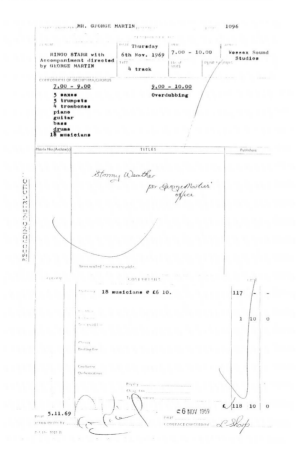

Friday 7 November

Wessex Sound Studios, London

Another session for Ringo's *Sentimental Journey*: recording the orchestral tracks for 'Stardust' (the 1929 Hoagy Carmichael song recorded by many major singers) between 7.00 and 10.00 pm. George Martin invoiced EMI £30 for this arrangement and his name was also noted on the recording documentation. However, the album sleeve credits Paul McCartney in this regard.

Friday 14 November

Trident Studios, London

A *Sentimental Journey* session: Ringo overdubbed his vocal onto 'Stardust' and recorded a basic track for 'Dream' (a 1945 hit for the Pied Pipers; newly arranged by George Martin). The session began at 4.00 pm but its end time wasn't noted.

Rough stereo mixes of two *Sentimental Journey* recordings, 'Dream' and 'Stardust', were produced by Geoff Emerick in Room Four at EMI Studios on Tuesday 18 November, 4.00 to 4.30 pm.

Tuesday 25 November

Apple Corps, London

Another big news day for John, in which he hoped for, and received, a huge media reaction from the act of returning his MBE medal to the Queen – his chauffeur delivered it to Buckingham Palace during the morning. John fielded a succession of calls and visits from journalists and broadcasters in his office at Apple, happy to be bagging more headlines for the peace crusade.

In addition to a number of news interviews, John was questioned by the BBC's David Bellan for broadcast in the two editions of the following morning's Radio 4 magazine programme *Today* (7.15–7.45 and 8.15–8.40).

Wednesday 26 November

Studio Two, EMI Studios, London

John was determined to see 'What's The New Mary Jane' and 'You Know My Name (Look Up The Number)' released. Though Beatles recordings and Lennon-McCartney song copyrights, they were really his work and his songs. If the Beatles wouldn't release them then he would, as a single under the Plastic Ono Band banner.

The intention of this 7.00 pm–3.00 am session, co-produced by John and Geoff Emerick, was two-fold: to edit the 30 April 1969 "best" mono mix of 'You Know My Name (Look Up The Number)' down from 6 mins 8 secs to a more acceptable duration for an A-side (it ended up 4 mins 19 secs), and to record new overdubs onto 'What's The New Mary Jane' for the B-side. The former task was easy, the latter much more complicated, with a number of mixes, edits and overdubs effected. But by 3.00 am the two sides of a Plastic Ono Band single were ready for pressing.

Discs were soon cut and Apple announced a rush-release date of Friday 5 December, catalogue number APPLES 1002. Apple also announced, rather cryptically, that the recordings featured John and Yoko singing "[with instrumental support from a group] of many of the greatest show business names of today". For reasons unknown (though it's likely that the other Beatles objected) the record never appeared. By Monday 1 December it was "on hold" and it never came off. But though 'What's The New Mary Jane' remains unissued, this 26 November 1969 edit of 'You Know My Name (Look Up The Number)' was released as the B-side of the Beatles' last British single, 'Let It Be', on Friday 6 March 1970.

Friday 28 November

Studio Two, EMI Studios, London

A *Sentimental Journey* session, recording take one of 'Blue Turning Grey Over You' (the 1930 Louis Armstrong hit, newly arranged by Oliver Nelson) between 5.00 and 6.30 pm; making a reduction mixdown of 'Stardust' (6.30–8.30); overdubbing Ringo's vocal onto this (8.30–10.00) and mixing it into stereo (10.00–12.00 pm).

Monday 1 December

London-area locations

Filming took place this day for a particularly interesting BBC documentary about Ringo Starr which, on Wednesday 10 December, comprised an entire edition of the BBC2 arts series *Line-Up* (sometimes called *Late Night Line-Up*), broadcast from 11.07 to 11.30 pm.

The object of the film was to promote *The Magic Christian*, although, strangely, it received no mention whatsoever in the final programme and there were no clip extracts. But the fact that Ringo was accorded such treatment on national TV the night before the royal world premiere of a feature-film in which he played a prominent role was link enough.

Shooting took place on location throughout this day, Ringo being accompanied and interviewed by the most regular of the *Line-Up* hosts, Tony Bilbow. The finished production showed Bilbow and Starr departing the Apple building in Savile Row and climbing into the back of Ringo's silver Mercedes-Benz, where they were filmed chatting intelligently and at length about a variety of worldly topics while the car wended its way past Buckingham Palace, over Battersea Bridge and past Battersea Power Station.

The action then switched to a rowing boat on a stretch of the River Thames somewhere in the rural London suburbs, with Ringo rowing and talking at the same time, filmed from the same boat and also from a second boat being rowed by the other members of the *Line-Up* production crew. Shooting finished as the winter sun was starting to set, which would have been around 4.00 pm.

Tuesday 2 December

'Tittenhurst', London Rd, Sunninghill, Ascot, Berkshire
and Colston Hall, Bristol
and Studio Two, EMI Studios, London

It was a measure of the imprint he left on the 1960s that when asked to choose the person whom he felt to have been the man of the decade, the sociologist and anthropologist Dr Desmond Morris chose John Lennon. Morris was one of three eminent people asked to make such a choice, the broadcaster Alistair Cooke selecting John F Kennedy and the writer Mary McCarthy opting for Ho Chi Minh. Having made their selections, each was commissioned by Associated TeleVision (ATV) to compile a 20-minute documentary to support his/her choice, the resulting one hour of material forming *Man Of The Decade*, networked by ATV on Tuesday 30 December (10.30–11.30 pm; John's section was the last, 11.10–11.30 pm).

John was naturally delighted to have been accorded such an honour, especially by the esteemed Morris, whom, as a 16-year-old, he had watched on television presenting Granada's children's programme *Zoo Time*. The cornerstone of the 20-minute section was an interview given by John, with Yoko, to Morris this day at 'Tittenhurst', out walking in the expansive, arboricultural grounds. (They filmed in the kitchen, too, but this footage wasn't used.) The 20 minutes also included short extracts of archive Beatles/Lennon film, which John was anxious to choose personally, getting together with Morris to do so in a Soho viewing theatre a few days earlier.

The clips John chose were: the Beatles performing 'Some Other Guy' at the Cavern Club; news footage of Beatlemania at Kennedy Airport on 7 February 1964; three sequences from *A Hard Day's Night* (the man on the train, the "press conference" and the 'If I Fell' performance); the Scotland Yard office sequence from *Help!* with Patrick Cargill; 'I'm Down' from *The Beatles At Shea Stadium*; 'Hey Jude' recording footage from *Music!*; 28 November 1968 news footage of John outside Marylebone Magistrates Court after being fined for drugs possession; a clip from the Amsterdam bed-in; two clips from the Montreal bed-in (John urging the Peoples Park students at Berkeley to adopt non-violent tactics, shown with footage of the subsequent rioting, and the recording of 'Give Peace A Chance'); and the 'Something' promotional film. Also shown was a clip of the 250,000 US anti-Vietnam War demonstrators marching on the White House on Moratorium Day, 15 November 1969, singing 'Give Peace A Chance'.

Bizarrely, considering the great rivalry which existed between the two broadcasting stations, Morris and the ATV crew were filmed interviewing John by a camera crew from the BBC, which was itself making a special documentary about the Lennons. This, in fact, was the first of a five-day shoot for the production, 'The World Of John And Yoko', screened in the BBC1 series *24 Hours* on Monday 15 December (10.30–11.05 pm), introduced by David Dimbleby. It was shown in colour, BBC1 having made the transition from monochrome on 15 November.

Royal Albert Hall in London headed by the American "white soul" husband and wife team Delaney & Bonnie, in which they were backed by a group called Friends led by Eric Clapton. Their rapport growing ever stronger, Eric persuaded George to join the tour as an anonymous member of Friends, and George accepted, knowing that this was a means for him to return to the concert stage without the headline-making Beatles comeback or indeed any kind of spotlight at all: he could just slip on at the back of the stage, scarcely recognisable anyway in his long flowing hair and beard, and play without fuss or bother, just the way he wanted it. Besides, George enjoyed Delaney & Bonnie's music so much that he had tried in May 1969 to release their album *Accept No Substitute* on Apple, although business complications had prevented it. And another attraction was that Ashton, Gardner and Dyke were among the tour's support acts, two of whom (not Gardner) were formerly in the Liverpool group the Remo Four and had played at George's invitation on his *Wonderwall* film soundtrack album.

So it was that George participated in a British package tour for the first time since 1965, the formula unchanged since then except that, with fewer acts on the bill, the star attraction could play 40 minutes instead of 20. Still, the tour played two "houses" per night over six consecutive nights at venues all visited by the Beatles during their 1963–65 touring heyday, the entourage staying each night in local hotels.

Also this day, at EMI Studios, Beatles tapes were being mixed. On 26 February 1970 Capitol Records issued the US album *Hey Jude*, a ten-song stereo-only Beatles compilation spanning 1964–1969. But as some of those ten had never been mixed into stereo such mixes had to be newly produced. Sessions today (2.30–5.30 pm) and on Friday 5 December were devoted to this purpose, 'Lady Madonna' and 'Rain' being done this afternoon.

'Octopus's Garden' was also mixed into stereo during this session, but for an entirely different purpose: on 14 December Ringo would be participating in the video-taping of a George Martin TV "spectacular" for Yorkshire Television, *With A Little Help From My Friends*, miming to a version of his *Abbey Road* composition. It had to be noticeably different from the Beatles' recording so that he didn't appear to be breaching the Musicians' Union miming ban. This new mix eliminated the Beatles' bass, piano and lead guitar tracks, ready for overdubbing on 8 December.

Wednesday 3 December

'Tittenhurst', Sunninghill, Ascot
and **Apple Corps, London**
and **Town Hall, Birmingham**

More shooting for the *24 Hours* documentary 'The World Of John And Yoko'. 'Tittenhurst' footage from this date that was included in the finished 50-minute production showed John and Yoko in bed, playing a mellotron, and John watching with rapt attention the vintage Granada clip of 'Some Other Guy' being projected onto a home-movie screen. The Lennons were then filmed sitting in the back of their London-bound white Rolls-Royce giving the day's

This was a remarkable production, for the BBC's cameras followed John and Yoko everywhere over the five days: into the recording studio, their home, their office, their car, their hotel, even into their bedroom and bathroom. In return for such exclusive access and co-operation, the Lennons persuaded the Corporation to draw-up a remarkable contract that required it to hand over all of the footage, whether used or not, and gave John and Yoko exclusive rights to exploit the material themselves in the future. Well into that future, 19 years on to be precise, a considerable amount of this *24 Hours* material was included by Yoko in her documentary feature-film *Imagine: John Lennon*.

Meanwhile, during this evening of Tuesday 2 December, George Harrison made his first stage appearance since the Beatles quit touring in August 1966. The previous night, 1 December, he had attended a package tour concert at the instructions to assistant Anthony Fawcett and then arriving at Apple.

Here, the *24 Hours* programme showed John discussing on the telephone his forthcoming trip to Toronto, in meetings with Fawcett and the Beatles' personal assistant Peter Brown, and giving interviews to Alan Smith of the *New Musical Express*, two people from Japan, disc-jockey/pop columnist Stuart Henry and the American writer Gloria Emerson, with whom John became engaged in a bitter argument. (This latter interview made for such fascinating viewing, and listening, that it was broadcast by BBC Radio 2 the night of the *24 Hours* programme, Monday 15 December, in *Late Night Extra*, 10.00–12.00 pm.)

George, meanwhile, spent the evening at the Town Hall in Birmingham, performing two "houses" on the Delaney & Bonnie package tour. He had last played this venue during the Beatles' May–June 1963 tour with Roy Orbison.

Thursday 4 December

Studio Two, EMI Studios, London
and **City Hall, Sheffield**

This day witnessed two separate solo sessions in EMI studio two. Between 9.30 am and 1.00 pm Johnnie Spence conducted a 17-piece orchestra through nine takes of 'Blue Turning Grey Over You', for *Sentimental Journey*. Ringo then overdubbed his vocal from 1.00 to 2.30 and the song was mixed into stereo 2.30–4.00 pm.

Three hours later – as George was about to play the first of two evening "houses" with Delaney & Bonnie at the City Hall in Sheffield – began a remarkable Plastic Ono Band recording session, filmed by the BBC for *24 Hours*. The POB on this occasion comprised John, Yoko and all the people one might expect to find at a John Lennon EMI recording session: Mal Evans, Anthony Fawcett, Geoff Emerick, Phil McDonald, Malcolm Davies, Eddie Klein and many others, all of whom *participated* in the long night's work (7.00 pm–1.40 am). Two "items" were recorded; the first was a long section of laughter, everybody sitting/standing in a circle, wearing red noses, guffawing uproariously and shouting out random thoughts, later overdubbed with percussion and chanting. The second "item" was a long whispering piece, each person queueing for a chance to whisper something into the microphone, Geoff Emerick causing considerable laughter when he whispered "Bill Livy's head". (Livy was on the technical staff at EMI Studios and was bald.)

Both 'Item 1' and 'Item 2' were then mixed into stereo and the mixes – together with five reels of studio/control room recordings which had been running throughout the session – were taken away by Mal Evans. John and Yoko announced their intention to make the tapes into a fourth *avant-garde* LP, following on from *Two Virgins*, *Life With The Lions* and *The Wedding Album* – one side would have featured the laughing, the other the whispering – but they must later have had a change of mind for the record didn't appear and was never again mentioned. If nothing else, though, the session allowed *24 Hours* viewers the chance to see some expectedly eccentric John and Yoko recording footage.

Friday 5 December

Market Square, Lavenham, Suffolk
and **Bull Hotel, Hall St, Long Melford, Suffolk**
and **City Hall, Newcastle-upon-Tyne**

The *24 Hours* production unit followed John and Yoko's Rolls-Royce out into the snow-covered Suffolk countryside this day, filming them en route and then in the market square in Lavenham while making a film, another of their "experimental" productions, *Apotheosis 2*. In this, they hunched together, shivering, covered from head to toe in an enormous black cape with only their eyes visible, while a hot-air balloon was inflated and launched into the sky, with the Lennons' ever-reliable "experimental" cameraman Nick Knowland on board, about to film for them glorious panoramic views of the local snowscape. (The snow was accidental – the filming was pre-arranged, and followed a previous *Apotheosis* shoot, in Hampshire, which had proven unsatisfactory.)

The *24 Hours* film showed John and Yoko waiting patiently for the balloon to go up, and, without their capes, checking into a local hotel for the night, the Bull in Long Melford.

There were three other celluloid exploits for the Lennons in 1969, this busiest of all years for them, for which dates cannot be pinpointed: *Honeymoon*, *Rape Part II* and *Self Portrait*, the last being a 42-minute slow-motion study of John's penis in various stages of erection, shown only at a handful of private screenings. Why he made the film is anyone's guess and it received no known public reviews – as Yoko said soon afterwards, "The critics wouldn't touch it".

Back to the evening of 5 December, George played two shows at the City Hall in Newcastle-upon-Tyne, standing unobtrusively at the back of the stage during Delaney & Bonnie's performances.

Back to the daytime of 5 December, 2.30–5.15 pm to be precise, stereo mixes of 'Hey Jude' and 'Revolution' were produced at EMI Studios for Capitol's *Hey Jude* album.

Saturday 6 December

Bull Hotel, Long Melford
and **Studio One, Wembley Studios, Wembley**
and **Empire Theatre, Liverpool**

The star, co-star and guest star of *The Magic Christian* – Peter Sellers, Ringo Starr and Spike Milligan – all appeared together on this day's edition of the London Weekend Television series *Frost On Saturday*, plugging the film which would have its world premiere the following Thursday. The programme, now in colour, was broadcast from 11.10 to 12.00 pm, and was taped earlier in the evening at Wembley Studios. In such illustrious company, a mini Goon reunion in effect, Ringo spoke only a little during the show, at one point delivering a brief, off-the-cuff vocal version of 'Octopus's Garden'. Clips from the film were also shown.

Earlier this day, shooting for the BBC's *24 Hours* production 'The World Of John And Yoko' was concluded when the Lennons were filmed in their Long Melford hotel room playing the game "fortunately/unfortunately".

George, meanwhile, with Delaney & Bonnie, was back where it had all started: on stage at the Empire Theatre in Liverpool, a quiet return home for one of the city's most famous sons.

Sunday 7 December

Studio E, Lime Grove Studios, London
and **Fairfield Hall, Croydon**

John, with Yoko, engaged in an unusual television appearance this evening, taking part in a live theological debate about evil in the BBC1 religious series *The Question Why*. The discussion was chaired by Malcolm Muggeridge, and it also featured Henry Cecil, Gerald Cohen, David Cooper, General Sir John Hackett, the Rev Christopher Neil-Smith, Paul Zeal and Canon Edward Carpenter. The programme was broadcast direct from Lime Grove Studios between 6.15 and 6.50 pm.

The Delaney & Bonnie package tour of Britain reached its seventh and final date this evening at the Fairfield Hall in Croydon, and the two "houses" were recorded for the live album *Delaney & Bonnie On Tour With Eric Clapton*, released in Britain on 29 May 1970. The songs, a mixture of new and old, soul and rock and roll, none composed by George, were 'Things Get Better', medley: 'Poor Elijah'/'Tribute To Robert Johnson', 'Only You Know And I Know', 'I Don't Want To Discuss It', 'That's What My Man Is For', 'Where There's A Will There's A Way', 'Comin' Home', medley: 'Long Tall Sally'/'Jenny Jenny'/'The Girl Can't Help It'/'Tutti Frutti'.

Monday 8 December

Studio Two, EMI Studios, London

The recording, in ten takes, 10.00 am–12.15 pm, of Ringo's new vocal overdub for 'Octopus's Garden' – with other musicians supplying bass, lead guitar and piano – for George Martin's *With A Little Help From My Friends* TV show (see 2 and 14 December).

Wednesday 10 – Friday 12 December

Falkoner Theatre, Falkoner Alle,
Copenhagen, Denmark

George's commitment to the Delaney & Bonnie concert tour extended even to these three dates in Copenhagen, returning to the city visited by the Beatles on 4 June 1964, when Jimmy Nicol was their substitute drummer. Only five years separated the two events; it could have been a lifetime.

Apart from their participation in John's forthcoming Lyceum concert in London (see 15 December), this was George's last date with Delaney & Bonnie, who returned to America delighted at having made such grand musical connections.

Sunday 14 December

Studio Four, The Television Centre,
Kirkstall Rd, Leeds, Yorkshire

Colour video-taping of the George Martin "spectacular" *With A Little Help From My Friends* took place this day at the studios of Yorkshire Television, the new (1968) ITV franchise holder for the north of England. (Granada, which formerly covered the area, now concentrated only on the north-west while Tyne Tees continued to programme the north-east region.) Ringo's contribution was the new vocal version of 'Octopus's Garden', to which he surreptitiously mimed before the cameras.

Also at YTV this day to contribute to the programme – shown by most regions 6.00–7.00 pm on Christmas Eve, Wednesday 24 December, and described in a press handout as "a fast-moving, colourful and musical show…forward-looking family entertainment heavily accentuated in music combined with comedy" – were Dudley Moore, the Hollies, Blue Mink, *Top Of The Pops* dancers Pan's People, Lulu, Spike Milligan and George Martin himself, conducting his 40-piece George Martin Orchestra. The show was produced by the fast-rising David Mallet, a lowly "runner" during the production of the Beatles' first promotional clips on 23 November 1965.

Monday 15 December

Apple Corps, London
and **Lyceum Ballroom, Wellington St, London**

And still *Get Back* dragged on. In June 1969 the delay was publicly blamed on the late production of a lavish book being prepared to accompany the LP. An August release date was then announced but quickly shelved. In late-July it was announced that a new LP (*Abbey Road*) would precede *Get Back* and that the latter would be issued in November, coinciding with the film. By August this had become December. By November it had become "the new year". In the meantime, acetate copies of some of Glyn Johns' spring 1969 mixes had reached US radio stations as a consequence of which a "bootleg" album had surfaced.

Film and book problems had undoubtedly caused a delay. But so had the Beatles' procrastinatory contempt for the whole project. If they did want it out at all they couldn't decide in which form. Added to which, they couldn't unanimously approve Glyn Johns' first *Get Back* album. Now, in December 1969, Johns was again commissioned to go away and produce a new Beatles album. There was but one new instruction: he must make it tie-in with the as-yet unissued film.

Based again at Olympic, Glyn Johns set to work on this date, 1.00–2.30 pm, continuing on 21 December and 5 and 8 January 1970, and attending EMI sessions on 3 and 4 January.

Meanwhile, over at the Apple HQ in central London, Ringo made an unusual radio recording: a two-minute appeal on behalf of the British Wireless for the Blind Fund, for broadcast by the BBC – as was the custom – on Christmas Day. It was transmitted at 10.15 that morning by Radio 1 as an insert into the 10.00 am–12.00 noon *Kenny Everett's Christmas Show*. (Sadly, however, it raised a mere £175, the least successful BBC charity appeal of the month.)

An altogether different task was tackled in the evening: the location recording by EMI of a Plastic Ono Band concert at the Lyceum Ballroom, the dance-hall situated just off The Strand in central London. Geoff Emerick produced the recording, which was engineered by Peter Bown and John Kurlander. They taped the entire concert, featuring the Hot Chocolate Band, the Pioneers, the Rascals, Jimmy Cliff, Black Velvet – even disc-jockey Emperor Rosko's between-acts records – before reaching the Plastic Ono Band's closing set of 'Cold Turkey' (nearly seven minutes) and 'Don't Worry Kyoko (Mummy's Only Looking For Her Hand In The Snow)' (an epic 16 minutes).

Organised to benefit UNICEF, the concert was named "Peace For Christmas" and John assembled an extended Plastic Ono Band at only 48 hours' notice – he later called it the Plastic Ono Supergroup – comprising (as well as he and Yoko), George, Eric Clapton, Klaus Voormann, Bobby Keys, Billy Preston, Keith Moon, Alan White, Jim Gordon and Delaney & Bonnie. This was the first appearance together of two Beatles on a British stage since 1 May 1966, and a little of the event was filmed by the newsreel cameras of Movietonews.

Between 8.00 and 10.00 pm on Wednesday 17 December, in the control room of studio one at EMI (a session which John missed, being back in Canada again), Geoff Emerick produced stereo mixes of the Plastic Ono Band's Lyceum concert, utilising the four-track band tapes and two-track audience tapes recorded two nights earlier. The performance wasn't issued on record until June 1972, however, when it appeared as part of John and Yoko's double-album *Some Time In New York City*, and for that purpose the four-track tapes were copied (at EMI Studios on 26 November 1970) and remixed with an overdub taped in New York in 1971: Nicky Hopkins on electric piano, replacing the original organ track.

Saturday 20 December

Department of Culture and Technology, University of Toronto, Toronto, Ontario, Canada,
and CBC Studio, Bay St, Toronto, Ontario, Canada

John had two TV engagements this pre-Christmas Saturday during his and Yoko's third visit to Canada in 1969 (the highlight of which was a long 23 December meeting with Prime Minister Trudeau in which John and Yoko were able to expound their peace message directly to a world leader for the first and only time).

The first was a film shoot for CBS-TV (the US company) in which John visited the University of Toronto office of the Canadian communications theorist Marshall McLuhan, author of *The Medium Is The Message*, and chatted together for 45 illuminating minutes. (No transmission information for this film is known.)

John then went to the Toronto TV studios of the Canadian Broadcasting Corporation and appeared on the live, networked *CBC Weekend*, a news, current events and public affairs programme, in which he and Rabbi Abraham Feinberg (one of the chorale on the Montreal bed-in 'Give Peace A Chance' recording) were interviewed by anchorman Lloyd Robertson. The show was broadcast from 10.15 to 11.15 pm local time.

Sunday 21 December

More *Get Back* mixing and editing by Glyn Johns, working from 2.00 until 4.00 this afternoon at Olympic Sound Studios in Barnes.

AS THE YEAR BEGAN, the Beatles knew that their time was up, that there would be no more group projects. The deepest imaginable rift had split them into two opposing camps, with Paul in one and John, George and Ringo in the other. In April, Paul would sum up the conflict as "personal differences, business differences, musical differences". The two sides scarcely fraternised with each other, and when, around February, Paul telephoned John to say that he was leaving the Beatles all that his former partner could reply was "Good! That makes two of us who have accepted it mentally."

For Paul, the final straw occurred when Allen Klein, supported by the other three Beatles, sought to impede the release of his first solo album, so that it wouldn't clash with a date supposedly fixed by Klein with United Artists for the release of the *Let It Be* film – the *Get Back* picture as was, which, like the album, was now more than a year out-of-date, unloved and unwanted except as a contractual filler with United Artists.

Although there were two sides to every argument, Paul regarded this as meddling with his individual activities; when Ringo appeared at his house one night to explain the situation, he threw him out, threatening to finish the group once and for all. Though the Beatles hadn't worked together for some months, the general public was unaware of just how much matters had deteriorated. Ringo's August 1968 decision to quit had been kept quiet, George's departure in January 1969 had leaked out but the depth of the disagreement had not, and when he returned a few days later it was assumed that all was rosy again. And when, in September 1969, John had informed the others that he wanted "a divorce", his decision was hushed-up because of delicate business negotiations.

The album *Let It Be* was finally issued in Britain on Friday 8 May, more than 16 months after starting out as *Get Back*; it was finished off with some drastic post-production mixing by Phil Spector. "A cheapskate epitaph, a cardboard tombstone, a glorified EP," one reviewer called it, and most others agreed, considering it patchy, over-produced and over-valued. George Martin was reportedly very upset when he heard what Phil Spector had done with the Beatles' sound, and Glyn Johns, the main man behind *Get Back*, has since heaped nothing but scorn and vitriol upon Spector's production.

Even Paul McCartney was publicly aggrieved, citing – in his affidavit seeking dissolution of the Beatles' partnership – Spector's extensive production job on 'The Long And Winding Road' and some other songs as an "intolerable interference" with his work. In court he substantiated with documents how he had attempted to get the album changed before its release but how his efforts were rebuffed. He also expressed public annoyance at the whole album package, which included a lavish book – no longer sold – that added

INTRODUCTION 1970 AND DIARY

John, without the others, on Top Of The Pops.

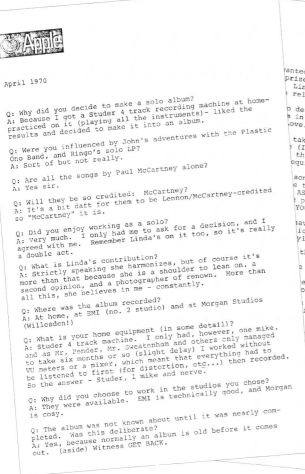

33 per cent to the retail price. It was only in November 1970 that the album could be bought without the marketing trimmings, the like of which had never before been employed by the Beatles.

In fairness to Phil Spector, he did precisely what John, George and Allen Klein had commissioned him to do: prepare an album to accompany the film – its world premiere was held in New York on 13 May, but none of the Beatles attended. Best producer in the world or not, he couldn't re-write or re-record the songs, which were mostly of second-class Beatles standard, recorded at a time of boredom, arguments and intense bad feeling within the group, recorded live on borrowed sound equipment, deliberately devoid of the superior studio polish so typical of their post-1965 output. In characteristically outspoken form, John said of Spector "He was given the shittiest load of badly recorded shit with a lousy feeling to it ever, and he made something out of it."

It was on Friday 10 April 1970 that the world was told that the Beatles had effectively broken up and would, in all likelihood, never again work together. It came as quite a shock. There was no announcement as such, but this was the inescapable conclusion drawn from a to-the-point written question-and-answer interview distributed with media review copies of *McCartney*, in which Paul made it perfectly plain that he saw no future for the group, did not miss the company of John, George or Ringo and wished henceforth to break free.

Around the world, virtually all other news items were relegated to second place in the morning newspapers, the evening newspapers, the radio and television bulletins.

John was both pleased and annoyed: pleased that, at last, the Beatles were drawing to a close, annoyed that Paul had been the one to break the news, as if it was all his idea. If at this time he had any regrets at all at the Beatles' passing, it was only that he hadn't announced it himself the previous September.

Because of contractual entanglements and horrific business problems the Beatles' corpse wasn't buried for some years, but the last rites were read on 10 April. It was, in so many senses, the end of an era, the like of which will never be repeated.

1970

JANUARY

Saturday 3 January

Studio Two, EMI Studios, London

The last time that the four Beatles were together inside EMI Studios was 20 August 1969. But that was not the group's final session. On this day – and again on 4 January – Paul, George and Ringo reunited at EMI to help complete *Get Back*. John was in Denmark on a four-week holiday.

During the Twickenham rehearsal section of the project (as seen in the *Let It Be* film), George played to Ringo a new song, 'I Me Mine', which he had composed only the night before. Since the sequence was to be included in the film it had to be properly recorded in order that it could appear on the accompanying *Let It Be* soundtrack album. So, working from 2.30 pm to 12.15 am, the three Beatles taped 16 takes of the rhythm track (acoustic and bass guitars, drums) and then added overdubs – electric piano, electric guitar, lead and backing vocals, an organ and a second acoustic guitar – onto the last of these.

The duration of the final recording was only 1 min 34 secs. After Phil Spector had overseen overdubs, re-produced and re-edited it for *Let It Be*, it was 2 mins 25 secs.

Sunday 4 January

Studio Two, EMI Studios, London

'Let It Be' was the one song on *Get Back* which already had an overdub: a guitar solo in the middle-eight section, taped on 30 April 1969. Several more overdubs were recorded in this 2.30 pm–4.00 am session.

The first was of harmony vocals by George, Paul and Linda McCartney onto the 31 January 1969 eight-track. This was then given three reduction mixdowns with simultaneous overdubs of two trumpets, two trombones and a tenor saxophone, arranged by George Martin. Onto the "best" of these was added a new and more stinging guitar solo by George, drums by Ringo, maracas by Paul, and – right at the end of the song – some more cellos. Stereo mixes ended the session and Glyn Johns took away all of the tapes from this and the previous night.

Note: the mix of 'Let It Be' used for the single release, issued in Britain on Friday 6 March, omitted this day's new lead guitar solo; the album version excluded the original 30 April 1969 solo, giving the misleading impression that the two were different takes.

Monday 5 January

Olympic Sound Studios, London

By the end of this 7.00–11.30 pm Olympic session, Glyn Johns had compiled a new 44-minute *Get Back* LP master tape. It lacked 'Teddy Boy' – because it would not be seen in the film and, presumably, because Paul had told him that he was presently re-recording the song for his first solo album (see 21 February 1970) – but it added the newly taped 'I Me Mine' and, for the same reason – that it would be seen in the film – it added 'Across The Universe'. (Both songs were mixed into stereo during this session.)

The culmination of 12 months' work, *Get Back* now looked like this – recording dates, 1969 unless stated, in parentheses. Side A: 'The One After 909' (30 January); 'Rocker' (22 January); 'Save The Last Dance For Me' (22 January); 'Don't Let Me Down' (22 January); 'Dig A Pony' (24 January); 'I've Got A Feeling' (24 January); 'Get Back' (28 January, the "single" version); 'Let It Be' (31 January and 30 April overdub, Glyn chose to ignore the 4 January upgrading). Side B: 'For You Blue' (25 January); 'Two Of Us' (24 January); 'Maggie Mae' (24 January); 'Dig It' (26 January); 'The Long And Winding Road' (31 January); 'I Me Mine' (3 January 1970); 'Across The Universe' (4–8 February 1968); 'Get Back (reprise)' (28 January).

This *Get Back*, like its predecessor, remains unreleased. The Beatles still couldn't agree on whether or not they liked it, and – additionally – John couldn't see why Glyn Johns wanted to be credited as producer, even without expecting a royalty. In March, Phil Spector was brought in to see what he could do.

Thursday 8 January

Olympic Sound Studios, London

A 9.00–11.00 pm session in which Glyn Johns tidied up *Get Back* by remixing 'Let It Be' (used for the single) and 'For You Blue', both in stereo.

Recently discovered studio documentation reveals that, before being mixed, this latter song first received a vocal overdub – so, obviously, George attended the session.

Wednesday 14 January

Olympic Sound Studios, London

A 2.30–5.30 pm session for Ringo's *Sentimental Journey*: overdubbing his vocal onto 'Love Is A Many Splendoured Thing' (a 1955 hit for the Four Aces; newly arranged by Quincy Jones) and also 'Sentimental Journey' (a 1945 hit sung by Doris Day; newly arranged by producer Richard Perry, with whom Ringo would work extensively in 1973–74). Both songs had been recorded up to vocal overdub stage by an orchestra in the USA (the dates not known) and the multi-track tapes had then been sent across to England. Rough stereo mixing from 5.30–6.00 pm concluded the session.

Tuesday 27 January

Studio Two, EMI Studios, London
and **NBC Television Studio, Alameda St, Burbank,**
Los Angeles, California, USA

The first-ever stereo mix of the Beatles' 'The Inner Light', done at Apple's request, was produced by Geoff Emerick between 10.00 and 11.30 am, although for no obvious use. (It wasn't issued until 1981.)

A few hours later, commencing at 7.00 pm and finishing at 4.00 am, the Plastic Ono Band started, completed and mixed a new single in EMI studio three: 'Instant Karma!', written earlier in the day by John. At the suggestion of George Harrison, Phil Spector produced the session, beginning a long working relationship with John and also George himself (and leading to his employment on the *Get Back* tapes – see 23 March).

'Instant Karma!' was recorded in ten takes of the basic track – acoustic guitar (John), drums (Alan White), bass (Klaus Voormann), electric piano (Billy Preston) and lead guitar (George) – taped from 7.00 to 12.00 pm, with considerable overdubs added from then until 3.00 am, most especially three tracks of a massed backing chorale/hand-claps comprising all of the above plus Yoko, Mal Evans and patrons from Hatchetts, a London night-club.

Four stereo mixes of the song were prepared from 3.00 to 4.00 am, completing the session, the fourth being used for the A-side of the single, rush-released in Britain on Friday 6 February. (The B-side, Yoko's 'Who Has Seen The Wind?' was taped privately, no date known.) For the American single, quite unbeknown to John, Phil Spector prepared a

new stereo mix in a Los Angeles studio a few days later – it was typical of the way the man worked.

In Los Angeles *this* day (27 January), in town to attend the 29 January local premiere of *The Magic Christian*, Ringo was happy to accept an invitation to video-tape an appearance on NBC's popular primetime comedy series *Rowan & Martin's Laugh-In*. It was shot in "beautiful downtown Burbank" in front of a studio audience, Ringo making a number of brief cameo appearances with the cast and other guest stars, including one where he joined Ruth Buzzi and Arte Johnson in their familiar park-bench setting.

The edition with Ringo was broadcast on US television on Monday 23 February (8.00–9.00 pm, EST), while viewers in Britain saw it on Sunday 12 April (BBC2, 7.25–8.15 pm, the 60-minute US edition coming down to 50 without commercials).

Ringo returned to Britain on Monday 2 February to resume recording sessions for *Sentimental Journey*. Before doing so, though, he filmed an interview for the Saturday lunchtime ABC-TV music series *Get It Together*, screened on 7 March (12.00 noon–12.30 pm, EST).

Tuesday 3 February

Studio Two, EMI Studios, London

A re-make of 'Love Is A Many Splendoured Thing' for *Sentimental Journey*. Arranger Quincy Jones conducted a 16-man band through eight takes, 2.30–4.30 pm; then from 4.30–6.30 pm Billy Preston overdubbed organ and Ringo added his vocal. The recording was mixed into stereo from 6.30 to 7.00 pm.

Thursday 5 February

Studio Two, EMI Studios, London

A re-recording of Ringo's vocal overdub onto take eight of 'Love Is A Many Splendoured Thing', 2.30–6.30 pm. (A 6 February session for this song, 7.00–10.00 pm in studio two, was cancelled. Quincy Jones was to have overdubbed a 25-piece orchestra onto the track. See 17 and 19 February.)

Friday 6 February

Apple Corps, London

An interview given by John and Yoko to David Bellan for the BBC Radio 1 series *Scene And Heard*. It was taped at Apple and an edited extract, 5 mins 40 secs in length, was included in the Sunday 15 February programme, broadcast 3.00–4.00 pm.

More of the interview was broadcast on the BBC World Service, comprising an entire edition of the series *Profile* on Thursday 28 May (2.15–2.30 pm, GMT).

Saturday 7 February

Studio One, Wembley Studios, Wembley

Showing off their newly scalped look to British TV viewers for the first time, John and Yoko taped an appearance on the London Weekend Television chat programme *The Simon Dee Show* this evening. They brought with them Michael X, the British Black Power leader with whom they had participated in a media event only the previous Wednesday at his "Black Centre" in Holloway, north London.

The fourth programme in Dee's new series (he was previously with the BBC), it was transmitted the following night, Sunday 8 February, 11.25 pm–12.15 am.

Monday 9 February

Studio Two, EMI Studios, London

A 2.30–7.00 pm session for Ringo's *Sentimental Journey*. The first task, 2.30–3.00 pm, was to record a simple mono demo of 'Whispering Grass' (the 1940 hit for the Ink Spots). The "best" was an edit of takes three and five, taken away by George Martin and handed later to Ron Goodwin, who would write the new arrangement.

From 3.00 to 6.00 pm Ringo overdubbed his lead vocal onto simultaneous eight-track reduction mixdowns of 'Have I Told You Lately That I Love You' (the 1945 composition popularised by Bing Crosby), newly arranged by Elmer Bernstein, recorded up to vocal overdub stage by an orchestra in the USA (the date unknown) and then sent across to England. The completed recording was mixed into stereo between 6.00 and 7.00 pm.

Tuesday 10 February

Studio Two, EMI Studios, London

Two distinct sessions in the same studio. Between 2.30 and 3.45 pm, Geoff Emerick produced three new mono mixes of 'Instant Karma!', eliminating one of John's two lead vocal tracks – done so that he could add a new vocal on top of the one remaining track (but otherwise mime to the record) for the Plastic Ono Band's next-day *Top Of The Pops* TV taping (see 11 February).

In the evening, studio two hosted another *Sentimental Journey* session, George Martin conducting his 15-piece orchestral arrangement as an overdub onto 'Dream' between 7.00 and 9.20 pm and mixing the recording into stereo from 9.20 to 10.30 pm.

Wednesday 11 February

Studio Eight, Television Centre, London
and Studio Two, EMI Studios, London

In person, the Beatles had appeared in the *Top Of The Pops* TV studio on just one occasion, 16 June 1966, performing 'Paperback Writer' and 'Rain'. Now, approaching four years later, John became the first to do so for a solo disc, 'Instant Karma!' The Plastic Ono Band this time comprised John himself (electric piano), Klaus Voormann (bass), one other man (bass/tambourine), Alan White (drums), Yoko (blind-folded knitting and card-holding) and Mal Evans (occasional tambourine).

However, despite performing in front of an audience (the typically motley collection of jigglers), their appearance – indeed this entire show – was pre-taped this evening for BBC1 transmission the next night, Thursday 12 February, from 7.15 to 8.00 pm. John and the band were on hand at the BBC's Television Centre in west London for a camera rehearsal at 3.30 pm and for the taping between 7.30 and 10.00 pm.

John and the POB actually shot two different versions – the second was included in *Top Of The Pops* a week later, Thursday 19 February, again transmitted on BBC1 from 7.15 to 8.00 pm. In both instances, John sang a new vocal on top of a single-track vocal and the instrumentation from the 27 January EMI recording.

Note: the Thursday 5 February edition of *Top Of The Pops* (BBC1, 7.15–8.00 pm) had featured 'Instant Karma!' accompanied by otherwise-mute 16mm film of John and Yoko supplied to the BBC by Apple. And on Thursday 5 March (7.15–8.00 pm) the first studio performance, as seen on 12 February, was repeated.

Back at EMI Studios this day, 'I'm A Fool To Care' (a 1954 hit for Les Paul with Mary Ford; newly arranged by Klaus Voormann) was recorded for Ringo's *Sentimental Journey* album. Klaus himself – before dashing over to the BBC to be with John – conducted a 15-man orchestra (one of whom was Billy Preston) from 2.30 to 5.30 pm, the "best" version being an edit (done between 5.30 and 6.30) of takes 19, 20 and 21, called 19. Ringo's vocal was overdubbed between 6.30 and 9.00, a stereo mix was produced from 9.00 to 10.00, a guitar track was overdubbed from 10.00 to 11.15 and an 11.15 to 11.45 stereo mix concluded the session.

Thursday 12 February

Studio Two, EMI Studios, London

Sentimental Journey recording of 'Let The Rest Of The World Go By' (a 1919 composition performed by Dick Haymes in the 1944 film *When Irish Eyes Are Smiling*; newly arranged by Les Reed). Reed conducted a 31-piece orchestra and nine singers between 7.00 and 9.00 pm, recording the first six takes in B-flat and five more in the key of C. Ringo overdubbed his vocal onto take six between 9.00 pm and 1.00 am and the recording was mixed into stereo between 1.00 and 1.30 am.

Tuesday 17 February

Studio Two, EMI Studios, London

Sentimental Journey overdubbing of a 15-piece string orchestra conducted by Francis Shaw onto 'I'm A Fool To Care' and 'Love Is A Many Splendoured Thing', 10.00 am–1.00 pm. The session actually began at 9.30 am, the first 30 minutes being spent producing a reduction mixdown of the former title to facilitate this work.

Wednesday 18 February

Studio Two, EMI Studios, London

Ringo re-recorded his vocal for 'Have I Told You Lately That I Love You' and 'Let The Rest Of The World Go By' between 2.30 and 5.30 pm and the latter song was mixed into stereo from 5.30 to 6.00.

Putting aside his work on *Sentimental Journey*, Ringo remained in EMI studio two for an exhilarating evening session that saw the first recording of his composition 'It Don't Come Easy', albeit under the working title 'You Gotta Pay Your Dues'. With George Martin producing but George Harrison on the studio floor directing the musicians, 20 basic

track takes were recorded from 7.00 pm to 12.30 am – George (acoustic guitar), Klaus Voormann (bass), drums (Ringo) and Stephen Stills (piano). From 12.30 until 4.00 George overdubbed two different electric guitar tracks, including a solo for the middle-eight section, and Ringo added lead vocals. The recording was then mixed into stereo from 4.00 until 4.30 am.

Note: this session and the following night's were incorrectly reported in the music press as having taken place at Apple Studios.

Thursday 19 February

Studio Two, EMI Studios, London

Two more Ringo sessions at EMI. The first, for *Sentimental Journey*, took place from 2.30 to 5.00 pm, and saw the overdubbing of eight singers, two flutes, an organ and a vibraphone onto 'Love Is A Many Splendoured Thing'. The second, 5.00 pm to 1.30 am, continued the recording of 'You

Gotta Pay Your Dues' ('It Don't Come Easy'), although George Harrison was not involved this time.

Ringo began by overdubbing another lead vocal onto the previous night's take 20, recorded from 5.00 to 6.00 pm. During a one hour break that followed, it was decided to re-make the song, takes 21 to 30 being taped between 7.00 and 11.00 pm, with two bass overdubs added to take 30 between 11.00 pm and 1.30 am. And that's where it rested, unfinished and unmixed. Ringo began a second re-make on 8 March.

Friday 20 February

Studio Two, EMI Studios, London

Stereo mixing of 'Love Is A Many Splendoured Thing', 'Dream', 'Sentimental Journey', 'I'm A Fool To Care', 'Let The Rest Of The World Go By' and 'Have I Told You Lately That I Love You'. These and three other already-mixed titles ('Night And Day', 'Stardust' and 'Blue Turning Grey Over You') were compiled into a *Sentimental Journey* master for the first time at the end of this 11.00 am–1.00 pm and 2.30–6.45 pm session, from which sample lacquer discs were cut.

Saturday 21 February

Studio Two, EMI Studios, London

Though very few knew it, and this extended even to his fellow Beatles and Apple personnel, Paul McCartney had been busy making his solo début album, too, recording at home in St John's Wood and then – under the pseudonym of Billy Martin – venturing out to Morgan Studios in nearby Willesden.

Recording began when Paul took delivery of a Studer four-track tape recorder at home. Working with a single microphone but without a console/mixer or VU meters he began just before Christmas 1969, the first song he taped, to test the Studer, being 'The Lovely Linda'. Others followed – 'That Would Be Something', two ad-libbed instrumentals: 'Valentine Day' and 'Momma Miss America (Rock & Roll Springtime)', 'Glasses' (a four-track recording of ringing wine glasses), 'Oo You', 'Teddy Boy' (see 24 January 1969), 'Junk' (see 30 May 1968) and its instrumental version 'Singalong Junk'. No documentation is available to supply dates and other details for these recordings.

Nor is there any available documentation about Billy Martin's secretive sessions at Morgan Studios, which probably took place in early February 1970, possibly beginning on the 10th. This was the work done there: start to finish eight-track recordings of the instrumentals 'Hot As Sun' and 'Kreen-Akrore' (work on the latter began on 12 February); four-track to eight-track copies of – and then overdubbing onto – 'Junk', 'Singalong Junk', 'Oo You' and 'Teddy Boy'; finished stereo mixing of 'Oo You', 'Teddy Boy', 'Junk' and 'Kreen-Akrore'; and the first but unused stereo mixes of 'The Lovely Linda', 'Glasses', 'Singalong Junk', and 'Momma Miss America (Rock & Roll Springtime)' – the subtitle in parentheses was dropped before release. The balance engineer at Morgan Studios was Robin Black. (All information about

these sessions has been collated from a remarkably detailed press release issued by Paul to promote the new album.)

Sessions switched to Abbey Road on this date. Paul still masquerading under the name Billy Martin and booking studio time directly rather than through Apple and AIR. The first task at EMI was to produce new stereo mixes of 'The Lovely Linda', 'Momma Miss America', 'Glasses' (which led directly into a tiny glimpse of a new but incomplete song, 'Suicide') and 'Singalong Junk', done from 12.00 noon to 2.45 and 3.45 to 8.00 pm.

Sunday 22 February

Studio Two, EMI Studios, London

This was, ostensibly, a mixing session, 12.00 noon to 10.00 pm, Paul taking to EMI Studios the previously-taped 'That Would Be Something' and 'Valentine Day' to be mixed into stereo for the first time. Once there, however, he also decided to record, taping from start right through to completion the two most acclaimed songs on the album, 'Every Night' and 'Maybe I'm Amazed'. Both were mixed into stereo, too, although 'Every Night' would be done again on 24 February.

Paul didn't issue a single from *McCartney* but its clear stand-out song was 'Maybe I'm Amazed' so it was to this soundtrack that he commissioned a four-minute promotional film for the album, produced by Charlie Jenkins in 35mm colour. The clip comprised a montage of homely photo stills, taken mostly by Linda, a few by Paul, and it was shown in the local area by London Weekend Television on Sunday 19 April (6.00–6.05 pm), in its own self-contained slot. In the USA the film was screened the same night by CBS in *The Ed Sullivan Show* (8.00–9.00 pm, EST).

Tuesday 24 February

Studios Two/One, EMI Studios, London

Two separate, simultaneous sessions at EMI: Paul (still as Billy Martin) in studio two, Ringo in studio one.

Between 10.00 am and 1.00 pm Paul mixed into stereo the Morgan Studios recording 'Hot As Sun' and made a copy of Sunday's "best" mix of 'Maybe I'm Amazed'. Then from 3.30 to 6.15 he remixed 'Every Night'.

Ringo's session, 3.30–7.15 pm, saw him overdub a new lead vocal onto simultaneous reduction mixdowns of 'Blue Turning Grey Over You'. Seven stereo mixes followed, six from different takes, the master being an edit of four of these.

Wednesday 25 February

Studio Two, EMI Studios, London
and De Lane Lea Sound Centre, Dean St, London

Paul's session at EMI began at 10.45 am with a 45-minute playback of various titles recorded for his début album. From 11.30 to 2.15 pm he taped the basic track for a new song, 'Man We Was Lonely', completing it in 12 takes. Then, after a one hour break, he continued from 3.15 to 9.00 pm overdubbing various instruments and adding vocals shared with Linda. Typically efficient, the song was mixed into stereo just once, between 9.00 am and 11.00 pm, and it was added to the LP master reel.

Ringo, meanwhile, was at De Lane Lea's new Soho studio, watching as a 20-piece orchestra, conducted by John Dankworth, recorded 'You Always Hurt The One You Love' (a 1944 hit for the Mills Brothers; newly arranged by Dankworth) for *Sentimental Journey*. It was taped, with Ringo's vocal, from 2.00 to 5.30 pm and mixed into stereo 5.30–7.30.

Saturday 28 February

New stereo mixes of George's 'For You Blue' were produced this day at EMI by Apple's Malcolm Davies – although it's not clear why. They weren't added to *Get Back* and weren't used on *Let It Be*. (Session timings not documented.)

Thursday 5 March

Morgan Studios, London

The recording of Ringo's *Sentimental Journey* was concluded with a two-day session at the north London studio where Paul had recently been taping and mixing tracks for his own début LP. Two songs were recorded in this session, for which a 36-part orchestra was recruited, each song conducted by its arranger: the first was 'Whispering Grass' (arranged by Ron Goodwin – see 9 February), the second 'Bye Bye Blackbird' (the 1926 song popularised by Eddie Cantor; newly arranged by Bee Gee Maurice Gibb). Ringo's overdubbed vocals completed this efficient 10.00 am–1.00 pm session.

Friday 6 March

Morgan Studios, London
and **Room Four, EMI Studios, London**

Overdubbing of sax (played by the song's arranger, John Dankworth), piano and drums onto 'You Always Hurt The One You Love', 10.00 am–12.00 noon at Morgan Studios, followed by a late-afternoon mixing session at EMI (beginning 5.30 pm, ending time not noted) that saw stereo masters prepared for 'Bye Bye Blackbird', 'Love Is A Many Splendoured Thing', 'Whispering Grass', and 'You Always Hurt The One You Love'.

With this, Ringo's début solo album was complete. Speedy processing at the pressing and sleeve printing factories (see also 15 March) ensured a quick release – on Friday 27 March in Britain.

Sunday 8 March

Trident Studios (?), London

The second re-make of Ringo's 'It Don't Come Easy', now with this title, following earlier attempts on 18 and 19 February. George Harrison again lent his production and guitar talents to the recording, but there is no available documentation to confirm absolutely a report that the session took place at Trident. It certainly wasn't at EMI.

Apple told the music press there were "absolutely no plans for the record to be released as a single at the present time", and they were right – it wasn't issued until 9 April 1971, following the taping of overdubs on 11 March (see next entry) and in October 1970.

Wednesday 11 March

Studio H25, Aeolian Hall, London
and **Trident Studios (?), London**

It had been some years – since the days of the old Light Programme, in fact – that BBC radio had been able to broadcast a special Beatles programme on a national "bank holiday". But for Easter Monday, 30 March 1970, Radio 1 was able to do just this in the form of *The Beatles Today*, thanks to the commitment of George Harrison. It was aired from 4.31 to 5.15 pm.

Remarkably for a latter-day interview, the programme was recorded at a BBC studio, Aeolian Hall in New Bond Street, central London, and George was interviewed there by Johnny Moran between 5.00 and 6.00 pm.

Subjects covered in *The Beatles Today* spanned a wide range: not just the state of the group but also a peer around the Apple Records roster, paying particular attention to such Harrison protégés as Jackie Lomax, Billy Preston, Doris Troy and the Radha Krishna Temple. The programme also happened to broadcast a long version of the Beatles' 'Dig It', running to 3 mins 13 secs, supplied to the BBC by Apple before the much pruned-down version was substituted for the *Let It Be* album release.

Two brief extracts from George's interview, 1 min 20 secs and 30 seconds, were included in the Sunday 15 March edition of the Radio 1 series *Scene And Heard* (3.00–4.00 pm), for which Moran was the regular host.

The recording of Ringo's 'It Don't Come Easy' continued this evening, probably at Trident Studios, with George Harrison producing.

Friday 13 March

A mono mix of 'Sentimental Journey', produced in EMI studio three by Chris Thomas from 12.00 noon to 1.30 pm. This wasn't for the album: it was made to assist in the shooting of a promotional film clip for the song (see 15 March).

Sunday 15 March

Talk of the Town, Cranbourn Street, London

Although EMI had no plans to extract a single from the album, Ringo came this day to the Talk of the Town, then the leading popular cabaret venue in central London, to film a clip for the title track, 'Sentimental Journey', which would be distributed to promote the album as a whole. Neil Aspinall directed the shoot, which began at 10.00 am, with John Gilbert producing.

Dressed in a smart blue suit topped off with an outlandish pink dickie-bow, Ringo trod the catwalk, dancing and singing in front of an invited audience (dining at candlelit tables), the Talk of the Town Orchestra especially conducted for the occasion by George Martin, a troupe of white-suited dancers and three backing vocalists (Doris Troy, Madeline Bell and Marsha Hunt) who stood on a platform which came down into prominence and then rose again during the clip.

'Sentimental Journey' was screened neither on *Top Of The Pops* nor any other BBC programme, but British viewers saw it on LWT's *Frost On Sunday* on 29 March when Ringo made a personal appearance in the studio (see that date for full details). In the USA, the clip was shown on *The Ed Sullivan Show* (CBS) on Sunday 17 May (8.00–9.00 pm, EST).

This promo shoot had one unexpected bonus: Ringo later revealed that the cover photograph of *Sentimental Journey* – in which he stood before a backdrop of his old neighbourhood in the Dingle area of Liverpool, in particular the Empress public house at the end of his street, Admiral Grove – was taken this day on the set at the Talk of the Town.

Monday 16 March

Studio Two, EMI Studios, London

Billy Martin's first appearance at EMI since 25 February. This was only a playback, however, of both the eight-track and stereo mix tapes for 'Oo You', recorded at Morgan Studios. Nothing was recorded or mixed in this 6.30–8.00 pm session.

Monday 23 March

Studio Three/Room Four, EMI Studios, London

Paul returned to EMI studio three, 3.00-7.00 pm to make and take finished copies of his *McCartney* master. The session was again booked under 'Billy Martin', the ruse now complete: he'd recorded in virtual secrecy what would otherwise have been one of the most clamoured after and anticipated of all albums. It was issued in Britain on Friday 17 April.

Meanwhile, over in Room Four of the same building, probably without Paul's knowledge, some well-worn tapes were once again being threaded onto machines. It was time for the enigmatic Phil Spector and *Let It Be* to enter, and for Glyn Johns and *Get Back* to exit.

Arguably the most famous record producer of all, Spector had been responsible for some of the classic songs of the rock era, Ike and Tina Turner's 'River Deep Mountain High', the Righteous Brothers' 'You've Lost That Lovin' Feelin'', the Crystals' 'Da Doo Ron Ron', the Ronettes' 'Be My Baby' and scores of others, many featuring his production speciality, the so-called "wall of sound". A former singer himself, however, Spector also brought the volatile temperament of an "artist" into the studio control room.

Following his baptism with 'Instant Karma!', Spector was invited by John, George and Allen Klein to "re-produce" the *Get Back* tapes, to assemble an album worthy of release to accompany the *Let It Be* movie. George attended most of these Easter 1970 mix sessions, in which Spector was assisted by EMI Studios' balance engineer Peter Bown.

Spector's stamp on *Let It Be* was to become more pronounced as time went by, and on this first day – none of the start/finish times for his EMI sessions was noted – he mixed two different versions of 'I've Got A Feeling', the rooftop recordings of 'Dig A Pony' (editing out the "all I want is" backing vocals) and 'The One After 909', he made an extended mix of 'I Me Mine' (see 3 January 1970) and had his first crack at mixing – again – the February 1968 recording of 'Across The Universe'.

Wednesday 25 March

Room Four, EMI Studios, London
and **Apple Corps, London**

Phil Spector's mix of 'Two Of Us' was probably his best achievement on the *Let It Be* material, done this day along with 'For You Blue' (incorporating George's new vocal from 8 January) and, interestingly, 'Teddy Boy', which, had it been included on the album, would have made it and the film differ when Spector's main task was to make them consistent, and would have clashed with Paul's new, solo recording of the song.

In his office at Apple this day, Ringo gave an interview to David Wigg for the Radio 1 series *Scene And Heard*. Extracts were broadcast over two editions, 5 mins 20 secs being used on Sunday 29 March and a further 2 mins 15 secs the following week, 5 April, both programmes transmitted from 3.00 to 4.00 pm.

Thursday 26 March

Room Four, EMI Studios, London

Phil Spector's sharpening of the Beatles' percussion sound came to a head with his 'Let It Be' mixes, adding such a degree of echo to Ringo's hi-hat that it became prominent. He also extended the duration by editing, and used only the 4 January 1970 guitar solo so that his mix was markedly different from the single.

Spector devoted much time to 'Get Back', using the "single" version as the basis for what most people believed to be an entirely different take, a delusion achieved by editing some extraneous chatter onto the start of the recording and crossfading its end with the applause and thanks that followed the tenth and final song from the Apple rooftop performance.

Also this day Spector remixed 'Maggie Mae' and, preceding a 1 April overdub session, 'The Long And Winding Road'.

Friday 27 March

Room Four, EMI Studios, London

Stereo mixing of 'Dig It' (using only 49 seconds of the 12 mins 25 secs original) and many short items of music or dialogue, only two of which, both spoken by John, made it onto the mastered album – the first was his "That was 'Can You Dig It' by Georgie Wood, now we'd like to do 'Hark The Angels Come'", which Spector crossfaded onto the end of 'Dig It' and thus introduced the album's next song, the hymnal 'Let It Be'. The second was John's *risqué* "'I Dig A Pygmy' by Charles Hawtrey and the Deaf Aids. Phase one, in which Doris gets her oats", which Spector used to open the LP.

Sunday 29 March

Studio Three, Wembley Studios, Wembley

Ringo's second appearance in four months on a David Frost show for London Weekend Television – this time *Frost On Sunday*, the last edition in the present series. On the former occasion (6 December 1969) he had been plugging *The Magic Christian*; this time the object of promotion was *Sentimental Journey*, and the programme included a screening of the promotional clip filmed on 15 March at the Talk of the Town. The show was transmitted live this Easter Sunday night from LWT's Wembley facility, 10.25–11.25 pm.

Monday 30 March

Room Four, EMI Studios, London

A session in which Phil Spector explored an interesting but ultimately rejected idea, in which he made a 16-second tape loop of the instrumental break in 'For You Blue' and overlaid numerous dialogue extracts from the film soundtrack, to which he had unlimited early access. In the end, however, only one tiny scrap of dialogue from the soundtrack – indeed from the entire Twickenham rehearsal sessions – made it onto the *Let It Be* LP: John's "Queen says no to pot-smoking FBI movement".

Tuesday 31 March

Studio B9, Broadcasting House, London

An appearance by Ringo on the live BBC Radio 2 programme *Open House*, transmitted from Broadcasting House in central London, 9.00 to 9.55 am. He chatted about *Sentimental Journey* and other subjects with the series' host, Pete Murray.

Wednesday 1 April

Studio One, EMI Studios, London

The apogee of Phil Spector's work on *Let It Be*: the overdub of lavish orchestral and choral tracks onto 'Across The Universe', 'The Long And Winding Road' and 'I Me Mine'.

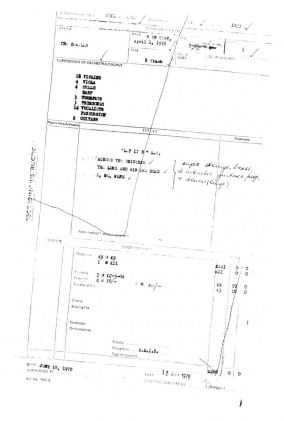

Ringo was the only Beatle to participate but the group's last recording session was still a momentous and unforgettable experience thanks to Spector, whose creative head was given full rein, in the process upsetting just about everyone: the balance and technical engineers, the orchestral conductors and the 50 musicians. Ringo ordered Spector to cool off, balance engineer Pete Bown stormed home (only returning after an apologetic phone call from Spector) and the orchestra downed instruments, albeit temporarily.

Spector himself did not write the orchestral scores. Richard Hewson arranged and conducted 'I Me Mine' and 'The Long And Winding Road' and Brian Rogers arranged and conducted 'Across The Universe', while John Barham notated the top lines and vocal harmonies for the latter two songs. However, the size and scope of the ensemble was pure Spector. Here was the "wall of sound" on a Beatles session: 18 violins, four violas, four cellos, a harp, three trumpets, three trombones, one set of drums (Ringo), two guitarists and 14 singers: a total of 50 contributors and a bill to EMI of a massive £1126 5s (£1126.25).

Thursday 2 April

Room Four, EMI Studios, London

Phil Spector's final task, mixing into stereo and editing 'The Long And Winding Road', 'I Me Mine' and 'Across The Universe'. The album was issued in Britain on Friday 8 May, more than 16 months after it had taken life as *Get Back*.

The film, meanwhile, opened in New York on 13 May and in London and Liverpool a week later, 20 May, none of the Beatles attending on any occasion. The hundreds of hours of January 1969 footage had been reduced to 210 minutes for the first rough cut, viewed by all four Beatles on Sunday 20 July 1969. It had then been cut further for release, down to 88 minutes, with a considerable amount of John and Yoko footage removed at the suggestion of Paul, George and Ringo. These three then had first sight of the final 88-minute version in October 1969, John and Yoko either not bothering or not able to attend. During all of this time the film, like the album, remained titled *Get Back*, and it was only in the spring of 1970 that it had switched to *Let It Be*.

Friday 10 April

Apple Corps, London

On the day that Paul's assertion that the Beatles had essentially split up was front-page headline news around the world, George was in his office at Apple being filmed by BBC cameras for an insert into the otherwise studio-based theological series *Fact Or Fantasy?*, broadcast by BBC1 in what has become known as British television's Sunday evening "God slot", in this instance 26 April, 6.15–6.50 pm. (The programme was also repeated, on Monday 27 April, BBC1, 12.50–1.25 pm.)

The subtitle of this edition was 'Prayer And Meditation' and George was questioned at some length about these subjects, the Krishna movement in particular, just under 11 minutes of edited interview going into the finished programme.

August 1971

Dear People:

The time has come for me to withdraw from the Beatles Fan Club. As you may know, the band split up over a year ago and has not played together since. Each of us is getting together his own career, and for this reason, I don't want to be involved with anything that continues the illusion that there is such a thing as the Beatles.

Those days are over. In the past, you have been great supporters, and the idea of this letter is to let you know how I want it to be in the future, in case you wanted to know. Now I'm not a Beatle any longer, and want to get back to where I once belonged — living my own life, having my own family, my privacy, and getting on with my own music.

Thanks for everything...

Paul, Child-Bride Linda, Boy Prodigy Heather and Baby Mary

THE BEATLES – A DISCOGRAPHY, 1962-1970

UK Singles

'My Bonnie'/'The Saints', 5 January 1962, Polydor NH 66833, [Tony Sheridan & the Beatles.]

'Love Me Do'/'PS I Love You', 5 October 1962, Parlophone 45-R 4949.

'Please Please Me'/'Ask Me Why', 11 January 1963, Parlophone 45-R 4983.

'From Me To You'/'Thank You Girl', 11 April 1963, Parlophone R 5015.

'She Loves You'/'I'll Get You', 23 August 1963, Parlophone R 5055.

'I Want To Hold Your Hand'/'This Boy', 29 November 1963, Parlophone R 5084.

'Can't Buy Me Love'/'You Can't Do That', 20 March 1964, Parlophone R 5114.

'A Hard Day's Night'/'Things We Said Today', 10 July 1964, Parlophone R 5160.

'I Feel Fine'/'She's A Woman', 27 November 1964, Parlophone R 5200.

'Ticket To Ride'/'Yes It Is', 9 April 1965, Parlophone R 5265.

'Help!'/'I'm Down', 23 July 1965, Parlophone R 5305.

'We Can Work It Out'/'Day Tripper', 3 December 1965, Parlophone R 5389.

'Paperback Writer'/'Rain', 10 June 1966, Parlophone R 5452.

'Eleanor Rigby'/'Yellow Submarine', 5 August 1966, Parlophone R 5493.

'Strawberry Fields Forever'/'Penny Lane', 17 February 1967, Parlophone R 5570.

'All You Need Is Love'/'Baby, You're A Rich Man', 7 July 1967, Parlophone R 5620.

'Hello, Goodbye'/'I Am The Walrus', 24 November 1967, Parlophone R 5655.

'Lady Madonna'/'The Inner Light', 15 March 1968, Parlophone R 5675.

'Hey Jude'/'Revolution', 30 August 1968, Apple [Parlophone] R 5722.

'Get Back'/'Don't Let Me Down', 11 April 1969, Apple [Parlophone] R 5777.

'The Ballad Of John And Yoko'/'Old Brown Shoe', 30 May 1969, Apple [Parlophone] R 5786.

'Something'/'Come Together', 31 October 1969, Apple [Parlophone] R 5814.

'Let It Be'/'You Know My Name (Look Up The Number)', 6 March 1970, Apple [Parlophone] R 5833.

UK EPs

Twist And Shout, 12 July 1963, Parlophone GEP 8882 (mono only).
A: 'Twist And Shout'; 'A Taste Of Honey'.
B: 'Do You Want To Know A Secret'; 'There's A Place'.

The Beatles' Hits, 6 September 1963, Parlophone GEP 8880 (mono only).
A: 'From Me To You'; 'Thank You Girl'.
B: 'Please Please Me'; 'Love Me Do'.

The Beatles (No 1), 1 November 1963, Parlophone GEP 8883 (mono only).
A: 'I Saw Her Standing There'; 'Misery'.
B: 'Anna (Go To Him)'; 'Chains'.

All My Loving, 7 February 1964, Parlophone GEP 8891 (mono only).
A: 'All My Loving'; 'Ask Me Why'.
B: 'Money (That's What I Want)'; 'PS I Love You'.

Long Tall Sally, 19 June 1964, Parlophone GEP 8913 (mono only).
A: 'Long Tall Sally'; 'I Call Your Name'.
B: 'Slow Down'; 'Matchbox'.

Extracts From The Film A Hard Day's Night, 6 November 1964, Parlophone GEP 8920 (mono only).
A: 'I Should Have Known Better'; 'If I Fell'.
B: 'Tell Me Why'; 'And I Love Her'.

Extracts From The Album A Hard Day's Night, 6 November 1964, Parlophone GEP 8924 (mono only).
A: 'Any Time At All'; 'I'll Cry Instead'.
B: 'Things We Said Today'; 'When I Get Home'.

Beatles For Sale, 6 April 1965, Parlophone GEP 8931 (mono only).
A: 'No Reply'; 'I'm A Loser'.
B: 'Rock And Roll Music'; 'Eight Days A Week'.

Beatles For Sale (No 2), 4 June 1965, Parlophone GEP 8938 (mono only).
A: 'I'll Follow The Sun'; 'Baby's In Black'.
B: 'Words Of Love'; 'I Don't Want To Spoil The Party'.

The Beatles' Million Sellers, 6 December 1965, Parlophone GEP 8946 (mono only).
A: 'She Loves You'; 'I Want To Hold Your Hand'.
B: 'Can't Buy Me Love'; 'I Feel Fine'.

Yesterday, 4 March 1966, Parlophone GEP 8948 (mono only).
A: 'Yesterday'; 'Act Naturally'.
B: 'You Like Me Too Much'; 'It's Only Love'.

Nowhere Man, 8 July 1966, Parlophone GEP 8952 (mono only).
A: 'Nowhere Man'; 'Drive My Car'.
B: 'Michelle'; 'You Won't See Me'.

Magical Mystery Tour, 8 December 1967, Parlophone MMT-1 (mono), SMMT-1 (stereo).
A: 'Magical Mystery Tour'; 'Your Mother Should Know'.
B: 'I Am The Walrus'.
C: 'The Fool On The Hill'; 'Flying'.
D: 'Blue Jay Way'.

UK Albums

Please Please Me, 22 March 1963, Parlophone PMC 1202 (mono), PCS 3042 (stereo).
A: 'I Saw Her Standing There'; 'Misery'; 'Anna (Go To Him)'; 'Chains'; 'Boys'; 'Ask Me Why'; 'Please Please Me'.
B: 'Love Me Do'; 'PS I Love You'; 'Baby It's You'; 'Do You Want To Know A Secret'; 'A Taste Of Honey'; 'There's A Place'; 'Twist And Shout'.

With The Beatles, 22 November 1963, Parlophone PMC 1206 (mono), PCS 3045 (stereo).
A: 'It Won't Be Long'; 'All I've Got To Do'; 'All My Loving'; 'Don't Bother Me'; 'Little Child'; 'Till There Was You'; 'Please Mister Postman'.
B: 'Roll Over Beethoven'; 'Hold Me Tight'; 'You Really Got A Hold On Me'; 'I Wanna Be Your Man'; '(There's A) Devil In Her Heart'; 'Not A Second Time'; 'Money (That's What I Want)'.

A Hard Day's Night, 10 July 1964, Parlophone PMC 1230 (mono), PCS 3058 (stereo).
A: 'A Hard Day's Night'; 'I Should Have Known Better'; 'If I Fell'; 'I'm Happy Just To Dance With You'; 'And I Love Her'; 'Tell Me Why'; 'Can't Buy Me Love'.
B: 'Any Time At All'; 'I'll Cry Instead'; 'Things We Said Today'; 'When I Get Home'; 'You Can't Do That'; 'I'll Be Back'.

Beatles For Sale, 4 December 1964, Parlophone PMC 1240 (mono), PCS 3062 (stereo).
A: 'No Reply'; 'I'm A Loser'; 'Baby's In Black'; 'Rock And Roll Music'; 'I'll Follow The Sun'; 'Mr Moonlight'; 'Kansas City'/'Hey-Hey-Hey-Hey!'.
B: 'Eight Days A Week'; 'Words Of Love'; 'Honey Don't'; 'Every Little Thing'; 'I Don't Want To Spoil The Party'; 'What You're Doing'; 'Everybody's Trying To Be My Baby'.

Help!, 6 August 1965, Parlophone PMC 1255 (mono), PCS 3071 (stereo).
A: 'Help!'; 'The Night Before'; 'You've Got To Hide Your Love Away'; 'I Need You'; 'Another Girl'; 'You're Going To Lose That Girl'; 'Ticket To Ride'.
B: 'Act Naturally'; 'It's Only Love'; 'You Like Me Too Much'; 'Tell Me What You See'; 'I've Just Seen A Face'; 'Yesterday'; 'Dizzy Miss Lizzy'.

Rubber Soul, 3 December 1965, Parlophone PMC 1267 (mono), PCS 3075 (stereo).
A: 'Drive My Car'; 'Norwegian Wood (This Bird Has Flown)'; 'You Won't See Me'; 'Nowhere Man'; 'Think For Yourself'; 'The Word'; 'Michelle'.
B: 'What Goes On'; 'Girl'; 'I'm Looking Through You'; 'In My Life'; 'Wait'; 'If I Needed Someone'; 'Run For Your Life'.

Revolver, 5 August 1966, Parlophone PMC 7009 (mono), PCS 7009 (stereo).
A: 'Taxman'; 'Eleanor Rigby'; 'I'm Only Sleeping'; 'Love You To'; 'Here, There And Everywhere'; 'Yellow Submarine'; 'She Said She Said'.
B: 'Good Day Sunshine'; 'And Your Bird Can Sing'; 'For No One'; 'Doctor Robert'; 'I Want To Tell You'; 'Got To Get You Into My Life'; 'Tomorrow Never Knows'.

A Collection Of Beatles Oldies, 9 December 1966, Parlophone PMC 7016 (mono), PCS 7016 (stereo).
A: 'She Loves You'; 'From Me To You'; 'We Can Work It Out'; 'Help!'; 'Michelle'; 'Yesterday'; 'I Feel Fine'; 'Yellow Submarine'.
B: 'Can't Buy Me Love'; 'Bad Boy'; 'Day Tripper'; 'A Hard Day's Night'; 'Ticket To Ride'; 'Paperback Writer'; 'Eleanor Rigby'; 'I Want To Hold Your Hand'.

Sgt Pepper's Lonely Hearts Club Band, 1 June 1967, Parlophone PMC 7027 (mono), PCS 7027 (stereo).
A: 'Sgt Pepper's Lonely Hearts Club Band'; 'With A Little Help From My Friends'; 'Lucy In The Sky With Diamonds'; 'Getting Better'; 'Fixing A Hole'; 'She's Leaving Home'; 'Being For The Benefit Of Mr Kite!'.
B: 'Within You Without You'; 'When I'm Sixty-Four'; 'Lovely Rita'; 'Good Morning Good Morning'; 'Sgt Pepper's Lonely Hearts Club Band (Reprise)'; 'A Day In The Life'.

The Beatles, 22 November 1968, Apple [Parlophone] PMC 7067-7068 (mono), PCS 7067-7068 (stereo).
A: 'Back In The USSR'; 'Dear Prudence'; 'Glass Onion'; 'Ob-La-Di, Ob-La-Da'; 'Wild Honey Pie'; 'The Continuing Story Of Bungalow Bill'; 'While My Guitar Gently Weeps'; 'Happiness Is A Warm Gun'.
B: 'Martha My Dear'; 'I'm So Tired'; 'Blackbird'; 'Piggies'; 'Rocky Raccoon'; 'Don't Pass Me By'; 'Why Don't We Do It In The Road'; 'I Will'; 'Julia'.
C: 'Birthday'; 'Yer Blues'; 'Mother Nature's Son'; 'Everybody's Got Something To Hide Except Me And My Monkey'; 'Sexy Sadie'; 'Helter Skelter'; 'Long Long Long'.
D: 'Revolution 1'; 'Honey Pie'; 'Savoy Truffle'; 'Cry Baby Cry'; 'Revolution 9'; 'Good Night'.

Yellow Submarine, 17 January 1969, Apple [Parlophone] PMC 7070 (mono), PCS 7070 (stereo).
A: 'Yellow Submarine'; 'Only A Northern Song'; 'All Together Now'; 'Hey Bulldog'; 'It's All Too Much'; 'All You Need Is Love'.
B: [Seven soundtrack instrumental cuts by the George Martin Orchestra.]

Abbey Road, 26 September 1969, Apple [Parlophone] PCS 7088 (stereo only).
A: 'Come Together'; 'Something'; 'Maxwell's Silver Hammer'; 'Oh! Darling'; 'Octopus's Garden'; 'I Want You (She's So Heavy)'.
B: 'Here Comes The Sun'; 'Because'; 'You Never Give Me Your Money'; 'Sun King'/'Mean Mr Mustard'; 'Polythene Pam'/'She Came In Through The Bathroom Window'; 'Golden Slumbers'/'Carry That Weight'; 'The End'; 'Her Majesty'.

Let It Be, 8 May 1970, Apple [Parlophone] PCS 7096 (stereo only).
A: 'Two Of Us'; 'Dig A Pony'; 'Across The Universe'; 'I Me Mine'; 'Dig It'; 'Let It Be'; 'Maggie Mae'.
B: 'I've Got A Feeling'; 'The One After 909'; 'The Long And Winding Road'; 'For You Blue'; 'Get Back'.

US Singles

'My Bonnie'/'The Saints', 23 April 1962, Decca 31382. [Tony Sheridan and the Beat Brothers.]

'Please Please Me'/'Ask Me Why', 25 February 1963, Vee Jay VJ 498.

'From Me To You'/'Thank You Girl', 27 May 1963, Vee Jay VJ 522.

'She Loves You'/'I'll Get You', 16 September 1963, Swan 4152.

'I Want To Hold Your Hand'/'I Saw Her Standing There', 26 December 1963, Capitol 5112.

'Please Please Me'/'From Me To You', 30 January 1964, Vee Jay VJ 581.

'Twist And Shout'/'There's A Place', 2 March 1964, Tollie 9001.

'Can't Buy Me Love'/'You Can't Do That', 16 March 1964, Capitol 5150.

'Do You Want To Know A Secret'/'Thank You Girl', 23 March 1964, Vee Jay VJ 587.

'Love Me Do'/'PS I Love You', 27 April 1964, Tollie 9008.

'Sie Liebt Dich'/'I'll Get You', 21 May 1964, Swan 4182.

'A Hard Day's Night'/'I Should Have Known Better', 13 July 1964, Capitol 5222.

'I'll Cry Instead'/'I'm Happy Just To Dance With You', 20 July 1964, Capitol 5234.

'And I Love Her'/'If I Fell', 20 July 1964, Capitol 5235.

'Matchbox'/'Slow Down', 24 August 1964, Capitol 5255.

'I Feel Fine'/'She's A Woman', 23 November 1964, Capitol 5327.

'Eight Days A Week'/'I Don't Want To Spoil The Party', 15 February 1965, Capitol 5371.

'Ticket To Ride'/'Yes It Is', 19 April 1965, Capitol 5476.

'Help!'/'I'm Down', 19 July 1965, Capitol 5476.

'Yesterday'/'Act Naturally', 13 September 1965, Capitol 5498.

'We Can Work It Out'/'Day Tripper', 6 December 1965, Capitol 5555.

'Nowhere Man'/'What Goes On', 21 February 1966, Capitol 5587.

'Paperback Writer'/'Rain', 30 May 1966, Capitol 5651.

'Eleanor Rigby'/'Yellow Submarine', 8 August 1966, Capitol 5715.

'Strawberry Fields Forever'/'Penny Lane', 13 February 1967, Capitol 5810.

'All You Need Is Love'/'Baby, You're A Rich Man', 17 July 1967, Capitol 5964.

'Hello, Goodbye'/'I Am The Walrus', 27 November 1967, Capitol 2056.

'Lady Madonna'/'The Inner Light', 18 March 1968, Capitol 2138.

'Hey Jude'/'Revolution', 26 August 1968, Apple [Capitol] 2276.

'Get Back'/'Don't Let Me Down', 5 May 1969, Apple [Capitol] 2490.

'The Ballad Of John And Yoko'/'Old Brown Shoe', 4 June 1969, Apple [Capitol] 2531.

'Something'/'Come Together', 6 October 1969, Apple [Capitol] 2654.

'Let It Be'/'You Know My Name (Look Up The Number)', 11 March 1970, Apple [Capitol] 2764.

'The Long And Winding Road'/'For You Blue', 11 May 1970, Apple [Capitol] 2832.

US Albums

Introducing The Beatles, 22 July 1963, Vee Jay VJLP 1062 (mono), SR 1062 (stereo).
A: 'I Saw Her Standing There'; 'Misery'; 'Anna (Go To Him)'; 'Chains'; 'Boys'; 'Love Me Do'.
B: 'PS I Love You'; 'Baby It's You'; 'Do You Want To Know A Secret'; 'A Taste Of Honey'; 'There's A Place'; 'Twist And Shout'.

Meet The Beatles!, 20 January 1964, Capitol T-2047 (mono), ST-2047 (stereo).
A: 'I Want To Hold Your Hand'; 'I Saw Her Standing There'; 'This Boy'; 'It Won't Be Long'; 'All I've Got To Do'; 'All My Loving'.
B: 'Don't Bother Me'; 'Little Child'; 'Till There Was You'; 'Hold Me Tight'; 'I Wanna Be Your Man'; 'Not A Second Time'.

Introducing The Beatles, 27 January 1964, Vee Jay VJLP 1062 (mono only).
A: 'I Saw Her Standing There'; 'Misery'; 'Anna (Go To Him)'; 'Chains'; 'Boys'; 'Ask Me Why'.
B: 'Please Please Me'; 'Baby It's You'; 'Do You Want To Know A Secret'; 'A Taste Of Honey'; 'There's A Place'; 'Twist And Shout'.

The Beatles' Second Album, 10 April 1964, Capitol T-2080 (mono), ST-2080 (stereo).
A: 'Roll Over Beethoven'; 'Thank You Girl'; 'You Really Got A Hold On Me'; '(There's A) Devil In Her Heart'; 'Money (That's What I Want)'; 'You Can't Do That'.
B: 'Long Tall Sally'; 'I Call Your Name'; 'Please Mister Postman'; 'I'll Get You'; 'She Loves You'.

A Hard Day's Night, 26 June 1964, United Artists UA 6366 (mono), UAS 6366 (stereo).
A: 'A Hard Day's Night'; 'Tell Me Why'; 'I'll Cry Instead'; 'I'm Happy Just To Dance With You'. [Plus two soundtrack instrumental cuts by George Martin & Orchestra.]
B: 'I Should Have Known Better'; 'If I Fell'; 'And I Love Her'; 'Can't Buy Me Love'. [Plus two soundtrack instrumental cuts by George Martin & Orchestra.]

Something New, 20 July 1964, Capitol T-2108 (mono), ST-2108 (stereo).
A: 'I'll Cry Instead'; 'Things We Said Today'; 'Any Time At All'; 'When I Get Home'; 'Slow Down'; 'Matchbox'.
B: 'Tell Me Why'; 'And I Love Her'; 'I'm Happy Just To Dance With You'; 'If I Fell'; 'Komm, Gib Mir Deine Hand'.

The Beatles' Story, 23 November 1964, Capitol TBO-2222 (mono), STBO-2222 (stereo).
A: interviews plus extracts from 'I Want To Hold Your Hand'; 'Slow Down'; 'This Boy'.
B: interviews plus extracts from 'You Can't Do That'; 'If I Fell'; 'And I Love Her'.
C: interviews plus extracts from 'A Hard Day's Night'; 'And I Love Her'.
D: interviews plus extracts from 'Twist And Shout' (live); 'Things We Said Today'; 'I'm Happy Just To Dance With You'; 'Little Child'; 'Long Tall Sally'; 'She Loves You'; 'Boys'.

Beatles '65, 15 December 1964, Capitol T-2228 (mono), ST-2228 (stereo).
A: 'No Reply'; 'I'm A Loser'; 'Baby's In Black'; 'Rock And Roll Music'; 'I'll Follow The Sun'; 'Mr Moonlight'.
B: 'Honey Don't'; 'I'll Be Back'; 'She's A Woman'; 'I Feel Fine'; 'Everybody's Trying To Be My Baby'.

The Early Beatles, 22 March 1965, Capitol T-2309 (mono), ST-2309 (stereo).
A: 'Love Me Do'; 'Twist And Shout'; 'Anna (Go To Him)'; 'Chains'; 'Boys'; 'Ask Me Why'.
B: 'Please Please Me'; 'PS I Love You'; 'Baby It's You'; 'A Taste Of Honey'; 'Do You Want To Know A Secret'.

Beatles VI, 14 June 1965, Capitol T-2358 (mono), ST-2358 (stereo).
A: 'Kansas City'/'Hey-Hey-Hey-Hey!'; 'Eight Days A Week'; 'You Like Me Too Much'; 'Bad Boy'; 'I Don't Want To Spoil The Party'; 'Words Of Love'.
B: 'What You're Doing'; 'Yes It Is'; 'Dizzy Miss Lizzy'; 'Tell Me What You See'; 'Every Little Thing'.

Help!, 13 August 1965, Capitol MAS-2386 (mono), SMAS-2386 (stereo).
A: 'Help!'; 'The Night Before'; 'You've Got To Hide Your Love Away'; 'I Need You'. [Plus three soundtrack instrumental cuts by George Martin & Orchestra.]
B: 'Another Girl'; 'Ticket To Ride'; 'You're Going To Lose That Girl'. [Plus three soundtrack instrumental cuts by George Martin & Orchestra.]

Rubber Soul, 6 December 1965, Capitol T-2442 (mono), ST-2442 (stereo).
A: 'I've Just Seen A Face'; 'Norwegian Wood (This Bird Has Flown)'; 'You Won't See Me'; 'Think For Yourself'; 'The Word'; 'Michelle'.
B: 'It's Only Love'; 'Girl'; 'I'm Looking Through You'; 'In My Life'; 'Wait'; 'Run For Your Life'.

"Yesterday"...And Today, 20 June 1966, Capitol T-2553 (mono), ST-2553 (stereo).
A: 'Drive My Car'; 'I'm Only Sleeping'; 'Nowhere Man'; 'Doctor Robert'; 'Yesterday'; 'Act Naturally'.
B: 'And Your Bird Can Sing'; 'If I Needed Someone'; 'We Can Work It Out'; 'What Goes On'; 'Day Tripper'.

Revolver, 8 August 1966, Capitol T-2576 (mono), ST-2576 (stereo).
A: 'Taxman'; 'Eleanor Rigby'; 'Love You To'; 'Here, There And Everywhere'; 'Yellow Submarine'; 'She Said She Said'.
B: 'Good Day Sunshine'; 'For No One'; 'I Want To Tell You'; 'Got To Get You Into My Life'; 'Tomorrow Never Knows'.

Sgt Pepper's Lonely Hearts Club Band, 2 June 1967, Capitol MAS-2653 (mono), SMAS-2653 (stereo).
– titles as UK release –

Magical Mystery Tour, 27 November 1967, Capitol MAL-2835 (mono), SMAL-2835 (stereo).
A: 'Magical Mystery Tour'; 'The Fool On The Hill'; 'Flying'; 'Blue Jay Way'; 'Your Mother Should Know'; 'I Am The Walrus'.
B: 'Hello, Goodbye'; 'Strawberry Fields Forever'; 'Penny Lane'; 'Baby, You're A Rich Man'; 'All You Need Is Love'.

The Beatles, 25 November 1968, Apple [Capitol] SWBO-101 (stereo only).
– titles as UK release –

Yellow Submarine, 13 January 1969, Apple [Capitol] SW-153 (stereo only).
– titles as UK release –

Abbey Road, 1 October 1969, Apple [Capitol] SO-383 (stereo only).
– titles as UK release –

Hey Jude, 26 February 1970, Apple [Capitol] SW-385 (stereo only).
A: 'Can't Buy Me Love'; 'I Should Have Known Better'; 'Paperback Writer'; 'Rain'; 'Lady Madonna'; 'Revolution'.
B: 'Hey Jude'; 'Old Brown Shoe'; 'Don't Let Me Down'; 'The Ballad Of John And Yoko'.

Let It Be, 18 May 1970, Apple [Capitol] AR-34001 (stereo only).
– titles as UK release –

THE BEATLES: PEAK CHART POSITIONS, 1962–1970

1. UK: singles

BBC The chart broadcast on the national BBC radio/TV networks
D The paper known at various points in the 1960s as *Disc*, *Disc Weekly* and *Disc And Music Echo*
MM *Melody Maker*
NME *New Musical Express*
RM The paper known at various points in the 1960s as *New Record Mirror* and *Record Mirror*
RR *Record Retailer*

Notes:
a The BBC compiled only a Top 20 at this point; 'Love Me Do' did not enter this.
b On 24 March 1963 *Record Mirror* ceased compiling its own chart and published instead the one compiled by *Record Retailer*.
c On 26 August 1967 *Disc And Music Echo* ceased compiling its own chart and published instead the one compiled by *Melody Maker*.
d Effective 13 February 1969 the BBC ceased compiling its own chart and united with *Record Retailer* to finance a new chart compiled by BMRB (British Market Research Bureau).

	BBC	D	MM	NME	RM	RR
Love Me Do	a	24	21	27	17	17
Please Please Me	1	1	1	1	1	2
From Me To You	1	1	1	1	b	1
She Loves You	1	1	1	1		1
I Want To Hold Your Hand	1	1	1	1		1
Can't Buy Me Love	1	1	1	1		1
A Hard Day's Night	1	1	1	1		1
I Feel Fine	1	1	1	1		1
Ticket To Ride	1	1	1	1		1
Help!	1	1	1	1		1
We Can Work It Out/ Day Tripper	1	1	1	1		1
Paperback Writer	1	1	1	1		1
Eleanor Rigby/ Yellow Submarine	1		1	1		1
Strawberry Fields Forever/Penny Lane	2	2	1	2		2
All You Need Is Love	1	1	1	1		1
Hello, Goodbye	1	c	1	1		1
Lady Madonna	1		2	1		1
Hey Jude	1		1	1		1
Get Back	d		1	1		1
The Ballad Of John And Yoko			1	1		1
Something			4	5		4
Let It Be			3	3		2

2. UK: EPs

Record Retailer was the only consistent publisher of a separate chart for the EP format. It ceased doing so on 30 November 1967.

	RR
Twist And Shout	1
The Beatles' Hits	1
The Beatles (No 1)	1
All My Loving	1
Long Tall Sally	1
Extracts From The Film A Hard Day's Night	1
Extracts From The Album A Hard Day's Night	8
Beatles For Sale	1
Beatles For Sale (No 2)	5
The Beatles' Million Sellers	1
Yesterday	1
Nowhere Man	4

3. UK: albums

Abbreviations and Notes as for UK singles.

	D	MM	NME	RR
Please Please Me	1	1	1	1
With The Beatles	1	1	1	1
A Hard Day's Night	1	1	1	1
Beatles For Sale	1	1	1	1
Help!	1	1	1	1
Rubber Soul	1	1	1	1
Revolver	1	1	1	1
A Collection Of Beatles Oldies	4	4	6	7
Sgt Pepper's Lonely Hearts Club Band	1	1	1	1
The Beatles	c	1	1	1
Yellow Submarine		4	3	3
Abbey Road	1	1	1	1
Let It Be	1	1	1	1

4. US: singles

B *Billboard*
C *Cashbox*
RW *Record World*

	B	C	RW
From Me To You	116	–	–
She Loves You	1	1	1
I Want To Hold Your Hand	1	1	1
Please Please Me (2nd issue)	3	3	3
Twist And Shout	2	1	1
Can't Buy Me Love	1	1	1
Do You Want To Know A Secret	2	3	3
Love Me Do	1	1	1
Sie Liebt Dich	97	–	–
A Hard Day's Night	1	1	1
I'll Cry Instead	25	22	28
And I Love Her	12	14	16
Matchbox	17	17	22
I Feel Fine	1	1	1
Eight Days A Week	1	1	1
Ticket To Ride	1	1	1
Help!	1	1	1
Yesterday	1	1	1
We Can Work It Out/Day Tripper	1	1	1
Nowhere Man	3	2	1
Paperback Writer	1	1	1
Eleanor Rigby/Yellow Submarine	2	1	1
Strawberry Fields Forever/ Penny Lane	1	1	1
All You Need Is Love	1	1	1
Hello, Goodbye	1	1	1
Lady Madonna	4	2	2
Hey Jude	1	1	1
Get Back	1	1	1
The Ballad Of John And Yoko	8	10	7
Something	1	1	1
Let It Be	1	1	1
The Long And Winding Road	1	1	1

5. US: albums

Meet The Beatles!	1	1	1
Introducing The Beatles (2nd issue)	2	2	1
The Beatles' Second Album	1	1	1
A Hard Day's Night	1	1	1
Something New	2	2	2
The Beatles' Story	7	7	13
Beatles '65	1	1	1
The Early Beatles	43	24	29
Beatles VI	1	1	1
Help!	1	1	1
Rubber Soul	1	1	1
"Yesterday"...And Today	1	1	1
Revolver	1	1	1
Sgt Pepper's Lonely Hearts Club Band	1	1	1
Magical Mystery Tour	1	1	1
The Beatles	1	1	1
Yellow Submarine	2	3	2
Abbey Road	1	1	1
Hey Jude	2	2	1
Let It Be	1	1	1

Long Tall Sally
Recording: 1/3/64
Mixing: 10/3/64, 4/6/64

Love Me Do (P)
Recording: 6/6/62, 4,11/9/62
Mixing: 6/6/62, 4,11/9/62, 25/2/63

Love You To (G)
Recording: 11,13/4/66
Mixing: 11,13/4/66, 16/5/66, 21/6/66

Lovely Rita (P)
Recording: 23,24/2/67, 7,21/3/67
Mixing: 21/3/67, 17/4/67

Lucy In The Sky With Diamonds (J)
Recording: 28/2/67, 1,2/3/67
Mixing: 2,3/3/67, 7/4/67

Maggie Mae
Recording: 24/1/69
Mixing: [see 4/3/69], 26/3/70

Magical Mystery Tour (P)
Recording: 25,26,27/4/67, 3/5/67, 7/11/67
Mixing: 27/4/67, 4/5/67, 6,7/11/67

Martha My Dear (P)
Recording: 4,5/10/68
Mixing: 5/10/68

Matchbox
Recording: 1/6/64
Mixing: 4,22/6/64

Maxwell's Silver Hammer (P)
Recording: 9,10,11/7/69, 6,25/8/69
Mixing: 10/7/69, 6,12,14/8/69

Mean Mr Mustard see Sun King/Mean Mr Mustard

Michelle (P)
Recording: 3/11/65
Mixing: 9,15/11/65

Misery (J-P)
Recording: 11,20/2/63
Mixing: 25/2/63

Money (That's What I Want)
Recording: 18,30/7/63, 30/9/63
Mixing: 21/8/63, 29/10/63

Mother Nature's Son (P)
Recording: 9,20/8/68
Mixing: 20/8/68, 12/10/68

Mr Moonlight
Recording: 14/8/64, 18/10/64
Mixing: 27/10/64, 4/11/64

The Night Before (P)
Recording: 17/2/65
Mixing: 18,23/2/65

No Reply (J)
Recording: 3/6/64, 30/9/64
Mixing: 16/10/64, 4/11/64

Norwegian Wood (This Bird Has Flown) (J)
Recording: 12,21/10/65
Mixing: 25,26/10/65

Not A Second Time (J)
Recording: 11/9/63
Mixing: 30/9/63, 29/10/63

Nowhere Man (J)
Recording: 21,22/10/65
Mixing: 25,26/10/65

Ob-La-Di, Ob-La-Da (P)
Recording: 3,4,5,8,9,11,15/7/68
Mixing: 8,11,15/7/68, 12/10/68

Octopus's Garden (R)
Recording: 26,29/4/69, 17,18/7/69
Mixing: 29/4/69, 18/7/69

Oh! Darling (P)
Recording: 27/1/69, 20,26/4/69, 17,18,22,23/7/69, 8,11/8/69
Mixing: 20/4/69, 1/5/69, 12/8/69

Old Brown Shoe (G)
Recording: 25/2/69, 16,18/4/69
Mixing: 25/2/69, 16,18/4/69

The One After 909 (J)
Recording: 5/3/63, 28,29,30/1/69
Mixing: 5/2/69, 23/3/70

Only A Northern Song (G)
Recording: 13,14/2/67, 20/4/67
Mixing: 14/2/67, 21/4/67, 29/10/68

Paperback Writer (P)
Recording: 13,14/4/66
Mixing: 14/4/66, 31/10/66

Penny Lane (P)
Recording: 29,30/12/66, 4,5,6,9,10,12,17/1/67
Mixing: 29,30/12/66, 9,12,17,25/1/67, 30/9/71 [see 7/11/67]

Piggies (G)
Recording: 19,20/9/68, 10/10/68
Mixing: 11/10/68

Please Mister Postman
Recording: 30/7/63
Mixing: 21/8/63, 29/10/63

Please Please Me (J)
Recording: 11/9/62, 26/11/62
Mixing: 30/11/62, 25/2/63

Polythene Pam/She Came In Through The Bathroom Window (J;P)
Recording: 25,28,30/7/69
Mixing: 30/7/69, 14/8/69

PS I Love You (P)
Recording: 6/6/62, 11/9/62
Mixing: 6/6/62, 11/9/62, 25/2/63

Rain (J)
Recording: 14,16/4/66
Mixing: 16/4/66, 2/12/69

Revolution (J)
Recording: 9,10,11,12/7/68
Mixing: 12,15/7/68, 5/12/69

Revolution 1 (J)
Recording: 30,31/5/68, 4,21/6/68
Mixing: 31/5/68, 4,21,25/6/68

Revolution 9 (J)
Recording: 10,11,20,21/6/68
Mixing: 21,25/6/68, 20,26/8/68

Rock And Roll Music
Recording: 18/10/64
Mixing: 26/10/64, 4/11/64

Rocky Raccoon (P)
Recording: 15/8/68
Mixing: 15/8/68, 10/10/68

Roll Over Beethoven
Recording: 30/7/63
Mixing: 21/8/63, 29/10/63

Run For Your Life (J)
Recording: 12/10/65
Mixing: 9,10/11/65

Savoy Truffle (G)
Recording: 3,5,11,14/10/68
Mixing: 14/10/68

Sexy Sadie (J)
Recording: 19,24/7/68, 13,21/8/68
Mixing: 21/8/68, 14/10/68

Sgt Pepper's Lonely Hearts Club Band (P)
Recording: 1,2/2/67, 3,6/3/67
Mixing: 2/2/67, 6/3/67

Sgt Pepper's Lonely Hearts Club Band (Reprise) (P)
Recording: 1/4/67
Mixing: 1,20/4/67

She Came In Through The Bathroom Window see Polythene Pam/She Came In Through The Bathroom Window

She Loves You (J-P)
Recording: 1/7/63
Mixing: 4/7/63, 8/11/66

She Said She Said (J)
Recording: 21/6/66
Mixing: 21,22/6/66

She's A Woman (P)
Recording: 8/10/64
Mixing: 12,21/10/64

She's Leaving Home (P)
Recording: 17,20/3/67
Mixing: 20/3/67, 17/4/67

Sie Liebt Dich (J-P)
Recording: 29/1/64
Mixing: 12/3/64

Slow Down
Recording: 1,4/6/64
Mixing: 4,22/6/64

Something (G)
Recording: 25/2/69, 16/4/69, 2,5/5/69, 11,16/7/69, 15/8/69
Mixing: 25/2/69, 6/5/69, 11/7/69, 19/8/69

Strawberry Fields Forever (J)
Recording: 24,28,29/11/66, 8,9,15,21/12/66
Mixing: 28,29/11/66, 9,15,22,29/12/66, 26/10/71 [see 7/11/67]

Sun King/Mean Mr Mustard (J)
Recording: 24,25,29/7/69
Mixing: 30/7/69, 14,21/8/69

A Taste Of Honey
Recording: 11/2/63
Mixing: 25/2/63

Taxman (G)
Recording: 20,21,22/4/66, 16/5/66
Mixing: 27/4/66, 16/5/66, 21/6/66

Tell Me What You See (P)
Recording: 18/2/65
Mixing: 20,23/2/65

Tell Me Why (J)
Recording: 27/2/64
Mixing: 3/3/64, 22/6/64

Thank You Girl (J-P)
Recording: 5,13/3/63
Mixing: 13/3/63

There's A Place (J)
Recording: 11/2/63
Mixing: 25/2/63

Things We Said Today (P)
Recording: 2,3/6/64
Mixing: 9,22/6/64

Think For Yourself (G)
Recording: 8/11/65
Mixing: 9/11/65

This Boy (J)
Recording: 17/10/63
Mixing: 21/10/63, 10/11/66

Ticket To Ride (J)
Recording: 15/2/65
Mixing: 18,23/2/65

Till There Was You
Recording: 18,30/7/63
Mixing: 21/8/63, 29/10/63

Tomorrow Never Knows (J)
Recording: 6,7,22/4/66
Mixing: 27/4/66, 6,22/6/66

Twist And Shout
Recording: 11/2/63
Mixing: 25/2/63

Two Of Us (P)
Recording: 24,25,31/1/69
Mixing: [see 4/3/69], 25/4/69, 25/3/70

Wait (P)
Recording: 17/6/65, 11/11/65
Mixing: 18/6/65, 15/11/65

We Can Work It Out (P)
Recording: 20,29/10/65
Mixing: 28,29/10/65, 10/11/65, 10/11/66

What Goes On (J)
Recording: 4/11/65
Mixing: 9/11/65

What You're Doing (P)
Recording: 29,30/9/64, 26/10/64
Mixing: 27/10/64

When I Get Home (J)
Recording: 2/6/64
Mixing: 4,22/6/64

When I'm Sixty-Four (P)
Recording: 6,8,20,21/12/66
Mixing: 21,29,30/12/66, 17/4/67

While My Guitar Gently Weeps (G)
Recording: 25/7/68, 16/8/68, 3,5,6/9/68
Mixing: 7,14/10/68

Why Don't We Do It In The Road (P)
Recording: 9,10/10/68
Mixing: 16-17/10/68

Wild Honey Pie (P)
Recording: 20/8/68
Mixing: 20/8/68, 13/10/68

With A Little Help From My Friends (J-P)
Recording: 29,30/3/67
Mixing: 31/3/67, 7/4/67

Within You Without You (G)
Recording: 15,22/3/67, 3/4/67
Mixing: 15,22/3/67, 3,4/4/67

The Word (J-P)
Recording: 10/11/65
Mixing: 11,15/11/65

Words Of Love
Recording: 18/10/64
Mixing: 26/10/64, 4/11/64

Yellow Submarine (P)
Recording: 26/5/66, 1/6/66
Mixing: 2,3,22/6/66

Yer Blues (J)
Recording: 13,14,20/8/68
Mixing: 14/8/68, 14/10/68

Yes It Is (J)
Recording: 16/2/65
Mixing: 18,23/2/65

Yesterday (P)
Recording: 14,17/6/65
Mixing: 17,18/6/65

You Can't Do That (J)
Recording: 25/2/64, 22/5/64
Mixing: 26/2/64, 10/3/64

You Know My Name (Look Up The Number) (J)
Recording: 17/5/67, 7,8/6/67, 30/4/69
Mixing: 7,9/6/67, 30/4/69, 26/11/69

You Like Me Too Much (G)
Recording: 17/2/65
Mixing: 18,23/2/65

You Never Give Me Your Money (P)
Recording: 6/5/69, 1,11,15,30,31/7/69, 5/8/69
Mixing: 15,30/7/69, 14/8/69

You Really Got A Hold On Me
Recording: 18/7/63, 17/10/63
Mixing: 21/8/63, 29/10/63

You Won't See Me (P)
Recording: 11/11/65
Mixing: 15/11/65

You're Going To Lose That Girl (J)
Recording: 19/2/65, 30/3/65
Mixing: 20,23/2/65, 2/4/65

You've Got To Hide Your Love Away (J)
Recording: 18/2/65
Mixing: 20,23/2/65

Your Mother Should Know (P)
Recording: 22,23/8/67, 16,29/9/67
Mixing: 30/9/67, 2/10/67, 6/11/67

The following are miscellaneous recordings and unreleased studio takes, demos, jams, etc, done by the Beatles at or for EMI, 1962 to 1970.

All Things Must Pass (G)
Demo recording: 25/2/69
Mixing: 25/2/69

Another Beatles Christmas Record (-)
Recording: 26/10/64
Mixing: 26/10/64

Anything (-)
Recording: 22/2/67

The Beatles' Christmas Record (-)
Recording: 17/10/63
Mixing: 17/10/63

The Beatles' Third Christmas Record (-)
Recording: 8/11/65
Mixing: 9/11/65

Besame Mucho (I)
Recording: 6/6/62
Mixing: 6/6/62

Besame Mucho (II)
Recording: 29/1/69

Billy's Song (I and II)
Recording: 28/1/69

Blues (-)
Recording: 23/1/69

Bye Bye Love
Recording: 25/1/69

Christmas Messages For Radios London and Caroline (-)
Recording: 6/12/66

Christmas Time Is Here Again (J-P-G-R)
Recording: 28/11/67
Mixing: 28/11/67

Come And Get It (P)
Demo recording: 24/7/69
Mixing: 24/7/69

Etcetera (P)
Demo recording: 20/8/68

God Save The Queen
Recording: 30/1/69
Mixing: 27/3/70

Going Up The Country
Recording: 22/1/69

Hollywood Bowl concert 1964
Recording: 23/8/64
Mixing: 27/8/64, 18/1/77

Hollywood Bowl concerts 1965
Recording: 29,30/8/65
Mixing: 18/1/77

How Do You Do It
Recording: 4/9/62
Mixing: 4/9/62

If You've Got Trouble (J-P)
Recording: 18/2/65
Mixing: 19,23/2/65

Isn't It A Pity (G)
Demo recording: 26/1/69

It's For You (P)
Demo recording: 3/6/64

Lady Madonna (jam) (P)
Recording: 31/1/69
Mixing: [see 4/3/69]

Leave My Kitten Alone
Recording: 14/8/64

Love Me Do (jam) (P)
Recording: 28/1/69

Mailman, Bring Me No More Blues
Recording: 29/1/69

Messages to Australia (-)
Recording: 12/9/63

Not Fade Away
Recording: 29/1/69

Not Guilty (G)
Recording: 7,8,9,12/8/68
Mixing: 12/8/68

Pantomime: Everywhere It's Christmas (-)
Recording: 25/11/66
Mixing: 2/12/66

Rocker (-)
Recording: 22/1/69
Mixing: [see 4/3/69]

Save The Last Dance For Me
Recording: 22/1/69
Mixing: [see 4/3/69]

Sgt Pepper album – concentric groove sounds (-)
Recording: 21/4/67

medley: Shake, Rattle And Roll/Kansas City/MissAnn/Lawdy Miss Clawdy/Blue Suede Shoes/You Really Got A Hold

On Me
Recording: 26/1/69
Mixing: [see 4/3/69]

She Came In Through The Bathroom Window (P)
Recording: 22/1/69

Shirley's Wild Accordion (J-P)
Recording: 12/10/67
Mixing: 12/10/67

Teddy Boy (P)
Recording: 24,28,29/1/69
Mixing: [see 4/3/69], 25/3/70

That Means A Lot (P)
Recording: 20/2/65, 30/3/65
Mixing: 20/2/65

The Tracks Of My Tears
Recording: 26/1/69

12-Bar Original (J-P-G-R)
Recording: 4/11/65
Mixing: 30/11/65

untitled pieces/effects (-)
Recording: 5/1/67, 9/5/67, 1,2/6/67, 1/11/67, 24/7/68, 25/1/69

The Walk
Recording: 27/1/69
Mixing: [see 4/3/69]

What's The New Mary Jane (J)
Recording: 14/8/68, 26/11/68
Mixing: 14/8/68, 26/9/68, 14/10/68, 11/9/69, 26/11/69

You'll Know What To Do (G)
Demo recording: 3/6/64

CHRONOLOGY OF UK RADIO APPEARANCES

This appendix lists the Beatles' British radio appearances to April 1970, excluding news coverage. (It is sorted in order of transmission date, not by recording date.)

Rec date	1st trans	Programme title	Station	Format
7/3/62	8/3/62	Teenager's Turn – Here We Go	BBC Light	ML
11/6/62	15/6/62	Teenager's Turn – Here We Go	BBC Light	ML
8/10/62	12/10/62	The Friday Spectacular	Luxembourg	MM/I
25/10/62	26/10/62	Teenager's Turn – Here We Go	BBC Light	ML
27/10/62	28/10/62	Sunday Spin	Hospital radio	I
16/11/62	23/11/62	The Friday Spectacular	Luxembourg	MM/I
27/11/62	4/12/62	The Talent Spot	BBC Light	ML
live	22/1/63	Pop Inn	BBC Light	I
16/1/63	25/1/63	Here We Go	BBC Light	ML
21/1/63	25/1/63	The Friday Spectacular	Luxembourg	MM/I
22/1/63	26/1/63	Saturday Club	BBC Light	ML
22/1/63	29/1/63	The Talent Spot	BBC Light	ML
live	20/2/63	Parade Of The Pops	BBC Light	ML
6/3/63	12/3/63	Here We Go	BBC Light	ML
11/3/63	15/3/63	The Friday Spectacular	Luxembourg	MM/I
live	16/3/63	Saturday Club	BBC Light	ML
21/3/63	28/3/63	On The Scene	BBC Light	ML
3/4/63	7/4/63	Easy Beat	BBC Light	ML/S
live	9/4/63	Pop Inn	BBC Light	I
live	18/4/63	Swinging Sound '63	BBC Light	ML
1/4/63	22/4/63	Side By Side	BBC Light	ML/S
1/4/63	13/5/63	Side By Side	BBC Light	ML/S
21/5/63	25/5/63	Saturday Club	BBC Light	ML/S
21/5/63	3/6/63	Steppin' Out	BBC Light	ML/S
24/5/63	4/6/63	Pop Go The Beatles (1)	BBC Light	ML/S
1/6/63	11/6/63	Pop Go The Beatles (2)	BBC Light	ML/S
1/6/63	18/6/63	Pop Go The Beatles (3)	BBC Light	ML/S
19/6/63	23/6/63	Easy Beat	BBC Light	ML/S
4/4/63	24/6/63	Side By Side	BBC Light	ML/S
17/6/63	25/6/63	Pop Go The Beatles (4)	BBC Light	ML/S
24/6/63	29/6/63	Saturday Club	BBC Light	ML/S
3/7/63	4/7/63	The Beat Show	BBC Light	ML
2/7/63	16/7/63	Pop Go The Beatles (5)	BBC Light	ML/S
17/7/63	21/7/63	Easy Beat	BBC Light	ML/S
10/7/63	23/7/63	Pop Go The Beatles (6)	BBC Light	ML/S
10/7/63	30/7/63	Pop Go The Beatles (7)	BBC Light	ML/S
16/7/63	6/8/63	Pop Go The Beatles (8)	BBC Light	ML/S
16/7/63	13/8/63	Pop Go The Beatles (9)	BBC Light	ML/S
16/7/63	20/8/63	Pop Go The Beatles (10)	BBC Light	ML/S
30/7/63	24/8/63	Saturday Club	BBC Light	ML/S
1/8/63	27/8/63	Pop Go The Beatles (11)	BBC Light	ML/S
30/7/63	30/8/63	Non Stop Pop	BBC Light	I
1/8/63	3/9/63	Pop Go The Beatles (12)	BBC Light	ML/S
3/9/63	10/9/63	Pop Go The Beatles (13)	BBC Light	ML/S
3/9/63	17/9/63	Pop Go The Beatles (14)	BBC Light	ML/S
3/9/63	24/9/63	Pop Go The Beatles (15)	BBC Light	ML/S
7/9/63	5/10/63	Saturday Club	BBC Light	ML
16/10/63	20/10/63	Easy Beat	BBC Light	ML/S
3/10/63	3/11/63	The Public Ear	BBC Light	I
9/10/63	3/11/63	The Ken Dodd Show	BBC Light	ML
4/11/63	10/11/63	The Royal Variety Performance	BBC Light	ML
20/11/63	20/11/63	Voice Of The North	BBC Home (L)	I
7/9/63	21/11/63	A World Of Sound	BBC Home	I (P)
20/11/63	27/11/63	Wacker, Mach Schau	BBC Home (L)	I (G)
29/11/63	n/k	Music Box	Hospital radio	I
17/12/63	21/12/63	Saturday Club	BBC Light	ML/S
7/12/63	25/12/63	Top Pops Of 1963	BBC Light	I
18/12/63	26/12/63	From Us To You	BBC Light	ML/S
5/1/64	12/1/64	The Public Ear	BBC Light	S (G/R)
7/2/64	8/2/64	Saturday Club	BBC Light	I
7/1/64	15/2/64	Saturday Club	BBC Light	ML/S
22/2/64	22/2/64	Saturday Club	BBC Light	I
17/3/64	18/3/64	Today	BBC Home	I (J)
18/3/64	22/3/64	The Public Ear	BBC Light	I/S
28/3/64	30/3/64	From Us To You	BBC Light	ML/S
31/3/64	4/4/64	Saturday Club	BBC Light	ML/S
19/3/64	12/4/64	Movie-Go-Round	BBC Light	I
20/3/64	12/4/64	Movie-Go-Round	BBC Light	I (R)
29/4/64	29/4/64	Scottish News	BBC Home (L)	I
31/3/64	2/5/64	A Slice Of Life	BBC Home	I (J)
1/5/64	18/5/64	From Us To You	BBC Light	ML/S
20/6/64	27/6/64	Roundabout	BBC Light	I
7/7/64	9/7/64	The Teen Scene	BBC Light	I (J)
14/7/64	16/7/64	Top Gear	BBC Light	ML/S
17/7/64	3/8/64	From Us To You	BBC Light	ML/S
12/8/64	13/8/64	The Teen Scene	BBC Light	I (R)
17/11/64	26/11/64	Top Gear	BBC Light	ML/S
28/11/64	29/11/64	The Teen Scene	BBC Light	I (J)
25/11/64	26/12/64	Saturday Club	BBC Light	ML/S
??/12/64	3/1-17/10/65	The Beatles	Luxembourg	I
19/3/65	20/3/65	Saturday Club	BBC Light	I
20/3/65	21/3-17/10/65	The Beatles	Luxembourg	I
live	13/4/65	Pop Inn	BBC Light	I
29/4/65	2/5-17/10/65	The Beatles	Luxembourg	I
26/5/65	7/6/65	The Beatles (Invite You To Take A Ticket To Ride)	BBC Light	ML/S
11/6/65	11/6/65	Late Night Extra	BBC Light	I (P)
16/6/65	21/6/65	Today	BBC Home	I (J)
20/6/65	27/6-17/10/65	The Beatles	Luxembourg	I
16/6/65	3/7/65	The World Of Books	BBC Home	I (J)
30/7/65	31/7/65	Lance A Gogo	BBC Light	I
15-20/8/65	30/8/65	The Beatles Abroad	BBC Light	I
29/11/65	25/12/65	Saturday Club	BBC Light	I
2/5/66	4/6/66	Saturday Club	BBC Light	I
8/7/66	8/7/66	Today	BBC Home	I (G/R)
1/8/66	6/8/66	David Frost At The Phonograph	BBC Light	I (P)
6/8/66	29/8/66	The Lennon And McCartney Songbook	BBC Light	I (J/P)
20/9/66	11/12/66	The Lively Arts	BBC Home	I (G)
20/3/67	27/3/67	The Ivor Novello Awards For 1966	BBC Light	I (J/P)
n/k	20/5/67	Where It's At	BBC Light	I(J/P/G)
n/k	1/7/67	Where It's At	BBC Light	I (P)
31/7/67	5/8/67	(farewell message)	Radio London	S (R)
13/9/67	30/9/67 7/10/67	Scene And Heard	BBC Radio 1	I (G)
14/9/67	14/10/67	Scene And Heard	BBC Radio 1	I (R)
n/k	25/11/67	Where It's At	BBC Radio 1	ML (P)
5/12/67	5/12/67	Late Night Extra	BBC Radio 1/2	I (J)
27/1/68	4/2/68	The Kenny Everett Show	BBC Radio 1	I (J)
6/6/68	9/6/68	The Kenny Everett Show	BBC Radio 1	I
6/8/68	6/8/68	Late Night Extra	BBC Radio 1/2	I (J)
20/11/68	21/11/68	–	Luxembourg	I (P)
live	11/12/68	Night Ride	BBC Radio 1/2	I (J)
21/1/69	25/1/69	Scene And Heard	BBC Radio 1	I (R)
4/3/69	8/3/69 12/4/69	Scene And Heard	BBC Radio 1	I (G)
1/4/69	1/4/69	Late Night Extra	BBC Radio 1/2	I (J)
3/4/69	3/4/69	The World At One	BBC Radio 4	I (G)
8/5/69	11/5/69 18/5/69	Scene And Heard	BBC Radio 1	I (J)
15/5/69	16/5/69	Light And Local	BBC Radio M'side	I(P)
n/k	22/6/69	The David Christian Show	Luxembourg	I (J)
14/8/69	20/9/69 27/9/69	Everett Is Here	BBC Radio 1	I (J)
19/9/69	21/9/69 28/9/69	Scene And Heard	BBC Radio 1	I (P)
n/k	26/9/69	–	Luxembourg	I (R)
n/k	27/9/69	–	Luxembourg	I (J)

CHRONOLOGY OF UK TELEVISION APPEARANCES

This appendix lists the Beatles' appearances on British television to April 1970, excluding news coverage and the screening of their promotional films/videos. (It is sorted in order of transmission date, not by filming/recording date.)

* originally made for a programme titled Know The North

KEY:

doc documentary	n/a not applicable
(G) George	n/k not known
I interview	(P) Paul
(J) John	(R) Ringo
(L) heard/shown locally only	S speech (but not interview)
ML music live	trans transmission
MM music mimed	

355

THE BEATLES' SESSION/LIVE PERFORMANCE RECORDINGS BROADCAST BY BBC RADIO

When the Beatles contributed in-studio music sessions for broadcast on BBC radio, they were, if only unwittingly, at the same time providing posterity with a cache of good-quality recordings to supplement EMI's priceless collection. A total of 275 different Beatles recordings were broadcast exclusively by the BBC, as shown in this at-a-glance A-Z.

Of special note are the 36 different songs – totalling 58 broadcast recordings – for which the group's *only* studio performance (excepting, in five instances, their Decca audition) was at the BBC, not EMI. These have also been extracted into a separate list at the end. Additionally, a BBC version which pre-dated the Beatles' EMI recording is denoted by an asterisk.

	Show	Recorded	Broadcast
All My Loving 1	Sat Club	17/12/63	21/12/63
All My Loving 2	FUTY	18/12/63	26/12/63
All My Loving 3	Sat Club	7/1/64	15/2/64
All My Loving 4	FUTY	28/2/64	30/3/64
And I Love Her	Top Gear	14/7/64	16/7/64
Anna (Go To Him) 1	PGTB 4	17/6/63	25/6/63
Anna (Go To Him) 2	PGTB 11	1/8/63	27/8/63
*Ask Me Why 1	Here We Go	11/6/62	15/6/62
Ask Me Why 2	Here We Go	16/1/63	25/1/63
Ask Me Why 3	Talent Spot	22/1/63	29/1/63
Ask Me Why 4	PGTB 15	3/9/63	24/9/63
Baby It's You 1	Side By Side	1/4/63	22/4/63
Baby It's You 2	PGTB 2	1/6/63	11/6/63
Beautiful Dreamer	Sat Club	22/1/63	26/1/63
Besame Mucho	Here We Go	11/6/62	15/6/62
Boys 1	Side By Side	1/4/63	13/5/63
Boys 2	Side By Side	4/4/63	24/6/63
Boys 3	Sat Club	21/5/63	25/5/63
Boys 4	PGTB 4	17/6/63	25/6/63
Boys 5	PGTB 14	3/9/63	17/9/63
Boys 6	FUTY	18/12/63	26/12/63
Boys 7	FUTY	17/7/64	3/8/64
Can't Buy Me Love 1	FUTY	28/2/64	30/3/64
Can't Buy Me Love 2	Sat Club	31/3/64	4/4/64
Can't Buy Me Love 3	FUTY	1/5/64	18/5/64
Carol	PGTB 5	2/7/63	16/7/63
*Chains 1	Here We Go	16/1/63	25/1/63
Chains 2	Side By Side	1/4/63	13/5/63
Chains 3	PGTB 4	17/6/63	25/6/63
Chains 4	PGTB 14	3/9/63	17/9/63
Clarabella	PGTB 5	2/7/63	16/7/63
Crying, Waiting, Hoping	PGTB 8	16/7/63	6/8/63
*(There's A) Devil In Her Heart 1	PGTB 10	16/7/63	20/8/63
(There's A) Devil In Her Heart 2	PGTB 15	3/9/63	24/9/63
Dizzy Miss Lizzy	Ticket	26/5/65	7/6/65
Do You Want To Know A Secret 1	Here We Go	6/3/63	12/3/63
Do You Want To Know A Secret 2	On The Scene	21/3/63	28/3/63
Do You Want To Know A Secret 3	Side By Side	1/4/63	22/4/63
Do You Want To Know A Secret 4	Sat Club	21/5/63	25/5/63
Do You Want To Know A Secret 5	PGTB 1	24/5/63	4/6/63
Do You Want To Know A Secret 6	PGTB 7	10/7/63	30/7/63
Don't Ever Change	PGTB 11	1/8/63	27/8/63
Dream Baby (How Long Must I Dream?)	Here We Go	7/3/62	8/3/62
*Everybody's Trying To Be My Baby 1	PGTB 1	24/5/63	4/6/63
*Everybody's Trying To Be My Baby 2	Sat Club	31/3/64	4/4/64
Everybody's Trying To Be My Baby 3	Top Gear	17/11/64	26/11/64
	Sat Club		26/12/64
Everybody's Trying To Be My Baby 4	Ticket	26/5/65	7/6/65
From Me To You 1	Side By Side	1/4/63	22/4/63
From Me To You 2	Side By Side	1/4/63	13/5/63
From Me To You 3	Easy Beat	3/4/63	7/4/63

	Show	Recorded	Broadcast
From Me To You 4	Side By Side	4/4/63	24/6/63
From Me To You 5	Swg Sound '63	live	18/4/63
From Me To You 6	Sat Club	21/5/63	25/5/63
From Me To You 7	Steppin' Out	21/5/63	3/6/63
From Me To You 8	PGTB 1	24/5/63	4/6/63
From Me To You 9	PGTB 3	1/6/63	18/6/63
From Me To You 10	Easy Beat	19/6/63	23/6/63
From Me To You 11	Sat Club	24/6/63	29/6/63
From Me To You 12	Beat Show	3/7/63	4/7/63
From Me To You 13	PGTB 12	1/8/63	3/9/63
From Me To You 14	PGTB 14	3/9/63	17/9/63
From Me To You 15	Easy Beat	16/10/63	20/10/63
From Me To You 16	Variety Perf	4/11/63	10/11/63
From Us To You 1	FUTY	18/12/63	26/12/63
From Us To You 2	FUTY	28/2/64	30/3/64
			18/5/64
			3/8/64
Glad All Over 1	PGTB 10	16/7/63	20/8/63
Glad All Over 2	Sat Club	30/7/63	24/8/63
Happy Birthday Saturday Club	Sat Club	7/9/63	5/10/63
A Hard Day's Night 1	Top Gear	14/7/64	16/7/64
A Hard Day's Night 2	FUTY	17/7/64	3/8/64
The Hippy Hippy Shake 1	Sat Club	live	16/3/63
The Hippy Hippy Shake 2	PGTB 1	24/5/63	4/6/63
The Hippy Hippy Shake 3	PGTB 7	10/7/63	30/7/63
The Hippy Hippy Shake 4	PGTB 13	3/9/63	10/9/63
The Hippy Hippy Shake 5	Sat Club	7/1/64	15/2/64
*Honey Don't 1	PGTB 12	1/8/63	3/9/63
*Honey Don't 2	FUTY	1/5/64	18/5/64
Honey Don't 3	Top Gear	17/11/64	26/11/64
Honey Don't 4	Ticket	26/5/65	7/6/65
The Honeymoon Song	PGTB 8	16/7/63	6/8/63
I Call Your Name	Sat Club	31/3/64	4/4/64
I Feel Fine	Top Gear	17/11/64	26/11/64
	Sat Club		26/12/64
I Forgot To Remember To Forget	FUTY	1/5/64	18/5/64
I Got A Woman 1	PGTB 9	16/7/63	13/8/63
I Got A Woman 2	Sat Club	31/3/64	4/4/64
I Got To Find My Baby 1	PGTB 2	1/6/63	11/6/63
I Got To Find My Baby 2	Sat Club	24/6/63	29/6/63
I Just Don't Understand	PGTB 10	16/7/63	13/8/63
I Saw Her Standing There 1	Sat Club	live	16/3/63
I Saw Her Standing There 2	Side By Side	1/4/63	22/4/63
I Saw Her Standing There 3	Sat Club	21/5/63	25/5/63
I Saw Her Standing There 4	Steppin' Out	21/5/63	3/6/63
I Saw Her Standing There 5	PGTB 4	17/6/63	25/6/63
I Saw Her Standing There 6	Easy Beat	17/7/63	21/7/63
I Saw Her Standing There 7	PGTB 15	3/9/63	24/9/63
I Saw Her Standing There 8	Sat Club	7/9/63	5/10/63
I Saw Her Standing There 9	Easy Beat	16/10/63	20/10/63
I Saw Her Standing There 10	FUTY	18/12/63	26/12/63
I Saw Her Standing There 11	FUTY	1/5/64	18/5/64
I Should Have Known Better 1	Top Gear	14/7/64	16/7/64
I Should Have Known Better 2	FUTY	17/7/64	3/8/64
I Wanna Be Your Man 1	Sat Club	7/1/64	15/2/64
I Wanna Be Your Man 2	FUTY	28/2/64	30/3/64
I Want To Hold Your Hand 1	Sat Club	17/12/63	21/12/63
I Want To Hold Your Hand 2	FUTY	18/12/63	26/12/63
I Want To Hold Your Hand 3	Sat Club	7/1/64	15/2/64
I'll Be On My Way	Side By Side	4/4/63	24/6/63
I'll Follow The Sun	Top Gear	17/11/64	26/11/64
I'll Get You 1	PGTB 9	16/7/63	13/8/63
I'll Get You 2	Sat Club	30/7/63	24/8/63
I'll Get You 3	PGTB 12	1/8/63	3/9/63
I'll Get You 4	PGTB 13	3/9/63	10/9/63
I'll Get You 5	Sat Club	7/9/63	5/10/63
I'm A Loser 1	Top Gear	17/11/64	26/11/64
	Sat Club		26/12/64
I'm A Loser 2	Ticket	26/5/65	7/6/65
I'm Gonna Sit Right Down And Cry (Over You)	PGTB 8	16/7/63	6/8/63
I'm Happy Just To Dance With You	FUTY	17/7/64	3/8/64

	Show	Recorded	Broadcast
I'm Talking About You	Sat Club	live	16/3/63
If I Fell 1	Top Gear	14/7/64	16/7/64
If I Fell 2	FUTY	17/7/64	3/8/64
Johnny B Goode	Sat Club	7/1/64	15/2/64
*Kansas City/Hey-Hey-Hey-Hey! 1	PGTB 8	16/7/63	6/8/63
*Kansas City/Hey-Hey-Hey-Hey! 2	FUTY	1/5/64	18/5/64
Kansas City/Hey-Hey-Hey-Hey! 3	Sat Club	25/11/64	26/12/64
Keep Your Hands Off My Baby	Sat Club	22/1/63	26/1/63
Lend Me Your Comb	PGTB 5	2/7/63	16/7/63
Lonesome Tears In My Eyes	PGTB 6	10/7/63	23/7/63
*Long Tall Sally 1	Side By Side	1/4/63	13/5/63
*Long Tall Sally 2	Sat Club	21/5/63	25/5/63
*Long Tall Sally 3	PGTB 9	16/7/63	13/8/63
*Long Tall Sally 4	Sat Club	30/7/63	24/8/63
Long Tall Sally 5	Sat Club	31/3/64	4/4/64
Long Tall Sally 6	Top Gear	14/7/64	16/7/64
Long Tall Sally 7	FUTY	17/7/64	3/8/64
Love Me Do 1	Here We Go	25/10/62	26/10/62
Love Me Do 2	Talent Spot	27/11/62	4/12/62
Love Me Do 3	Sat Club	22/1/63	26/1/63
Love Me Do 4	Parade Pops	live	20/2/63
Love Me Do 5	Side By Side	4/4/63	24/6/63
Love Me Do 6	PGTB 2	1/6/63	11/6/63
Love Me Do 7	PGTB 6	10/7/63	23/7/63
Love Me Do 8	PGTB 13	3/9/63	10/9/63
Love Me Do 9	Easy Beat	16/10/63	20/10/63
Lucille 1	PGTB 14	3/9/63	17/9/63
Lucille 2	Sat Club	7/9/63	5/10/63
*Matchbox 1	PGTB 7	10/7/63	30/7/63
*Matchbox 2	FUTY	1/5/64	18/5/64
Memphis, Tennessee 1	Here We Go	7/3/62	8/3/62
Memphis, Tennessee 2	PGTB 3	1/6/63	18/6/63
Memphis, Tennessee 3	Sat Club	24/6/63	29/6/63
Memphis, Tennessee 4	PGTB 7	10/7/63	30/7/63
Memphis, Tennessee 5	Sat Club	7/9/63	5/10/63
Misery 1	Here We Go	6/3/63	12/3/63
Misery 2	Sat Club	live	16/3/63
Misery 3	On The Scene	21/3/63	28/3/63
Misery 4	Side By Side	1/4/63	22/4/63
Misery 5	Easy Beat	3/4/63	7/4/63
Misery 6	PGTB 1	24/5/63	4/6/63
Misery 7	PGTB 14	3/9/63	17/9/63
*Money (That's What I Want) 1	Sat Club	21/5/63	25/5/63
*Money (That's What I Want) 2	PGTB 3	1/6/63	18/6/63
*Money (That's What I Want) 3	Sat Club	24/6/63	29/6/63
Money (That's What I Want) 4	PGTB 12	1/8/63	3/9/63
Money (That's What I Want) 5	FUTY	18/12/63	26/12/63
Money (That's What I Want) 6	Sat Club	7/1/64	15/2/64
The Night Before	Ticket	26/5/65	7/6/65
Nothin' Shakin' (But The Leaves On The Trees)	PGTB 6	10/7/63	23/7/63
Ooh! My Soul	PGTB 11	1/8/63	27/8/63
A Picture Of You	Here We Go	11/6/62	15/6/62
*Please Mister Postman 1	Here We Go	7/3/62	8/3/62
*Please Mister Postman 2	PGTB 7	10/7/63	30/7/63
Please Mister Postman 3	FUTY	28/2/64	30/3/64
Please Please Me 1	Here We Go	16/1/63	25/1/63
Please Please Me 2	Sat Club	22/1/63	26/1/63
Please Please Me 3	Talent Spot	22/1/63	29/1/63
Please Please Me 4	Parade Pops	live	20/2/63
Please Please Me 5	Here We Go	6/3/63	12/3/63
Please Please Me 6	Sat Club	live	16/3/63
Please Please Me 7	On The Scene	21/3/63	28/3/63
Please Please Me 8	Side By Side	1/4/63	22/4/63
Please Please Me 9	Easy Beat	3/4/63	7/4/63
Please Please Me 10	Steppin' Out	21/5/63	3/6/63
Please Please Me 11	PGTB 9	16/7/63	13/8/63
Please Please Me 12	Easy Beat	16/10/63	20/10/63
Pop Go The Beatles	PGTB 1-15	24/5/63	4/6-24/9/63

PS I Love You 1	Here We Go	25/10/62	26/10/62
PS I Love You 2	Talent Spot	27/11/62	4/12/62
PS I Love You 3	PGTB 4	17/6/63	25/6/63
Rock And Roll Music	Sat Club	25/11/64	26/12/64
*Roll Over Beethoven 1	Steppin' Out	21/5/63	3/6/63
*Roll Over Beethoven 2	Sat Club	24/6/63	29/6/63
Roll Over Beethoven 3	PGTB 12	1/8/63	3/9/63
Roll Over Beethoven 4	Sat Club	17/12/63	21/12/63
Roll Over Beethoven 5	FUTY	18/12/63	26/12/63
Roll Over Beethoven 6	Sat Club	7/1/64	15/2/64
Roll Over Beethoven 7	FUTY	28/2/64	30/3/64
She Loves You 1	PGTB 9	16/7/63	13/8/63
	PGTB 10		20/8/63
She Loves You 2	Sat Club	30/7/63	24/8/63
She Loves You 3	PGTB 11	1/8/63	27/8/63
She Loves You 4	PGTB 13	3/9/63	10/9/63
She Loves You 5	PGTB 15	3/9/63	24/9/63
She Loves You 6	Sat Club	7/9/63	5/10/63
She Loves You 7	Ken Dodd	9/10/63	3/11/63
			6/11/63
			1/2/64
She Loves You 8	Easy Beat	16/10/63	20/10/63
She Loves You 9	Sat Club	17/12/63	21/12/63
She Loves You 10	FUTY	18/12/63	26/12/63
She's A Woman 1	Top Gear	17/11/64	26/11/64
	Sat Club		26/12/64
She's A Woman 2	Ticket	26/5/65	7/6/65
A Shot Of Rhythm And Blues 1	PGTB 3	1/6/63	18/6/63
A Shot Of Rhythm And Blues 2	Easy Beat	17/7/63	21/7/63
A Shot Of Rhythm And Blues 3	PGTB 11	1/8/63	27/8/63
Side By Side	Side By Side	1/4/63	22/4/63
			13/5/63
			24/6/63
*Slow Down	PGTB 10	16/7/63	20/8/63
So How Come (No One Loves Me)	PGTB 6	10/7/63	23/7/63
Soldier Of Love (Lay Down Your Arms)	PGTB 5	2/7/63	16/7/63
Some Other Guy 1	Sat Club	22/1/63	26/1/63
Some Other Guy 2	Talent Spot	22/1/63	29/1/63
Some Other Guy 3	Easy Beat	19/6/63	23/6/63
Sure To Fall (In Love With You) 1	PGTB 3	1/6/63	18/6/63
Sure To Fall (In Love With You) 2	PGTB 15	3/9/63	24/9/63
Sure To Fall (In Love With You) 3	Sat Club	31/3/64	4/4/64
Sure To Fall (In Love With You) 4	FUTY	1/5/64	18/5/64
Sweet Little Sixteen	PGTB 6	10/7/63	23/7/63
*A Taste Of Honey 1	Here We Go	25/10/62	26/10/62
A Taste Of Honey 2	Side By Side	1/4/63	13/5/63
A Taste Of Honey 3	PGTB 3	1/6/63	18/6/63
A Taste Of Honey 4	Easy Beat	19/6/63	23/6/63
A Taste Of Honey 5	Beat Show	3/7/63	4/7/63
A Taste Of Honey 6	PGTB 6	10/7/63	23/7/63
A Taste Of Honey 7	PGTB 13	3/9/63	10/9/63
Thank You Girl 1	Side By Side	1/4/63	13/5/63
Thank You Girl 2	Steppin' Out	21/5/63	3/6/63
Thank You Girl 3	Easy Beat	19/6/63	23/6/63
That's All Right (Mama)	PGTB 5	2/7/63	16/7/63
There's A Place 1	PGTB 5	2/7/63	16/7/63
There's A Place 2	Easy Beat	17/7/63	21/7/63
There's A Place 3	PGTB 12	1/8/63	3/9/63
Things We Said Today 1	Top Gear	14/7/64	16/7/64
Things We Said Today 2	FUTY	17/7/64	3/8/64
This Boy 1	Sat Club	17/12/63	21/12/63
This Boy 2	FUTY	28/2/64	30/3/64
Ticket To Ride	Ticket	26/5/65	7/6/65
*Till There Was You 1	PGTB 2	1/6/63	11/6/63
*Till There Was You 2	Sat Club	24/6/63	29/6/63
*Till There Was You 3	PGTB 7	10/7/63	30/7/63
Till There Was You 4	PGTB 13	3/9/63	10/9/63
Till There Was You 5	Variety Perf	4/11/63	10/11/63
Till There Was You 6	Sat Club	17/12/63	21/12/63
Till There Was You 7	FUTY	18/12/63	26/12/63
Till There Was You 8	FUTY	28/2/64	30/3/64

To Know Her Is To Love Her	PGTB 8	16/7/63	6/8/63
Too Much Monkey Business 1	Sat Club	live	16/3/63
Too Much Monkey Business 2	Side By Side	4/4/63	24/6/63
Too Much Monkey Business 3	PGTB 2	1/6/63	11/6/63
Too Much Monkey Business 4	PGTB 13	3/9/63	10/9/63
*Twist And Shout 1	Talent Spot	27/11/62	4/12/62
Twist And Shout 2	Swg Sound '63	live	18/4/63
Twist And Shout 3	PGTB 4	17/6/63	25/6/63
Twist And Shout 4	Beat Show	3/7/63	4/7/63
Twist And Shout 5	PGTB 8	16/7/63	6/8/63
Twist And Shout 6	Easy Beat	17/7/63	21/7/63
Twist And Shout 7	Sat Club	30/7/63	24/8/63
Twist And Shout 8	PGTB 11	1/8/63	27/8/63
Twist And Shout 9	PGTB 15	3/9/63	24/9/63
Twist And Shout 10	Variety Perf	4/11/63	10/11/63
*Words Of Love	PGTB 10	16/7/63	20/8/63
You Can't Do That 1	FUTY	28/2/64	30/3/64
You Can't Do That 2	Sat Club	31/3/64	4/4/64
You Can't Do That 3	FUTY	1/5/64	18/5/64
You Can't Do That 4	Top Gear	14/7/64	16/7/64
*You Really Got A Hold On Me 1	PGTB 1	24/5/63	4/6/63
*You Really Got A Hold On Me 2	PGTB 9	16/7/63	13/8/63
You Really Got A Hold On Me 3	Sat Club	30/7/63	24/8/63
You Really Got A Hold On Me 4	PGTB 14	3/9/63	17/9/63
Youngblood	PGTB 2	1/6/63	11/6/63

ABBREVIATIONS:

FUTY	From Us To You
Ken Dodd	The Ken Dodd Show
Parade Pops	Parade Of The Pops
PGTB	Pop Go The Beatles (edition number adjacent)
Sat Club	Saturday Club
Swg Sound '63	Swinging Sound '63
Ticket	The Beatles (Invite You To Take A Ticket To Ride)
Variety Perf	Royal Variety Performance

THE SPECIAL 36

Of the 275 different Beatles recordings broadcast by BBC radio, the following 58, of 36 songs, merit special attention because they were not taped by the group for issue on record. Thirty-five are "covers", one – 'I'll Be On My Way' – is a Lennon-McCartney original, otherwise available only as an EMI recording by Billy J Kramer with the Dakotas. Good quality tapes still exist for most, though not all, of the 36, and it was principally from these that, at December 1991, EMI was preparing an album for first-time commercial release.

Beautiful Dreamer
Besame Mucho
Carol
Clarabella
Crying, Waiting, Hoping
Don't Ever Change
Dream Baby (How Long Must I Dream?)
Glad All Over [two different versions]
The Hippy Hippy Shake [five different versions]
The Honeymoon Song
I Forgot To Remember To Forget
I Got A Woman [two different versions]
I Got To Find My Baby [two different versions]
I Just Don't Understand
I'll Be On My Way
I'm Gonna Sit Right Down And Cry (Over You)
I'm Talking About You
Johnny B Goode
Keep Your Hands Off My Baby
Lend Me Your Comb
Lonesome Tears In My Eyes

Lucille [two different versions]
Memphis, Tennessee [five different versions]
Nothin' Shakin' (But The Leaves On The Trees)
Ooh! My Soul
A Picture Of You
A Shot Of Rhythm And Blues [three different versions]
So How Come (No One Loves Me)
Soldier Of Love (Lay Down Your Arms)
Some Other Guy [three different versions]
Sure To Fall (In Love With You) [four different versions]
Sweet Little Sixteen
That's All Right (Mama)
To Know Her Is To Love Her
Too Much Monkey Business [four different versions]
Youngblood

Additionally, there are three theme tunes – From Us To You [two different versions], Pop Go The Beatles and Side By Side – two recordings of Honey Don't (1 August 1963 and 1 May 1964) which feature John Lennon on lead vocal, rather than Ringo who sang the Beatles' EMI recording, and a few ditties such as Happy Birthday Saturday Club and the Chrimble Mudley.

OTHER ENGAGEMENTS PLAYED

The chronology of the Beatles' live engagements in this book's diary sections is complete from 1962; before then, however, it lacks a number of appearances which were neither advertised nor noted down at the time and for which only locations – not dates – are known.

The principal "grey area" is 1957-59; the Quarry Men were little more than a fun group, formed by schoolboys, and almost all of their engagements were arranged through friends and contacts, not promoters and contracts, so details of only a scant few bookings have been preserved.

What follows is a list of these "missing" engagements. Unless otherwise stated, all are Liverpool-area venues.

1957-59

From mid-1956 until early-1958 regular skiffle group contests were held as interval attractions at the larger ballrooms and theatres on Merseyside, providing not just "an opportunity to become known" (precisely to whom it was never made clear) but, more importantly perhaps, free entertainment for promoters – keen combos, from April 1957 often including the Quarry Men, eagerly queued up for their big chance. Venues included the Pavilion Theatre, Aintree; the Grafton and Locarno Ballrooms, both in West Derby Road; the Pavilion Theatre, Lodge Lane; and the Rialto Ballroom, Upper Parliament Street/Stanhope Street.

Other regular audition venues for the Quarry Men, based in south Liverpool, included the Wilson Hall, Garston and the Winter Gardens Ballroom, Heald Street, Garston. In September 1958 one winner at this latter venue was "rock and roll comedian" Jimmy Tarbuck, while two months later another contest was won by Ronald Wycherley, later to achieve fame as Billy Fury. The Winter Gardens Ballroom also opened up for regular Tuesday rock nights on 30 April 1957, though it rarely advertised who was performing.

The Quarry Men almost certainly played at the Cavern Club on more than the two occasions listed in the diary, but since the venue's newspaper advertisements rarely gave more than "plus skiffle interval", "plus mystery skiffle group" or other such non-descript statements, precise dates are impossible to research.

Their line-up including members of the St Peter's Parish Church Youth Club, Woolton, the Quarry Men undoubtedly secured a few engagements there, in addition to playing at the church's 6 July 1957 garden fête. Two people recall John Lennon storming out of the club one particular evening because his microphone repeatedly broke down.

Both St Barnabas Church Hall, Penny Lane, and Holyoake Hall, Smithdown Road, Wavertree, held regular unadvertised Saturday-night skiffle sessions with interval attractions. The Quarry Men attended on a handful of occasions.

The Quarry Men played during the sixth-formers' dance at John's school, Quarry Bank High, Harthill Road, Woolton, in July 1957.

The group played one Friday night in November 1957 (either 1, 8, 15, 22 or 29) at the Haig Dance Club, Haig Avenue, Moreton, Wirral, Cheshire.

The Quarry Men played at the Morgue Skiffle Cellar on several occasions after it opened on 13 March 1958. (See that entry.)

In mid-1958 the Quarry Men had an unsuccessful Saturday-night audition at the Lowlands Club, Hayman's Green, in the West Derby area of Liverpool. This venue was situated close by the Casbah Coffee Club which opened more than a year later.

Paul McCartney has recalled that one of John "Duff" Lowe's few engagements as a member of the Quarry Men, indeed perhaps his only one, took place at the Stevedors' and Dockers' Union Club premises in Window Lane, Garston, known locally as the Blue Union Club. The exact date of this mid-1958 appearance cannot be traced.

Harry Harrison, George's father, was a bus driver and chairman of several social committees, and booked the Quarry Men whenever an opportunity arose. In addition to the party listed in the diary for 1 January 1959 the group also played at busmen's social clubs in Picton Road, Wavertree; and Finch Lane, near Huyton.

The Quarry Men played at the Prescot Cables club in Hope Street, Prescot, Lancashire, sometime early in 1959. It was after this engagement that drummer Colin Hanton quit the group.

Other known miscellaneous Quarry Men engagements: several family celebrations; one ten-minute interval appearance in the club house at Lee Park Golf Course, off Childwall Valley Road; Childwall Labour Club; Gateacre Labour Club; various local working men's clubs; St Anne's Club in Litherland; the youth club of St Luke's Church, Stanley Road, Bootle; and birthday parties in Ford (north Liverpool) and Smithdown Lane, Edge Hill.

1960

The only semi-regular performances of the Quarry Men/Beatals in Spring 1960, probably in early May, were the Friday afternoon Students' Union dances in the school hall of the Liverpool College of Art, Hope Street, during John Lennon and Stuart Sutcliffe's final year of education there. Any record of the dates has long since vanished. As the group were without sufficient amplifiers (they numbered a new guitarist, of course) the union was prevailed upon to provide one, on the proviso that it never left the building; it did – the Beatles used the amp, albeit irregularly, until 1962.

The Beatals played during an interval break one Sunday afternoon in early-1960 at the original Cassanova Club, situated above the Temple Restaurant in Temple Street, central Liverpool. The venue was opened on 10 January 1960 by Cass and the Cassanovas, frustrated at the lack of opportunities to play in the city, and it operated on Thursday, Friday and Saturday nights, and Sunday afternoons.

In addition to their occasional Monday night appearances at the Jacaranda Coffee Bar between the end of May and mid-August 1960, the Silver Beatles may well have fulfilled other unannounced and unadvertised dates there during this period as owner Allan Williams saw fit, especially with the permanent absence from late-June of his resident group, the Royal Caribbean Steel Band. On one occasion, probably in late-June, the Silver Beatles backed Royston Ellis, the teenage "beat poet", while he recited some of his work, allegedly shocking the not yet worldly-wise group with his overtly homosexual prose.

For one week in early July 1960 the Silver Beatles fulfilled their infamous strip club booking at the New Cabaret Artistes, 174a Upper Parliament Street. The exact dates are not known.

On very rare occasions (probably just once or twice in mid-1960) the Silver Beatles played for an afternoon in the cellar of a shebeen run by Allan Williams' business partner, Lord Woodbine: the New Colony Club, situated in a semi-derelict house at 80 Berkley Street, in the heart of Liverpool's vice area.

The precise dates for the Beatles' few, sporadic and unannounced 1960 appearances at the Top Ten Club in Hamburg are now lost for ever, if they were ever noted down at all. In addition to impromptu jamming with Tony Sheridan and his group, the Jets, the Beatles also performed there alone on one or two occasions towards the conclusion of their initial stay in Hamburg, at the end of November 1960.

1961

In the three months prior to April 1961, between the group's first and second trips to Hamburg, the Beatles found time in their increasingly busy schedule to play two small venues in Southport, Lancashire, 20 miles up the coast from Liverpool. One was the ATC Club, Birkdale, where they reportedly received the grand sum of £1 10s (£1.50) between them; the second was at the Labour Club, Devonshire Road, High Park. Neither was advertised and dates cannot be found.

The Beatles are understood to have played in at least two Liverpool labour clubs in 1961, although no record of such engagements has survived and nor were the bookings advertised. Another early-1961 appearance – no date known – is said to have taken place at Halewood Village Hall.

After a lunchtime session in the Cavern Club the Beatles occasionally moved on to an afternoon drinking establishment, the Starline Club in Windsor Street, for extra rehearsals, and refreshment. Apparently they also fulfilled one or two evening performances there too, but these were unadvertised and not noted down.

The author has been unable to confirm rumour of a late-1961 appearance by the Beatles at a Sunday afternoon dance in the hall at Allerton Synagogue in Booker Avenue, West Allerton.

Several people recall the Beatles playing a Sunday night engagement at the CI (Catholic Institute), St Edward's College, Sandfield Park, near the West Derby area of Liverpool. The engagement was not advertised and all CI records have since been destroyed. The engagement is likely to have been between October and December 1961, however. What is known is that the Beatles played badly and were not re-booked.

One Sunday evening towards the end of the year the Beatles played at the Glenpark Club in Lord Street, Southport.

British disc-jockey and TV personality Jimmy Savile recalls the Beatles playing on two occasions at the Three Coins Club in Fountain Street, Manchester, Lancashire. Only one of these, the second date, was advertised, but as the first was for a fee of just £5 this would seem to place it in the pre-Epstein period. Since the Three Coins did not open for business until 14 October 1961, and they only engaged live groups on a Sunday, this perhaps further narrows the date down to 5 November.

Another possible Manchester booking for which no date is traceable took place at the Embassy Club, situated in Rochdale Road. British comedian Bernard Manning, whose family have operated this and other Manchester club venues since the late 1950s, has stated that the Beatles once performed there for a £14 fee, which would seem to date it in the pre-Epstein 1961 period.

ENGAGEMENTS NOT PLAYED

This section lists live performance bookings for the Beatles (in their various forms) which the group did not or could not fulfil, and alleged appearances which, contrary to rumour, did not take place.

1958

The Quarry Men were advertised to appear at Wilson Hall in Garston on Thursday 9 January 1958 but promoter Charlie McBain switched them to a dance the following night at New Clubmoor Hall, Norris Green.

Although they attempted to secure early-1958 bookings at the Attic Skiffle Club in Islington, central Liverpool, the Quarry Men never appeared there.

The Quarry Men only once performed at St Peter's Parish Church Fête, Woolton: on 6 July 1957. Entertainment at the 1958 event, held on 5 July, was supplied solely by the Band of the Cheshire Yeomanry.

1960

The Silver Beetles' first official, advertised engagement was at Lathom Hall in Seaforth on Saturday 21 May 1960. The group did not show, however, being 367 miles away, in Inverness, at the time.

A 6 August 1960 booking for the Silver Beatles at the Grosvenor Ballroom in Liscard, Wallasey, was cancelled owing to complaints from nearby residents about the clientele's noise and hooliganism.

1961

An 18 February 1961 booking for the Beatles at the Cassanova Club, central Liverpool, was re-scheduled for the 28th, and their place was taken by Rory Storm and the Hurricanes.

The Beatles' 29 July 1961 appearance at Blair Hall in Walton was originally scheduled for Holyoake Hall in Wavertree.

A night-time booking at the Cavern Club on 5 September 1961 was cancelled.

Although dance promoter Lewis Buckley wrote to the Beatles in late-1961 and offered them engagements in Crewe and/or Northwich, Cheshire, it is certain that the group were unable to accommodate him. Buckley also approached other Liverpool groups like Rory Storm and the Hurricanes and had more success. The Beatles did play for Buckley, but not until Brian Epstein was established as their manager.

1962

A series of planned engagements for the Beatles in Chester in March 1962 was cancelled; it was another five months before the group made their début in the Cheshire city.

There is no evidence to support a claim that the Beatles played at the Kraal Club in New Brighton, Cheshire, in 1962. Most Liverpool rock groups played there but not the Beatles. Nor did they play at the Silver Blades Ice Rink in Prescot Road, central Liverpool, during 1962 or any other year, contrary to local rumour.

A number of the Beatles' Cavern Club bookings in 1962 were either postponed, cancelled or re-arranged:

Their 9 June "Welcome Home" night was originally planned for 6 June but was re-arranged because of their first recording session at EMI.

On 8 August they were excused a night-time booking so that they could play in Doncaster.

An advertised lunchtime booking for 21 August was switched to the following day at the request of Granada Television, which filmed them then.

On 29 August they were excused a night-time booking so that they could play in Morecambe.

A lunchtime booking on 5 September was switched to the 6th because the Beatles were still travelling home from London after the previous day's EMI recording session.

On 8 October they were excused a lunchtime booking so that they could travel to London to record for Radio Luxembourg.

On 23 November they were excused a lunchtime booking so that they could travel to London to audition for BBC Television.

On 2 December they were excused a night-time booking so that they could play in Peterborough.

The Beatles did not perform live in Nuneaton, Warwickshire, despite claims to that effect in the Beatles' first-ever press release, issued to promote 'Love Me Do'. The only beat venue in that town was the Co-operative Ballroom, and the promoter has confirmed that he never presented them.

The Beatles' 6 October 1962 Horticultural Society dance at Hulme Hall, Port Sunlight, was originally arranged to take place at the village's Golden Primrose Restaurant, Old Chester Road.

The Beatles were originally engaged to perform at the Jubilee Hall in Dukinfield, Cheshire, on 17 November 1962 but this was cancelled and they played instead in Coventry.

Brian Epstein's grand whole-page advertisement in *Mersey Beat* in December 1962 mentioned that the Beatles had played in Blackpool. This was not strictly true. The Beatles were provisionally booked for a short season in late-1962 at the Picador Club in Bloomfield Road, Blackpool, but this was cancelled by the manager of the club after what he perceived to be a poor appearance by the group on the Granada Television show *People And Places*. Epstein may, however, have been referring to the Beatles' 25 August booking in nearby Fleetwood.

The Beatles did not play at the Klic Klic Klub in Stanley Street, Southport, Lancashire, in 1962, despite local rumour to the contrary. The Klub actually opened for business on 12 January 1963, and even then the Beatles never played there.

1963

A provisional booking for the Beatles to appear at the Town Hall in Congleton, Cheshire, on 19 January 1963, never reached fruition, although rumours continued to circulate that they would do so at some point.

The Beatles were provisionally engaged to play at the Emporium Ballroom in Doncaster on 23 January 1963, but this was postponed and never re-arranged. Instead, the group performed at the Cavern on this night. (The Emporium Ballroom was a new name for Doncaster's Co-op Ballroom, played by the Beatles on 8 August 1962.)

The Beatles' 26 January 1963 show at the El Rio Club, Macclesfield, was originally booked for the previous Saturday, 19 January, but was re-arranged when Brian Epstein slotted in a visit to Whitchurch on that date.

The Beatles were provisionally engaged to perform at the Astoria Ballroom in Middlesbrough on 29 January 1963 but negotiations were never completed. Eden Kane entertained the Astoria clientele that night.

In late-January 1963 the promoters of Saturday-night beat music dances at Clipstone Welfare Hall in Mansfield, Nottinghamshire, included the Beatles' name in a newspaper advertisement listing their forthcoming attractions. But they were a little premature with their announcement since a contract had yet to be signed and the Beatles never did fulfil a booking there.

When the Beatles' February/March 1963 tour with Helen Shapiro was first announced, in November 1962, it included visits to the Gaumont Cinema in Hanley on 9 February and De Montfort Hall, Leicester, on 10 February. The Hanley concert was later re-arranged for 3 March, with the Empire Theatre, Sunderland, slotted in its place, while the plan for a Leicester concert was dropped altogether in favour of a show at the Embassy Cinema in promoter Arthur Howes' home town of Peterborough. (The Beatles didn't play at this concert anyway – refer to diary entry for 9 February 1963.)

The Beatles' 12 February 1963 engagement at the Azena Ballroom in Sheffield was originally booked to take place at St Aidan's Church Hall but local police advised that it should be moved to a venue which could safely contain the expected large turn-out.

Contrary to local rumour, the Beatles did not play at the Peppermint Lounge ballroom in central

Liverpool, which opened on 7 March 1963. They did play there in February 1961, however, when it was known as Sampson and Barlow's New Ballroom and as the Cassanova Club.

An agreement that the Beatles would play at the 1963 May Ball of Christ College, Oxford University, was scrapped when it was realised that it would interfere with the Beatles' holiday plans, which started on 28 April.

When the Beatles' May/June 1963 tour with Roy Orbison (originally Duane Eddy) was first announced, at the beginning of March, it included a 24 May visit to the Granada Cinema in Harrow, Middlesex, and a 30 May visit to the Granada Cinema in Kingston-upon-Thames, Surrey. Neither of these concerts took place, and the tour visited Walthamstow and Manchester on those dates. The Walthamstow booking had initially been set for 3 June, for which the Granada Cinema in Woolwich was inserted into the schedule.

The Beatles did not appear in Margate, Kent, on 18 June 1963, despite claims that they did. Nor did they appear at the Princess Theatre in Torquay, Devon, on 14 July 1963, as first announced in the music press in February. This was changed to 18 August to allow the Beatles to appear in Blackpool; Gerry and the Pacemakers fulfilled the Torquay date.

The 21 June 1963 concert at the Odeon Cinema, Guildford, was originally planned for the Dome Theatre, Brighton, Sussex.

A concert set for the ABC Cinema, Great Yarmouth, on 1 September 1963 was cancelled several weeks earlier to enable the Beatles to tape an appearance for the ABC Television show *Big Night Out*, transmitted on 7 September.

The 7 September 1963 concert at Fairfield Hall, Croydon, was originally arranged for the Broadway Cinema in Letchworth, Hertfordshire. Brian Epstein objected.

The Beatles' appearance at the (Victory) Memorial Hall in Northwich, Cheshire, on 14 September 1963 is often erroneously credited to the Civic Hall, Nantwich, Cheshire.

In February 1963, when promoter Arthur Howes first announced the Beatles' series of summer dates at seaside resorts, the list included three optional Sunday-night appearances at the Queen's Theatre in Blackpool, Lancashire, on 15, 22 and 29 September. These were cancelled to make way for a holiday period, although Brian Epstein did later accept an afternoon booking for the Beatles in London on 15 September.

A Beatles appearance planned for the Music Hall in Shrewsbury, Shropshire, on 18 October 1963 was cancelled soon after it was announced, in August.

1964

The Beatles did not appear live at the Empire Theatre, Liverpool, for a week's residency between 30 March and 6 April 1964. This engagement was cancelled soon after the initial press announcement in late-1963. Audiences at the Empire that week saw Frank Ifield instead.

The Beatles did not appear at the Futurist Theatre in Scarborough on 12 July 1964. Shortly after the initial press announcement the booking was re-arranged for 9 August. The Beatles played on 12 July at the Hippodrome Theatre in Brighton.

When the Beatles' August/September 1964 North American tour was first planned it did not

include the concerts in Indiana, Boston, Pittsburgh, Cleveland and, of course, Kansas City. The Coliseum, Seattle show on 21 August was, at that time, set for the Municipal Stadium; the Olympia Stadium, Detroit concert was planned for Cobo Hall; the Jacksonville concert on 11 September was lined up for either Gator Bowl or the Coliseum (the former was finally selected); and the charity show at the Paramount Theatre, New York, was at that early planning stage down to take place at the Metropolitan Opera. One show was scrapped altogether: a concert set for Colt Stadium, Houston, Texas, on 19 September. This date was eventually selected for rest at a Missouri ranch.

When the Beatles' October/November 1964 British tour was first announced, at the end of April, it included visits to the Odeon Cinemas in Hammersmith on 23 October, Lewisham on 24 October and Southend-on-Sea on 31 October. In mid-June these dates were re-arranged for Kilburn, Walthamstow and Ipswich respectively. The New Victoria Theatre in London had also been mooted as a venue for the 23 October show.

1965

The Beatles did not play a concert in Jerez de la Frontera, Spain, on 1 July 1965, despite frequent reports to the contrary. They visited the sherry city, but did not perform.

When the Beatles' August 1965 North American tour was first announced, at the beginning of February, the location of the concert on 20 August – Detroit or Chicago – was still undecided. The latter was eventually chosen. That first draft of the itinerary also detailed a concert in Mexico City, Mexico, on 28 August, later switched to the

southern California city of San Diego.

The Beatles played only one night at Shea Stadium, New York – on 15 August 1965. Common belief that they gave a second show there during this tour, on 16 August, is incorrect.

The Beatles' two London concerts, on 10 and 11 December 1965, were at one time mooted for the Royal Albert Hall and the Empire Pool, Wembley, respectively. The Odeon Cinema, Hammersmith, and the Astoria Cinema, Finsbury Park, were selected instead. The date of 6 December was kept free but tentatively set aside for a concert in either Leicester, Bristol or Leeds should promoter Arthur Howes have persuaded the Beatles to relent and perform that day. The Beatles didn't relent. The concert at the Gaumont Cinema in Sheffield on 8 December was originally scheduled for the nearby City Hall.

1966

When the Beatles' August 1966 North American tour was first announced, in April, the 14 August show was set for the State Fairgrounds, Louisville, Kentucky. It was later switched to Cleveland Stadium, Cleveland, Ohio. The group's 18 August Boston, Massachusetts concert, at Suffolk Downs Racetrack, was originally intended for the city's Fenway Park.

Again, the Beatles played only one night at Shea Stadium, New York, on the 1966 tour – on 23 August. Widely published reports erroneously state that they also played there on 24 August.

WHERE THEY PLAYED

This index cross-refers with the diary sections and Other Engagements Played appendix (abbreviated here to OEP) to list the venues for all live "concert" (but not audience radio or TV) performances played by the Beatles or solo members of the Beatles until April 1970.

The full postal address of a venue will be found under its first entry. A figure in parentheses indicates the number of separate dates this venue was played on a given page, if more than once; *p* indicates postponed, *c* cancelled.

Location	Venue	Pages
Wallasey: Liscard	Grosvenor Ballroom	27(2), 28(8), 29, 40, 41, 46
Wallasey: New Brighton	Tower Ballroom	48, 49(2), 50, 51(2), 63, 64(2), 66(4), 69, 71, 72, 73, 74(2), 75, 79(2), 80, 83, 84, 85, 112
West Kirby	Thistle Café	64
CUMBERLAND		
Carlisle	ABC Cinema	99, 130
DERBYSHIRE		
Buxton	Pavilion Gardens Ballroom	106, 125
DEVONSHIRE		
Exeter	ABC Cinema	104, 129, 176
Plymouth	ABC Cinema	129, 176
Torquay	Princess Theatre	119
DURHAM		
Stockton-on-Tees	Globe Cinema	130, 174
Sunderland	Empire Theatre	99, 130
	Rink Ballroom	109
ESSEX		
Romford	ABC Cinema	104
	Odeon Cinema	112
Southend-on-Sea	Odeon Cinema	111, 133
GLOUCESTERSHIRE		
Cheltenham	Odeon Cinema	127
Gloucester	Regal Cinema	104
Lydney	Town Hall	76
Stroud	Subscription Rooms	68, 76
HAMPSHIRE		
Aldershot	The Palais Ballroom	50
Bournemouth	Gaumont Cinema	119(6), 167, 176
	Winter Gardens Theatre	129
Portsmouth	Guildhall	105, 128p, 132
Portsmouth: Southsea	Savoy Ballroom	106
Southampton	Gaumont Cinema	110, 133, 176
KENT		
Chatham	Invicta Ballroom	96
Margate	Winter Gardens	116(6)
LANCASHIRE		
Blackburn	King George's Hall	112
Blackpool	ABC Theatre	116(2), 118, 119, 121
	Opera House	167, 168
	Queen's Theatre	117, 118
Bootle	St John's Hall	38, 39, 41, 66, 74
	St Luke's Church	OEP
Darwen	Co-operative Hall	98
Fleetwood	Marine Hall Ballroom	76
Leigh	Casino Ballroom	101
Liverpool	Cabaret Club	74
	The Cassanova Club (first)	OEP
	The Cassanova Club (second)	39, 40(3), 41(3)
	Cavern Club	14, 16, 39, 40, 41(4), 42(8), 43(13), 44(12), 45(8), 46(12), 47(8), 48(9), 49(16), 50, 51(13), 63(11), 64(10), 65(6), 66(12), 67(5), 68(14), 69(6), 70, 71(11), 72(7), 73(11), 74(12), 75(7), 76(6), 78(4), 79(9), 80(9), 81(6), 83(4), 84(3), 85(3), 86(5), 95, 96, 97(2), 98(4), 100 106, 118, OEP
	David Lewis Club	47
	Empire Theatre	14, 17(3), 82, 104, 111, 132, 135, 176, 209, 337

Location	Venue	Pages
	Grafton Rooms	74, 95, 112, 118, OEP
	Jacaranda Coffee Bar	27, 28, OEP
	Lewis's department store	84
	Liverpool College of Art	OEP
	Liverpool Jazz Society	41(2), 42(3)
	Locarno Ballroom	100, OEP
	Merseyside Civil Service Club	39, 48, 49(3)
	New Cabaret Artistes	OEP
	New Colony Club	OEP
	Odd Spot Club	68, 75
	Odeon Cinema	132
	Pavilion Theatre	69, OEP
	Rialto Ballroom	78, 80, OEP
	Rosebery Street	14
	MV Royal Iris	45, 73, 74, 80
	St Barnabas Church Hall	OEP
	Starline Club	OEP
	Storyville Jazz Club	66, 67, 68
Liverpool: Aintree	Aintree Institute	38(6), 39(3), 40(4), 41(4), 43(2), 44(4), 45(2), 46(3), 47, 49, 64
	Pavilion Theatre	OEP
Liverpool: (West) Allerton	Allerton Synagogue	OEP
Liverpool: Broadgreen	The Morgue Skiffle Cellar	16, OEP
Liverpool: Childwall	Childwall Labour Club	OEP
	Lee Park Golf Course	OEP
Liverpool: Crosby	Alexandra Hall	38
Liverpool: Croxteth	Mossway Hall	42
Liverpool: Edge Hill	Smithdown Lane	OEP
Liverpool: Ford	(venue not known)	OEP
Liverpool: Garston	Stevedors' and Dockers' Union Club	OEP
	Wilson Hall	15, 16(3), OEP
	Winter Gardens Ballroom	OEP
Liverpool: Gateacre	Gateacre Labour Club	OEP
Liverpool: Halewood	Village Hall	OEP
Liverpool: Huyton	Finch Lane bus depot	OEP
	Hambleton Hall	38, 39(2), 40(2), 41, 42, 44, 45, 46(2), 47, 49(2), 51, 63
Liverpool Knotty Ash	Village Hall	46(3), 47(2), 48, 49, 68
Liverpool: Litherland	St Anne's Club	OEP
	Town Hall	29, 38(2), 39, 40(3), 41(2), 43(3), 44, 46(4), 47, 48(2)
Liverpool: Maghull	Albany Cinema	46
Liverpool: Norris Green	New Clubmoor Hall (Conservative Club)	15(2), 16
Liverpool: Old Swan	Stanley Abattoir Social Club	15
Liverpool: Seaforth	Lathom Hall	26, 38(3), 39(6), 40
Liverpool: Speke	Upton Green	16
Liverpool: Tuebrook	St John's Hall	40, 41, 43(3), 44(4), 45, 46
Liverpool: Walton	Blair Hall	39, 43(4)
Liverpool: Wavertree	Holyoake Hall	43(2), OEP
	Picton Road bus depot	OEP
Liverpool: West Derby	Casbah Coffee Club	17(7), 29(2), 38, 39(2), 40(2), 41(2), 42(2), 44(2), 45, 46(2), 47, 49(3), 51, 63(2), 64(2), 65(2), 66(2), 67(2), 68(2), 69(3), 72
	Lowlands Club	OEP
	St Edward's College	OEP
Liverpool: Woolton	Quarry Bank High School	OEP
	St Peter's Parish Church	14, OEP
	Woolton Village Club	17

Location	Venue	Pages
Manchester	Embassy Club	OEP
	Oasis Club	65, 80, 86, 101
	Odeon Cinema	111
	Southern Sporting Club	112
	Three Coins Club	98, OEP
Manchester: Ardwick	ABC Cinema	129, 173, 209
	Hippodrome Theatre	17
Middleton	Co-operative Hall	106
Morecambe	Floral Hall Ballroom	76, 96
Nelson	Imperial Ballroom	109, 118
Newton-le-Willows: Earlestown	Town Hall	84
Oldham	Astoria Ballroom	100
Prescot	Prescot Cables Club	OEP
Preston	Public Hall	81, 122
St Helens	Plaza Ballroom	72, 73(3), 102
Southport	Cambridge Hall	74
	Floral Hall	66, 83, 109, 124
	Glenpark Club	OEP
	Kingsway Club	64(2), 65, 66, 67(2), 68, 74
	Odeon Cinema	101, 119(6)
	Queen's Hotel	85
Southport: Birkdale	ATC Club	OEP
Southport: High Park	Labour Club	OEP
Urmston	Abbotsfield Park	118
Warrington	Bell Hall	73
Widnes	Queen's Hall	76, 78, 79, 81, 100
Wigan	ABC Cinema	173
LEICESTERSHIRE		
Leicester	De Montfort Hall	105, 130, 173
LINCOLNSHIRE		
Lincoln	ABC Cinema	130
LONDON		
London	The Blue Gardenia Club	50
	Grosvenor House Hotel	131
	London Palladium Theatre	167
	Lyceum Ballroom	338
	Pigalle Club	108
	Prince of Wales Theatre	127, 160
	Royal Albert Hall	107, 122
London: East Ham	Granada Cinema	103, 128
London: Finsbury Park	Astoria Cinema	135(6), 142(10), 176, 209
	Majestic Ballroom	109
London: Hammersmith	Odeon Cinema	179(6), 183(14), 209
London: Kilburn	Gaumont State Cinema/Ballroom	106, 175
London: Lewisham	Odeon Cinema	104, 133
London: Leyton	Swimming Baths	106
London: Tooting	Granada Cinema	111
London: Walthamstow	Granada Cinema	110, 175
London: Wimbledon	Wimbledon Palais	133
London: Woolwich	Granada Cinema	112
MIDDLESEX		
Wembley	Empire Pool	108, 158, 188, 220
NORFOLK		
Great Yarmouth	ABC Cinema	114, 117
Norwich	Grosvenor Rooms	109
NORTHAMPTONSHIRE		
Northampton	ABC Cinema	104, 128
Peterborough	Embassy Cinema	84, 104
NORTHUMBERLAND		
Newcastle-upon-Tyne	City Hall	104, 112, 130, 209, 337
	Majestic Ballroom	98, 114
NOTTINGHAMSHIRE		
Mansfield	Granada Cinema	101, 104
Nottingham	Elizabethan Ballroom	103
	Odeon Cinema	110, 133, 176

OXFORDSHIRE
Oxford | Carfax Assembly Rooms | 100

SHROPSHIRE
Shrewsbury | Granada Cinema | 101
| Music Hall | 86, 109
Whitchurch | Town Hall | 96

SOMERSET
Bath | Pavilion | 112
Taunton | Gaumont Cinema | 101, 121
Weston-super-
Mare | Odeon Cinema | 117(6)

STAFFORDSHIRE
Hanley | Gaumont Cinema | 102, 110
Old Hill | Plaza Ballroom | 95, 116
Smethwick | Smethwick Baths
| Ballroom | 83
Stoke-on-Trent | King's Hall | 98, 108
Tamworth | Assembly Rooms | 98
Trentham | Trentham Gardens | 124
West Bromwich | Adelphi Ballroom | 83
Wolverhampton | Gaumont Cinema | 104, 129

SUFFOLK
Ipswich | Gaumont Cinema | 110, 176

SURREY
Croydon | Fairfield Hall | 109, 121, 338
Guildford | Odeon Cinema | 113
West Croydon | ABC Cinema | 104

SUSSEX
Brighton | Hippodrome Theatre | 112, 166, 175

WARWICKSHIRE
Birmingham | Hippodrome Theatre | 103, 128
| Odeon Cinema | 173, 209
| Town Hall | 112, 336
Birmingham:
King's Heath | Ritz Ballroom | 95p, 100
Coventry | Coventry Theatre | 101, 129
| Matrix Hall | 83
Sutton Coldfield | Maney Hall | 98

WILTSHIRE
Salisbury | City Hall | 112
Swindon | McIlroy's Ballroom | 73

WORCESTERSHIRE
Tenbury Wells | Bridge Hotel | 107
Worcester | Gaumont Cinema | 111, 121

YORKSHIRE
Bradford | Gaumont Cinema | 98, 135, 173
Doncaster | Co-op Ballroom | 74
| Gaumont Cinema | 98, 104, 133
| St James Street Baths | 100
Harrogate | The Royal Hall | 103
Huddersfield | ABC Cinema | 130
Hull | ABC Cinema | 130, 174
| Majestic Ballroom | 81, 100
Leeds | Odeon Cinema | 112, 127, 175
| Queen's Hall | 114
Middlesbrough | Astoria Ballroom | 114
Scarborough | Futurist Theatre | 133, 167
Sheffield | City Hall | 101, 104, 111, 127,

176, 337
| Gaumont Cinema | 209
Sheffield: Gleadless | Azena Ballroom | 100
Wakefield | Regal Cinema | 99
York | Rialto Theatre | 101, 103, 111, 130

UNITED KINGDOM: NORTHERN IRELAND
Belfast | King's Hall | 176
| Ritz Cinema | 128

UNITED KINGDOM: SCOTLAND
Aberdeen | Beach Ballroom | 95
Alloa | Town Hall | 26
Bridge of Allan | Museum Hall | 95
Dingwall | Town Hall | 95
Dundee | Caird Hall | 124, 175
Edinburgh | ABC Cinema | 159, 174
Elgin | Two Red Shoes Ballroom | 95
Forres | Town Hall | 27
Fraserburgh | Dalrymple Hall | 26
Glasgow | Concert Hall | 123
| Odeon Cinema | 112, 159, 175, 209
Inverness | Northern Meeting
| Ballroom | 26
Keith | Longmore Hall | 95c
| St Thomas' Hall | 27
Kirkcaldy | Carlton Theatre | 123
Nairn | Regal Ballroom | 27
Peterhead | Rescue Hall | 27

UNITED KINGDOM: WALES
Abergavenny | Town Hall | 113
Cardiff | Capitol Cinema | 111, 176, 209
Llandudno | Odeon Cinema | 118(6)
Mold | Assembly Hall | 97
Prestatyn | Royal Lido Ballroom | 84
Rhyl | Regent Dansette | 73
| Ritz Ballroom | 117(2)

UNITED STATES OF AMERICA (by state)
CALIFORNIA
Los Angeles | Dodger Stadium | 230
| Hollywood Bowl | 169, 201(2)
San Diego | Balboa Stadium | 201
San Francisco | Candlestick Park | 230
| Cow Palace | 168, 202

COLORADO
Denver | Red Rocks Amphitheatre | 170

DISTRICT OF COLUMBIA
Washington DC | DC Stadium | 229
| Washington Coliseum | 146

FLORIDA
Jacksonville | Gator Bowl | 171

GEORGIA
Atlanta | Atlanta Stadium | 200

ILLINOIS
Chicago | International
| Amphitheatre | 171, 228
| White Sox Park | 201

INDIANA
Indianapolis | Indiana State Fair
| Coliseum | 170

LOUISIANA
New Orleans | City Park Stadium | 171

MARYLAND
Baltimore | Civic Center | 171

MASSACHUSETTS
Boston | Boston Garden | 171
| Suffolk Downs Racetrack | 229

MICHIGAN
Detroit | Olympia Stadium | 171, 228

MINNESOTA
Minneapolis | Metropolitan Stadium | 201

MISSOURI
Kansas City | Municipal Stadium | 171
St Louis | Busch Stadium | 229

NEVADA
Las Vegas | Convention Center | 169

NEW JERSEY
Atlantic City | Convention Hall | 170

NEW YORK
New York | Carnegie Hall | 146
| Forest Hills Tennis
| Stadium | 170(2)
| Paramount Theatre | 172
| William A Shea Municipal
| Stadium [Shea Stadium] | 199, 229

OHIO
Cincinnati | Cincinnati Gardens | 170
| Crosley Field | 229
Cleveland | Cleveland Stadium | 229
| Public Auditorium | 171

OREGON
Portland | Memorial Coliseum | 201

PENNSYLVANIA
Philadelphia | Convention Hall | 170
| John F Kennedy Stadium | 229
Pittsburgh | Civic Arena | 171

TENNESSEE
Memphis | Mid-South Coliseum | 229

TEXAS
Dallas | Dallas Memorial
| Auditorium | 171
Houston | Sam Houston Coliseum | 200

WASHINGTON
Seattle | Coliseum | 169, 229

WISCONSIN
Milwaukee | Milwaukee Arena | 171

WEST GERMANY
Essen | Grugahalle | 227
Hamburg | Ernst Merck Halle | 227
| Indra Club | 28(48)
| Kaiserkeller | 28(58)
| Star-Club | 69(48), 83(14), 86(13)
| Top Ten Club | 42(92), OEP
Munich | Circus-Krone-Bau | 226

WHAT THEY PLAYED

This appendix is an attempt to catalogue, alphabetically, the Beatles' live performance repertoire, from their Quarry Men birth in 1957 via Johnny and the Moondogs, the Beatals, the Silver Beetles and the Silver Beatles, through to the Beatles and their decision in 1966 to cease giving concerts. The list is set out in this manner:

Song title | Beatles' singer, if known
Year(s) they performed this song live
Composer(s) | Influential recording artist
(year)

Although it is complete for the years 1964-66, the list is almost certainly incomplete for the period 1957-63. Additionally, while information in the section "Year(s) they performed this song live" is known to be correct for 1964 to 1966, prior to this – while logical judgement and every reliable source has been utilised – the year(s) given for certain songs may not be entirely accurate.

In most instances, Lennon-McCartney compositions are thus written. Relatively few of their songs were 50:50 collaborations, however, and where the identity of the main writer is known his name appears in upper case.

Act Naturally | Ringo
1965
Russell-Morrison | Buck Owens (1963)

Ain't She Sweet | John
1957, 1958, 1959, 1960, 1961, 1962
Yellen-Ager | [footnote]

Ain't That A Shame | ?
1958, 1959, 1960, 1961
Domino-Bartholomew | Fats Domino (1955)

All My Loving | Paul
1963, 1964
Lennon-McCARTNEY | —

All Over Again | ?
1960, 1961, 1962
Cash | Johnny Cash (1958)

All Shook Up | Paul
1957, 1958, 1959, 1960
Blackwell-Presley | Elvis Presley (1957)

Almost Grown | John?
1960, 1961, 1962
Berry | Chuck Berry (1959)

Anna (Go To Him) | John
1962, 1963
Alexander | Arthur Alexander (1962)

Apache (Instrumental)
1960
Lordan The Shadows (1960)

Are You Lonesome Tonight Paul?
1961
Turk-Handman Elvis Presley (1961)

Ask Me Why John
1962, 1963
LENNON-McCartney —

Baby Blue John?
1960, 1961, 1962
Vincent-Jones Gene Vincent and his Blue Caps
(1958)

Baby I Don't Care (You're So Square) ?
1960, 1961
Leiber-Stoller Elvis Presley(1957) or
Buddy Holly (1958)

Baby It's You John
1962, 1963
David-Bacharach-Williams The Shirelles (1961)

Baby Let's Play House ?
1960, 1961, 1962
Gunter Elvis Presley (1955)

Baby's In Black John/Paul
1964, 1965, 1966
Lennon-McCartney —

Bad Boy John
1960, 1961, 1962
Williams Larry Williams (1959)

Beautiful Dreamer Paul
1962, 1963
Foster Slim Whitman (1954)?

Be-Bop-A-Lula John
1957, 1958, 1959, 1960, 1961, 1962
Vincent-Davis Gene Vincent and his Blue
Caps (1956)

Begin The Beguine Paul?
1960
Porter Pat Boone (1957)

Besame Mucho Paul
1961, 1962
Velazquez-Skylar The Coasters (1960)

Better Luck Next Time ?
1960, 1961, 1962
Berlin June Christy (1957)?

Blue Moon Of Kentucky Paul
1957, 1958, 1959, 1960, 1961
Monroe Elvis Presley (1954)

Blue Suede Shoes John
1957, 1958, 1959, 1960, 1961, 1962
Perkins Carl Perkins (1956) and Elvis Presley
(1956)

Bony Moronie John
1957, 1958, 1959, 1960, 1961
Williams Larry Williams (1957)

Boppin' The Blues John
1959, 1960, 1961, 1962
Perkins-Griffin Carl Perkins (1956)

Boys Pete Best (1961-62); Ringo (1962-64)
1961, 1962, 1963, 1964
Dixon-Farrell The Shirelles (1960)

Bring It On Home To Me ?
1962
Cooke Sam Cooke (1962)

Buzz Buzz A Diddle-It ?
1961, 1962
Slay-Crewe Freddy Cannon (1961)

Can't Believe You Wanna Leave ?
1960, 1961, 1962
Price Little Richard (1957) or Gene Vincent and
his Blue Caps (1959)

Can't Buy Me Love Paul
1964, 1965
Lennon-McCARTNEY —

Carol John
1960, 1961, 1962
Berry Chuck Berry (1958)

Cathy's Clown ?
1960, 1961, 1962
Everly-Everly The Everly Brothers (1960)

Catswalk (Instrumental)
1958, 1959, 1960, 1961, 1962
McCartney [footnote]

Chains John/Paul/George
1963
Goffin-King The Cookies (1962)

Clarabella Paul
1960, 1961, 1962
Pingatore The Jodimars (1956)

C'mon Everybody ?
1959, 1960, 1961, 1962
Cochran-Capehart Eddie Cochran (1959)

Come Go With Me John
1957, 1958, 1959
Quick The Del-Vikings (1957)

Coquette ?
1960, 1961
Lombardo-Green-Kahn Fats Domino (1958)

Corrine, Corrina ?
1960, 1961, 1962
Trad arr McCoy-Chatman- Williams-Parish
Lonnie Donegan (1960)

Crackin' Up Paul
1960, 1961
McDaniel Bo Diddley (1959)

Cry For A Shadow (Instrumental)
1961
Lennon-Harrison —

Crying, Waiting, Hoping George
1960, 1961, 1962
Holly Buddy Holly (1959)

The Cumberland Gap John
1957, 1958, 1959
Traditional Lonnie Donegan and his Skiffle Group
(1957)

Dance In The Street ?
1960, 1961, 1962
Davis-Welch Gene Vincent and his Blue Caps
(1958)

Darktown Strutters Ball George
1960, 1961, 1962
Brooks Joe Brown and the Bruvvers (1960)

Day Tripper John/Paul
1965, 1966
LENNON-McCartney —

(There's A) Devil In Her Heart George
1962, 1963
Drapkin The Donays (1962) [footnote]

Diamonds (Instrumental)
1963
Lordan Jet Harris and Tony Meehan (1963)

Dizzy Miss Lizzy John
1960, 1961, 1962, 1965
Williams Larry Williams (1958)

Do You Want To Dance John
1959, 1960, 1961, 1962
Freeman Bobby Freeman (1958)

Do You Want To Know A Secret George
1963
LENNON-McCartney —

Don't Be Cruel (To A Heart Paul?
That's True)
1959, 1960, 1961
Blackwell-Presley Elvis Presley (1956)

Don't Ever Change George
1962
Goffin-King The Crickets (1962)

Don't Forbid Me Paul
1960, 1961
Singleton Pat Boone (1957)

Don't Let The Sun Catch You Crying Paul
1960
Greene Ray Charles (1960) [footnote]

Down The Line ?
1960, 1961, 1962
Orbison Jerry Lee Lewis (1958)

Dream George
1962
Miller Cliff Richard and the Shadows (1961)

Dream Baby (How Long Paul
Must I Dream?)
1962
Walker Roy Orbison (1962)

España Cañi (Spanish (Instrumental)
Gypsy Dance)
1960
Marquina ? (first recorded 1951)

Everybody's Trying To Be George
My Baby
1961, 1962, 1964, 1965
Perkins Carl Perkins (1958)

Everyday ?
1957, 1958, 1959, 1960, 1961, 1962
Hardin-Petty Buddy Holly and the Crickets (1957)

Falling In Love Again (Can't Help It) Paul
1961, 1962
Hollander Marlene Dietrich (1930)

A Fool For You ?
1960, 1961, 1962
Charles Ray Charles (1959)

Fool Number One ?
1961, 1962
Fulton Brenda Lee (1961)

Fools Like Me John
1960, 1961, 1962
Clement-Maddux Jerry Lee Lewis (1959)

Freight Train John
1957, 1958, 1959
Trad arr Cotten or Trad arr James-Williams
Chas McDevitt Skiffle Group
featuring Nancy Whiskey (1957)

From Me To You John/Paul
1963, 1964
Lennon-McCartney —

Glad All Over George
1960, 1961, 1962
Schroeder-Tepper-Bennett Carl Perkins (1957)
[footnote]

Gone, Gone, Gone ?
1960, 1961, 1962
Perkins Carl Perkins (1959)

Good Golly Miss Molly Paul
1960, 1961
Blackwell-Marascalco Little Richard (1958)

Good Rockin' Tonight ?
1958, 1959, 1960, 1961, 1962
Brown Elvis Presley (1954)

Great Balls Of Fire ?
1960, 1961
Hammer-Blackwell Jerry Lee Lewis (1957)

Guitar Boogie (Instrumental)
1957, 1958, 1959
Smith Arthur Smith and his Crackerjacks (1946)

Hallelujah I Love Her So Paul
1960, 1961, 1962
Charles Ray Charles (1956) and Eddie
Cochran (1960)

A Hard Day's Night John
1964, 1965
LENNON-McCartney —

Harry Lime (Instrumental)
(*Third Man* Theme)
1960
Karas Anton Karas (1949) [footnote]

Heartbreak Hotel ?
1957, 1958, 1959, 1960, 1961
Axton-Durden-Presley Elvis Presley (1956)

Heavenly ?
1960, 1961
Twitty-Nance Conway Twitty (1959) or Emile
Ford and the Checkmates (1960)

Hello Little Girl John
1957, 1958, 1959, 1960, 1961, 1962
LENNON-McCartney —

Help! John
1965
LENNON-McCartney —

Hey Ba-Ba-Re-Bop Paul
1960, 1961
Hamner-Hampton Lionel Hampton and
his Orchestra (1946)

Hey! Baby Paul
1962
Channel-Cobb Bruce Channel (1962)

Hey, Good Lookin' John?
1960, 1961, 1962
Williams Gene Vincent and his Blue Caps
(1958)

Hey Let's Twist Paul?
1962
Glover-Dee-Levy Joey Dee and the Starliters
(1962)

High School Confidential Paul
1958, 1959, 1960, 1961
Lewis-Hargrave Jerry Lee Lewis (1958)

The Hippy Hippy Shake Paul
1961, 1962, 1963
Romero Chan Romero (1959)

(Marie's The Name Of) His Latest Flame ?
1961, 1962
Pomus-Shuman Elvis Presley (1961)

Hit The Road Jack ?
1961, 1962
Mayfield Ray Charles (1961)

Hold Me Tight Paul
1961, 1962, 1963
Lennon-McCARTNEY —

Home ?
1957, 1958, 1959, 1960
Van Steeden-Clarkson-Clarkson [footnote]

Honey Don't John (1962-64);
Ringo (1964-65)
1962, 1963, 1964, 1965
Perkins Carl Perkins (1956)

Honey Hush ?
1960
Turner   Joe Turner (1953) or Johnny Burnette
and the Rock 'n' Roll Trio (1957)

The Honeymoon Song Paul
1960, 1961, 1962
Theodorakis-Sansom   Marino Marini and his
Quartet (1959)

Honky Tonk Blues John
1957, 1958, 1959
Williams   Hank Williams (1952)

Hot As Sun (Instrumental)
1957, 1958, 1959
McCartney   —

Hound Dog John
1957, 1958, 1959, 1960, 1961
Leiber-Stoller   Elvis Presley (1956)

A House With Love In It ?
1960, 1961
Lippman-Dee   Vera Lynn (1956)?

How Do You Do It John
1962
Murray   [footnote]

How High The Moon Paul?
1960, 1961
Lewis-Hamilton   Les Paul with Mary Ford (1951)

(Baby) Hully Gully John
1960, 1961, 1962
Smith-Goldsmith   The Olympics (1959)

I Fancy Me Chances John/Paul
1962
Lennon-McCartney   —

I Feel Fine John
1964, 1965, 1966
LENNON-McCartney   —

I Feel So Bad Paul
1961, 1962
Willis   Elvis Presley (1961)

I Forgot To Remember To Forget George
1960, 1961, 1962
Kesler-Feathers   Elvis Presley (1955)

I Got A Woman John
1960, 1961, 1962
Charles-Richards   Elvis Presley (1956)

I Got To Find My Baby John
1961, 1962
Berry   Chuck Berry (1960)

I Just Don't Understand John
1961, 1962
Wilkin-Westberry   Ann-Margret (1961)

I Know ?
1959, 1960, 1961
Domino-Bartholomew   Fats Domino (1955)

I Lost My Little Girl Paul
1957, 1958, 1959
Lennon-McCARTNEY   —

I Remember ?
1960, 1961
Cochran-Capehart   Eddie Cochran (1959)

I Remember You Paul
1962
Mercer-Schertzinger   Frank Ifield (1962)

I Saw Her Standing There Paul
1962, 1963, 1964
Lennon-McCARTNEY   —

I Should Have Known Better John
1964
LENNON-McCartney   —

I Wanna Be Your Man Ringo
1963, 1964, 1965, 1966
Lennon-McCartney   —

I Want To Hold Your Hand John/Paul
1963, 1964
Lennon-McCartney   —

I Will Always Be In Love With You John
1960, 1961
Ruby-Green-Stept   Fats Domino (1960)?

I Wish I Could Shimmy John
Like My Sister Kate
1961, 1962
Piron   The Olympics (1961)

I Wonder If I Care As Much ?
1959, 1960, 1961
Everly-Everly   The Everly Brothers (1957)

I'll Be On My Way Paul/John
1961, 1962
Lennon-McCARTNEY   —

I'll Follow The Sun Paul
1959, 1960, 1961
Lennon-McCARTNEY   —

I'll Never Let You Go (Little Darlin') ?
1960, 1961, 1962
Autry-Wakely   Elvis Presley (1958)

I'm A Loser John
1964, 1965
LENNON-McCartney   —

I'm Down Paul
1965, 1966
Lennon-McCARTNEY   —

I'm Gonna Be A Wheel Someday Paul
1960, 1961
Bartholomew-Hayes-Domino   Fats Domino (1959)

I'm Gonna Sit Right Down John
And Cry (Over You)
1960, 1961, 1962, 1963
Thomas-Biggs   Elvis Presley (1956)

I'm Happy Just To Dance With You George
1964
LENNON-McCartney   —

I'm Henry The Eighth I Am George
1961, 1962
Murray-Weston   Joe Brown and the Bruvvers
(1961)

I'm In Love Again Paul
1960, 1961
Domino-Bartholomew   Fats Domino (1956)

I'm Talking About You John
1962
Berry   Chuck Berry (1961)

If I Fell John/Paul
1964
LENNON-McCartney   —

If I Needed Someone George
1965, 1966
Harrison   —

If You Gotta Make A Fool Paul
Of Somebody
1962
Clark   James Ray (1961)

In Spite Of All The Danger John
1958, 1959
McCartney-Harrison   —

It'll Be Me ?
1959, 1960, 1961
Clement   Jerry Lee Lewis (1957)

It's A Long Way To Tipperary ?
1960
Judge-Williams   Traditional

It's Now Or Never Paul
1960, 1961, 1962
DiCapua-Schroeder-Gold-Capurro   Elvis Presley
(1960)

It's So Easy ?
1958, 1959, 1960, 1961, 1962
Holly-Petty   Buddy Holly and the Crickets (1958)

Jailhouse Rock John
1958, 1959, 1960
Leiber-Stoller   Elvis Presley (1958)

Jambalaya (On The Bayou) ?
1960, 1961
Williams   Hank Williams (1952) or Jerry Lee
Lewis (1959)

Johnny B Goode John
1958, 1959, 1960, 1961, 1962
Berry   Chuck Berry (1958)

Just Because Paul
1960, 1961
Shelton-Shelton-Robin   Elvis Presley (1956)
[footnote]

Just Fun ?
1957, 1958, 1959
Lennon-McCartney   —

Kansas City/Hey-Hey-Hey-Hey! Paul
1961, 1962, 1964
Leiber-Stoller/Penniman   Little Richard (1959)
[footnote]

Keep Looking That Way ?
1957, 1958, 1959
Lennon-McCartney   —

Keep Your Hands Off My Baby John
1963
Goffin-King   Little Eva (1963)

Lawdy Miss Clawdy ?
1957, 1958, 1959, 1960, 1961, 1962
Price   Elvis Presley (1956)

Lazy River John
1959, 1960, 1961
Carmichael-Arodin   Gene Vincent and his Blue Caps
(1956)

Leave My Kitten Alone John
1961, 1962
John-Turner-McDougal   Johnny Preston (1961)

Lend Me Your Comb John/Paul
1957, 1958, 1959, 1960, 1961, 1962
Twomey-Wise-Weisman   Carl Perkins (1957)

Let's Stomp ?
1963
Goldstein-Feldman-Gottehrer   Bobby Comstock (1963)

Like Dreamers Do Paul
1957, 1958, 1959, 1960, 1961, 1962
Lennon-McCARTNEY   —

Little Queenie Paul
1960, 1961, 1962, 1963
Berry   Chuck Berry (1959)

Livin' Lovin' Wreck ?
1961, 1962
Blackwell   Jerry Lee Lewis (1961)

The Loco–Motion ?
1962, 1963
Goffin-King   Little Eva (1962)

Lonesome Tears In My Eyes John
1961, 1962
Burnette-Burnette-Burlison-Mortimer   The Johnny
Burnette Trio (1956)

Long Tall Sally Paul
1957, 1958, 1959, 1960, 1961, 1962, 1963, 1964,
1965, 1966
Johnson-Penniman-Blackwell   Little Richard (1956)

Looking Glass (Instrumental)
1957, 1958, 1959
Lennon-McCartney   —

Love Is A Swingin' Thing ?
1962
Owens-Dixon   The Shirelles (1962)

Love Love Love George?
1961
McRae-Wyche-David   Bobby Vee (1961)

Love Me Do Paul
1962, 1963
Lennon-McCARTNEY   —

Love Me Tender Stuart Sutcliffe
1960, 1961
Presley-Matson   Elvis Presley (1956)

Love Of My Life ?
1960, 1961, 1962
Bryant-Bryant   The Everly Brothers (1959)

Love Of The Loved Paul
1960, 1961, 1962
Lennon-McCARTNEY   —

Loving You Stuart Sutcliffe
1959, 1960
Leiber-Stoller   Elvis Presley (1957)

Lucille Paul
1957, 1958, 1959, 1960, 1961, 1962
Penniman-Collins   Little Richard (1957)

Maggie May John
1957, 1958, 1959
Traditional   The Vipers Skiffle Group (1957)

Mailman Blues ?
1957, 1958, 1959
Price   Lloyd Price (1954)

Mailman, Bring Me No More Blues ?
1961, 1962
Roberts-Katz-Clayton   Buddy Holly and the Crickets
(1957)

Main Title Theme (Instrumental)
(*The Man With The Golden Arm*)
1962
Bernstein   Jet Harris (1962)

Mama Said ?
1962
Dixon-Denson   The Shirelles (1961)

Matchbox Pete Best(1960-62); John (1962)
1960, 1961, 1962
Perkins   Carl Perkins (1957)

Maybe Baby ?
1958, 1959, 1960, 1961
Holly-Petty   Buddy Holly and the Crickets (1958)

Maybellene John
1959, 1960, 1961
Berry-Freed-Fratto   Chuck Berry (1955)

Mean Woman Blues ?
1957, 1958, 1959, 1960, 1961, 1962
De Metruis   Jerry Lee Lewis (1957) or
Elvis Presley (1957)

Memphis, Tennessee John
1960, 1961, 1962
Berry   Chuck Berry (1959)

Midnight Shift ?
1960, 1961, 1962
Lee-Ainsworth   Buddy Holly and the Crickets (1956)

Midnight Special (Prisoner's Song) ?
1957, 1958, 1959, 1960
Traditional   Lonnie Donegan and his Skiffle
Group (1957)

Mighty Man ?
1961, 1962
Jones   Davy Jones (1960)

Misery John/Paul
1963
Lennon-McCartney —

Miss Ann Paul
1960, 1961
Johnson-Penniman Little Richard (1956)

Money (That's What I Want) John
1960, 1961, 1962, 1963, 1964
Gordy-Bradford Barret Strong (1959)

Moonglow And The Theme From *Picnic* ?
1957, 1958, 1959, 1960
Hudson-De Lange-Mills-Duning-Allen
The McGuire Sisters (1956)?

More Than I Can Say ?
1961, 1962
Allison-Curtis The Crickets (1960) or
Bobby Vee (1961)

Movin' And Groovin' (Instrumental)
1959, 1960
Hazlewood-Eddy Duane Eddy and the
Rebels (1959)

Mr Moonlight John
1962, 1963
Johnson Dr Feelgood and the Interns (1962)

My Bonnie Lies Over The Ocean John
1962
Trad arr Sheridan Tony Sheridan and the Beatles
(1961) [footnote]

Mystery Train John
1957, 1958, 1959
Parker-Phillips Elvis Presley (1955)

New Orleans ?
1961
Guida-Royster [Gary] US Bonds (1961)

No Other Baby John
1958, 1959
Bishop-Watson The Vipers Skiffle Group (1958)

Nobody But You ?
1962
Bonner-Bonarrigo The Lafayettes (1962)

Nothin' Shakin' (But The Leaves George
On The Trees)
1960, 1961, 1962
Colacrai-Fontaine-Lampert-Cleveland
Eddie Fontaine (1958)

Nowhere Man John
1965, 1966
LENNON-McCartney —

The One After 909 John
1957, 1958, 1959, 1960, 1961, 1962
LENNON-McCartney —

One Track Mind ?
1961, 1962
Rene-Lewis Bobby Lewis (1961)

Ooh! My Soul Paul
1960, 1961, 1962, 1963
Penniman Little Richard (1958)

Open (Your Lovin' Arms) George
1962
Knox Buddy Knox (1962)

Over The Rainbow John
1960, 1961, 1962
Harburg-Arlen Gene Vincent and his
Blue Caps (1959)

Paperback Writer Paul
1966
Lennon-McCARTNEY —

Party John
1957, 1958, 1959, 1960
Robinson Elvis Presley (1957) [footnote]

Peaches And Cream John
1960, 1961
Williams Larry Williams (1959)

Peanut Butter John
1961, 1962
Barnum-Cooper-Smith-Goldsmith
The Marathons (1961)

Peggy Sue John
1957, 1958, 1959, 1960, 1961, 1962
Holly-Allison-Petty Buddy Holly (1957)

Peppermint Twist Pete Best
1962
Dee-Glover Joey Dee and the Starliters (1962)

A Picture Of You George
1962
Beveridge-Oakman Joe Brown and the
Bruvvers (1962)

Pinwheel Twist Paul
1962
Lennon-McCARTNEY —

Please Mister Postman John
1961, 1962
Holland-Bateman-Gorman-Dobbins-Garrett
The Marvelettes (1961)

Please Please Me John/Paul
1962, 1963, 1964
LENNON-McCartney —

PS I Love You Paul
1962, 1963
Lennon-McCARTNEY —

Quarter To Three ?
1961, 1962
Barge-Guida-Anderson [Gary] US Bonds (1961)

Railroad Bill John
1957, 1958, 1959, 1960, 1961
Traditional Lonnie Donegan and his
Skiffle Group (1956)

Raining In My Heart Paul?
1959, 1960, 1961, 1962
Bryant-Bryant Buddy Holly (1959)

Ramrod (Instrumental)
1958, 1959, 1960
Casey Duane Eddy and the Rebels (1958)

Raunchy (Instrumental)
1958, 1959, 1960
Justis-Manker Bill Justis and his Orchestra
(1957)

Ready Teddy John
1959, 1960, 1961
Blackwell-Marascalco Little Richard (1956)

Red Hot John
1961, 1962
Emerson Ronnie Hawkins (1959)

Red Sails In The Sunset Paul
1960, 1961, 1962
Kennedy-Williams Joe Turner (1959) or Emile
Ford and the Checkmates (1960)

Reelin' And Rockin' ?
1960, 1961
Berry Chuck Berry (1958)

Reminiscing George
1962, 1963
Curtis Buddy Holly (1962)

Rip It Up John
1959, 1960, 1961
Blackwell-Marascalco Little Richard (1956)

Road Runner ?
1961, 1962
McDaniel Bo Diddley (1960)

Rock And Roll Music John
1959, 1960, 1961, 1962, 1963, 1964, 1965, 1966
Berry Chuck Berry (1957)

Rock Island Line John
1957, 1958, 1959
Ledbetter Lonnie Donegan and his Skiffle Group
(1954)

Roll Over Beethoven John (1957-61);
George (1961-64)
1957, 1958, 1959, 1960, 1961, 1962, 1963, 1964
Berry Chuck Berry (1956)

Runaway ?
1961, 1962
Shannon-Crook Del Shannon (1961)

San Francisco Bay Blues George
1960, 1961
Fuller Ramblin' Jack Elliott (1960)

Save The Last Dance For Me John
1961, 1962
Pomus-Shuman The Drifters (1960)

Say Mama John
1960, 1961
Meeks-Earl Gene Vincent and his
Blue Caps (1959)

Searchin' Paul
1957, 1958, 1959, 1960, 1961, 1962
Leiber-Stoller The Coasters (1957)

Send Me Some Lovin' John
1959, 1960, 1961, 1962
Marascalco-Blackwell Little Richard (1957)

September In The Rain Paul
1961, 1962
Dubin-Warren Dinah Washington (1961)

September Song ?
1960
Anderson-Weill Johnny Ray (1959)?

Shakin' All Over ?
1960, 1961
Heath Johnny Kidd and the Pirates (1960)

Sharing You George
1962
Goffin-King Bobby Vee (1962)

She Loves You John/Paul
1963, 1964
Lennon-McCartney —

She's A Woman Paul
1964, 1965, 1966
Lennon-McCARTNEY —

The Sheik Of Araby George
1961, 1962
Smith-Snyder-Wheeler Joe Brown and the
Bruvvers (1961)

Sheila George
1962, 1963
Roe Tommy Roe (1962)

Shimmy Shimmy John/Paul
1960, 1961, 1962
Massey-Schubert Bobby Freeman (1960)

Short Fat Fanny John
1958, 1959, 1960, 1961
Williams Larry Williams (1957)

A Shot Of Rhythm And Blues John
1962
Thompson Arthur Alexander (1962)

Shout John/Paul/George
1960, 1961
Isley-Isley-Isley The Isley Brothers (1959)

Slow Down John
1960, 1961, 1962
Williams Larry Williams (1958)

So How Come (No One Loves Me) George
1961, 1962
Bryant The Everly Brothers (1960)

Soldier Of Love John
(Lay Down Your Arms)
1962
Cason-Moon Arthur Alexander (1962)

Some Other Guy John/Paul
1962, 1963
Leiber-Stoller-Barrett Ritchie Barrett (1962)

Stand By Me John
1961, 1962
King-Leiber-Stoller Ben E King (1961)

Stay ?
1960, 1961, 1962
Williams Maurice Williams and the Zodiacs (1960)

Sticks And Stones ?
1960, 1961
Turner Ray Charles (1960)

Summertime ?
1958, 1959, 1960, 1961
Gershwin Gene Vincent and his Blue Caps (1958)

Sure To Fall (In Love With You) Paul
1957, 1958, 1959, 1960, 1961, 1962
Perkins-Claunch-Cantrell Carl Perkins (1956)

Sweet Little Sixteen John
1957, 1958, 1959, 1960, 1961, 1962
Berry Chuck Berry (1956)

Take Good Care Of My Baby George
1961, 1962
Goffin-King Bobby Vee (1961)

A Taste Of Honey Paul
1962, 1963
Marlow-Scott Lenny Welch (1962)

Teenage Heaven ?
1960, 1961
Cochran-Capehart Eddie Cochran (1959)

Tennessee John
1957, 1958, 1959, 1960, 1961
Perkins Carl Perkins (1956)

Tequila (Instrumental)
1959, 1960
Rio The Champs (1958)

Thank You Girl John/Paul
1963
Lennon-McCartney —

That'll Be The Day John
1957, 1958, 1959, 1960
Holly-Allison-Petty Buddy Holly and
the Crickets (1957)

That's All Right (Mama) Paul
1957, 1958, 1959, 1960, 1961, 1962
Crudup Elvis Presley (1954)

That's My Woman ?
1957, 1958, 1959
Lennon-McCartney

That's When Your Heartaches Begin Paul
1959, 1960, 1961
Fisher-Raskin-Hill Elvis Presley (1957)

There's A Place John
1963
LENNON-McCartney —

There's No One In The Whole ?
Wide World
1962
Pavey-Schroeder Jackie Lee and the
Raindrops (1962)

Things We Said Today Paul
1964
Lennon-McCARTNEY

Think It Over ?
1958, 1959, 1960, 1961, 1962
Holly-Allison-Petty Buddy Holly and the
Crickets (1958)

Thinking Of Linking ?
1957, 1958, 1959
Lennon-McCartney —

Thirty Days John
1960, 1961
Berry Chuck Berry (1955) [footnote]

This Boy John/Paul/George
1963, 1964
LENNON-McCartney —

Three Cool Cats George
1959, 1960, 1961, 1962, 1963
Leiber-Stoller The Coasters (1959)

Three Steps To Heaven ?
1960, 1961, 1962
Cochran Eddie Cochran (1960)

Three–Thirty Blues (Instrumental)
1960, 1961
Hazlewood-Eddy Duane Eddy and the
Rebels (1959)

Thumbin' A Ride Paul
1961, 1962
Leiber-Stoller The Coasters (1961)

Ticket To Ride John
1965
LENNON-McCartney —

Till There Was You Paul
1961, 1962, 1963, 1964
Willson Peggy Lee (1961)

Time ?
1961, 1962
Kaye-Springer Craig Douglas (1961)

Time Will Bring You Everything John?
1960, 1961, 1962
Vincent-Peak Gene Vincent and
his Blue Caps (1958)

Tip Of My Tongue Paul
1962
Lennon-McCARTNEY —

To Know Her Is To Love Her John
1960, 1961, 1962
Spector The Teddy Bears (1958) [footnote]

Tonight Is So Right For Love ?
1960, 1961, 1962
Wayne-Silver Elvis Presley (1960)

Too Bad About Sorrows ?
1957, 1958, 1959
Lennon-McCartney —

Too Much Monkey Business John
1960, 1961, 1962
Berry Chuck Berry (1956)

True Love ?
1960
Porter Bing Crosby and Grace Kelly (1956)
or Elvis Presley (1957)

Tutti Frutti Paul
1960, 1961, 1962
Penniman-LaBostrie Little Richard (1957)

Twenty Flight Rock Paul
1957, 1958, 1959, 1960, 1961, 1962
Cochran-Fairchild Eddie Cochran (1957)

Twist And Shout John
1962, 1963, 1964, 1965
Russell-Medley The Isley Brothers (1962)

Vacation Time ?
1960, 1961
Berry Chuck Berry (1958)

Walk Don't Run (Instrumental)
1960, 1961
Smith The Ventures (1960)

Walk Right In Paul?
1963
Cannon-Woods-Darling-Svanoe The Rooftop
Singers (1963)

Watch Your Step John ?
1961, 1962
Parker Bobby Parker (1961)

The Wayward Wind ?
1960, 1961
Lebowsky-Newman Gene Vincent and his
Blue Caps (1958)

We Can Work It Out Paul
1965
Lennon-McCARTNEY —

Wedding Bells John?
1960, 1961
Fain-Kahal-Raskin Gene Vincent and his
Blue Caps (1957)

Weep No More My Baby ?
1960, 1961
Arnette-O'Dell-Murphy-Paterno Johnny Kidd
and the Pirates (1960)

Well... (Baby Please Don't Go) John
1960, 1961, 1962
Ward The Olympics (1958)

What A Crazy World George
We're Living In
1962
Klein Joe Brown and the Bruvvers (1962)

What'd I Say Paul
1960, 1961, 1962
Charles Ray Charles (1959)

When ?
1958
Reardon-Evans The Kalin Twins (1958)

When I'm Sixty–Four Paul
1960, 1961, 1962
Lennon-McCARTNEY —

When My Little Girl Is Smiling ?
1962
Goffin-King The Drifters (1962)

When The Saints Go Marching In ?
1958, 1959, 1962
Traditional Jerry Lee Lewis (1958) or
Fats Domino (1959) [footnote]

Where Have You Been All My Life? John
1962
Mann-Weil Arthur Alexander (1962)

Whole Lotta Shakin' Goin' On ?
1957, 1958, 1959, 1960, 1961, 1962
Williams-David Jerry Lee Lewis (1957)

Wild Cat Paul
1960, 1961
Schroeder-Gold Gene Vincent and his
Blue Caps (1959)

Wild In The Country Pete Best
1961, 1962
Peretti-Creatore-Weiss Elvis Presley (1961)

Will You Love Me Tomorrow? John
1961, 1962
Goffin-King The Shirelles (1961)

Winston's Walk (Instrumental)
1957, 1958, 1959
Lennon-McCartney —

Wooden Heart Paul
1961, 1962
Twomey-Wise-Weisman-Kaempfert
Elvis Presley (1960) [footnote]

Words Of Love John/George
1958, 1959, 1960, 1961, 1962
Holly Buddy Holly (1957)

The World Is Waiting John/Paul
For The Sunrise
1960
Lockhart-Seitz Les Paul with Mary Ford (1953)

Worried Man Blues John
1957, 1958, 1959
Traditional Lonnie Donegan and his Skiffle Group
(1955) or The Vipers Skiffle Group
(1957) [footnote]

Ya Ya John
1961, 1962
Robinson-Lewis-Dorsey Lee Dorsey (1961)

Yakety Yak ?
1960
Leiber-Stoller The Coasters (1958)

Years Roll Along ?
1957, 1958, 1959
Lennon-McCartney —

Yesterday Paul
1965, 1966
Lennon-McCARTNEY —

You Are My Sunshine ?
1960
Davis-Mitchell ?

You Can't Do That John
1964
LENNON-McCartney —

You Don't Know What You Got ?
1961
Hampton-Burton Ral Donner (1961)

You Don't Understand Me John
1960, 1961, 1962
Massey Bobby Freeman (1960)

You Really Got A Hold On Me John
1962, 1963
Robinson [Smokey Robinson and] The Miracles
(1962)

You Were Meant For Me ?
1957, 1958, 1959, 1960
Freed-Brown ?

You Win Again John
1958, 1959, 1960, 1961
Williams Hank Williams (1952) or
Jerry Lee Lewis (1958)

Youngblood George
1958, 1959, 1960, 1961, 1962
Leiber-Stoller-Pomus The Coasters (1957)

Your Feet's Too Big Paul
1961, 1962
Benson-Fisher Fats Waller (1939) or
Chubby Checker (1961)

Your True Love George
1958, 1959, 1960, 1961, 1962
Perkins Carl Perkins (1957)

Footnotes:

AIN'T SHE SWEET
The version most likely to have prompted the Beatles' performance of this song would be Gene Vincent and his Blue Caps' 1956 recording. But since John's vocal rendition was different from Vincent's, it would seem that he arranged his own, unique version. He may have also been influenced by Duffy Power's 1959 recording.

CATSWALK
When this was first released on record, in 1967 by the Chris Barber Band, it was re-titled 'Catcall'.

(THERE'S A) DEVIL IN HER HEART
The Donays were an all-girl group so this was originally '(There's A) Devil In His Heart'.

DON'T LET THE SUN CATCH YOU CRYING
This is not the song taken into the charts by Gerry and the Pacemakers in 1964.

GLAD ALL OVER
This is not the song taken into the charts by the Dave Clark Five in 1963.

HARRY LIME (THIRD MAN THEME)
Chet Atkins, a favourite of the Beatles, and George in particular, released a version of this in July 1960 which may have led them to perform it after this date.

HOME
The Mills Brothers released a version of this in June 1960, which may have influenced the Beatles, although they also performed it before this date.

HOW DO YOU DO IT
This is the Mitch Murray composition that so nearly became the Beatles' début single. Though they made their dislike for it clear at EMI, the Beatles are known to have performed the song in live appearances for a short time in the summer of 1962, a few months before Gerry and the Pacemakers took their recording to number one.

JUST BECAUSE
This composition has no relation to the Lloyd Price song of the same title cut in 1957. (Paul recorded a cover version of the Presley song in 1987, John a version of Price's in 1973.)

KANSAS CITY/HEY-HEY-HEY-HEY!
This medley of two songs recorded separately by Little Richard in 1959 was not the Beatles' idea: Richard himself cut them together that same year and it is this version the Beatles performed and (in 1964) recorded.

MY BONNIE LIES OVER THE OCEAN
The 1961 Sheridan/Beatles recording of this song – under the title 'My Bonnie' – credited the composer as "Trad arr Sheridan", although it was written by Charles T Pratt (under the pseudonyms J T Wood and H T Fulmer) in 1881. A rock-era version of the song was first realised on disc in 1958 by Ray Charles.

PARTY
The correct title of the song more popularly known as 'Let's Have A Party'.

THIRTY DAYS
Sometimes performed as 'Forty Days'.

TO KNOW HER IS TO LOVE HER
Originally written and recorded as 'To Know Him Is To Love Her'.

WHEN THE SAINTS GO MARCHING IN
The Beatles may have also been influenced by the first rock-era version of this, titled 'The Saints Rock 'n' Roll', by Bill Haley and the Comets in 1956. The 1961 Sheridan/Beatles recording of this song – under the title 'The Saints' – credited the composer as "Trad arr Sheridan" and it was this version the Beatles performed live in 1962.

WOODEN HEART
Like Presley's version, Paul sang the lyrics in part-German, part-English. For obvious reasons, this was a particular favourite with Hamburg audiences.

WORRIED MAN BLUES
Also known as 'It Takes A Worried Man To Sing A Worried Song'.